Defect
Detect

DUmps Binaries Logs INternals
School of Security

Windows Memory Dump Analysis Extended

Extensions
Database and Event Stream Processing
Data Science and Visualization
Machine Learning and AI

Second Edition

Dmitry Vostokov
Software Diagnostics Services

Extended Windows Memory Dump Analysis: Using and Writing WinDbg Extensions, Database and Event Stream Processing, Data Science and Visualization, Machine Learning and AI, Second Edition

Published by OpenTask, Republic of Ireland

OpenTask books and magazines are available through booksellers and distributors worldwide. For further information or comments, send requests to press@opentask.com.

A CIP catalog record for this book is available from the British Library.

ISBN-13: 978-1-912636-51-8 (Paperback)

Revision 2.00 (November 2024)

Contents

About the Author

Dmitry Vostokov is an internationally recognized expert, speaker, educator, scientist, inventor, and author. He founded the pattern-oriented software diagnostics, forensics, and prognostics discipline (Systematic Software Diagnostics) and Software Diagnostics Institute (DA+TA: DumpAnalysis.org + TraceAnalysis.org). Vostokov has also authored over 50 books on software diagnostics, anomaly detection and analysis, software and memory forensics, root cause analysis and problem solving, memory dump analysis, debugging, software trace and log analysis, reverse engineering, and malware analysis. He has over 30 years of experience in software architecture, design, development, and maintenance in various industries, including leadership, technical, and people management roles. Dmitry founded OpenTask Iterative and Incremental Publishing (OpenTask.com) and Software Diagnostics Technology and Services (former Memory Dump Analysis Services) PatternDiagnostics.com. In his spare time, he explores Software Narratology and Quantum Software Diagnostics. His interest areas are theoretical software diagnostics and its mathematical and computer science foundations, application of formal logic, semiotics, artificial intelligence, machine learning, and data mining to diagnostics and anomaly detection, software diagnostics engineering and diagnostics-driven development, diagnostics workflow and interaction. Recent interest areas also include functional programming, cloud native computing, monitoring, observability, visualization, security, automation, applications of category theory to software diagnostics, development and big data, and diagnostics of artificial intelligence.

Introduction

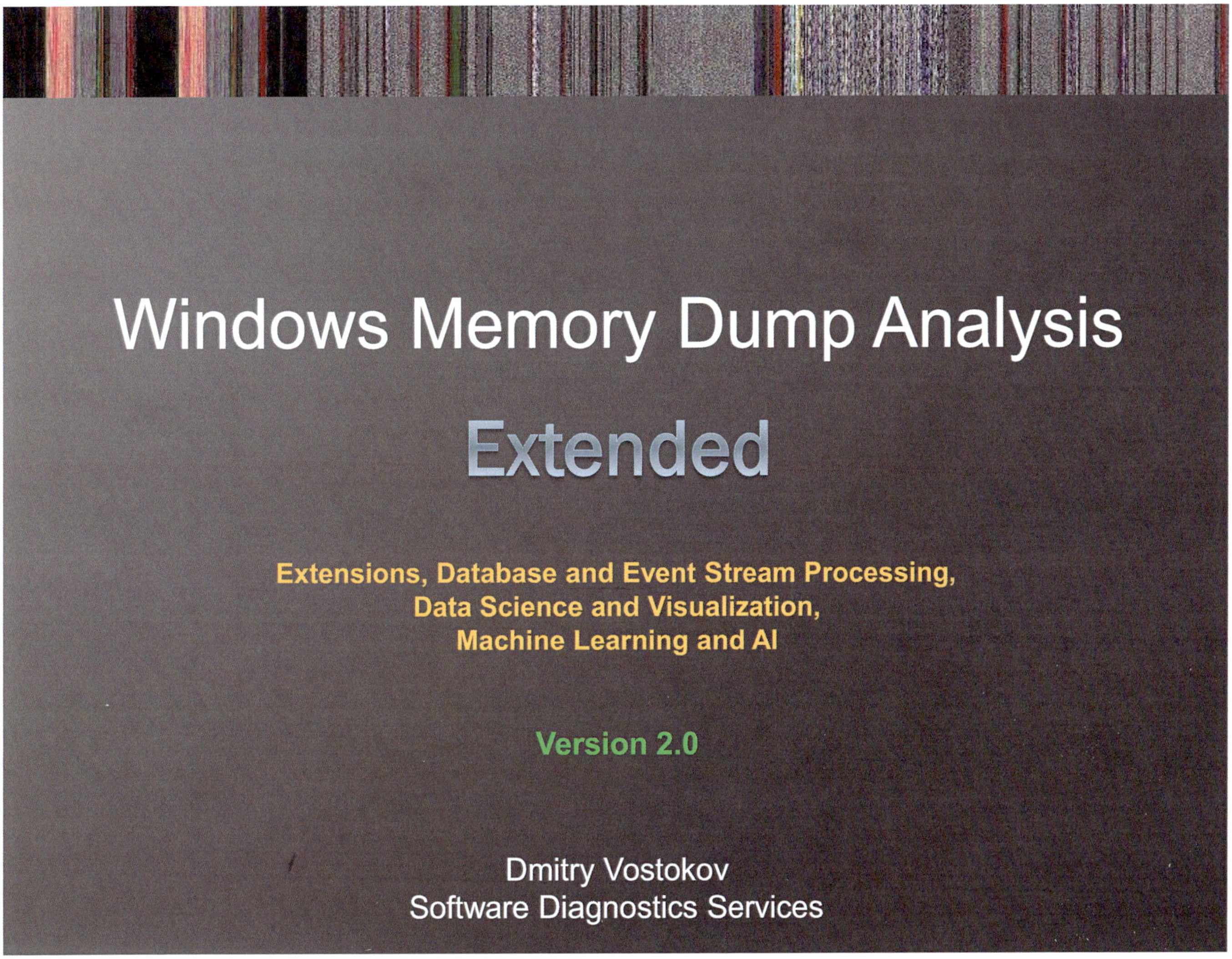
Windows Memory Dump Analysis
Extended
Extensions, Database and Event Stream Processing,
Data Science and Visualization,
Machine Learning and AI
Version 2.0
Dmitry Vostokov
Software Diagnostics Services

Hello Everyone, my name is Dmitry Vostokov, and I teach this training course.

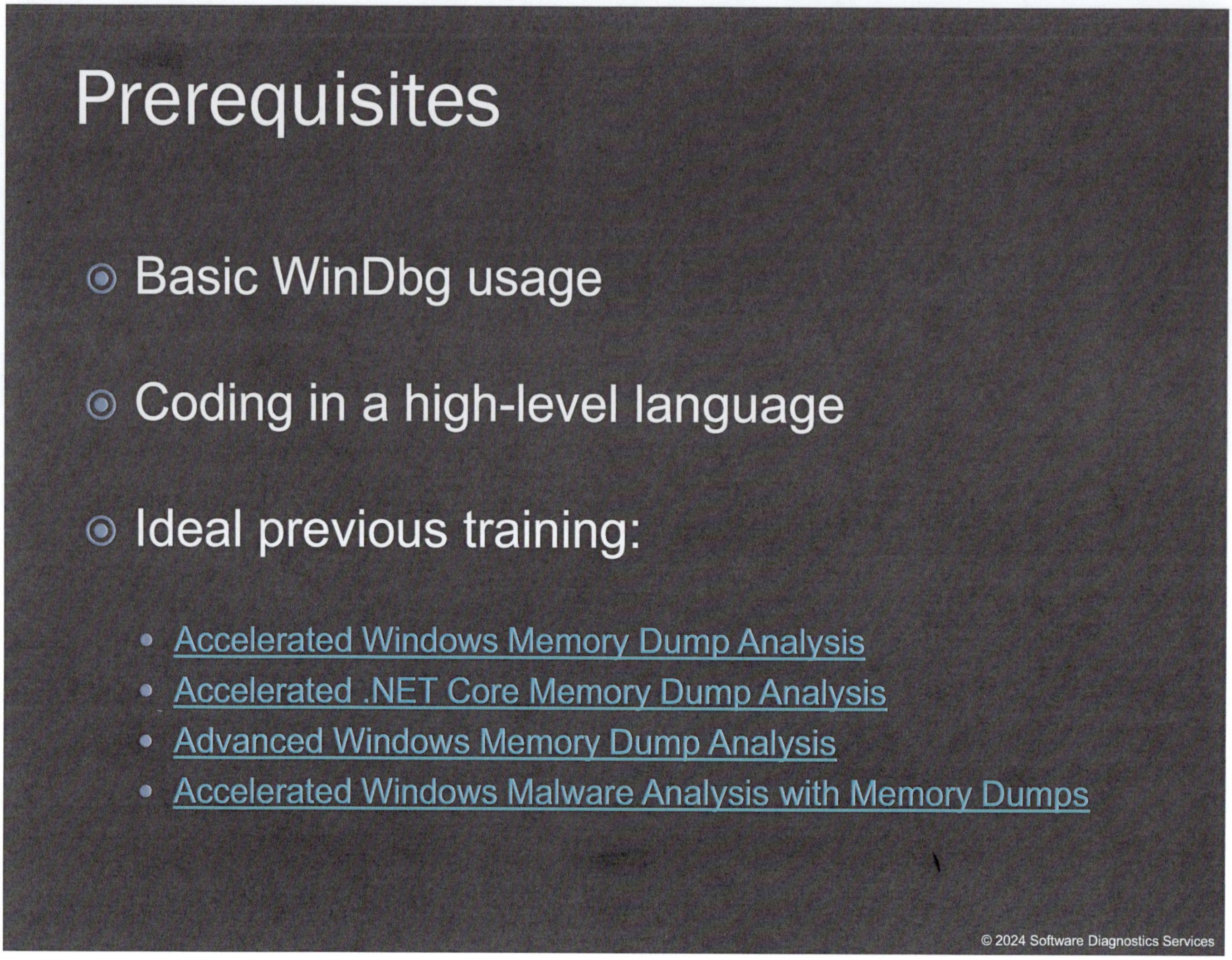
Prerequisites
Basic WinDbg usage
Coding in a high-level language
Ideal previous training:
Accelerated Windows Memory Dump Analysis
Accelerated .NET Core Memory Dump Analysis
Advanced Windows Memory Dump Analysis
Accelerated Windows Malware Analysis with Memory Dumps
© 2024 Software Diagnostics Services

This course presupposes that you already have basic experience using the WinDbg app or classic WinDbg from the Debugging Tools for Windows. Some WinDbg exercises also assume your familiarity with Python, and if not, you can still follow and learn a bit of Python that way. Writing WinDbg extensions assumes you are familiar with C, C++ and its Standard Library, and optionally, Rust. This course is a follow-up course for other Accelerated or Advanced courses.

Accelerated Windows Memory Dump Analysis
http://www.patterndiagnostics.com/accelerated-windows-memory-dump-analysis-book

Accelerated .NET Core Memory Dump Analysis
http://www.patterndiagnostics.com/accelerated-net-memory-dump-analysis-book

Advanced Windows Memory Dump Analysis
http://www.patterndiagnostics.com/advanced-windows-memory-dump-analysis-book

Accelerated Windows Malware Analysis with Memory Dumps
https://www.patterndiagnostics.com/accelerated-windows-malware-analysis-book

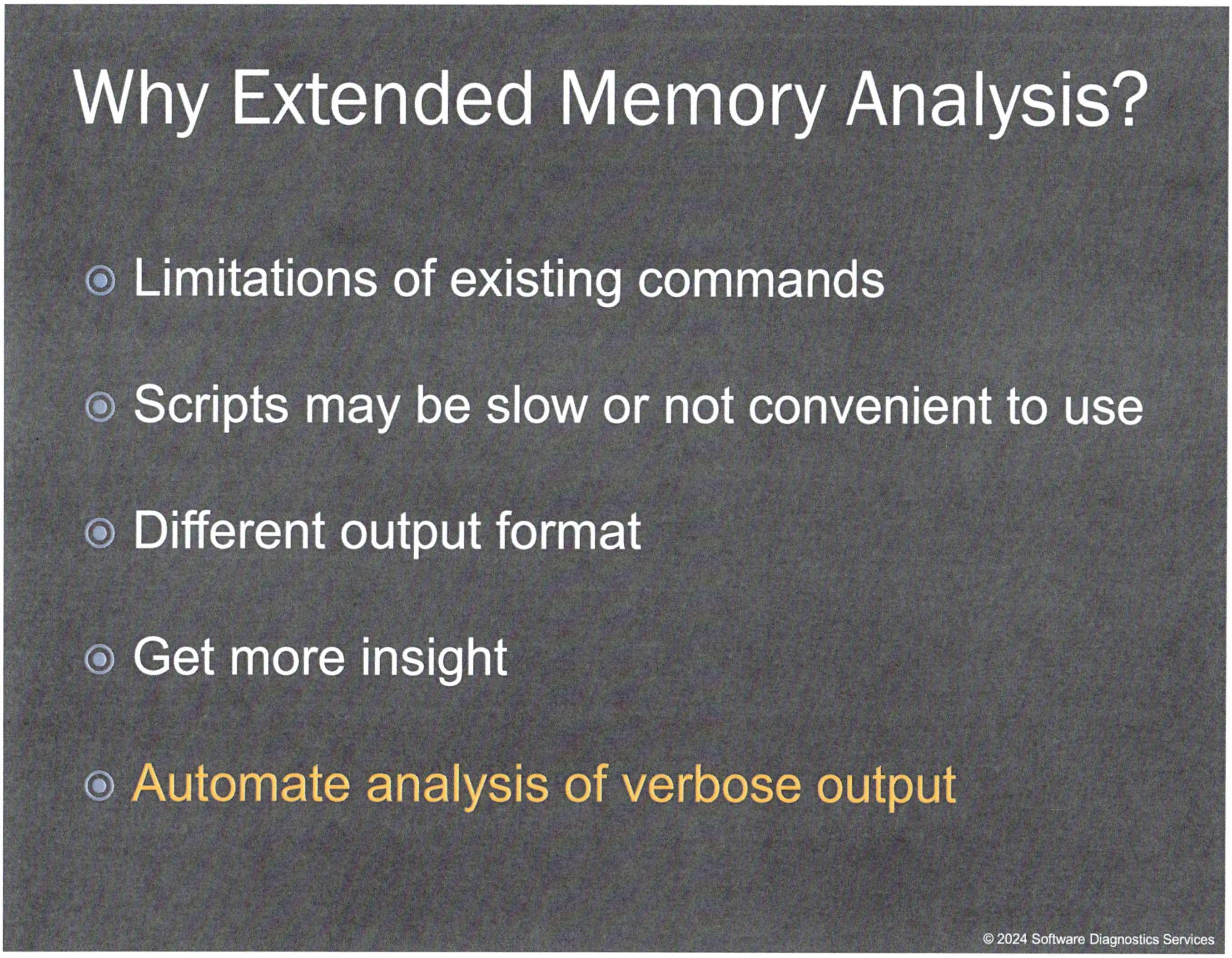

Why Extended Memory Analysis?
Limitations of existing commands
Scripts may be slow or not convenient to use
Different output format
Get more insight
Automate analysis of verbose output
© 2024 Software Diagnostics Services

Many extensions and their commands are included in the WinDbg app or classic WinDbg debugger from Debugging Tools for Windows. However some of them are slow or have an output format that is not easy to analyze by a human. Existing WinDbg scripting capabilities may be inconvenient to develop and use in some cases, especially if you prefer a different language and a different data model. Since we get textual data from a debugger, we may also want to apply modern data processing, analysis, and visualization methods to get additional insight into past system behavior. The output from some commands may be really verbose, especially when we analyze and compare multiple memory dumps. In such cases, machine learning and AI methods may be beneficial to automate manual laborious analysis. In this and the next slides, I highlight what's new in the second edition of this course.

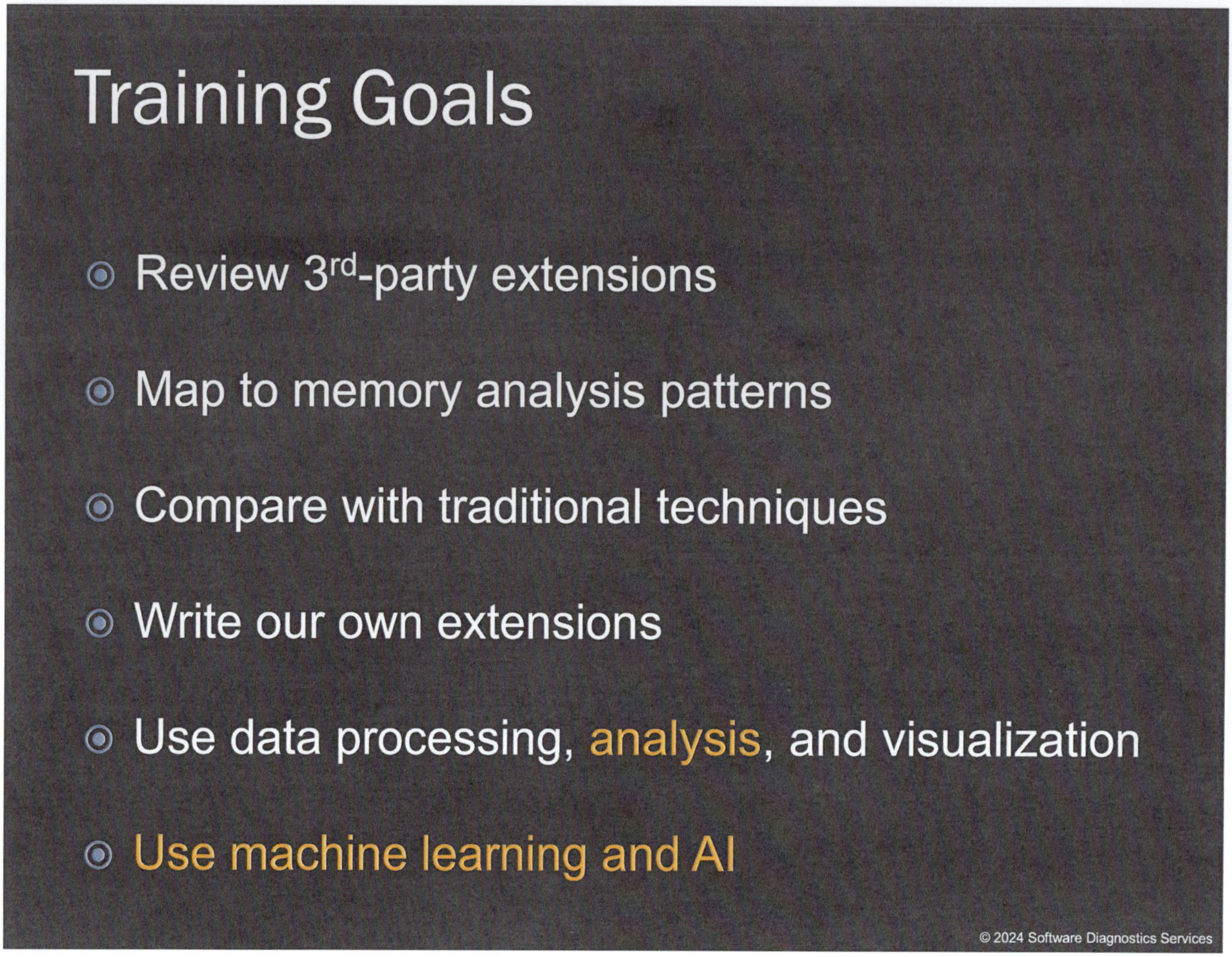

Training Goals
Review 3rd-party extensions
Map to memory analysis patterns
Compare with traditional techniques
Write our own extensions
Use data processing, analysis, and visualization
Use machine learning and AI
© 2024 Software Diagnostics Services

Based on the need, we have the following goals. First, we review existing 3rd-party extensions, and in the process, we map their commands to existing memory analysis patterns. We also compare them to traditional commands and techniques. Then, we learn to write our own extensions in C, C++, and Rust. We also take a look at data processing, analysis, and visualization methods that we can leverage for memory dump analysis. And, finally, we look at machine learning and AI methods to aid laborious analysis of complex cases.

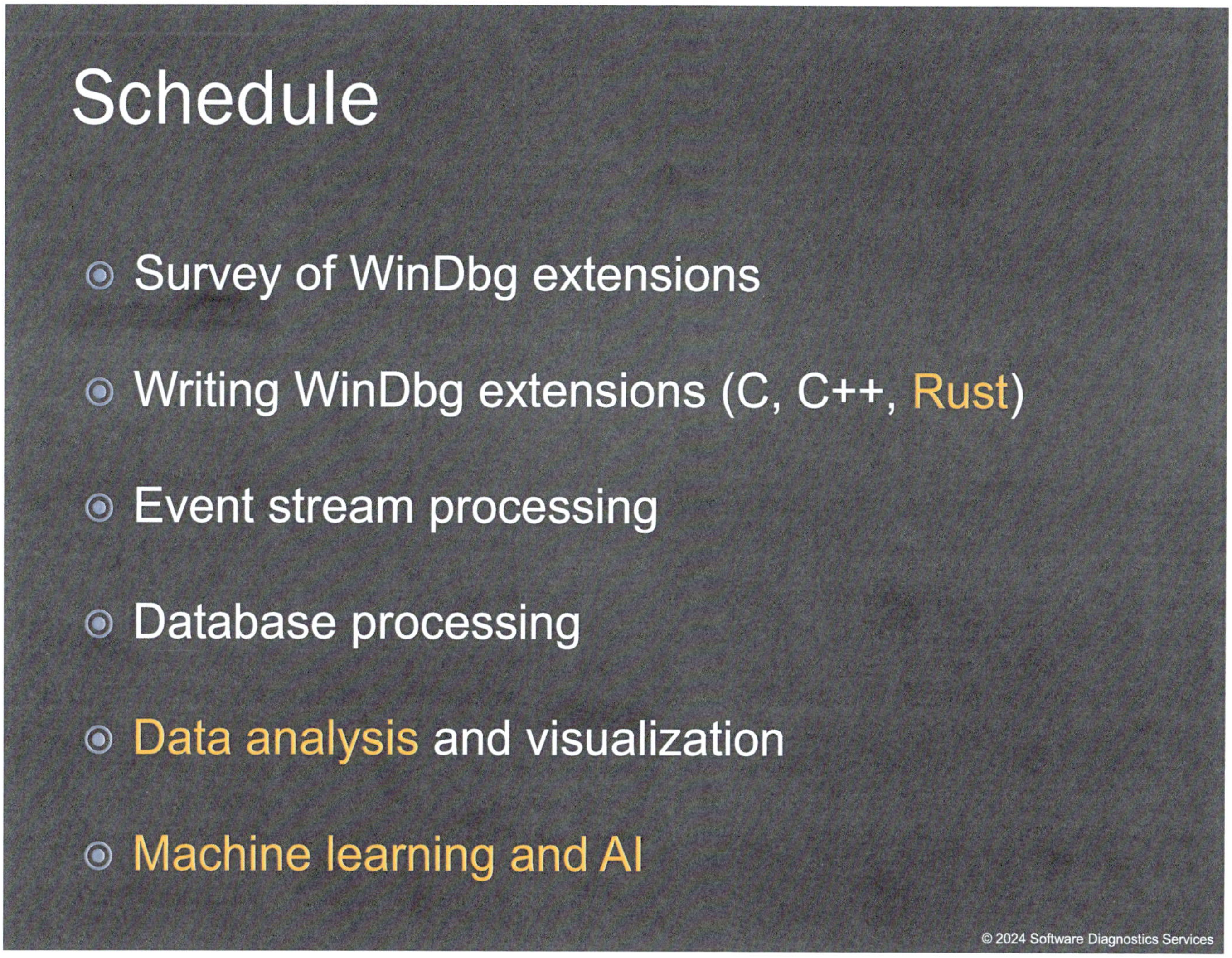

Schedule
Survey of WinDbg extensions
Writing WinDbg extensions (C, C++, Rust)
Event stream processing
Database processing
Data analysis and visualization
Machine learning and AI
© 2024 Software Diagnostics Services

This training consists of 6 parts.

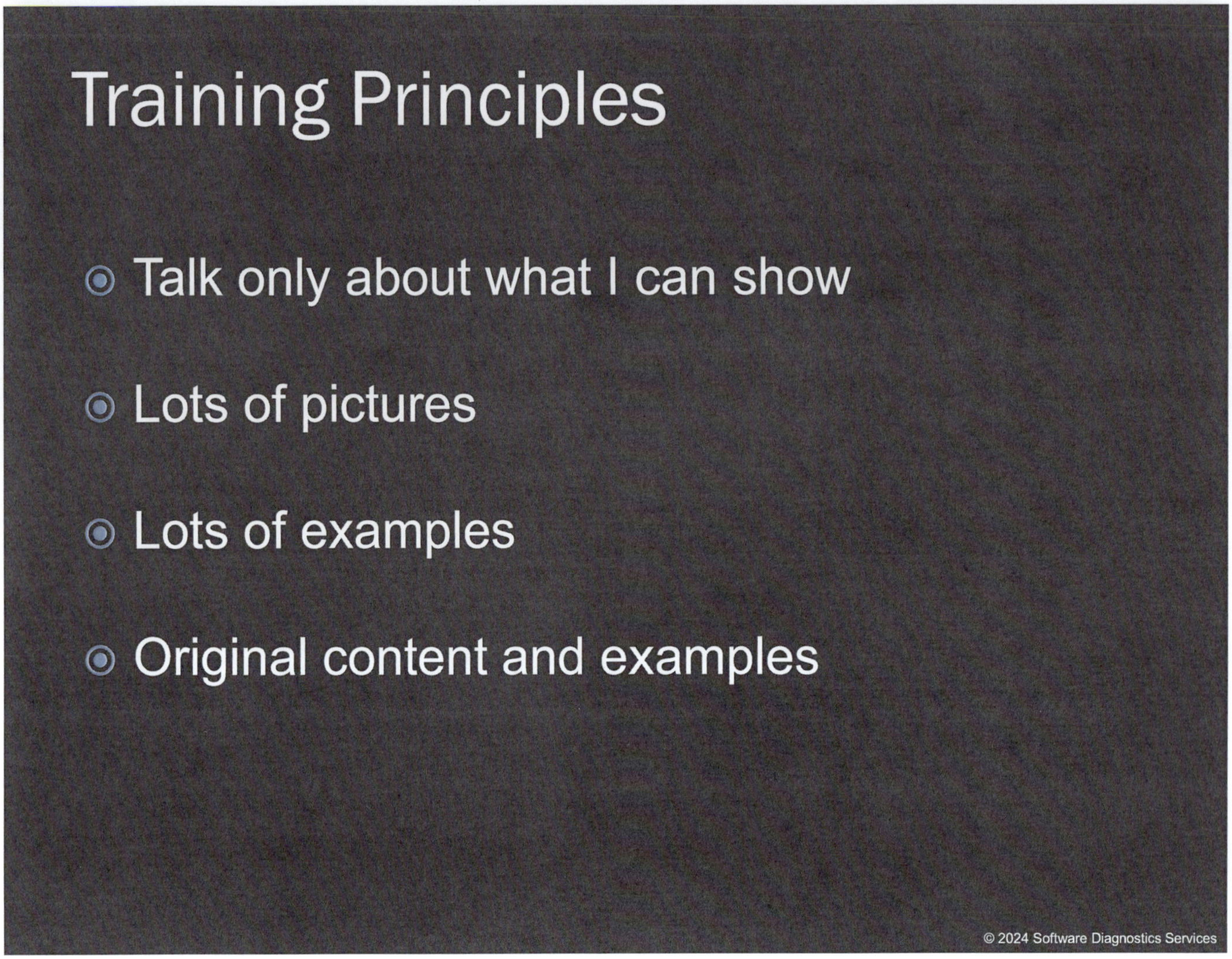
Training Principles
Talk only about what I can show
Lots of pictures
Lots of examples
Original content and examples
© 2024 Software Diagnostics Services

There were many training formats to consider, and I decided that the best way was to concentrate on hands-on exercises. Specifically, for this training, I developed 25 of them.

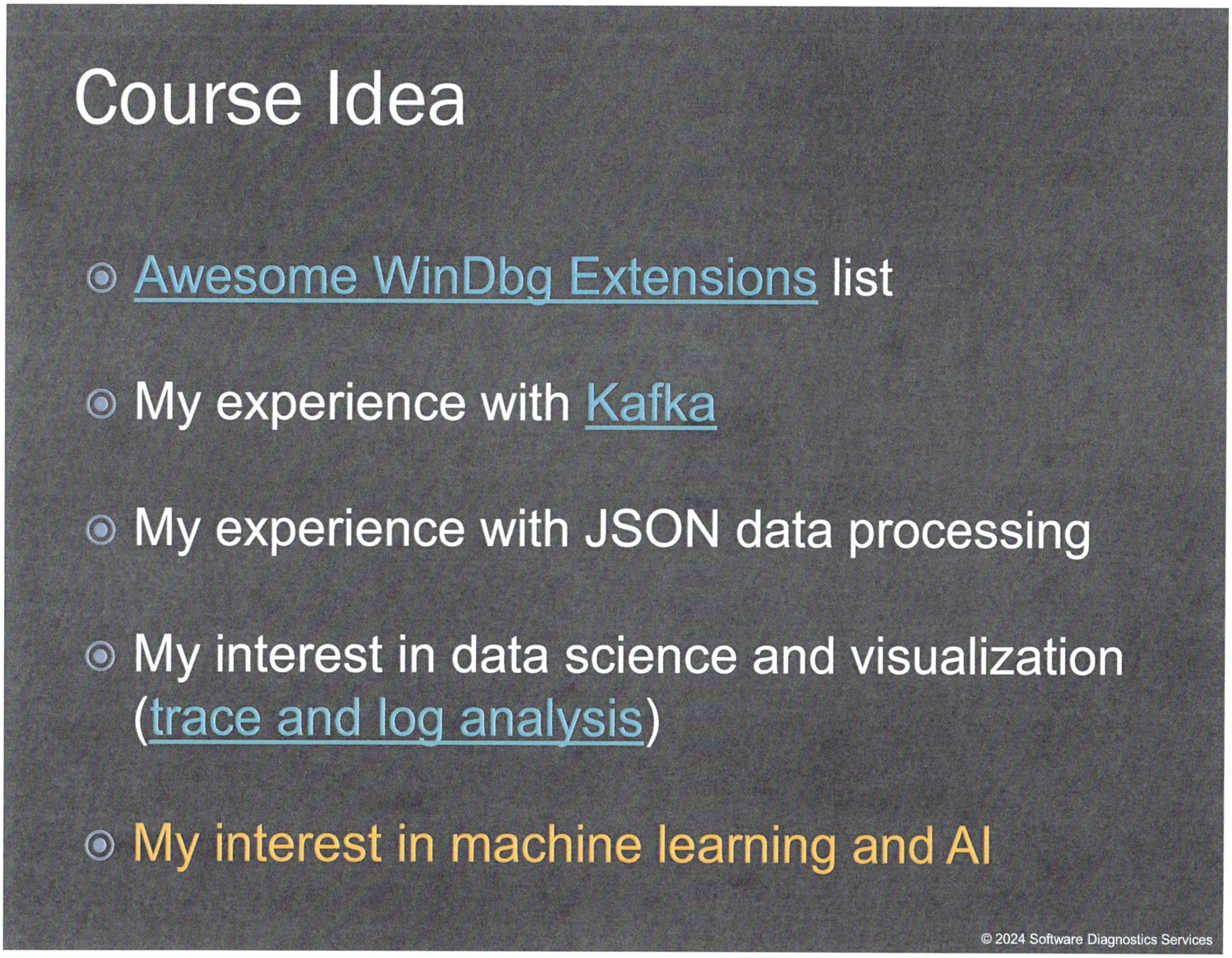

Course Idea
Awesome WinDbg Extensions list
My experience with Kafka
My experience with JSON data processing
My interest in data science and visualization (trace and log analysis)
My interest in machine learning and AI
© 2024 Software Diagnostics Services

The idea of this course came to me when I saw the Awesome WinDbg Extensions[1] GitHub repository. I immediately thought it would be good to investigate extensions and scripts not listed in my shorter list on WinDbg.org. So, the idea of the new course was born. I also wrote extensions in the past, mainly for my private use, except for one publicly available. And I thought it would be good to add a writing extensions tutorial to this new training. Last 7 years, I have been working with JSON data format and its processing, and for the last 4 years, using Kafka[2] log storing and streaming platform. Considering my interest in data science related to trace and log analysis[3] (I also added a few related memory dump analysis patterns) and visualization, I decided to add such topics to the course, too. Finally, while working with complex cases involving multiple memory and laborious analysis of verbose WinDbg output, I decided to include a few machine learning and AI methods.

---

[1] https://github.com/anhkgg/awesome-windbg-extensions

[2] https://kafka.apache.org/

[3] https://www.patterndiagnostics.com/trace-log-analysis-pattern-reference

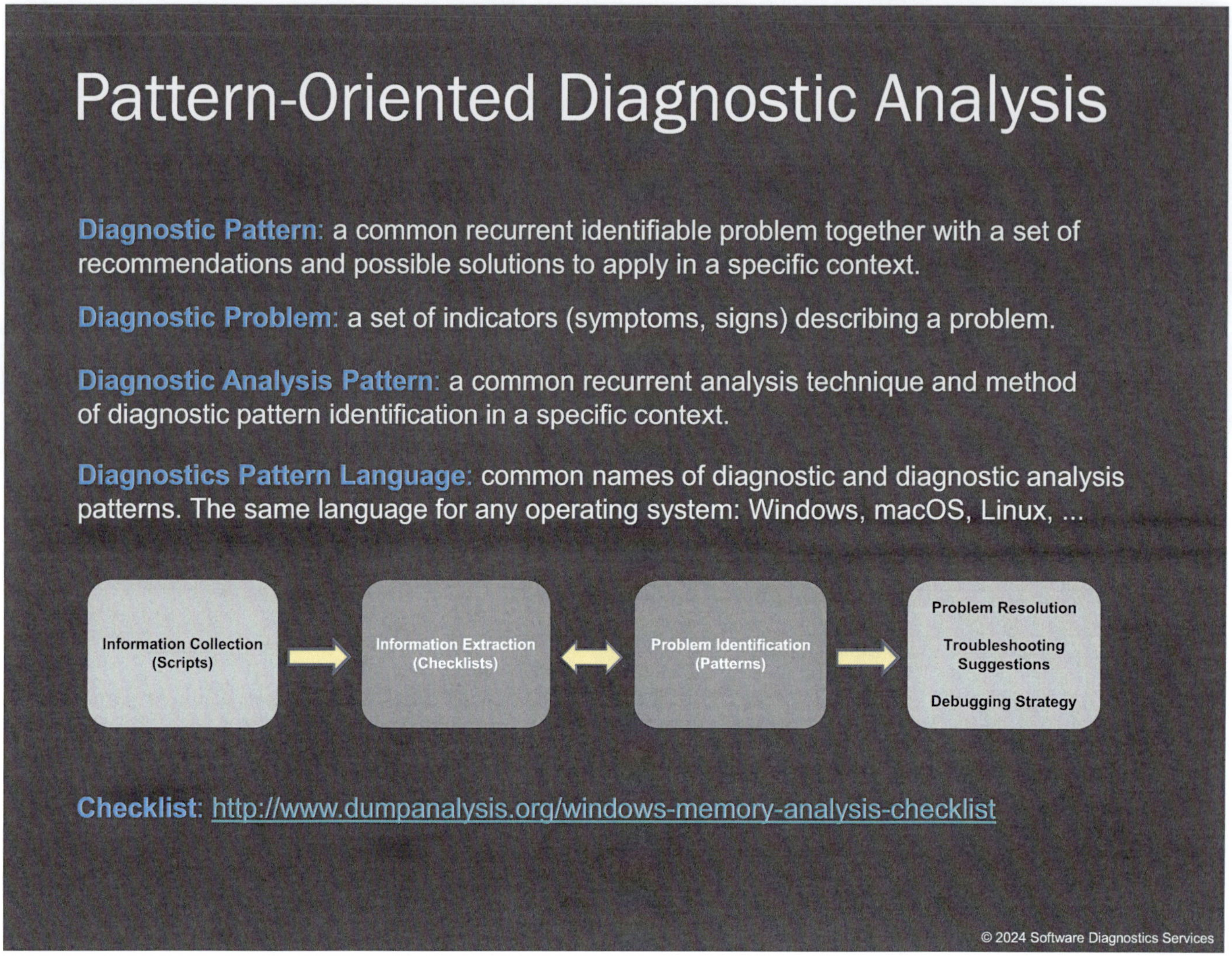

Pattern-Oriented Diagnostic Analysis
Diagnostic Pattern: a common recurrent identifiable problem together with a set of recommendations and possible solutions to apply in a specific context.
Diagnostic Problem: a set of indicators (symptoms, signs) describing a problem.
Diagnostic Analysis Pattern: a common recurrent analysis technique and method of diagnostic pattern identification in a specific context.
Diagnostics Pattern Language: common names of diagnostic and diagnostic analysis patterns. The same language for any operating system: Windows, macOS, Linux, ...
Information Collection (Scripts)
Information Extraction (Checklists)
Problem Identification (Patterns)
Problem Resolution
Troubleshooting Suggestions
Debugging Strategy
Checklist: http://www.dumpanalysis.org/windows-memory-analysis-checklist
© 2024 Software Diagnostics Services

Checklist: http://www.dumpanalysis.org/windows-memory-analysis-checklist

A few words about logs, checklists, and patterns: memory dump analysis is usually an analysis of a text for the presence of patterns. We run commands, and they output text; then, we look at that textual output, and when we find something suspicious, we execute more commands. Here, checklists can be very useful. One such checklist is provided as a link. In many cases (for example, process memory leaks, raw stack analysis, and complete memory dumps), it is beneficial to collect information into one log file by running several commands at once (like a script) and then do the first-order analysis.

Practice Exercises

Links

- Applications:

Download links are in the exercise E0.

- Exercise Transcripts:

Included in this book.

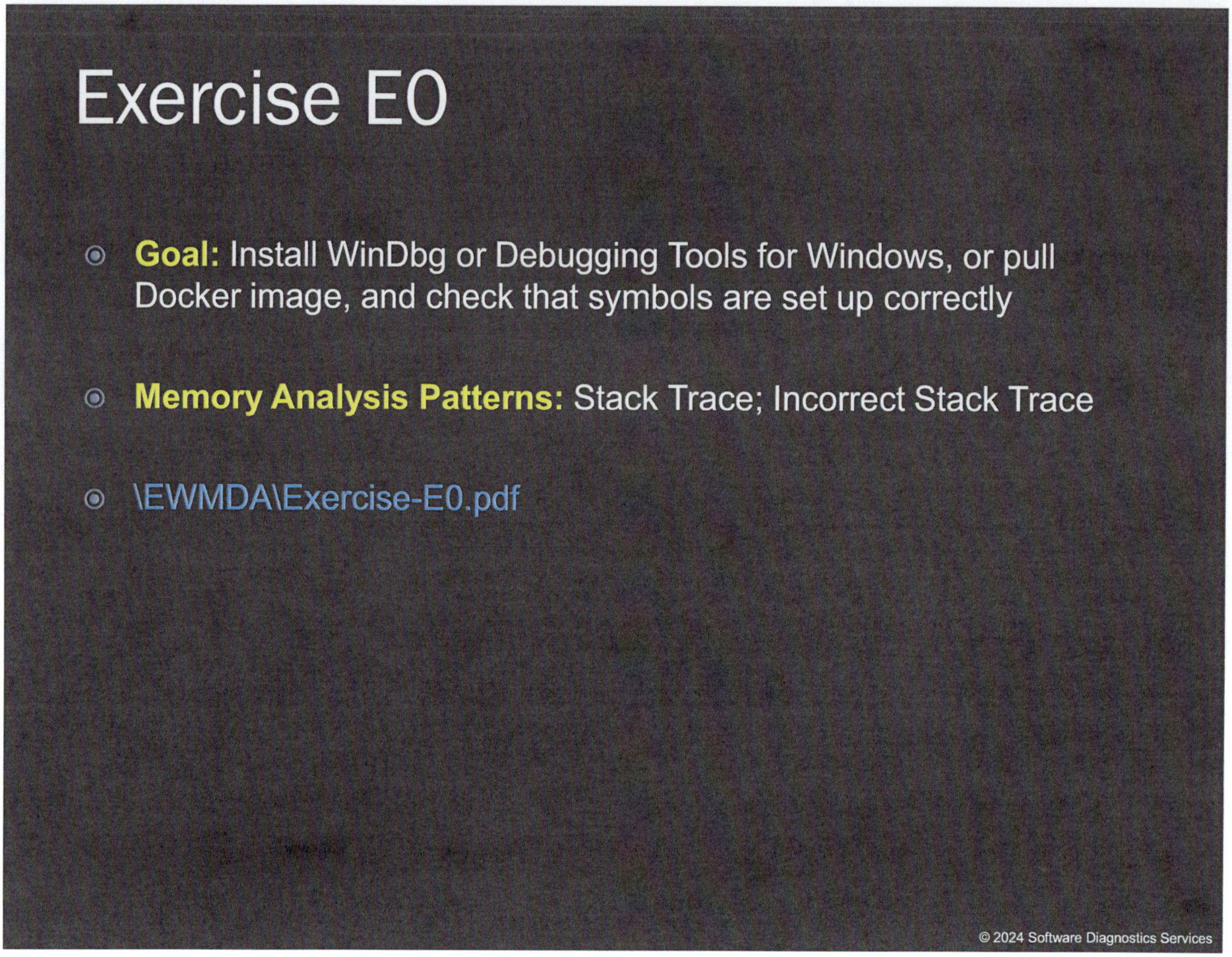
Exercise E0
Goal: Install WinDbg or Debugging Tools for Windows, or pull Docker image, and check that symbols are set up correctly
Memory Analysis Patterns: Stack Trace; Incorrect Stack Trace
\EWMDA\Exercise-E0.pdf
© 2024 Software Diagnostics Services

Exercise E0: Download, set up, and verify your WinDbg or Debugging Tools for Windows installation or Docker Debugging Tools for Windows image

Goal: Install WinDbg or Debugging Tools for Windows, or pull Docker image, and check that symbols are set up correctly.

Memory Analysis Patterns: Stack Trace; Incorrect Stack Trace.

1. Download memory dump files if you haven't done that already and unpack the archive:

https://www.patterndiagnostics.com/Training/EWMDA/EWMDA-Dumps.zip

2. Install WinDbg (or upgrade existing WinDbg Preview) from https://learn.microsoft.com/en-gb/windows-hardware/drivers/debugger. Run WinDbg.

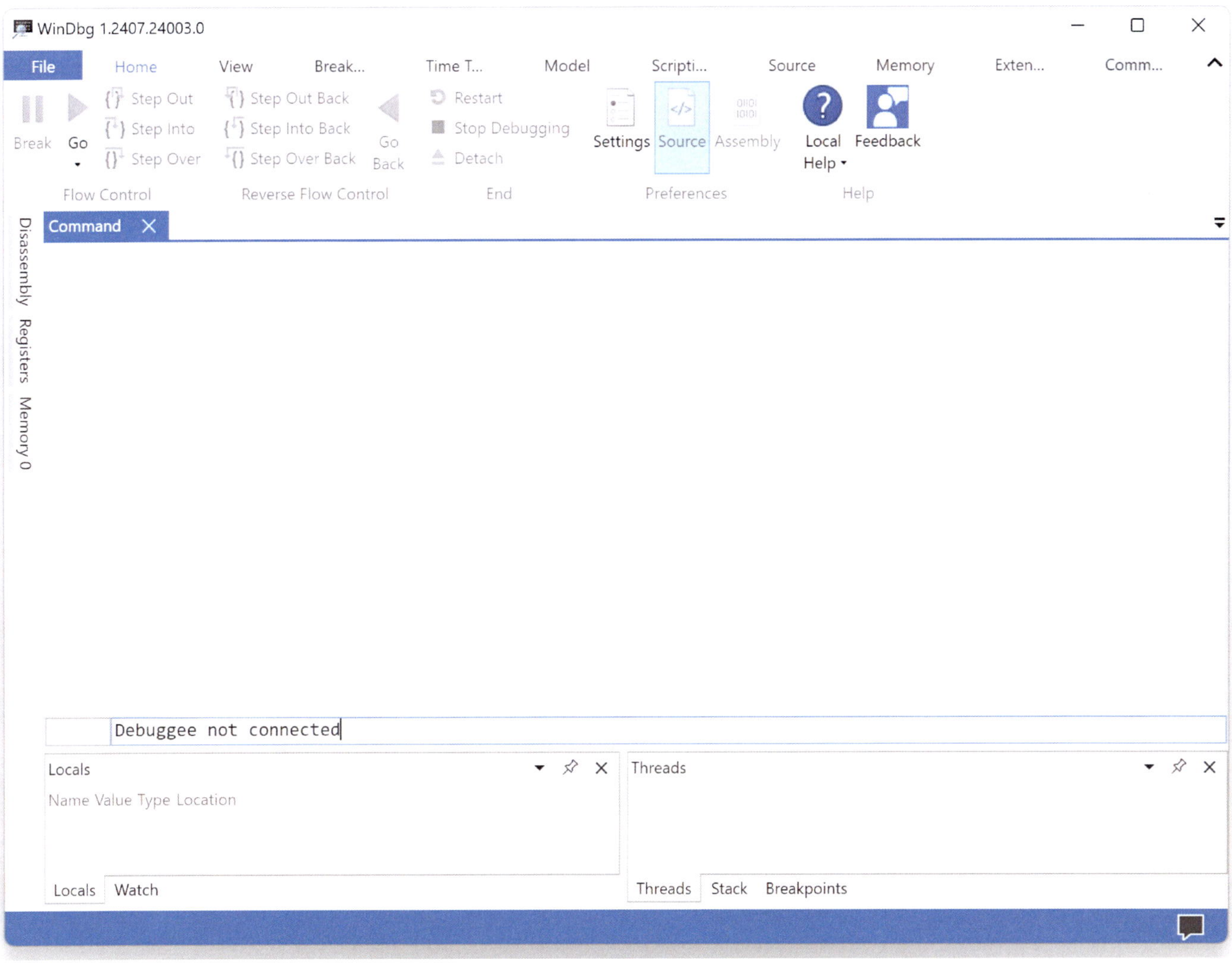

3. Open \EWMDA-Dumps\Process\x64\wordpad.DMP:

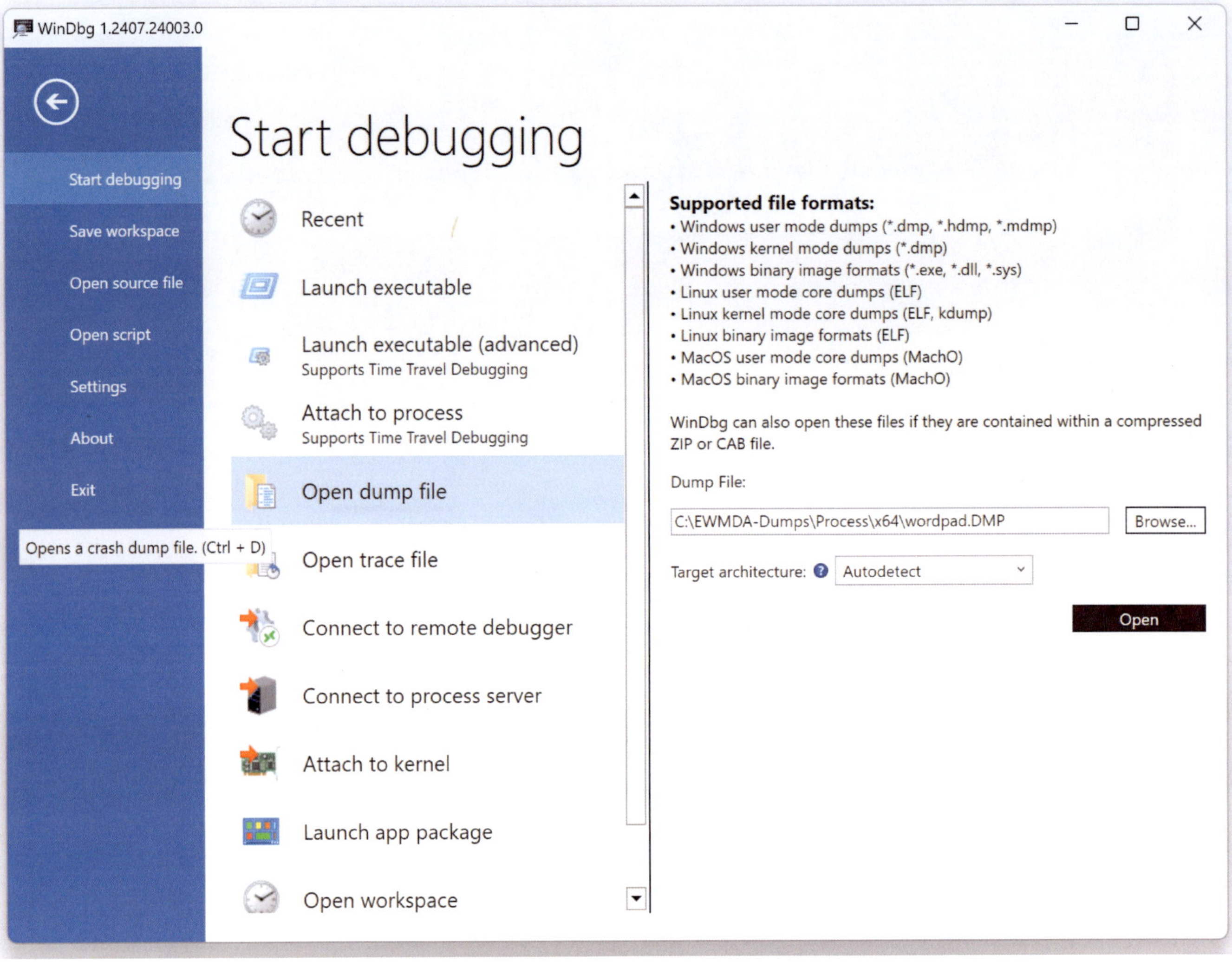

4. We get the dump file loaded:

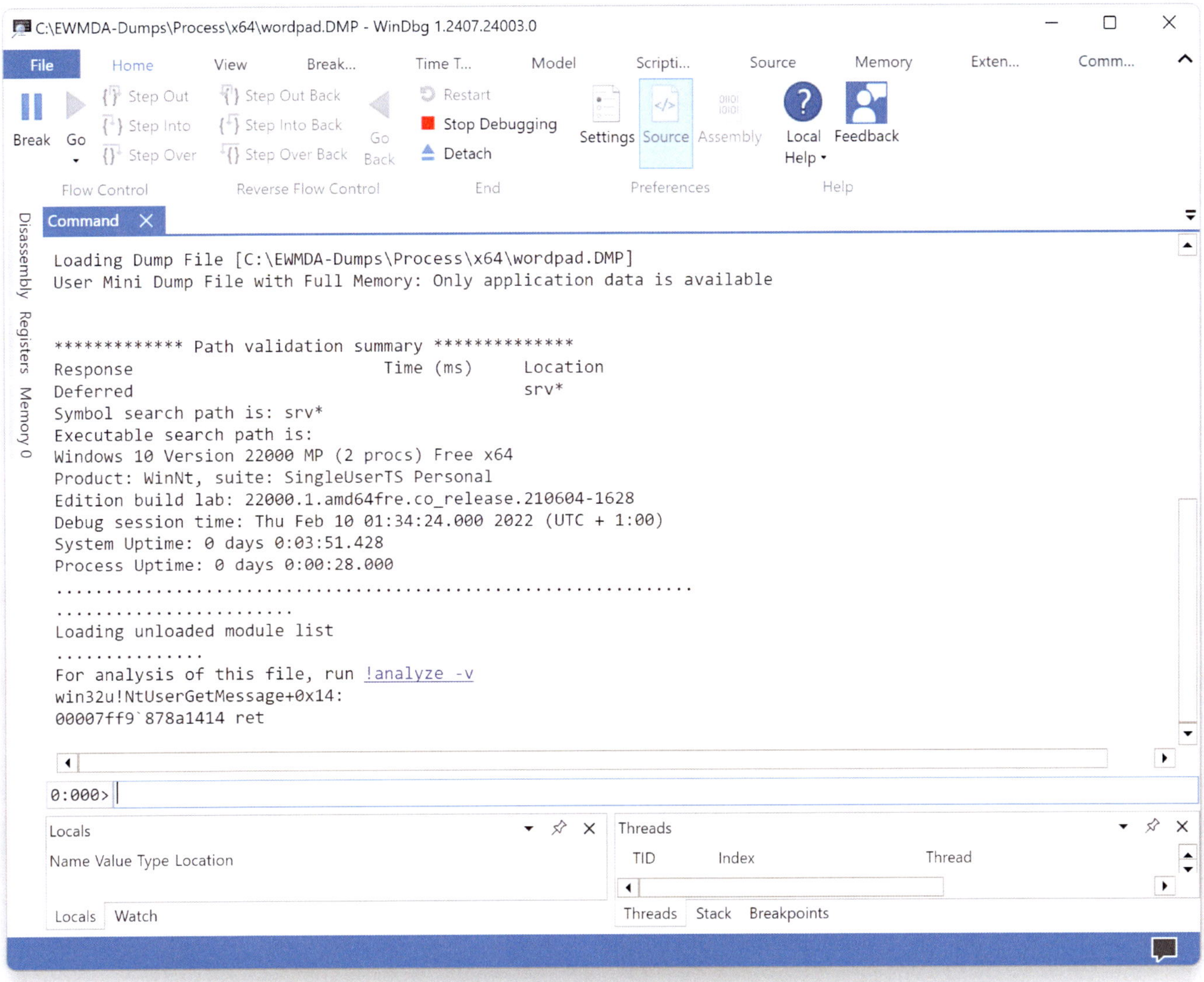
C:\EWMDA-Dumps\Process\x64\wordpad.DMP - WinDbg 1.2407.24003.0
File
Home
View
Break...
Time T...
Model
Scripti...
Source
Memory
Exten...
Comm...
Break
Go
Step Out
Step Into
Step Over
Step Out Back
Step Into Back
Step Over Back
Go Back
Restart
Stop Debugging
Detach
Settings
Source
Assembly
Local Help
Feedback
Flow Control
Reverse Flow Control
End
Preferences
Help
Disassembly
Registers
Memory 0
Command
Loading Dump File [C:\EWMDA-Dumps\Process\x64\wordpad.DMP]
User Mini Dump File with Full Memory: Only application data is available
************* Path validation summary **************
Response Time (ms) Location
Deferred srv*
Symbol search path is: srv*
Executable search path is:
Windows 10 Version 22000 MP (2 procs) Free x64
Product: WinNt, suite: SingleUserTS Personal
Edition build lab: 22000.1.amd64fre.co_release.210604-1628
Debug session time: Thu Feb 10 01:34:24.000 2022 (UTC + 1:00)
System Uptime: 0 days 0:03:51.428
Process Uptime: 0 days 0:00:28.000
Loading unloaded module list
For analysis of this file, run !analyze -v
win32u!NtUserGetMessage+0x14:
00007ff9`878a1414 ret
0:000>
Locals
Name Value Type Location
Locals
Watch
Threads
TID
Index
Thread
Threads
Stack
Breakpoints

5. We can execute the **k** command to get the stack trace:

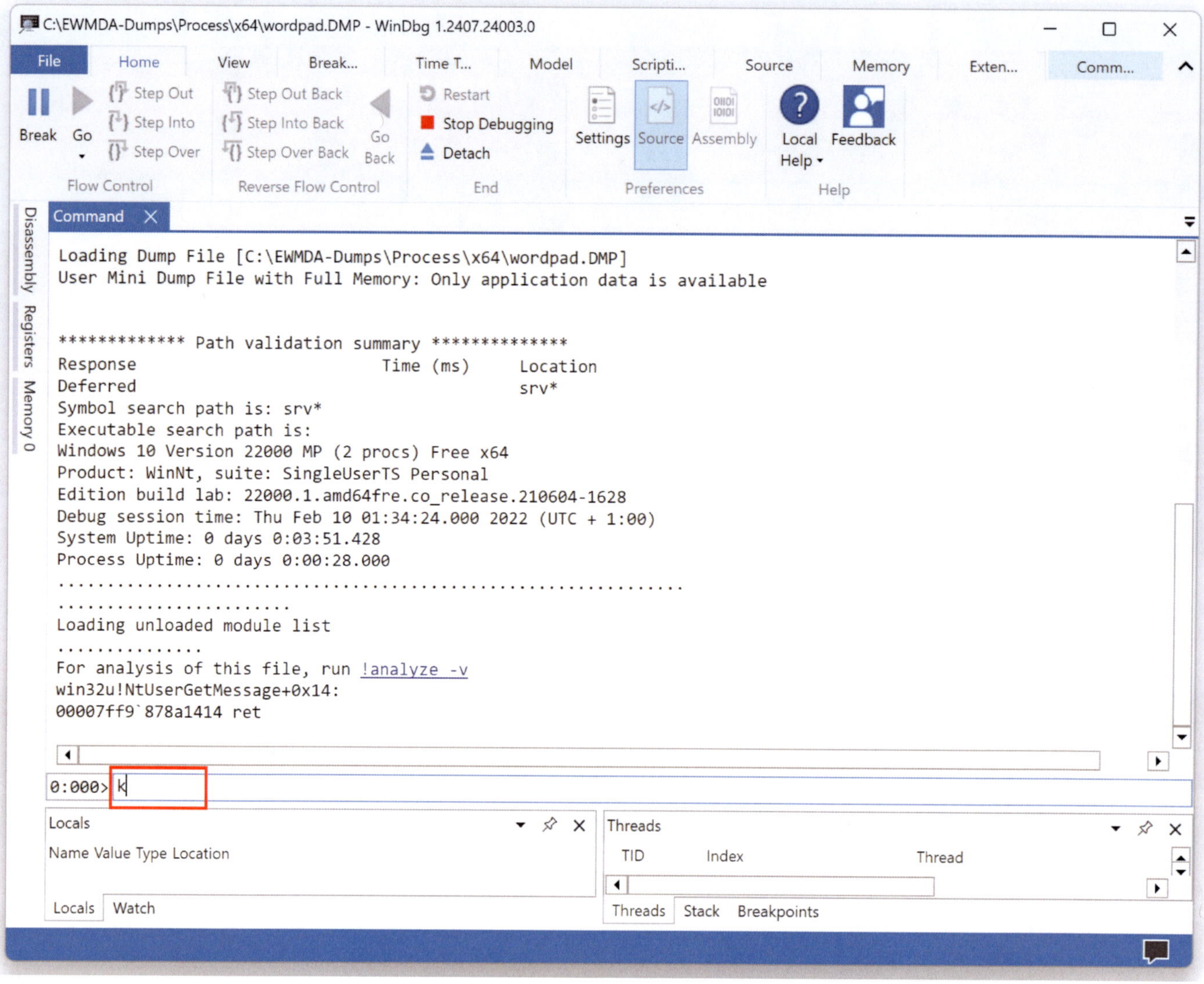

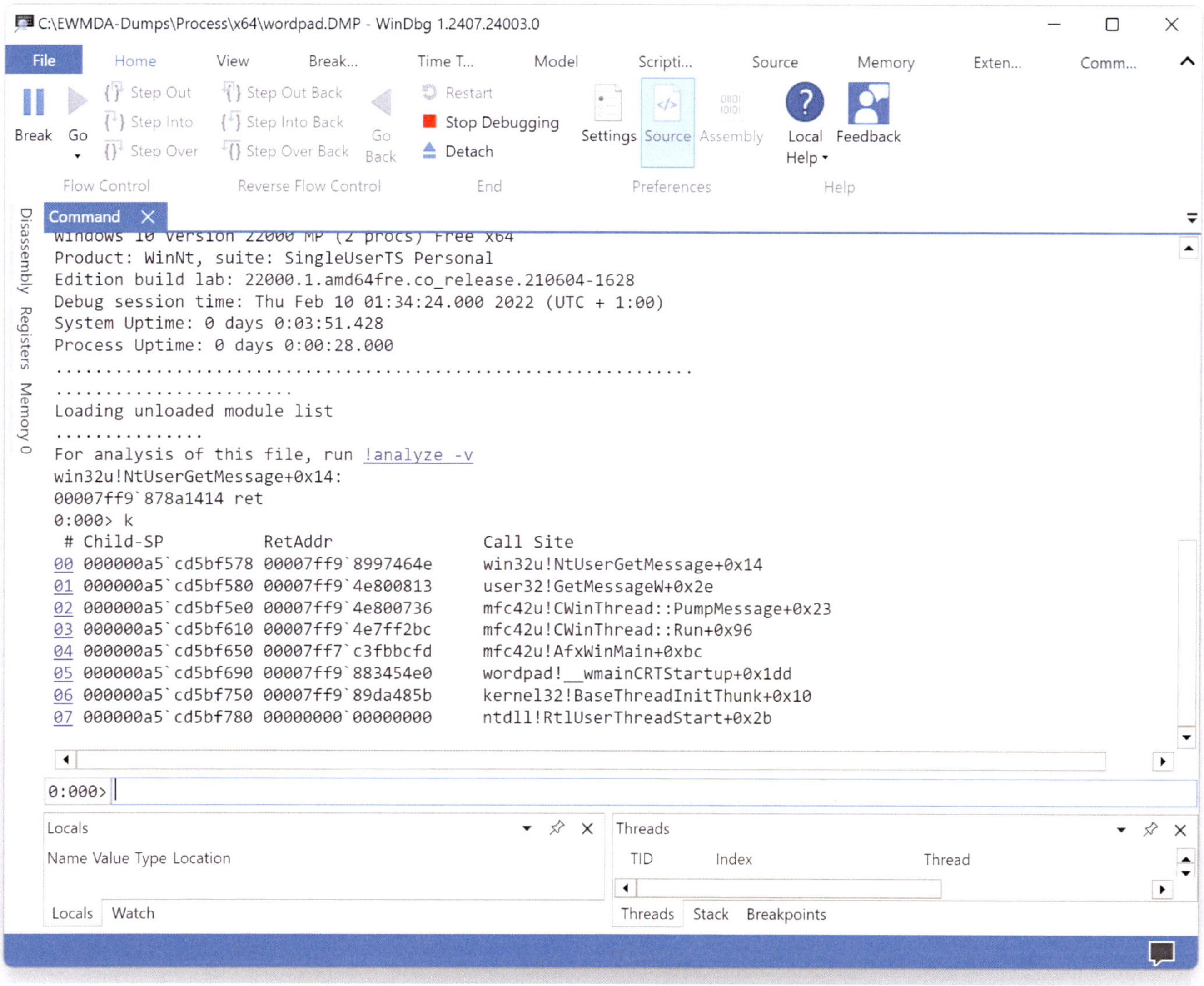

6. The output of the **k** command should be this:

```
0:000> k
 # Child-SP          RetAddr               Call Site
00 000000a5`cd5bf578 00007ff9`8997464e     win32u!NtUserGetMessage+0x14
01 000000a5`cd5bf580 00007ff9`4e800813     user32!GetMessageW+0x2e
02 000000a5`cd5bf5e0 00007ff9`4e800736     mfc42u!CWinThread::PumpMessage+0x23
03 000000a5`cd5bf610 00007ff9`4e7ff2bc     mfc42u!CWinThread::Run+0x96
04 000000a5`cd5bf650 00007ff7`c3fbbcfd     mfc42u!AfxWinMain+0xbc
05 000000a5`cd5bf690 00007ff9`883454e0     wordpad!__wmainCRTStartup+0x1dd
06 000000a5`cd5bf750 00007ff9`89da485b     kernel32!BaseThreadInitThunk+0x10
07 000000a5`cd5bf780 00000000`00000000     ntdll!RtlUserThreadStart+0x2b
```

If it has this form below with a large offset, then your symbol files were not set up correctly – **Incorrect Stack Trace** pattern:

```
0:000> k
 # Child-SP          RetAddr               Call Site
00 000000a5`cd5bf578 00007ff9`8997464e     win32u!NtUserGetMessage+0x14
01 000000a5`cd5bf580 00007ff9`4e800813     user32!GetMessageW+0x2e
02 000000a5`cd5bf5e0 00007ff9`4e800736     mfc42u!Ordinal5730+0x23
03 000000a5`cd5bf610 00007ff9`4e7ff2bc     mfc42u!Ordinal6054+0x96
04 000000a5`cd5bf650 00007ff7`c3fbbcfd     mfc42u!Ordinal1584+0xbc
05 000000a5`cd5bf690 00007ff9`883454e0     wordpad+0xbcfd
06 000000a5`cd5bf750 00007ff9`89da485b     kernel32!BaseThreadInitThunk+0x10
07 000000a5`cd5bf780 00000000`00000000     ntdll!RtlUserThreadStart+0x2b
```

7. [Required for Exercise EW2 but optional for others] Download and install the recommended version of Debugging Tools for Windows (See windbg.org for quick links, WinDbg Quick Links \ Download Debugging Tools for Windows). For this part, we use WinDbg 10.0.26100.1 from Windows SDK 10.0.26100 for Windows 11, version 24H2.

8. Launch WinDbg from Windows Kits \ WinDbg (X64).

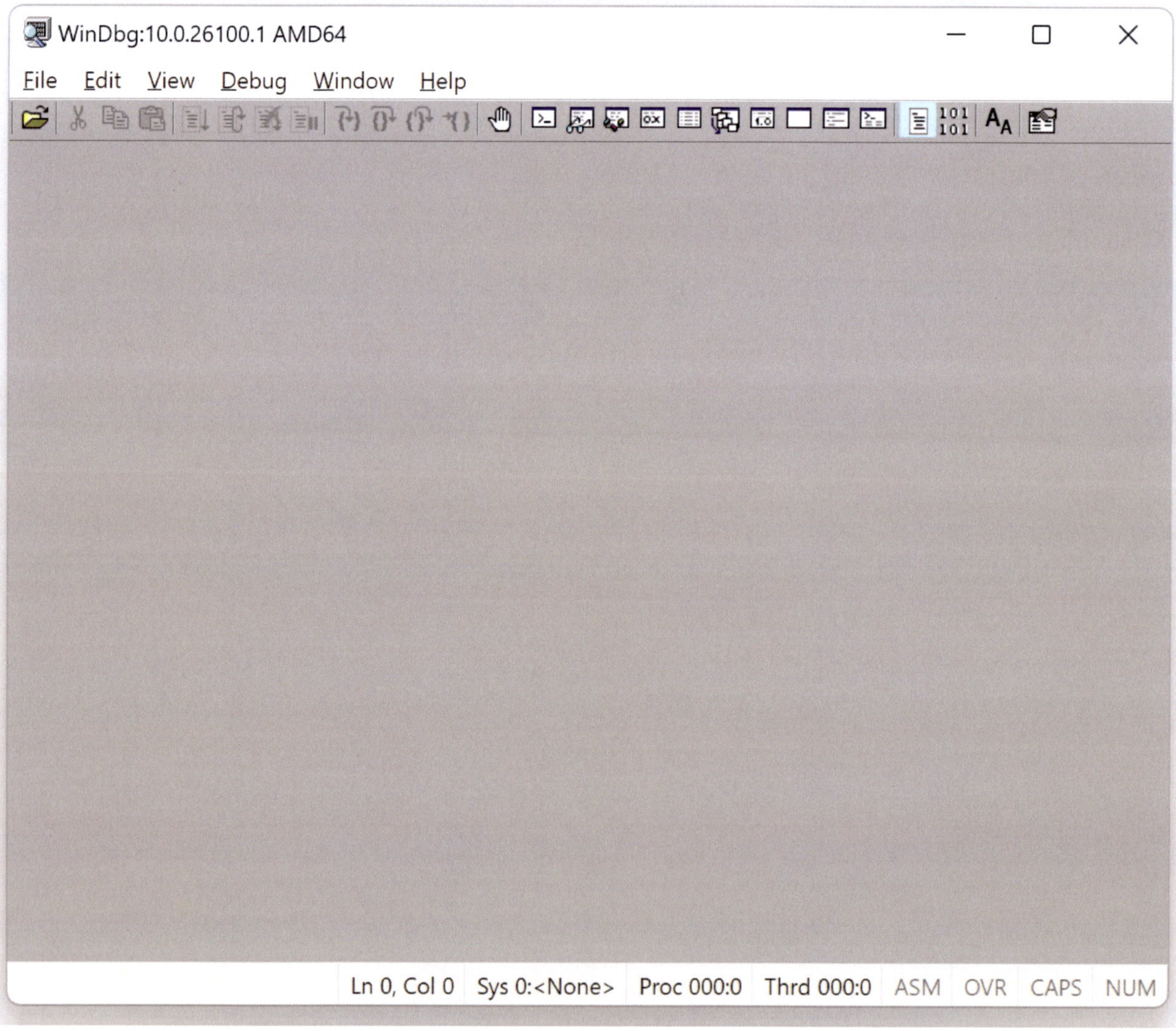

9. Open \EWMDA-Dumps\Process\x64\wordpad.DMP:

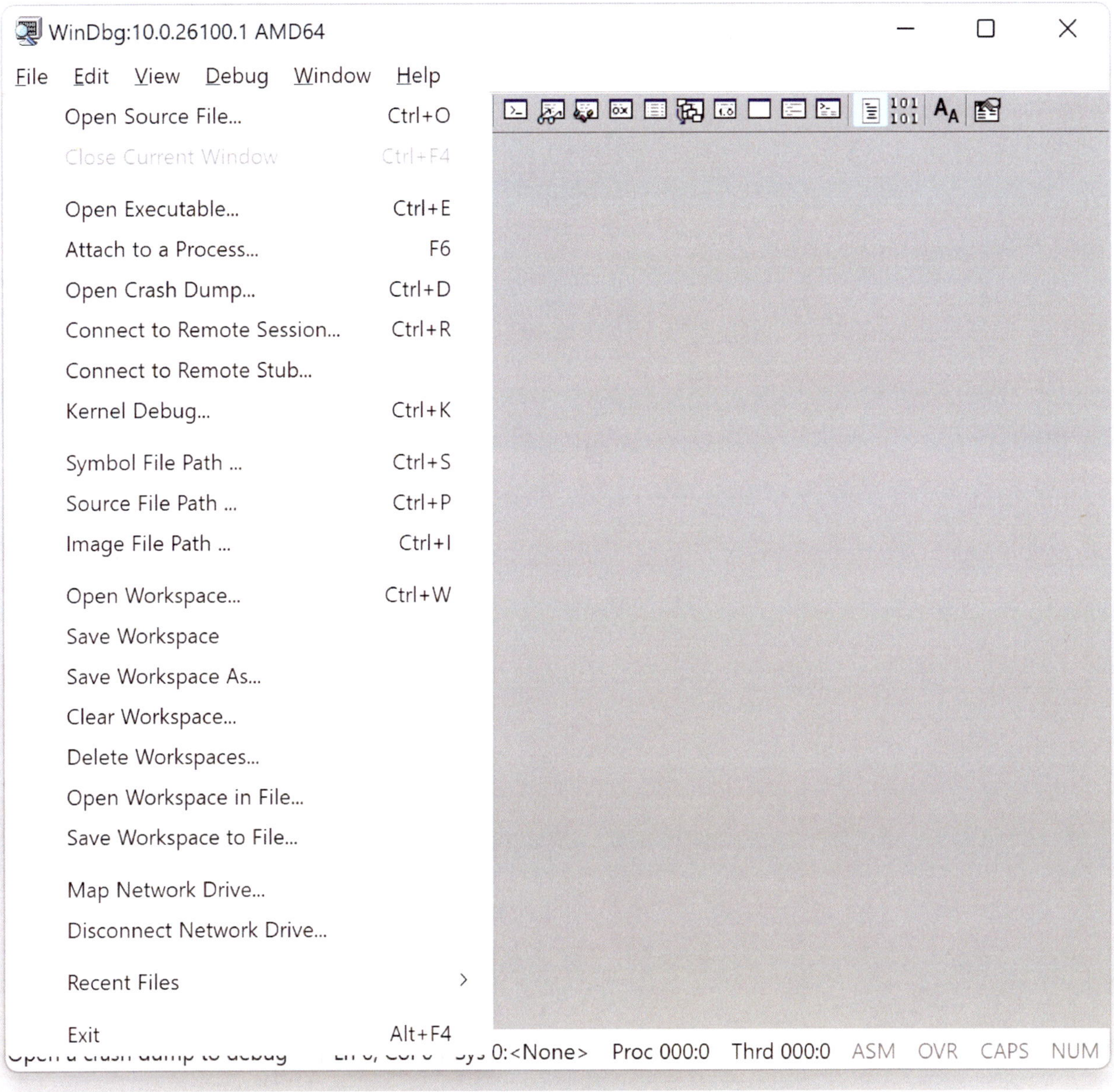

10. We get the dump file loaded:

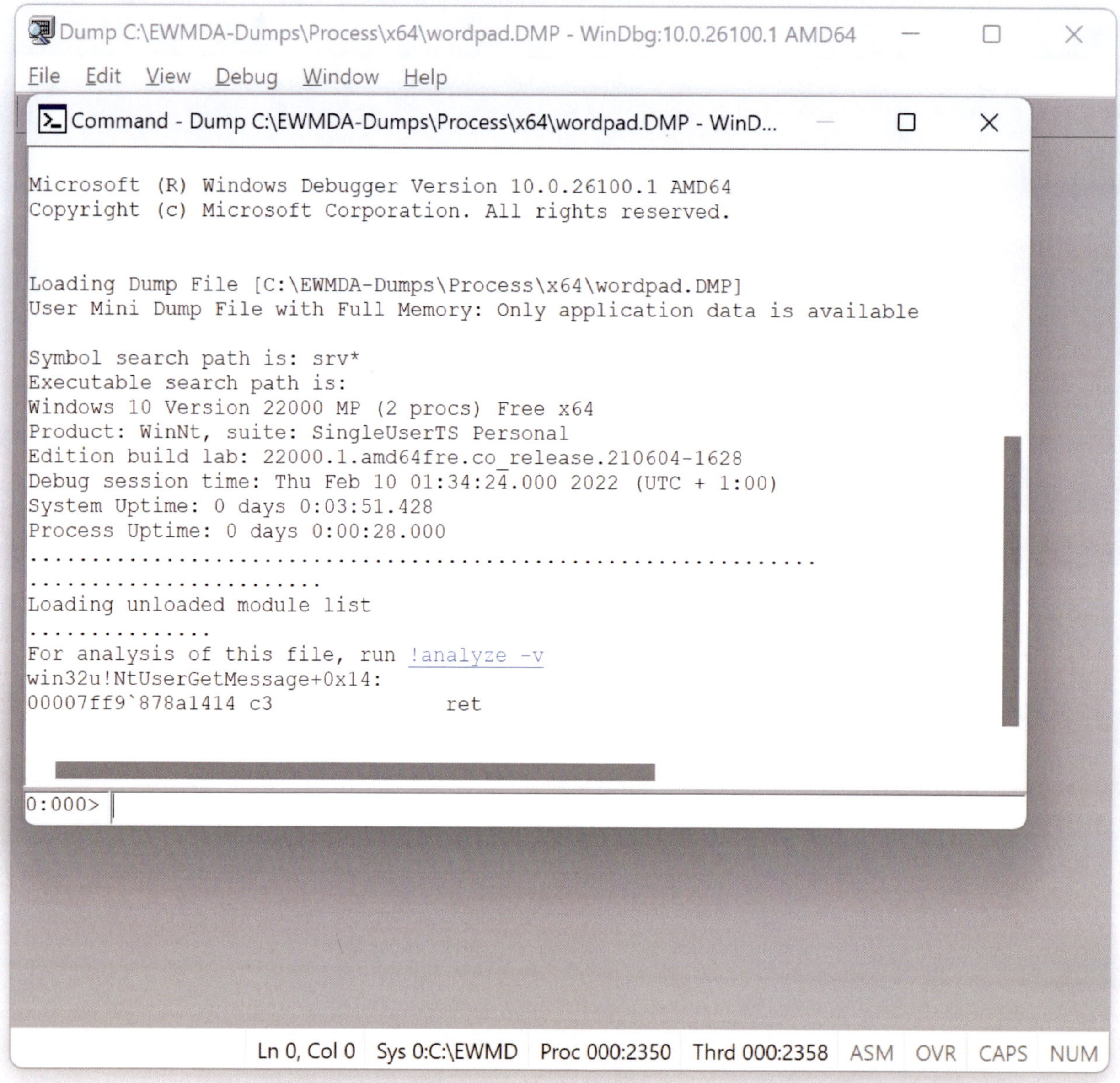
Dump C:\EWMDA-Dumps\Process\x64\wordpad.DMP - WinDbg:10.0.26100.1 AMD64
File Edit View Debug Window Help
Command - Dump C:\EWMDA-Dumps\Process\x64\wordpad.DMP - WinD...
Microsoft (R) Windows Debugger Version 10.0.26100.1 AMD64
Copyright (c) Microsoft Corporation. All rights reserved.
Loading Dump File [C:\EWMDA-Dumps\Process\x64\wordpad.DMP]
User Mini Dump File with Full Memory: Only application data is available
Symbol search path is: srv*
Executable search path is:
Windows 10 Version 22000 MP (2 procs) Free x64
Product: WinNt, suite: SingleUserTS Personal
Edition build lab: 22000.1.amd64fre.co_release.210604-1628
Debug session time: Thu Feb 10 01:34:24.000 2022 (UTC + 1:00)
System Uptime: 0 days 0:03:51.428
Process Uptime: 0 days 0:00:28.000
Loading unloaded module list
For analysis of this file, run !analyze -v
win32u!NtUserGetMessage+0x14:
00007ff9`878a1414 c3 ret
0:000>
Ln 0, Col 0
Sys 0:C:\EWMD
Proc 000:2350
Thrd 000:2358
ASM
OVR
CAPS
NUM

11. Type the **k** command to verify the correctness of the stack trace:

```
Command - Dump C:\EWMDA-Dumps\Process\x64\wordpad.DMP - WinDbg:10.0.26100.1 AMD64

Microsoft (R) Windows Debugger Version 10.0.26100.1 AMD64
Copyright (c) Microsoft Corporation. All rights reserved.


Loading Dump File [C:\EWMDA-Dumps\Process\x64\wordpad.DMP]
User Mini Dump File with Full Memory: Only application data is available

Symbol search path is: srv*
Executable search path is:
Windows 10 Version 22000 MP (2 procs) Free x64
Product: WinNt, suite: SingleUserTS Personal
Edition build lab: 22000.1.amd64fre.co_release.210604-1628
Debug session time: Thu Feb 10 01:34:24.000 2022 (UTC + 1:00)
System Uptime: 0 days 0:03:51.428
Process Uptime: 0 days 0:00:28.000
................................................................
........................
Loading unloaded module list
...............
For analysis of this file, run !analyze -v
win32u!NtUserGetMessage+0x14:
00007ff9`878a1414 c3              ret

0:000> k
```

```
Command - Dump C:\EWMDA-Dumps\Process\x64\wordpad.DMP - WinDbg:10.0.26100.1 AMD64
Executable search path is:
Windows 10 Version 22000 MP (2 procs) Free x64
Product: WinNt, suite: SingleUserTS Personal
Edition build lab: 22000.1.amd64fre.co_release.210604-1628
Debug session time: Thu Feb 10 01:34:24.000 2022 (UTC + 1:00)
System Uptime: 0 days 0:03:51.428
Process Uptime: 0 days 0:00:28.000
................................................................
........................
Loading unloaded module list
...............
For analysis of this file, run !analyze -v
win32u!NtUserGetMessage+0x14:
00007ff9`878a1414 c3              ret
0:000> k
 # Child-SP          RetAddr               Call Site
00 000000a5`cd5bf578 00007ff9`8997464e     win32u!NtUserGetMessage+0x14
01 000000a5`cd5bf580 00007ff9`4e800813     user32!GetMessageW+0x2e
02 000000a5`cd5bf5e0 00007ff9`4e800736     mfc42u!CWinThread::PumpMessage+0x23
03 000000a5`cd5bf610 00007ff9`4e7ff2bc     mfc42u!CWinThread::Run+0x96
04 000000a5`cd5bf650 00007ff7`c3fbbcfd     mfc42u!AfxWinMain+0xbc
05 000000a5`cd5bf690 00007ff9`883454e0     wordpad!__wmainCRTStartup+0x1dd
06 000000a5`cd5bf750 00007ff9`89da485b     kernel32!BaseThreadInitThunk+0x10
07 000000a5`cd5bf780 00000000`00000000     ntdll!RtlUserThreadStart+0x2b

0:000>
```

12. [Optional] Another approach is to use a Docker container image that contains preinstalled WinDbg x64 with symbol files for this course's memory dump files:

```
C:\EWMDA-Dumps>docker pull patterndiagnostics/windbg:10.0.26100.1-ewmda

C:\EWMDA-Dumps>docker run -it -v C:\EWMDA-Dumps:C:\EWMDA-Dumps
patterndiagnostics/windbg:10.0.26100.1-ewmda

Microsoft Windows [Version 10.0.20348.2655]
(c) Microsoft Corporation. All rights reserved.

C:\WinDbg>windbg C:\EWMDA-Dumps\Process\x64\wordpad.DMP

************* Preparing the environment for Debugger Extensions Gallery repositories
**************
   ExtensionRepository : Implicit
   UseExperimentalFeatureForNugetShare : true
   AllowNugetExeUpdate : true
   NonInteractiveNuget : true
   AllowNugetMSCredentialProviderInstall : true
   AllowParallelInitializationOfLocalRepositories : true

   EnableRedirectToV8JsProvider : false

   -- Configuring repositories
      ----> Repository : LocalInstalled, Enabled: true
      ----> Repository : UserExtensions, Enabled: true

>>>>>>>>>>>>> Preparing the environment for Debugger Extensions Gallery repositories completed,
duration 0.000 seconds

************* Waiting for Debugger Extensions Gallery to Initialize **************

>>>>>>>>>>>>> Waiting for Debugger Extensions Gallery to Initialize completed, duration 0.094
seconds
   ----> Repository : UserExtensions, Enabled: true, Packages count: 0
   ----> Repository : LocalInstalled, Enabled: true, Packages count: 29

Microsoft (R) Windows Debugger Version 10.0.26100.1 AMD64
Copyright (c) Microsoft Corporation. All rights reserved.

Loading Dump File [C:\EWMDA-Dumps\Process\x64\wordpad.DMP]
User Mini Dump File with Full Memory: Only application data is available


************* Path validation summary **************
Response                         Time (ms)     Location
OK                                             C:\WinDbg\mss
Symbol search path is: C:\WinDbg\mss
Executable search path is:
Windows 10 Version 22000 MP (2 procs) Free x64
Product: WinNt, suite: SingleUserTS Personal
Edition build lab: 22000.1.amd64fre.co_release.210604-1628
Debug session time: Thu Feb 10 01:34:24.000 2022 (UTC + 1:00)
System Uptime: 0 days 0:03:51.428
Process Uptime: 0 days 0:00:28.000
................................................................
.......................
```

```
Loading unloaded module list
...............
For analysis of this file, run !analyze -v
win32u!NtUserGetMessage+0x14:
00007ff9`878a1414 c3              ret
0:000>

0:000> k
Child-SP          RetAddr           Call Site
000000a5`cd5bf578 00007ff9`8997464e win32u!NtUserGetMessage+0x14
000000a5`cd5bf580 00007ff9`4e800813 user32!GetMessageW+0x2e
000000a5`cd5bf5e0 00007ff9`4e800736 mfc42u!CWinThread::PumpMessage+0x23
000000a5`cd5bf610 00007ff9`4e7ff2bc mfc42u!CWinThread::Run+0x96
000000a5`cd5bf650 00007ff7`c3fbbcfd mfc42u!AfxWinMain+0xbc
000000a5`cd5bf690 00007ff9`883454e0 wordpad!__wmainCRTStartup+0x1dd
000000a5`cd5bf750 00007ff9`89da485b kernel32!BaseThreadInitThunk+0x10
000000a5`cd5bf780 00000000`00000000 ntdll!RtlUserThreadStart+0x2b

0:000> q
quit:
NatVis script unloaded from 'C:\Program Files\Windows
Kits\10\Debuggers\x64\Visualizers\atlmfc.natvis'
NatVis script unloaded from 'C:\Program Files\Windows
Kits\10\Debuggers\x64\Visualizers\ObjectiveC.natvis'
NatVis script unloaded from 'C:\Program Files\Windows
Kits\10\Debuggers\x64\Visualizers\concurrency.natvis'
NatVis script unloaded from 'C:\Program Files\Windows
Kits\10\Debuggers\x64\Visualizers\cpp_rest.natvis'
NatVis script unloaded from 'C:\Program Files\Windows
Kits\10\Debuggers\x64\Visualizers\stl.natvis'
NatVis script unloaded from 'C:\Program Files\Windows
Kits\10\Debuggers\x64\Visualizers\Windows.Data.Json.natvis'
NatVis script unloaded from 'C:\Program Files\Windows
Kits\10\Debuggers\x64\Visualizers\Windows.Devices.Geolocation.natvis'
NatVis script unloaded from 'C:\Program Files\Windows
Kits\10\Debuggers\x64\Visualizers\Windows.Devices.Sensors.natvis'
NatVis script unloaded from 'C:\Program Files\Windows
Kits\10\Debuggers\x64\Visualizers\Windows.Media.natvis'
NatVis script unloaded from 'C:\Program Files\Windows
Kits\10\Debuggers\x64\Visualizers\windows.natvis'
NatVis script unloaded from 'C:\Program Files\Windows
Kits\10\Debuggers\x64\Visualizers\winrt.natvis'

C:\WinDbg>exit

C:\EWMDA-Dumps>
```

If you find any symbol problems, please use the Contact form on www.patterndiagnostics.com to report them.

We recommend exiting WinDbg after each exercise.

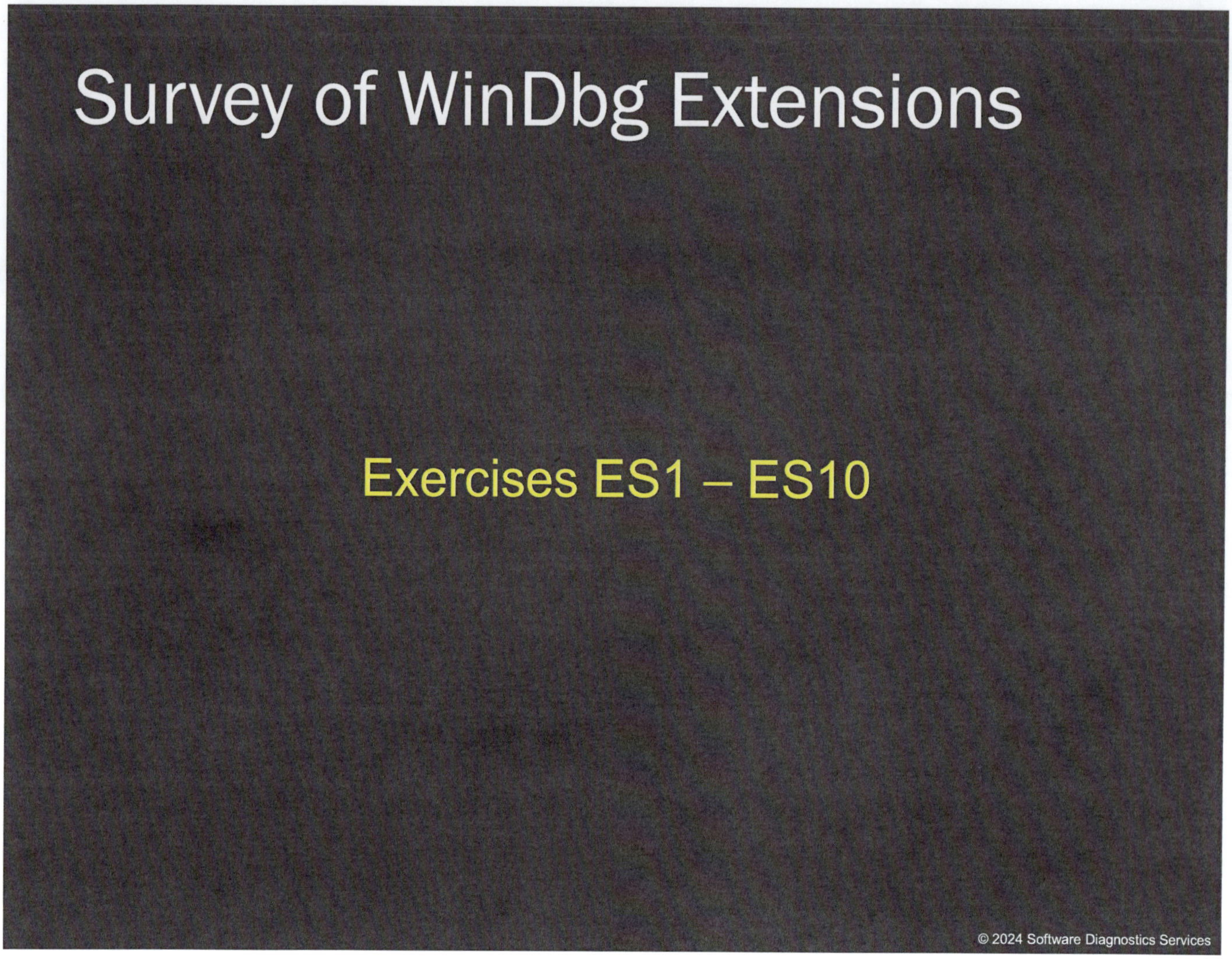
Survey of WinDbg Extensions
Exercises ES1 – ES10
© 2024 Software Diagnostics Services

For this part, I created ten hands-on exercises. We use complete memory dumps for all exercises except ES10.

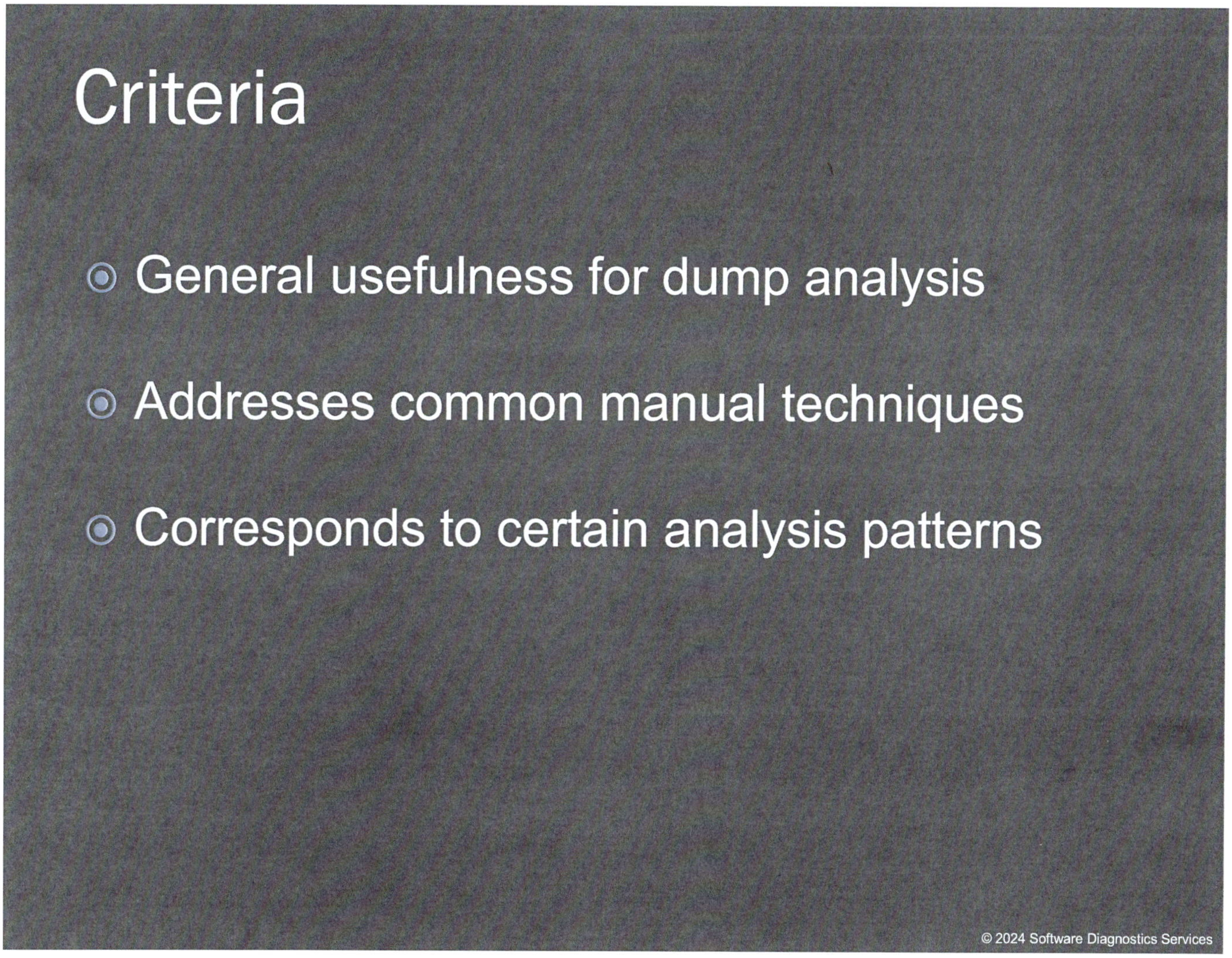
Criteria
General usefulness for dump analysis
Addresses common manual techniques
Corresponds to certain analysis patterns
© 2024 Software Diagnostics Services

Instead of covering all extensions, I selected a few based on some criteria. And, for selected extensions, I covered only selected extension commands based on some criteria again. First, an extension needs to be useful for memory dump analysis. So, I skipped some that are geared toward live debugging. Also, an extension must address common manual techniques or drawbacks of classical commands. Finally, an extension command needs to correspond to existing memory analysis patterns, although, in some cases, an extension command may create a new analysis pattern name or provide a pattern variant of an existing analysis pattern.

Exercise ES1

- **Goal:** Explore Patterns WinDbg extension
- \EWMDA\Exercise-ES1.pdf

Patterns
https://www.patterndiagnostics.com/patterns-extension

Exercise ES1: Explore Patterns WinDbg Extension

Goal: Explore the patterns[4] WinDbg extension

1. Launch WinDbg.

2. Open \EWMDA-Dumps\Complete\x64\MEMORY-W11.DMP.

3. We get the dump file loaded:

```
Microsoft (R) Windows Debugger Version 10.0.27668.1000 AMD64
Copyright (c) Microsoft Corporation. All rights reserved.


Loading Dump File [C:\EWMDA-Dumps\Complete\x64\MEMORY-W11.DMP]
Kernel Bitmap Dump File: Full address space is available


************* Path validation summary **************
Response                         Time (ms)     Location
Deferred                                       srv*
Symbol search path is: srv*
Executable search path is:
Windows 10 Kernel Version 22000 MP (2 procs) Free x64
Product: WinNt, suite: TerminalServer SingleUserTS Personal
Edition build lab: 22000.1.amd64fre.co_release.210604-1628
Kernel base = 0xfffff806`61e00000 PsLoadedModuleList = 0xfffff806`62a296b0
Debug session time: Sat Nov 13 23:17:16.607 2021 (UTC + 1:00)
System Uptime: 0 days 0:03:06.813
Loading Kernel Symbols
..............................................................
...............................................................
...............................................................
..
Loading User Symbols
..................................
Loading unloaded module list
........
For analysis of this file, run !analyze -v
nt!KeBugCheckEx:
fffff806`62215590 mov     qword ptr [rsp+8],rcx ss:0018:ffffbe82`96f64670=000000000000000a
```

4. We load the x64 version of the *patterns* extension:

```
0: kd> .load C:\EWMDA-Dumps\patterns\x64\patterns
```

[4] The latest version can be downloaded from: https://www.patterndiagnostics.com/patterns-extension.

5. We can also check if it was loaded successfully:

```
0: kd> .chain
Extension DLL search Path:
[...]
Extension DLL chain:
    C:\EWMDA-Dumps\patterns\x64\patterns: image 2.1.0.0, API 0.1.0, built Sun Sep  8 12:42:15 2024
        [path: C:\EWMDA-Dumps\patterns\x64\patterns.dll]
    DbgEngCoreDMExt: image 10.0.27668.1000, API 0.0.0,
        [path: C:\Program Files\WindowsApps\Microsoft.WinDbg_1.2407.24003.0_x64__8wekyb3d8bbwe\amd64\winext\DbgEngCoreDMExt.dll]
    wdfkd: image 10.0.27668.1000, API 1.0.0,
        [path: C:\Program Files\WindowsApps\Microsoft.WinDbg_1.2407.24003.0_x64__8wekyb3d8bbwe\amd64\winext\wdfkd.dll]
    MachOBinComposition: image 10.0.27668.1000, API 0.0.0,
        [path: C:\Program Files\WindowsApps\Microsoft.WinDbg_1.2407.24003.0_x64__8wekyb3d8bbwe\amd64\winext\MachOBinComposition.dll]
    ELFBinComposition: image 10.0.27668.1000, API 0.0.0,
        [path: C:\Program Files\WindowsApps\Microsoft.WinDbg_1.2407.24003.0_x64__8wekyb3d8bbwe\amd64\winext\ELFBinComposition.dll]
    dbghelp: image 10.0.27668.1000, API 10.0.6,
        [path: C:\Program Files\WindowsApps\Microsoft.WinDbg_1.2407.24003.0_x64__8wekyb3d8bbwe\amd64\dbghelp.dll]
    exts: image 10.0.27668.1000, API 1.0.0,
        [path: C:\Program Files\WindowsApps\Microsoft.WinDbg_1.2407.24003.0_x64__8wekyb3d8bbwe\amd64\WINXP\exts.dll]
    kext: image 10.0.27668.1000, API 1.0.0,
        [path: C:\Program Files\WindowsApps\Microsoft.WinDbg_1.2407.24003.0_x64__8wekyb3d8bbwe\amd64\winext\kext.dll]
    kdexts: image 10.0.27668.1000, API 1.0.0,
        [path: C:\Program Files\WindowsApps\Microsoft.WinDbg_1.2407.24003.0_x64__8wekyb3d8bbwe\amd64\winxp\kdexts.dll]
```

6. Since the extension is on top, we can use **!help** instead of **!patterns.help**:

```
0: kd> !help
Patterns Debugger Extension DLL (Version 2.1.0.0 [std]). Copyright © 2015-2024 Software Diagnostics
Services. All rights reserved.

Commands:
    lst               - Shows the current list of memory analysis pattern categories
    lst category      - Shows the current list of memory analysis patterns for the specified category
    sdl abbreviation  - Opens a pattern description from Software Diagnostics Library
    chk               - Shows the current memory analysis checklist categories
    chk category      - Shows the current memory analysis checklist for the specified category
    eula              - Shows license terms
```

7. The extension supports DML hyperlinks when possible (for example, in the GUI debugger version such as WinDbg, so the console-based Docker environment doesn't have it). **!chk** command outputs Memory Analysis Checklist[5] categories:

```
0: kd> !chk
The following memory analysis checklist categories are available:

General [G]
Application [A]
System [S]
BSOD [B]
.NET [.]
```

8. In the DML version, we can click on a category and also use the Back link, but for non-DML environments, we need to specify a category for the **!chk** command:

```
0: kd> !chk S
Memory Analysis Checklist for System Hang:

Default analysis (!analyze -v -hang)
ERESOURCE contention (!locks)
```

[5] https://www.dumpanalysis.org/windows-memory-analysis-checklist

```
Processes and virtual memory including session space (!vm 4)
Important services are present and not hanging (for example, terminal or IMA services for
Citrix environments)
Pools (!poolused)
Waiting threads (!stacks)
Critical system queues (!exqueue f)
I/O (!irpfind)
The list of all thread stack traces (!process 0 3f)
LPC/ALPC chain for suspected threads (!lpc message or !alpc /m after search for "Waiting for
reply to LPC" or "Waiting for reply to ALPC" in !process 0 3f output)
Mutants (search for "Mutants - owning thread" in !process 0 3f output)
Critical sections for suspected processes (!cs -l -o -s)
Sessions, session processes (!session, !sprocess)
Processes (size, handle table size) (!process 0 0)
Running threads (!running)
Ready threads (!ready)
DPC queues (!dpcs)
The list of APCs (!apc)
Internal queued spinlocks (!qlocks)
Computer name (dS srv!srvcomputername)
File cache, VACB (!filecache)
File objects for blocked thread IRPs (!irp -> !fileobj)
Network (!ndiskd.miniports and !ndiskd.pktpools)
Disk (!scsikd.classext -> !scsikd.classext class_device 2)
Modules rdbss, mrxdav, mup, mrxsmb in stack traces
Functions Ntfs!Ntfs* and nt!Fs* in stack traces

Back
```

Note: The extension uses the currently published checklist at the time of this writing. It may be amended in the future, so please download the most recent version of the extension for your practical analysis needs.

9. The **!lst** command lists analysis pattern categories, and we can navigate back and forth in the DML version. In the non-DML version, we need to specify the category as a parameter:

```
0: kd> !lst
Memory Analysis Pattern Categories:

Hooksware Patterns [H]
Wait Chain Patterns [W]
DLL Link Patterns [L]
Memory Consumption Patterns [M]
Dynamic Memory Corruption Patterns [C]
Deadlock and Livelock Patterns [D]
Contention Patterns [N]
Stack Overflow Patterns [O]
.NET / CLR / Managed Space Patterns [.]
Stack Trace Patterns [S]
Symbol Patterns [Y]
Exception Patterns [E]
Meta-Memory Dump Patterns [-]
Module Patterns [!]
Optimization Patterns [I]
Thread Patterns [T]
Process Patterns [P]
Executive Resource Patterns [X]
Falsity and Coincidence Patterns [F]
```

```
RPC, LPC and ALPC Patterns [R]
Hidden Artifact Patterns [A]
Pointer Patterns [*]
Frame Patterns [+]
CPU Consumption Patterns [^]
Region Patterns [#]
Malware Analysis Patterns [@]

0: kd> !lst S
Stack Trace Patterns:

Stack Trace [STTR]
Stack Trace Collection (unmanaged space) [STCU]
Special Stack Trace [SSTR]
Exception Stack Trace [ESTR]
Dual Stack Trace [DSTR]
Truncated Stack Trace [TSTR]
Managed Stack Trace [MSTR]
Incorrect Stack Trace [ISTR]
Stack Trace Set [STSE]
Stack Trace Collection (managed space) [STCM]
Stack Trace Collection (predicate) [STCP]
Empty Stack Trace [EMST]
Stack Trace Collection (I/O requests) [STCI]
Stack Trace Change [STCH]
First Fault Stack Trace [FFST]
Critical Stack Trace [CSTR]
RIP Stack Trace [RSTR]
Glued Stack Trace [GSTR]
Rough Stack Trace (unmanaged space) [RSTU]
Past Stack Trace [PSTR]
Stack Trace (I/O request) [STIO]
Stack Trace (file system filters) [STFS]
Stack Trace (database) [STDB]
Variable Subtrace [VASU]
Technology-Specific Subtrace (COM interface invocation) [TSCI]
Technology-Specific Subtrace (dynamic memory) [TSDM]
Technology-Specific Subtrace (JIT .NET code) [TSJN]
Technology-Specific Subtrace (COM client call) [TSCC]
Internal Stack Trace [INST]
Stack Trace Collection (CPUs) [STCC]
Stack Trace Surface [STSU]
Hidden Stack Trace [HSTR]
Constant Subtrace [COSU]
Stack Trace Signature [STSI]
Quotient Stack Trace [QSTR]
Module Stack Trace [MOST]
Coincidental Frames [COFR]
Least Common Frame [LCFR]
Foreign Module Frame [FMFR]
Unified Stack Trace [USTR]
Aggregated Frames [AGFR]
Stack Trace (I/O devices) [SIOD]
Stack Trace Motif [STMO]
Stack Trace Race [STRA]
Source Stack Trace [SRCS]
Hidden Stack [HIST]
Interrupt Stack [INTS]
Frame Trace [FRTR]
```

```
False Frame [FAFR]
Procedure Call Chain [PCCH]
Rough Stack Trace (managed space) [RSTM]
Rough Stack Trace Collection (unmanaged space) [RSCU]
Caller-n-Callee [CNCA]
Shadow Stack Trace [SHST]
Foreign Stack [FSTA]
Annotated Stack Trace [ANST]

Back
```

10. If we click on an individual analysis pattern in the DML-based version, the default web browser should open the appropriate link from the Software Diagnostics Library[6] (which requires prior login). In the non-DML version, we need to use the **!sdl** command with the corresponding four-letter pattern tag:

```
0: kd> !sdl RSCU
```

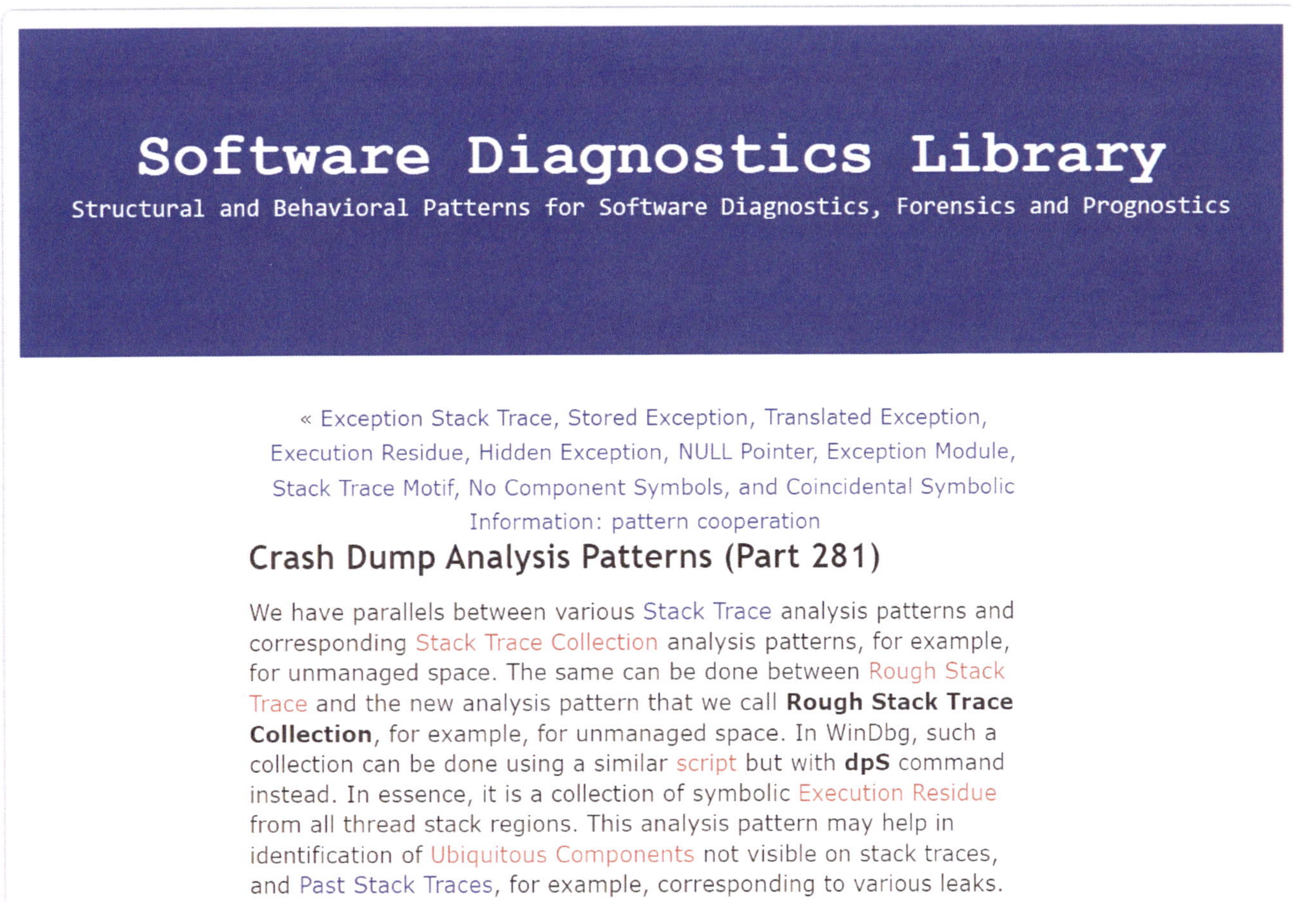

Software Diagnostics Library

Structural and Behavioral Patterns for Software Diagnostics, Forensics and Prognostics

« Exception Stack Trace, Stored Exception, Translated Exception, Execution Residue, Hidden Exception, NULL Pointer, Exception Module, Stack Trace Motif, No Component Symbols, and Coincidental Symbolic Information: pattern cooperation

Crash Dump Analysis Patterns (Part 281)

We have parallels between various Stack Trace analysis patterns and corresponding Stack Trace Collection analysis patterns, for example, for unmanaged space. The same can be done between Rough Stack Trace and the new analysis pattern that we call **Rough Stack Trace Collection**, for example, for unmanaged space. In WinDbg, such a collection can be done using a similar script but with **dpS** command instead. In essence, it is a collection of symbolic Execution Residue from all thread stack regions. This analysis pattern may help in identification of Ubiquitous Components not visible on stack traces, and Past Stack Traces, for example, corresponding to various leaks.

11. We can unload the extension anytime if we no longer need it:

```
0: kd> .unload C:\EWMDA-Dumps\patterns\x64\patterns
```

Note: We recommend exiting WinDbg after each exercise to avoid possible confusion and glitches.

[6] https://www.dumpanalysis.org/blog

Exercise ES2

- **Goal:** Explore MEX WinDbg extension
- **Memory Analysis Patterns:** Zombie Processes; Instrumentation Information; Blocked Thread (Software); Active Thread; Suspended Thread; Wait Chain (ALPC); Input Thread; Exception Stack Trace; Stack Trace Collection (Predicate); Stack Trace Collection (CPUs); Spiking Thread; Execution Residue (Unmanaged Space)
- \EWMDA\Exercise-ES2.pdf

MEX

https://www.microsoft.com/en-us/download/details.aspx?id=53304

Exercise ES2: Explore MEX WinDbg Extension

Goal: Explore the MEX[7] WinDbg extension.

Memory Analysis Patterns: Zombie Processes; Instrumentation Information; Blocked Thread (Software); Active Thread; Suspended Thread; Wait Chain (ALPC); Input Thread; Exception Stack Trace; Stack Trace Collection (Predicate); Stack Trace Collection (CPUs); Spiking Thread; Execution Residue (Unmanaged Space).

1. Launch WinDbg.

2. Open \EWMDA-Dumps\Complete\x64\MEMORY-W11.DMP.

3. We get the dump file loaded:

```
Microsoft (R) Windows Debugger Version 10.0.27668.1000 AMD64
Copyright (c) Microsoft Corporation. All rights reserved.


Loading Dump File [C:\EWMDA-Dumps\Complete\x64\MEMORY-W11.DMP]
Kernel Bitmap Dump File: Full address space is available


************* Path validation summary **************
Response                         Time (ms)     Location
Deferred                                       srv*
Symbol search path is: srv*
Executable search path is:
Windows 10 Kernel Version 22000 MP (2 procs) Free x64
Product: WinNt, suite: TerminalServer SingleUserTS Personal
Edition build lab: 22000.1.amd64fre.co_release.210604-1628
Kernel base = 0xfffff806`61e00000 PsLoadedModuleList = 0xfffff806`62a296b0
Debug session time: Sat Nov 13 23:17:16.607 2021 (UTC + 1:00)
System Uptime: 0 days 0:03:06.813
Loading Kernel Symbols
...............................................................
................................................................
................................................................
..
Loading User Symbols
..................................
Loading unloaded module list
........
For analysis of this file, run !analyze -v
nt!KeBugCheckEx:
fffff806`62215590 mov     qword ptr [rsp+8],rcx ss:0018:ffffbe82`96f64670=000000000000000a
```

4. We open a log file:

```
0: kd> .logopen C:\EWMDA-Dumps\Complete\x64\ES2.log
Opened log file 'C:\EWMDA-Dumps\Complete\x64\ES2.log'
```

[7] https://www.microsoft.com/en-us/download/details.aspx?id=53304

5. To use Microsoft MEX Debugging Extension, you can either download it from Microsoft (if you haven't done it previously) or use the already supplied module in the dump archive. For the former, after downloading, extracting, and unzipping, we copy \x64*mex.dll* to some location, for example, to the WinDbg installation folder (for example, *C:\Program Files (x86)\Windows Kits\10\Debuggers\x64*) or some other location if you use WinDbg app). In this exercise transcript, we use the latter approach.

```
0: kd> .load C:\EWMDA-Dumps\Mex\x64\mex
Mex External 3.0.0.7172 Loaded!
```

```
0: kd> !mex.help
Mex currently has 255 extensions available.  Please specify a keyword to search.
Or browse by category:

All PowerShell[6] SystemCenter[3] Networking[12] Process[5] Mex[2] Kernel[27] DotNet[32] Decompile[15] Utility[40] Thread[27] Binaries[6] General[22]
```

```
0: kd> !mex.help -all
[...]
```

6. We can use some commands as a replacement to broken or less detailed classic WinDbg commands, for example **!sprocess**:

```
0: kd> !sprocess 1 3f
Dumping Session 1
```

We can see the list of session 1 processes and also their bitness by using the MEX extension **tasklist** command:

```
0: kd> !mex.tasklist -s 1
PID             Address          Name                           Ses
=============   ================ ============================== ===
0x250  0n592    ffffc38c30880140 csrss.exe                        1
0x2b8  0n696    ffffc38c3041e080 winlogon.exe                     1
0x348  0n840    ffffc38c304a61c0 fontdrvhost.exe                  1
0x288  0n648    ffffc38c30331080 dwm.exe                          1
0x1214 0n4628   ffffc38c32414080 sihost.exe                       1
0x1228 0n4648   ffffc38c32413080 svchost.exe(CDPUserSvc)          1
0x1268 0n4712   ffffc38c32455080 svchost.exe(WpnUserService)      1
0x12d8 0n4824   ffffc38c324a4080 taskhostw.exe                    1
0xfcc  0n4044   ffffc38c326e2080 explorer.exe                     1
0x1514 0n5396   ffffc38c32691080 svchost.exe(cbdhsvc)             1
0x14d0 0n5328   ffffc38c32b62080 StartMenuExperienceHost.exe      1
0x153c 0n5436   ffffc38c32b5c080 SearchHost.exe                   1
0x13a8 0n5032   ffffc38c32c98080 RuntimeBroker.exe                1
0x1638 0n5688   ffffc38c32c6d080 svchost.exe(UdkUserSvc)          1
0x11d0 0n4560   ffffc38c32d28080 RuntimeBroker.exe                1
0x1868 0n6248   ffffc38c32e14080 dllhost.exe                      1
0x1b14 0n6932   ffffc38c33040080 YourPhone.exe                    1
0x1a14 0n6676   ffffc38c33228080 ctfmon.exe                       1
0x1a2c 0n6700   ffffc38c33231080 TabTip.exe                       1
0x1cf8 0n7416   ffffc38c332ce080 MiniSearchHost.exe               1
0x1df4 0n7668   ffffc38c333be080 TextInputHost.exe                1
0x1ea0 0n7840   ffffc38c323af080 smartscreen.exe                  1
0x1f4c 0n8012   ffffc38c335340c0 SecurityHealthSystray.exe        1
0x1f9c 0n8092   ffffc38c3353f0c0 vmtoolsd.exe                     1
0x1fcc 0n8140   ffffc38c33541080 vm3dservice.exe                  1
0x1fe0 0n8160   ffffc38c32e6e080 OneDrive.exe                     1
0x1e74 0n7796   ffffc38c336ee080 Cortana.exe                      1
```

```
0x1f2c 0n7980 ffffc38c3374a080 RuntimeBroker.exe                1
0x4cc  0n1228 ffffc38c33622080 svchost.exe(NPSMSvc)             1
0x6e0  0n1760 ffffc38c3329b080 svchost.exe(AarSvc)              1
0x2088 0n8328 ffffc38c32e6f080 svchost.exe(UnistackSvcGroup)    1
0x2258 0n8792 ffffc38c324020c0 RuntimeBroker.exe                1
0x1284 0n4740 ffffc38c334020c0 AppA.exe*32                      1
0x1224 0n4644 ffffc38c3010b0c0 conhost.exe                      1
0x9d4  0n2516 ffffc38c2e16b080 notmyfault64.exe                 1
============= ================ ============================== ===
PID           Address          Name                           Ses

Warning! Zombie process(es) detected (not displayed). Count: 7 [zombie report]
```

Note: For the complete list or **tasklist** command options, please use the **-?** parameter.

We can list zombie processes or get a shorter report about them using these commands:

```
0: kd> !mex.tasklist -z
PID           Address          Name                 Ses Thd Obj Handles Obj Pointers
============= ================ ==================== === === =========== ============
0x12bc 0n4796 ffffc38c324a2080 taskhostw.exe          1   0           0            1
0x13ac 0n5036 ffffc38c326dd080 userinit.exe           1   0           1            1
0x12b0 0n4784 ffffc38c34d020c0 MoNotificationUx.exe   1   0           1        32765
0x2110 0n8464 ffffc38c32dd8080 MoNotificationUx.exe   1   0           1        32765
0x14e0 0n5344 ffffc38c336ce080 MoNotificationUx.exe   1   0           1        32765
0x219c 0n8604 ffffc38c2e168080 MoNotificationUx.exe   1   0           1        32765
0x540  0n1344 ffffc38c32249080 TabTip.exe             1   0           1        32763
============= ================ ==================== === === =========== ============
PID           Address          Name                 Ses Thd Obj Handles Obj Pointers

0: kd> !mex.tasklist -z -r
Count Name                 Ses Thd Obj Handles Obj Pointers
===== ==================== === === =========== ============
    1 TabTip.exe             1   0           1        32763
    1 taskhostw.exe          1   0           0            1
    1 userinit.exe           1   0           1            1
    4 MoNotificationUx.exe   1   0           1        32765
===== ==================== === === =========== ============
Count Name                 Ses Thd Obj Handles Obj Pointers
    7
```

Sometimes, we are interested in *svchost.exe* to service name translation:

```
0: kd> !mex.tasklist -svc
PID           Address          Name
============= ================ ========================================
0x0    0n0    fffff80662b32b00 Idle
0x4    0n4    ffffc38c2c4ed040 System
0x64   0n100  ffffc38c2c515080 Registry
0x178  0n376  ffffc38c2ea83040 smss.exe
0x200  0n512  ffffc38c2e75e140 csrss.exe
0x248  0n584  ffffc38c3087b080 wininit.exe
0x250  0n592  ffffc38c30880140 csrss.exe
0x290  0n656  ffffc38c308a3100 services.exe
0x298  0n664  ffffc38c3040d0c0 lsass.exe
0x2b8  0n696  ffffc38c3041e080 winlogon.exe
0x340  0n832  ffffc38c304a41c0 fontdrvhost.exe
```

```
0x348  0n840  ffffc38c304a61c0 fontdrvhost.exe
0x350  0n848  ffffc38c304a9080 svchost.exe(-p)
0x3b0  0n944  ffffc38c30522080 WUDFHost.exe
0x3cc  0n972  ffffc38c30570080 svchost.exe(-p)
0x1c8  0n456  ffffc38c305e8080 svchost.exe(LSM)
0x288  0n648  ffffc38c30331080 dwm.exe
0x450  0n1104 ffffc38c3039b080 svchost.exe(gpsvc)
0x458  0n1112 ffffc38c303a0080 svchost.exe(-p)
0x468  0n1128 ffffc38c30399080 svchost.exe(lmhosts)
0x470  0n1136 ffffc38c303c2080 svchost.exe(BTAGService)
0x498  0n1176 ffffc38c303e00c0 svchost.exe(BthAvctpSvc)
0x4b4  0n1204 ffffc38c30909080 svchost.exe(bthserv)
0x4ec  0n1260 ffffc38c3091f080 svchost.exe(NcbService)
0x4f8  0n1272 ffffc38c30922080 svchost.exe(TimeBrokerSvc)
0x59c  0n1436 ffffc38c316020c0 svchost.exe(Schedule)
0x5bc  0n1468 ffffc38c31616080 svchost.exe(DispBrokerDesktopSvc)
0x5dc  0n1500 ffffc38c3161c080 svchost.exe(ProfSvc)
0x614  0n1556 ffffc38c3166a080 svchost.exe(DisplayEnhancementService)
0x63c  0n1596 ffffc38c31691080 svchost.exe(nsi)
0x648  0n1608 ffffc38c316240c0 svchost.exe(UserManager)
0x670  0n1648 ffffc38c316a40c0 svchost.exe(DeviceAssociationService)
0x69c  0n1692 ffffc38c2c509080 svchost.exe(netprofm)
0x6cc  0n1740 ffffc38c2c5db080 svchost.exe(SensorService)
0x708  0n1800 ffffc38c2c5c8080 svchost.exe(SensrSvc)
0x758  0n1880 ffffc38c317880c0 svchost.exe(TabletInputService)
0x780  0n1920 ffffc38c2c562080 svchost.exe(FontCache)
0x7b0  0n1968 ffffc38c2c553080 svchost.exe(camsvc)
0x81c  0n2076 ffffc38c2c51a080 svchost.exe(-p)
0x840  0n2112 ffffc38c2c518080 svchost.exe(EventLog)
0x8a8  0n2216 ffffc38c3188d080 svchost.exe(EventSystem)
0x8b0  0n2224 ffffc38c318900c0 svchost.exe(SysMain)
0x8c0  0n2240 ffffc38c318a7080 svchost.exe(Themes)
0x8f8  0n2296 ffffc38c318aa040 MemCompression
0x948  0n2376 ffffc38c319660c0 svchost.exe(Dhcp)
0x958  0n2392 ffffc38c31969080 svchost.exe(SENS)
0x97c  0n2428 ffffc38c31906080 svchost.exe(AudioEndpointBuilder)
0x9cc  0n2508 ffffc38c30557080 svchost.exe(WinHttpAutoProxySvc)
0xa18  0n2584 ffffc38c319c0080 svchost.exe(-p)
0xa50  0n2640 ffffc38c31a0f080 svchost.exe(-p)
0xa60  0n2656 ffffc38c31a31080 svchost.exe(-p)
0xa84  0n2692 ffffc38c31a460c0 svchost.exe(ShellHWDetection)
0xacc  0n2764 ffffc38c31ae00c0 svchost.exe(StateRepository)
0xaf8  0n2808 ffffc38c31aed0c0 audiodg.exe
0xb14  0n2836 ffffc38c31aea080 spoolsv.exe
0xb44  0n2884 ffffc38c31b31080 svchost.exe(-p)
0xb8c  0n2956 ffffc38c31b43080 svchost.exe(LanmanWorkstation)
0x9f0  0n2544 ffffc38c31bd1080 svchost.exe(-p)
0xa34  0n2612 ffffc38c31bd0080 svchost.exe(-p)
0xb58  0n2904 ffffc38c31bd7080 svchost.exe(DPS)
0xc1c  0n3100 ffffc38c31bc2080 svchost.exe(iphlpsvc)
0xc4c  0n3148 ffffc38c31cb9080 svchost.exe(SstpSvc)
0xc68  0n3176 ffffc38c31ce60c0 svchost.exe(LanmanServer)
0xc78  0n3192 ffffc38c31cf5080 svchost.exe(TrkWks)
0xc80  0n3200 ffffc38c31cb6080 VGAuthService.exe
0xc8c  0n3212 ffffc38c31d61080 vmtoolsd.exe
0xc98  0n3224 ffffc38c31d62080 MsMpEng.exe
0xca4  0n3236 ffffc38c31d64080 svchost.exe(Winmgmt)
0xcb4  0n3252 ffffc38c31d77080 svchost.exe(WpnService)
0xe18  0n3608 ffffc38c31f350c0 svchost.exe(netsvcs)
```

```
0xe34  0n3636 ffffc38c31f29080 dllhost.exe
0xe88  0n3720 ffffc38c31f4f080 svchost.exe(RmSvc)
0xf94  0n3988 ffffc38c320e60c0 dllhost.exe
0xcf4  0n3316 ffffc38c321c0080 AggregatorHost.exe
0xc64  0n3172 ffffc38c322330c0 WmiPrvSE.exe
0x10a0 0n4256 ffffc38c323130c0 msdtc.exe
0x117c 0n4476 ffffc38c3238e080 svchost.exe(AppXSvc)
0x1214 0n4628 ffffc38c32414080 sihost.exe
0x1228 0n4648 ffffc38c32413080 svchost.exe(CDPUserSvc)
0x1268 0n4712 ffffc38c32455080 svchost.exe(WpnUserService)
0x12d8 0n4824 ffffc38c324a4080 taskhostw.exe
0x107c 0n4220 ffffc38c3260e080 svchost.exe(TokenBroker)
0xc2c  0n3116 ffffc38c3260b080 VSSVC.exe
0xfcc  0n4044 ffffc38c326e2080 explorer.exe
0x11b4 0n4532 ffffc38c326e5080 svchost.exe(CDPSvc)
0x1514 0n5396 ffffc38c32691080 svchost.exe(cbdhsvc)
0x1568 0n5480 ffffc38c327c9080 svchost.exe(Appinfo)
0x16c0 0n5824 ffffc38c327c6080 WmiPrvSE.exe
0x177c 0n6012 ffffc38c32995080 SearchIndexer.exe
0x1784 0n6020 ffffc38c32996080 svchost.exe(BITS)
0x17d0 0n6096 ffffc38c32adc080 svchost.exe(SSDPSRV)
0x14d0 0n5328 ffffc38c32b62080 StartMenuExperienceHost.exe
0x153c 0n5436 ffffc38c32b5c080 SearchHost.exe
0x13a8 0n5032 ffffc38c32c98080 RuntimeBroker.exe
0x1638 0n5688 ffffc38c32c6d080 svchost.exe(UdkUserSvc)
0x11d0 0n4560 ffffc38c32d28080 RuntimeBroker.exe
0x1868 0n6248 ffffc38c32e14080 dllhost.exe
0x19ac 0n6572 ffffc38c32397080 svchost.exe(LicenseManager)
0x1a70 0n6768 ffffc38c31ba80c0 svchost.exe(ClipSVC)
0x1b14 0n6932 ffffc38c33040080 YourPhone.exe
0x12e0 0n4832 ffffc38c331020c0 svchost.exe(wlidsvc)
0x1a14 0n6676 ffffc38c33228080 ctfmon.exe
0x1a2c 0n6700 ffffc38c33231080 TabTip.exe
0x1838 0n6200 ffffc38c32ee70c0 MsMpEngCP.exe
0x1c30 0n7216 ffffc38c33288080 svchost.exe(lfsvc)
0x1cf8 0n7416 ffffc38c332ce080 MiniSearchHost.exe
0x1d40 0n7488 ffffc38c332d20c0 NisSrv.exe
0x1db4 0n7604 ffffc38c332c7080 svchost.exe(WdiSystemHost)
0x1df4 0n7668 ffffc38c333be080 TextInputHost.exe
0x1e34 0n7732 ffffc38c334570c0 svchost.exe(PcaSvc)
0x1ea0 0n7840 ffffc38c323af080 smartscreen.exe
0x1f4c 0n8012 ffffc38c335340c0 SecurityHealthSystray.exe
0x1f58 0n8024 ffffc38c334e0080 SecurityHealthService.exe
0x1f9c 0n8092 ffffc38c3353f0c0 vmtoolsd.exe
0x1fcc 0n8140 ffffc38c33541080 vm3dservice.exe
0x1fe0 0n8160 ffffc38c32e6e080 OneDrive.exe
0x1e74 0n7796 ffffc38c336ee080 Cortana.exe
0x1f2c 0n7980 ffffc38c3374a080 RuntimeBroker.exe
0x4cc  0n1228 ffffc38c33622080 svchost.exe(NPSMSvc)
0x500  0n1280 ffffc38c336f8080 svchost.exe(wuauserv)
0x6e0  0n1760 ffffc38c3329b080 svchost.exe(AarSvc)
0xcd4  0n3284 ffffc38c332a0080 svchost.exe(DoSvc)
0xfb0  0n4016 ffffc38c306ab0c0 svchost.exe(StorSvc)
0x2088 0n8328 ffffc38c32e6f080 svchost.exe(UnistackSvcGroup)
0x2258 0n8792 ffffc38c324020c0 RuntimeBroker.exe
0x23b4 0n9140 ffffc38c335c70c0 SgrmBroker.exe
0x23dc 0n9180 ffffc38c2e19f0c0 sppsvc.exe
0x23fc 0n9212 ffffc38c32e020c0 svchost.exe(UsoSvc)
0x1300 0n4864 ffffc38c33ade0c0 MoUsoCoreWorker.exe
```

```
0x2048 0n8264 ffffc38c2ecc80c0 svchost.exe(W32Time)
0xdd8  0n3544 ffffc38c337240c0 svchost.exe(wscsvc)
0x1e98 0n7832 ffffc38c337ba0c0 UsoClient.exe
0x1284 0n4740 ffffc38c334020c0 AppA.exe*32
0x1224 0n4644 ffffc38c3010b0c0 conhost.exe
0x9d4  0n2516 ffffc38c2e16b080 notmyfault64.exe
============= ================ ======================================
PID           Address          Name

Warning! Zombie process(es) detected (not displayed). Count: 7 [zombie report]
```

Note: If you want to see command lines, use the **-cl** parameter. Nicely summarized additional information, such as whether *gflags.exe* was used, whether blocked, running, suspended, or waiting-for-ALPC threads exist (including overall thread count), can be seen with the **-a** parameter (pay attention to **!! Rn Ry Bk Lc IO Er** columns). It also shows PIDs in both hex and decimal formats. Consider this as a column-based **!process 0 3f**. Some columns may not show information for recent Windows versions.

7. We can get the list of all ALPC receiver threads and threads waiting for a reply using these commands:

```
0: kd> !mex.wrlpcreceive
Process                  PID Thread             Id CSwitches  User Kernel State        Time Reason       Wait Function
======================== ==== ================ ==== ========= ===== ====== ======= ========= ============ ======================================================
System                     4 ffffc38c2ea81040  174        66     0   31ms Waiting    33s.500 WrLpcReceive nt!AlpcpSignalAndWait+0x13d
csrss.exe                200 ffffc38c2e3af580  210       618  31ms   78ms Waiting      656ms WrLpcReceive CSRSRV!CsrApiRequestThread+0x106
csrss.exe                200 ffffc38c308720c0  23c         3     0      0 Waiting 2m:48.765 WrLpcReceive CSRSRV!CsrSbApiRequestThread+0x34
csrss.exe                200 ffffc38c3087e140  26c       889 125ms  188ms Waiting          0 WrLpcReceive CSRSRV!CsrApiRequestThread+0x106
csrss.exe                200 ffffc38c303b2080  460       559  63ms   16ms Waiting     1s.140 WrLpcReceive CSRSRV!CsrApiRequestThread+0x106
csrss.exe                250 ffffc38c30887080  268       410  47ms   94ms Waiting     3s.156 WrLpcReceive CSRSRV!CsrApiRequestThread+0x106
csrss.exe                250 ffffc38c30411080  2b0         3     0      0 Waiting 2m:48.125 WrLpcReceive CSRSRV!CsrSbApiRequestThread+0x34
csrss.exe                250 ffffc38c3041d080  2f0       383  94ms   63ms Waiting     3s.250 WrLpcReceive CSRSRV!CsrApiRequestThread+0x106
csrss.exe                250 ffffc38c30327080  318         4     0      0 Waiting 2m:41.750 WrLpcReceive winsrvext!AutoRotationRequestThread+0xc2
csrss.exe                250 ffffc38c308bf080  39c       354  31ms   47ms Waiting     3s.250 WrLpcReceive CSRSRV!CsrApiRequestThread+0x106
lsass.exe                298 ffffc38c30421080  2c4         1     0      0 Waiting 2m:48.093 WrLpcReceive lsass!LsapRmServerThread+0x66
dwm.exe                  288 ffffc38c316820c0  668       153     0   31ms Waiting 2m:43.734 WrLpcReceive DispBroker!DispBroker::AlpcServer::ProcessMessage+0x7b
svchost.exe (FontCache)  780 ffffc38c2c542080  4e0       175     0   31ms Waiting     3s.406 WrLpcReceive fntcache!AlpcServer::ProcessMessage+0xe1
svchost.exe (Themes)     8c0 ffffc38c31894080  8f0       215     0   16ms Waiting     3s.093 WrLpcReceive themeservice!CAPIConnection::Listen+0x81
ctfmon.exe              1a14 ffffc38c321af080 1b38       188     0   16ms Waiting     2s.828 WrLpcReceive MSCTF!CCtfServerPort::ServerLoop+0x18f
Count: 15
```

Note: The command takes some time to execute since it has to scan all threads.

```
0: kd> !mex.wrlpcreply
Process                  PID Thread             Id CSwitches   User Kernel State        Time Reason     Waiting On                                                     Wait Function
======================== ==== ================ ==== ========= ====== ====== ======= ========= ========== =============================================================== ===================================================================
csrss.exe                200 ffffc38c3081f080  22c         7      0      0 Waiting 2m:24.937 WrLpcReply Thread: ffffc38c30594080 in svchost.exe (LSM) (0n456)               winsrvext!TerminalServerRequestThread+0x304
csrss.exe                250 ffffc38c3040c080  2a0        38      0      0 Waiting 2m:25.109 WrLpcReply Thread: ffffc38c30594080 in svchost.exe (LSM) (0n456)               winsrvext!TerminalServerRequestThread+0x304
svchost.exe (netprofm)   69c ffffc38c32abf080 1368         3      0      0 Waiting 2m:13.796 WrLpcReply Thread: ffffc38c32ac7080 in svchost.exe (SSDPSRV) (0n6096)          ssdpapi!GetNotificationLoop+0x84
svchost.exe (SensrSvc)   708 ffffc38c2ea5d080  89c         1      0      0 Waiting 2m:42.359 WrLpcReply Thread: ffffc38c30327080 in csrss.exe (0n592)                       RotMgr!CRotationManager::AutoRotationClientHandler+0xd7
svchost.exe (AppXSvc)   117c ffffc38c323b9080 1bb8      8047 2s.766 1s.203 Waiting      46ms WrLpcReply Thread: ffffc38c3038d080 in svchost.exe (StateRepository) (0n2764) combase!CMessageCall::RpcSendRequestReceiveResponse+0xb9
svchost.exe (BITS)      1784 ffffc38c3301e080 1a48         1      0      0 Waiting 2m:04.562 WrLpcReply Thread: ffffc38c32ab4080 in svchost.exe (SSDPSRV) (0n6096)          SSDPAPI!GetNotificationLoop+0x84
SearchHost.exe          153c ffffc38c3282b080 1540       151   47ms   16ms Waiting 1m:00.281 WrLpcReply Message queued                                                     twinapi_appcore!PsmpHandleQuiesceRequest+0x307
SearchHost.exe          153c ffffc38c33032080 19c0        11      0   16ms Waiting 2m:05.562 WrLpcReply Thread: ffffc38c32e92080 in dllhost.exe (0n6248)                     edgehtml!WebPlatStorageEventsManager::BackgroundThreadProc+0x15c
SearchHost.exe          153c ffffc38c3223b080 1018        12      0      0 Waiting 1m:57.359 WrLpcReply Thread: ffffc38c32e96040 in dllhost.exe (0n6248)                     edgehtml!WebPlatStorageEventsManager::BackgroundThreadProc+0x15c
RuntimeBroker.exe       13a8 ffffc38c32c4d080 1350       133      0   63ms Waiting 1m:09.156 WrLpcReply Thread: ffffc38c31ec9080 in SearchHost.exe (0n5436)                  combase!CMessageCall::RpcSendRequestReceiveResponse+0xb9
RuntimeBroker.exe       2258 ffffc38c3301a040 226c        99      0   16ms Waiting   30s.609 WrLpcReply Message queued to YourPhone.exe (0n6932)                         combase!CMessageCall::RpcSendRequestReceiveResponse+0xb9
Count: 11
```

8. A standard way to list all stack traces is to use the **!for_each_thread** command, where we can customize stack trace output, for example:

```
0: kd> !for_each_thread ".thread /r /p @#Thread; kc"
```

Note: We can use this script to list all processes and threads, including 32-bit stack traces when it is possible:

```
!for_each_thread "!thread @#Thread 3f;.thread /w @#Thread; .reload; kb 256; .effmach AMD64"
```

Mex **!ForEachThread** (**!fet**) can also be used for this purpose. Use the **-?** option to see the syntax. The advantage of it is the ability to apply commands to a particular process (we don't need to exclude other processes in the body of the

!for_each_thread command) and also include terminated threads (we choose *AppA.exe*32* process address from the previous output):

```
0: kd> !mex.fet -t -p ffffc38c334020c0 "!thread @#Thread 3f; .thread /w @#Thread; .reload; kL 256; .effmach AMD64"
[...]
Changing to thread: ffffc38c2ecd4080
THREAD ffffc38c2ecd4080  Cid 1284.200c  Teb: 0000000000e5f000 Win32Thread: ffffc38c2e156be0 WAIT: (WrUserRequest) UserMode Non-Alertable
    ffffc38c34d76440  QueueObject
Not impersonating
DeviceMap                 ffffac8a09519470
Owning Process            ffffc38c334020c0       Image:         AppA.exe
Attached Process          N/A            Image:         N/A
Wait Start TickCount      11514          Ticks: 442 (0:00:00:06.906)
Context Switch Count      757            IdealProcessor: 1
UserTime                  00:00:00.000
KernelTime                00:00:00.046
Win32 Start Address ucrtbase!thread_start<unsigned int (__stdcall*)(void *),1> (0x0000000075bb67e0)
Stack Init ffffbe8295d80c70 Current ffffbe8295d80410
Base ffffbe8295d81000 Limit ffffbe8295d7b000 Call 0000000000000000
Priority 10 BasePriority 8 PriorityDecrement 0 IoPriority 2 PagePriority 5
Child-SP          RetAddr           Call Site
ffffbe82`95d80450 fffff806`62132457     nt!KiSwapContext+0x76
ffffbe82`95d80590 fffff806`62134309     nt!KiSwapThread+0x3a7
ffffbe82`95d80670 fffff806`6212e224     nt!KiCommitThreadWait+0x159
ffffbe82`95d80710 fffff806`6208ef60     nt!KeWaitForSingleObject+0x234
ffffbe82`95d80800 ffffbd43`fb63b466     nt!KeWaitForMultipleObjects+0x540
ffffbe82`95d80900 ffffbd43`fb63b0cf     win32kfull!xxxRealSleepThread+0x2c6
ffffbe82`95d80a20 ffffbd43`fb5c1864     win32kfull!xxxSleepThread2+0xb3
ffffbe82`95d80a70 ffffbd43`fad09562     win32kfull!NtUserWaitMessage+0x44
ffffbe82`95d80ab0 fffff806`62227b75     win32k!NtUserWaitMessage+0x16
ffffbe82`95d80ae0 00000000`76fe1cf3     nt!KiSystemServiceCopyEnd+0x25 (TrapFrame @ ffffbe82`95d80ae0)
00000000`031beb48 00000000`76fe1cb4     wow64cpu!CpupSyscallStub+0x13
00000000`031beb50 00000000`76fe1d75     wow64cpu!Thunk0Arg+0x5
00000000`031bec00 00007ffc`863de06d     wow64cpu!BTCpuSimulate+0xbb5
00000000`031bec40 00007ffc`863dd8ad     wow64!RunCpuSimulation+0xd
00000000`031bec70 00007ffc`8851a958     wow64!Wow64LdrpInitialize+0x12d
00000000`031bef20 00007ffc`8851a843     ntdll!_LdrpInitialize+0xdc
00000000`031befa0 00007ffc`8851a76e     ntdll!LdrpInitializeInternal+0x6b
00000000`031bf220 00000000`00000000     ntdll!LdrInitializeThunk+0xe

Implicit thread is now ffffc38c`2ecd4080
WARNING: WOW context retrieval requires
switching to the thread's process context.
Use .process /p ffffc38c`2e16b080 to switch back.
Implicit process is now ffffc38c`334020c0
x86 context set
Loading Kernel Symbols
...............................................................
................................................................
................................................................
..
Loading User Symbols
.......
Loading unloaded module list
........
Loading Wow64 Symbols
..........................

************* Symbol Loading Error Summary **************
Module name            Error
SharedUserData         No error - symbol load deferred

You can troubleshoot most symbol related issues by turning on symbol loading diagnostics (!sym noisy) and repeating the command that caused symbols to be loaded.
You should also verify that your symbol search path (.sympath) is correct.
 # ChildEBP          RetAddr
00 032bfa58 74e7e889     win32u!NtUserWaitMessage+0xc
01 032bfaa0 74e7e768     USER32!DialogBox2+0x10a
02 032bfad0 74ecb218     USER32!InternalDialogBox+0xd7
03 032bfb9c 74ec9f80     USER32!SoftModalMessageBox+0x718
04 032bfcf8 74ecaa87     USER32!MessageBoxWorker+0x314
05 032bfd80 74ecaaf5     USER32!MessageBoxTimeoutW+0x187
Unable to load image C:\MemoryDumps\AppA.exe, Win32 error 0n2
*** WARNING: Unable to verify checksum for AppA.exe
06 032bfda0 000211e4     USER32!MessageBoxW+0x45
07 032bfdd8 0002181a     AppA!thread_D+0x24
08 (Inline) --------     AppA!std::_Invoker_functor::_Call+0x7
09 (Inline) --------     AppA!std::invoke+0x7
0a 032bfdf4 75bb6823     AppA!std::thread::_Invoke<std::tuple<void (__cdecl*)(void)>,0>+0x2a
0b 032bfe2c 75ca6739     ucrtbase!thread_start<unsigned int (__stdcall*)(void *),1>+0x43
0c 032bfe3c 77058aff     KERNEL32!BaseThreadInitThunk+0x19
0d 032bfe94 77058acd     ntdll_76ff0000!__RtlUserThreadStart+0x2b
0e 032bfea4 00000000     ntdll_76ff0000!_RtlUserThreadStart+0x1b
Effective machine: x64 (AMD64)
[...]
```

9. If we try to search for RPC threads using the **!stacks** command to filter stack traces, we fail since the command doesn't switch to the proper process context to show correct user space thread stacks. To search for such threads, we can use the MEX extension command **!UniqueStacks**:

```
0: kd> !mex.us -a RPCRT4
Process: svchost.exe @ ffffc38c2c509080
==================================================================
1 thread: ffffc38c32abf080
    fffff8066221d056 nt!KiSwapContext+0x76
    fffff80662132457 nt!KiSwapThread+0x3a7
    fffff80662134309 nt!KiCommitThreadWait+0x159
    fffff8066212e224 nt!KeWaitForSingleObject+0x234
    fffff806620c443d nt!AlpcpSignalAndWait+0x13d
    fffff8066254da56 nt!AlpcpReceiveSynchronousReply+0x56
    fffff8066254d5af nt!AlpcpProcessSynchronousRequest+0x36f
    fffff8066254ca86 nt!NtAlpcSendWaitReceivePort+0x1d6
    fffff80662227b75 nt!KiSystemServiceCopyEnd+0x25
    00007ffc885444d4 ntdll!NtAlpcSendWaitReceivePort+0x14
    00007ffc86587232 RPCRT4!LRPC_BASE_CCALL::DoSendReceive+0x112
    00007ffc865842cb RPCRT4!LRPC_CCALL::SendReceive+0x5b
    00007ffc865aeb09 RPCRT4!I_RpcSendReceive+0x79
    00007ffc865d20b6 RPCRT4!NdrSendReceive+0x36
    00007ffc8663c690 RPCRT4!NdrpClientCall3+0x7d0
    00007ffc8663dd38 RPCRT4!NdrClientCall3+0xe8
    00007ffc79752914 ssdpapi!GetNotificationLoop+0x84
    00007ffc876b54e0 KERNEL32!BaseThreadInitThunk+0x10
    00007ffc884a485b ntdll!RtlUserThreadStart+0x2b

Threads matching filter: 1 out of 32

Process: svchost.exe @ ffffc38c31ae00c0
[...]
```

The search command also goes through 32-bit stack traces:

```
0: kd> !mex.us -a MessageBox
Unable to load image C:\Program Files\VMware\VMware Tools\VMware VGAuth\VGAuthService.exe, Win32 error 0n2
Unable to load image C:\Program Files\VMware\VMware Tools\VMware VGAuth\glib-2.0.dll, Win32 error 0n2
Unable to load image C:\Program Files\VMware\VMware Tools\plugins\vmsvc\guestInfo.dll, Win32 error 0n2
Unable to load image C:\Program Files\VMware\VMware Tools\vmtoolsd.exe, Win32 error 0n2
Unable to load image C:\Program Files\VMware\VMware Tools\glib-2.0.dll, Win32 error 0n2
Unable to load image C:\Program Files\VMware\VMware Tools\plugins\vmsvc\diskWiper.dll, Win32 error 0n2
Unable to load image C:\Program Files\VMware\VMware Tools\plugins\vmsvc\hwUpgradeHelper.dll, Win32 error 0n2
Unable to load image C:\ProgramData\Microsoft\Windows Defender\Platform\4.18.2110.6-0\mpsvc.dll, Win32 error 0n2
Unable to load image C:\ProgramData\Microsoft\Windows Defender\Definition Updates\{E6F01128-A5A7-4CBF-AB31-D669E2FA0EA5}\mpengine.dll, Win32 error 0n2
Unable to load image C:\ProgramData\Microsoft\Windows Defender\Platform\4.18.2110.6-0\mpclient.dll, Win32 error 0n2
Unable to load image C:\ProgramData\Microsoft\Windows Defender\Platform\4.18.2110.6-0\mprtp.dll, Win32 error 0n2
Unable to load image c:\windows\system32\appxdeploymentserver.dll, Win32 error 0n2
Unable to load image C:\WINDOWS\system32\vm3dum64_10.dll, Win32 error 0n2
Unable to load image C:\Program Files\WindowsApps\Microsoft.YourPhone_1.21092.149.0_x64__8wekyb3d8bbwe\YourPhone.dll, Win32 error 0n2
*** WARNING: Unable to verify checksum for YourPhone.dll
Unable to load image C:\ProgramData\Microsoft\Windows Defender\Definition Updates\{E6F01128-A5A7-4CBF-AB31-D669E2FA0EA5}\mpengine.dll, Win32 error 0n2
Unable to load image C:\ProgramData\Microsoft\Windows Defender\Scans\MsMpEngCP.exe, Win32 error 0n2
Unable to load image C:\ProgramData\Microsoft\Windows Defender\Platform\4.18.2110.6-0\NisSrv.exe, Win32 error 0n2
Unable to load image C:\Program Files\VMware\VMware Tools\plugins\vmusr\dndcp.dll, Win32 error 0n2
Unable to load image C:\Program Files\VMware\VMware Tools\plugins\vmusr\desktopEvents.dll, Win32 error 0n2
Unable to load image C:\Program Files\VMware\VMware Tools\plugins\vmusr\unity.dll, Win32 error 0n2
Unable to load image C:\Program Files\VMware\VMware Tools\glib-2.0.dll, Win32 error 0n2
Unable to load image C:\Windows\System32\vm3dservice.exe, Win32 error 0n2
Unable to load image C:\Users\dumpa\AppData\Local\Microsoft\OneDrive\21.205.1003.0005\OneDriveTelemetryStable.dll, Win32 error 0n2
Unable to load image C:\Users\dumpa\AppData\Local\Microsoft\OneDrive\21.205.1003.0005\FileSyncClient.dll, Win32 error 0n2
Unable to load image C:\Users\dumpa\AppData\Local\Microsoft\OneDrive\21.205.1003.0005\SyncEngine.DLL, Win32 error 0n2
Unable to load image C:\Users\dumpa\AppData\Local\Microsoft\OneDrive\21.205.1003.0005\LoggingPlatform.dll, Win32 error 0n2
Unable to load image C:\Program Files\WindowsApps\Microsoft.549981C3F5F10_3.2109.6305.0_x64__8wekyb3d8bbwe\Cortana.dll, Win32 error 0n2
*** WARNING: Unable to verify checksum for Cortana.dll
Unable to load image C:\WINDOWS\system32\sppsvc.exe, Win32 error 0n2
Process: AppA.exe @ ffffc38c334020c0
==================================================================
1 thread: ffffc38c2ecd4080
```

```
    fffff8066221d056 nt!KiSwapContext+0x76
    fffff80662132457 nt!KiSwapThread+0x3a7
    fffff80662134309 nt!KiCommitThreadWait+0x159
    fffff8066212e224 nt!KeWaitForSingleObject+0x234
    fffff8066208ef60 nt!KeWaitForMultipleObjects+0x540
    ffffbd43fb63b466 win32kfull!xxxRealSleepThread+0x2c6
    ffffbd43fb63b0cf win32kfull!xxxSleepThread2+0xb3
    ffffbd43fb5c1864 win32kfull!NtUserWaitMessage+0x44
    ffffbd43fad09562 win32k!NtUserWaitMessage+0x16
    fffff80662227b75 nt!KiSystemServiceCopyEnd+0x25
    000000007657112c win32u!NtUserWaitMessage+0xc
    0000000074e7e889 USER32!DialogBox2+0x10a
    0000000074e7e768 USER32!InternalDialogBox+0xd7
    0000000074ecb218 USER32!SoftModalMessageBox+0x718
    0000000074ec9f80 USER32!MessageBoxWorker+0x314
    0000000074ecaa87 USER32!MessageBoxTimeoutW+0x187
    0000000074ecaaf5 USER32!MessageBoxW+0x45
    00000000000211e4 AppA+0x11e4
    000000000002181a AppA+0x181a
    0000000075bb6823 ucrtbase!thread_start<unsigned int (__stdcall*)(void *),1>+0x43
    0000000075ca6739 KERNEL32!BaseThreadInitThunk+0x19
    0000000077058aff ntdll_76ff0000!__RtlUserThreadStart+0x2b
    0000000077058acd ntdll_76ff0000!_RtlUserThreadStart+0x1b

Threads matching filter: 1 out of 9
```

The command can also search for exception or bugcheck processing threads and also for non-waiting threads:

```
0: kd> !mex.us -a -crash
Process: notmyfault64.exe @ ffffc38c2e16b080
==============================================================
1 thread: ffffc38c33ac3080
    fffff80662215590 nt!KeBugCheckEx
    fffff806622281a9 nt!KiBugCheckDispatch+0x69
    fffff80662224300 nt!KiPageFault+0x440
    fffff80660571981 myfault+0x1981
    fffff80660571d3d myfault+0x1d3d
    fffff80660571ea1 myfault+0x1ea1
    fffff80662102f65 nt!IofCallDriver+0x55
    fffff8066256b532 nt!IopSynchronousServiceTail+0x1d2
```

```
    fffff8066256acbf nt!IopXxxControlFile+0x5df
    fffff8066256a6c6 nt!NtDeviceIoControlFile+0x56
    fffff80662227b75 nt!KiSystemServiceCopyEnd+0x25
    00007ffc88543444 ntdll!NtDeviceIoControlFile+0x14
    00007ffc85c23edb KERNELBASE!DeviceIoControl+0x6b
    00007ffc876b5f91 KERNEL32!DeviceIoControlImplementation+0x81
    00007ff7be36342f notmyfault64+0x342f
    00007ffc87fd484b USER32!UserCallDlgProcCheckWow+0x14b
    00007ffc87fd409b USER32!DefDlgProcWorker+0xcb
    00007ffc880197c9 USER32!DefDlgProcA+0x39
    00007ffc87fd1c4c USER32!UserCallWinProcCheckWow+0x33c
    00007ffc87fd179c USER32!DispatchClientMessage+0x9c
    00007ffc87fe4b4d USER32!_fnDWORD+0x3d
    00007ffc885472b4 ntdll!KiUserCallbackDispatcherContinue
    00007ffc85b21434 win32u!NtUserMessageCall+0x14
    00007ffc87fd08cf USER32!SendMessageWorker+0x12f
    00007ffc87fd0737 USER32!SendMessageW+0x137
    00007ffc73c550bf COMCTL32!Button_ReleaseCapture+0xbb
    00007ffc73c88822 COMCTL32!Button_WndProc+0x802
    00007ffc87fd1c4c USER32!UserCallWinProcCheckWow+0x33c
    00007ffc87fd0ea6 USER32!DispatchMessageWorker+0x2a6
    00007ffc87fd6084 USER32!IsDialogMessageW+0x104
    00007ffc73c35f9f COMCTL32!Prop_IsDialogMessage+0x4b
    00007ffc73c35e48 COMCTL32!_RealPropertySheet+0x2c0
    00007ffc73c35abd COMCTL32!_PropertySheet+0x49
    00007ffc73d00953 COMCTL32!PropertySheetA+0x53
    00007ff7be364cd0 notmyfault64+0x4cd0
    00007ff7be365292 notmyfault64+0x5292
    00007ffc876b54e0 KERNEL32!BaseThreadInitThunk+0x10
    00007ffc884a485b ntdll!RtlUserThreadStart+0x2b

Threads matching filter: 1 out of 3
```

```
0: kd> !mex.us -a -nw
Process: Idle @ fffff80662b32b00
============================================================
2 threads: ffffc38c2c48e300 ffffc38c2c58a080
    fffff8066221d056 nt!KiSwapContext+0x76
    fffff80662132457 nt!KiSwapThread+0x3a7
    fffff806621be45c nt!KiExecuteDpcDelegate+0x5c
    fffff80662219644 nt!KiStartSystemThread+0x34

Threads matching filter: 2 out of 4

Process: System @ ffffc38c2c4ed040
============================================================
2 threads: ffffc38c2c524080 ffffc38c2c5bd080
    fffff8066221d056 nt!KiSwapContext+0x76
    fffff80662132457 nt!KiSwapThread+0x3a7
    fffff80662134309 nt!KiCommitThreadWait+0x159
    fffff806620548cf nt!KeWaitForGate+0xcf
    fffff806621c6cd2 nt!KiExecuteDpc+0x92
    fffff806620478f5 nt!PspSystemThreadStartup+0x55
    fffff80662219644 nt!KiStartSystemThread+0x34

22 threads: ffffc38c2ef89040 ffffc38c2cda5080 ffffc38c31bbc080 ffffc38c2cd94080 ffffc38c2c541080 ffffc38c325ca040 ffffc38c3168c040 ffffc38c2e6f1040 ffffc38c2c519080 ffffc38c2cd1b480 ...
    fffff8066221d056 nt!KiSwapContext+0x76
    fffff80662132457 nt!KiSwapThread+0x3a7
    fffff80662134309 nt!KiCommitThreadWait+0x159
    fffff8066211d679 nt!KeRemovePriQueue+0x259
    fffff8066211cfd3 nt!ExpWorkerThread+0xd3
    fffff806620478f5 nt!PspSystemThreadStartup+0x55
    fffff80662219644 nt!KiStartSystemThread+0x34

Threads matching filter: 24 out of 130

Process: svchost.exe @ ffffc38c31ae00c0
============================================================
1 thread: ffffc38c3038d080
    fffff806624f2074 nt!CmpReportNotifyHelper+0xf4
    fffff806624f1f3d nt!CmpReportNotifyForKcbStack+0x45
    fffff80662512c54 nt!CmpCreateChild+0x66c
    fffff8066257dbc3 nt!CmpDoParseKey+0x22b3
    fffff8066257b4ef nt!CmpParseKey+0x2df
    fffff80662572562 nt!ObpLookupObjectName+0x652
    fffff806625719d1 nt!ObOpenObjectByNameEx+0x1f1
    fffff8066251abd0 nt!CmCreateKey+0x480
    fffff8066251a732 nt!NtCreateKey+0x52
    fffff80662227b75 nt!KiSystemServiceCopyEnd+0x25
    00007ffc88543704 ntdll!NtCreateKey+0x14
    00007ffc85c29e86 KERNELBASE!Wow64NtCreateKey+0xae
    00007ffc85c4a071 KERNELBASE!BaseRegCreateMultipartKey+0x139
    00007ffc85c2a2e6 KERNELBASE!LocalBaseRegCreateKey+0x382
    00007ffc85c24675 KERNELBASE!RegCreateKeyExInternalW+0x145
```

```
    00007ffc85c23b4b KERNELBASE!RegCreateKeyExW+0x4b
    00007ffc79dc3744 windows_staterepositorycore!SRCacheContext_CreateSubContext+0x84
    00007ffc78552887 windows_staterepository!StateRepository::Entity::CacheApplicationUser::Cache_Add+0x17c7
    00007ffc785423e4 windows_staterepository!StateRepository::CacheManagement::_Update_JournalEntry_ApplicationUser+0xd4
    00007ffc785420a7 windows_staterepository!StateRepository::CacheManagement::_Update_JournalEntry+0x487
    00007ffc7854143c windows_staterepository!StateRepository::CacheManagement::_Update+0x5ec
    00007ffc785426c6 windows_staterepository!StateRepository::CacheManagement::Update+0x1a
    00007ffc785427c4 windows_staterepository!StateRepository::CacheManagement::Update+0x94
    00007ffc78542b1c windows_staterepository!Windows::Internal::StateRepository::Management::RepositoryManagerServer::Cache_Update+0x2dc
    00007ffc865d23e3 RPCRT4!Invoke+0x73
    00007ffc8663b68c RPCRT4!Ndr64StubWorker+0xb7c
    00007ffc8659e5b2 RPCRT4!NdrStubCall3+0xd2
    00007ffc86d862ab combase!CStdStubBuffer_Invoke+0x8b                                                                  (onecore\com\combase\ndr\ndrole\stub.cxx @ 1480)
    00007ffc865b40a5 RPCRT4!CStdStubBuffer_Invoke+0x45
    (Inline)         combase!InvokeStubWithExceptionPolicyAndTracing::__l6::<lambda_c9f3956a20c9da92a64affc24fdd69ec>::operator()+0x22   (onecore\com\combase\dcomrem\channelb.cxx @ 1161)
    00007ffc86d2191d combase!ObjectMethodExceptionHandlingAction<<lambda_c9f3956a20c9da92a64affc24fdd69ec> >+0x4d    (onecore\com\combase\dcomrem\excepn.hxx @ 94)
    (Inline)         combase!InvokeStubWithExceptionPolicyAndTracing+0xda                                                (onecore\com\combase\dcomrem\channelb.cxx @ 1159)
    00007ffc86d216b7 combase!DefaultStubInvoke+0x257                                                                     (onecore\com\combase\dcomrem\channelb.cxx @ 1228)
    00007ffc86d8cbf8 combase!SyncServerCall::StubInvoke+0x38                                                             (onecore\com\combase\dcomrem\ServerCall.hpp @ 787)
    (Inline)         combase!StubInvoke+0x2d8                                                                            (onecore\com\combase\dcomrem\channelb.cxx @ 1510)
    00007ffc86d6b46b combase!ServerCall::ContextInvoke+0x46b                                                             (onecore\com\combase\dcomrem\ctxchnl.cxx @ 1425)
    (Inline)         combase!CServerChannel::ContextInvoke+0x84                                                          (onecore\com\combase\dcomrem\ctxchnl.cxx @ 1332)
    00007ffc86d6fdf1 combase!DefaultInvokeInApartment+0xc1                                                               (onecore\com\combase\dcomrem\callctrl.cxx @ 3299)
    00007ffc86d613a3 combase!ComInvokeWithLockAndIPID+0xa13                                                              (onecore\com\combase\dcomrem\channelb.cxx @ 2241)
    (Inline)         combase!ThreadInvokeReturnHresult+0x188                                                             (onecore\com\combase\dcomrem\channelb.cxx @ 7195)
    00007ffc86d5eac9 combase!ThreadInvoke+0x1b9                                                                          (onecore\com\combase\dcomrem\channelb.cxx @ 7303)
    00007ffc865b2c72 RPCRT4!DispatchToStubInCNoAvrf+0x22
    00007ffc8657748f RPCRT4!RPC_INTERFACE::DispatchToStubWorker+0x1af
    00007ffc86577098 RPCRT4!RPC_INTERFACE::DispatchToStubWithObject+0x188
    00007ffc865874b5 RPCRT4!LRPC_SCALL::DispatchRequest+0x175
    00007ffc86586b07 RPCRT4!LRPC_SCALL::HandleRequest+0x837
    00007ffc8658618b RPCRT4!LRPC_SASSOCIATION::HandleRequest+0x24b
    00007ffc86585e61 RPCRT4!LRPC_ADDRESS::HandleRequest+0x181
    00007ffc86585a97 RPCRT4!LRPC_ADDRESS::ProcessIO+0x897
    00007ffc8658c179 RPCRT4!LrpcIoComplete+0xc9
    00007ffc884c1fd0 ntdll!TppAlpcpExecuteCallback+0x280
    00007ffc884b6cb8 ntdll!TppWorkerThread+0x448
    00007ffc876b54e0 KERNEL32!BaseThreadInitThunk+0x10
    00007ffc884a485b ntdll!RtlUserThreadStart+0x2b

Threads matching filter: 1 out of 16
```

Note: The option **-a** searches all processes. For illustration, we sometimes omit it to search the current process of interest only if it takes too long otherwise. All such examples are very slow for complete memory dumps and, therefore, it is recommended to get all threads and their stack traces once, and then do second-order filtering and searching on the resulted textual output.

10. To see stack traces from threads running on CPUs, you can use these MEX extension commands:

```
0: kd> !mex.running
Process                      PID Thread           Id   Pri Base Pri Next CPU CSwitches User  Kernel State   Time Reason
============================ === ================ ==== === ======== ======== ========= ===== ======= ======= ==== =============
notmyfault64.exe             9d4 ffffc38c33ac3080 2038  12        8        0      1135  16ms    94ms Running    0 WrPreempted
svchost.exe (StateRepository) acc ffffc38c3038d080 1f80  10       10        1      1321 234ms    63ms Running    0 WrDispatchInt

Count: 2 | Show Unique Stacks
```

```
0: kd> !mex.us -cpu
1 thread: ffffc38c3038d080
    fffff806624f2074 nt!CmpReportNotifyHelper+0xf4
    fffff806624f1f3d nt!CmpReportNotifyForKcbStack+0x45
    fffff80662512c54 nt!CmpCreateChild+0x66c
    fffff8066257dbc3 nt!CmpDoParseKey+0x22b3
    fffff8066257b4ef nt!CmpParseKey+0x2df
    fffff80662572562 nt!ObpLookupObjectName+0x652
    fffff806625719d1 nt!ObOpenObjectByNameEx+0x1f1
    fffff8066251abd0 nt!CmCreateKey+0x480
    fffff8066251a732 nt!NtCreateKey+0x52
    fffff80662227b75 nt!KiSystemServiceCopyEnd+0x25
    00007ffc88543704 ntdll!NtCreateKey+0x14
    00007ffc85c29e86 KERNELBASE!Wow64NtCreateKey+0xae
    00007ffc85c4a071 KERNELBASE!BaseRegCreateMultipartKey+0x139
    00007ffc85c2a2e6 KERNELBASE!LocalBaseRegCreateKey+0x382
    00007ffc85c24675 KERNELBASE!RegCreateKeyExInternalW+0x145
    00007ffc85c23b4b KERNELBASE!RegCreateKeyExW+0x4b
    00007ffc79dc3744 windows_staterepositorycore!SRCacheContext_CreateSubContext+0x84
    00007ffc78552887 windows_staterepository!StateRepository::Entity::CacheApplicationUser::Cache_Add+0x17c7
    00007ffc785423e4 windows_staterepository!StateRepository::CacheManagement::_Update_JournalEntry_ApplicationUser+0xd4
    00007ffc785420a7 windows_staterepository!StateRepository::CacheManagement::_Update_JournalEntry+0x487
    00007ffc7854143c windows_staterepository!StateRepository::CacheManagement::_Update+0x5ec
    00007ffc785426c6 windows_staterepository!StateRepository::CacheManagement::Update+0x1a
    00007ffc785427c4 windows_staterepository!StateRepository::CacheManagement::Update+0x94
    00007ffc78542b1c windows_staterepository!Windows::Internal::StateRepository::Management::RepositoryManagerServer::Cache_Update+0x2dc
    00007ffc865d23e3 RPCRT4!Invoke+0x73
    00007ffc8663b68c RPCRT4!Ndr64StubWorker+0xb7c
    00007ffc8659e5b2 RPCRT4!NdrStubCall3+0xd2
    00007ffc86d862ab combase!CStdStubBuffer_Invoke+0x8b                                                                  (onecore\com\combase\ndr\ndrole\stub.cxx @ 1480)
    00007ffc865b40a5 RPCRT4!CStdStubBuffer_Invoke+0x45
    (Inline)         combase!InvokeStubWithExceptionPolicyAndTracing::__l6::<lambda_c9f3956a20c9da92a64affc24fdd69ec>::operator()+0x22   (onecore\com\combase\dcomrem\channelb.cxx @ 1161)
    00007ffc86d2191d combase!ObjectMethodExceptionHandlingAction<<lambda_c9f3956a20c9da92a64affc24fdd69ec> >+0x4d    (onecore\com\combase\dcomrem\excepn.hxx @ 94)
    (Inline)         combase!InvokeStubWithExceptionPolicyAndTracing+0xda                                                (onecore\com\combase\dcomrem\channelb.cxx @ 1159)
    00007ffc86d216b7 combase!DefaultStubInvoke+0x257                                                                     (onecore\com\combase\dcomrem\channelb.cxx @ 1228)
    00007ffc86d8cbf8 combase!SyncServerCall::StubInvoke+0x38                                                             (onecore\com\combase\dcomrem\ServerCall.hpp @ 787)
    (Inline)         combase!StubInvoke+0x2d8                                                                            (onecore\com\combase\dcomrem\channelb.cxx @ 1510)
    00007ffc86d6b46b combase!ServerCall::ContextInvoke+0x46b                                                             (onecore\com\combase\dcomrem\ctxchnl.cxx @ 1425)
    (Inline)         combase!CServerChannel::ContextInvoke+0x84                                                          (onecore\com\combase\dcomrem\ctxchnl.cxx @ 1332)
    00007ffc86d6fdf1 combase!DefaultInvokeInApartment+0xc1                                                               (onecore\com\combase\dcomrem\callctrl.cxx @ 3299)
    00007ffc86d613a3 combase!ComInvokeWithLockAndIPID+0xa13                                                              (onecore\com\combase\dcomrem\channelb.cxx @ 2241)
    (Inline)         combase!ThreadInvokeReturnHresult+0x188                                                             (onecore\com\combase\dcomrem\channelb.cxx @ 7195)
    00007ffc86d5eac9 combase!ThreadInvoke+0x1b9                                                                          (onecore\com\combase\dcomrem\channelb.cxx @ 7303)
    00007ffc865b2c72 RPCRT4!DispatchToStubInCNoAvrf+0x22
```

```
    00007ffc8657748f RPCRT4!RPC_INTERFACE::DispatchToStubWorker+0x1af
    00007ffc86577098 RPCRT4!RPC_INTERFACE::DispatchToStubWithObject+0x188
    00007ffc865874b5 RPCRT4!LRPC_SCALL::DispatchRequest+0x175
    00007ffc86586b07 RPCRT4!LRPC_SCALL::HandleRequest+0x837
    00007ffc8658618b RPCRT4!LRPC_SASSOCIATION::HandleRequest+0x24b
    00007ffc86585e61 RPCRT4!LRPC_ADDRESS::HandleRequest+0x181
    00007ffc86585a97 RPCRT4!LRPC_ADDRESS::ProcessIO+0x897
    00007ffc8658c179 RPCRT4!LrpcIoComplete+0xc9
    00007ffc884c1fd0 ntdll!TppAlpcpExecuteCallback+0x280
    00007ffc884b6cb8 ntdll!TppWorkerThread+0x448
    00007ffc876b54e0 KERNEL32!BaseThreadInitThunk+0x10
    00007ffc884a485b ntdll!RtlUserThreadStart+0x2b

1 thread: ffffc38c33ac3080
    fffff80662215590 nt!KeBugCheckEx
    fffff806622281a9 nt!KiBugCheckDispatch+0x69
    fffff80662224300 nt!KiPageFault+0x440
    fffff80660571981 myfault+0x1981
    fffff80660571d3d myfault+0x1d3d
    fffff80660571ea1 myfault+0x1ea1
    fffff80662102f65 nt!IofCallDriver+0x55
    fffff8066256b532 nt!IopSynchronousServiceTail+0x1d2
    fffff8066256acbf nt!IopXxxControlFile+0x5df
    fffff8066256a6c6 nt!NtDeviceIoControlFile+0x56
    fffff80662227b75 nt!KiSystemServiceCopyEnd+0x25
    00007ffc88543444 ntdll!NtDeviceIoControlFile+0x14
    00007ffc85c23edb KERNELBASE!DeviceIoControl+0x6b
    00007ffc876b5f91 KERNEL32!DeviceIoControlImplementation+0x81
    00007ff7be36342f notmyfault64+0x342f
    00007ffc87fd484b USER32!UserCallDlgProcCheckWow+0x14b
    00007ffc87fd409b USER32!DefDlgProcWorker+0xcb
    00007ffc880197c9 USER32!DefDlgProcA+0x39
    00007ffc87fd1c4c USER32!UserCallWinProcCheckWow+0x33c
    00007ffc87fd179c USER32!DispatchClientMessage+0x9c
    00007ffc87fe4b4d USER32!_fnDWORD+0x3d
    00007ffc885472b4 ntdll!KiUserCallbackDispatcherContinue
    00007ffc85b21434 win32u!NtUserMessageCall+0x14
    00007ffc87fd08cf USER32!SendMessageWorker+0x12f
    00007ffc87fd0737 USER32!SendMessageW+0x137
    00007ffc73c550bf COMCTL32!Button_ReleaseCapture+0xbb
    00007ffc73c88822 COMCTL32!Button_WndProc+0x802
    00007ffc87fd1c4c USER32!UserCallWinProcCheckWow+0x33c
    00007ffc87fd0ea6 USER32!DispatchMessageWorker+0x2a6
    00007ffc87fd6084 USER32!IsDialogMessageW+0x104
    00007ffc73c35f9f COMCTL32!Prop_IsDialogMessage+0x4b
    00007ffc73c35e48 COMCTL32!_RealPropertySheet+0x2c0
    00007ffc73c35abd COMCTL32!_PropertySheet+0x49
    00007ffc73d00953 COMCTL32!PropertySheetA+0x53
    00007ff7be364cd0 notmyfault64+0x4cd0
    00007ff7be365292 notmyfault64+0x5292
    00007ffc876b54e0 KERNEL32!BaseThreadInitThunk+0x10
    00007ffc884a485b ntdll!RtlUserThreadStart+0x2b

2 stack(s) with 2 threads displayed (2 Total threads)
```

Note: We use the **!mex.running** command to differentiate it from the preloaded **!kdexts.running** (which doesn't show the correct user space portion of stack traces).

11. To sort threads by kernel and user mode CPU consumption, use these commands:

```
0: kd> !mex.runaway2 -a -k
Showing top 10 threads
Thread ID          Kernel Time           User Time             Total Time
=============================================================================
ffffc38c2c508080 | 0 days 0:00:13.016 | 0 days 0:00:00.000 | 0 days 0:00:13.016
ffffc38c2e3b0080 | 0 days 0:00:07.297 | 0 days 0:00:06.094 | 0 days 0:00:13.391
ffffc38c3282c080 | 0 days 0:00:05.469 | 0 days 0:00:20.750 | 0 days 0:00:26.219
ffffc38c3270d080 | 0 days 0:00:05.250 | 0 days 0:00:02.422 | 0 days 0:00:07.672
ffffc38c308f0080 | 0 days 0:00:03.094 | 0 days 0:00:00.000 | 0 days 0:00:03.094
ffffc38c321ad080 | 0 days 0:00:02.859 | 0 days 0:00:01.234 | 0 days 0:00:04.093
ffffc38c31897080 | 0 days 0:00:02.391 | 0 days 0:00:02.922 | 0 days 0:00:05.313
ffffc38c30333080 | 0 days 0:00:02.328 | 0 days 0:00:00.828 | 0 days 0:00:03.156
ffffc38c32621080 | 0 days 0:00:02.203 | 0 days 0:00:00.594 | 0 days 0:00:02.797
ffffc38c2c58f080 | 0 days 0:00:02.000 | 0 days 0:00:00.750 | 0 days 0:00:02.750
=============================================================================
Thread ID          Kernel Time           User Time             Total Time
```

```
0: kd> !mex.runaway2 -a -u
Showing top 10 threads
Thread ID          User Time             Kernel Time           Total Time
=============================================================================
ffffc38c3282c080 | 0 days 0:00:20.750 | 0 days 0:00:05.469 | 0 days 0:00:26.219
ffffc38c2e3b0080 | 0 days 0:00:06.094 | 0 days 0:00:07.297 | 0 days 0:00:13.391
ffffc38c31f82040 | 0 days 0:00:05.375 | 0 days 0:00:01.891 | 0 days 0:00:07.266
ffffc38c31897080 | 0 days 0:00:02.922 | 0 days 0:00:02.391 | 0 days 0:00:05.313
```

```
ffffc38c323b9080 | 0 days 0:00:02.766 | 0 days 0:00:01.203 | 0 days 0:00:03.969
ffffc38c3270d080 | 0 days 0:00:02.422 | 0 days 0:00:05.250 | 0 days 0:00:07.672
ffffc38c32e31040 | 0 days 0:00:02.203 | 0 days 0:00:00.547 | 0 days 0:00:02.750
ffffc38c30917080 | 0 days 0:00:01.828 | 0 days 0:00:00.156 | 0 days 0:00:01.984
ffffc38c2ef61080 | 0 days 0:00:01.594 | 0 days 0:00:00.625 | 0 days 0:00:02.219
ffffc38c328f0080 | 0 days 0:00:01.422 | 0 days 0:00:00.297 | 0 days 0:00:01.719
===============================================================================
Thread ID           User Time            Kernel Time          Total Time

0: kd> !mex.runaway2 -v -u
Showing top 10 threads
Process          Thread ID          User Time            Kernel Time          Total Time           Time %   CPU %    Current Function
=============================================================================================================================================================
vmtoolsd.exe   | ffffc38c3282c080 | 0 days 0:00:20.750 | 0 days 0:00:05.469 | 0 days 0:00:26.219 | 11.16  | 5.58   | win32u!NtUserMsgWaitForMultipleObjectsEx+0x14
explorer.exe   | ffffc38c2e3b0080 | 0 days 0:00:06.094 | 0 days 0:00:07.297 | 0 days 0:00:13.391 | 3.28   | 1.64   | win32u!NtUserMsgWaitForMultipleObjectsEx+0x14
MsMpEngCP.exe  | ffffc38c31f82040 | 0 days 0:00:05.375 | 0 days 0:00:01.891 | 0 days 0:00:07.266 | 2.89   | 1.44   | Failed to get Current Function- this is a work in progress.
svchost.exe    | ffffc38c31897080 | 0 days 0:00:02.922 | 0 days 0:00:02.391 | 0 days 0:00:05.313 | 1.57   | 0.79   | sysmain!PfSvcMainThreadWorker+0xf02
svchost.exe    | ffffc38c323b9080 | 0 days 0:00:02.766 | 0 days 0:00:01.203 | 0 days 0:00:03.969 | 1.49   | 0.74   | combase!CMessageCall::RpcSendRequestReceiveResponse+0xb9
explorer.exe   | ffffc38c3270d080 | 0 days 0:00:02.422 | 0 days 0:00:05.250 | 0 days 0:00:07.672 | 1.3    | 0.65   | win32u!NtUserMsgWaitForMultipleObjectsEx+0x14
MsMpEng.exe    | ffffc38c32e31040 | 0 days 0:00:02.203 | 0 days 0:00:00.547 | 0 days 0:00:02.750 | 1.18   | 0.59   | Failed to get Current Function- this is a work in progress.
MsMpEngCP.exe  | ffffc38c30917080 | 0 days 0:00:01.828 | 0 days 0:00:00.156 | 0 days 0:00:01.984 | 0.98   | 0.49   | Failed to get Current Function- this is a work in progress.
svchost.exe    | ffffc38c2ef61080 | 0 days 0:00:01.594 | 0 days 0:00:00.625 | 0 days 0:00:02.219 | 0.86   | 0.43   | KERNELBASE!SleepConditionVariableSRW+0x29
svchost.exe    | ffffc38c328f0080 | 0 days 0:00:01.422 | 0 days 0:00:00.297 | 0 days 0:00:01.719 | 0.76   | 0.38   | Failed to get Current Function- this is a work in progress.
=============================================================================================================================================================
Process          Thread ID          User Time            Kernel Time          Total Time           Time %   CPU %    Current Function
```

12. We can also use regular expressions for stack traces, treating them as a multiline string (**-m**):

```
0: kd> .thread /r /p
Implicit thread is now ffffc38c`33ac3080
Implicit process is now ffffc38c`2e16b080
Loading User Symbols
..................................

************* Symbol Loading Error Summary **************
Module name            Error
vsock                  The system cannot find the file specified
vmci                   The system cannot find the file specified
WdFilter               The system cannot find the file specified
vm3dmp                 The system cannot find the file specified
vmmemctl               The system cannot find the file specified
vmhgfs                 The system cannot find the file specified
myfault                The system cannot find the file specified

You can troubleshoot most symbol related issues by turning on symbol loading diagnostics (!sym
noisy) and repeating the command that caused symbols to be loaded.
You should also verify that your symbol search path (.sympath) is correct.

0: kd> !mex.us -m (.*)BugCheck(.*)PageFault(.*)
1 thread [stats]: ffffc38c33ac3080
    fffff80662215590 nt!KeBugCheckEx
    fffff806622281a9 nt!KiBugCheckDispatch+0x69
    fffff80662224300 nt!KiPageFault+0x440
    fffff80660571981 myfault+0x1981
    fffff80660571d3d myfault+0x1d3d
    fffff80660571ea1 myfault+0x1ea1
    fffff80662102f65 nt!IofCallDriver+0x55
    fffff8066256b532 nt!IopSynchronousServiceTail+0x1d2
    fffff8066256acbf nt!IopXxxControlFile+0x5df
    fffff8066256a6c6 nt!NtDeviceIoControlFile+0x56
    fffff80662227b75 nt!KiSystemServiceCopyEnd+0x25
    00007ffc88543444 ntdll!NtDeviceIoControlFile+0x14
    00007ffc85c23edb KERNELBASE!DeviceIoControl+0x6b
    00007ffc876b5f91 KERNEL32!DeviceIoControlImplementation+0x81
    00007ff7be36342f notmyfault64+0x342f
    00007ffc87fd484b USER32!UserCallDlgProcCheckWow+0x14b
```

```
    00007ffc87fd409b USER32!DefDlgProcWorker+0xcb
    00007ffc880197c9 USER32!DefDlgProcA+0x39
    00007ffc87fd1c4c USER32!UserCallWinProcCheckWow+0x33c
    00007ffc87fd179c USER32!DispatchClientMessage+0x9c
    00007ffc87fe4b4d USER32!_fnDWORD+0x3d
    00007ffc885472b4 ntdll!KiUserCallbackDispatcherContinue
    00007ffc85b21434 win32u!NtUserMessageCall+0x14
    00007ffc87fd08cf USER32!SendMessageWorker+0x12f
    00007ffc87fd0737 USER32!SendMessageW+0x137
    00007ffc73c550bf COMCTL32!Button_ReleaseCapture+0xbb
    00007ffc73c88822 COMCTL32!Button_WndProc+0x802
    00007ffc87fd1c4c USER32!UserCallWinProcCheckWow+0x33c
    00007ffc87fd0ea6 USER32!DispatchMessageWorker+0x2a6
    00007ffc87fd6084 USER32!IsDialogMessageW+0x104
    00007ffc73c35f9f COMCTL32!Prop_IsDialogMessage+0x4b
    00007ffc73c35e48 COMCTL32!_RealPropertySheet+0x2c0
    00007ffc73c35abd COMCTL32!_PropertySheet+0x49
    00007ffc73d00953 COMCTL32!PropertySheetA+0x53
    00007ff7be364cd0 notmyfault64+0x4cd0
    00007ff7be365292 notmyfault64+0x5292
    00007ffc876b54e0 KERNEL32!BaseThreadInitThunk+0x10
    00007ffc884a485b ntdll!RtlUserThreadStart+0x2b

Threads matching filter: 1 out of 3
```

13. There's a very useful command to analyze execution residue in both kernel and user space thread stack regions. It splits data by frames and combines **dps**, **dpa**, and **dpu** functionality (we removed UNICODE and ASCII noise for clarity):

```
0: kd> !mex.irs
Frame  Function                        Stack Address      Value              Symbol                          Unicode    Ansi
==============================================================================================================================
    0 | nt!KeBugCheckEx               |                  |                  | --- frame start ---           |          |
      |                               |                  |                  | --- frame end ---             |          |
    1 | nt!KiBugCheckDispatch+0x69    |                  |                  | --- frame start ---           |          |
      |                               | ffffbe8296f64670 | 000000000000000a |                               |          |
      |                               | ffffbe8296f64678 | ffffac8a0d8ea010 |                               |          |
      |                               | ffffbe8296f64680 | 0000000000000002 |                               |          |
      |                               | ffffbe8296f64688 | 0000000000000000 |                               |          |
      |                               | ffffbe8296f64690 | fffff80660571981 | myfault+0x1981                |          |
      |                               | ffffbe8296f64698 | 0000000000000000 |                               |          |
      |                               | ffffbe8296f646a0 | 0000000000000000 |                               |          |
      |                               | ffffbe8296f646a8 | 0000000000000000 |                               |          |
      |                               | ffffbe8296f646b0 | 0000000000000000 |                               |          |
      |                               | ffffbe8296f646b8 | 0000000000000000 |                               |          |
      |                               | ffffbe8296f646c0 | 0000000000000000 |                               |          |
      |                               | ffffbe8296f646c8 | 0000000000000000 |                               |          |
      |                               | ffffbe8296f646d0 | 0000000000000000 |                               |          |
      |                               | ffffbe8296f646d8 | 0000000000000000 |                               |          |
      |                               | ffffbe8296f646e0 | 0000000000000000 |                               |          |
      |                               | ffffbe8296f646e8 | 0000000000000000 |                               |          |
      |                               | ffffbe8296f646f0 | 0000000000000000 |                               |          |
      |                               | ffffbe8296f646f8 | 0000000000000000 |                               |          |
      |                               | ffffbe8296f64700 | 0000000000000000 |                               |          |
      |                               | ffffbe8296f64708 | 0000000000000000 |                               |          |
      |                               | ffffbe8296f64710 | 0000000000000000 |                               |          |
      |                               | ffffbe8296f64718 | 0000000000000000 |                               |          |
      |                               | ffffbe8296f64720 | 0000000000000000 |                               |          |
      |                               | ffffbe8296f64728 | 0000000000000000 |                               |          |
      |                               | ffffbe8296f64730 | 0000000000000000 |                               |          |
      |                               | ffffbe8296f64738 | 0000000000000000 |                               |          |
      |                               | ffffbe8296f64740 | 0000000000000000 |                               |          |
      |                               | ffffbe8296f64748 | 0000000000000000 |                               |          |
      |                               | ffffbe8296f64750 | 0000000000000000 |                               |          |
      |                               | ffffbe8296f64758 | ffffbd43fa8b2468 | win32kbase!gDomainHookLock    |          |
      |                               | ffffbe8296f64760 | fffffc571d9ef0d5 |                               |          |
      |                               | ffffbe8296f64768 | ffffbd43fa619191 | win32kbase!ThreadUnlock1+0x71 |          |
      |                               | ffffbe8296f64770 | ffffac8a0d8ea010 |                               |          |
      |                               | ffffbe8296f64778 | ffffc38c31efb390 |                               |          |
      |                               | ffffbe8296f64780 | ffffc38c31efb360 |                               |          |
      |                               | ffffbe8296f64788 | ffffc38c31efb370 |                               |          |
      |                               | ffffbe8296f64790 | ffffc38c2c4792d0 |                               |          |
      |                               | ffffbe8296f64798 | 0000000000000001 |                               |          |
      |                               | ffffbe8296f647a0 | ffffc38c34dd8690 |                               |          |
      |                               | ffffbe8296f647a8 | fffff80662224300 | nt!KiPageFault+0x440          |          |
      |                               |                  |                  | --- frame end ---             |          |
    2 | nt!KiPageFault+0x440          |                  |                  | --- frame start ---           |          |
      |                               | ffffbe8296f647b0 | 0000000000000000 |                               |          |
      |                               | ffffbe8296f647b8 | ffffbd11c0e0c2b8 |                               |          |
      |                               | ffffbe8296f647c0 | ffff2703d5aecdf2 |                               |          |
      |                               | ffffbe8296f647c8 | ffffbd11c253e710 |                               |          |
      |                               | ffffbe8296f647d0 | 0000000000000f4d |                               |          |
      |                               | ffffbe8296f647d8 | 00001f8001000000 |                               |          |
      |                               | ffffbe8296f647e0 | 0000000000001000 |                               |          |
      |                               | ffffbe8296f647e8 | ffffac8a0d8e7000 |                               |          |
      |                               | ffffbe8296f647f0 | ffffac8a0d480000 |                               |          |
```

```
  |                                 | ffffbe8296f647f8 | ffffac8a0d480000 |                                 |     |
  |                                 | ffffbe8296f64800 | ffffc38c2c402000 |                                 |     | UMDu
  |                                 | ffffbe8296f64808 | fffff80662a5f540 | nt!ExPoolState+0x4580           |     |
  |                                 | ffffbe8296f64810 | ffffac8a0d8e7000 |                                 |     |
  |                                 | ffffbe8296f64820 | 0000000000000000 |                                 |     |
  |                                 | ffffbe8296f64828 | 0000000000000000 |                                 |     |
  |                                 | ffffbe8296f64830 | 0000000000000000 |                                 |     |
  |                                 | ffffbe8296f64838 | 0000000000000000 |                                 |     |
  |                                 | ffffbe8296f64840 | 0000000000000000 |                                 |     |
  |                                 | ffffbe8296f64848 | 0000000000000000 |                                 |     |
  |                                 | ffffbe8296f64850 | 0000000000000000 |                                 |     |
  |                                 | ffffbe8296f64858 | 0000000000000000 |                                 |     |
  |                                 | ffffbe8296f64860 | 0000000000000000 |                                 |     |
  |                                 | ffffbe8296f64868 | 0000000000000000 |                                 |     |
  |                                 | ffffbe8296f64870 | 0000000000000000 |                                 |     |
  |                                 | ffffbe8296f64878 | 0000000000000000 |                                 |     |
  |                                 | ffffbe8296f64880 | ffffac8a0d8ea010 |                                 |     |
  |                                 | ffffbe8296f64888 | 0000000000000000 |                                 |     |
  |                                 | ffffbe8296f64890 | 0000000000000103 |                                 |     |
  |                                 | ffffbe8296f64898 | 0000000000000000 |                                 |     |
  |                                 | ffffbe8296f648a0 | 0000000000000001 |                                 |     |
  |                                 | ffffbe8296f648a8 | 0000000000000000 |                                 |     |
  |                                 | ffffbe8296f648b0 | 0000000000000800 |                                 |     |
  |                                 | ffffbe8296f648b8 | fffff8066286b964 | nt!ExAllocatePoolWithTag+0x64   |     |
  |                                 | ffffbe8296f648c0 | 0000000000000000 |                                 |     |
  |                                 | ffffbe8296f648c8 | 0000000000000000 |                                 |     |
  |                                 | ffffbe8296f648d0 | 0000000000000001 |                                 |     |
  |                                 | ffffbe8296f648d8 | ffffc38c31efb370 |                                 |     |
  |                                 | ffffbe8296f648e0 | ffffc38c34dd8690 |                                 |     |
  |                                 | ffffbe8296f648e8 | ffffc38c2c4792d0 |                                 |     |
  |                                 | ffffbe8296f648f0 | ffffc38c31efb390 |                                 |     |
  |                                 | ffffbe8296f648f8 | ffffc38c31efb360 |                                 |     |
  |                                 | ffffbe8296f64900 | ffffac8a0d8e7010 |                                 |     |
  |                                 | ffffbe8296f64908 | ffffbe8296f64bb1 |                                 |     |
  |                                 | ffffbe8296f64910 | 0000000000000000 |                                 |     |
  |                                 | ffffbe8296f64918 | fffff80660571981 | myfault+0x1981                  |     |
  |                                 | ffffbe8296f64920 | 0000000000000010 |                                 |     |
  |                                 | ffffbe8296f64928 | 0000000000050282 |                                 |     |
  |                                 | ffffbe8296f64930 | ffffbe8296f64940 |                                 |     |
  |                                 | ffffbe8296f64938 | 0000000000000018 |                                 |     |
  |                                 |                  |                  | --- frame end ---               |     |
3 | myfault+0x1981                  |                  |                  | --- frame start ---             |     |
  |                                 | ffffbe8296f64940 | ffffbe8296f64d10 |                                 |     |
  |                                 | ffffbe8296f64948 | fffff8066d8cee70 |                                 |     |
  |                                 | ffffbe8296f64950 | 0000000000000000 |                                 |     |
  |                                 | ffffbe8296f64958 | ffffc38c306d4f70 |                                 |     |
  |                                 | ffffbe8296f64960 | 0000000000000000 |                                 |     |
  |                                 | ffffbe8296f64968 | fffff80660571d3d | myfault+0x1d3d                  |     |
  |                                 |                  |                  | --- frame end ---               |     |
4 | myfault+0x1d3d                  |                  |                  | --- frame start ---             |     |
  |                                 | ffffbe8296f64970 | 0000000000001000 |                                 |     |
  |                                 | ffffbe8296f64978 | 0000000000000000 |                                 |     |
  |                                 | ffffbe8296f64980 | ffffc38c33ac3080 |                                 |     |
  |                                 | ffffbe8296f64988 | ffffbd11c0e0c010 |                                 |     |
  |                                 | ffffbe8296f64990 | 0000000000000000 |                                 |     |
  |                                 | ffffbe8296f64998 | 0000000000000000 |                                 |     |
  |                                 | ffffbe8296f649a0 | ffffc38c306d4f10 |                                 |     |
  |                                 | ffffbe8296f649a8 | fffff8066212df2c | nt!ExReleaseResourceAndLeaveC...|     |
  |                                 | ffffbe8296f649b0 | ffffc38c306d4f10 |                                 |     |
  |                                 | ffffbe8296f649b8 | fffff8066d8cee70 |                                 |     |
  |                                 | ffffbe8296f649c0 | fffff8066d8cee70 |                                 |     |
  |                                 | ffffbe8296f649c8 | fffff80600000000 |                                 |     |
  |                                 | ffffbe8296f649d0 | ffffbd43fa8b2468 | win32kbase!gDomainHookLock      |     |
  |                                 | ffffbe8296f649d8 | ffffbd11c0e0c010 |                                 |     |
  |                                 | ffffbe8296f649e0 | 0000000000000000 |                                 |     |
  |                                 | ffffbe8296f649e8 | ffffc38c306d4f70 |                                 |     |
  |                                 | ffffbe8296f649f0 | 0000000000000000 |                                 |     |
  |                                 | ffffbe8296f649f8 | 0000000000000000 |                                 |     |
  |                                 | ffffbe8296f64a00 | ffffbd11c0e0c010 |                                 |     |
  |                                 | ffffbe8296f64a08 | ffffbd43fa6a305e | win32kbase!tagDomLock::UnLock...|     |
  |                                 | ffffbe8296f64a10 | 0000000000000001 |                                 |     |
  |                                 | ffffbe8296f64a18 | ffffbe8296f64b18 |                                 |     |
  |                                 | ffffbe8296f64a20 | 0000000000000000 |                                 |     |
  |                                 | ffffbe8296f64a28 | ffffc38c306d4f70 |                                 |     |
  |                                 | ffffbe8296f64a30 | ffffbe8296f64a78 |                                 |     |
  |                                 | ffffbe8296f64a38 | ffffbd43fb5dfa63 | win32kfull!FreeDelayedHooks+0xe3|     |
  |                                 | ffffbe8296f64a40 | ffffbe8296f64bb0 |                                 |     |
  |                                 | ffffbe8296f64a48 | 00000000cd56fd8b |                                 |     |
  |                                 | ffffbe8296f64a50 | 0000000000000001 |                                 |     |
  |                                 | ffffbe8296f64a58 | fffff806621036ea | nt!RtlHashBytes2+0x1a           |     |
  |                                 | ffffbe8296f64a60 | ffffbd43fa8b2468 | win32kbase!gDomainHookLock      |     |
  |                                 | ffffbe8296f64a68 | ffffbd43fb5cec01 | win32kfull!GetJournallingQueu...|     |
  |                                 | ffffbe8296f64a70 | ffffbd43fa8af108 | win32kbase!gDomainDummyLock     |     |
  |                                 | ffffbe8296f64a78 | 9948a42f5fd49696 |                                 |     |
  |                                 | ffffbe8296f64a80 | 0000000000000000 |                                 |     |
  |                                 | ffffbe8296f64a88 | fffff806624a42fd | nt!AstGetHashedBitNumbers+0xc1  |     |
  |                                 | ffffbe8296f64a90 | ffff6a98d8ef3384 |                                 |     |
  |                                 | ffffbe8296f64a98 | ffffbd11c0e0c000 |                                 |     |
  |                                 | ffffbe8296f64aa0 | 0000000000000001 |                                 |     |
  |                                 | ffffbe8296f64aa8 | fffff80660571ea1 | myfault+0x1ea1                  |     |
  |                                 |                  |                  | --- frame end ---               |     |
5 | myfault+0x1ea1                  |                  |                  | --- frame start ---             |     |
  |                                 | ffffbe8296f64ab0 | ffffc38c31efb360 |                                 |     |
  |                                 | ffffbe8296f64ac0 | ffffc38c2c4792d0 |                                 |     |
  |                                 | ffffbe8296f64ac8 | 0000000000005fd4 |                                 |     |
  |                                 | ffffbe8296f64ad0 | 0000000000000000 |                                 |     |
  |                                 | ffffbe8296f64ad8 | fffff80600000000 |                                 |     |
  |                                 | ffffbe8296f64ae0 | 00005fd483360018 |                                 |     |
  |                                 | ffffbe8296f64ae8 | ffffc38c31efb390 |                                 |     |
  |                                 | ffffbe8296f64af0 | ffffc38c2c4792d0 |                                 |     |
  |                                 | ffffbe8296f64af8 | fffff8066256df14 | nt!AstLogIoctl+0x1d4            |     |
  |                                 | ffffbe8296f64b00 | 0000000000000001 |                                 |     |
  |                                 | ffffbe8296f64b08 | fffff80662102f65 | nt!IofCallDriver+0x55           |     |
  |                                 |                  |                  | --- frame end ---               |     |
6 | nt!IofCallDriver+0x55           |                  |                  | --- frame start ---             |     |
  |                                 | ffffbe8296f64b10 | ffffc38c31efb360 |                                 |     |
  |                                 | ffffbe8296f64b18 | 0000000000000002 |                                 |     |
  |                                 | ffffbe8296f64b20 | 0000000000000000 |                                 |     |
  |                                 | ffffbe8296f64b28 | 0000000000000000 |                                 |     |
  |                                 | ffffbe8296f64b30 | 0000000000000000 |                                 |     |
  |                                 | ffffbe8296f64b38 | ffffc38c34dd8690 |                                 |     |
  |                                 | ffffbe8296f64b40 | 0000000083360018 |                                 |     |
  |                                 | ffffbe8296f64b48 | fffff8066256b532 | nt!IopSynchronousServiceTail+...|     |
  |                                 |                  |                  | --- frame end ---               |     |
7 | nt!IopSynchronousServiceTail+...|                  |                  | --- frame start ---             |     |
  |                                 | ffffbe8296f64b50 | 0000000000000001 |                                 |     |
  |                                 | ffffbe8296f64b58 | ffffc38c31efb360 |                                 |     |
  |                                 | ffffbe8296f64b60 | ffffbe8296f64bb1 |                                 |     |
```

```
   |                                   | ffffbe8296f64b68 | fffff80662102d23 | nt!IopAllocateIrpPrivate+0x183     |   |
   |                                   | ffffbe8296f64b70 | ffffc38c2e16b080 |                                    |   |
   |                                   | ffffbe8296f64b78 | ffffbd4300000000 |                                    |   |
   |                                   | ffffbe8296f64b80 | ffffc30000000000 |                                    |   |
   |                                   | ffffbe8296f64b88 | ffffc38c34dd8690 |                                    |   |
   |                                   | ffffbe8296f64b90 | 0000000000000000 |                                    |   |
   |                                   | ffffbe8296f64b98 | 0000000000000001 |                                    |   |
   |                                   | ffffbe8296f64ba0 | 0000000000000000 |                                    |   |
   |                                   | ffffbe8296f64ba8 | 0000000000000001 |                                    |   |
   |                                   | ffffbe8296f64bb0 | ffffc38c34dd8690 |                                    |   |
   |                                   | ffffbe8296f64bb8 | fffffc571d9efd95 |                                    |   |
   |                                   | ffffbe8296f64bc0 | 0000000000000000 |                                    |   |
   |                                   | ffffbe8296f64bc8 | 0000000000000001 |                                    |   |
   |                                   | ffffbe8296f64bd0 | 0000000000000000 |                                    |   |
   |                                   | ffffbe8296f64bd8 | 0000000000000001 |                                    |   |
   |                                   | ffffbe8296f64be0 | ffffc38c34dd8690 |                                    |   |
   |                                   | ffffbe8296f64be8 | ffffc38c31efb360 |                                    |   |
   |                                   | ffffbe8296f64bf0 | ffffbe8296f64ea0 |                                    |   |
   |                                   | ffffbe8296f64bf8 | fffff8066256acbf | nt!IopXxxControlFile+0x5df         |   |
   |                                   |                  |                  | --- frame end ---                  |   |
 8 | nt!IopXxxControlFile+0x5df        |                  |                  | --- frame start ---                |   |
   |                                   | ffffbe8296f64c00 | ffffc38c00000000 |                                    |   |
   |                                   | ffffbe8296f64c08 | ffffbe8296f64ea0 |                                    |   |
   |                                   | ffffbe8296f64c10 | 0000000083360018 |                                    |   |
   |                                   | ffffbe8296f64c18 | 0000000083360018 |                                    |   |
   |                                   | ffffbe8296f64c20 | ffffbe8296f64c01 |                                    |   |
   |                                   | ffffbe8296f64c28 | ffffbd43fb690901 | win32kfull!ClientImmProcessKe...   |   |
   |                                   | ffffbe8296f64c30 | fffff80600000002 |                                    |   |
   |                                   | ffffbe8296f64c38 | ffffbd43fa643fb8 | win32kbase!UserSessionSwitchL...   |   |
   |                                   | ffffbe8296f64c40 | 0000000000000000 |                                    |   |
   |                                   | ffffbe8296f64c48 | 0000000000000001 |                                    |   |
   |                                   | ffffbe8296f64c50 | 0000000000000000 |                                    |   |
   |                                   | ffffbe8296f64c58 | 00000000fa619100 |                                    |   |
   |                                   | ffffbe8296f64c60 | 0000000000000100 |                                    |   |
   |                                   | ffffbe8296f64c68 | ffffc38c34dd8690 |                                    |   |
   |                                   | ffffbe8296f64c70 | 0000000000000000 |                                    |   |
   |                                   | ffffbe8296f64c78 | ffffc38c2c4792d0 |                                    |   |
   |                                   | ffffbe8296f64c80 | 00000000000002b1 |                                    |   |
   |                                   | ffffbe8296f64c88 | 0000000000000000 |                                    |   |
   |                                   | ffffbe8296f64c90 | 0000000000000000 |                                    |   |
   |                                   | ffffbe8296f64c98 | 0000000000000000 |                                    |   |
   |                                   | ffffbe8296f64ca0 | 0000000000000000 |                                    |   |
   |                                   | ffffbe8296f64ca8 | ffffc38c34dd8690 |                                    |   |
   |                                   | ffffbe8296f64cb0 | ffffc38c31efb360 |                                    |   |
   |                                   | ffffbe8296f64cb8 | ffffbd1183360018 |                                    |   |
   |                                   | ffffbe8296f64cc0 | 0012019f00000000 |                                    |   |
   |                                   | ffffbe8296f64cc8 | ffffbd43fb67b3a8 | win32kfull!NtUserMessageCall+...   |   |
   |                                   | ffffbe8296f64cd0 | ffffc38c33ac3080 |                                    |   |
   |                                   | ffffbe8296f64cd8 | fffff8066d8cee70 |                                    |   |
   |                                   | ffffbe8296f64ce0 | ffffbd11c0e0c010 |                                    |   |
   |                                   | ffffbe8296f64ce8 | fffff8066d8cfd20 |                                    |   |
   |                                   | ffffbe8296f64cf0 | 0000000000000000 |                                    |   |
   |                                   | ffffbe8296f64cf8 | fffff806000002b1 |                                    |   |
   |                                   | ffffbe8296f64d00 | 0000000000000001 |                                    |   |
   |                                   | ffffbe8296f64d08 | 0000000000000111 |                                    |   |
   |                                   | ffffbe8296f64d10 | 0000000000020454 |                                    |   |
   |                                   | ffffbe8296f64d18 | 0000000000020454 |                                    |   |
   |                                   | ffffbe8296f64d20 | ffffbe8296f64dc8 |                                    |   |
   |                                   | ffffbe8296f64d28 | 0000003f0731ec28 |                                    |   |
   |                                   | ffffbe8296f64d30 | ffffc38c33ac3080 |                                    |   |
   |                                   | ffffbe8296f64d38 | fffff8066256a6c6 | nt!NtDeviceIoControlFile+0x56      |   |
   |                                   |                  |                  | --- frame end ---                  |   |
 9 | nt!NtDeviceIoControlFile+0x56     |                  |                  | --- frame start ---                |   |
   |                                   | ffffbe8296f64d40 | 0000000000000000 |                                    |   |
   |                                   | ffffbe8296f64d48 | 0000000000000000 |                                    |   |
   |                                   | ffffbe8296f64d50 | 0000000000000000 |                                    |   |
   |                                   | ffffbe8296f64d58 | 0000000000000000 |                                    |   |
   |                                   | ffffbe8296f64d60 | 0000003f0731ec60 |                                    |   |
   |                                   | ffffbe8296f64d68 | 0000000083360001 |                                    |   |
   |                                   | ffffbe8296f64d70 | 0000000000000000 |                                    |   |
   |                                   | ffffbe8296f64d78 | ffffc38c00000000 |                                    |   |
   |                                   | ffffbe8296f64d80 | 0000000000000000 |                                    |   |
   |                                   | ffffbe8296f64d88 | 0000000000000000 |                                    |   |
   |                                   | ffffbe8296f64d90 | ffffbe8200000001 |                                    |   |
   |                                   | ffffbe8296f64d98 | fffff8066d8cfd20 |                                    |   |
   |                                   | ffffbe8296f64da0 | 0000000000000000 |                                    |   |
   |                                   | ffffbe8296f64da8 | fffff80662227b75 | nt!KiSystemServiceCopyEnd+0x25     |   |
   |                                   |                  |                  | --- frame end ---                  |   |
10 | nt!KiSystemServiceCopyEnd+0x25    |                  |                  | --- frame start ---                |   |
   |                                   |                  |                  | --- frame end ---                  |   |
11 | ntdll!NtDeviceIoControlFile+0x14  |                  |                  | --- frame start ---                |   |
   |                                   | 0000003f0731ec08 | 00007ffc85c23edb | KERNELBASE!DeviceIoControl+0x6b    |   |
   |                                   |                  |                  | --- frame end ---                  |   |
12 | KERNELBASE!DeviceIoControl+0x6b   |                  |                  | --- frame start ---                |   |
   |                                   | 0000003f0731ec10 | 000000000002043c |                                    |   |
   |                                   | 0000003f0731ec18 | 0000003f0731ef49 |                                    |   |
   |                                   | 0000003f0731ec20 | 000001e9bdfc0000 |                                    |   |
   |                                   | 0000003f0731ec28 | 0000000000000000 |                                    |   |
   |                                   | 0000003f0731ec30 | 0000003f0731ec60 |                                    |   |
   |                                   | 0000003f0731ec38 | 0000000083360018 |                                    |   |
   |                                   | 0000003f0731ec40 | 0000000000000000 |                                    |   |
   |                                   | 0000003f0731ec48 | 0000000000000000 |                                    |   |
   |                                   | 0000003f0731ec50 | 0000000000000000 |                                    |   |
   |                                   | 0000003f0731ec58 | 000001e900000000 |                                    |   |
   |                                   | 0000003f0731ec60 | 0000000000000000 |                                    |   |
   |                                   | 0000003f0731ec68 | 00007ffc87fd0737 | USER32!SendMessageW+0x137          |   |
   |                                   | 0000003f0731ec70 | 0000000000000000 |                                    |   |
   |                                   | 0000003f0731ec78 | 00007ffc876b5f91 | KERNEL32!DeviceIoControlImple...   |   |
   |                                   |                  |                  | --- frame end ---                  |   |
13 | KERNEL32!DeviceIoControlImple...  |                  |                  | --- frame start ---                |   |
   |                                   | 0000003f0731ec80 | 0000000083360018 |                                    |   |
   |                                   | 0000003f0731ec88 | 0000000000000000 |                                    |   |
   |                                   | 0000003f0731ec90 | 0000000000000000 |                                    |   |
   |                                   | 0000003f0731ec98 | 00007ffc880199f9 | USER32!IsDlgButtonChecked+0x9      |   |
   |                                   | 0000003f0731eca0 | 0000000000000000 |                                    |   |
   |                                   | 0000003f0731eca8 | 0000000000000000 |                                    |   |
   |                                   | 0000003f0731ecb0 | 0000003f0731ed10 |                                    |   |
   |                                   | 0000003f0731ecb8 | 0000000000000000 |                                    |   |
   |                                   | 0000003f0731ecc0 | 0000000000000000 |                                    |   |
   |                                   | 0000003f0731ecc8 | 00007ff7be36342f | notmyfault64+0x342f                |   |
   |                                   |                  |                  | --- frame end ---                  |   |
14 | notmyfault64+0x342f               |                  |                  | --- frame start ---                |   |
   |                                   | 0000003f0731ecd0 | 0000000000020454 |                                    |   |
   |                                   | 0000003f0731ecd8 | 0000003f0731ed69 |                                    |   |
   |                                   | 0000003f0731ece0 | 0000003f0731ed69 |                                    |   |
   |                                   | 0000003f0731ece8 | 0000000000000000 |                                    |   |
   |                                   | 0000003f0731ecf0 | 0000000000000000 |                                    |   |
   |                                   | 0000003f0731ecf8 | 000001e900000000 |                                    |   |
```

```
   |                              | 0000003f0731ed00 | 0000003f0731ed10 |                                |                      |
   |                              | 0000003f0731ed08 | 0000000000000000 |                                |                      |
   |                              | 0000003f0731ed10 | 0000000000000000 |                                |                      |
   |                              | 0000003f0731ed18 | 31007ffc00000001 |                                |                      |
   |                              | 0000003f0731ed20 | 000001e9bdfc0328 |                                |                      |
   |                              | 0000003f0731ed28 | 000001e9bdfc0150 |                                |                      |
   |                              | 0000003f0731ed30 | 0000000000000040 |                                |                      |
   |                              | 0000003f0731ed38 | 00000000000000d0 |                                |                      |
   |                              | 0000003f0731ed40 | 000001e9bdfd0b10 |                                |                      |
   |                              | 0000003f0731ed48 | 000001e9bdfc0000 |                                |                      |
   |                              | 0000003f0731ed50 | 000001e9bdfd0b10 |                                |                      |
   |                              | 0000003f0731ed58 | 000001e9be011250 |                                |                      |
   |                              | 0000003f0731ed60 | 0000003f0731eeb0 |                                |                      |
   |                              | 0000003f0731ed68 | 0000000000000033 |                                |                      |
   |                              | 0000003f0731ed70 | 0000000000000003 |                                |                      |
   |                              | 0000003f0731ed78 | 000001e9be0116a0 |                                | &Crash               | &
   |                              | 0000003f0731ed80 | 0000000000000000 |                                |                      |
   |                              | 0000003f0731ed88 | 0000000000000006 |                                |                      |
   |                              | 0000003f0731ed90 | 0000000000000001 |                                |                      |
   |                              | 0000003f0731ed98 | 00007ffc87fd4a0a | USER32!_BeginIfHookedDManipHo... |                    |
   |                              | 0000003f0731eda0 | 0000000000000020 |                                |                      |
   |                              | 0000003f0731eda8 | 00007ffc884c7551 | ntdll!RtlFreeHeap+0x51         |                      |
   |                              | 0000003f0731edb0 | 0000df49902013e5 |                                |                      |
   |                              | 0000003f0731edb8 | 0000000000000000 |                                |                      |
   |                              | 0000003f0731edc0 | 0000003f0731ef28 |                                |                      |
   |                              | 0000003f0731edc8 | 00007ffc87fd484b | USER32!UserCallDlgProcCheckWo... |                    |
   |                              |                  |                  | --- frame end ---              |                      |
15 | USER32!UserCallDlgProcCheckWo... |              |                  | --- frame start ---            |                      |
   |                              | 0000003f0731edd0 | 0000000000000001 |                                |                      |
   |                              | 0000003f0731edd8 | 0000000000000001 |                                |                      |
   |                              | 0000003f0731ede0 | 0000000000000001 |                                |                      |
   |                              | 0000003f0731ede8 | 0000000000000002 |                                |                      |
   |                              | 0000003f0731edf0 | 000001e9be2c6e80 |                                |                      |
   |                              | 0000003f0731edf8 | 00007ffc87fd24b5 | USER32!_GetWindowLongPtr+0x65  |                      |
   |                              | 0000003f0731ee00 | 0000003f40000040 |                                |                      |
   |                              | 0000003f0731ee08 | 00007ffc885c906b | ntdll!RtlFindLowerBoundInSort... |                    |
   |                              | 0000003f0731ee10 | 0000000000000000 |                                |                      |
   |                              | 0000003f0731ee18 | 8000601000000000 |                                |                      |
   |                              | 0000003f0731ee20 | 0000000000000000 |                                |                      |
   |                              | 0000003f0731ee28 | 00007ffc00000000 |                                |                      |
   |                              | 0000003f0731ee30 | 00007ff7be3632d0 | notmyfault64+0x32d0            |                      |
   |                              | 0000003f0731ee38 | 0000000000000010 |                                |                      |
   |                              | 0000003f0731ee40 | 0000000000000048 |                                |                      |
   |                              | 0000003f0731ee48 | 000001e900000001 |                                |                      |
   |                              | 0000003f0731ee50 | 0000000000000000 |                                |                      |
   |                              | 0000003f0731ee58 | 0000000000000000 |                                |                      |
   |                              | 0000003f0731ee60 | 0000000000000030 |                                |                      |
   |                              | 0000003f0731ee68 | ffffffffffffffff |                                |                      |
   |                              | 0000003f0731ee70 | ffffffffffffffff |                                |                      |
   |                              | 0000003f0731ee78 | 00007ffc87fd47b6 | USER32!UserCallDlgProcCheckWo... |                    |
   |                              | 0000003f0731ee80 | 0000000000000000 |                                |                      |
   |                              | 0000003f0731ee88 | 0000000000000000 |                                |                      |
   |                              | 0000003f0731ee90 | 0000000000000001 |                                |                      |
   |                              | 0000003f0731ee98 | 000000000004046e |                                |                      |
   |                              | 0000003f0731eea0 | 00000000000003f9 |                                |                      |
   |                              | 0000003f0731eea8 | 00007ffc87fd409b | USER32!DefDlgProcWorker+0xcb   |                      |
   |                              |                  |                  | --- frame end ---              |                      |
16 | USER32!DefDlgProcWorker+0xcb |                  |                  | --- frame start ---            |                      |
   |                              | 0000003f0731eeb0 | 0000000000000000 |                                |                      |
   |                              | 0000003f0731eeb8 | 00007ff7be3632d0 | notmyfault64+0x32d0            |                      |
   |                              | 0000003f0731eec0 | 0000000000000111 |                                |                      |
   |                              | 0000003f0731eec8 | 000001e9be6d6f60 |                                |                      |
   |                              | 0000003f0731eed0 | 00000000000003f9 |                                |                      |
   |                              | 0000003f0731eed8 | 000000000004046e |                                |                      |
   |                              | 0000003f0731eee0 | 0000000000000001 |                                |                      |
   |                              | 0000003f0731eee8 | 0000003f0731eef0 |                                |                      |
   |                              | 0000003f0731eef0 | 0000000000000000 |                                |                      |
   |                              | 0000003f0731eef8 | 00007ffc87fd24b5 | USER32!_GetWindowLongPtr+0x65  |                      |
   |                              | 0000003f0731ef00 | 000000000004046e |                                |                      |
   |                              | 0000003f0731ef08 | 0000000000000000 |                                |                      |
   |                              | 0000003f0731ef10 | 0000f4b332e88b6a |                                |                      |
   |                              | 0000003f0731ef18 | 000001e9be00ea00 |                                |                      |
   |                              | 0000003f0731ef20 | 0000378a5b8abd5e |                                |                      |
   |                              | 0000003f0731ef28 | 0000000000000000 |                                |                      |
   |                              | 0000003f0731ef30 | 0000000000000000 |                                |                      |
   |                              | 0000003f0731ef38 | 0000000000000111 |                                |                      |
   |                              | 0000003f0731ef40 | 0000000000000000 |                                |                      |
   |                              | 0000003f0731ef48 | 00000000000003f9 |                                |                      |
   |                              | 0000003f0731ef50 | 0000000000000111 |                                |                      |
   |                              | 0000003f0731ef58 | 000000000004046e |                                |                      |
   |                              | 0000003f0731ef60 | 0000003f0731f2c8 |                                |                      |
   |                              | 0000003f0731ef68 | 00007ffc880197c9 | USER32!DefDlgProcA+0x39        |                      |
   |                              |                  |                  | --- frame end ---              |                      |
17 | USER32!DefDlgProcA+0x39      |                  |                  | --- frame start ---            |                      |
   |                              | 0000003f0731ef70 | 000000000004046e |                                |                      |
   |                              | 0000003f0731ef78 | 00000000000000f3 |                                |                      |
   |                              | 0000003f0731ef80 | 000000000004046e |                                |                      |
   |                              | 0000003f0731ef88 | 0000000000000000 |                                |                      |
   |                              | 0000003f0731ef90 | 000037fe00000001 |                                |                      |
   |                              | 0000003f0731ef98 | 00007ffc884deec7 | ntdll!RtlDeactivateActivation... |                    |
   |                              | 0000003f0731efa0 | 0000000080006010 |                                |                      |
   |                              | 0000003f0731efa8 | 00007ffc87fd1c4c | USER32!UserCallWinProcCheckWo... |                    |
   |                              |                  |                  | --- frame end ---              |                      |
18 | USER32!UserCallWinProcCheckWo... |              |                  | --- frame start ---            |                      |
   |                              | 0000003f0731efb0 | 0000000000000001 |                                |                      |
   |                              | 0000003f0731efb8 | 0000000000000000 |                                |                      |
   |                              | 0000003f0731efc0 | 0000000000000001 |                                |                      |
   |                              | 0000003f0731efc8 | 0000000000000000 |                                |                      |
   |                              | 0000003f0731efd0 | 000001e9be011048 |                                |                      | L
   |                              | 0000003f0731efd8 | 0000000000000000 |                                |                      |
   |                              | 0000003f0731efe0 | 0000000000000021 |                                |                      |
   |                              | 0000003f0731efe8 | 00007ffc85c33f79 | KERNELBASE!OpenEventW+0x99     |                      |
   |                              | 0000003f0731eff0 | 0000000000000000 |                                |                      |
   |                              | 0000003f0731eff8 | 0000000000000000 |                                |                      |
   |                              | 0000003f0731f000 | 8000601000000000 |                                |                      |
   |                              | 0000003f0731f008 | 0000000000000000 |                                |                      |
   |                              | 0000003f0731f010 | 0000000000000000 |                                |                      |
   |                              | 0000003f0731f018 | 0000000000000000 |                                |                      |
   |                              | 0000003f0731f020 | 0000000000000000 |                                |                      |
   |                              | 0000003f0731f028 | 0000000000000000 |                                |                      |
   |                              | 0000003f0731f030 | 0000000000000000 |                                |                      |
   |                              | 0000003f0731f038 | 0000000000000000 |                                |                      |
   |                              | 0000003f0731f040 | 0000000000000000 |                                |                      |
   |                              | 0000003f0731f048 | 00007ffc82bf2a84 | apphelp!Insp_WindowHook+0x74   |                      |
   |                              | 0000003f0731f050 | 00006d04dd5fc651 |                                |                      |
   |                              | 0000003f0731f058 | 00007ffc82bf2a10 | apphelp!Insp_WindowHook        |                      |
   |                              | 0000003f0731f060 | 0000000000000000 |                                |                      |
   |                              | 0000003f0731f068 | 0000000000000000 |                                |                      |
```

```
   |                              | 0000003f0731f070 | 000037fefbb00d9e |                                  |                    |
   |                              | 0000003f0731f078 | 0000000000000215 |                                  |                    |
   |                              | 0000003f0731f080 | 00007ffc885430e0 | ntdll!NtdllDialogWndProc_A       |                    |
   |                              | 0000003f0731f088 | 0000000000000000 |                                  |                    |
   |                              | 0000003f0731f090 | 0000000000000048 |                                  |                    |
   |                              | 0000003f0731f098 | 0000000000000001 |                                  |                    |
   |                              | 0000003f0731f0a0 | 0000000000000000 |                                  |                    |
   |                              | 0000003f0731f0a8 | 0000000000000000 |                                  |                    |
   |                              | 0000003f0731f0b0 | 0000000000000030 |                                  |                    |
   |                              | 0000003f0731f0b8 | ffffffffffffffff |                                  |                    |
   |                              | 0000003f0731f0c0 | ffffffffffffffff |                                  |                    |
   |                              | 0000003f0731f0c8 | 00007ffc87fd1aed | USER32!UserCallWinProcCheckWo... |                    |
   |                              | 0000003f0731f0d0 | 0000000000000000 |                                  |                    |
   |                              | 0000003f0731f0d8 | 0000f4b332e8954a |                                  |                    |
   |                              | 0000003f0731f0e0 | 0000000000000000 |                                  |                    |
   |                              | 0000003f0731f0e8 | 0000000000000000 |                                  |                    |
   |                              | 0000003f0731f0f0 | 0000000000000000 |                                  |                    |
   |                              | 0000003f0731f0f8 | 0000000000000000 |                                  |                    |
   |                              | 0000003f0731f100 | 0000000000000000 |                                  |                    |
   |                              | 0000003f0731f108 | 0000000080000000 |                                  |                    |
   |                              | 0000003f0731f110 | 0000000000000388 |                                  |                    |
   |                              | 0000003f0731f118 | 00007ffc87fd179c | USER32!DispatchClientMessage+... |                    |
   |                              |                  |                  | --- frame end ---                |                    |
19 | USER32!DispatchClientMessage+... |              |                  | --- frame start ---              |                    |
   |                              | 0000003f0731f120 | 0000313008652f97 |                                  |                    |
   |                              | 0000003f0731f128 | 00007ffc885430e0 | ntdll!NtdllDialogWndProc_A       |                    |
   |                              | 0000003f0731f130 | 0000000000020454 |                                  |                    |
   |                              | 0000003f0731f138 | 00007ffc00000111 |                                  |                    |
   |                              | 0000003f0731f140 | 00000000000003f9 |                                  |                    |
   |                              | 0000003f0731f148 | 000000000004046e |                                  |                    |
   |                              | 0000003f0731f150 | 0000003f00000001 |                                  |                    |
   |                              | 0000003f0731f158 | 00007ffc00000001 |                                  |                    |
   |                              | 0000003f0731f160 | 0000000000000000 |                                  |                    |
   |                              | 0000003f0731f168 | 0000000000000000 |                                  |                    |
   |                              | 0000003f0731f170 | 0000000000000000 |                                  |                    |
   |                              | 0000003f0731f178 | 00007ffc87fe4b4d | USER32!_fnDWORD+0x3d             |                    |
   |                              |                  |                  | --- frame end ---                |                    |
20 | USER32!_fnDWORD+0x3d         |                  |                  | --- frame start ---              |                    |
   |                              | 0000003f0731f180 | 0000000000000000 |                                  |                    |
   |                              | 0000003f0731f188 | 0000000000000000 |                                  |                    |
   |                              | 0000003f0731f190 | 00000000000003f9 |                                  |                    |
   |                              | 0000003f0731f198 | 00000000000c0000 |                                  |                    |
   |                              | 0000003f0731f1a0 | 00007ffc885430e0 | ntdll!NtdllDialogWndProc_A       |                    |
   |                              | 0000003f0731f1a8 | 0000000000000000 |                                  |                    |
   |                              | 0000003f0731f1b0 | 0000003f0731f238 |                                  |                    |
   |                              | 0000003f0731f1b8 | 0000000000000000 |                                  |                    |
   |                              | 0000003f0731f1c0 | 0000000000000000 |                                  |                    |
   |                              | 0000003f0731f1c8 | 00007ffc88055000 | USER32!apfnDispatch              |                    |
   |                              | 0000003f0731f1d0 | 00007ffc87fd1f1b | USER32!UserCallWinProcCheckWo... |                    |
   |                              | 0000003f0731f1d8 | 00007ffc885472b4 | ntdll!KiUserCallbackDispatche... |                    |
   |                              |                  |                  | --- frame end ---                |                    |
21 | ntdll!KiUserCallbackDispatche... |              |                  | --- frame start ---              |                    |
   |                              | 0000003f0731f1e0 | 0000000000000000 |                                  |                    |
   |                              | 0000003f0731f1e8 | 0000000000000000 |                                  |                    |
   |                              | 0000003f0731f1f0 | 0000000000000000 |                                  |                    |
   |                              | 0000003f0731f1f8 | 0000000000000000 |                                  |                    |
   |                              | 0000003f0731f200 | 0000003f0731f238 |                                  |                    |
   |                              | 0000003f0731f208 | 0000000200000030 |                                  |                    |
   |                              | 0000003f0731f210 | 00007ffc85b21434 | win32u!NtUserMessageCall+0x14    |                    |
   |                              | 0000003f0731f218 | 00007ffc8804caf8 | USER32!fnHkINLPCWPRETSTRUCTW+... |                    |
   |                              | 0000003f0731f220 | 0000000000000000 |                                  |                    |
   |                              | 0000003f0731f228 | 0000003f0731f268 |                                  |                    |
   |                              | 0000003f0731f230 | 000000000004046e |                                  |                    |
   |                              | 0000003f0731f238 | 000001e9be6d6f60 |                                  |                    |
   |                              | 0000003f0731f240 | 0000000000000111 |                                  |                    |
   |                              | 0000003f0731f248 | 00000000000003f9 |                                  |                    |
   |                              | 0000003f0731f250 | 000000000004046e |                                  |                    |
   |                              | 0000003f0731f258 | 00007ffc885430e0 | ntdll!NtdllDialogWndProc_A       |                    |
   |                              | 0000003f0731f260 | 00007ffc88543250 | ntdll!NtdllDispatchMessage_W     |                    |
   |                              |                  |                  | --- frame end ---                |                    |
22 | win32u!NtUserMessageCall+0x14 |                 |                  | --- frame start ---              |                    |
   |                              | 0000003f0731f268 | 00007ffc87fd08cf | USER32!SendMessageWorker+0x12f   |                    |
   |                              |                  |                  | --- frame end ---                |                    |
23 | USER32!SendMessageWorker+0x12f |                |                  | --- frame start ---              |                    |
   |                              | 0000003f0731f270 | 0000000000000000 |                                  |                    |
   |                              | 0000003f0731f278 | 00007ffc87fe4b65 | USER32!_fnDWORD+0x55             |                    |
   |                              | 0000003f0731f280 | 0000000000000000 |                                  |                    |
   |                              | 0000003f0731f288 | 0000000000000000 |                                  |                    |
   |                              | 0000003f0731f290 | 0000000000000000 |                                  |                    |
   |                              | 0000003f0731f298 | ffffffff000002b1 |                                  |                    |
   |                              | 0000003f0731f2a0 | 00007ffc00000000 |                                  |                    |
   |                              | 0000003f0731f2a8 | 000000000000000f |                                  |                    |
   |                              | 0000003f0731f2b0 | 0000000000020454 |                                  |                    |
   |                              | 0000003f0731f2b8 | 0000000000000000 |                                  |                    |
   |                              | 0000003f0731f2c0 | 0000000000000000 |                                  |                    |
   |                              | 0000003f0731f2c8 | 000000000004046e |                                  |                    |
   |                              | 0000003f0731f2d0 | 0000000000000111 |                                  |                    |
   |                              | 0000003f0731f2d8 | 0000000000000000 |                                  |                    |
   |                              | 0000003f0731f2e0 | 00000000000003f9 |                                  |                    |
   |                              | 0000003f0731f2e8 | 0000000050010001 |                                  |                    |
   |                              | 0000003f0731f2f0 | 0000000000020454 |                                  |                    |
   |                              | 0000003f0731f2f8 | 000001e9be6d6f60 |                                  |                    |
   |                              | 0000003f0731f300 | 0000000000000000 |                                  |                    |
   |                              | 0000003f0731f308 | 00007ffc87fd0737 | USER32!SendMessageW+0x137        |                    |
   |                              |                  |                  | --- frame end ---                |                    |
24 | USER32!SendMessageW+0x137    |                  |                  | --- frame start ---              |                    |
   |                              | 0000003f0731f310 | 00007ffc85b2b2d4 | win32u!NtUserReleaseCapture+0x14 |                    |
   |                              | 0000003f0731f318 | 0000000000000000 |                                  |                    |
   |                              | 0000003f0731f320 | 00000000000003f9 |                                  |                    |
   |                              | 0000003f0731f328 | 000000000004046e |                                  |                    |
   |                              | 0000003f0731f330 | 000001e900000000 |                                  |                    |
   |                              | 0000003f0731f338 | 00007ffc73c55120 | COMCTL32!Button_NotifyParent+... |                    |
   |                              | 0000003f0731f340 | 0000000000020454 |                                  |                    |
   |                              | 0000003f0731f348 | 0000000000000000 |                                  |                    |
   |                              | 0000003f0731f350 | 000000000004046e |                                  |                    |
   |                              | 0000003f0731f358 | 000001e9be027260 |                                  |                    |
   |                              | 0000003f0731f360 | 00000000000b0025 |                                  |                    |
   |                              | 0000003f0731f368 | 00007ffc73c550bf | COMCTL32!Button_ReleaseCaptur... |                    |
   |                              |                  |                  | --- frame end ---                |                    |
25 | COMCTL32!Button_ReleaseCaptur... |              |                  | --- frame start ---              |                    |
   |                              | 0000003f0731f370 | 000001e9be027260 |                                  |                    |
   |                              | 0000003f0731f378 | 0000000000000001 |                                  |                    |
   |                              | 0000003f0731f380 | 0000000050010001 |                                  |                    |
   |                              | 0000003f0731f388 | 0000000000000001 |                                  |                    |
   |                              | 0000003f0731f390 | 000001e9be027260 |                                  |                    |
   |                              | 0000003f0731f398 | 00007ffc73c88822 | COMCTL32!Button_WndProc+0x802    |                    |
   |                              |                  |                  | --- frame end ---                |                    |
26 | COMCTL32!Button_WndProc+0x802 |                 |                  | --- frame start ---              |                    |
```

```
   |                              | 0000003f0731f3a0 | 0000000000000202 |                                |                                        |
   |                              | 0000003f0731f3a8 | 0000003f0731f449 |                                |                                        |
   |                              | 0000003f0731f3b0 | 0000000000000000 |                                |                                        |
   |                              | 0000003f0731f3b8 | 0000000000000000 |                                |                                        |
   |                              | 0000003f0731f3c0 | 0000000000000000 |                                |                                        |
   |                              | 0000003f0731f3c8 | 00007ffc884dfba3 | ntdll!RtlActivateActivationCo... |                                      |
   |                              | 0000003f0731f3d0 | 0000000b00000025 |                                |                                        |
   |                              | 0000003f0731f3d8 | 0000000000000000 |                                |                                        |
   |                              | 0000003f0731f3e0 | 0000000000000000 |                                |                                        |
   |                              | 0000003f0731f3e8 | 0000000000000000 |                                |                                        |
   |                              | 0000003f0731f3f0 | 000000170000004b |                                |                                        |
   |                              | 0000003f0731f3f8 | 0000003f0731f5b8 |                                |                                        |
   |                              | 0000003f0731f400 | 0000000000000001 |                                |                                        |
   |                              | 0000003f0731f408 | 00007ffc8804caf8 | USER32!fnHkINLPCWPRETSTRUCTW+... |                                      |
   |                              | 0000003f0731f410 | 0000000000000000 |                                |                                        |
   |                              | 0000003f0731f418 | 00007ffc73c88020 | COMCTL32!Button_WndProc        |                    | @USVWATAUAVAWH    |
   |                              | 0000003f0731f420 | 000000000004046e |                                |                                        |
   |                              | 0000003f0731f428 | 00000000000000f4 |                                |                                        |
   |                              | 0000003f0731f430 | 00007ffc73c88020 | COMCTL32!Button_WndProc        |                    | @USVWATAUAVAWH    |
   |                              | 0000003f0731f438 | 0000000000000001 |                                |                                        |
   |                              | 0000003f0731f440 | 0000000000000048 |                                |                                        |
   |                              | 0000003f0731f448 | 0000000000000001 |                                |                                        |
   |                              | 0000003f0731f450 | 00006d04dd5fda51 |                                |                                        |
   |                              | 0000003f0731f458 | 0000000000000000 |                                |                                        |
   |                              | 0000003f0731f460 | 0000000000000070 |                                |                                        |
   |                              | 0000003f0731f468 | 0000000000000000 |                                |                                        |
   |                              | 0000003f0731f470 | 0000000000000000 |                                |                                        |
   |                              | 0000003f0731f478 | 0000000000000202 |                                |                                        |
   |                              | 0000003f0731f480 | 0000000000000000 |                                |                                        |
   |                              | 0000003f0731f488 | 0000000080006010 |                                |                                        |
   |                              | 0000003f0731f490 | 0000000000000000 |                                |                                        |
   |                              | 0000003f0731f498 | 0000000000000001 |                                |                                        |
   |                              | 0000003f0731f4a0 | 0000000000000002 |                                |                                        |
   |                              | 0000003f0731f4a8 | 00007ffc87fd1c4c | USER32!UserCallWinProcCheckWo... |                                      |
   |                              |                  |                  | --- frame end ---              |                                        |
27 | USER32!UserCallWinProcCheckWo... |              |                  | --- frame start ---            |                                        |
   |                              | 0000003f0731f4b0 | 0000000000000000 |                                |                                        |
   |                              | 0000003f0731f4b8 | 0000000080000000 |                                |                                        |
   |                              | 0000003f0731f4c0 | 0000000000000001 |                                |                                        |
   |                              | 0000003f0731f4c8 | 0000000000000000 |                                |                                        |
   |                              | 0000003f0731f4d0 | 0000000000000087 |                                |                                        |
   |                              | 0000003f0731f4d8 | 00007ffc73c88020 | COMCTL32!Button_WndProc        |                                        |
   |                              | 0000003f0731f4e0 | 000000000004046e |                                |                                        |
   |                              | 0000003f0731f4e8 | 00007ffc0000000f |                                |                                        |
   |                              | 0000003f0731f4f0 | 0000000000000000 |                                |                                        |
   |                              | 0000003f0731f4f8 | 0000000000000000 |                                |                                        |
   |                              | 0000003f0731f500 | 8000601000000000 |                                |                                        |
   |                              | 0000003f0731f508 | 0000000000000000 |                                |                                        |
   |                              | 0000003f0731f510 | 0000000000000000 |                                |                                        |
   |                              | 0000003f0731f518 | 0000000008652ee7 |                                |                                        |
   |                              | 0000003f0731f520 | 0000000000000000 |                                |                                        |
   |                              | 0000003f0731f528 | 0000000000000000 |                                |                                        |
   |                              | 0000003f0731f530 | 0000000000000000 |                                |                                        |
   |                              | 0000003f0731f538 | 0000000000000000 |                                |                                        |
   |                              | 0000003f0731f540 | 0000000000000000 |                                |                                        |
   |                              | 0000003f0731f548 | 0000000000000000 |                                |                                        |
   |                              | 0000003f0731f550 | 0000000000000000 |                                |                                        |
   |                              | 0000003f0731f558 | 00007ffc87fe60fa | USER32!CtfHookProcWorker+0x2a  |                                        |
   |                              | 0000003f0731f560 | 0000000000000000 |                                |                                        |
   |                              | 0000003f0731f568 | 0000000000000000 |                                |                                        |
   |                              | 0000003f0731f570 | 0000000000000000 |                                |                                        |
   |                              | 0000003f0731f578 | 00007ffc88055000 | USER32!apfnDispatch            |                                        |
   |                              | 0000003f0731f580 | 00007ffc73c88020 | COMCTL32!Button_WndProc        |                                        |
   |                              | 0000003f0731f590 | 0000000000000048 |                                |                                        |
   |                              | 0000003f0731f598 | 0000000000000001 |                                |                                        |
   |                              | 0000003f0731f5a0 | 0000000000000000 |                                |                                        |
   |                              | 0000003f0731f5a8 | 0000000000000000 |                                |                                        |
   |                              | 0000003f0731f5b0 | 0000000000000030 |                                |                                        |
   |                              | 0000003f0731f5b8 | ffffffffffffffff |                                |                                        |
   |                              | 0000003f0731f5c0 | ffffffffffffffff |                                |                                        |
   |                              | 0000003f0731f5c8 | 00007ffc87fd1aed | USER32!UserCallWinProcCheckWo... |                                      |
   |                              | 0000003f0731f5d0 | 0000000000000000 |                                |                                        |
   |                              | 0000003f0731f5d8 | 00007ffc87fc1da6 | USER32!_fnHkINLPMOUSEHOOKSTRU... |                                      |
   |                              | 0000003f0731f5e0 | 0000000000000000 |                                |                                        |
   |                              | 0000003f0731f5e8 | 0000003f07458800 |                                |                                        |
   |                              | 0000003f0731f5f0 | 0000000000000000 |                                |                                        |
   |                              | 0000003f0731f5f8 | 0000000000000000 |                                |                                        |
   |                              | 0000003f0731f600 | 0000003f0731f7a8 |                                |                                        |
   |                              | 0000003f0731f608 | 000001e9be6d88e0 |                                |                                        |
   |                              | 0000003f0731f610 | 00007ffc73c88020 | COMCTL32!Button_WndProc        |                                        |
   |                              |                  |                  | --- frame end ---              |                                        |
28 | USER32!DispatchMessageWorker+... |              |                  | --- frame start ---            |                                        |
   |                              | 0000003f0731f620 | 0000000000000000 |                                |                                        |
   |                              | 0000003f0731f628 | 00007ffc73c88020 | COMCTL32!Button_WndProc        |                                        |
   |                              | 0000003f0731f630 | 000000000004046e |                                |                                        |
   |                              | 0000003f0731f638 | 00007ffc00000202 |                                |                                        |
   |                              | 0000003f0731f640 | 0000000000000000 |                                |                                        |
   |                              | 0000003f0731f648 | 00000000000b0025 |                                |                                        |
   |                              | 0000003f0731f650 | 0000003f00000001 |                                |                                        |
   |                              | 0000003f0731f658 | 0000002c00000001 |                                |                                        |
   |                              | 0000003f0731f660 | 000000000004046e |                                |                                        |
   |                              | 0000003f0731f668 | 0000000000000202 |                                |                                        |
   |                              | 0000003f0731f670 | 0000000000000009 |                                |                                        |
   |                              | 0000003f0731f678 | 000001e9be6d88e0 |                                |                                        |
   |                              | 0000003f0731f680 | 0000000000000000 |                                |                                        |
   |                              | 0000003f0731f688 | 0000000000020450 |                                |                                        |
   |                              | 0000003f0731f690 | 0000003f0731f7a8 |                                |                                        |
   |                              | 0000003f0731f698 | 00007ffc87fd6084 | USER32!IsDialogMessageW+0x104  |                                        |
   |                              |                  |                  | --- frame end ---              |                                        |
29 | USER32!IsDialogMessageW+0x104 |                 |                  | --- frame start ---            |                                        |
   |                              | 0000003f0731f6a0 | 00007ffc73c88020 | COMCTL32!Button_WndProc        |                    | @USVWATAUAVAWH    |
   |                              | 0000003f0731f6a8 | 0000000000000000 |                                |                                        |
   |                              | 0000003f0731f6b0 | 000001e9be6d3570 |                                |                                        |
   |                              | 0000003f0731f6b8 | 000000000004046e |                                |                                        |
   |                              | 0000003f0731f6c0 | 0000000000000001 |                                |                                        |
   |                              | 0000003f0731f6c8 | 0000000000000000 |                                |                                        |
   |                              | 0000003f0731f6d0 | 0000000000000001 |                                |                                        |
   |                              | 0000003f0731f6d8 | 0000000000000000 |                                |                                        |
   |                              | 0000003f0731f6e0 | 0000000000000000 |                                |                                        |
   |                              | 0000003f0731f6e8 | 000000000000ffff |                                |                                        |
   |                              | 0000003f0731f6f0 | 0000003f0731f7a8 |                                |                                        |
   |                              | 0000003f0731f6f8 | 00007ffc73c35f9f | COMCTL32!Prop_IsDialogMessage... |                                      |
   |                              |                  |                  | --- frame end ---              |                                        |
30 | COMCTL32!Prop_IsDialogMessage... |              |                  | --- frame start ---            |                                        |
   |                              | 0000003f0731f700 | 000001e9bdfe6080 |                                |                                        |
   |                              | 0000003f0731f708 | 0000003f0731f7a9 |                                |                                        |
   |                              | 0000003f0731f710 | 0000000000000100 |                                |                                        |
   |                              | 0000003f0731f718 | 0000000000020450 |                                |                                        |
```

```
   |                               | 0000003f0731f720 | 00000000ffffffff |                                 |                 |
   |                               | 0000003f0731f728 | 0000000000020450 |                                 |                 |
   |                               | 0000003f0731f730 | 000001e9bdfe6080 |                                 |                 |
   |                               | 0000003f0731f738 | 00007ffc73c35e48 | COMCTL32!_RealPropertySheet+0... |                |
   |                               |                  |                  | --- frame end ---               |                 |
31 | COMCTL32!_RealPropertySheet+0... |               |                  | --- frame start ---             |                 |
   |                               | 0000003f0731f740 | 000001e9bdfd09e0 |                                 |                 |
   |                               | 0000003f0731f748 | 0000003f0731f7a9 |                                 |                 |
   |                               | 0000003f0731f750 | 0000000000000000 |                                 |                 |
   |                               | 0000003f0731f758 | 1002ccdb00000001 |                                 |                 |
   |                               | 0000003f0731f760 | 000001e9bdfe6080 |                                 |                 |
   |                               | 0000003f0731f768 | 00007ffc73c37675 | COMCTL32!_CreatePropertySheet... |                |
   |                               | 0000003f0731f770 | 0000003f0731f784 |                                 |                 |
   |                               | 0000003f0731f778 | 0000000000000001 |                                 |                 |
   |                               | 0000003f0731f780 | 0000000007310809 |                                 |                 |
   |                               | 0000003f0731f788 | 000001e9000000fe |                                 |                 |
   |                               | 0000003f0731f790 | 000001e9bdfd09e0 |                                 |                 |
   |                               | 0000003f0731f798 | 000001e9bdfd28c0 |                                 |                 |
   |                               | 0000003f0731f7a0 | 0000000000000000 |                                 |                 |
   |                               | 0000003f0731f7a8 | 000000000004046e |                                 |                 |
   |                               | 0000003f0731f7b0 | 0000000000000202 |                                 |                 |
   |                               | 0000003f0731f7b8 | 0000000000000000 |                                 |                 |
   |                               | 0000003f0731f7c0 | 00000000000b0025 |                                 |                 |
   |                               | 0000003f0731f7c8 | 000001c10002d9bc |                                 |                 |
   |                               | 0000003f0731f7d0 | 000000000000021e |                                 |                 |
   |                               | 0000003f0731f7d8 | 00006d04dd5fdeb1 |                                 |                 |
   |                               | 0000003f0731f7e0 | 0000000000000000 |                                 |                 |
   |                               | 0000003f0731f7e8 | 00007ff7be360000 | notmyfault64                    |                 |
   |                               | 0000003f0731f7f0 | 0000000000000000 |                                 |                 |
   |                               | 0000003f0731f7f8 | 0000000000000000 |                                 |                 |
   |                               | 0000003f0731f800 | 0000003f0731f9e0 |                                 |                 |
   |                               | 0000003f0731f808 | 00007ffc73c35abd | COMCTL32!_PropertySheet+0x49    |                 |
   |                               |                  |                  | --- frame end ---               |                 |
32 | COMCTL32!_PropertySheet+0x49  |                  |                  | --- frame start ---             |                 |
   |                               | 0000003f0731f810 | 0000003f0731f860 |                                 | `               | `
   |                               | 0000003f0731f818 | 0000003f0731f860 |                                 | `               | `
   |                               | 0000003f0731f820 | 0000000083360018 |                                 |                 |
   |                               | 0000003f0731f828 | 000001e9bdfe6080 |                                 |                 |
   |                               | 0000003f0731f830 | 000001e9bdfe50c0 |                                 |                 |
   |                               | 0000003f0731f838 | 00007ffc73d00953 | COMCTL32!PropertySheetA+0x53    |                 |
   |                               |                  |                  | --- frame end ---               |                 |
33 | COMCTL32!PropertySheetA+0x53  |                  |                  | --- frame start ---             |                 |
   |                               | 0000003f0731f840 | 000001e9bdfe6080 |                                 |                 |
   |                               | 0000003f0731f848 | 0000003f0731f940 |                                 | `               | `
   |                               | 0000003f0731f850 | 00007ffc87f9d130 | SHELL32!_imp_CommandLineToArgvW |                 |
   |                               | 0000003f0731f858 | 0000000000000000 |                                 |                 |
   |                               | 0000003f0731f860 | 0280018800000060 |                                 |                 |
   |                               | 0000003f0731f868 | 0000000000000000 |                                 |                 |
   |                               | 0000003f0731f870 | 00007ff7be360000 | notmyfault64                    |                 | MZ
   |                               | 0000003f0731f878 | 0000000000000000 |                                 |                 |
   |                               | 0000003f0731f880 | 000001e9bdfe3c60 |                                 | Not My Fault    | N
   |                               | 0000003f0731f888 | 0000000000000003 |                                 |                 |
   |                               | 0000003f0731f890 | 0000000000000000 |                                 |                 |
   |                               | 0000003f0731f898 | 0000003f0731fa40 |                                 | h               | h
   |                               | 0000003f0731f8a0 | 00007ff7be364130 | notmyfault64+0x4130             |                 |
   |                               | 0000003f0731f8a8 | 0000000000000000 |                                 |                 |
   |                               | 0000003f0731f8b0 | 0000000000000000 |                                 |                 |
   |                               | 0000003f0731f8b8 | 0000000000000000 |                                 |                 |
   |                               | 0000003f0731f8c0 | 00006d04dd5fd1b1 |                                 |                 |
   |                               | 0000003f0731f8c8 | 0000000000000000 |                                 |                 |
   |                               | 0000003f0731f8d0 | 0000000000000000 |                                 |                 |
   |                               | 0000003f0731f8d8 | 00007ff7be364cd0 | notmyfault64+0x4cd0             |                 |
   |                               |                  |                  | --- frame end ---               |                 |
34 | notmyfault64+0x4cd0           |                  |                  | --- frame start ---             |                 |
   |                               | 0000003f0731f8e0 | 0000003f0731f9e0 |                                 |                 |
   |                               | 0000003f0731f8e8 | 0000000083360018 |                                 |                 |
   |                               | 0000003f0731f8f0 | 0000000000000000 |                                 |                 |
   |                               | 0000003f0731f8f8 | 0000003f0731f9e0 |                                 |                 |
   |                               | 0000003f0731f900 | 00007ff7be360000 | notmyfault64                    |                 | MZ
   |                               | 0000003f0731f908 | 00000000000a1000 |                                 |                 |
   |                               | 0000003f0731f910 | 0000000001000000 |                                 |                 |
   |                               | 0000003f0731f918 | 0000000000680066 |                                 |                 |
   |                               | 0000003f0731f920 | 0000000000000001 |                                 |                 |
   |                               | 0000003f0731f928 | 007600650044005c |                                 |                 |
   |                               | 0000003f0731f930 | 005c006500630069 |                                 |                 |
   |                               | 0000003f0731f938 | 0064007200610048 |                                 |                 |
   |                               | 0000003f0731f940 | 0200018800000060 |                                 |                 |
   |                               | 0000003f0731f948 | 0000000000000000 |                                 |                 |
   |                               | 0000003f0731f950 | 00007ff7be360000 | notmyfault64                    |                 | MZ
   |                               | 0000003f0731f958 | 0000000000000000 |                                 |                 |
   |                               | 0000003f0731f960 | 00007ff7be3de290 | notmyfault64+0x7e290            |                 | Not My Fault
   |                               | 0000003f0731f968 | 0000000000000003 |                                 |                 |
   |                               | 0000003f0731f970 | 0000000000000000 |                                 |                 |
   |                               | 0000003f0731f978 | 0000003f0731fa40 |                                 | h               | h
   |                               | 0000003f0731f980 | 00007ff7be364130 | notmyfault64+0x4130             |                 |
   |                               | 0000003f0731f988 | 0000000000000000 |                                 |                 |
   |                               | 0000003f0731f990 | 0000000000000000 |                                 |                 |
   |                               | 0000003f0731f998 | 0000000000000000 |                                 |                 |
   |                               | 0000003f0731f9a0 | 0000000600000094 |                                 |                 |
   |                               | 0000003f0731f9a8 | 000023f000000002 |                                 |                 |
   |                               | 0000003f0731f9b0 | 0000000000000002 |                                 |                 |
   |                               | 0000003f0731f9b8 | 0000000000000000 |                                 |                 |
   |                               | 0000003f0731f9c0 | 0000000000000000 |                                 |                 |
   |                               | 0000003f0731f9c8 | 0000000000000000 |                                 |                 |
   |                               | 0000003f0731f9d0 | 0000000000000000 |                                 |                 |
   |                               | 0000003f0731f9d8 | 0000000000000000 |                                 |                 |
   |                               | 0000003f0731f9e0 | 0000000000000000 |                                 |                 |
   |                               | 0000003f0731f9e8 | 0000000000000000 |                                 |                 |
   |                               | 0000003f0731f9f0 | 0000000000000000 |                                 |                 |
   |                               | 0000003f0731f9f8 | 0000000000000000 |                                 |                 |
   |                               | 0000003f0731fa00 | 0000000000000000 |                                 |                 |
   |                               | 0000003f0731fa08 | 0000000000000000 |                                 |                 |
   |                               | 0000003f0731fa10 | 0000000000000000 |                                 |                 |
   |                               | 0000003f0731fa18 | 0000000000000000 |                                 |                 |
   |                               | 0000003f0731fa20 | 0000000000000000 |                                 |                 |
   |                               | 0000003f0731fa28 | 0000000000000000 |                                 |                 |
   |                               | 0000003f0731fa30 | 0000000000000000 |                                 |                 |
   |                               | 0000003f0731fa38 | 0000000000001010 |                                 |                 |
   |                               | 0000003f0731fa40 | 0000000000000068 |                                 |                 |
   |                               | 0000003f0731fa48 | 00007ff7be360000 | notmyfault64                    |                 | MZ
   |                               | 0000003f0731fa50 | 00007ff7be3ca730 | notmyfault64+0x6a730            |                 | CRASH
   |                               | 0000003f0731fa58 | 0000000000000000 |                                 |                 |
   |                               | 0000003f0731fa60 | 0000000000000000 |                                 |                 |
   |                               | 0000003f0731fa68 | 00007ff7be3632d0 | notmyfault64+0x32d0             |                 |
   |                               | 0000003f0731fa70 | 0000000000000000 |                                 |                 |
   |                               | 0000003f0731fa78 | 0000000000000000 |                                 |                 |
   |                               | 0000003f0731fa80 | 0000000000000000 |                                 |                 |
   |                               | 0000003f0731fa88 | 0000000000000000 |                                 |                 |
```

```
     |                                  | 0000003f0731fa90 | 0000000000000000 |                                  |                      |
     |                                  | 0000003f0731fa98 | 0000000000000000 |                                  |                      |
     |                                  | 0000003f0731faa0 | 0000000000000000 |                                  |                      |
     |                                  | 0000003f0731faa8 | 0000000000000068 |                                  |                      |
     |                                  | 0000003f0731fab0 | 00007ff7be360000 | notmyfault64                     |                      | MZ
     |                                  | 0000003f0731fab8 | 00007ff7be3ca738 | notmyfault64+0x6a738             |                      | HANG
     |                                  | 0000003f0731fac0 | 0000000000000000 |                                  |                      |
     |                                  | 0000003f0731fac8 | 0000000000000000 |                                  |                      |
     |                                  | 0000003f0731fad0 | 00007ff7be363c60 | notmyfault64+0x3c60              |                      |
     |                                  | 0000003f0731fad8 | 0000000000000000 |                                  |                      |
     |                                  | 0000003f0731fae0 | 0000000000000000 |                                  |                      |
     |                                  | 0000003f0731fae8 | 0000000000000000 |                                  |                      |
     |                                  | 0000003f0731faf0 | 0000000000000000 |                                  |                      |
     |                                  | 0000003f0731faf8 | 0000000000000000 |                                  |                      |
     |                                  | 0000003f0731fb00 | 0000000000000000 |                                  |                      |
     |                                  | 0000003f0731fb08 | 0000000000000000 |                                  |                      |
     |                                  | 0000003f0731fb10 | 0000000000000068 |                                  |                      |
     |                                  | 0000003f0731fb18 | 00007ff7be360000 | notmyfault64                     |                      | MZ
     |                                  | 0000003f0731fb20 | 00007ff7be3ca740 | notmyfault64+0x6a740             |                      | LEAK
     |                                  | 0000003f0731fb28 | 0000000000000000 |                                  |                      |
     |                                  | 0000003f0731fb30 | 0000000000000000 |                                  |                      |
     |                                  | 0000003f0731fb38 | 00007ff7be363df0 | notmyfault64+0x3df0              |                      |
     |                                  | 0000003f0731fb40 | 0000000000000000 |                                  |                      |
     |                                  | 0000003f0731fb48 | 0000000000000000 |                                  |                      |
     |                                  | 0000003f0731fb50 | 0000000000000000 |                                  |                      |
     |                                  | 0000003f0731fb58 | 0000000000000000 |                                  |                      |
     |                                  | 0000003f0731fb60 | 0000000000000000 |                                  |                      |
     |                                  | 0000003f0731fb68 | 0000000000000000 |                                  |                      |
     |                                  | 0000003f0731fb70 | 0000000000000000 |                                  |                      |
     |                                  | 0000003f0731fb78 | 00007ff7be3a3c9d | notmyfault64+0x43c9d             |                      |
     |                                  | 0000003f0731fb80 | 0000df49902007d5 |                                  |                      |
     |                                  | 0000003f0731fb88 | 0000000000000000 |                                  |                      |
     |                                  | 0000003f0731fb90 | 0000000000000000 |                                  |                      |
     |                                  | 0000003f0731fb98 | 0000000000000000 |                                  |                      |
     |                                  | 0000003f0731fba0 | 0000000000000000 |                                  |                      |
     |                                  | 0000003f0731fba8 | 00007ff7be365292 | notmyfault64+0x5292              |                      |
     |                                  |                  |                  | --- frame end ---                |                      |
  35 | notmyfault64+0x5292              |                  |                  | --- frame start ---              |                      |
     |                                  | 0000003f0731fbb0 | 0000000000000001 |                                  |                      |
     |                                  | 0000003f0731fbb8 | 0000000000000001 |                                  |                      |
     |                                  | 0000003f0731fbc0 | 0000000000000000 |                                  |                      |
     |                                  | 0000003f0731fbc8 | 0000000000000000 |                                  |                      |
     |                                  | 0000003f0731fbd0 | 0000000000000000 |                                  |                      |
     |                                  | 0000003f0731fbd8 | 0000000000000000 |                                  |                      |
     |                                  | 0000003f0731fbe0 | 0000000000000000 |                                  |                      |
     |                                  | 0000003f0731fbe8 | 00007ffc876b54e0 | KERNEL32!BaseThreadInitThunk+... |                      |
     |                                  |                  |                  | --- frame end ---                |                      |
  36 | KERNEL32!BaseThreadInitThunk+... |                  |                  | --- frame start ---              |                      |
     |                                  | 0000003f0731fbf0 | 0000000000000000 |                                  |                      |
     |                                  | 0000003f0731fbf8 | 0000000000000000 |                                  |                      |
     |                                  | 0000003f0731fc00 | 0000000000000000 |                                  |                      |
     |                                  | 0000003f0731fc08 | 0000000000000000 |                                  |                      |
     |                                  | 0000003f0731fc10 | 0000000000000000 |                                  |                      |
     |                                  | 0000003f0731fc18 | 00007ffc884a485b | ntdll!RtlUserThreadStart+0x2b    |                      |
     |                                  |                  |                  | --- frame end ---                |                      |
  37 | ntdll!RtlUserThreadStart+0x2b    |                  |                  | --- frame start ---              |                      |
     |                                  | 0000003f0731fc20 | 0000000000000000 |                                  |                      |
     |                                  | 0000003f0731fc28 | 0000000000000000 |                                  |                      |
     |                                  | 0000003f0731fc30 | 0000000000000000 |                                  |                      |
     |                                  | 0000003f0731fc38 | 0000000000000000 |                                  |                      |
     |                                  | 0000003f0731fc40 | 0000000000000000 |                                  |                      |
     |                                  | 0000003f0731fc48 | 0000000000000000 |                                  |                      |
     |                                  | 0000003f0731fc50 | 0000000000000000 |                                  |                      |
     |                                  | 0000003f0731fc58 | 0000000000000000 |                                  |                      |
     |                                  | 0000003f0731fc60 | 000004f0fffffb30 |                                  |                      |
     |                                  | 0000003f0731fc68 | 000004d0fffffb30 |                                  |                      |
     |                                  | 0000003f0731fc70 | 0000000000000021 |                                  |                      |
     |                                  | 0000003f0731fc78 | 0000000000000000 |                                  |                      |
     |                                  | 0000003f0731fc80 | 0000000000000000 |                                  |                      |
     |                                  | 0000003f0731fc88 | 0000000000000000 |                                  |                      |
     |                                  | 0000003f0731fc90 | 0000000000000000 |                                  |                      |
     |                                  | 0000003f0731fc98 | 0000000000000000 |                                  |                      |
     |                                  |                  |                  | --- frame end ---                |                      |
===============================================================================================================================================
Frame  Function                           Stack Address      Value              Symbol                             Unicode                Ansi
```

14. We close logging before exiting WinDbg:

```
0: kd> .logclose
Closing open log file C:\EWMDA-Dumps\Complete\x64\ES2.log
```

Exercise ES3

- **Goal:** Explore DbgKit WinDbg extension

- **Memory Analysis Patterns:** Module Collection; Historical Information; Driver Device Collection; Stack Trace (I/O devices); Stack Trace Collection (I/O drivers); System Object; Value References; Zombie Processes; Virtualized Process (WOW64); Stack Trace Collection; Environment Hint; Deviant Token; Raw Pointer; Out-of-Module Pointer

- \EWMDA\Exercise-ES3.pdf

Exercise ES3: Explore DbgKit WinDbg Extension

Goal: Explore the DbgKit WinDbg extension.

Memory Analysis Patterns: Module Collection; Historical Information; Driver Device Collection; Stack Trace (I/O devices); Stack Trace Collection (I/O drivers); System Object; Value References; Zombie Processes; Virtualized Process (WOW64); Stack Trace Collection; Environment Hint; Deviant Token; Raw Pointer; Out-of-Module Pointer.

1. Launch WinDbg. This extension is not included for a Docker setup version of exercises since it uses GUI.

2. Open \EWMDA-Dumps\Complete\x64\MEMORY-W11.DMP.

3. We get the dump file loaded:

```
Microsoft (R) Windows Debugger Version 10.0.27668.1000 AMD64
Copyright (c) Microsoft Corporation. All rights reserved.


Loading Dump File [C:\EWMDA-Dumps\Complete\x64\MEMORY-W11.DMP]
Kernel Bitmap Dump File: Full address space is available


************* Path validation summary **************
Response                         Time (ms)     Location
Deferred                                       srv*
Symbol search path is: srv*
Executable search path is:
Windows 10 Kernel Version 22000 MP (2 procs) Free x64
Product: WinNt, suite: TerminalServer SingleUserTS Personal
Edition build lab: 22000.1.amd64fre.co_release.210604-1628
Kernel base = 0xfffff806`61e00000 PsLoadedModuleList = 0xfffff806`62a296b0
Debug session time: Sat Nov 13 23:17:16.607 2021 (UTC + 1:00)
System Uptime: 0 days 0:03:06.813
Loading Kernel Symbols
...............................................................
................................................................
................................................................
..
Loading User Symbols
...................................
Loading unloaded module list
........
For analysis of this file, run !analyze -v
nt!KeBugCheckEx:
fffff806`62215590 mov     qword ptr [rsp+8],rcx ss:0018:ffffbe82`96f64670=000000000000000a
```

4. We open a log file:

```
0: kd> .logopen C:\EWMDA-Dumps\Complete\x64\ES3.log
Opened log file 'C:\EWMDA-Dumps\Complete\x64\ES3.log'
```

5. For this training, we put the extension in the dump archive because the original link to download it or check for updates was no longer available. We load the extension:

```
0: kd> .load C:\EWMDA-Dumps\DbgKit\x64\dbgkit

0: kd> !help

DbgKit 3.1
Copyright © 2016 Andrey Bazhan
http://www.andreybazhan.com

help - Displays this list
st   - Displays system service table
ps   - Displays information about processes
mm   - Displays physical memory usage information
dv   - Displays information about devices
ob   - Displays information about objects
bp   - Enables, disables and removes breakpoints
```

6. We first try the **!mm** command, which launches the Memory Explorer window that you may need to bring to the foreground (it may take some time until the PFN (Page Frame Numbers) database is built):

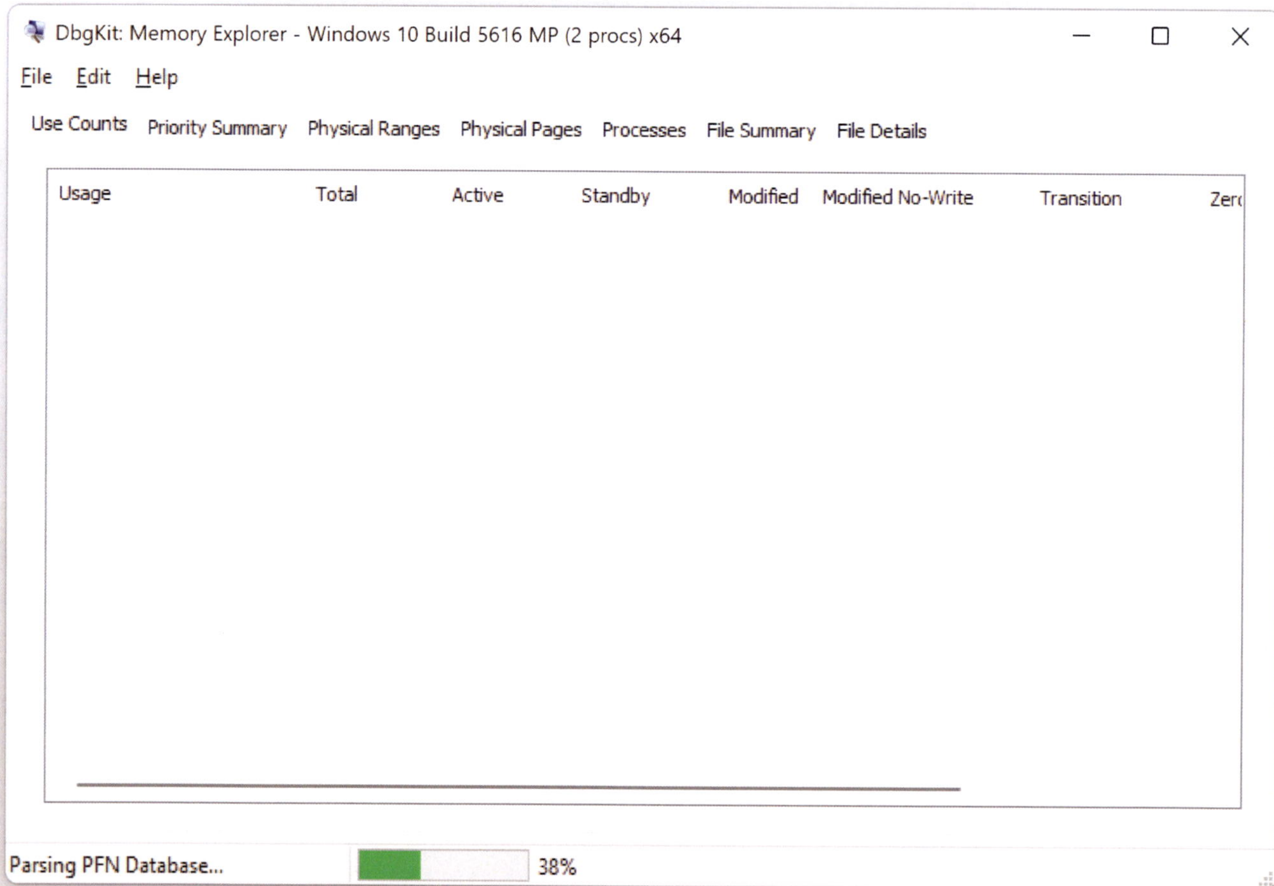

7. We can check the File Summary tab and search for the file name of interest:

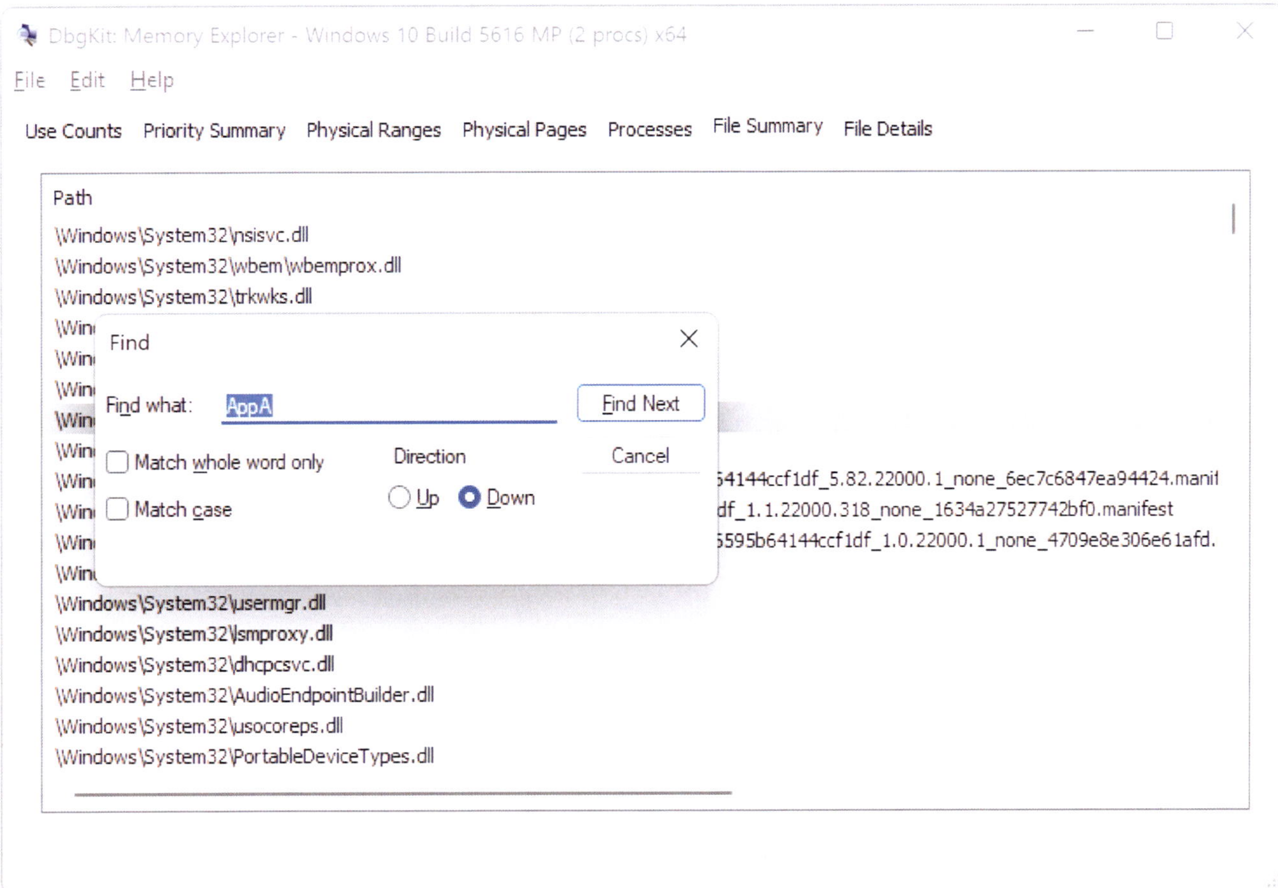

8. For any file, we can use a context right-click menu to explore its object and other structures:

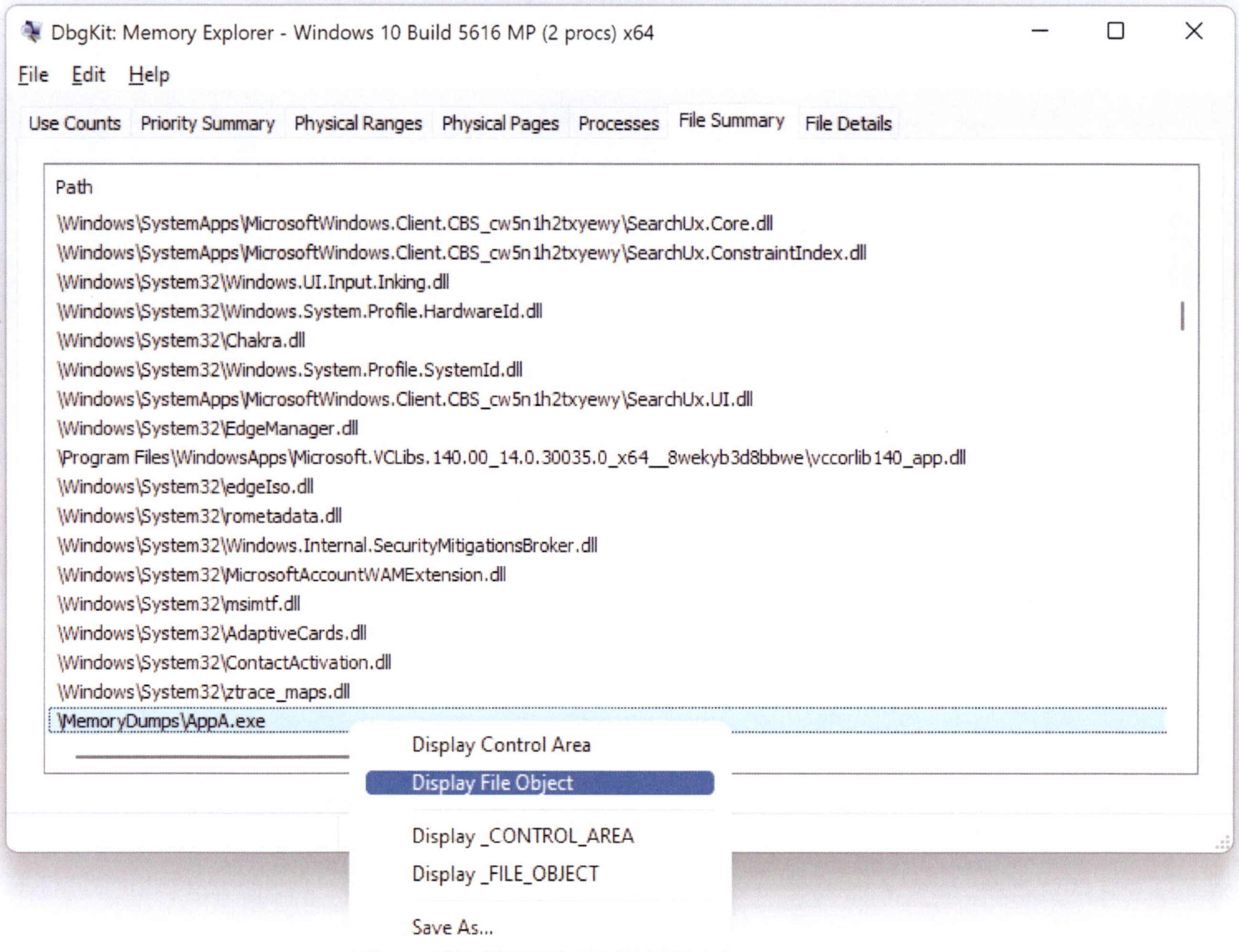

The output is redirected to the WinDbg window:

```
Device Object: 0xffffc38c2cee4860   \Driver\volmgr
Vpb: 0xffffc38c2cea2b90
Event signalled
Access: Read SharedRead SharedDelete

Flags:  0x44442
	Synchronous IO
	Cache Supported
	Queue Irps to Thread
	Cleanup Complete
	Handle Created

FsContext: 0xffffac8a0ba9a170	FsContext2: 0xffffac8a08dc5710
CurrentByteOffset: 0
Cache Data:
  Section Object Pointers: ffffc38c33b0d758
  Shared Cache Map: 00000000
```

```
nt!_FILE_OBJECT ffffc38c33b746f0

   +0x000 Type             : 0n5
   +0x002 Size             : 0n216
   +0x008 DeviceObject     : 0xffffc38c`2cee4860 _DEVICE_OBJECT
   +0x010 Vpb              : 0xffffc38c`2cea2b90 _VPB
   +0x018 FsContext        : 0xffffac8a`0ba9a170 Void
   +0x020 FsContext2       : 0xffffac8a`08dc5710 Void
   +0x028 SectionObjectPointer : 0xffffc38c`33b0d758 _SECTION_OBJECT_POINTERS
   +0x030 PrivateCacheMap  : (null)
   +0x038 FinalStatus      : 0n0
   +0x040 RelatedFileObject : (null)
   +0x048 LockOperation    : 0 ''
   +0x049 DeletePending    : 0 ''
   +0x04a ReadAccess       : 0x1 ''
   +0x04b WriteAccess      : 0 ''
   +0x04c DeleteAccess     : 0 ''
   +0x04d SharedRead       : 0x1 ''
   +0x04e SharedWrite      : 0 ''
   +0x04f SharedDelete     : 0x1 ''
   +0x050 Flags            : 0x44442
   +0x058 FileName         : _UNICODE_STRING "\MemoryDumps\AppA.exe"
   +0x068 CurrentByteOffset : _LARGE_INTEGER 0x0
   +0x070 Waiters          : 0
   +0x074 Busy             : 0
   +0x078 LastLock         : (null)
   +0x080 Lock             : _KEVENT
   +0x098 Event            : _KEVENT
   +0x0b0 CompletionContext : (null)
   +0x0b8 IrpListLock      : 0
   +0x0c0 IrpList          : _LIST_ENTRY [ 0xffffc38c`33b747b0 - 0xffffc38c`33b747b0 ]
   +0x0d0 FileObjectExtension : (null)
```

9. We can also save any file of interest (actually, its available pages in memory to a binary file for further investigation by other tools):

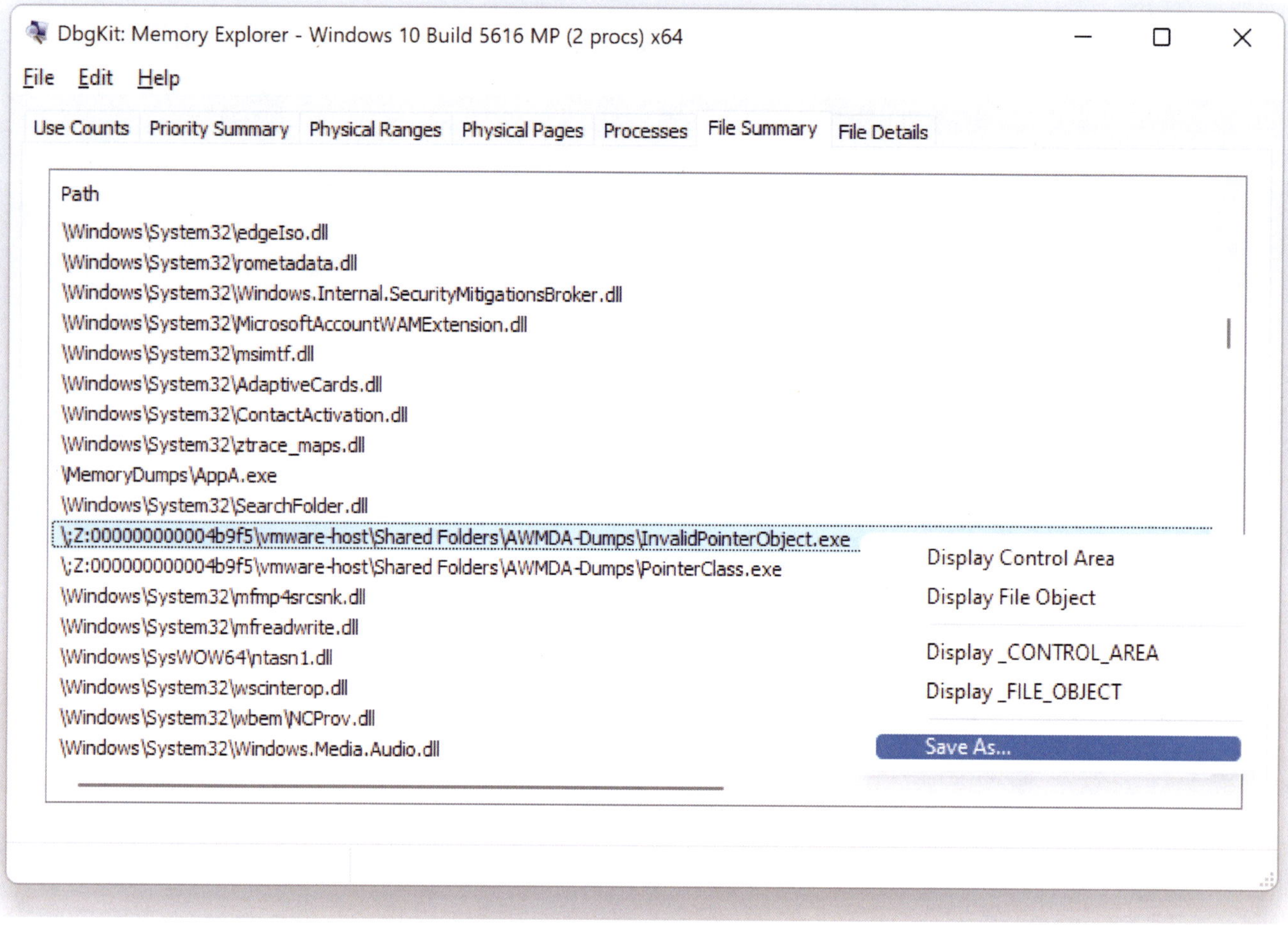

10. Fine-grained details about file pages are available in the File Details tab, where we can inspect file page details and see the contents of memory (redirected to WinDbg window):

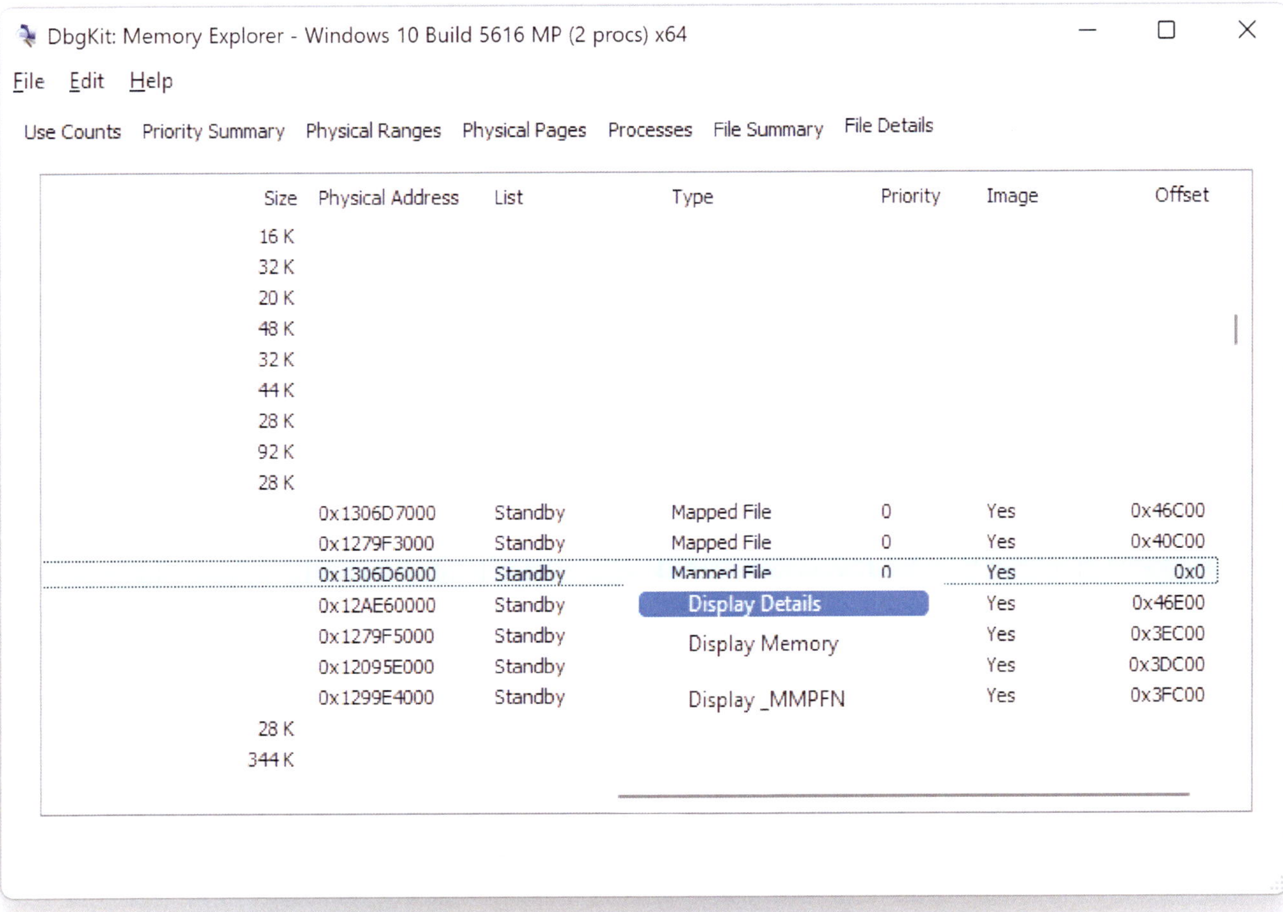


```
PFN 001306D6 at address FFFF840003914820
flink       001306D7  blink / share count 0012FF65  pteaddress FFFFAC8A0AF94C80
reference count 0000    used entry count  01A0      Cached    color 0   Priority 5
restore pte C38C2E8989A00430  containing page 1272F8  Standby     P
 Shared

  #1306d6000 4d 5a 90 00 03 00 00 00-04 00 00 00 ff ff 00 00 MZ..............
  #1306d6010 b8 00 00 00 00 00 00 00-40 00 00 00 00 00 00 00 ........@.......
  #1306d6020 00 00 00 00 00 00 00 00-00 00 00 00 00 00 00 00 ................
  #1306d6030 00 00 00 00 00 00 00 00-00 00 00 f8 00 00 00 ................
  #1306d6040 0e 1f ba 0e 00 b4 09 cd-21 b8 01 4c cd 21 54 68 ........!..L.!Th
  #1306d6050 69 73 20 70 72 6f 67 72-61 6d 20 63 61 6e 6e 6f is program canno
  #1306d6060 74 20 62 65 20 72 75 6e-20 69 6e 20 44 4f 53 20 t be run in DOS
  #1306d6070 6d 6f 64 65 2e 0d 0d 0a-24 00 00 00 00 00 00 00 mode....$.......
  #1306d6080 39 a5 a2 38 7d c4 cc 6b-7d c4 cc 6b 7d c4 cc 6b 9..8}..k}..k}..k
  #1306d6090 26 ac cf 6a 77 c4 cc 6b-26 ac c8 6a 6f c4 cc 6b &..jw..k&..jo..k
  #1306d60a0 26 ac c9 6a db c4 cc 6b-76 ab c8 6a 6d c4 cc 6b &..j...kv..jm..k
  #1306d60b0 76 ab cf 6a 74 c4 cc 6b-76 ab c9 6a 2d c4 cc 6b v..jt..kv..j-..k
  #1306d60c0 26 ac cd 6a 7e c4 cc 6b-7d c4 cd 6b 21 c4 cc 6b &..j~..k}..k!..k
  #1306d60d0 bb ab c5 6a 7c c4 cc 6b-bb ab 33 6b 7c c4 cc 6b ...j|..k..3k|..k
  #1306d60e0 bb ab ce 6a 7c c4 cc 6b-52 69 63 68 7d c4 cc 6b ...j|..kRich}..k
  #1306d60f0 00 00 00 00 00 00 00 00-50 45 00 00 64 86 07 00 ........PE..d...
```

```
#1306d6100 3f 93 ac 5e 00 00 00 00-00 00 00 00 f0 00 22 00 ?..^..........".
#1306d6110 0b 02 0e 19 00 d8 02 00-00 ba 01 00 00 00 00 00 ................
#1306d6120 44 e0 00 00 00 10 00 00-00 00 39 49 f7 7f 00 00 D.........9I....
#1306d6130 00 10 00 00 00 02 00 00-06 00 00 00 00 00 00 00 ................
#1306d6140 06 00 00 00 00 00 00 00-00 d0 04 00 00 04 00 00 ................
#1306d6150 00 00 00 00 03 00 60 81-00 00 10 00 00 00 00 00 ......`.........
#1306d6160 00 10 00 00 00 00 00 00-00 00 10 00 00 00 00 00 ................
#1306d6170 00 10 00 00 00 00 00 00-00 00 00 00 10 00 00 00 ................
#1306d6180 00 00 00 00 00 00 00 00-1c 32 04 00 28 00 00 00 .........2..(...
#1306d6190 00 b0 04 00 e0 01 00 00-00 70 04 00 d8 2d 00 00 .........p...-..
#1306d61a0 00 00 00 00 00 00 00 00-00 c0 04 00 64 0d 00 00 ............d...
#1306d61b0 40 f3 03 00 70 00 00 00-00 00 00 00 00 00 00 00 @...p...........
#1306d61c0 00 00 00 00 00 00 00 00-00 00 00 00 00 00 00 00 ................
#1306d61d0 b0 f3 03 00 30 01 00 00-00 00 00 00 00 00 00 00 ....0...........
#1306d61e0 00 f0 02 00 90 02 00 00-00 00 00 00 00 00 00 00 ................
#1306d61f0 00 00 00 00 00 00 00 00-00 00 00 00 00 00 00 00 ................
#1306d6200 2e 74 65 78 74 00 00 00-cc d7 02 00 00 10 00 00 .text...........
#1306d6210 00 d8 02 00 00 04 00 00-00 00 00 00 00 00 00 00 ................
#1306d6220 00 00 00 00 20 00 00 60-2e 72 64 61 74 61 00 00 .... ..`.rdata..
#1306d6230 b8 4a 01 00 00 f0 02 00-00 4c 01 00 00 dc 02 00 .J........L.....
#1306d6240 00 00 00 00 00 00 00 00-00 00 00 00 40 00 00 40 ............@..@
#1306d6250 2e 64 61 74 61 00 00 00-f0 2c 00 00 00 40 04 00 .data....,...@..
#1306d6260 00 14 00 00 00 28 04 00-00 00 00 00 00 00 00 00 .....(..........
#1306d6270 00 00 00 00 40 00 00 c0-2e 70 64 61 74 61 00 00 ....@....pdata..
#1306d6280 d8 2d 00 00 00 70 04 00-00 2e 00 00 00 3c 04 00 .-...p.......<..
#1306d6290 00 00 00 00 00 00 00 00-00 00 00 00 40 00 00 40 ............@..@
#1306d62a0 5f 52 44 41 54 41 00 00-00 01 00 00 00 a0 04 00 _RDATA..........
#1306d62b0 00 02 00 00 00 6a 04 00-00 00 00 00 00 00 00 00 .....j..........
#1306d62c0 00 00 00 00 40 00 00 40-2e 72 73 72 63 00 00 00 ....@..@.rsrc...
#1306d62d0 e0 01 00 00 00 b0 04 00-00 02 00 00 00 6c 04 00 .............l..
#1306d62e0 00 00 00 00 00 00 00 00-00 00 00 00 40 00 00 40 ............@..@
#1306d62f0 2e 72 65 6c 6f 63 00 00-64 0d 00 00 00 c0 04 00 .reloc..d.......
#1306d6300 00 0e 00 00 00 6e 04 00-00 00 00 00 00 00 00 00 .....n..........
#1306d6310 00 00 00 00 40 00 00 42-00 00 00 00 00 00 00 00 ....@..B........
#1306d6320 00 00 00 00 00 00 00 00-00 00 00 00 00 00 00 00 ................
#1306d6330 00 00 00 00 00 00 00 00-00 00 00 00 00 00 00 00 ................
#1306d6340 00 00 00 00 00 00 00 00-00 00 00 00 00 00 00 00 ................
#1306d6350 00 00 00 00 00 00 00 00-00 00 00 00 00 00 00 00 ................
#1306d6360 00 00 00 00 00 00 00 00-00 00 00 00 00 00 00 00 ................
#1306d6370 00 00 00 00 00 00 00 00-00 00 00 00 00 00 00 00 ................
#1306d6380 00 00 00 00 00 00 00 00-00 00 00 00 00 00 00 00 ................
#1306d6390 00 00 00 00 00 00 00 00-00 00 00 00 00 00 00 00 ................
#1306d63a0 00 00 00 00 00 00 00 00-00 00 00 00 00 00 00 00 ................
#1306d63b0 00 00 00 00 00 00 00 00-00 00 00 00 00 00 00 00 ................
#1306d63c0 00 00 00 00 00 00 00 00-00 00 00 00 00 00 00 00 ................
#1306d63d0 00 00 00 00 00 00 00 00-00 00 00 00 00 00 00 00 ................
#1306d63e0 00 00 00 00 00 00 00 00-00 00 00 00 00 00 00 00 ................
#1306d63f0 00 00 00 00 00 00 00 00-00 00 00 00 00 00 00 00 ................
#1306d6400 00 00 00 00 00 00 00 00-00 00 00 00 00 00 00 00 ................
#1306d6410 00 00 00 00 00 00 00 00-00 00 00 00 00 00 00 00 ................
#1306d6420 00 00 00 00 00 00 00 00-00 00 00 00 00 00 00 00 ................
#1306d6430 00 00 00 00 00 00 00 00-00 00 00 00 00 00 00 00 ................
#1306d6440 00 00 00 00 00 00 00 00-00 00 00 00 00 00 00 00 ................
#1306d6450 00 00 00 00 00 00 00 00-00 00 00 00 00 00 00 00 ................
#1306d6460 00 00 00 00 00 00 00 00-00 00 00 00 00 00 00 00 ................
#1306d6470 00 00 00 00 00 00 00 00-00 00 00 00 00 00 00 00 ................
#1306d6480 00 00 00 00 00 00 00 00-00 00 00 00 00 00 00 00 ................
#1306d6490 00 00 00 00 00 00 00 00-00 00 00 00 00 00 00 00 ................
#1306d64a0 00 00 00 00 00 00 00 00-00 00 00 00 00 00 00 00 ................
```

```
#1306d64b0 00 00 00 00 00 00 00 00-00 00 00 00 00 00 00 00 ................
#1306d64c0 00 00 00 00 00 00 00 00-00 00 00 00 00 00 00 00 ................
#1306d64d0 00 00 00 00 00 00 00 00-00 00 00 00 00 00 00 00 ................
#1306d64e0 00 00 00 00 00 00 00 00-00 00 00 00 00 00 00 00 ................
#1306d64f0 00 00 00 00 00 00 00 00-00 00 00 00 00 00 00 00 ................
#1306d6500 00 00 00 00 00 00 00 00-00 00 00 00 00 00 00 00 ................
#1306d6510 00 00 00 00 00 00 00 00-00 00 00 00 00 00 00 00 ................
#1306d6520 00 00 00 00 00 00 00 00-00 00 00 00 00 00 00 00 ................
#1306d6530 00 00 00 00 00 00 00 00-00 00 00 00 00 00 00 00 ................
#1306d6540 00 00 00 00 00 00 00 00-00 00 00 00 00 00 00 00 ................
#1306d6550 00 00 00 00 00 00 00 00-00 00 00 00 00 00 00 00 ................
#1306d6560 00 00 00 00 00 00 00 00-00 00 00 00 00 00 00 00 ................
#1306d6570 00 00 00 00 00 00 00 00-00 00 00 00 00 00 00 00 ................
#1306d6580 00 00 00 00 00 00 00 00-00 00 00 00 00 00 00 00 ................
#1306d6590 00 00 00 00 00 00 00 00-00 00 00 00 00 00 00 00 ................
#1306d65a0 00 00 00 00 00 00 00 00-00 00 00 00 00 00 00 00 ................
#1306d65b0 00 00 00 00 00 00 00 00-00 00 00 00 00 00 00 00 ................
#1306d65c0 00 00 00 00 00 00 00 00-00 00 00 00 00 00 00 00 ................
#1306d65d0 00 00 00 00 00 00 00 00-00 00 00 00 00 00 00 00 ................
#1306d65e0 00 00 00 00 00 00 00 00-00 00 00 00 00 00 00 00 ................
#1306d65f0 00 00 00 00 00 00 00 00-00 00 00 00 00 00 00 00 ................
#1306d6600 00 00 00 00 00 00 00 00-00 00 00 00 00 00 00 00 ................
#1306d6610 00 00 00 00 00 00 00 00-00 00 00 00 00 00 00 00 ................
#1306d6620 00 00 00 00 00 00 00 00-00 00 00 00 00 00 00 00 ................
#1306d6630 00 00 00 00 00 00 00 00-00 00 00 00 00 00 00 00 ................
#1306d6640 00 00 00 00 00 00 00 00-00 00 00 00 00 00 00 00 ................
#1306d6650 00 00 00 00 00 00 00 00-00 00 00 00 00 00 00 00 ................
#1306d6660 00 00 00 00 00 00 00 00-00 00 00 00 00 00 00 00 ................
#1306d6670 00 00 00 00 00 00 00 00-00 00 00 00 00 00 00 00 ................
#1306d6680 00 00 00 00 00 00 00 00-00 00 00 00 00 00 00 00 ................
#1306d6690 00 00 00 00 00 00 00 00-00 00 00 00 00 00 00 00 ................
#1306d66a0 00 00 00 00 00 00 00 00-00 00 00 00 00 00 00 00 ................
#1306d66b0 00 00 00 00 00 00 00 00-00 00 00 00 00 00 00 00 ................
#1306d66c0 00 00 00 00 00 00 00 00-00 00 00 00 00 00 00 00 ................
#1306d66d0 00 00 00 00 00 00 00 00-00 00 00 00 00 00 00 00 ................
#1306d66e0 00 00 00 00 00 00 00 00-00 00 00 00 00 00 00 00 ................
#1306d66f0 00 00 00 00 00 00 00 00-00 00 00 00 00 00 00 00 ................
#1306d6700 00 00 00 00 00 00 00 00-00 00 00 00 00 00 00 00 ................
#1306d6710 00 00 00 00 00 00 00 00-00 00 00 00 00 00 00 00 ................
#1306d6720 00 00 00 00 00 00 00 00-00 00 00 00 00 00 00 00 ................
#1306d6730 00 00 00 00 00 00 00 00-00 00 00 00 00 00 00 00 ................
#1306d6740 00 00 00 00 00 00 00 00-00 00 00 00 00 00 00 00 ................
#1306d6750 00 00 00 00 00 00 00 00-00 00 00 00 00 00 00 00 ................
#1306d6760 00 00 00 00 00 00 00 00-00 00 00 00 00 00 00 00 ................
#1306d6770 00 00 00 00 00 00 00 00-00 00 00 00 00 00 00 00 ................
#1306d6780 00 00 00 00 00 00 00 00-00 00 00 00 00 00 00 00 ................
#1306d6790 00 00 00 00 00 00 00 00-00 00 00 00 00 00 00 00 ................
#1306d67a0 00 00 00 00 00 00 00 00-00 00 00 00 00 00 00 00 ................
#1306d67b0 00 00 00 00 00 00 00 00-00 00 00 00 00 00 00 00 ................
#1306d67c0 00 00 00 00 00 00 00 00-00 00 00 00 00 00 00 00 ................
#1306d67d0 00 00 00 00 00 00 00 00-00 00 00 00 00 00 00 00 ................
#1306d67e0 00 00 00 00 00 00 00 00-00 00 00 00 00 00 00 00 ................
#1306d67f0 00 00 00 00 00 00 00 00-00 00 00 00 00 00 00 00 ................
#1306d6800 00 00 00 00 00 00 00 00-00 00 00 00 00 00 00 00 ................
#1306d6810 00 00 00 00 00 00 00 00-00 00 00 00 00 00 00 00 ................
#1306d6820 00 00 00 00 00 00 00 00-00 00 00 00 00 00 00 00 ................
#1306d6830 00 00 00 00 00 00 00 00-00 00 00 00 00 00 00 00 ................
#1306d6840 00 00 00 00 00 00 00 00-00 00 00 00 00 00 00 00 ................
#1306d6850 00 00 00 00 00 00 00 00-00 00 00 00 00 00 00 00 ................
```

```
#1306d6860 00 00 00 00 00 00 00 00-00 00 00 00 00 00 00 00 ................
#1306d6870 00 00 00 00 00 00 00 00-00 00 00 00 00 00 00 00 ................
#1306d6880 00 00 00 00 00 00 00 00-00 00 00 00 00 00 00 00 ................
#1306d6890 00 00 00 00 00 00 00 00-00 00 00 00 00 00 00 00 ................
#1306d68a0 00 00 00 00 00 00 00 00-00 00 00 00 00 00 00 00 ................
#1306d68b0 00 00 00 00 00 00 00 00-00 00 00 00 00 00 00 00 ................
#1306d68c0 00 00 00 00 00 00 00 00-00 00 00 00 00 00 00 00 ................
#1306d68d0 00 00 00 00 00 00 00 00-00 00 00 00 00 00 00 00 ................
#1306d68e0 00 00 00 00 00 00 00 00-00 00 00 00 00 00 00 00 ................
#1306d68f0 00 00 00 00 00 00 00 00-00 00 00 00 00 00 00 00 ................
#1306d6900 00 00 00 00 00 00 00 00-00 00 00 00 00 00 00 00 ................
#1306d6910 00 00 00 00 00 00 00 00-00 00 00 00 00 00 00 00 ................
#1306d6920 00 00 00 00 00 00 00 00-00 00 00 00 00 00 00 00 ................
#1306d6930 00 00 00 00 00 00 00 00-00 00 00 00 00 00 00 00 ................
#1306d6940 00 00 00 00 00 00 00 00-00 00 00 00 00 00 00 00 ................
#1306d6950 00 00 00 00 00 00 00 00-00 00 00 00 00 00 00 00 ................
#1306d6960 00 00 00 00 00 00 00 00-00 00 00 00 00 00 00 00 ................
#1306d6970 00 00 00 00 00 00 00 00-00 00 00 00 00 00 00 00 ................
#1306d6980 00 00 00 00 00 00 00 00-00 00 00 00 00 00 00 00 ................
#1306d6990 00 00 00 00 00 00 00 00-00 00 00 00 00 00 00 00 ................
#1306d69a0 00 00 00 00 00 00 00 00-00 00 00 00 00 00 00 00 ................
#1306d69b0 00 00 00 00 00 00 00 00-00 00 00 00 00 00 00 00 ................
#1306d69c0 00 00 00 00 00 00 00 00-00 00 00 00 00 00 00 00 ................
#1306d69d0 00 00 00 00 00 00 00 00-00 00 00 00 00 00 00 00 ................
#1306d69e0 00 00 00 00 00 00 00 00-00 00 00 00 00 00 00 00 ................
#1306d69f0 00 00 00 00 00 00 00 00-00 00 00 00 00 00 00 00 ................
#1306d6a00 00 00 00 00 00 00 00 00-00 00 00 00 00 00 00 00 ................
#1306d6a10 00 00 00 00 00 00 00 00-00 00 00 00 00 00 00 00 ................
#1306d6a20 00 00 00 00 00 00 00 00-00 00 00 00 00 00 00 00 ................
#1306d6a30 00 00 00 00 00 00 00 00-00 00 00 00 00 00 00 00 ................
#1306d6a40 00 00 00 00 00 00 00 00-00 00 00 00 00 00 00 00 ................
#1306d6a50 00 00 00 00 00 00 00 00-00 00 00 00 00 00 00 00 ................
#1306d6a60 00 00 00 00 00 00 00 00-00 00 00 00 00 00 00 00 ................
#1306d6a70 00 00 00 00 00 00 00 00-00 00 00 00 00 00 00 00 ................
#1306d6a80 00 00 00 00 00 00 00 00-00 00 00 00 00 00 00 00 ................
#1306d6a90 00 00 00 00 00 00 00 00-00 00 00 00 00 00 00 00 ................
#1306d6aa0 00 00 00 00 00 00 00 00-00 00 00 00 00 00 00 00 ................
#1306d6ab0 00 00 00 00 00 00 00 00-00 00 00 00 00 00 00 00 ................
#1306d6ac0 00 00 00 00 00 00 00 00-00 00 00 00 00 00 00 00 ................
#1306d6ad0 00 00 00 00 00 00 00 00-00 00 00 00 00 00 00 00 ................
#1306d6ae0 00 00 00 00 00 00 00 00-00 00 00 00 00 00 00 00 ................
#1306d6af0 00 00 00 00 00 00 00 00-00 00 00 00 00 00 00 00 ................
#1306d6b00 00 00 00 00 00 00 00 00-00 00 00 00 00 00 00 00 ................
#1306d6b10 00 00 00 00 00 00 00 00-00 00 00 00 00 00 00 00 ................
#1306d6b20 00 00 00 00 00 00 00 00-00 00 00 00 00 00 00 00 ................
#1306d6b30 00 00 00 00 00 00 00 00-00 00 00 00 00 00 00 00 ................
#1306d6b40 00 00 00 00 00 00 00 00-00 00 00 00 00 00 00 00 ................
#1306d6b50 00 00 00 00 00 00 00 00-00 00 00 00 00 00 00 00 ................
#1306d6b60 00 00 00 00 00 00 00 00-00 00 00 00 00 00 00 00 ................
#1306d6b70 00 00 00 00 00 00 00 00-00 00 00 00 00 00 00 00 ................
#1306d6b80 00 00 00 00 00 00 00 00-00 00 00 00 00 00 00 00 ................
#1306d6b90 00 00 00 00 00 00 00 00-00 00 00 00 00 00 00 00 ................
#1306d6ba0 00 00 00 00 00 00 00 00-00 00 00 00 00 00 00 00 ................
#1306d6bb0 00 00 00 00 00 00 00 00-00 00 00 00 00 00 00 00 ................
#1306d6bc0 00 00 00 00 00 00 00 00-00 00 00 00 00 00 00 00 ................
#1306d6bd0 00 00 00 00 00 00 00 00-00 00 00 00 00 00 00 00 ................
#1306d6be0 00 00 00 00 00 00 00 00-00 00 00 00 00 00 00 00 ................
#1306d6bf0 00 00 00 00 00 00 00 00-00 00 00 00 00 00 00 00 ................
#1306d6c00 00 00 00 00 00 00 00 00-00 00 00 00 00 00 00 00 ................
```

```
#1306d6c10 00 00 00 00 00 00 00 00-00 00 00 00 00 00 00 00 ................
#1306d6c20 00 00 00 00 00 00 00 00-00 00 00 00 00 00 00 00 ................
#1306d6c30 00 00 00 00 00 00 00 00-00 00 00 00 00 00 00 00 ................
#1306d6c40 00 00 00 00 00 00 00 00-00 00 00 00 00 00 00 00 ................
#1306d6c50 00 00 00 00 00 00 00 00-00 00 00 00 00 00 00 00 ................
#1306d6c60 00 00 00 00 00 00 00 00-00 00 00 00 00 00 00 00 ................
#1306d6c70 00 00 00 00 00 00 00 00-00 00 00 00 00 00 00 00 ................
#1306d6c80 00 00 00 00 00 00 00 00-00 00 00 00 00 00 00 00 ................
#1306d6c90 00 00 00 00 00 00 00 00-00 00 00 00 00 00 00 00 ................
#1306d6ca0 00 00 00 00 00 00 00 00-00 00 00 00 00 00 00 00 ................
#1306d6cb0 00 00 00 00 00 00 00 00-00 00 00 00 00 00 00 00 ................
#1306d6cc0 00 00 00 00 00 00 00 00-00 00 00 00 00 00 00 00 ................
#1306d6cd0 00 00 00 00 00 00 00 00-00 00 00 00 00 00 00 00 ................
#1306d6ce0 00 00 00 00 00 00 00 00-00 00 00 00 00 00 00 00 ................
#1306d6cf0 00 00 00 00 00 00 00 00-00 00 00 00 00 00 00 00 ................
#1306d6d00 00 00 00 00 00 00 00 00-00 00 00 00 00 00 00 00 ................
#1306d6d10 00 00 00 00 00 00 00 00-00 00 00 00 00 00 00 00 ................
#1306d6d20 00 00 00 00 00 00 00 00-00 00 00 00 00 00 00 00 ................
#1306d6d30 00 00 00 00 00 00 00 00-00 00 00 00 00 00 00 00 ................
#1306d6d40 00 00 00 00 00 00 00 00-00 00 00 00 00 00 00 00 ................
#1306d6d50 00 00 00 00 00 00 00 00-00 00 00 00 00 00 00 00 ................
#1306d6d60 00 00 00 00 00 00 00 00-00 00 00 00 00 00 00 00 ................
#1306d6d70 00 00 00 00 00 00 00 00-00 00 00 00 00 00 00 00 ................
#1306d6d80 00 00 00 00 00 00 00 00-00 00 00 00 00 00 00 00 ................
#1306d6d90 00 00 00 00 00 00 00 00-00 00 00 00 00 00 00 00 ................
#1306d6da0 00 00 00 00 00 00 00 00-00 00 00 00 00 00 00 00 ................
#1306d6db0 00 00 00 00 00 00 00 00-00 00 00 00 00 00 00 00 ................
#1306d6dc0 00 00 00 00 00 00 00 00-00 00 00 00 00 00 00 00 ................
#1306d6dd0 00 00 00 00 00 00 00 00-00 00 00 00 00 00 00 00 ................
#1306d6de0 00 00 00 00 00 00 00 00-00 00 00 00 00 00 00 00 ................
#1306d6df0 00 00 00 00 00 00 00 00-00 00 00 00 00 00 00 00 ................
#1306d6e00 00 00 00 00 00 00 00 00-00 00 00 00 00 00 00 00 ................
#1306d6e10 00 00 00 00 00 00 00 00-00 00 00 00 00 00 00 00 ................
#1306d6e20 00 00 00 00 00 00 00 00-00 00 00 00 00 00 00 00 ................
#1306d6e30 00 00 00 00 00 00 00 00-00 00 00 00 00 00 00 00 ................
#1306d6e40 00 00 00 00 00 00 00 00-00 00 00 00 00 00 00 00 ................
#1306d6e50 00 00 00 00 00 00 00 00-00 00 00 00 00 00 00 00 ................
#1306d6e60 00 00 00 00 00 00 00 00-00 00 00 00 00 00 00 00 ................
#1306d6e70 00 00 00 00 00 00 00 00-00 00 00 00 00 00 00 00 ................
#1306d6e80 00 00 00 00 00 00 00 00-00 00 00 00 00 00 00 00 ................
#1306d6e90 00 00 00 00 00 00 00 00-00 00 00 00 00 00 00 00 ................
#1306d6ea0 00 00 00 00 00 00 00 00-00 00 00 00 00 00 00 00 ................
#1306d6eb0 00 00 00 00 00 00 00 00-00 00 00 00 00 00 00 00 ................
#1306d6ec0 00 00 00 00 00 00 00 00-00 00 00 00 00 00 00 00 ................
#1306d6ed0 00 00 00 00 00 00 00 00-00 00 00 00 00 00 00 00 ................
#1306d6ee0 00 00 00 00 00 00 00 00-00 00 00 00 00 00 00 00 ................
#1306d6ef0 00 00 00 00 00 00 00 00-00 00 00 00 00 00 00 00 ................
#1306d6f00 00 00 00 00 00 00 00 00-00 00 00 00 00 00 00 00 ................
#1306d6f10 00 00 00 00 00 00 00 00-00 00 00 00 00 00 00 00 ................
#1306d6f20 00 00 00 00 00 00 00 00-00 00 00 00 00 00 00 00 ................
#1306d6f30 00 00 00 00 00 00 00 00-00 00 00 00 00 00 00 00 ................
#1306d6f40 00 00 00 00 00 00 00 00-00 00 00 00 00 00 00 00 ................
#1306d6f50 00 00 00 00 00 00 00 00-00 00 00 00 00 00 00 00 ................
#1306d6f60 00 00 00 00 00 00 00 00-00 00 00 00 00 00 00 00 ................
#1306d6f70 00 00 00 00 00 00 00 00-00 00 00 00 00 00 00 00 ................
#1306d6f80 00 00 00 00 00 00 00 00-00 00 00 00 00 00 00 00 ................
#1306d6f90 00 00 00 00 00 00 00 00-00 00 00 00 00 00 00 00 ................
#1306d6fa0 00 00 00 00 00 00 00 00-00 00 00 00 00 00 00 00 ................
#1306d6fb0 00 00 00 00 00 00 00 00-00 00 00 00 00 00 00 00 ................
```

```
#1306d6fc0 00 00 00 00 00 00 00 00-00 00 00 00 00 00 00 00 ................
#1306d6fd0 00 00 00 00 00 00 00 00-00 00 00 00 00 00 00 00 ................
#1306d6fe0 00 00 00 00 00 00 00 00-00 00 00 00 00 00 00 00 ................
#1306d6ff0 00 00 00 00 00 00 00 00-00 00 00 00 00 00 00 00 ................
```

11. We close the Memory Explorer window and bring the Device Explorer window by using the **!dv** command (we may need to bring the window to the foreground):

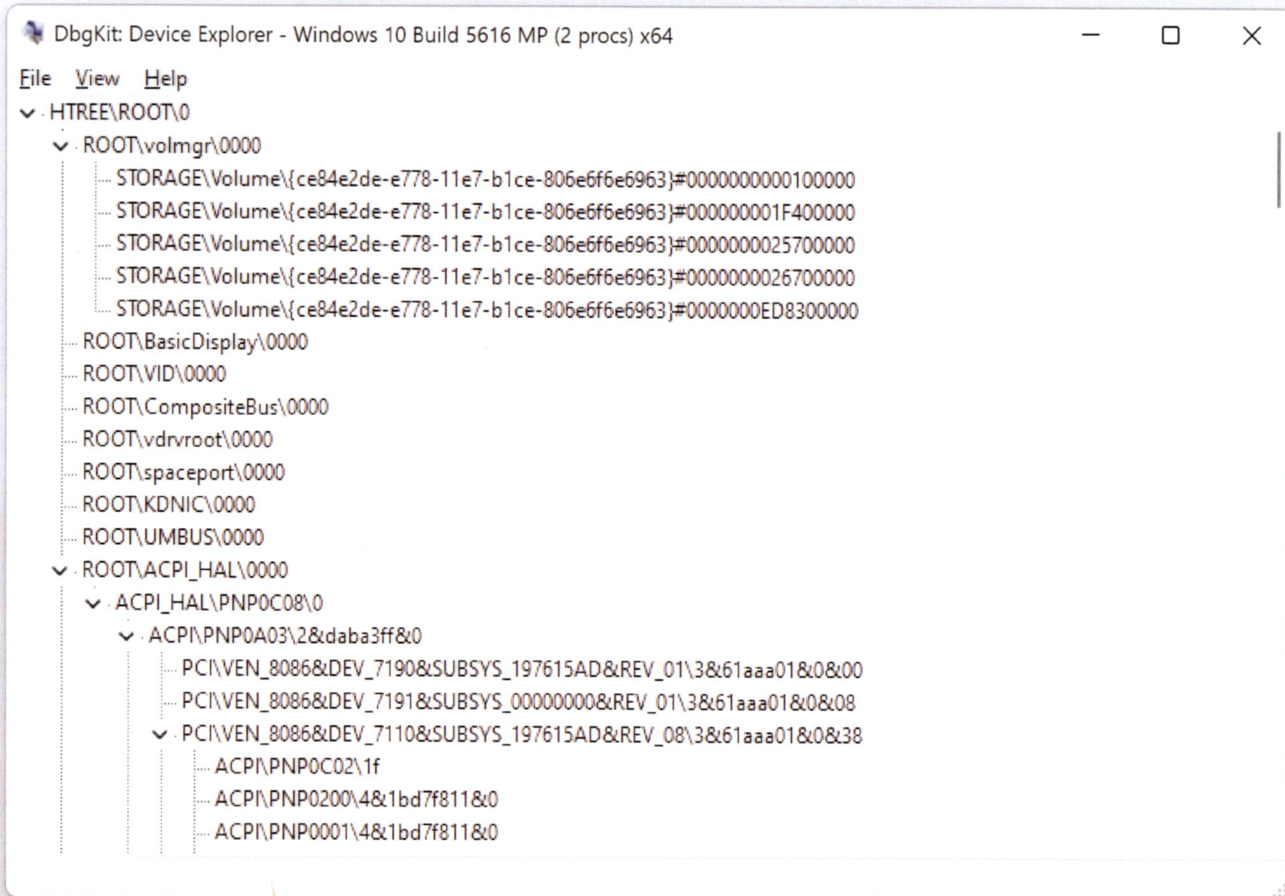

12. For the chosen device, we can use the context menu to explore the device stack, device and driver objects (the latter may take some time as it also outputs all driver's device objects) with the output redirected to the WinDbg window (Display Driver Object may take some time):

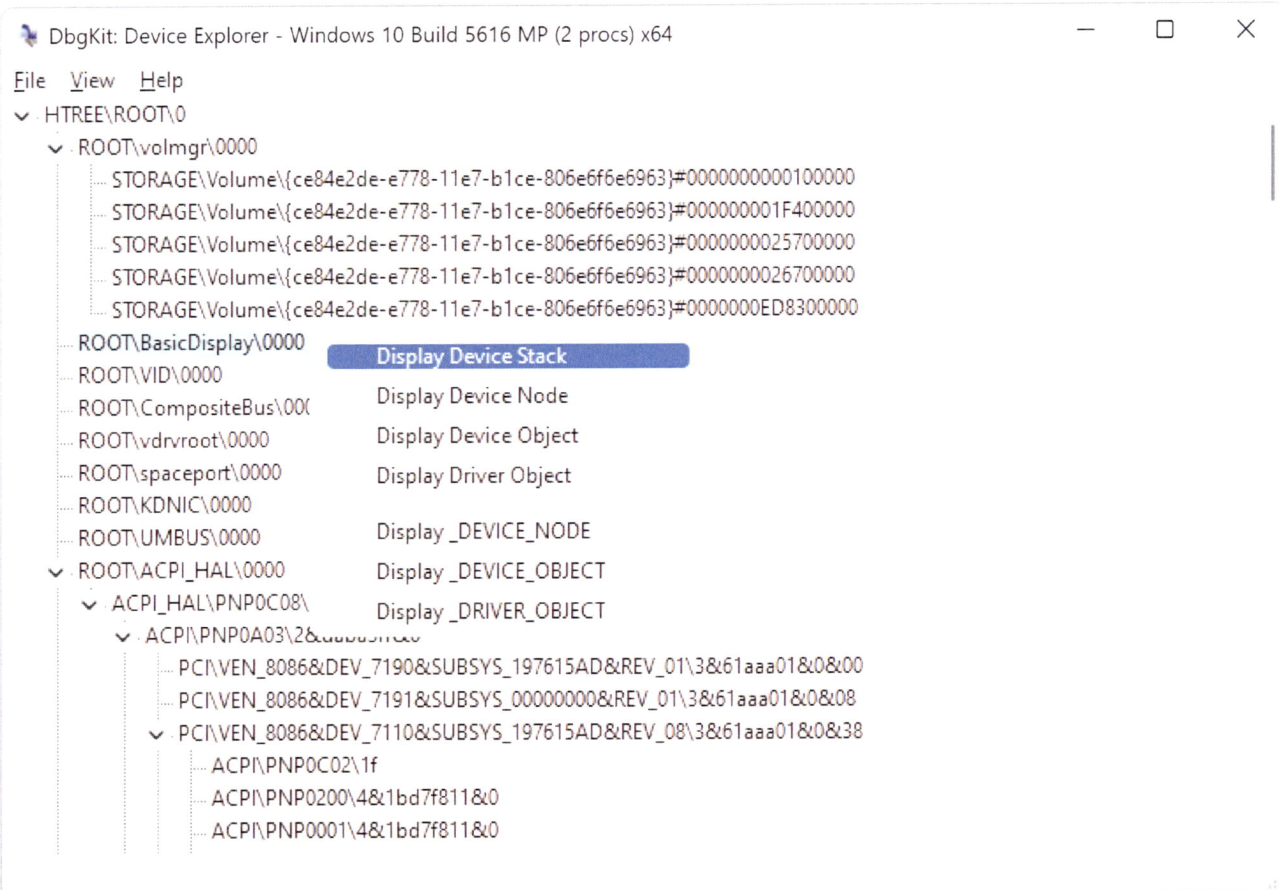


```
  !DevObj          !DrvObj              !DevExt          ObjectName
  ffffc38c30210030  \Driver\BasicDisplayffffc38c30210180
> ffffc38c2c52ad80  \Driver\PnpManager ffffc38c2c52aed0  00000002
!DevNode ffffc38c2c519ab0 :
  DeviceInst is "ROOT\BasicDisplay\0000"
  ServiceName is "BasicDisplay"

Device object (ffffc38c2c52ad80) is for:
 00000002 \Driver\PnpManager DriverObject ffffc38c2c477e20
Current Irp 00000000 RefCount 0 Type 00000004 Flags 00001040
SecurityDescriptor ffffac8a0461d1a0 DevExt ffffc38c2c52aed0 DevObjExt ffffc38c2c52aed8 DevNode
ffffc38c2c519ab0
ExtensionFlags (0000000000)
Characteristics (0x00000180)  FILE_AUTOGENERATED_DEVICE_NAME, FILE_DEVICE_SECURE_OPEN
AttachedDevice (Upper) ffffc38c30210030 \Driver\BasicDisplay
Device queue is not busy.

Driver object (ffffc38c2c477e20) is for:
 \Driver\PnpManager

Driver Extension List: (id , addr)
```

```
Device Object list:
ffffc38c2c53dd90  ffffc38c2c53db50  ffffc38c2c53d5e0  ffffc38c2c53d070
ffffc38c2c53ba00  ffffc38c2c539d80  ffffc38c2c4e7d80  ffffc38c2c521db0
ffffc38c2c537d80  ffffc38c2c532d80  ffffc38c2c530d80  ffffc38c2c52ed80
ffffc38c2c52cd80  ffffc38c2c52ad80  ffffc38c2c4e5d80  ffffc38c2c611e20


DriverEntry:    fffff806628f0080  nt!PipPnPDriverEntry
DriverStartIo: 00000000
DriverUnload:  00000000
AddDevice:      fffff806624b6860  nt!ArbPreprocessEntry

Dispatch routines:
[00] IRP_MJ_CREATE                      fffff80662033c40   nt!IopInvalidDeviceRequest
[01] IRP_MJ_CREATE_NAMED_PIPE           fffff80662033c40   nt!IopInvalidDeviceRequest
[02] IRP_MJ_CLOSE                       fffff80662033c40   nt!IopInvalidDeviceRequest
[03] IRP_MJ_READ                        fffff80662033c40   nt!IopInvalidDeviceRequest
[04] IRP_MJ_WRITE                       fffff80662033c40   nt!IopInvalidDeviceRequest
[05] IRP_MJ_QUERY_INFORMATION           fffff80662033c40   nt!IopInvalidDeviceRequest
[06] IRP_MJ_SET_INFORMATION             fffff80662033c40   nt!IopInvalidDeviceRequest
[07] IRP_MJ_QUERY_EA                    fffff80662033c40   nt!IopInvalidDeviceRequest
[08] IRP_MJ_SET_EA                      fffff80662033c40   nt!IopInvalidDeviceRequest
[09] IRP_MJ_FLUSH_BUFFERS               fffff80662033c40   nt!IopInvalidDeviceRequest
[0a] IRP_MJ_QUERY_VOLUME_INFORMATION    fffff80662033c40   nt!IopInvalidDeviceRequest
[0b] IRP_MJ_SET_VOLUME_INFORMATION      fffff80662033c40   nt!IopInvalidDeviceRequest
[0c] IRP_MJ_DIRECTORY_CONTROL           fffff80662033c40   nt!IopInvalidDeviceRequest
[0d] IRP_MJ_FILE_SYSTEM_CONTROL         fffff80662033c40   nt!IopInvalidDeviceRequest
[0e] IRP_MJ_DEVICE_CONTROL              fffff80662033c40   nt!IopInvalidDeviceRequest
[0f] IRP_MJ_INTERNAL_DEVICE_CONTROL     fffff80662033c40   nt!IopInvalidDeviceRequest
[10] IRP_MJ_SHUTDOWN                    fffff80662033c40   nt!IopInvalidDeviceRequest
[11] IRP_MJ_LOCK_CONTROL                fffff80662033c40   nt!IopInvalidDeviceRequest
[12] IRP_MJ_CLEANUP                     fffff80662033c40   nt!IopInvalidDeviceRequest
[13] IRP_MJ_CREATE_MAILSLOT             fffff80662033c40   nt!IopInvalidDeviceRequest
[14] IRP_MJ_QUERY_SECURITY              fffff80662033c40   nt!IopInvalidDeviceRequest
[15] IRP_MJ_SET_SECURITY                fffff80662033c40   nt!IopInvalidDeviceRequest
[16] IRP_MJ_POWER                       fffff80662190e80   nt!IopPowerDispatch
[17] IRP_MJ_SYSTEM_CONTROL              fffff8066274dd10   nt!IopSystemControlDispatch
[18] IRP_MJ_DEVICE_CHANGE               fffff80662033c40   nt!IopInvalidDeviceRequest
[19] IRP_MJ_QUERY_QUOTA                 fffff80662033c40   nt!IopInvalidDeviceRequest
[1a] IRP_MJ_SET_QUOTA                   fffff80662033c40   nt!IopInvalidDeviceRequest
[1b] IRP_MJ_PNP                         fffff806625db920   nt!IopPnPDispatch


Device Object stacks:

!devstack ffffc38c2c53dd90 :
  !DevObj           !DrvObj             !DevExt           ObjectName
  ffffc38c2ece3be0  \Driver\rdpbus      ffffc38c2ece3d30  RdpBus
> ffffc38c2c53dd90  \Driver\PnpManager ffffc38c2c53dee0  0000000f
!DevNode ffffc38c2c53f350 :
  DeviceInst is "ROOT\RDPBUS\0000"
  ServiceName is "rdpbus"

!devstack ffffc38c2c53db50 :
  !DevObj           !DrvObj             !DevExt           ObjectName
  ffffc38c2ece2250  \Driver\swenum      ffffc38c2ece23a0
> ffffc38c2c53db50  \Driver\PnpManager ffffc38c2c53dca0  0000000e
!DevNode ffffc38c2c53f020 :
  DeviceInst is "ROOT\SYSTEM\0000"
```

```
  ServiceName is "swenum"

!devstack ffffc38c2c53d5e0 :
  !DevObj           !DrvObj            !DevExt           ObjectName
  ffffc38c3020bb70  \Driver\mssmbios   ffffc38c3020bcc0
> ffffc38c2c53d5e0  \Driver\PnpManager ffffc38c2c53d730  0000000d
!DevNode ffffc38c2c53d7d0 :
  DeviceInst is "ROOT\mssmbios\0000"
  ServiceName is "mssmbios"

!devstack ffffc38c2c53d070 :
  !DevObj           !DrvObj            !DevExt           ObjectName
  ffffc38c30206d10  \Driver\NdisVirtualBusffffc38c3020ac70
> ffffc38c2c53d070  \Driver\PnpManager ffffc38c2c53d1c0  0000000c
!DevNode ffffc38c2c53d260 :
  DeviceInst is "ROOT\NdisVirtualBus\0000"
  ServiceName is "NdisVirtualBus"

!devstack ffffc38c2c53ba00 :
  !DevObj           !DrvObj            !DevExt           ObjectName
  ffffc38c2cd83d40 Unable to load image \SystemRoot\System32\drivers\vmci.sys, Win32 error 0n2
 \Driver\vmci       ffffc38c2cd83e90  VMCIHostDev
> ffffc38c2c53ba00  \Driver\PnpManager ffffc38c2c53bb50  0000000b
!DevNode ffffc38c2c53bbf0 :
  DeviceInst is "ROOT\VMWVMCIHOSTDEV\0000"
  ServiceName is "vmci"

!devstack ffffc38c2c539d80 :
  !DevObj           !DrvObj            !DevExt           ObjectName
  ffffc38c2ecdf030  \Driver\BasicRenderffffc38c2ecdf180
> ffffc38c2c539d80  \Driver\PnpManager ffffc38c2c539ed0  0000000a
!DevNode ffffc38c2c53b680 :
  DeviceInst is "ROOT\BasicRender\0000"
  ServiceName is "BasicRender"

!devstack ffffc38c2c4e7d80 :
  !DevObj           !DrvObj            !DevExt           ObjectName
  ffffc38c2c541ae0  \Driver\ACPI_HAL   ffffc38c2c541c30
> ffffc38c2c4e7d80  \Driver\PnpManager ffffc38c2c4e7ed0  00000009
!DevNode ffffc38c2c53b350 :
  DeviceInst is "ROOT\ACPI_HAL\0000"

!devstack ffffc38c2c521db0 :
  !DevObj           !DrvObj            !DevExt           ObjectName
  ffffc38c2cdd6490  \Driver\umbus      ffffc38c2ea86310
> ffffc38c2c521db0  \Driver\PnpManager ffffc38c2c521f00  00000008
!DevNode ffffc38c2c53b020 :
  DeviceInst is "ROOT\UMBUS\0000"
  ServiceName is "umbus"

!devstack ffffc38c2c537d80 :
  !DevObj           !DrvObj            !DevExt           ObjectName
  ffffc38c2e6ee4d0  \Driver\kdnic      ffffc38c2e6ee620
> ffffc38c2c537d80  \Driver\PnpManager ffffc38c2c537ed0  00000007
!DevNode ffffc38c2c521a30 :
  DeviceInst is "ROOT\KDNIC\0000"
  ServiceName is "kdnic"

!devstack ffffc38c2c532d80 :
```

```
  !DevObj           !DrvObj             !DevExt           ObjectName
  ffffc38c2cd720a0  \Driver\spaceport   ffffc38c2cd721f0  Spaceport
> ffffc38c2c532d80  \Driver\PnpManager  ffffc38c2c532ed0  00000006
!DevNode ffffc38c2c51fab0 :
  DeviceInst is "ROOT\spaceport\0000"
  ServiceName is "spaceport"

!devstack ffffc38c2c530d80 :
  !DevObj           !DrvObj             !DevExt           ObjectName
  ffffc38c2cd62d20  \Driver\vdrvroot    ffffc38c2cde0f40
> ffffc38c2c530d80  \Driver\PnpManager  ffffc38c2c530ed0  00000005
!DevNode ffffc38c2c51dab0 :
  DeviceInst is "ROOT\vdrvroot\0000"
  ServiceName is "vdrvroot"

!devstack ffffc38c2c52ed80 :
  !DevObj           !DrvObj             !DevExt           ObjectName
  ffffc38c2cd92490  \Driver\CompositeBusffffc38c2ea82310
> ffffc38c2c52ed80  \Driver\PnpManager  ffffc38c2c52eed0  00000004
!DevNode ffffc38c2c51bab0 :
  DeviceInst is "ROOT\CompositeBus\0000"
  ServiceName is "CompositeBus"

!devstack ffffc38c2c52cd80 :
  !DevObj           !DrvObj             !DevExt           ObjectName
  ffffc38c3020fbe0  \Driver\Vid         ffffc38c30211b80
> ffffc38c2c52cd80  \Driver\PnpManager  ffffc38c2c52ced0  00000003
!DevNode ffffc38c2c4e3ab0 :
  DeviceInst is "ROOT\VID\0000"
  ServiceName is "Vid"

!devstack ffffc38c2c52ad80 :
  !DevObj           !DrvObj             !DevExt           ObjectName
  ffffc38c30210030  \Driver\BasicDisplayffffc38c30210180
> ffffc38c2c52ad80  \Driver\PnpManager  ffffc38c2c52aed0  00000002
!DevNode ffffc38c2c519ab0 :
  DeviceInst is "ROOT\BasicDisplay\0000"
  ServiceName is "BasicDisplay"

!devstack ffffc38c2c4e5d80 :
  !DevObj           !DrvObj             !DevExt           ObjectName
  ffffc38c2cd7b7e0  \Driver\volmgr      ffffc38c2cd7b930  VolMgrControl
> ffffc38c2c4e5d80  \Driver\PnpManager  ffffc38c2c4e5ed0  00000001
!DevNode ffffc38c2c510ab0 :
  DeviceInst is "ROOT\volmgr\0000"
  ServiceName is "volmgr"

!devstack ffffc38c2c611e20 :
  !DevObj           !DrvObj             !DevExt           ObjectName
> ffffc38c2c611e20  \Driver\PnpManager  00000000
!DevNode ffffc38c2c50eab0 :
  DeviceInst is "HTREE\ROOT\0"

Processed 16 device objects.
```

13. We close the Device Explorer window and bring the Object Explorer window by using the **!ob** command (we may need to bring the window to the foreground), where we can use the context menu to explore object details (redirected to the WinDbg window):

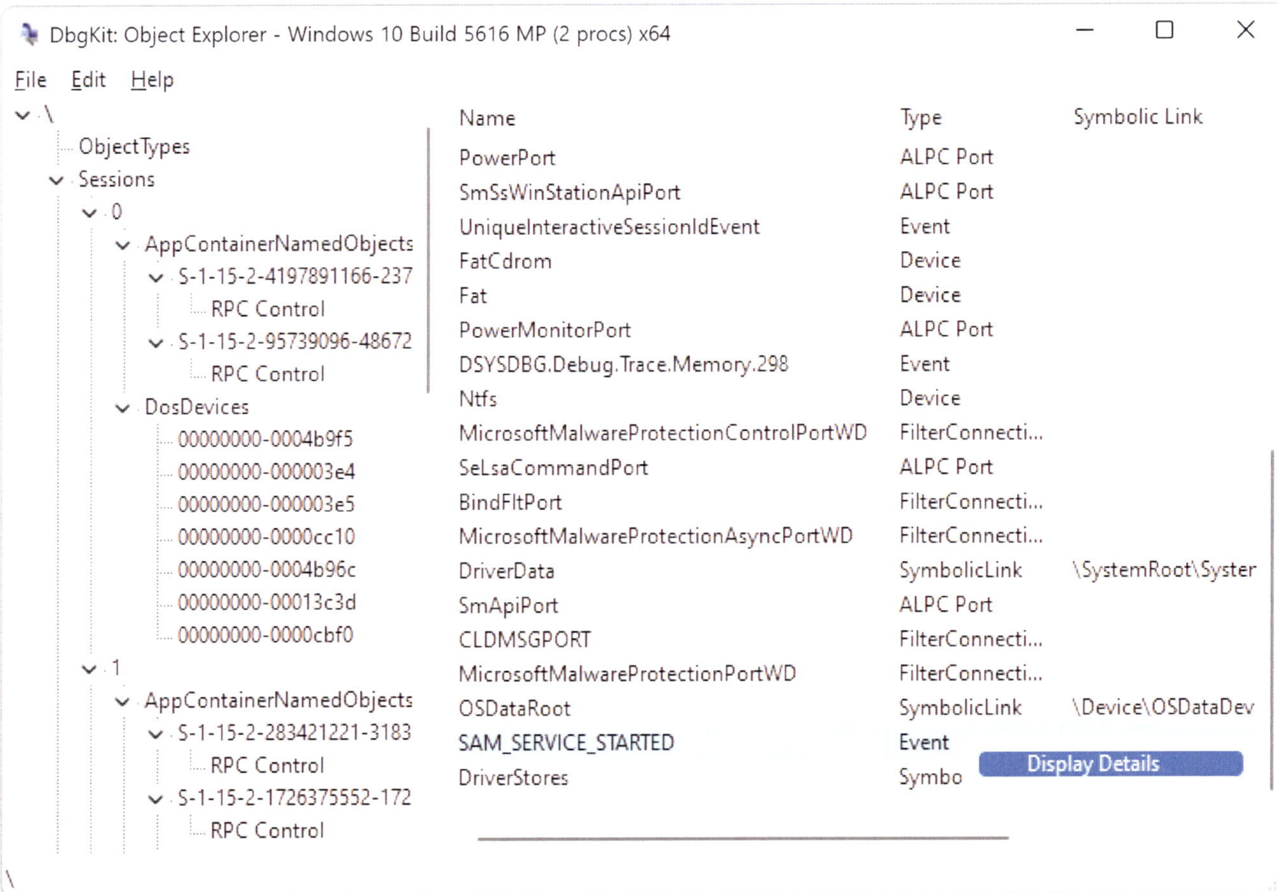


```
Object: ffffc38c2cc91510  Type: (ffffc38c2c4ec560) Event
    ObjectHeader: ffffc38c2cc914e0 (new version)
    HandleCount: 1  PointerCount: 32769
    Directory Object: ffffac8a0420ec50  Name: \SAM_SERVICE_STARTED
Optional Headers:
    NameInfo(ffffc38c2cc914e0)
    QuotaInfo(ffffc38c2cc914e0) PPool: 8001, NPPool: 0
      SecurityDescriptor: 1, SDQuotaBlock: 0000000000000000
```

14. We close the Object Explorer window and try to bring the Process Explorer window using the **!ps** command. Unfortunately, it doesn't work for the version of the WinDbg app we use in this edition:

```
0: kd> !ps
================================================================
=                                                              =
================================================================
= [0x0] : TypeError: Cannot read properties of null (readin... =
================================================================
```

Fortunately, it works in the WinDbg classic:

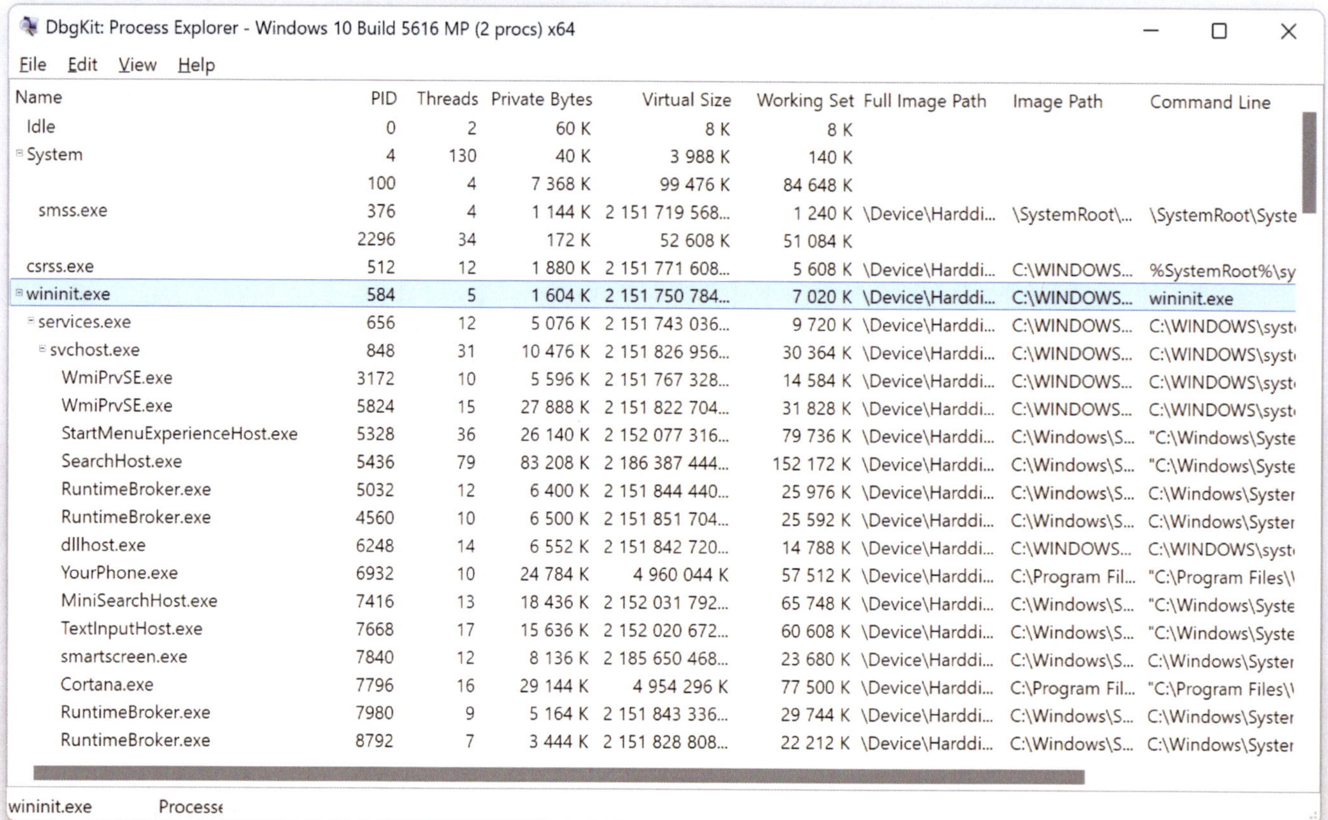

DbgKit: Process Explorer - Windows 10 Build 5616 MP (2 procs) x64

File Edit View Help

Name	PID	Threads	Private Bytes	Virtual Size	Working Set	Full Image Path	Image Path	Command Line
Idle	0	2	60 K	8 K	8 K			
System	4	130	40 K	3 988 K	140 K			
	100	4	7 368 K	99 476 K	84 648 K			
smss.exe	376	4	1 144 K	2 151 719 568...	1 240 K	\Device\Harddi...	\SystemRoot\...	\SystemRoot\Syste
	2296	34	172 K	52 608 K	51 084 K			
csrss.exe	512	12	1 880 K	2 151 771 608...	5 608 K	\Device\Harddi...	C:\WINDOWS...	%SystemRoot%\sy
wininit.exe	584	5	1 604 K	2 151 750 784...	7 020 K	\Device\Harddi...	C:\WINDOWS...	wininit.exe
services.exe	656	12	5 076 K	2 151 743 036...	9 720 K	\Device\Harddi...	C:\WINDOWS...	C:\WINDOWS\syst
svchost.exe	848	31	10 476 K	2 151 826 956...	30 364 K	\Device\Harddi...	C:\WINDOWS...	C:\WINDOWS\syst
WmiPrvSE.exe	3172	10	5 596 K	2 151 767 328...	14 584 K	\Device\Harddi...	C:\WINDOWS...	C:\WINDOWS\syst
WmiPrvSE.exe	5824	15	27 888 K	2 151 822 704...	31 828 K	\Device\Harddi...	C:\WINDOWS...	C:\WINDOWS\syst
StartMenuExperienceHost.exe	5328	36	26 140 K	2 152 077 316...	79 736 K	\Device\Harddi...	C:\Windows\S...	"C:\Windows\Syste
SearchHost.exe	5436	79	83 208 K	2 186 387 444...	152 172 K	\Device\Harddi...	C:\Windows\S...	"C:\Windows\Syste
RuntimeBroker.exe	5032	12	6 400 K	2 151 844 440...	25 976 K	\Device\Harddi...	C:\Windows\S...	C:\Windows\Syster
RuntimeBroker.exe	4560	10	6 500 K	2 151 851 704...	25 592 K	\Device\Harddi...	C:\Windows\S...	C:\Windows\Syster
dllhost.exe	6248	14	6 552 K	2 151 842 720...	14 788 K	\Device\Harddi...	C:\WINDOWS...	C:\WINDOWS\syst
YourPhone.exe	6932	10	24 784 K	4 960 044 K	57 512 K	\Device\Harddi...	C:\Program Fil...	"C:\Program Files\
MiniSearchHost.exe	7416	13	18 436 K	2 152 031 792...	65 748 K	\Device\Harddi...	C:\Windows\S...	"C:\Windows\Syste
TextInputHost.exe	7668	17	15 636 K	2 152 020 672...	60 608 K	\Device\Harddi...	C:\Windows\S...	"C:\Windows\Syste
smartscreen.exe	7840	12	8 136 K	2 185 650 468...	23 680 K	\Device\Harddi...	C:\Windows\S...	C:\Windows\Syster
Cortana.exe	7796	16	29 144 K	4 954 296 K	77 500 K	\Device\Harddi...	C:\Program Fil...	"C:\Program Files\
RuntimeBroker.exe	7980	9	5 164 K	2 151 843 336...	29 744 K	\Device\Harddi...	C:\Windows\S...	C:\Windows\Syster
RuntimeBroker.exe	8792	7	3 444 K	2 151 828 808...	22 212 K	\Device\Harddi...	C:\Windows\S...	C:\Windows\Syster

wininit.exe Processe

In the table header, we can use the context menu to select columns:

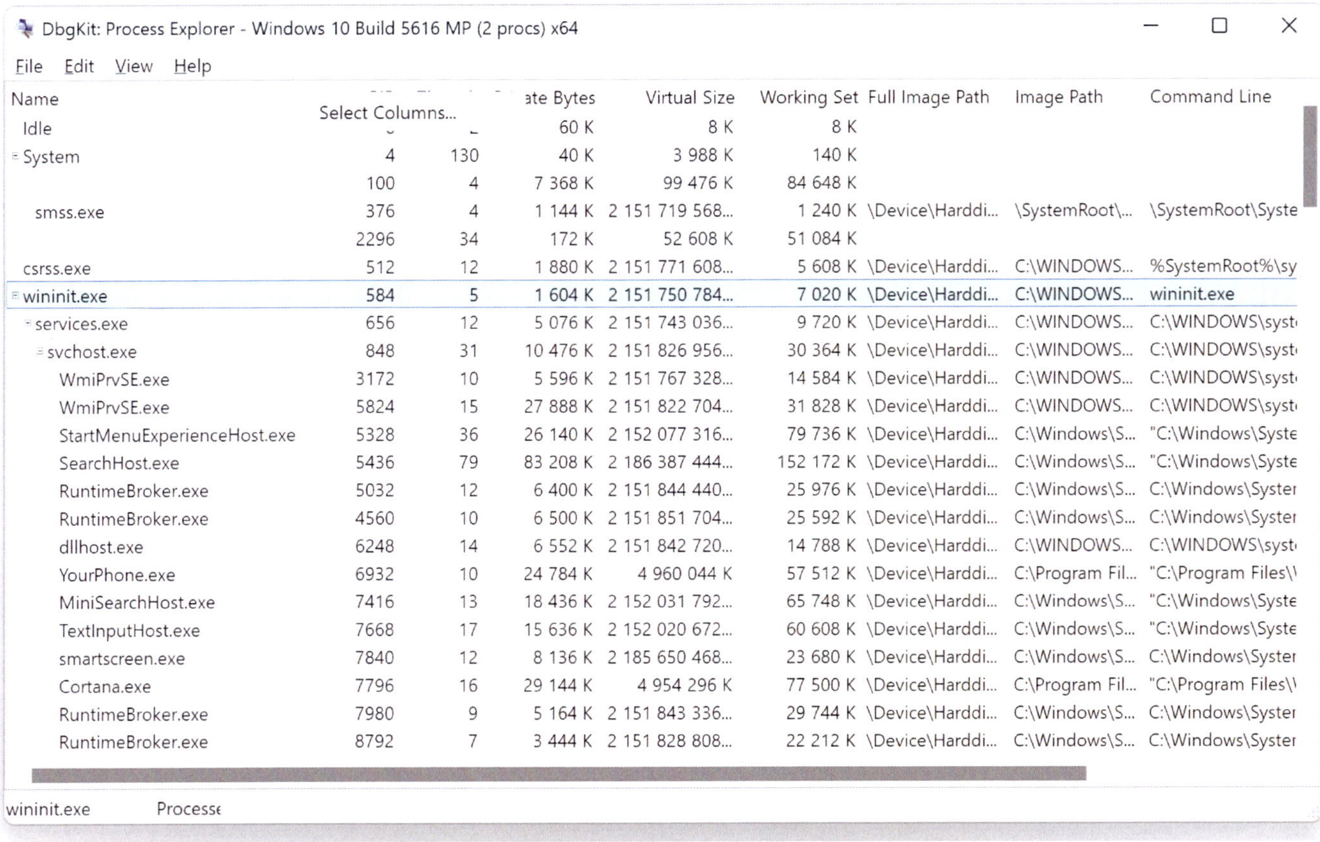

DbgKit: Process Explorer - Windows 10 Build 5616 MP (2 procs) x64

File Edit View Help

Select Columns...

Name			ate Bytes	Virtual Size	Working Set	Full Image Path	Image Path	Command Line
Idle			60 K	8 K	8 K			
System	4	130	40 K	3 988 K	140 K			
	100	4	7 368 K	99 476 K	84 648 K			
smss.exe	376	4	1 144 K	2 151 719 568...	1 240 K	\Device\Harddi...	\SystemRoot\...	\SystemRoot\Syste
	2296	34	172 K	52 608 K	51 084 K			
csrss.exe	512	12	1 880 K	2 151 771 608...	5 608 K	\Device\Harddi...	C:\WINDOWS...	%SystemRoot%\sy
wininit.exe	584	5	1 604 K	2 151 750 784...	7 020 K	\Device\Harddi...	C:\WINDOWS...	wininit.exe
services.exe	656	12	5 076 K	2 151 743 036...	9 720 K	\Device\Harddi...	C:\WINDOWS...	C:\WINDOWS\syst
svchost.exe	848	31	10 476 K	2 151 826 956...	30 364 K	\Device\Harddi...	C:\WINDOWS...	C:\WINDOWS\syst
WmiPrvSE.exe	3172	10	5 596 K	2 151 767 328...	14 584 K	\Device\Harddi...	C:\WINDOWS...	C:\WINDOWS\syst
WmiPrvSE.exe	5824	15	27 888 K	2 151 822 704...	31 828 K	\Device\Harddi...	C:\WINDOWS...	C:\WINDOWS\syst
StartMenuExperienceHost.exe	5328	36	26 140 K	2 152 077 316...	79 736 K	\Device\Harddi...	C:\Windows\S...	"C:\Windows\Syste
SearchHost.exe	5436	79	83 208 K	2 186 387 444...	152 172 K	\Device\Harddi...	C:\Windows\S...	"C:\Windows\Syste
RuntimeBroker.exe	5032	12	6 400 K	2 151 844 440...	25 976 K	\Device\Harddi...	C:\Windows\S...	C:\Windows\Syster
RuntimeBroker.exe	4560	10	6 500 K	2 151 851 704...	25 592 K	\Device\Harddi...	C:\Windows\S...	C:\Windows\Syster
dllhost.exe	6248	14	6 552 K	2 151 842 720...	14 788 K	\Device\Harddi...	C:\WINDOWS...	C:\WINDOWS\syst
YourPhone.exe	6932	10	24 784 K	4 960 044 K	57 512 K	\Device\Harddi...	C:\Program Fil...	"C:\Program Files\
MiniSearchHost.exe	7416	13	18 436 K	2 152 031 792...	65 748 K	\Device\Harddi...	C:\Windows\S...	"C:\Windows\Syste
TextInputHost.exe	7668	17	15 636 K	2 152 020 672...	60 608 K	\Device\Harddi...	C:\Windows\S...	"C:\Windows\Syste
smartscreen.exe	7840	12	8 136 K	2 185 650 468...	23 680 K	\Device\Harddi...	C:\Windows\S...	C:\Windows\Syster
Cortana.exe	7796	16	29 144 K	4 954 296 K	77 500 K	\Device\Harddi...	C:\Program Fil...	"C:\Program Files\
RuntimeBroker.exe	7980	9	5 164 K	2 151 843 336...	29 744 K	\Device\Harddi...	C:\Windows\S...	C:\Windows\Syster
RuntimeBroker.exe	8792	7	3 444 K	2 151 828 808...	22 212 K	\Device\Harddi...	C:\Windows\S...	C:\Windows\Syster

wininit.exe Processe

We deselect Full Image Path and select Image Type to see 32-bit processes:

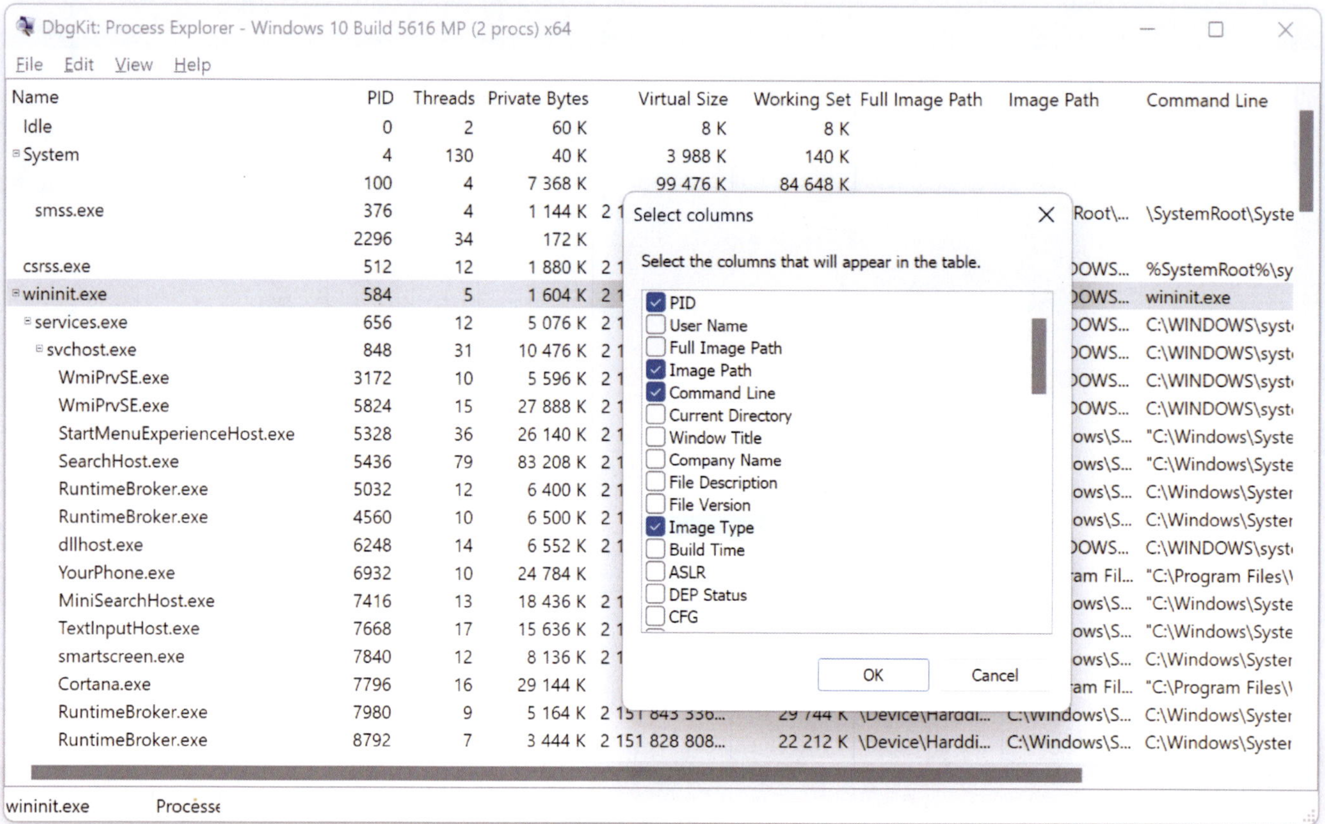
DbgKit: Process Explorer - Windows 10 Build 5616 MP (2 procs) x64
File Edit View Help
Name PID Threads Private Bytes Virtual Size Working Set Full Image Path Image Path Command Line
Idle 0 2 60 K 8 K 8 K
System 4 130 40 K 3 988 K 140 K
100 4 7 368 K 99 476 K 84 648 K
smss.exe 376 4 1 144 K
2296 34 172 K
csrss.exe 512 12 1 880 K
wininit.exe 584 5 1 604 K
services.exe 656 12 5 076 K
svchost.exe 848 31 10 476 K
WmiPrvSE.exe 3172 10 5 596 K
WmiPrvSE.exe 5824 15 27 888 K
StartMenuExperienceHost.exe 5328 36 26 140 K
SearchHost.exe 5436 79 83 208 K
RuntimeBroker.exe 5032 12 6 400 K
RuntimeBroker.exe 4560 10 6 500 K
dllhost.exe 6248 14 6 552 K
YourPhone.exe 6932 10 24 784 K
MiniSearchHost.exe 7416 13 18 436 K
TextInputHost.exe 7668 17 15 636 K
smartscreen.exe 7840 12 8 136 K
Cortana.exe 7796 16 29 144 K
RuntimeBroker.exe 7980 9 5 164 K
RuntimeBroker.exe 8792 7 3 444 K 2 151 828 808... 22 212 K \Device\Harddi... C:\Windows\S... C:\Windows\Syster
Select columns
Select the columns that will appear in the table.
PID
User Name
Full Image Path
Image Path
Command Line
Current Directory
Window Title
Company Name
File Description
File Version
Image Type
Build Time
ASLR
DEP Status
CFG
OK
Cancel
wininit.exe Processe

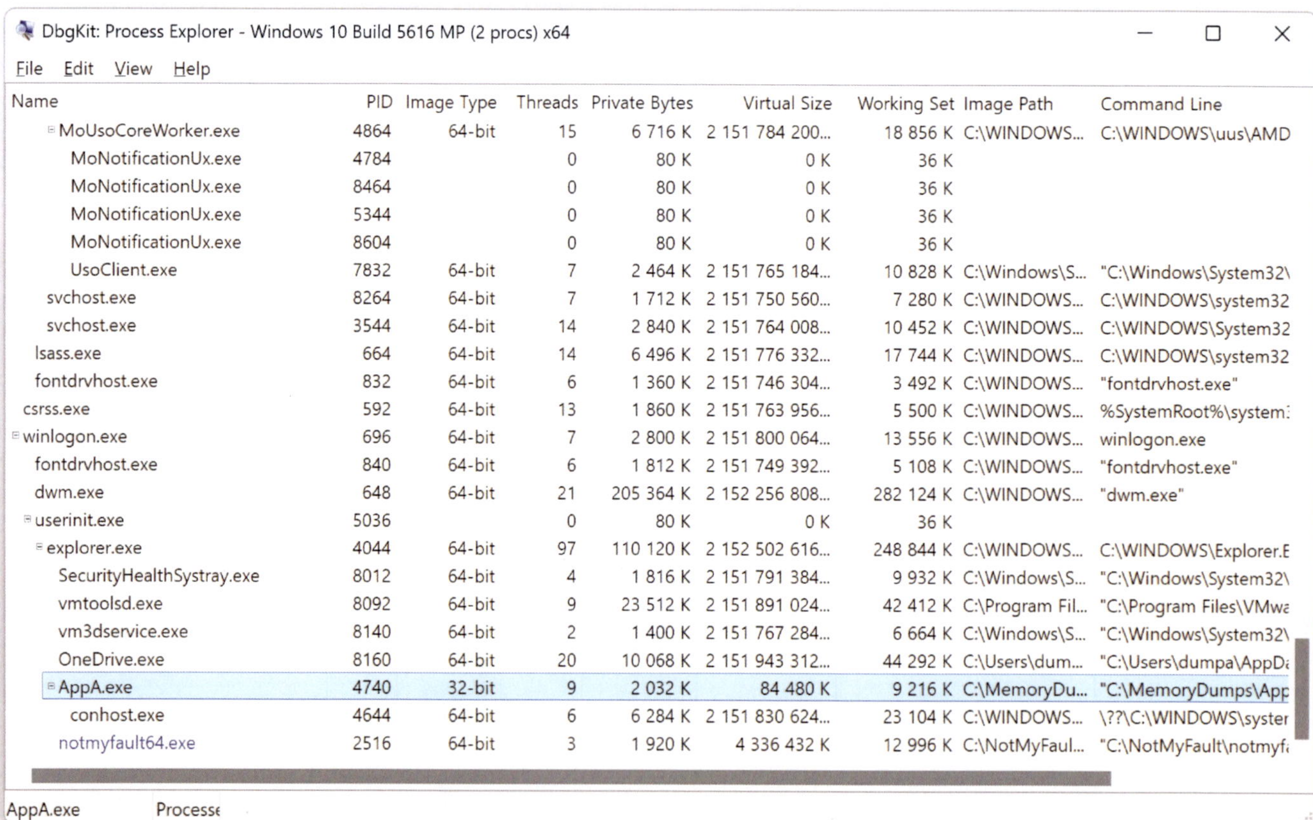
DbgKit: Process Explorer - Windows 10 Build 5616 MP (2 procs) x64
File Edit View Help
Name PID Image Type Threads Private Bytes Virtual Size Working Set Image Path Command Line
MoUsoCoreWorker.exe 4864 64-bit 15 6 716 K 2 151 784 200... 18 856 K C:\WINDOWS... C:\WINDOWS\uus\AMD
MoNotificationUx.exe 4784 0 80 K 0 K 36 K
MoNotificationUx.exe 8464 0 80 K 0 K 36 K
MoNotificationUx.exe 5344 0 80 K 0 K 36 K
MoNotificationUx.exe 8604 0 80 K 0 K 36 K
UsoClient.exe 7832 64-bit 7 2 464 K 2 151 765 184... 10 828 K C:\Windows\S... "C:\Windows\System32\
svchost.exe 8264 64-bit 7 1 712 K 2 151 750 560... 7 280 K C:\WINDOWS... C:\WINDOWS\system32
svchost.exe 3544 64-bit 14 2 840 K 2 151 764 008... 10 452 K C:\WINDOWS... C:\WINDOWS\System32
lsass.exe 664 64-bit 14 6 496 K 2 151 776 332... 17 744 K C:\WINDOWS... C:\WINDOWS\system32
fontdrvhost.exe 832 64-bit 6 1 360 K 2 151 746 304... 3 492 K C:\WINDOWS... "fontdrvhost.exe"
csrss.exe 592 64-bit 13 1 860 K 2 151 763 956... 5 500 K C:\WINDOWS... %SystemRoot%\system:
winlogon.exe 696 64-bit 7 2 800 K 2 151 800 064... 13 556 K C:\WINDOWS... winlogon.exe
fontdrvhost.exe 840 64-bit 6 1 812 K 2 151 749 392... 5 108 K C:\WINDOWS... "fontdrvhost.exe"
dwm.exe 648 64-bit 21 205 364 K 2 152 256 808... 282 124 K C:\WINDOWS... "dwm.exe"
userinit.exe 5036 0 80 K 0 K 36 K
explorer.exe 4044 64-bit 97 110 120 K 2 152 502 616... 248 844 K C:\WINDOWS... C:\WINDOWS\Explorer.E
SecurityHealthSystray.exe 8012 64-bit 4 1 816 K 2 151 791 384... 9 932 K C:\Windows\S... "C:\Windows\System32\
vmtoolsd.exe 8092 64-bit 9 23 512 K 2 151 891 024... 42 412 K C:\Program Fil... "C:\Program Files\VMwa
vm3dservice.exe 8140 64-bit 2 1 400 K 2 151 767 284... 6 664 K C:\Windows\S... "C:\Windows\System32\
OneDrive.exe 8160 64-bit 20 10 068 K 2 151 943 312... 44 292 K C:\Users\dum... "C:\Users\dumpa\AppD
AppA.exe 4740 32-bit 9 2 032 K 84 480 K 9 216 K C:\MemoryDu... "C:\MemoryDumps\App
conhost.exe 4644 64-bit 6 6 284 K 2 151 830 624... 23 104 K C:\WINDOWS... \??\C:\WINDOWS\syster
notmyfault64.exe 2516 64-bit 3 1 920 K 4 336 432 K 12 996 K C:\NotMyFaul... "C:\NotMyFault\notmyf
AppA.exe Processe

It is possible to sort by a column and come back to the process tree structure by clicking on the column header (we choose the Threads column):

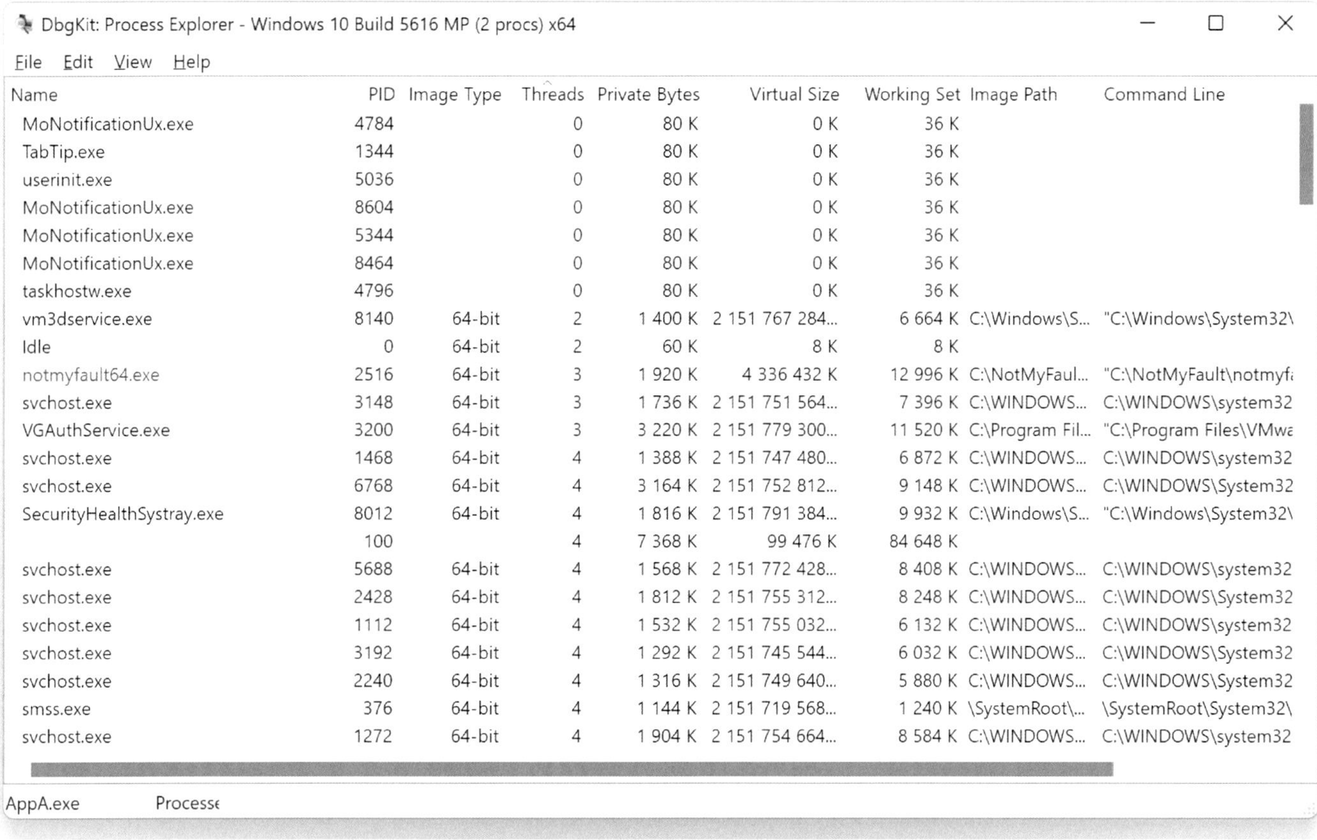
DbgKit: Process Explorer - Windows 10 Build 5616 MP (2 procs) x64

File Edit View Help

Name	PID	Image Type	Threads	Private Bytes	Virtual Size	Working Set	Image Path	Command Line
MoNotificationUx.exe	4784		0	80 K	0 K	36 K		
TabTip.exe	1344		0	80 K	0 K	36 K		
userinit.exe	5036		0	80 K	0 K	36 K		
MoNotificationUx.exe	8604		0	80 K	0 K	36 K		
MoNotificationUx.exe	5344		0	80 K	0 K	36 K		
MoNotificationUx.exe	8464		0	80 K	0 K	36 K		
taskhostw.exe	4796		0	80 K	0 K	36 K		
vm3dservice.exe	8140	64-bit	2	1 400 K	2 151 767 284...	6 664 K	C:\Windows\S...	"C:\Windows\System32\
Idle	0	64-bit	2	60 K	8 K	8 K		
notmyfault64.exe	2516	64-bit	3	1 920 K	4 336 432 K	12 996 K	C:\NotMyFaul...	"C:\NotMyFault\notmyfa
svchost.exe	3148	64-bit	3	1 736 K	2 151 751 564...	7 396 K	C:\WINDOWS...	C:\WINDOWS\system32
VGAuthService.exe	3200	64-bit	3	3 220 K	2 151 779 300...	11 520 K	C:\Program Fil...	"C:\Program Files\VMwa
svchost.exe	1468	64-bit	4	1 388 K	2 151 747 480...	6 872 K	C:\WINDOWS...	C:\WINDOWS\system32
svchost.exe	6768	64-bit	4	3 164 K	2 151 752 812...	9 148 K	C:\WINDOWS...	C:\WINDOWS\System32
SecurityHealthSystray.exe	8012	64-bit	4	1 816 K	2 151 791 384...	9 932 K	C:\Windows\S...	"C:\Windows\System32\
	100		4	7 368 K	99 476 K	84 648 K		
svchost.exe	5688	64-bit	4	1 568 K	2 151 772 428...	8 408 K	C:\WINDOWS...	C:\WINDOWS\system32
svchost.exe	2428	64-bit	4	1 812 K	2 151 755 312...	8 248 K	C:\WINDOWS...	C:\WINDOWS\System32
svchost.exe	1112	64-bit	4	1 532 K	2 151 755 032...	6 132 K	C:\WINDOWS...	C:\WINDOWS\system32
svchost.exe	3192	64-bit	4	1 292 K	2 151 745 544...	6 032 K	C:\WINDOWS...	C:\WINDOWS\System32
svchost.exe	2240	64-bit	4	1 316 K	2 151 749 640...	5 880 K	C:\WINDOWS...	C:\WINDOWS\System32
smss.exe	376	64-bit	4	1 144 K	2 151 719 568...	1 240 K	\SystemRoot\...	\SystemRoot\System32\
svchost.exe	1272	64-bit	4	1 904 K	2 151 754 664...	8 584 K	C:\WINDOWS...	C:\WINDOWS\system32

AppA.exe Processe

We then select the 32-bit *AppA.exe* process and use the context menu to Set Context and then Display Details to dump process information (similar to the **!process** command output) to the WinDbg window:

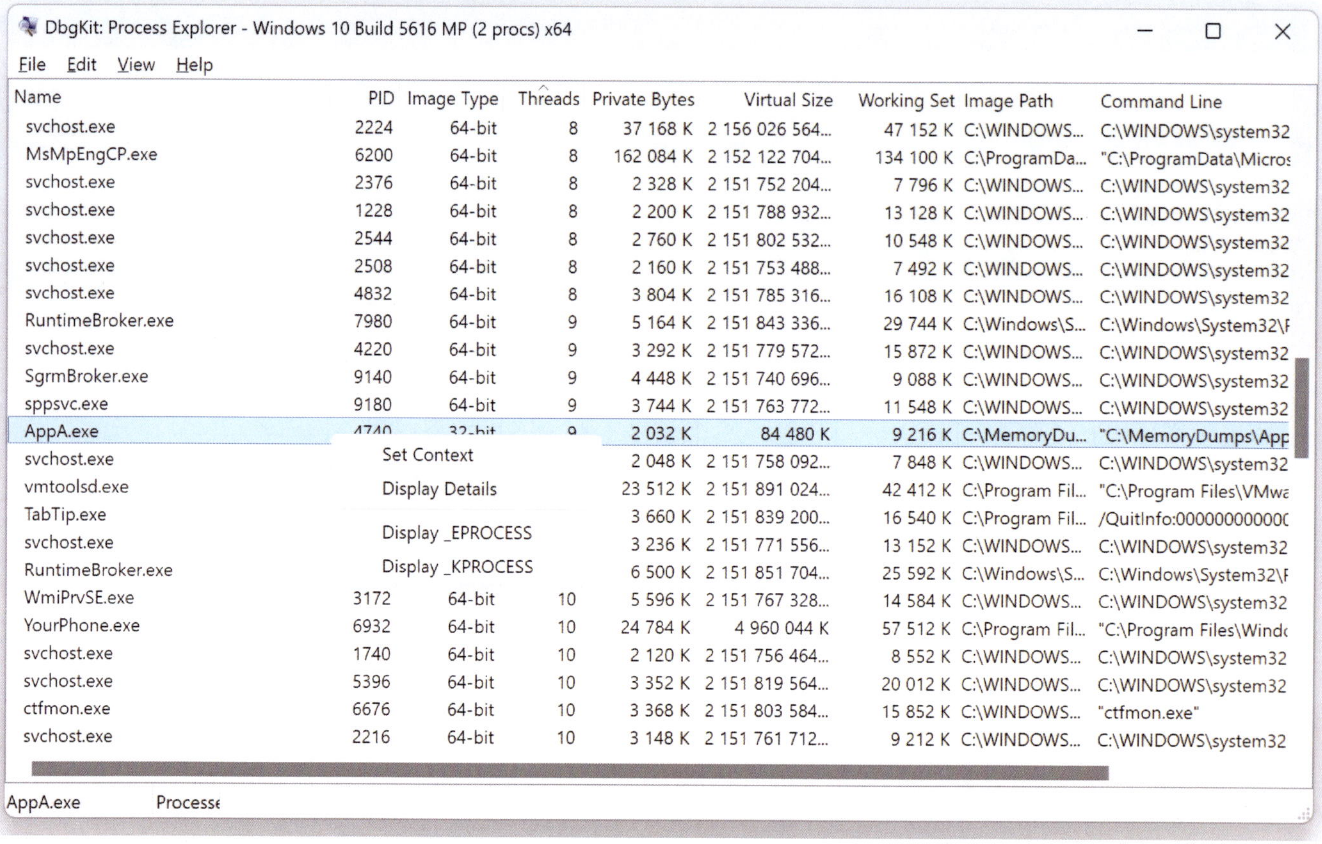

DbgKit: Process Explorer - Windows 10 Build 5616 MP (2 procs) x64

File Edit View Help

Name	PID	Image Type	Threads	Private Bytes	Virtual Size	Working Set	Image Path	Command Line
svchost.exe	2224	64-bit	8	37 168 K	2 156 026 564...	47 152 K	C:\WINDOWS...	C:\WINDOWS\system32
MsMpEngCP.exe	6200	64-bit	8	162 084 K	2 152 122 704...	134 100 K	C:\ProgramDa...	"C:\ProgramData\Micros
svchost.exe	2376	64-bit	8	2 328 K	2 151 752 204...	7 796 K	C:\WINDOWS...	C:\WINDOWS\system32
svchost.exe	1228	64-bit	8	2 200 K	2 151 788 932...	13 128 K	C:\WINDOWS...	C:\WINDOWS\system32
svchost.exe	2544	64-bit	8	2 760 K	2 151 802 532...	10 548 K	C:\WINDOWS...	C:\WINDOWS\system32
svchost.exe	2508	64-bit	8	2 160 K	2 151 753 488...	7 492 K	C:\WINDOWS...	C:\WINDOWS\system32
svchost.exe	4832	64-bit	8	3 804 K	2 151 785 316...	16 108 K	C:\WINDOWS...	C:\WINDOWS\system32
RuntimeBroker.exe	7980	64-bit	9	5 164 K	2 151 843 336...	29 744 K	C:\Windows\S...	C:\Windows\System32\I
svchost.exe	4220	64-bit	9	3 292 K	2 151 779 572...	15 872 K	C:\WINDOWS...	C:\WINDOWS\system32
SgrmBroker.exe	9140	64-bit	9	4 448 K	2 151 740 696...	9 088 K	C:\WINDOWS...	C:\WINDOWS\system32
sppsvc.exe	9180	64-bit	9	3 744 K	2 151 763 772...	11 548 K	C:\WINDOWS...	C:\WINDOWS\system32
AppA.exe	4740	32-bit	9	2 032 K	84 480 K	9 216 K	C:\MemoryDu...	"C:\MemoryDumps\App
svchost.exe				2 048 K	2 151 758 092...	7 848 K	C:\WINDOWS...	C:\WINDOWS\system32
vmtoolsd.exe				23 512 K	2 151 891 024...	42 412 K	C:\Program Fil...	"C:\Program Files\VMwa
TabTip.exe				3 660 K	2 151 839 200...	16 540 K	C:\Program Fil...	/QuitInfo:00000000000C
svchost.exe				3 236 K	2 151 771 556...	13 152 K	C:\WINDOWS...	C:\WINDOWS\system32
RuntimeBroker.exe				6 500 K	2 151 851 704...	25 592 K	C:\Windows\S...	C:\Windows\System32\I
WmiPrvSE.exe	3172	64-bit	10	5 596 K	2 151 767 328...	14 584 K	C:\WINDOWS...	C:\WINDOWS\system32
YourPhone.exe	6932	64-bit	10	24 784 K	4 960 044 K	57 512 K	C:\Program Fil...	"C:\Program Files\Windo
svchost.exe	1740	64-bit	10	2 120 K	2 151 756 464...	8 552 K	C:\WINDOWS...	C:\WINDOWS\system32
svchost.exe	5396	64-bit	10	3 352 K	2 151 819 564...	20 012 K	C:\WINDOWS...	C:\WINDOWS\system32
ctfmon.exe	6676	64-bit	10	3 368 K	2 151 803 584...	15 852 K	C:\WINDOWS...	"ctfmon.exe"
svchost.exe	2216	64-bit	10	3 148 K	2 151 761 712...	9 212 K	C:\WINDOWS...	C:\WINDOWS\system32

Set Context

Display Details

Display _EPROCESS

Display _KPROCESS

AppA.exe Processe

```
Setting the process context to AppA.exe
Implicit process is now ffffc38c`334020c0
Loading User Symbols
.......

PROCESS ffffc38c334020c0
    SessionId: 1  Cid: 1284    Peb: 00e45000  ParentCid: 0fcc
    DirBase: 03d77002  ObjectTable: ffffac8a0b2a7200  HandleCount: 145.
    Image: AppA.exe
    VadRoot ffffc38c2e156b40 Vads 97 Clone 0 Private 362. Modified 18. Locked 0.
    DeviceMap ffffac8a09519470
    Token                             ffffac8a0b35c770
    ElapsedTime                       00:00:27.018
    UserTime                          00:00:00.000
    KernelTime                        00:00:00.000
    QuotaPoolUsage[PagedPool]         153864
    QuotaPoolUsage[NonPagedPool]      13448
    Working Set Sizes (now,min,max)  (2362, 50, 345) (9448KB, 200KB, 1380KB)
    PeakWorkingSetSize                2304
    VirtualSize                       82 Mb
    PeakVirtualSize                   98 Mb
    PageFaultCount                    2448
    MemoryPriority                    BACKGROUND
    BasePriority                      8
    CommitCharge                      508
    Job                               ffffc38c317de060

        THREAD ffffc38c3340b080  Cid 1284.128c  Teb: 0000000000e47000 Win32Thread: ffffc38c2e155970 WAIT: (UserRequest) UserMode Non-Alertable
            ffffc38c31883080  Thread
        Not impersonating
        DeviceMap                 ffffac8a09519470
        Owning Process            ffffc38c334020c0       Image:         AppA.exe
        Attached Process          N/A            Image:         N/A
        Wait Start TickCount      10273          Ticks: 1683 (0:00:00:26.296)
        Context Switch Count      89             IdealProcessor: 1
        UserTime                  00:00:00.000
        KernelTime                00:00:00.015
Unable to load image C:\MemoryDumps\AppA.exe, Win32 error 0n2
*** WARNING: Unable to verify checksum for AppA.exe
        Win32 Start Address AppA (0x0000000000021ad5)
        Stack Init ffffbe8294e97c70 Current ffffbe8294e97650
        Base ffffbe8294e98000 Limit ffffbe8294e92000 Call 0000000000000000
        Priority 8  BasePriority 8  IoPriority 2  PagePriority 5
Unable to load image \??\C:\WINDOWS\system32\drivers\myfault.sys, Win32 error 0n2
        Child-SP          RetAddr               : Args to Child                                                           : Call Site
        ffffbe82`94e97690 fffff806`62132457     : ffff8400`0000000a 00000000`ffffffff ffffbe82`00000000 ffffc38c`2e3b0158 : nt!KiSwapContext+0x76
        ffffbe82`94e977d0 fffff806`62134309     : ffffbe82`94e97ae0 00000000`00000000 ffffbe82`94e979b0 00000000`00000000 : nt!KiSwapThread+0x3a7
        ffffbe82`94e978b0 fffff806`6212e224     : 00000000`00000000 fffff806`00000000 ffffc38c`00000000 00000000`00000000 : nt!KiCommitThreadWait+0x159
        ffffbe82`94e97950 fffff806`6256a5eb     : ffffc38c`31883080 00000000`00000006 00000000`00000001 00000000`00000000 : nt!KeWaitForSingleObject+0x234
        ffffbe82`94e97a40 fffff806`6256a51a     : ffffc38c`3340b080 00000000`00000000 00000000`00000000 00000000`01220a38 : nt!ObWaitForSingleObject+0xbb
        ffffbe82`94e97aa0 fffff806`62227b75     : ffffc38c`3340b080 00000000`00000000 00000000`00000000 00000000`00000000 : nt!NtWaitForSingleObject+0x6a
        ffffbe82`94e97ae0 00000000`76fe1cf3     : 00000000`76fe1b56 00000023`7706530c 00007ffc`863d0023 00000000`00000000 : nt!KiSystemServiceCopyEnd+0x25 (TrapFrame @ ffffbe82`94e97ae0)
        00000000`00d6e988 00000000`76fe1b56     : 00000023`7706530c 00007ffc`863d0023 00000000`00000000 00000000`010ffaf0 : wow64cpu!CpupSyscallStub+0x13
```

```
00000000`00d6e990 00000000`76fe1d75     : 00000000`010ff824 00007ffc`863dc6ec 00000000`00020108 00007ffc`863de163 : wow64cpu!Thunk0ArgReloadState+0x5
00000000`00d6ea40 00007ffc`863de06d     : 00000000`00e46000 00000000`00020108 00000000`00000000 00000000`00d6f470 : wow64cpu!BTCpuSimulate+0xbb5
00000000`00d6ea80 00007ffc`863dd8ad     : 00000000`00000000 00000000`01126a28 00000000`00000000 00000000`00000000 : wow64!RunCpuSimulation+0xd
00000000`00d6eab0 00007ffc`8857f66d     : 00000000`00020108 00007ffc`885d4758 00000000`00e45000 00007ffc`885d0740 : wow64!Wow64LdrpInitialize+0x12d
00000000`00d6ed60 00007ffc`8856d558     : 00000000`00000000 00000000`00000000 00000000`00000000 00000000`00000001 : ntdll!LdrpInitializeProcess+0x16d1
00000000`00d6f120 00007ffc`8851a843     : 00000000`00000000 00007ffc`884a0000 00000000`00e47000 00000000`00e45050 : ntdll!_LdrpInitialize+0x52cdc
00000000`00d6f1a0 00007ffc`8851a76e     : 00000000`00d6f470 00000000`00000000 00000000`00d6f470 00000000`00000000 : ntdll!LdrpInitializeInternal+0x6b
00000000`00d6f420 00000000`00000000     : 00000000`00000000 00000000`00000000 00000000`00000000 00000000`00000000 : ntdll!LdrInitializeThunk+0xe

THREAD ffffc38c3205c080  Cid 1284.1680  Teb: 0000000000e4b000 Win32Thread: 0000000000000000 WAIT: (WrQueue) UserMode Alertable
    ffffc38c34d73b00  QueueObject
Not impersonating
DeviceMap                 ffffac8a09519470
Owning Process            ffffc38c334020c0       Image:         AppA.exe
Attached Process          N/A            Image:         N/A
Wait Start TickCount      10292          Ticks: 1664 (0:00:00:26.000)
Context Switch Count      6              IdealProcessor: 0
UserTime                  00:00:00.000
KernelTime                00:00:00.000
Win32 Start Address 0x0000000077021940
Stack Init ffffbe82985fec70 Current ffffbe82985fe360
Base ffffbe82985ff000 Limit ffffbe82985f9000 Call 0000000000000000
Priority 8  BasePriority 8  IoPriority 2  PagePriority 5
Child-SP          RetAddr               : Args to Child                                                           : Call Site
ffffbe82`985fe3a0 fffff806`62132457     : ffffbe82`00000008 fffff806`ffffffff ffffc38c`00000000 ffffc38c`3203f158 : nt!KiSwapContext+0x76
ffffbe82`985fe4e0 fffff806`62134309     : 00000000`00e67000 00007fff`ffff0000 00000000`00000000 ffffac8a`0d49a340 : nt!KiSwapThread+0x3a7
ffffbe82`985fe5c0 fffff806`62136d66     : ffffc38c`00000000 00000007`00000000 ffffffff`00000000 00000000`00000000 : nt!KiCommitThreadWait+0x159
ffffbe82`985fe660 fffff806`62136778     : ffffc38c`34d73b00 ffffac8a`0d49a301 00000000`00000001 00000000`00000000 : nt!KeRemoveQueueEx+0x2b6
ffffbe82`985fe710 fffff806`62138fdc     : ffffc38c`00000000 ffffc38c`336d6750 ffffc38c`336d6750 ffffbe82`985feb60 : nt!IoRemoveIoCompletion+0x98
ffffbe82`985fe830 fffff806`62227b75     : 00000000`00000000 00000000`00000000 00000000`00000000 00000000`00e4b000 : nt!NtWaitForWorkViaWorkerFactory+0x39c
ffffbe82`985fea70 00007ffc`88546f14     : 00007ffc`863da76a 00000000`011de301 00000000`00000000 00000002`00000000 : nt!KiSystemServiceCopyEnd+0x25 (TrapFrame @ ffffbe82`985feae0)
00000000`011de3d8 00007ffc`863da76a     : 00000000`011de301 00000000`00000000 00000002`00000000 00007ffc`00000004 : ntdll!NtWaitForWorkViaWorkerFactory+0x14
00000000`011de3e0 00007ffc`863d77ca     : 00000000`00000000 00000000`00e4d000 00007ffc`863da650 00000000`00e4b000 : wow64!whNtWaitForWorkViaWorkerFactory+0x11a
00000000`011de470 00000000`76fe17ba     : 00000023`7706649c 00000000`00000023 00000000`01221bf0 00000000`014df898 : wow64!Wow64SystemServiceEx+0x15a
00000000`011ded30 00000000`76fe1d75     : 00000000`014df5cc 00007ffc`863dc6ec 00000000`00000000 00007ffc`863de163 : wow64cpu!ServiceNoTurbo+0xb
00000000`011dede0 00007ffc`863de06d     : 00000000`0121ffc0 00000000`00000000 00000000`00000000 00000000`011df450 : wow64cpu!BTCpuSimulate+0xbb5
00000000`011dee20 00007ffc`863dd8ad     : 00000000`00000000 00000000`00000001 00000000`00000000 00000000`00000000 : wow64!RunCpuSimulation+0xd
00000000`011dee50 00007ffc`8851a958     : 00000000`00000000 00000000`00000000 00000000`00000001 00000000`00000000 : wow64!Wow64LdrpInitialize+0x12d
00000000`011df100 00007ffc`8851a843     : 00000000`00000000 00007ffc`884a0000 00000000`00e4b000 00000000`00000000 : ntdll!_LdrpInitialize+0xdc
00000000`011df180 00007ffc`8851a76e     : 00000000`011df450 00000000`00000000 00000000`011df450 00000000`00000000 : ntdll!LdrpInitializeInternal+0x6b
00000000`011df400 00000000`00000000     : 00000000`00000000 00000000`00000000 00000000`00000000 00000000`00000000 : ntdll!LdrInitializeThunk+0xe

THREAD ffffc38c32e6b080  Cid 1284.167c  Teb: 0000000000e4f000 Win32Thread: 0000000000000000 WAIT: (WrQueue) UserMode Alertable
    ffffc38c34d73b00  QueueObject
Not impersonating
DeviceMap                 ffffac8a09519470
Owning Process            ffffc38c334020c0       Image:         AppA.exe
Attached Process          N/A            Image:         N/A
Wait Start TickCount      10292          Ticks: 1664 (0:00:00:26.000)
Context Switch Count      11             IdealProcessor: 1
UserTime                  00:00:00.000
KernelTime                00:00:00.000
Win32 Start Address 0x0000000077021940
Stack Init ffffbe8296a92c70 Current ffffbe8296a92360
Base ffffbe8296a93000 Limit ffffbe8296a8d000 Call 0000000000000000
Priority 9  BasePriority 8  IoPriority 2  PagePriority 5
Child-SP          RetAddr               : Args to Child                                                           : Call Site
ffffbe82`96a923a0 fffff806`62132457     : 00000000`00000008 fffff806`ffffffff 00000000`00000000 ffffc38c`3197b118 : nt!KiSwapContext+0x76
ffffbe82`96a924e0 fffff806`62134309     : 00000000`00000000 00000000`00000000 00000000`00000000 00000000`00000000 : nt!KiSwapThread+0x3a7
ffffbe82`96a925c0 fffff806`62136d66     : 00000000`00000000 ffffbe82`00000000 00000000`00000000 00000000`00000000 : nt!KiCommitThreadWait+0x159
ffffbe82`96a92660 fffff806`62136778     : ffffc38c`34d73b00 00000000`00000001 00000000`00000001 00000000`00000000 : nt!KeRemoveQueueEx+0x2b6
ffffbe82`96a92710 fffff806`62138fdc     : 00000000`00000000 00000000`00000000 00000000`00000000 00000000`00000000 : nt!IoRemoveIoCompletion+0x98
ffffbe82`96a92830 fffff806`62227b75     : ffffc38c`333de2e0 00000000`00000000 00000000`00000000 ffffc38c`2ecd41c0 : nt!NtWaitForWorkViaWorkerFactory+0x39c
ffffbe82`96a92a70 00007ffc`88546f14     : 00007ffc`863da76a 00000000`0151e401 00000000`00000000 00000002`00000000 : nt!KiSystemServiceCopyEnd+0x25 (TrapFrame @ ffffbe82`96a92ae0)
00000000`0151e488 00007ffc`863da76a     : 00000000`0151e401 00000000`00000000 00000002`00000000 00000000`00000004 : ntdll!NtWaitForWorkViaWorkerFactory+0x14
00000000`0151e490 00007ffc`863d77ca     : 00000000`00000000 00000000`00e51000 00007ffc`863da650 00000000`00e4f000 : wow64!whNtWaitForWorkViaWorkerFactory+0x11a
00000000`0151e520 00000000`76fe17ba     : 00000023`7706477c 00000000`00000023 00000000`01221e88 00000000`0161fdc0 : wow64!Wow64SystemServiceEx+0x15a
00000000`0151ede0 00000000`76fe1d75     : 00000000`0161faf4 00007ffc`863dc6ec 00000000`00000000 00007ffc`863de163 : wow64cpu!ServiceNoTurbo+0xb
00000000`0151ee90 00007ffc`863de06d     : 00000000`0121ffc0 00000000`00000000 00000000`00000000 00000000`0151f500 : wow64cpu!BTCpuSimulate+0xbb5
00000000`0151eed0 00007ffc`863dd8ad     : 00000000`00000000 00000000`00000001 00000000`00000000 00000000`00000000 : wow64!RunCpuSimulation+0xd
00000000`0151ef00 00007ffc`8851a958     : 00000000`00000000 00000000`00000000 00000000`00000001 00000000`00000000 : wow64!Wow64LdrpInitialize+0x12d
00000000`0151f1b0 00007ffc`8851a843     : 00000000`00000000 00007ffc`884a0000 00000000`00e4f000 00000000`00000000 : ntdll!_LdrpInitialize+0xdc
00000000`0151f230 00007ffc`8851a76e     : 00000000`0151f500 00000000`00000000 00000000`0151f500 00000000`00000000 : ntdll!LdrpInitializeInternal+0x6b
00000000`0151f4b0 00000000`00000000     : 00000000`00000000 00000000`00000000 00000000`00000000 00000000`00000000 : ntdll!LdrInitializeThunk+0xe

THREAD ffffc38c31883080  Cid 1284.2058  Teb: 0000000000e53000 Win32Thread: 0000000000000000 WAIT: (DelayExecution) UserMode Non-Alertable
    ffffffffffffffff  NotificationEvent
Not impersonating
DeviceMap                 ffffac8a09519470
Owning Process            ffffc38c334020c0       Image:         AppA.exe
Attached Process          N/A            Image:         N/A
Wait Start TickCount      10273          Ticks: 1683 (0:00:00:26.296)
Context Switch Count      4              IdealProcessor: 0
UserTime                  00:00:00.000
KernelTime                00:00:00.000
Win32 Start Address 0x0000000075bb67e0
Stack Init ffffbe8295795c70 Current ffffbe8295795720
Base ffffbe8295796000 Limit ffffbe8295790000 Call 0000000000000000
Priority 8  BasePriority 8  IoPriority 2  PagePriority 5
Child-SP          RetAddr               : Args to Child                                                           : Call Site
ffffbe82`95795760 fffff806`62132457     : 00000000`0000000a fffffb00`ffffffff 00000000`00000000 ffffc38c`32e6b158 : nt!KiSwapContext+0x76
ffffbe82`957958a0 fffff806`62134309     : ffffc38c`31883080 fffff806`620d6e97 00000000`00000000 00000000`5fb1a500 : nt!KiSwapThread+0x3a7
ffffbe82`95795980 fffff806`62137fc6     : 00000000`00000000 00000000`00000000 00000000`0000009b 00000000`866d786a : nt!KiCommitThreadWait+0x159
ffffbe82`95795a20 fffff806`6257fdaf     : 00000000`02dffda0 00000000`00000000 00000000`00000000 00000000`00000002 : nt!KeDelayExecutionThread+0x416
ffffbe82`95795ab0 fffff806`62227b75     : ffffc38c`31883080 00000000`00000000 ffffffff`d941c980 ffffc38c`00000000 : nt!NtDelayExecution+0x5f
ffffbe82`95795ae0 00000000`76fe1cf3     : 00000000`76fe1bd2 00000000`77066d50 00000000`00000023 00000000`00000202 : nt!KiSystemServiceCopyEnd+0x25 (TrapFrame @ ffffbe82`95795ae0)
00000000`02dfea28 00000000`76fe1bd2     : 00000000`77066d50 00000000`00000023 00000000`00000202 00000000`02efffd4 : wow64cpu!CpupSyscallStub+0x13
00000000`02dfea30 00000000`76fe1d75     : 00000000`02effd08 00007ffc`863dc6ec 00000000`00000000 00007ffc`863de163 : wow64cpu!Thunk2ArgNSpNSpReloadState+0xc
00000000`02dfeae0 00007ffc`863de06d     : 00000000`012282d0 00000000`00000000 00000000`00000000 00000000`02dff150 : wow64cpu!BTCpuSimulate+0xbb5
00000000`02dfeb20 00007ffc`863dd8ad     : 00000000`00000000 00000000`00000001 00000000`00000000 00000000`00000000 : wow64!RunCpuSimulation+0xd
00000000`02dfeb50 00007ffc`8851a958     : 00000000`00000000 00000000`00000000 00000000`00000001 00000000`00000000 : wow64!Wow64LdrpInitialize+0x12d
00000000`02dfee00 00007ffc`8851a843     : 00000000`00000000 00007ffc`884a0000 00000000`00e53000 00000000`00000000 : ntdll!_LdrpInitialize+0xdc
00000000`02dfee80 00007ffc`8851a76e     : 00000000`02dff150 00000000`00000000 00000000`02dff150 00000000`00000000 : ntdll!LdrpInitializeInternal+0x6b
00000000`02dff100 00000000`00000000     : 00000000`00000000 00000000`00000000 00000000`00000000 00000000`00000000 : ntdll!LdrInitializeThunk+0xe

THREAD ffffc38c2c52f080  Cid 1284.205c  Teb: 0000000000e57000 Win32Thread: 0000000000000000 WAIT: (DelayExecution) UserMode Non-Alertable
    ffffffffffffffff  NotificationEvent
Not impersonating
DeviceMap                 ffffac8a09519470
Owning Process            ffffc38c334020c0       Image:         AppA.exe
Attached Process          N/A            Image:         N/A
Wait Start TickCount      10273          Ticks: 1683 (0:00:00:26.296)
Context Switch Count      3              IdealProcessor: 1
UserTime                  00:00:00.000
KernelTime                00:00:00.000
Win32 Start Address 0x0000000075bb67e0
Stack Init ffffbe8295d9cc70 Current ffffbe8295d9c720
Base ffffbe8295d9d000 Limit ffffbe8295d97000 Call 0000000000000000
```

```
Priority 8  BasePriority 8  IoPriority 2  PagePriority 5
Child-SP          RetAddr               : Args to Child                                                           : Call Site
ffffbe82`95d9c760 fffff806`62132457     : 00000800`0000000b fffffb7d`ffffffff 00000000`00000000 ffffc38c`31802198 : nt!KiSwapContext+0x76
ffffbe82`95d9c8a0 fffff806`62134309     : ffffc38c`2c52f080 fffff806`620d6e97 00000000`00000000 00000000`5fb1a500 : nt!KiSwapThread+0x3a7
ffffbe82`95d9c980 fffff806`62137fc6     : 00000000`00000000 00000000`00000000 00000000`000000c1 00000000`8705f5a3 : nt!KiCommitThreadWait+0x159
ffffbe82`95d9ca20 fffff806`6257fdaf     : 00000000`02f3fda0 00000000`0303fa9c 00000000`0303fa00 00000000`00000002 : nt!KeDelayExecutionThread+0x416
ffffbe82`95d9cab0 fffff806`62227b75     : ffffc38c`2c52f080 00000000`00000006 ffffffff`d8a93300 ffffc38c`00000000 : nt!NtDelayExecution+0x5f
ffffbe82`95d9cae0 00000000`76fe1cf3     : 00000000`76fe1bd2 00000023`77065ccc 00000000`00000023 00000000`fffffffa : nt!KiSystemServiceCopyEnd+0x25 (TrapFrame @ ffffbe82`95d9cae0)
00000000`02f3ed78 00000000`76fe1bd2     : 00000023`77065ccc 00000000`00000023 00000000`fffffffa 00000000`0303fb8c : wow64cpu!CpupSyscallStub+0x13
00000000`02f3ed80 00000000`76fe1d75     : 00000000`0303f8c0 00007ffc`863dc6ec 00000000`00000000 00007ffc`863de163 : wow64cpu!Thunk2ArgNSpNSpReloadState+0xc
00000000`02f3ee30 00007ffc`863de06d     : 00000000`01228390 00000000`00000000 00000000`00000000 00000000`02f3f4a0 : wow64cpu!BTCpuSimulate+0xbb5
00000000`02f3ee70 00007ffc`863dd8ad     : 00000000`00000000 00000000`00000001 00000000`00000000 00000000`00000000 : wow64!RunCpuSimulation+0xd
00000000`02f3eea0 00007ffc`8851a958     : 00000000`00000000 00000000`00000000 00000000`00000001 00000000`00000000 : wow64!Wow64LdrpInitialize+0x12d
00000000`02f3f150 00007ffc`8851a843     : 00000000`00000000 00007ffc`884a0000 00000000`00e57000 00000000`00000000 : ntdll!_LdrpInitialize+0xdc
00000000`02f3f1d0 00007ffc`8851a76e     : 00000000`02f3f4a0 00000000`00000000 00000000`02f3f4a0 00000000`00000000 : ntdll!LdrpInitializeInternal+0x6b
00000000`02f3f450 00000000`00000000     : 00000000`00000000 00000000`00000000 00000000`00000000 00000000`00000000 : ntdll!LdrInitializeThunk+0xe

THREAD ffffc38c318020c0  Cid 1284.2044  Teb: 0000000000e5b000 Win32Thread: 0000000000000000 WAIT: (DelayExecution) UserMode Non-Alertable
    ffffffffffffffff  NotificationEvent
Not impersonating
DeviceMap                 ffffac8a09519470
Owning Process            ffffc38c334020c0       Image:         AppA.exe
Attached Process          N/A            Image:         N/A
Wait Start TickCount      10273          Ticks: 1683 (0:00:00:26.296)
Context Switch Count      3              IdealProcessor: 0
UserTime                  00:00:00.000
KernelTime                00:00:00.000
Win32 Start Address 0x0000000075bb67e0
Stack Init ffffbe8295d5dc70 Current ffffbe8295d5d720
Base ffffbe8295d5e000 Limit ffffbe8295d58000 Call 0000000000000000
Priority 8  BasePriority 8  IoPriority 2  PagePriority 5
Child-SP          RetAddr               : Args to Child                                                           : Call Site
ffffbe82`95d5d760 fffff806`62132457     : 00000000`0000000b fffffb00`ffffffff 00000000`00000000 ffffc38c`337ea158 : nt!KiSwapContext+0x76
ffffbe82`95d5d8a0 fffff806`62134309     : ffffc38c`318020c0 fffff806`620d6e97 00000000`00000000 00000000`5fb1a500 : nt!KiSwapThread+0x3a7
ffffbe82`95d5d980 fffff806`62137fc6     : 00000000`00000000 00000000`00000000 00000000`000000e7 00000000`879e9296 : nt!KiCommitThreadWait+0x159
ffffbe82`95d5da20 fffff806`6257fdaf     : 00000000`0307fda0 00000000`00000000 00000000`00000000 00000000`00000002 : nt!KeDelayExecutionThread+0x416
ffffbe82`95d5dab0 fffff806`62227b75     : ffffc38c`318020c0 00000000`00000000 ffffffff`d8109c80 ffffc38c`00000000 : nt!NtDelayExecution+0x5f
ffffbe82`95d5dae0 00000000`76fe1cf3     : 00000000`76fe1bd2 00000000`77066d50 00000000`00000023 00000000`00000202 : nt!KiSystemServiceCopyEnd+0x25 (TrapFrame @ ffffbe82`95d5dae0)
00000000`0307eae8 00000000`76fe1bd2     : 00000000`77066d50 00000000`00000023 00000000`00000202 00000000`0317f828 : wow64cpu!CpupSyscallStub+0x13
00000000`0307eaf0 00000000`76fe1d75     : 00000000`0317f55c 00007ffc`863dc6ec 00000000`00000000 00007ffc`863de163 : wow64cpu!Thunk2ArgNSpNSpReloadState+0xc
00000000`0307eba0 00007ffc`863de06d     : 00000000`01228590 00000000`00000000 00000000`00000000 00000000`0307f210 : wow64cpu!BTCpuSimulate+0xbb5
00000000`0307ebe0 00007ffc`863dd8ad     : 00000000`00000000 00000000`00000001 00000000`00000000 00000000`00000000 : wow64!RunCpuSimulation+0xd
00000000`0307ec10 00007ffc`8851a958     : 00000000`00000000 00000000`00000000 00000000`00000001 00000000`00000000 : wow64!Wow64LdrpInitialize+0x12d
00000000`0307eec0 00007ffc`8851a843     : 00000000`00000000 00007ffc`884a0000 00000000`00e5b000 00000000`00000000 : ntdll!_LdrpInitialize+0xdc
00000000`0307ef40 00007ffc`8851a76e     : 00000000`0307f210 00000000`00000000 00000000`0307f210 00000000`00000000 : ntdll!LdrpInitializeInternal+0x6b
00000000`0307f1c0 00000000`00000000     : 00000000`00000000 00000000`00000000 00000000`00000000 00000000`00000000 : ntdll!LdrInitializeThunk+0xe

THREAD ffffc38c2ecd4080  Cid 1284.200c  Teb: 0000000000e5f000 Win32Thread: ffffc38c2e156be0 WAIT: (WrUserRequest) UserMode Non-Alertable
    ffffc38c34d76440  QueueObject
Not impersonating
DeviceMap                 ffffac8a09519470
Owning Process            ffffc38c334020c0       Image:         AppA.exe
Attached Process          N/A            Image:         N/A
Wait Start TickCount      11514          Ticks: 442 (0:00:00:06.906)
Context Switch Count      757            IdealProcessor: 1
UserTime                  00:00:00.000
KernelTime                00:00:00.046
Win32 Start Address 0x0000000075bb67e0
Stack Init ffffbe8295d80c70 Current ffffbe8295d80410
Base ffffbe8295d81000 Limit ffffbe8295d7b000 Call 0000000000000000
Priority 10  BasePriority 8  IoPriority 2  PagePriority 5
Child-SP          RetAddr               : Args to Child                                                           : Call Site
ffffbe82`95d80450 fffff806`62132457     : 00000000`00000009 00000000`ffffffff 00000000`00000000 ffffc38c`32e2d158 : nt!KiSwapContext+0x76
ffffbe82`95d80590 fffff806`62134309     : ffffbe82`00000000 fffff806`620d4bfc ffffbe82`95d80770 00000000`00000000 : nt!KiSwapThread+0x3a7
ffffbe82`95d80670 fffff806`6212e224     : 00000000`00000000 00000000`00000000 00000000`00000000 00000000`00000000 : nt!KiCommitThreadWait+0x159
ffffbe82`95d80710 fffff806`6208ef60     : ffffc38c`34d76440 ffffbd43`0000000d 00000000`00000001 ffffc38c`306d3a00 : nt!KeWaitForSingleObject+0x234
ffffbe82`95d80800 ffffbd43`fb63b466     : ffffbd11`c2413010 ffffbd11`c2413010 00000000`00000001 00000000`00e5f000 : nt!KeWaitForMultipleObjects+0x540
ffffbe82`95d80900 ffffbd43`fb63b0cf     : ffffbd11`c2413010 ffffbd11`00000000 00000000`00000001 00000000`00000000 : win32kfull!xxxRealSleepThread+0x2c6
ffffbe82`95d80a20 ffffbd43`fb5c1864     : ffffc38c`2ecd4080 ffffbe82`95d80b60 00000000`00000000 00000000`00000020 : win32kfull!xxxSleepThread2+0xb3
ffffbe82`95d80a70 ffffbd43`fad09562     : 00000000`00e5f000 00000000`00000000 00000000`00000000 00000000`032bfa70 : win32kfull!NtUserWaitMessage+0x44
ffffbe82`95d80ab0 fffff806`62227b75     : 00000040`40000a00 00000000`00000000 00000000`031bfda0 ffffbe82`95d80b60 : win32k!NtUserWaitMessage+0x16
ffffbe82`95d80ae0 00000000`76fe1cf3     : 00000000`76fe1cb4 00000023`7657109c 00000000`00000023 00000000`032bfa70 : nt!KiSystemServiceCopyEnd+0x25 (TrapFrame @ ffffbe82`95d80ae0)
00000000`031beb48 00000000`76fe1cb4     : 00000023`7657109c 00000000`00000023 00000000`032bfa70 00000000`032bf9b8 : wow64cpu!CpupSyscallStub+0x13
00000000`031beb50 00000000`76fe1d75     : 00000000`032bfbdc 00007ffc`863dc6ec 00000000`00000000 00007ffc`863de163 : wow64cpu!Thunk0Arg+0x5
00000000`031bec00 00007ffc`863de06d     : 00000000`01228490 00000000`00000000 00000000`00000000 00000000`031bf270 : wow64cpu!BTCpuSimulate+0xbb5
00000000`031bec40 00007ffc`863dd8ad     : 00000000`00000000 00000000`00000001 00000000`00000000 00000000`00000000 : wow64!RunCpuSimulation+0xd
00000000`031bec70 00007ffc`8851a958     : 00000000`00000000 00000000`00000000 00000000`00000001 00000000`00000000 : wow64!Wow64LdrpInitialize+0x12d
00000000`031bef20 00007ffc`8851a843     : 00000000`00000000 00007ffc`884a0000 00000000`00e5f000 00000000`00000000 : ntdll!_LdrpInitialize+0xdc
00000000`031befa0 00007ffc`8851a76e     : 00000000`031bf270 00000000`00000000 00000000`031bf270 00000000`00000000 : ntdll!LdrpInitializeInternal+0x6b
00000000`031bf220 00000000`00000000     : 00000000`00000000 00000000`00000000 00000000`00000000 00000000`00000000 : ntdll!LdrInitializeThunk+0xe

THREAD ffffc38c337ea080  Cid 1284.12ec  Teb: 0000000000e63000 Win32Thread: 0000000000000000 WAIT: (DelayExecution) UserMode Non-Alertable
    ffffffffffffffff  NotificationEvent
Not impersonating
DeviceMap                 ffffac8a09519470
Owning Process            ffffc38c334020c0       Image:         AppA.exe
Attached Process          N/A            Image:         N/A
Wait Start TickCount      10273          Ticks: 1683 (0:00:00:26.296)
Context Switch Count      3              IdealProcessor: 0
UserTime                  00:00:00.000
KernelTime                00:00:00.000
Win32 Start Address 0x0000000075bb67e0
Stack Init ffffbe8295c76c70 Current ffffbe8295c76720
Base ffffbe8295c77000 Limit ffffbe8295c71000 Call 0000000000000000
Priority 8  BasePriority 8  IoPriority 2  PagePriority 5
Child-SP          RetAddr               : Args to Child                                                           : Call Site
ffffbe82`95c76760 fffff806`62132457     : 00000000`0000000b fffffb00`ffffffff 00000000`00000000 ffffc38c`2e89c158 : nt!KiSwapContext+0x76
ffffbe82`95c768a0 fffff806`62134309     : ffffc38c`337ea080 fffff806`620d6e97 00000000`00000000 00000000`5fb1a500 : nt!KiSwapThread+0x3a7
ffffbe82`95c76980 fffff806`62137fc6     : 00000000`00000000 00000000`00000000 00000000`000000e7 00000000`879e963a : nt!KiCommitThreadWait+0x159
ffffbe82`95c76a20 fffff806`6257fdaf     : 00000000`032ffda0 00000000`00000000 00000000`00000000 00000000`00000002 : nt!KeDelayExecutionThread+0x416
ffffbe82`95c76ab0 fffff806`62227b75     : ffffc38c`337ea080 00000000`00000000 ffffffff`d8109c80 ffffc38c`00000000 : nt!NtDelayExecution+0x5f
ffffbe82`95c76ae0 00000000`76fe1cf3     : 00000000`76fe1bd2 00000000`77066d50 00000000`00000023 00000000`00000202 : nt!KiSystemServiceCopyEnd+0x25 (TrapFrame @ ffffbe82`95c76ae0)
00000000`032fec38 00000000`76fe1bd2     : 00000000`77066d50 00000000`00000023 00000000`00000202 00000000`033ffbf0 : wow64cpu!CpupSyscallStub+0x13
00000000`032fec40 00000000`76fe1d75     : 00000000`033ff924 00007ffc`863dc6ec 00000000`00000000 00007ffc`863de163 : wow64cpu!Thunk2ArgNSpNSpReloadState+0xc
00000000`032fecf0 00007ffc`863de06d     : 00000000`01228530 00000000`00000000 00000000`00000000 00000000`032ff360 : wow64cpu!BTCpuSimulate+0xbb5
00000000`032fed30 00007ffc`863dd8ad     : 00000000`00000000 00000000`00000001 00000000`00000000 00000000`00000000 : wow64!RunCpuSimulation+0xd
00000000`032fed60 00007ffc`8851a958     : 00000000`00000000 00000000`00000000 00000000`00000001 00000000`00000000 : wow64!Wow64LdrpInitialize+0x12d
00000000`032ff010 00007ffc`8851a843     : 00000000`00000000 00007ffc`884a0000 00000000`00e63000 00000000`00000000 : ntdll!_LdrpInitialize+0xdc
00000000`032ff090 00007ffc`8851a76e     : 00000000`032ff360 00000000`00000000 00000000`032ff360 00000000`00000000 : ntdll!LdrpInitializeInternal+0x6b
00000000`032ff310 00000000`00000000     : 00000000`00000000 00000000`00000000 00000000`00000000 00000000`00000000 : ntdll!LdrInitializeThunk+0xe

THREAD ffffc38c2e89c080  Cid 1284.0aa0  Teb: 0000000000e67000 Win32Thread: 0000000000000000 WAIT: (DelayExecution) UserMode Non-Alertable
    ffffffffffffffff  NotificationEvent
Not impersonating
DeviceMap                 ffffac8a09519470
Owning Process            ffffc38c334020c0       Image:         AppA.exe
Attached Process          N/A            Image:         N/A
Wait Start TickCount      10273          Ticks: 1683 (0:00:00:26.296)
```

```
Context Switch Count      3                 IdealProcessor: 1
UserTime                  00:00:00.000
KernelTime                00:00:00.000
Win32 Start Address 0x0000000075bb67e0
Stack Init ffffbe82966f9c70 Current ffffbe82966f9720
Base ffffbe82966fa000 Limit ffffbe82966f4000 Call 0000000000000000
Priority 8  BasePriority 8  IoPriority 2  PagePriority 5
Child-SP          RetAddr               : Args to Child                                                           : Call Site
ffffbe82`966f9760 fffff806`62132457     : 00000000`0000000b fffffb00`ffffffff 00000000`00000000 ffffc38c`2ecd4158 : nt!KiSwapContext+0x76
ffffbe82`966f98a0 fffff806`62134309     : ffffc38c`2e89c080 fffff806`620d6e97 00000000`00000000 00000000`5fb1a500 : nt!KiSwapThread+0x3a7
ffffbe82`966f9980 fffff806`62137fc6     : 00000000`00000000 00000000`00000000 00000000`000000e7 00000000`879e9982 : nt!KiCommitThreadWait+0x159
ffffbe82`966f9a20 fffff806`6257fdaf     : 00000000`0343fda0 00000000`00000000 00000000`00000000 00000000`00000002 : nt!KeDelayExecutionThread+0x416
ffffbe82`966f9ab0 fffff806`62227b75     : ffffc38c`2e89c080 00000000`00000000 ffffffff`d8109c80 ffffc38c`00000000 : nt!NtDelayExecution+0x5f
ffffbe82`966f9ae0 00000000`76fe1cf3     : 00000000`76fe1bd2 00000000`77066d50 00000000`00000023 00000000`00000202 : nt!KiSystemServiceCopyEnd+0x25 (TrapFrame @ ffffbe82`966f9ae0)
00000000`0343ed38 00000000`76fe1bd2     : 00000000`77066d50 00000000`00000023 00000000`00000202 00000000`0353fd28 : wow64cpu!CpupSyscallStub+0x13
00000000`0343ed40 00000000`76fe1d75     : 00000000`0353fa5c 00007ffc`863dc6ec 00000000`00000000 00007ffc`863de163 : wow64cpu!Thunk2ArgNSpNSpReloadState+0xc
00000000`0343edf0 00007ffc`863de06d     : 00000000`01228350 00000000`00000000 00000000`00000000 00000000`0343f460 : wow64cpu!BTCpuSimulate+0xbb5
00000000`0343ee30 00007ffc`863dd8ad     : 00000000`00000000 00000000`00000001 00000000`00000000 00000000`00000000 : wow64!RunCpuSimulation+0xd
00000000`0343ee60 00007ffc`8851a958     : 00000000`00000000 00000000`00000000 00000000`00000001 00000000`00000000 : wow64!Wow64LdrpInitialize+0x12d
00000000`0343f110 00007ffc`8851a843     : 00000000`00000000 00007ffc`884a0000 00000000`00e67000 00000000`00000000 : ntdll!_LdrpInitialize+0xdc
00000000`0343f190 00007ffc`8851a76e     : 00000000`0343f460 00000000`00000000 00000000`0343f460 00000000`00000000 : ntdll!LdrpInitializeInternal+0x6b
00000000`0343f410 00000000`00000000     : 00000000`00000000 00000000`00000000 00000000`00000000 00000000`00000000 : ntdll!LdrInitializeThunk+0xe
```

15. Double-clicking on our process line launches the process information window with additional tabs. We select the Handles tab and dump details about a handle table entry by using the context menu:

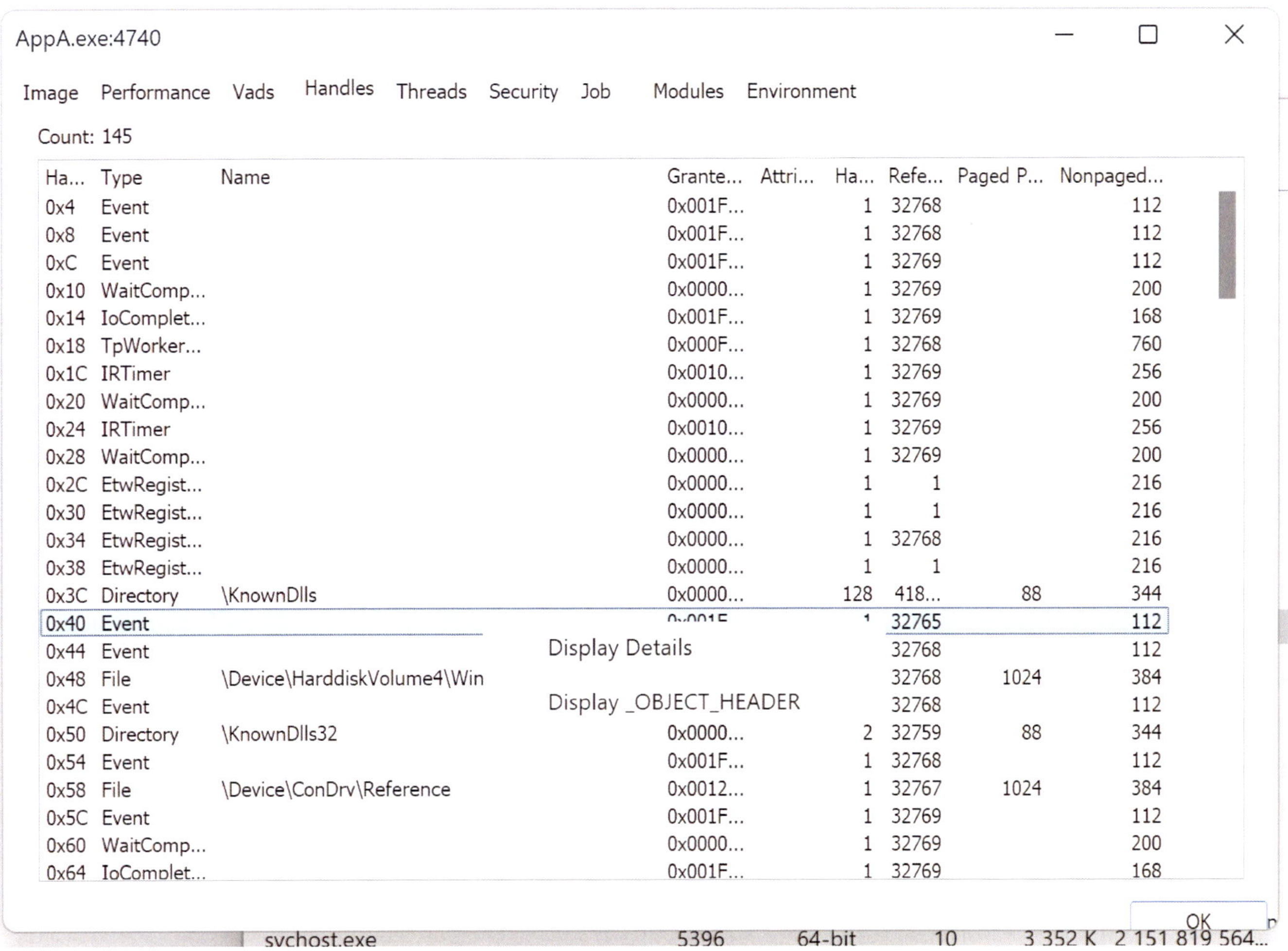


```
Object: ffffc38c333ddfe0  Type: (ffffc38c2c4ec560) Event
    ObjectHeader: ffffc38c333ddfb0 (new version)
    HandleCount: 1  PointerCount: 32765
Optional Headers:
    QuotaInfo(ffffc38c333ddfb0) PPool: 7ffd, NPPool: 0
      SecurityDescriptor: 1, SDQuotaBlock: 0000000000000000

nt!_OBJECT_HEADER ffffc38c333ddfb0

   +0x000 PointerCount      : 0n32765
```

```
+0x008 HandleCount       : 0n1
+0x008 NextToFree        : 0x00000000`00000001 Void
+0x010 Lock              : _EX_PUSH_LOCK
+0x018 TypeIndex         : 0xb ''
+0x019 TraceFlags        : 0 ''
+0x019 DbgRefTrace       : 0y0
+0x019 DbgTracePermanent : 0y0
+0x01a InfoMask          : 0x8 ''
+0x01b Flags             : 0 ''
+0x01b NewObject         : 0y0
+0x01b KernelObject      : 0y0
+0x01b KernelOnlyAccess : 0y0
+0x01b ExclusiveObject   : 0y0
+0x01b PermanentObject   : 0y0
+0x01b DefaultSecurityQuota : 0y0
+0x01b SingleHandleEntry : 0y0
+0x01b DeletedInline     : 0y0
+0x01c Reserved          : 0
+0x020 ObjectCreateInfo : 0xffffc38c`304b5900 _OBJECT_CREATE_INFORMATION
+0x020 QuotaBlockCharged : 0xffffc38c`304b5900 Void
+0x028 SecurityDescriptor : (null)
+0x030 Body              : _QUAD
```

We continue exploring other tabs, for example:

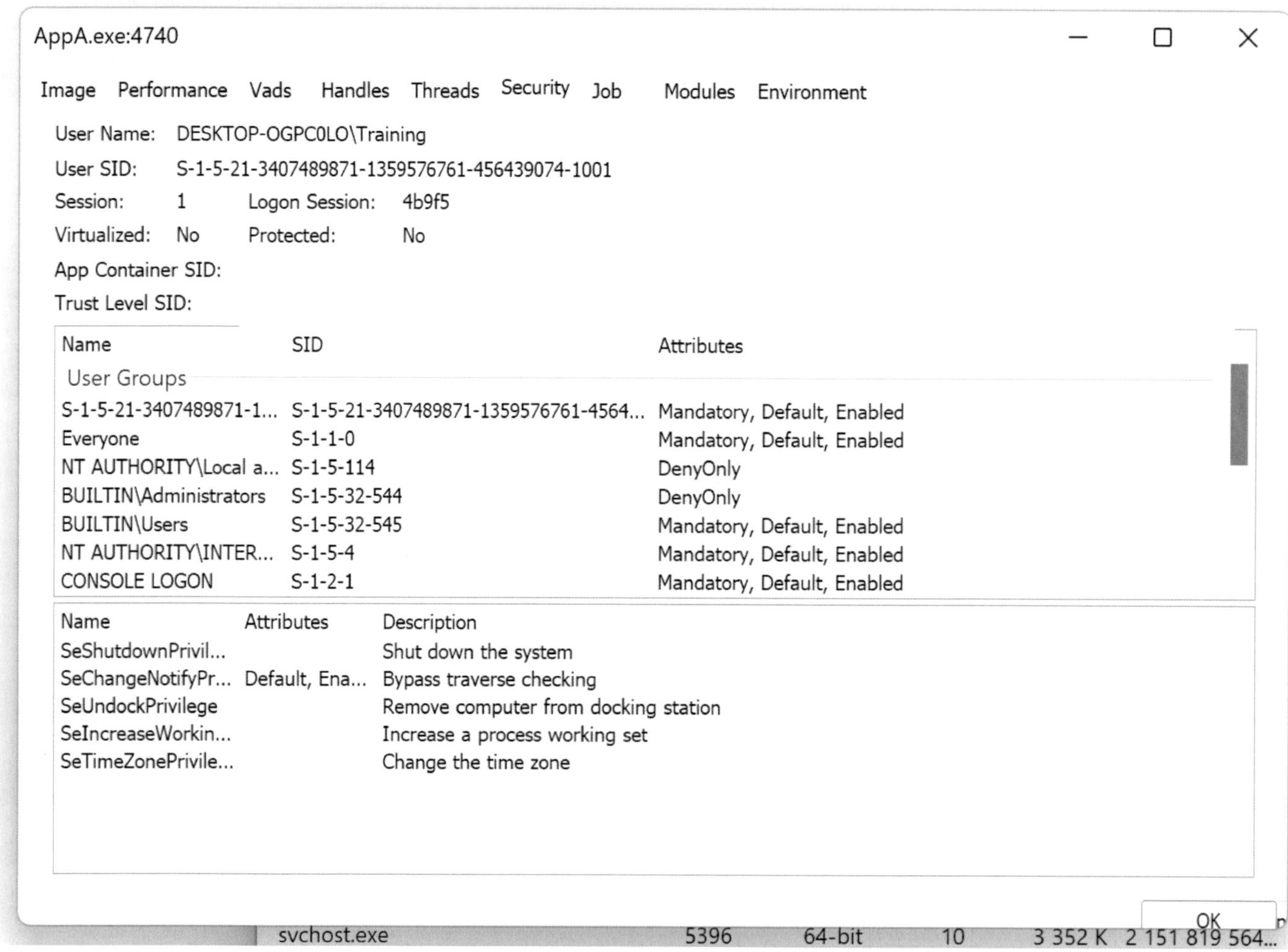

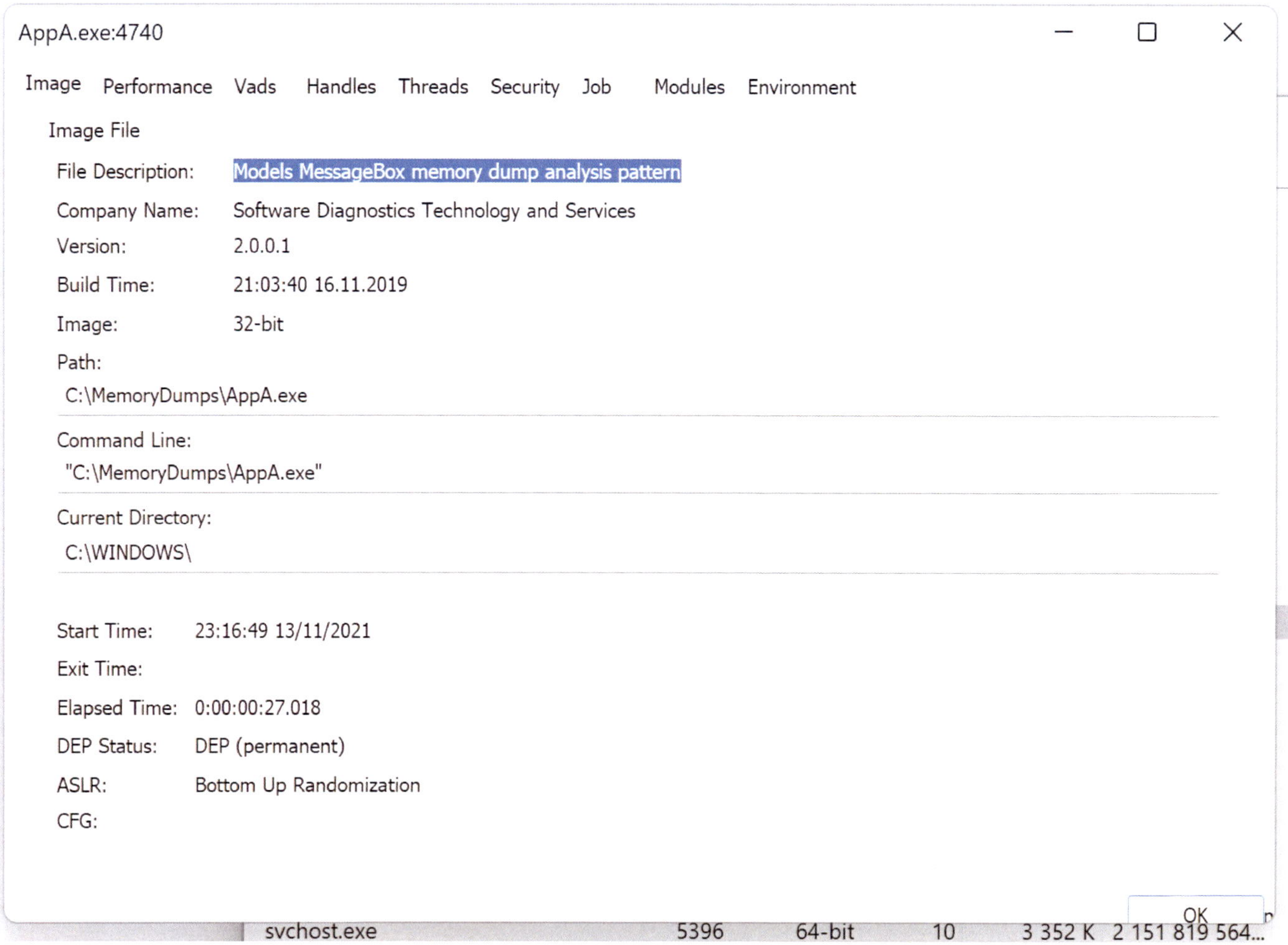
AppA.exe:4740
Image Performance Vads Handles Threads Security Job Modules Environment
Image File
File Description: Models MessageBox memory dump analysis pattern
Company Name: Software Diagnostics Technology and Services
Version: 2.0.0.1
Build Time: 21:03:40 16.11.2019
Image: 32-bit
Path:
C:\MemoryDumps\AppA.exe
Command Line:
"C:\MemoryDumps\AppA.exe"
Current Directory:
C:\WINDOWS\
Start Time: 23:16:49 13/11/2021
Exit Time:
Elapsed Time: 0:00:00:27.018
DEP Status: DEP (permanent)
ASLR: Bottom Up Randomization
CFG:
OK
svchost.exe 5396 64-bit 10 3 352 K 2 151 819 564...

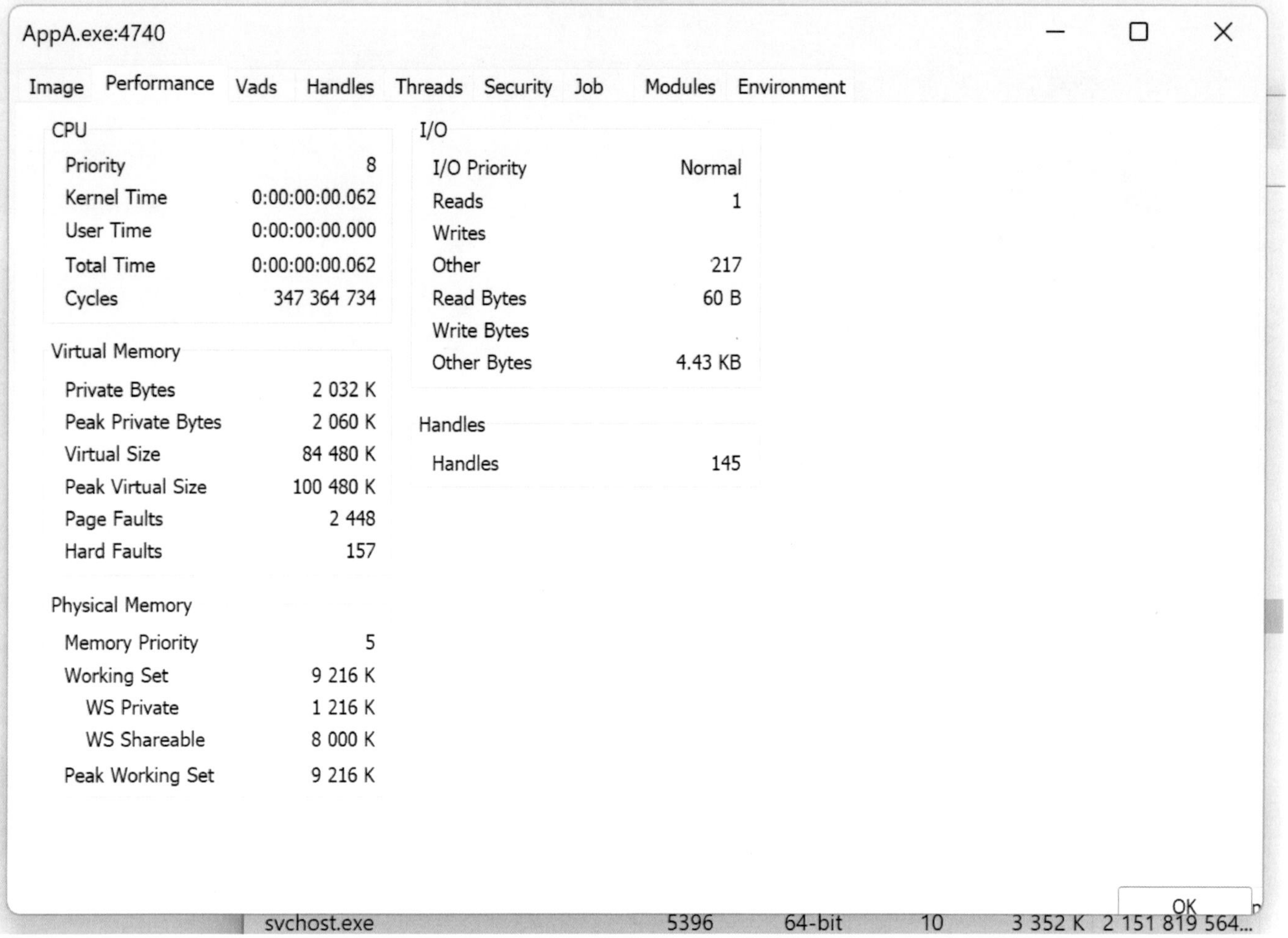
AppA.exe:4740
Image
Performance
Vads
Handles
Threads
Security
Job
Modules
Environment
CPU
Priority 8
Kernel Time 0:00:00:00.062
User Time 0:00:00:00.000
Total Time 0:00:00:00.062
Cycles 347 364 734
Virtual Memory
Private Bytes 2 032 K
Peak Private Bytes 2 060 K
Virtual Size 84 480 K
Peak Virtual Size 100 480 K
Page Faults 2 448
Hard Faults 157
Physical Memory
Memory Priority 5
Working Set 9 216 K
WS Private 1 216 K
WS Shareable 8 000 K
Peak Working Set 9 216 K
I/O
I/O Priority Normal
Reads 1
Writes
Other 217
Read Bytes 60 B
Write Bytes
Other Bytes 4.43 KB
Handles
Handles 145
OK
svchost.exe 5396 64-bit 10 3 352 K 2 151 819 564...

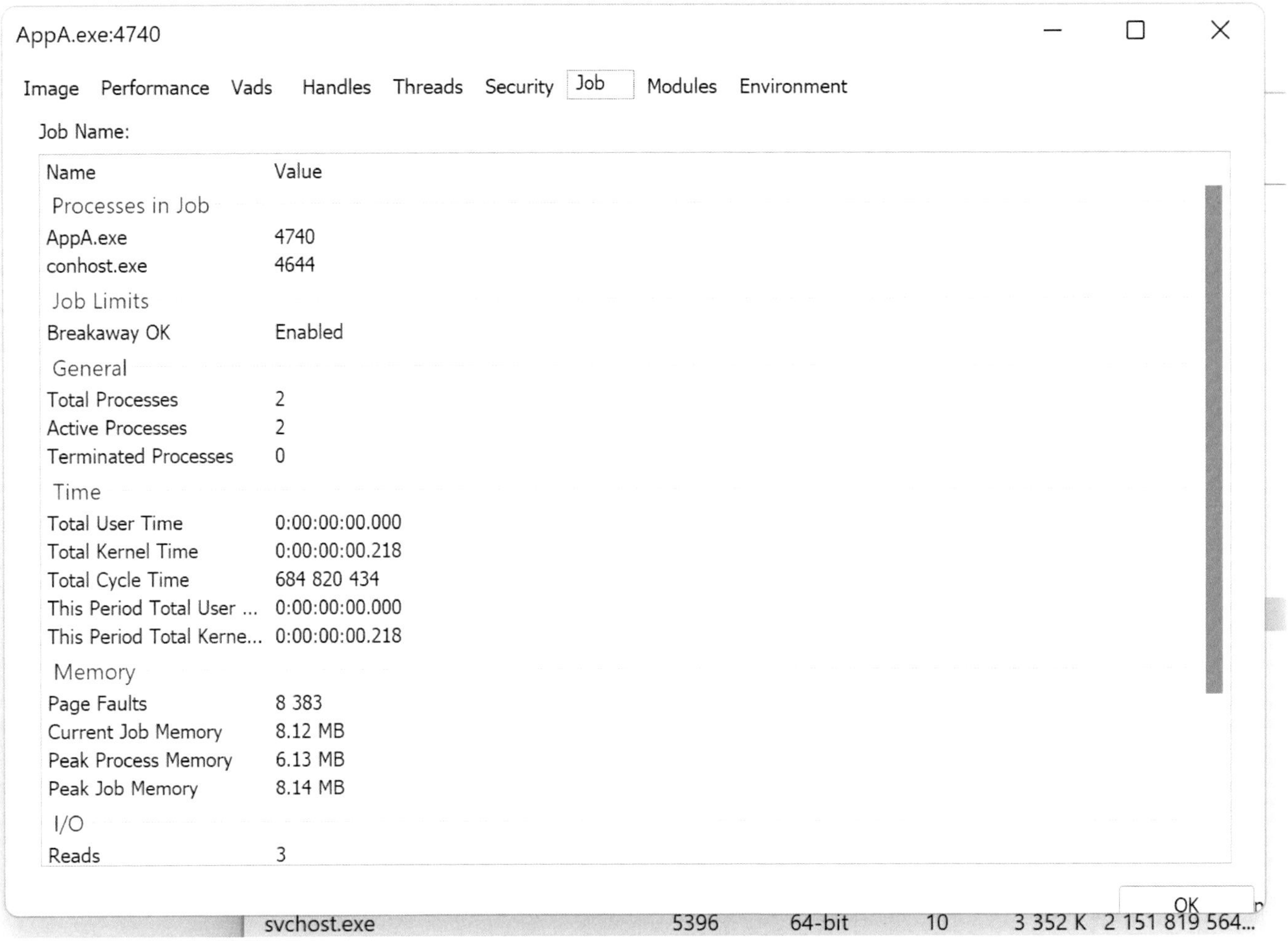
AppA.exe:4740
Image
Performance
Vads
Handles
Threads
Security
Job
Modules
Environment
Job Name:
Name
Value
Processes in Job
AppA.exe 4740
conhost.exe 4644
Job Limits
Breakaway OK Enabled
General
Total Processes 2
Active Processes 2
Terminated Processes 0
Time
Total User Time 0:00:00:00.000
Total Kernel Time 0:00:00:00.218
Total Cycle Time 684 820 434
This Period Total User ... 0:00:00:00.000
This Period Total Kerne... 0:00:00:00.218
Memory
Page Faults 8 383
Current Job Memory 8.12 MB
Peak Process Memory 6.13 MB
Peak Job Memory 8.14 MB
I/O
Reads 3
OK
svchost.exe 5396 64-bit 10 3 352 K 2 151 819 564...

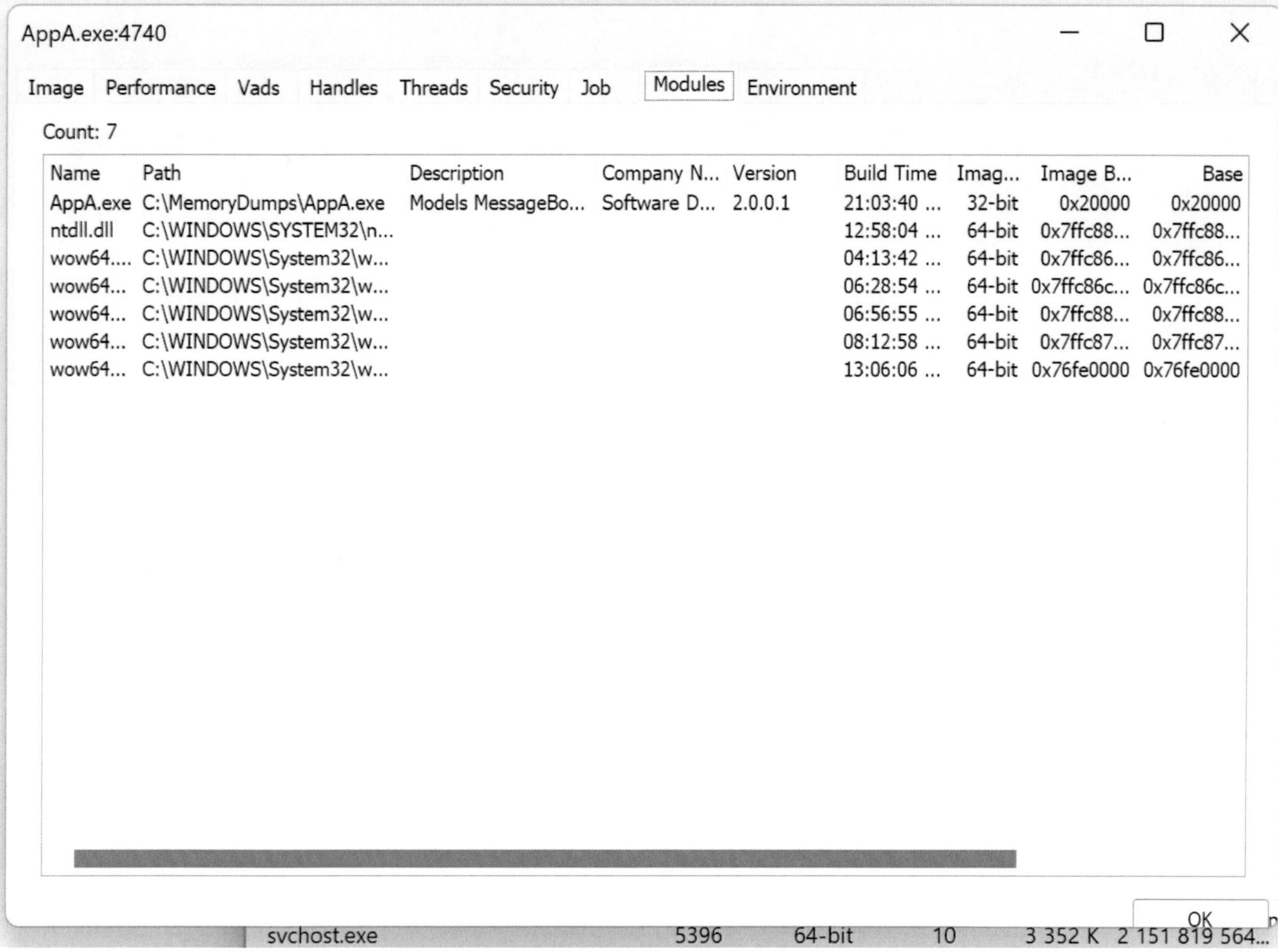

Name	Path	Description	Company N...	Version	Build Time	Imag...	Image B...	Base
AppA.exe	C:\MemoryDumps\AppA.exe	Models MessageBo...	Software D...	2.0.0.1	21:03:40 ...	32-bit	0x20000	0x20000
ntdll.dll	C:\WINDOWS\SYSTEM32\n...				12:58:04 ...	64-bit	0x7ffc88...	0x7ffc88...
wow64....	C:\WINDOWS\System32\w...				04:13:42 ...	64-bit	0x7ffc86...	0x7ffc86...
wow64...	C:\WINDOWS\System32\w...				06:28:54 ...	64-bit	0x7ffc86c...	0x7ffc86c...
wow64...	C:\WINDOWS\System32\w...				06:56:55 ...	64-bit	0x7ffc88...	0x7ffc88...
wow64...	C:\WINDOWS\System32\w...				08:12:58 ...	64-bit	0x7ffc87...	0x7ffc87...
wow64...	C:\WINDOWS\System32\w...				13:06:06 ...	64-bit	0x76fe0000	0x76fe0000

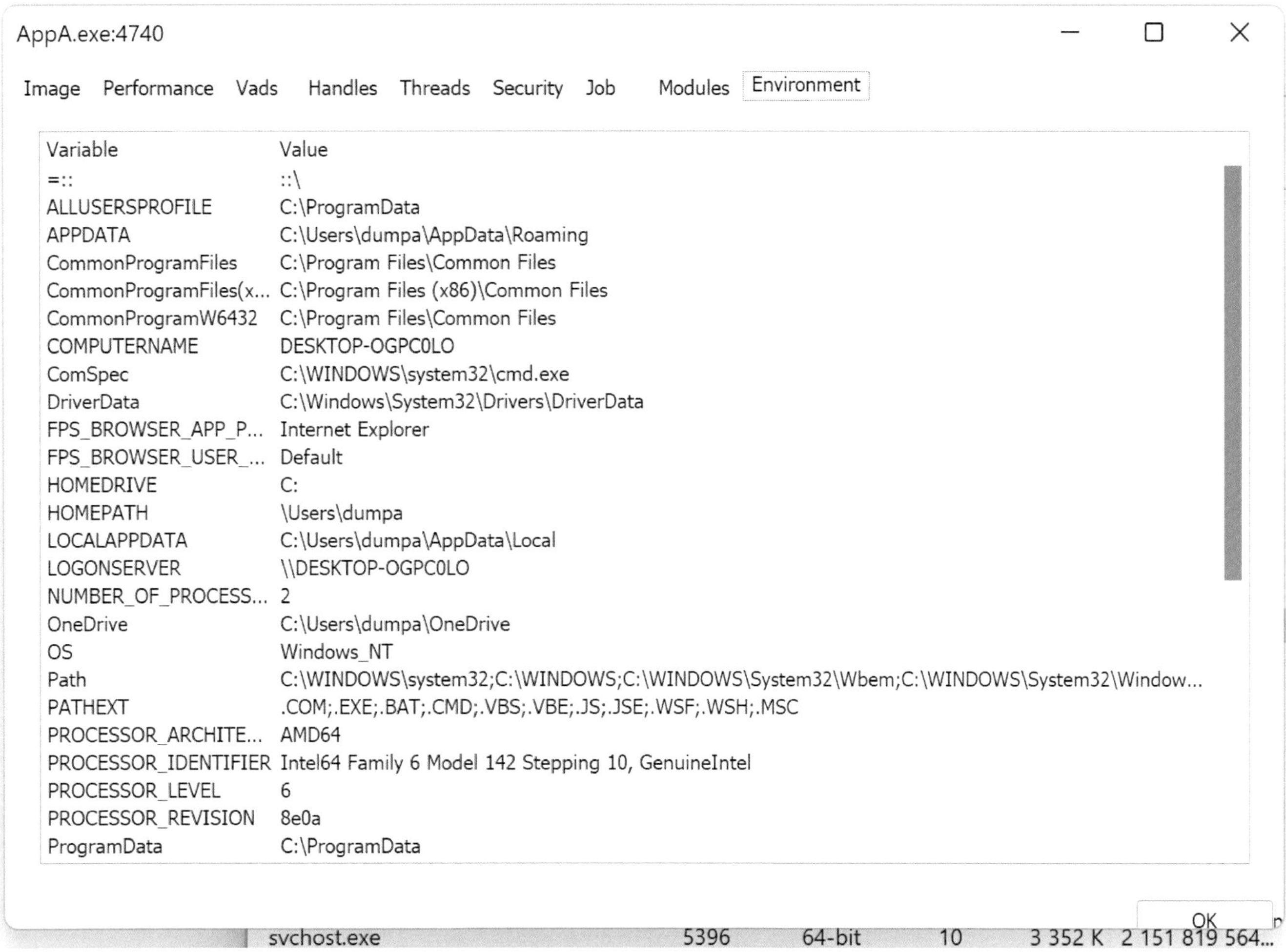
AppA.exe:4740
Image Performance Vads Handles Threads Security Job Modules Environment
Variable Value
=:: ::\
ALLUSERSPROFILE C:\ProgramData
APPDATA C:\Users\dumpa\AppData\Roaming
CommonProgramFiles C:\Program Files\Common Files
CommonProgramFiles(x... C:\Program Files (x86)\Common Files
CommonProgramW6432 C:\Program Files\Common Files
COMPUTERNAME DESKTOP-OGPC0LO
ComSpec C:\WINDOWS\system32\cmd.exe
DriverData C:\Windows\System32\Drivers\DriverData
FPS_BROWSER_APP_P... Internet Explorer
FPS_BROWSER_USER_... Default
HOMEDRIVE C:
HOMEPATH \Users\dumpa
LOCALAPPDATA C:\Users\dumpa\AppData\Local
LOGONSERVER \\DESKTOP-OGPC0LO
NUMBER_OF_PROCESS... 2
OneDrive C:\Users\dumpa\OneDrive
OS Windows_NT
Path C:\WINDOWS\system32;C:\WINDOWS;C:\WINDOWS\System32\Wbem;C:\WINDOWS\System32\Window...
PATHEXT .COM;.EXE;.BAT;.CMD;.VBS;.VBE;.JS;.JSE;.WSF;.WSH;.MSC
PROCESSOR_ARCHITE... AMD64
PROCESSOR_IDENTIFIER Intel64 Family 6 Model 142 Stepping 10, GenuineIntel
PROCESSOR_LEVEL 6
PROCESSOR_REVISION 8e0a
ProgramData C:\ProgramData
OK
svchost.exe 5396 64-bit 10 3 352 K 2 151 819 564...

Note: We skipped the Threads tab as it didn't show 32-bit stack trace details for this process.

16. Edit \ Find... Process Explorer menu allows us to find references to particular handles or modules whose names contain the specified string:

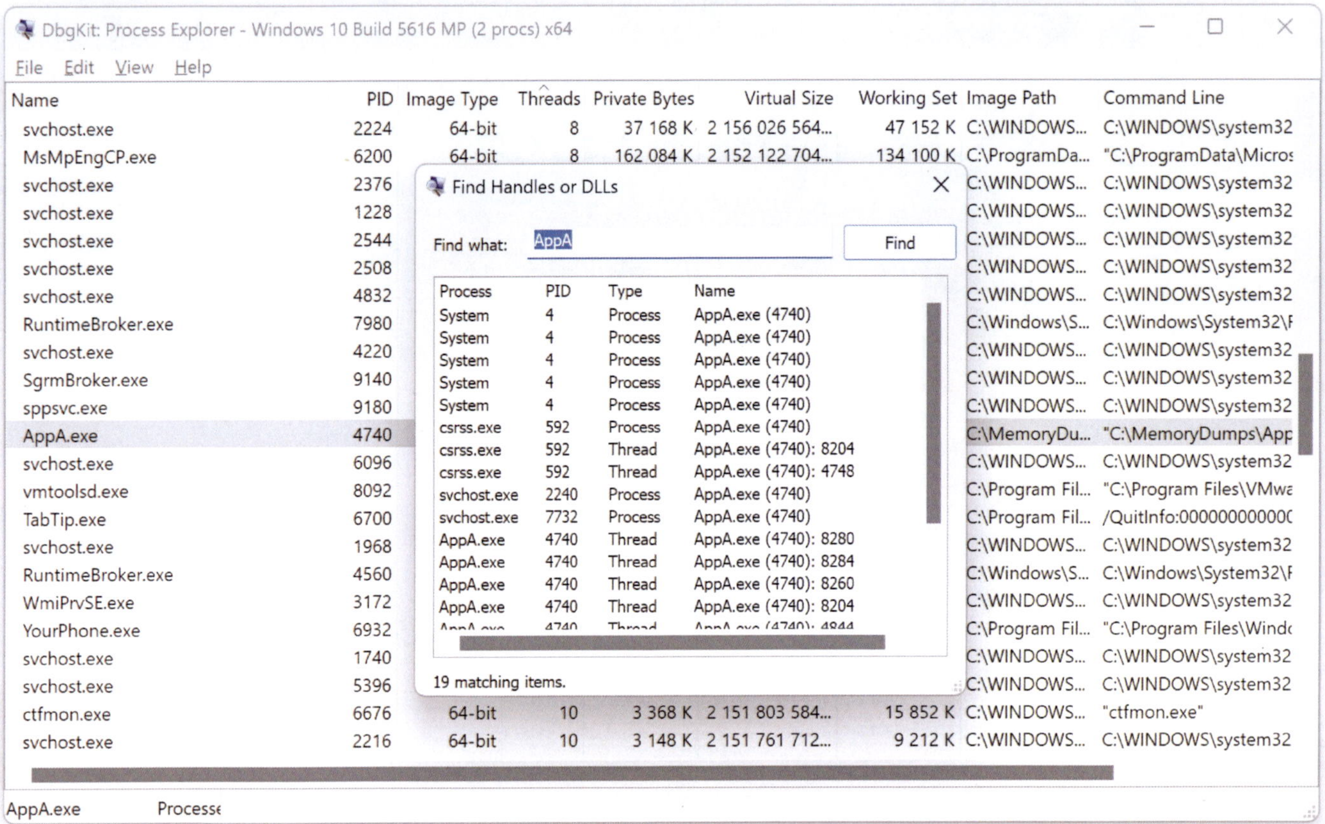

Double-clicking list entry brings the corresponding process handle or module list location:

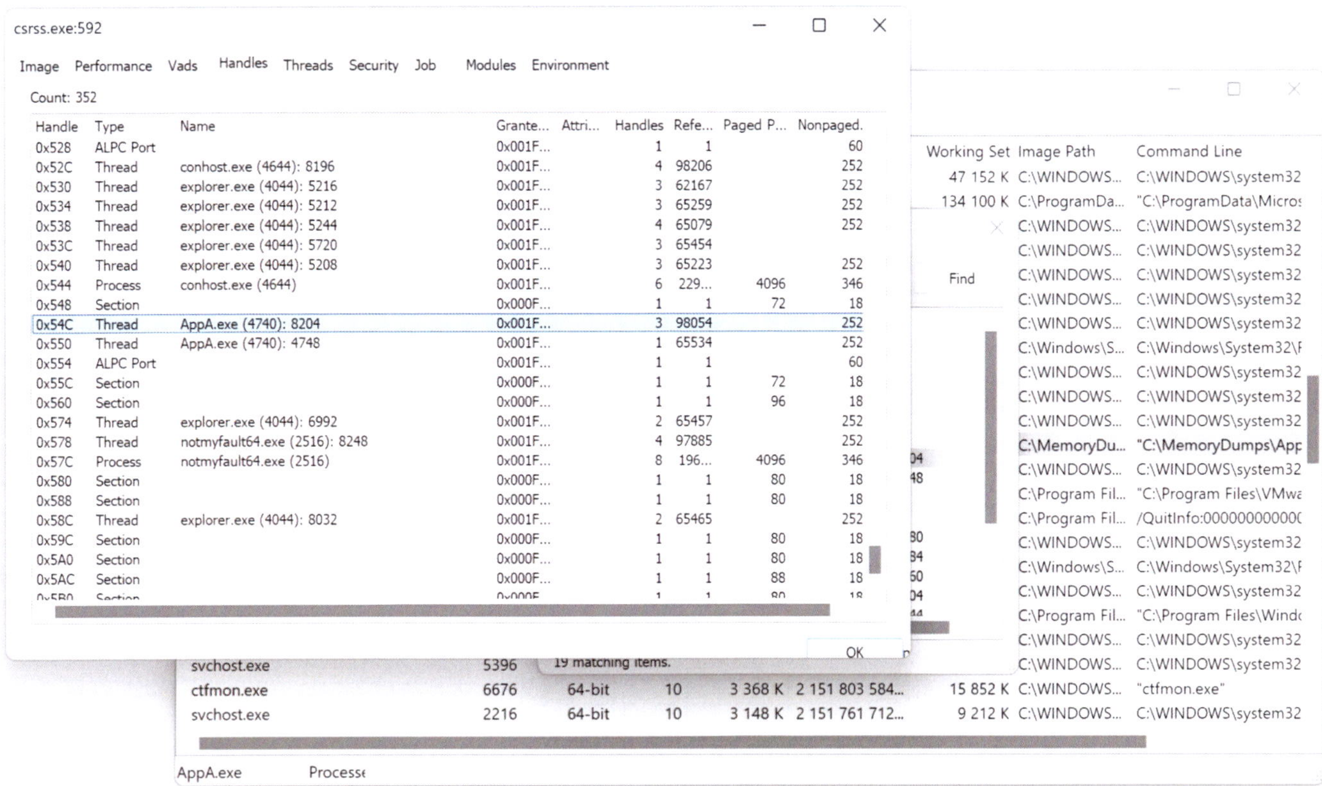

17. Finally, the **!st** command unpacks system service table information to check for any non-nt pointers:

```
0: kd> !st

000:   fffff8066209dea0    nt!NtAccessCheck
001:   fffff80662035150    nt!NtWorkerFactoryWorkerReady
002:   fffff806624b4df0    nt!NtAcceptConnectPort
003:   fffff8066277bae0    nt!NtMapUserPhysicalPagesScatter
004:   fffff8066256a4b0    nt!NtWaitForSingleObject
005:   fffff80662219260    nt!NtCallbackReturn
006:   fffff80662580090    nt!NtReadFile
007:   fffff8066256a670    nt!NtDeviceIoControlFile
008:   fffff806624ee280    nt!NtWriteFile
009:   fffff8066257fe30    nt!NtRemoveIoCompletion
00a:   fffff806624ed0d0    nt!NtReleaseSemaphore
00b:   fffff8066254b5b0    nt!NtReplyWaitReceivePort
00c:   fffff80662524710    nt!NtReplyPort
00d:   fffff8066256ff60    nt!NtSetInformationThread
00e:   fffff8066246ff60    nt!NtSetEvent
00f:   fffff8066256b880    nt!NtClose
010:   fffff806625225f0    nt!NtQueryObject
011:   fffff806624f6520    nt!NtQueryInformationFile
012:   fffff806624762e0    nt!NtOpenKey
013:   fffff80662472f50    nt!NtEnumerateValueKey
014:   fffff8066258a1b0    nt!NtFindAtom
015:   fffff806624e7c50    nt!NtQueryDefaultLocale
016:   fffff8066257aa80    nt!NtQueryKey
017:   fffff80662554c40    nt!NtQueryValueKey
018:   fffff806624e2c90    nt!NtAllocateVirtualMemory
```

```
019:    fffff806625825e0    nt!NtQueryInformationProcess
01a:    fffff80662486720    nt!NtWaitForMultipleObjects32
01b:    fffff806624bf2c0    nt!NtWriteFileGather
01c:    fffff806624e0280    nt!NtSetInformationProcess
01d:    fffff8066251a6e0    nt!NtCreateKey
01e:    fffff80662575c80    nt!NtFreeVirtualMemory
01f:    fffff80662763940    nt!NtImpersonateClientOfPort
020:    fffff806624fabe0    nt!NtReleaseMutant
021:    fffff806624f8570    nt!NtQueryInformationToken
022:    fffff8066248d660    nt!NtRequestWaitReplyPort
023:    fffff80662576aa0    nt!NtQueryVirtualMemory
024:    fffff806624f56b0    nt!NtOpenThreadToken
025:    fffff8066255e8c0    nt!NtQueryInformationThread
026:    fffff8066255f3d0    nt!NtOpenProcess
027:    fffff806620981f0    nt!NtSetInformationFile
028:    fffff806625633a0    nt!NtMapViewOfSection
029:    fffff806624f0050    nt!NtAccessCheckAndAuditAlarm
02a:    fffff80662589660    nt!NtUnmapViewOfSection
02b:    fffff8066254b5d0    nt!NtReplyWaitReceivePortEx
02c:    fffff80662599a80    nt!NtTerminateProcess
02d:    fffff806627f8a20    nt!NtSetEventBoostPriority
02e:    fffff8066249fff0    nt!NtReadFileScatter
02f:    fffff806624f56d0    nt!NtOpenThreadTokenEx
030:    fffff8066255f9f0    nt!NtOpenProcessTokenEx
031:    fffff8066248a940    nt!NtQueryPerformanceCounter
032:    fffff8066255b890    nt!NtEnumerateKey
033:    fffff806625055e0    nt!NtOpenFile
034:    fffff8066257fd50    nt!NtDelayExecution
035:    fffff806624e5a80    nt!NtQueryDirectoryFile
036:    fffff80662582440    nt!NtQuerySystemInformation
037:    fffff806625d4540    nt!NtOpenSection
038:    fffff806627f8810    nt!NtQueryTimer
039:    fffff80662486870    nt!NtFsControlFile
03a:    fffff80662546a40    nt!NtWriteVirtualMemory
03b:    fffff80662495710    nt!NtCloseObjectAuditAlarm
03c:    fffff8066258b020    nt!NtDuplicateObject
03d:    fffff806625061f0    nt!NtQueryAttributesFile
03e:    fffff80662476b90    nt!NtClearEvent
03f:    fffff80662546a70    nt!NtReadVirtualMemory
040:    fffff806625d4470    nt!NtOpenEvent
041:    fffff80662542a10    nt!NtAdjustPrivilegesToken
042:    fffff80662560310    nt!NtDuplicateToken
043:    fffff80662215cc0    nt!NtContinue
044:    fffff806625dcfe0    nt!NtQueryDefaultUILanguage
045:    fffff806624c4410    nt!NtQueueApcThread
046:    fffff8066200c550    nt!NtYieldExecution
047:    fffff806627ff950    nt!NtAddAtom
048:    fffff806624d2170    nt!NtCreateEvent
049:    fffff806624f6e40    nt!NtQueryVolumeInformationFile
04a:    fffff806625640d0    nt!NtCreateSection
04b:    fffff80662497be0    nt!NtFlushBuffersFile
04c:    fffff806625b1180    nt!NtApphelpCacheControl
04d:    fffff806627aa6c0    nt!NtCreateProcessEx
04e:    fffff806627aa760    nt!NtCreateThread
04f:    fffff80662596ec0    nt!NtIsProcessInJob
050:    fffff80662574e50    nt!NtProtectVirtualMemory
051:    fffff806624813f0    nt!NtQuerySection
052:    fffff806624928c0    nt!NtResumeThread
053:    fffff80662546720    nt!NtTerminateThread
```

```
054:    fffff80662763a40    nt!NtReadRequestData
055:    fffff80662505650    nt!NtCreateFile
056:    fffff806624aa5b0    nt!NtQueryEvent
057:    fffff80662763bc0    nt!NtWriteRequestData
058:    fffff80662477800    nt!NtOpenDirectoryObject
059:    fffff806624980f0    nt!NtAccessCheckByTypeAndAuditAlarm
05a:    fffff806627f54e0    nt!NtQuerySystemTime
05b:    fffff806624729c0    nt!NtWaitForMultipleObjects
05c:    fffff80662465ef0    nt!NtSetInformationObject
05d:    fffff80662479770    nt!NtCancelIoFile
05e:    fffff8066209ec30    nt!NtTraceEvent
05f:    fffff806625a34f0    nt!NtPowerInformation
060:    fffff806624f0440    nt!NtSetValueKey
061:    fffff806620c0050    nt!NtCancelTimer
062:    fffff8066216fd80    nt!NtSetTimer
063:    fffff80662036420    nt!NtAccessCheckByType
064:    fffff806623ef6b0    nt!NtAccessCheckByTypeResultList
065:    fffff806627c8430    nt!NtAccessCheckByTypeResultListAndAuditAlarm
066:    fffff806627c84e0    nt!NtAccessCheckByTypeResultListAndAuditAlarmByHandle
067:    fffff806627ffa70    nt!NtAcquireCrossVmMutant
068:    fffff806624bc070    nt!NtAcquireProcessActivityReference
069:    fffff80662497f70    nt!NtAddAtomEx
06a:    fffff806627fc540    nt!NtAddBootEntry
06b:    fffff806627fc570    nt!NtAddDriverEntry
06c:    fffff80662499e50    nt!NtAdjustGroupsToken
06d:    fffff806625dd710    nt!NT_DISK::GetPnpProperty
06e:    fffff806627b0690    nt!NtAlertResumeThread
06f:    fffff806627b07b0    nt!NtAlertThread
070:    fffff8066254bc30    nt!NtAlertThreadByThreadId
071:    fffff80662475120    nt!NtAllocateLocallyUniqueId
072:    fffff806624b4010    nt!NtAllocateReserveObject
073:    fffff8066277b210    nt!NtAllocateUserPhysicalPages
074:    fffff8066277b230    nt!NtAllocateUserPhysicalPagesEx
075:    fffff80662599f40    nt!NtAllocateUuids
076:    fffff806624e2920    nt!NtAllocateVirtualMemoryEx
077:    fffff806625271f0    nt!NtAlpcAcceptConnectPort
078:    fffff806624c07f0    nt!NtAlpcCancelMessage
079:    fffff80662524a90    nt!NtAlpcConnectPort
07a:    fffff806625248b0    nt!NtAlpcConnectPortEx
07b:    fffff8066249ea40    nt!NtAlpcCreatePort
07c:    fffff8066252bf90    nt!NtAlpcCreatePortSection
07d:    fffff806624a4dc0    nt!NtAlpcCreateResourceReserve
07e:    fffff80662528cf0    nt!NtAlpcCreateSectionView
07f:    fffff80662529900    nt!NtAlpcCreateSecurityContext
080:    fffff8066252bea0    nt!NtAlpcDeletePortSection
081:    fffff8066266a690    nt!NtAlpcDeleteResourceReserve
082:    fffff8066252c870    nt!NtAlpcDeleteSectionView
083:    fffff80662529800    nt!NtAlpcDeleteSecurityContext
084:    fffff80662523a20    nt!NtAlpcDisconnectPort
085:    fffff80662763d10    nt!NtAlpcImpersonateClientContainerOfPort
086:    fffff806624f7bb0    nt!NtAlpcImpersonateClientOfPort
087:    fffff80662526ee0    nt!NtAlpcOpenSenderProcess
088:    fffff8066247f7e0    nt!NtAlpcOpenSenderThread
089:    fffff8066246ea40    nt!NtAlpcQueryInformation
08a:    fffff8066252b9f0    nt!NtAlpcQueryInformationMessage
08b:    fffff80662763f60    nt!NtAlpcRevokeSecurityContext
08c:    fffff8066254c8b0    nt!NtAlpcSendWaitReceivePort
08d:    fffff806625a28f0    nt!NtAlpcSetInformation
08e:    fffff806625e36e0    nt!NtAreMappedFilesTheSame
```

```
08f:    fffff80662596be0    nt!NtAssignProcessToJobObject
090:    fffff806620d3df0    nt!NtAssociateWaitCompletionPacket
091:    fffff8066221eaa0    nt!NtCallEnclave
092:    fffff806624a9e80    nt!NtCancelIoFileEx
093:    fffff80662734db0    nt!NtCancelSynchronousIoFile
094:    fffff80662167900    nt!NtCancelTimer2
095:    fffff8066202f0a0    nt!NtCancelWaitCompletionPacket
096:    fffff806627ac670    nt!NtChangeProcessState
097:    fffff806627ac860    nt!NtChangeThreadState
098:    fffff806621d9280    nt!NtCommitComplete
099:    fffff806621d92a0    nt!NtCommitEnlistment
09a:    fffff80662455ee0    nt!NtCommitRegistryTransaction
09b:    fffff806621d92c0    nt!NtCommitTransaction
09c:    fffff8066270b740    nt!NtCompactKeys
09d:    fffff8066248be50    nt!NtCompareObjects
09e:    fffff806624c0ec0    nt!NtCompareSigningLevels
09f:    fffff80662494e00    nt!NtCompareTokens
0a0:    fffff806624b6860    nt!ArbPreprocessEntry
0a1:    fffff8066270ba10    nt!NtCompressKey
0a2:    fffff80662523ac0    nt!NtConnectPort
0a3:    fffff80662215cd0    nt!NtContinueEx
0a4:    fffff80662803800    nt!NtConvertBetweenAuxiliaryCounterAndPerformanceCounter
0a5:    fffff806627f8970    nt!NtCreateCrossVmEvent
0a6:    fffff806627ffb40    nt!NtCreateCrossVmMutant
0a7:    fffff80662726760    nt!NtCreateDebugObject
0a8:    fffff8066247c040    nt!NtCreateDirectoryObject
0a9:    fffff8066247c020    nt!NtCreateDirectoryObjectEx
0aa:    fffff80662778590    nt!NtCreateEnclave
0ab:    fffff806621d92e0    nt!NtCreateEnlistment
0ac:    fffff806625dd710    nt!NT_DISK::GetPnpProperty
0ad:    fffff806624c6ae0    nt!NtCreateIRTimer
0ae:    fffff80662492d10    nt!NtCreateIoCompletion
0af:    fffff806627368c0    nt!NtCreateIoRing
0b0:    fffff806625966c0    nt!NtCreateJobObject
0b1:    fffff806625dd640    nt!ArbAddReserved
0b2:    fffff80662519e50    nt!NtCreateKeyTransacted
0b3:    fffff8066263c0f0    nt!NtCreateKeyedEvent
0b4:    fffff806624d9f00    nt!NtCreateLowBoxToken
0b5:    fffff8066245a9f0    nt!NtCreateMailslotFile
0b6:    fffff8066247eb70    nt!NtCreateMutant
0b7:    fffff806624a90d0    nt!NtCreateNamedPipeFile
0b8:    fffff80662631d00    nt!NtCreatePagingFile
0b9:    fffff806627b0d50    nt!NtCreatePartition
0ba:    fffff8066249e9f0    nt!NtCreatePort
0bb:    fffff806624d7400    nt!NtCreatePrivateNamespace
0bc:    fffff806627aa630    nt!NtCreateProcess
0bd:    fffff806627aca50    nt!NtCreateProcessStateChange
0be:    fffff80662803930    nt!NtCreateProfile
0bf:    fffff80662803a10    nt!NtCreateProfileEx
0c0:    fffff806624bdcf0    nt!NtCreateRegistryTransaction
0c1:    fffff806621d9300    nt!NtCreateResourceManager
0c2:    fffff80662769980    nt!NtCreateSectionEx
0c3:    fffff8066258def0    nt!NtCreateSemaphore
0c4:    fffff8066247c390    nt!NtCreateSymbolicLinkObject
0c5:    fffff806624eaa10    nt!NtCreateThreadEx
0c6:    fffff806627acc60    nt!NtCreateThreadStateChange
0c7:    fffff8066258fa80    nt!NtCreateTimer
0c8:    fffff806625a31a0    nt!NtCreateTimer2
0c9:    fffff806627c9ab0    nt!NtCreateToken
```

```
0ca:   fffff80662541580   nt!NtCreateTokenEx
0cb:   fffff806621d9320   nt!NtCreateTransaction
0cc:   fffff806621d9340   nt!NtCreateTransactionManager
0cd:   fffff80662504340   nt!NtCreateUserProcess
0ce:   fffff806624847d0   nt!NtCreateWaitCompletionPacket
0cf:   fffff8066249e9a0   nt!NtCreateWaitablePort
0d0:   fffff806625077f0   nt!NtCreateWnfStateName
0d1:   fffff806625a2e20   nt!NtCreateWorkerFactory
0d2:   fffff80662726970   nt!NtDebugActiveProcess
0d3:   fffff80662726b90   nt!NtDebugContinue
0d4:   fffff80662469310   nt!NtDeleteAtom
0d5:   fffff806627fc5a0   nt!NtDeleteBootEntry
0d6:   fffff806627fc730   nt!NtDeleteDriverEntry
0d7:   fffff806625f9700   nt!NtDeleteFile
0d8:   fffff80662517b70   nt!NtDeleteKey
0d9:   fffff806627c85a0   nt!NtDeleteObjectAuditAlarm
0da:   fffff806625e1390   nt!NtDeletePrivateNamespace
0db:   fffff8066250da20   nt!NtDeleteValueKey
0dc:   fffff80662646940   nt!NtDeleteWnfStateData
0dd:   fffff80662507230   nt!NtDeleteWnfStateName
0de:   fffff806625dd710   nt!NT_DISK::GetPnpProperty
0df:   fffff806625f45c0   nt!NtDisableLastKnownGood
0e0:   fffff806627f5d40   nt!NtDisplayString
0e1:   fffff80662434e10   nt!NtDrawText
0e2:   fffff806625f3440   nt!NtEnableLastKnownGood
0e3:   fffff806627fc8c0   nt!NtEnumerateBootEntries
0e4:   fffff806627fcf20   nt!NtEnumerateDriverEntries
0e5:   fffff806627fd3e0   nt!NtEnumerateSystemEnvironmentValuesEx
0e6:   fffff806621d9360   nt!NtEnumerateTransactionObject
0e7:   fffff806624789b0   nt!NtExtendSection
0e8:   fffff806627cb210   nt!NtFilterBootOption
0e9:   fffff806624a9a00   nt!NtFilterToken
0ea:   fffff806625dd710   nt!NT_DISK::GetPnpProperty
0eb:   fffff80662497c10   nt!NtFlushBuffersFileEx
0ec:   fffff806626473d0   nt!NtFlushInstallUILanguage
0ed:   fffff806624b6860   nt!ArbPreprocessEntry
0ee:   fffff80662476350   nt!NtFlushKey
0ef:   fffff8066215e6a0   nt!NtFlushProcessWriteBuffers
0f0:   fffff8066259e360   nt!NtFlushVirtualMemory
0f1:   fffff806624b6860   nt!ArbPreprocessEntry
0f2:   fffff8066277b250   nt!NtFreeUserPhysicalPages
0f3:   fffff8066270bbd0   nt!NtFreezeRegistry
0f4:   fffff806621d9380   nt!NtFreezeTransactions
0f5:   fffff80662496270   nt!NtGetCachedSigningLevel
0f6:   fffff80662507fc0   nt!NtGetCompleteWnfStateSubscription
0f7:   fffff806624c1c00   nt!NtGetContextThread
0f8:   fffff806627aaf80   nt!NtGetCurrentProcessorNumber
0f9:   fffff806627aafe0   nt!NtGetCurrentProcessorNumberEx
0fa:   fffff80662794d50   nt!NtGetDevicePowerState
0fb:   fffff80662496580   nt!NtGetMUIRegistryInfo
0fc:   fffff806624acc10   nt!NtGetNextProcess
0fd:   fffff806624b1670   nt!NtGetNextThread
0fe:   fffff806625b50f0   nt!NtGetNlsSectionPtr
0ff:   fffff806621d93a0   nt!NtGetNotificationResourceManager
100:   fffff8066214d9f0   nt!NtGetWriteWatch
101:   fffff8066246a630   nt!NtImpersonateAnonymousToken
102:   fffff806624909d0   nt!NtImpersonateThread
103:   fffff80662778a90   nt!NtInitializeEnclave
104:   fffff8066249cfb0   nt!NtInitializeNlsFiles
```

```
105:    fffff806624c5470    nt!NtInitializeRegistry
106:    fffff806625e7180    nt!NtInitiatePowerAction
107:    fffff806625f0f50    nt!NtIsSystemResumeAutomatic
108:    fffff806624c3820    nt!NtIsUILanguageComitted
109:    fffff8066264bff0    nt!NtListenPort
10a:    fffff806624a63e0    nt!NtLoadDriver
10b:    fffff80662778d70    nt!NtLoadEnclaveData
10c:    fffff8066264c790    nt!NtLoadKey
10d:    fffff806625f9d80    nt!NtLoadKey2
10e:    fffff806624c4d10    nt!NtLoadKey3
10f:    fffff8066251bf10    nt!NtLoadKeyEx
110:    fffff806624edd70    nt!NtLockFile
111:    fffff806625f4e70    nt!NtLockProductActivationKeys
112:    fffff806625f6fc0    nt!NtLockRegistryKey
113:    fffff8066206b380    nt!NtLockVirtualMemory
114:    fffff806624c5ba0    nt!NtMakePermanentObject
115:    fffff806624bc550    nt!NtMakeTemporaryObject
116:    fffff806624a2630    nt!NtManageHotPatch
117:    fffff806624d0af0    nt!NtManagePartition
118:    fffff806628027d0    nt!NtMapCMFModule
119:    fffff8066277b810    nt!NtMapUserPhysicalPages
11a:    fffff806624b8dd0    nt!NtMapViewOfSectionEx
11b:    fffff806627fd6a0    nt!NtModifyBootEntry
11c:    fffff806627fd6d0    nt!NtModifyDriverEntry
11d:    fffff8066249fcc0    nt!NtNotifyChangeDirectoryFile
11e:    fffff8066249fd20    nt!NtNotifyChangeDirectoryFileEx
11f:    fffff80662533ab0    nt!NtNotifyChangeKey
120:    fffff80662533b20    nt!NtNotifyChangeMultipleKeys
121:    fffff8066247b2f0    nt!NtNotifyChangeSession
122:    fffff806621d93c0    nt!NtOpenEnlistment
123:    fffff806625dd710    nt!NT_DISK::GetPnpProperty
124:    fffff80662734b00    nt!NtOpenIoCompletion
125:    fffff806625d37d0    nt!NtOpenJobObject
126:    fffff80662574050    nt!NtOpenKeyEx
127:    fffff8066270bc90    nt!NtOpenKeyTransacted
128:    fffff80662519fb0    nt!NtOpenKeyTransactedEx
129:    fffff80662803e60    nt!NtOpenKeyedEvent
12a:    fffff806625d42f0    nt!NtOpenMutant
12b:    fffff8066249f330    nt!NtOpenObjectAuditAlarm
12c:    fffff80662649930    nt!NtOpenPartition
12d:    fffff806624d6d90    nt!NtOpenPrivateNamespace
12e:    fffff8066255f3b0    nt!NtOpenProcessToken
12f:    fffff8066270bcb0    nt!NtOpenRegistryTransaction
130:    fffff806621d93e0    nt!NtOpenResourceManager
131:    fffff806625d43c0    nt!NtOpenSemaphore
132:    fffff806624bfa40    nt!NtOpenSession
133:    fffff80662472b10    nt!NtOpenSymbolicLinkObject
134:    fffff8066247fa10    nt!NtOpenThread
135:    fffff806627f8760    nt!NtOpenTimer
136:    fffff806621d9400    nt!NtOpenTransaction
137:    fffff806621d9420    nt!NtOpenTransactionManager
138:    fffff806625acbe0    nt!NtPlugPlayControl
139:    fffff806621d9440    nt!NtPrePrepareComplete
13a:    fffff806621d9460    nt!NtPrePrepareEnlistment
13b:    fffff806621d9480    nt!NtPrepareComplete
13c:    fffff806621d94a0    nt!NtPrepareEnlistment
13d:    fffff80662543250    nt!NtPrivilegeCheck
13e:    fffff80662602270    nt!NtPrivilegeObjectAuditAlarm
13f:    fffff806624b1cb0    nt!NtPrivilegedServiceAuditAlarm
```

```
140:    fffff806621d94c0    nt!NtPropagationComplete
141:    fffff806621d94e0    nt!NtPropagationFailed
142:    fffff806628046f0    nt!NtPssCaptureVaSpaceBulk
143:    fffff806624ed010    nt!NtPulseEvent
144:    fffff80662803a80    nt!NtQueryAuxiliaryCounterFrequency
145:    fffff806627fd700    nt!NtQueryBootEntryOrder
146:    fffff806627fd980    nt!NtQueryBootOptions
147:    fffff80662165220    nt!NtQueryDebugFilterState
148:    fffff806624e5b10    nt!NtQueryDirectoryFileEx
149:    fffff8066252ccb0    nt!NtQueryDirectoryObject
14a:    fffff806627fdc90    nt!NtQueryDriverEntryOrder
14b:    fffff80662490e20    nt!NtQueryEaFile
14c:    fffff80662505200    nt!NtQueryFullAttributesFile
14d:    fffff8066249d4a0    nt!NtQueryInformationAtom
14e:    fffff80662734ea0    nt!NtQueryInformationByName
14f:    fffff806621d9500    nt!NtQueryInformationEnlistment
150:    fffff80662591710    nt!NtQueryInformationJobObject
151:    fffff80662763970    nt!NtQueryInformationPort
152:    fffff806621d9520    nt!NtQueryInformationResourceManager
153:    fffff806621d9540    nt!NtQueryInformationTransaction
154:    fffff806621d9560    nt!NtQueryInformationTransactionManager
155:    fffff8066243d250    nt!NtQueryInformationWorkerFactory
156:    fffff806625dd000    nt!NtQueryInstallUILanguage
157:    fffff806625e1020    nt!NtQueryIntervalProfile
158:    fffff80662734c20    nt!NtQueryIoCompletion
159:    fffff80662736e00    nt!NtQueryIoRingCapabilities
15a:    fffff80662472420    nt!NtQueryLicenseValue
15b:    fffff8066250cae0    nt!NtQueryMultipleValueKey
15c:    fffff806627ffbf0    nt!NtQueryMutant
15d:    fffff8066270bdf0    nt!NtQueryOpenSubKeys
15e:    fffff8066270c030    nt!NtQueryOpenSubKeysEx
15f:    fffff806625dd650    nt!CmpCleanUpHigherLayerKcbCachesPreCallback
160:    fffff806627376b0    nt!NtQueryQuotaInformationFile
161:    fffff806624e39e0    nt!NtQuerySecurityAttributesToken
162:    fffff80662476660    nt!NtQuerySecurityObject
163:    fffff806624b25e0    nt!NtQuerySecurityPolicy
164:    fffff806627ff7c0    nt!NtQuerySemaphore
165:    fffff806624f8170    nt!NtQuerySymbolicLinkObject
166:    fffff806627fdfc0    nt!NtQuerySystemEnvironmentValue
167:    fffff806624b83f0    nt!NtQuerySystemEnvironmentValueEx
168:    fffff8066248ce80    nt!NtQuerySystemInformationEx
169:    fffff806624b5170    nt!NtQueryTimerResolution
16a:    fffff80662509090    nt!NtQueryWnfStateData
16b:    fffff8066249d980    nt!NtQueryWnfStateNameInformation
16c:    fffff806624c5070    nt!NtQueueApcThreadEx
16d:    fffff80662547170    nt!NtQueueApcThreadEx2
16e:    fffff80662215fd0    nt!NtRaiseException
16f:    fffff806624a8390    nt!NtRaiseHardError
170:    fffff806621d9580    nt!NtReadOnlyEnlistment
171:    fffff806623882e0    nt!NtReadVirtualMemoryEx
172:    fffff806621d95a0    nt!NtRecoverEnlistment
173:    fffff806621d95c0    nt!NtRecoverResourceManager
174:    fffff806621d95e0    nt!NtRecoverTransactionManager
175:    fffff806621d9b00    nt!NtRegisterProtocolAddressInformation
176:    fffff806624bc880    nt!NtRegisterThreadTerminatePort
177:    fffff80662803f60    nt!NtReleaseKeyedEvent
178:    fffff806620c3ad0    nt!NtReleaseWorkerFactoryWorker
179:    fffff806624736c0    nt!NtRemoveIoCompletionEx
17a:    fffff80662726d90    nt!NtRemoveProcessDebug
```

```
17b:    fffff8066270c390    nt!NtRenameKey
17c:    fffff806621d9b20    nt!NtRenameTransactionManager
17d:    fffff8066270c810    nt!NtReplaceKey
17e:    fffff8066244fcc0    nt!NtReplacePartitionUnit
17f:    fffff80662763aa0    nt!NtReplyWaitReplyPort
180:    fffff806624a3990    nt!NtRequestPort
181:    fffff806624d27b0    nt!NtResetEvent
182:    fffff806624ca730    nt!NtResetWriteWatch
183:    fffff8066270cb70    nt!NtRestoreKey
184:    fffff806627b0830    nt!NtResumeProcess
185:    fffff806621688f0    nt!NtRevertContainerImpersonation
186:    fffff806621d9600    nt!NtRollbackComplete
187:    fffff806621d9620    nt!NtRollbackEnlistment
188:    fffff8066245a080    nt!NtRollbackRegistryTransaction
189:    fffff806621d9640    nt!NtRollbackTransaction
18a:    fffff806621d9b80    nt!NtRollforwardTransactionManager
18b:    fffff806624533e0    nt!NtSaveKey
18c:    fffff80662453400    nt!NtSaveKeyEx
18d:    fffff8066270cdd0    nt!NtSaveMergedKeys
18e:    fffff80662523b10    nt!NtSecureConnectPort
18f:    fffff806626499f0    nt!NtSerializeBoot
190:    fffff806627fe2e0    nt!NtSetBootEntryOrder
191:    fffff806627fe4f0    nt!NtSetBootOptions
192:    fffff806624c3f50    nt!NtSetCachedSigningLevel
193:    fffff806624c3f80    nt!NtSetCachedSigningLevel2
194:    fffff806627af460    nt!NtSetContextThread
195:    fffff80662626300    nt!NtSetDebugFilterState
196:    fffff8066264a5d0    nt!NtSetDefaultHardErrorPort
197:    fffff806625dc8c0    nt!NtSetDefaultLocale
198:    fffff806625dc8a0    nt!NtSetDefaultUILanguage
199:    fffff806627fe700    nt!NtSetDriverEntryOrder
19a:    fffff806627370d0    nt!NtSetEaFile
19b:    fffff806625dd710    nt!NT_DISK::GetPnpProperty
19c:    fffff806625dd710    nt!NT_DISK::GetPnpProperty
19d:    fffff80662052a10    nt!NtSetIRTimer
19e:    fffff80662726f00    nt!NtSetInformationDebugObject
19f:    fffff806621d9660    nt!NtSetInformationEnlistment
1a0:    fffff80662736ea0    nt!NtSetInformationIoRing
1a1:    fffff80662592bd0    nt!NtSetInformationJobObject
1a2:    fffff8066255e480    nt!NtSetInformationKey
1a3:    fffff806621d9680    nt!NtSetInformationResourceManager
1a4:    fffff80662781d70    nt!NtSetInformationSymbolicLink
1a5:    fffff80662467300    nt!NtSetInformationToken
1a6:    fffff806621d96a0    nt!NtSetInformationTransaction
1a7:    fffff806621d9b40    nt!NtSetInformationTransactionManager
1a8:    fffff8066253cce0    nt!NtSetInformationVirtualMemory
1a9:    fffff806620a3cd0    nt!NtSetInformationWorkerFactory
1aa:    fffff806625e10f0    nt!NtSetIntervalProfile
1ab:    fffff8066254be00    nt!NtSetIoCompletion
1ac:    fffff80662474090    nt!NtSetIoCompletionEx
1ad:    fffff806621d8fc0    nt!BvgaSetVirtualFrameBuffer
1ae:    fffff806625dd710    nt!NT_DISK::GetPnpProperty
1af:    fffff806625dd710    nt!NT_DISK::GetPnpProperty
1b0:    fffff80662737dc0    nt!NtSetQuotaInformationFile
1b1:    fffff8066248c0d0    nt!NtSetSecurityObject
1b2:    fffff806627fe910    nt!NtSetSystemEnvironmentValue
1b3:    fffff806624b8510    nt!NtSetSystemEnvironmentValueEx
1b4:    fffff80662538b70    nt!NtSetSystemInformation
1b5:    fffff8066284f7e0    nt!NtSetSystemPowerState
```

```
1b6:   fffff806627f5560    nt!NtSetSystemTime
1b7:   fffff8066259c1a0    nt!NtSetThreadExecutionState
1b8:   fffff80662167ed0    nt!NtSetTimer2
1b9:   fffff806620cf470    nt!NtSetTimerEx
1ba:   fffff80662539730    nt!NtSetTimerResolution
1bb:   fffff8066263ddb0    nt!NtSetUuidSeed
1bc:   fffff806625e3ba0    nt!NtSetVolumeInformationFile
1bd:   fffff8066249dcf0    nt!NtSetWnfProcessNotificationEvent
1be:   fffff80662434f90    nt!NtShutdownSystem
1bf:   fffff80662046fe0    nt!NtShutdownWorkerFactory
1c0:   fffff80662045160    nt!NtSignalAndWaitForSingleObject
1c1:   fffff806621d9b60    nt!NtSinglePhaseReject
1c2:   fffff80662803af0    nt!NtStartProfile
1c3:   fffff80662803d60    nt!NtStopProfile
1c4:   fffff806623559a0    nt!NtSubmitIoRing
1c5:   fffff80662508c30    nt!NtSubscribeWnfStateChange
1c6:   fffff806627b08b0    nt!NtSuspendProcess
1c7:   fffff806624bd100    nt!NtSuspendThread
1c8:   fffff806624b7f10    nt!NtSystemDebugControl
1c9:   fffff806627793a0    nt!NtTerminateEnclave
1ca:   fffff806625997a0    nt!NtTerminateJobObject
1cb:   fffff806624a1880    nt!NtTestAlert
1cc:   fffff8066270d070    nt!NtThawRegistry
1cd:   fffff806621d96c0    nt!NtThawTransactions
1ce:   fffff806624fda40    nt!NtTraceControl
1cf:   fffff806627fec30    nt!NtTranslateFilePath
1d0:   fffff8066216dcf0    nt!DefaultAddProfileSource
1d1:   fffff8066273db40    nt!NtUnloadDriver
1d2:   fffff80662470160    nt!NtUnloadKey
1d3:   fffff80662470070    nt!NtUnloadKey2
1d4:   fffff806624701b0    nt!NtUnloadKeyEx
1d5:   fffff806624ed9c0    nt!NtUnlockFile
1d6:   fffff8066214bd80    nt!NtUnlockVirtualMemory
1d7:   fffff806625896d0    nt!NtUnmapViewOfSectionEx
1d8:   fffff80662507650    nt!NtUnsubscribeWnfStateChange
1d9:   fffff80662508690    nt!NtUpdateWnfStateData
1da:   fffff806625dd710    nt!NT_DISK::GetPnpProperty
1db:   fffff806624c6f20    nt!NtWaitForAlertByThreadId
1dc:   fffff80662727090    nt!NtWaitForDebugEvent
1dd:   fffff80662804330    nt!NtWaitForKeyedEvent
1de:   fffff80662138c40    nt!NtWaitForWorkViaWorkerFactory
1df:   fffff806625dd710    nt!NT_DISK::GetPnpProperty
1e0:   fffff806625dd710    nt!NT_DISK::GetPnpProperty
```

18. We close logging before exiting WinDbg:

```
0: kd> .logclose
Closing open log C:\EWMDA-Dumps\Complete\x64\ES3.log
```

Exercise ES4

- **Goal:** Explore win32kext WinDbg extension
- **Memory Analysis Patterns:** Handle Limit (GDI, Kernel Space); Wait Chain (Window Messaging)
- \EWMDA\Exercise-ES4.pdf

win32kext
https://github.com/progmboy/win32kext

Exercise ES4: Explore win32kext WinDbg Extension

Goal: Explore the win32kext[8] WinDbg extension.

Memory Analysis Patterns: Handle Limit (GDI, Kernel Space); Wait Chain (Window Messaging).

1. Launch WinDbg.

2. Open \EWMDA-Dumps\Complete\x64\MEMORY-WM.DMP.

3. We get the dump file loaded:

```
Microsoft (R) Windows Debugger Version 10.0.27668.1000 AMD64
Copyright (c) Microsoft Corporation. All rights reserved.


Loading Dump File [C:\EWMDA-Dumps\Complete\x64\MEMORY-WM.DMP]
Kernel Bitmap Dump File: Full address space is available


************* Path validation summary **************
Response                         Time (ms)     Location
Deferred                                       srv*
Symbol search path is: srv*
Executable search path is:
Windows 10 Kernel Version 22000 MP (2 procs) Free x64
Product: WinNt, suite: TerminalServer SingleUserTS Personal
Edition build lab: 22000.1.amd64fre.co_release.210604-1628
Kernel base = 0xfffff804`04a00000 PsLoadedModuleList = 0xfffff804`05629bc0
Debug session time: Sat Feb 19 15:26:18.655 2022 (UTC + 1:00)
System Uptime: 0 days 0:06:04.659
Loading Kernel Symbols
..............................................................
...............................................................
...............................................................
..
Loading User Symbols
...................................
Loading unloaded module list
........
For analysis of this file, run !analyze -v
nt!KeBugCheckEx:
fffff804`04e16220 mov     qword ptr [rsp+8],rcx ss:0018:ffffa784`8ee7d680=000000000000000a
```

4. We open a log file:

```
1: kd> .logopen C:\EWMDA-Dumps\Complete\x64\ES4.log
Opened log file 'C:\EWMDA-Dumps\Complete\x64\ES4.log'
```

[8] https://github.com/progmboy/win32kext

5. We built the extension from the GitHub repo using Visual C++ 2022 and included it in the dump archive. We can load it now:

```
1: kd> .load C:\EWMDA-Dumps\win32kext\x64\win32kext

1: kd> !help
=================================================================
win32k debugger extentions:
author: pgboy
-----------------------------------------------------------------

gh     [object handle]              -- HMGR entry of handle (GDI object like DC/BITMAP/PALETTE etc)
uh     [object handle]              -- USER entry of handle (USER object like WINDOW/MENU etc)
duh    [-h]                        -- Dump USER entry of handle (USER object like WINDOW/MENU etc)
dgh    [-h]                        -- Dump HMGR entry of handle (GDI object like DC/BITMAP/PALETTE etc)
dpsurf [SURFACE ptr]                -- SURFACE
dpso   [SURFOBJ ptr]                -- SURFACE struct from SURFOBJ
dr     [REGION ptr]                 -- REGION
cr     [REGION ptr]                 -- check REGION
dppal  [PALETTE ptr]                -- PALETTE
=================================================================
```

6. The **!duh** command dumps user objects such as windows (USER32.DLL API such as *CreateWindow*), and the **!dgh** command dumps graphical objects as fonts (GDI32.DLL API as *CreateFont*):

```
1: kd> !duh
Total 0x580 handles
handle=0x00010002 object=0xffff80401f90000 process=0xffff8008ae887140 type=(01)Window
handle=0x00010003 object=0xffff80401fb0000 process=0xffff8008ae887140 type=(03)Cursor
handle=0x00010004 object=0xffff80401f90150 process=0xffff8008ae887140 type=(01)Window
handle=0x00010005 object=0xffff80401fb00a0 process=0xffff8008ae887140 type=(03)Cursor
handle=0x00010006 object=0xffff80401f902a0 process=0xffff8008ae887140 type=(01)Window
handle=0x00010007 object=0xffff80401fb0140 process=0xffff8008ae887140 type=(03)Cursor
handle=0x00010008 object=0xffff80401f903f0 process=0xffff8008ae887140 type=(01)Window
handle=0x00010009 object=0xffff80401fb01e0 process=0xffff8008ae887140 type=(03)Cursor
handle=0x0001000a object=0xffff80401f90540 process=0xffff8008ae887140 type=(01)Window
handle=0x0001000b object=0xffff80401fb0280 process=0xffff8008ae887140 type=(03)Cursor
handle=0x0001000c object=0xffff80401f90690 process=0xffff8008ae887140 type=(01)Window
handle=0x0001000d object=0xffff80401fb0320 process=0xffff8008ae887140 type=(03)Cursor
handle=0x0001000e object=0xffff80401f907e0 process=0xffff8008ae887140 type=(01)Window
handle=0x0001000f object=0xffff80401fb03c0 process=0xffff8008ae887140 type=(03)Cursor
handle=0x00010010 object=0xffff80401f90930 process=0xffff8008ae887140 type=(01)Window
handle=0x00010011 object=0xffff80401fb0460 process=0xffff8008ae887140 type=(03)Cursor
can not read win32kbase!gpKernelHandleTable at fffff9511c55cb50
user control-c break

1: kd> !duh -h
Usage: !duh [args]

args list:
-p [process] filter object by process
-t [type id] filter object by type id
   valid type:
   id:1 - Window
   id:2 - Menu
   id:3 - Cursor
   id:4 - DeferWindowPos
```

```
   id:5 - WindowHook
   id:6 - MemoryHandle
   id:7 - CPD
   id:8 - AcceleratorTable
   id:9 - CsDde
   id:10 - Conversation
   id:11 - pxs
   id:12 - Monitor
   id:13 - Keyboard
   id:14 - KeyboardLayout
   id:15 - EventHook
   id:16 - Timer
   id:17 - InputContext
   id:18 - HidData
   id:20 - TouchInputInfo
   id:21 - GestureInfo
   id:23 - BaseWindow
example:
!duh
    will dump user object in system
!duh -p 0xffffffff13450080
    will dump user object create by process 0xffffffff13450080
!duh -t 1
    will dump all window object
!duh -t 1 -p 0xffffffff13450080
    will dump all window object create by process 0xffffffff13450080

1: kd> !dgh
Handle:0x0004000a Object=0xfffff80402190000 Type=Rgn(4) entry=0xfffff804020000f0 processx=0x0
Handle:0x0088000b Object=0xfffff80401ba0000 Type=Palette(8) entry=0xfffff80402000108 processx=0x0
Handle:0x0008000c Object=0xfffff80401ba0090 Type=Palette(8) entry=0xfffff80402000120 processx=0x0
Handle:0x0008000d Object=0xfffff80401ba0120 Type=Palette(8) entry=0xfffff80402000138 processx=0x0
Handle:0x0008000e Object=0xfffff80401ba01b0 Type=Palette(8) entry=0xfffff80402000150 processx=0x0
Handle:0x0085000f Object=0xfffff80401b50000 Type=Bitmap(5) entry=0xfffff80402000168 processx=0x0
Handle:0x00900010 Object=0xfffff80401b80000 Type=Brush(16) entry=0xfffff80402000180 processx=0x0
Handle:0x00900011 Object=0xfffff80401b800a0 Type=Brush(16) entry=0xfffff80402000198 processx=0x0
Handle:0x00900012 Object=0xfffff80401b80140 Type=Brush(16) entry=0xfffff804020001b0 processx=0x0
Handle:0x00900013 Object=0xfffff80401b801e0 Type=Brush(16) entry=0xfffff804020001c8 processx=0x0
Handle:0x00900014 Object=0xfffff80401b80280 Type=Brush(16) entry=0xfffff804020001e0 processx=0x0
Handle:0x00900015 Object=0xfffff80401b80320 Type=Brush(16) entry=0xfffff804020001f8 processx=0x0
Handle:0x00b00016 Object=0xfffff80401b90000 Type=Brush(16) entry=0xfffff80402000210 processx=0x0
Handle:0x00b00017 Object=0xfffff80401b900c0 Type=Brush(16) entry=0xfffff80402000228 processx=0x0
Handle:0x00b00018 Object=0xfffff80401b90180 Type=Brush(16) entry=0xfffff80402000240 processx=0x0
Handle:0x00b00019 Object=0xfffff80401b90240 Type=Brush(16) entry=0xfffff80402000258 processx=0x0
Handle:0x0010001a Object=0xfffff80401b803c0 Type=Brush(16) entry=0xfffff80402000270 processx=0x0
Handle:0x0010001b Object=0xfffff80401b80460 Type=Brush(16) entry=0xfffff80402000288 processx=0x0
Handle:0x0190001c Object=0xfffff80401b805a0 Type=Brush(16) entry=0xfffff804020002a0 processx=0x0
Handle:0x0005001d Object=0xfffff80401b50580 Type=Bitmap(5) entry=0xfffff804020002b8 processx=0x0
Handle:0x0010001e Object=0xfffff80401b80500 Type=Brush(16) entry=0xfffff804020002d0 processx=0x0
Handle:0x0089001f Object=0xfffff90600603940 Type=ColorSpace(9) entry=0xfffff804020002e8 processx=0x0
Handle:0x008a0020 Object=0xfffff9060060bce0 Type=Font(10) entry=0xfffff80402000300 processx=0x0
Handle:0x038a0021 Object=0xfffff9060060c010 Type=Font(10) entry=0xfffff80402000318 processx=0x1
Handle:0x008a0022 Object=0xfffff9060060c2b0 Type=Font(10) entry=0xfffff80402000330 processx=0x0
Handle:0x008a0023 Object=0xfffff9060060c550 Type=Font(10) entry=0xfffff80402000348 processx=0x0
Handle:0x008a0024 Object=0xfffff9060060c7f0 Type=Font(10) entry=0xfffff80402000360 processx=0x0
can not read win32kbase!gpHandleManager at fffff906006028a0
user control-c break

1: kd> !dgh -h
Usage: !dgh [args]

args list:
```

```
-p [process] filter object by process
-t [type id] filter object by type id
   valid type:
   id:1 - DC
   id:2 - ColorTransform
   id:4 - Rgn
   id:5 - Bitmap
   id:7 - Path
   id:8 - Palette
   id:9 - ColorSpace
   id:10 - Font
   id:14 - ColorTransform
   id:15 - Sprite
   id:16 - Brush
   id:18 - LogicSurface
   id:19 - Space
   id:21 - ServerMetafile
   id:28 - Driver
   id:138 - Font2
example:
!dgh
    will dump gdi object in system
!dgh -p 0xffffffff13450080
    will dump gdi object create by process 0xffffffff13450080
!dgh -t 5
    will dump all bitmap object
!dgh -t 1 -p 0xffffffff13450080
    will dump all bitmap object create by process 0xffffffff13450080
```

7. **!uh** and **!gh** show information about specific handles. We illustrate their usefulness in the window messaging chain example. We see this thread (it could also be from the output of the **!process 0 3f** command or the problem description mentioning a particular process, hanging, where we look at its stack traces):

```
1: kd> !thread ffff8008afcc6080 3f
THREAD ffff8008afcc6080  Cid 20d0.10e8  Teb: 000000aa3c2e9000 Win32Thread: ffff8008b34cab70 WAIT:
(WrUserRequest) UserMode Non-Alertable
    ffff8008b35b9d80  QueueObject
Not impersonating
DeviceMap                 ffffbc06b0049df0
Owning Process            ffff8008ad7ca080       Image:         AppF.exe
Attached Process          N/A            Image:         N/A
Wait Start TickCount      22929          Ticks: 409 (0:00:00:06.390)
Context Switch Count      916            IdealProcessor: 1  NoStackSwap
UserTime                  00:00:00.015
KernelTime                00:00:00.062
Unable to load image C:\Work\AppF.exe, Win32 error 0n2
*** WARNING: Unable to verify checksum for AppF.exe
Win32 Start Address AppF (0x00007ff6074515b8)
Stack Init ffffa7848cb6bc70 Current ffffa7848cb6aff0
Base ffffa7848cb6c000 Limit ffffa7848cb66000 Call 0000000000000000
Priority 10 BasePriority 8 PriorityDecrement 0 IoPriority 2 PagePriority 5
Unable to load image \??\C:\WINDOWS\system32\drivers\myfault.sys, Win32 error 0n2
Child-SP          RetAddr           Call Site
ffffa784`8cb6b030 fffff804`04d327f7     nt!KiSwapContext+0x76
ffffa784`8cb6b170 fffff804`04d346a9     nt!KiSwapThread+0x3a7
ffffa784`8cb6b250 fffff804`04d2e5c4     nt!KiCommitThreadWait+0x159
ffffa784`8cb6b2f0 fffff804`04c8efe0     nt!KeWaitForSingleObject+0x234
ffffa784`8cb6b3e0 fffff951`1d3aafd6     nt!KeWaitForMultipleObjects+0x540
ffffa784`8cb6b4e0 fffff951`1d3aa222     win32kfull!xxxRealSleepThread+0x2c6
ffffa784`8cb6b600 fffff951`1d3a8efd     win32kfull!xxxInterSendMsgEx+0xd72
```

```
ffffa784`8cb6b770 fffff951`1d400594      win32kfull!xxxSendTransformableMessageTimeout+0x38d
ffffa784`8cb6b8f0 fffff951`1d3f3da7      win32kfull!xxxWrapSendMessage+0x24
ffffa784`8cb6b950 fffff951`1d3eaefc      win32kfull!NtUserfnDWORD+0x67
ffffa784`8cb6b990 fffff951`1bd77305      win32kfull!NtUserMessageCall+0x1bc
ffffa784`8cb6ba20 fffff804`04e28775      win32k!NtUserMessageCall+0x3d
ffffa784`8cb6ba70 00007ffe`4b031434      nt!KiSystemServiceCopyEnd+0x25 (TrapFrame @ ffffa784`8cb6bae0)
000000aa`3c4ff778 00007ffe`4cd608cf      win32u!NtUserMessageCall+0x14
000000aa`3c4ff780 00007ffe`4cd60737      USER32!SendMessageWorker+0x12f
000000aa`3c4ff820 00007ff6`0745127e      USER32!SendMessageW+0x137
000000aa`3c4ff880 00007ffe`4cd61c4c      AppF+0x127e
000000aa`3c4ff920 00007ffe`4cd60ea6      USER32!UserCallWinProcCheckWow+0x33c
000000aa`3c4ffa90 00007ff6`074511bd      USER32!DispatchMessageWorker+0x2a6
000000aa`3c4ffb10 00007ff6`0745154a      AppF+0x11bd
000000aa`3c4ffc00 00007ffe`4bb954e0      AppF+0x154a
000000aa`3c4ffc40 00007ffe`4d1c485b      KERNEL32!BaseThreadInitThunk+0x10
000000aa`3c4ffc70 00000000`00000000      ntdll!RtlUserThreadStart+0x2b
```

We notice that the AppF thread is blocked in the *SendMessage* call. We try to disassemble the caller return address backward to find a possible window handle argument, but we find that it was dynamically returned by *FindWindow* in a volatile register RAX:

```
1: kd> .thread /r /p ffff8008afcc6080
Implicit thread is now ffff8008`afcc6080
Implicit process is now ffff8008`ad7ca080
Loading User Symbols
..............................

************* Symbol Loading Error Summary **************
Module name            Error
myfault                The system cannot find the file specified

You can troubleshoot most symbol related issues by turning on symbol loading diagnostics (!sym
noisy) and repeating the command that caused symbols to be loaded.
You should also verify that your symbol search path (.sympath) is correct.

1: kd> ub 00007ff6`0745127e
Unable to load image C:\Work\AppF.exe, Win32 error 0n2
*** WARNING: Unable to verify checksum for AppF.exe
AppF+0x1255:
00007ff6`07451255 488d15c4450100  lea     rdx,[AppF+0x15820 (00007ff6`07465820)]
00007ff6`0745125c 488d0dbd450100  lea     rcx,[AppF+0x15820 (00007ff6`07465820)]
00007ff6`07451263 ff1517d00000    call    qword ptr [AppF+0xe280 (00007ff6`0745e280)]
00007ff6`07451269 4533c9          xor     r9d,r9d
00007ff6`0745126c ba11010000      mov     edx,111h
00007ff6`07451271 488bc8          mov     rcx,rax
00007ff6`07451274 458d4168        lea     r8d,[r9+68h]
00007ff6`07451278 ff15facf0000    call    qword ptr [AppF+0xe278 (00007ff6`0745e278)]

1: kd> dps 00007ff6`0745e278 L1
00007ff6`0745e278  00007ffe`4cd60600 USER32!SendMessageW

1: kd> dps 00007ff6`0745e280 L1
00007ff6`0745e280  00007ffe`4cd75b90 USER32!FindWindowW
```

Instead, we can find possible window handle patterns as execution residue in the stack region around "send window"-related calls:

```
1: kd> kv
 *** Stack trace for last set context - .thread/.cxr resets it
 # Child-SP          RetAddr           : Args to Child                                                           : Call Site
00 ffffa784`8cb6b030 fffff804`04d327f7 : ffffa784`0000000a 00000000`ffffffff 00000000`00000000 ffff8008`b0747158 : nt!KiSwapContext+0x76
01 ffffa784`8cb6b170 fffff804`04d346a9 : ffffa784`8cb6b2f0 00000000`00000000 ffffa784`8cb6b350 00000000`00000006 : nt!KiSwapThread+0x3a7
02 ffffa784`8cb6b250 fffff804`04d2e5c4 : 00000000`00000000 00000000`00000000 00000000`00000000 00000000`00000000 : nt!KiCommitThreadWait+0x159
03 ffffa784`8cb6b2f0 fffff804`04c8efe0 : ffff8008`b35b9d80 fffff951`0000000d 00000000`00000001 ffff8008`aa0a4400 : nt!KeWaitForSingleObject+0x234
04 ffffa784`8cb6b3e0 fffff951`1d3aafd6 : fffff906`0086b010 fffff906`0086b010 fffff804`0f5d1150 00000000`00000004 : nt!KeWaitForMultipleObjects+0x540
05 ffffa784`8cb6b4e0 fffff951`1d3aa222 : ffff8008`b35bf500 fffff804`00000000 00000000`00000000 ffff8008`00000000 : win32kfull!xxxRealSleepThread+0x2c6
06 ffffa784`8cb6b600 fffff951`1d3a8efd : fffff804`0f5d1150 00000000`00000001 00000000`00000068 00000000`00000000 : win32kfull!xxxInterSendMsgEx+0xd72
07 ffffa784`8cb6b770 fffff951`1d400594 : fffff804`0f5d1150 fffff951`1c2f3ad8 00000000`00000000 00000000`00000001 :
win32kfull!xxxSendTransformableMessageTimeout+0x38d
08 ffffa784`8cb6b8f0 fffff951`1d3f3da7 : 00000000`00000000 fffff951`1c2f5c40 fffff804`0f5d1150 00000000`0005044c : win32kfull!xxxWrapSendMessage+0x24
09 ffffa784`8cb6b950 fffff951`1d3eaefc : fffff804`0f5d1150 00000000`0005044c 000000aa`3c4ff701 00000000`00000000 : win32kfull!NtUserfnDWORD+0x67
0a ffffa784`8cb6b990 fffff951`1bd77305 : ffffa784`8cb6ba88 00000000`0005044c 00000000`00000068 ffff8008`afcc6080 : win32kfull!NtUserMessageCall+0x1bc
0b ffffa784`8cb6ba20 fffff804`04e28775 : 00000000`00000000 00000000`00000000 00000000`00000000 fffff804`0f5cf930 : win32k!NtUserMessageCall+0x3d
0c ffffa784`8cb6ba70 00007ffe`4b031434 : 00007ffe`4cd608cf 00000000`00000003 00000000`000000a1 00000000`00000001 : nt!KiSystemServiceCopyEnd+0x25
(TrapFrame @ ffffa784`8cb6bae0)
0d 000000aa`3c4ff778 00007ffe`4cd608cf : 00000000`00000003 00000000`000000a1 00000000`00000001 00000000`00000005 : win32u!NtUserMessageCall+0x14
0e 000000aa`3c4ff780 00007ffe`4cd60737 : 000000aa`3c4ff810 00000000`00000000 00000000`00000068 00000000`00000000 : USER32!SendMessageWorker+0x12f
0f 000000aa`3c4ff820 00007ff6`0745127e : 00000000`00030464 00007ff6`07469d00 00000000`80006010 00000000`00000000 : USER32!SendMessageW+0x137
10 000000aa`3c4ff880 00007ffe`4cd61c4c : 00000000`00000000 00000000`00000001 00000000`00000001 00000000`00000000 : AppF+0x127e
11 000000aa`3c4ff920 00007ffe`4cd60ea6 : 00000000`02010005 00007ff6`07451200 00000000`00030464 00007ffe`00000111 : USER32!UserCallWinProcCheckWow+0x33c
12 000000aa`3c4ffa90 00007ff6`074511bd : 00007ff6`07451200 00000000`0001047a 00000000`00000001 00007ff6`07450000 : USER32!DispatchMessageWorker+0x2a6
13 000000aa`3c4ffb10 00007ff6`0745154a : 00000000`00000001 00000000`00000000 00000000`00000000 00000000`00000000 : AppF+0x11bd
14 000000aa`3c4ffc00 00007ffe`4bb954e0 : 00000000`00000000 00000000`00000000 00000000`00000000 00000000`00000000 : AppF+0x154a
15 000000aa`3c4ffc40 00007ffe`4d1c485b : 00000000`00000000 00000000`00000000 00000000`00000000 00000000`00000000 : KERNEL32!BaseThreadInitThunk+0x10
16 000000aa`3c4ffc70 00000000`00000000 : 00000000`00000000 00000000`00000000 00000000`00000000 00000000`00000000 : ntdll!RtlUserThreadStart+0x2b
```

We check the window handle validity and then get the owner process:

```
1: kd> !uh 0005044c
Object Handle      0x5044c
Object Type        Window(1)
Create Flag        0x239
Object             0xfffff8040f5d1150
pOwner             0xfffff906022d67a0
process            0xffff8008b10ed080
```

```
1: kd> !process 0xffff8008b10ed080 0
PROCESS ffff8008b10ed080
    SessionId: 1  Cid: 1060    Peb: ea3dd8f000  ParentCid: 144c
    DirBase: 6f792002  ObjectTable: ffffbc06b557ea00  HandleCount: 144.
    Image: AppG.exe
```

8. We close logging before exiting WinDbg:

```
1: kd> .logclose
Closing open log file C:\EWMDA-Dumps\Complete\x64\ES4.log
```

Exercise ES5

- **Goal:** Explore SwishDbgExt WinDbg extension
- **Memory Analysis Patterns:** Historical Information; Missing Thread (Kernel Space); Driver Device Collection; Patched Code; Out-of-Module Pointer; Self-Diagnosis (Registry); System Object; Namespace
- \EWMDA\Exercise-ES5.pdf

SwishDbgExt
https://github.com/comaeio/SwishDbgExt

Exercise ES5: Explore SwishDbgExt WinDbg Extension

Goal: Explore the SwishDbgExt[9] WinDbg extension.

Memory Analysis Patterns: Historical Information; Missing Thread (Kernel Space); Driver Device Collection; Patched Code; Out-of-Module Pointer; Self-Diagnosis (Registry); System Object; Namespace.

1. Launch WinDbg.

2. Open \EWMDA-Dumps\Complete\x64\MEMORY-W11.DMP.

3. We get the dump file loaded:

```
Microsoft (R) Windows Debugger Version 10.0.27668.1000 AMD64
Copyright (c) Microsoft Corporation. All rights reserved.


Loading Dump File [C:\EWMDA-Dumps\Complete\x64\MEMORY-W11.DMP]
Kernel Bitmap Dump File: Full address space is available


************* Path validation summary **************
Response                         Time (ms)     Location
Deferred                                       srv*
Symbol search path is: srv*
Executable search path is:
Windows 10 Kernel Version 22000 MP (2 procs) Free x64
Product: WinNt, suite: TerminalServer SingleUserTS Personal
Edition build lab: 22000.1.amd64fre.co_release.210604-1628
Kernel base = 0xfffff806`61e00000 PsLoadedModuleList = 0xfffff806`62a296b0
Debug session time: Sat Nov 13 23:17:16.607 2021 (UTC + 1:00)
System Uptime: 0 days 0:03:06.813
Loading Kernel Symbols
...............................................................
................................................................
................................................................
..
Loading User Symbols
...................................
Loading unloaded module list
........
For analysis of this file, run !analyze -v
nt!KeBugCheckEx:
fffff806`62215590 mov     qword ptr [rsp+8],rcx ss:0018:ffffbe82`96f64670=000000000000000a
```

4. We open a log file:

```
0: kd> .logopen C:\EWMDA-Dumps\Complete\x64\ES5.log
Opened log file 'C:\EWMDA-Dumps\Complete\x64\ES5.log'
```

[9] https://github.com/comaeio/SwishDbgExt

5. We built the extension from the GitHub repo using Visual C++ 2022 and included it in the dump archive. We can load it now:

```
0: kd> .load C:\EWMDA-Dumps\SwishDbgExt\x64\SwishDbgExt
       SwishDbgExt  - Incident Response & Digital Forensics Debugging Extension
       SwishDbgExt Copyright (C) 2018 Comae Technologies DMCC - www.comae.com
       SwishDbgExt Copyright (C) 2014-2018 Matthieu Suiche (@msuiche)

       This program comes with ABSOLUTELY NO WARRANTY; for details type `show w'.
       This is free software, and you are welcome to redistribute it
       under certain conditions; type `show c' for details.

0: kd> !SwishDbgExt.help
Commands for C:\EWMDA-Dumps\SwishDbgExt\x64\SwishDbgExt.dll:
  !help              - Displays information on available extension commands
  !ms_callbacks      - Display callback functions
  !ms_checkcodecave - Look for used code cave
  !ms_consoles       - Display console command's history
  !ms_credentials    - Display user's credentials (based on gentilwiki's
                       mimikatz)
  !ms_drivers        - Display list of drivers
  !ms_dump           - Dump memory space on disk
  !ms_exqueue        - Display Ex queued workers
  !ms_fixit          - Reset segmentation in WinDbg (Fix "16.kd>")
  !ms_gdt            - Display GDT
  !ms_hivelist       - Display list of registry hives
  !ms_idt            - Display IDT
  !ms_lxss           - Display lsxx entries
  !ms_malscore       - Analyze a memory space and returns a Malware Score Index
                       (MSI) - (based on Frank Boldewin's work)
  !ms_mbr            - Scan Master Boot Record (MBR)
  !ms_netstat        - Display network information (sockets, connections, ...)
  !ms_object         - Display list of object
  !ms_pools          - Display list of big pools for suspicious allocations
  !ms_process        - Display list of processes
  !ms_readkcb        - Read key control block
  !ms_readknode      - Read key node
  !ms_readkvalue     - Read key value
  !ms_regcheck       - Scan for suspicious registry entries
  !ms_scanndishook   - Scan and display suspicious NDIS hooks
  !ms_services       - Display list of services
  !ms_ssdt           - Display service descriptor table (SDT) functions
  !ms_store          - Display information related to the Store Manager
                       (ReadyBoost)
  !ms_timers         - Display list of KTIMER
  !ms_vacbs          - Display list of cached VACBs
  !ms_verbose        - Turn verbose mode on/off
  !ms_yarascan       - Scan process memory using yara rules
!help <cmd> will give more information for a particular command
```

We now show examples of commands we found useful not only for memory forensics but for software diagnostics in general.

6. Various callbacks, such as process notification functions, can be listed using this command:

```
0: kd> !ms_callbacks

[*] IopFsNotifyChangeQueueHead:
     Object: 0xFFFFAC8A04360F40 Driver Object: 0xFFFFC38C2CE0ECE0 Procedure: 0xFFFFF806615C8D00 (FLTMGR!FltpFsNotification)

[*] PnpProfileNotifyList:
     Object: 0xFFFFAC8A04B88E20 Driver Object: 0xFFFFC38C2ECDD7E0 Session: 0x0 Procedure: 0xFFFFF80669DCF0C0
(i8042prt!I8xProfileNotificationCallback)
     Object: 0xFFFFAC8A04B89900 Driver Object: 0xFFFFC38C2EA7BDD0 Session: 0x0 Procedure: 0xFFFFF80669F6C180
(HDAudBus!HdAudBusProfileChangeCallback)

[*] PspCreateProcessNotifyRoutine:
     Procedure: 0xFFFFF80666D08790 (cng!CngCreateProcessNotifyRoutine)
Unable to load image \SystemRoot\system32\drivers\wd\WdFilter.sys, Win32 error 0n2
     Procedure: 0xFFFFF80667745E00 (WdFilter+0x45e00)
     Procedure: 0xFFFFF80666B3B4B0 (ksecdd!KsecCreateProcessNotifyRoutine)
     Procedure: 0xFFFFF80667D7C100 (tcpip!CreateProcessNotifyRoutineEx)
     Procedure: 0xFFFFF806682FD990 (iorate!IoRateProcessCreateNotify)
     Procedure: 0xFFFFF80666C797D0 (CI!I_PEProcessNotify)
     Procedure: 0xFFFFF8066951B320 (dxgkrnl!DxgkProcessNotify)
Unable to load image \SystemRoot\system32\DRIVERS\vm3dmp.sys, Win32 error 0n2
     Procedure: 0xFFFFF80669E79EC0 (vm3dmp+0x9ec0)
Unable to load image \SystemRoot\system32\drivers\peauth.sys, Win32 error 0n2
     Procedure: 0xFFFFF8066AE3ACF0 (peauth+0x3acf0)

[*] PspLoadImageNotifyRoutine:
     Procedure: 0xFFFFF806677467B0 (WdFilter+0x467b0)
     Procedure: 0xFFFFF80669D1E550 (ahcache!CitmpLoadImageCallback)

[*] PspCreateThreadNotifyRoutine:
     Procedure: 0xFFFFF80667747540 (WdFilter+0x47540)
     Procedure: 0xFFFFF806677472A0 (WdFilter+0x472a0)

[*] CallbackListHead:
     Procedure: 0xFFFFF806677376A0 (WdFilter+0x376a0)
     Procedure: 0xFFFFF806625B1330 (nt!VrpRegistryCallback)

[*] KeBugCheckCallbackListHead:
     Procedure: 0xFFFFF8066810C090 (fvevol!FveBugcheckHandler)

[*] KiNmiCallbackListHead:

[*] AlpcpLogCallbackListHead:

[*] EmpCallbackListHead:
     GUID: {BF67CD9D-B8D1-4BED-BFDA-1DEE5963BE6B} Procedure: 0xFFFFF806623D0030 (nt!PopEmUpdateDeviceConstraintCallback)
     GUID: {84D99F45-0B07-46CF-BABD-1981C86E3025} Procedure: 0xFFFFF806623D4910 (nt!PopEmModuleAddressMatchCallback)
     GUID: {13925944-2A6A-4E3C-AC97-37735C19393D} Procedure: 0x0000000000000000 ()
     GUID: {C31600A9-8AED-442C-8013-8903D6E89BF8} Procedure: 0xFFFFF80666F85DF0 (ACPI!ACPIDeviceIdMutiStringMatchCallback)
     GUID: {33204598-9949-4AD1-B41E-A4A0F705DC12} Procedure: 0xFFFFF80666F58F80 (ACPI!ACPIDeviceMatchCallback)
     GUID: {C2569BEF-5980-4120-8582-9D0774DCF86D} Procedure: 0xFFFFF80666F55F00 (ACPI!ACPINsObjMatchCallback)
     GUID: {1E66F3D7-0FC9-4829-AA45-C430EA96A434} Procedure: 0xFFFFF80667077E30 (pci!PciQueryRuleCallback)
     GUID: {B9EB207B-E0C8-4C01-A575-49DD7D510B46} Procedure: 0xFFFFF8066708E820 (pci!PciSetMpsSizeCallback)
     GUID: {898A8E39-096C-4A25-87E5-5BB0ED1D6704} Procedure: 0xFFFFF8066708E790 (pci!PciSetD0DelayCallback)
     GUID: {F79DE8DC-F3D1-4802-9C4B-6BF742D65FBD} Procedure: 0xFFFFF8066708E7D0 (pci!PciSetHackflagsCallback)
     GUID: {DFBFD6FE-435A-419E-8F2C-9B13A3C04C9E} Procedure: 0xFFFFF80667075570 (pci!PciDeviceMatchCallback)
     GUID: {D2E7862C-B8FA-4274-9BD1-59BA8DA0A7C2} Procedure: 0xFFFFF80662634CA0 (nt!EmCpuMatchCallback)
     GUID: {76C5EAB2-5420-43F7-BD26-50BA9E2CD742} Procedure: 0xFFFFF806627D9BD0 (nt!WmiMatchSMBiosSysInfo)
     GUID: {59229CA6-17A7-4E11-9EDA-DF0E93D7AF3A} Procedure: 0xFFFFF8066272AC10 (nt!EmRemoveBadS3PagesCallback)
     GUID: {24453286-BDE8-46BC-85D1-1982EDF3E212} Procedure: 0xFFFFF8066272AC80 (nt!EmSystemArchitectureCallback)
     GUID: {9D991181-C86A-4517-9FE7-32290377B564} Procedure: 0xFFFFF806624B6860 (nt!ArbPreprocessEntry)
     GUID: {8026FF68-3BD0-4BA4-A1D4-DE724F781B78} Procedure: 0xFFFFF806625DD700 (nt!EmTrueCallback)
     GUID: {A380467C-D907-4716-8B9B-17584E34256C} Procedure: 0x0000000000000000 ()
     GUID: {182A2B31-D5B8-45EF-BB6D-646EBAEDD8F1} Procedure: 0xFFFFF8066272AB90 (nt!EmMatchDate)
     GUID: {6F8D0C6D-B6FB-4584-8B34-F39422CFA61A} Procedure: 0x0000000000000000 ()
     GUID: {78BC9E89-552A-4AB8-9231-132E09E235B2} Procedure: 0x0000000000000000 ()
     GUID: {7CD2B230-6CEA-4957-B5D7-CFA977C22B18} Procedure: 0xFFFFF806621CF040 (nt!HalMatchAcpiFADTBootArch)
     GUID: {BF51DEF4-AC9C-44F3-ADE7-26DD13E756D3} Procedure: 0xFFFFF80662300A90 (nt!HalMatchAcpiRevision)
     GUID: {BEAE4D5F-2203-4856-94BB-C772A2C7624A} Procedure: 0xFFFFF80662300990 (nt!HalMatchAcpiCreatorRevision)
     GUID: {7E8FAE0F-7591-4EB6-9554-1D0699873111} Procedure: 0xFFFFF80662300A10 (nt!HalMatchAcpiOemRevision)
     GUID: {E0E45284-F266-4048-9A5E-7D4007C9C5AB} Procedure: 0xFFFFF806621CD420 (nt!HalMatchAcpiOemTableId)
     GUID: {2960716F-B0D8-41C9-9BB4-EE8BA248F86E} Procedure: 0xFFFFF806621AC3B0 (nt!HalMatchAcpiOemId)

[*] Tcpip driver IOCTL dispatch table:
    | IPSEC | DevObj: 0xFFFFC38C2CDC96D0 | IoctlDispatch: 0xFFFFF80667F56AF0 | tcpip!IPSecDispatchDevCtl |
    |   KFD | DevObj: 0xFFFFC38C2CDC94A0 | IoctlDispatch: 0xFFFFF80667DB1D30 | tcpip!KfdDispatchDevCtl |
    |   ALE | DevObj: 0xFFFFC38C2CDC9270 | IoctlDispatch: 0xFFFFF80667DC57B0 | tcpip!WfpAleDispatchControl |
    |  EQOS | DevObj: 0xFFFFC38C2E0E4D10 | IoctlDispatch: 0xFFFFF80667F4FB40 | tcpip!EQoSDispatchControl |
    |   IDP | DevObj: 0xFFFFC38C2E0E8D10 | IoctlDispatch: 0xFFFFF80667F77260 | tcpip!IdpDispatchIoctl |
```

```
[*]  Object Callbacks:
PreCallback Procedure: 0xFFFFF80667743C30 (WdFilter+0x43c30)

[*]  Object Callbacks:
PreCallback Procedure: 0xFFFFF80667743C30 (WdFilter+0x43c30)

[*] PspSiloMonitorList Callbacks:
     [0x0003] CreateCallback  Procedure: 0xFFFFF80666C5F430 (CI!CiCreateSiloNotification)
     [0x0005] CreateCallback  Procedure: 0xFFFFF80667CB9440 (NETIO!NsiContainerCreateCallback)
     [0x0005] DestroyCallback Procedure: 0xFFFFF80667CB9540 (NETIO!NsiContainerTerminateCallback)
     [0x0006] CreateCallback  Procedure: 0xFFFFF8066720ACC0 (pcw!PCW_SILO_CONTEXT::SiloCreateCallback)
     [0x0008] CreateCallback  Procedure: 0xFFFFF80666B3E790 (ksecdd!KsecdCreateSiloNotification)
     [0x0008] DestroyCallback Procedure: 0xFFFFF80666B42100 (ksecdd!KsecdTerminateSiloNotification)
     [0x0009] CreateCallback  Procedure: 0xFFFFF806682DB5E0 (mup!MupiContainerCreateNotify)
     [0x0009] DestroyCallback Procedure: 0xFFFFF806682DB810 (mup!MupiContainerTerminateNotify)
     [0x000b] CreateCallback  Procedure: 0xFFFFF806694092B0 (Msfs!MsSiloCreateNotify)
     [0x000b] DestroyCallback Procedure: 0xFFFFF80669409360 (Msfs!MsSiloTerminateNotify)
     [0x000c] CreateCallback  Procedure: 0xFFFFF8066A764DC0 (afd!AfdPodSiloCreateCallback)
     [0x000c] DestroyCallback Procedure: 0xFFFFF8066A76D8B0 (afd!AfdPodSiloTerminateCallback)
     [0x000d] CreateCallback  Procedure: 0xFFFFF80669B4EAC0 (rdbss!RxpSiloCreateNotification)
     [0x000d] DestroyCallback Procedure: 0xFFFFF80669B4EEB0 (rdbss!RxpSiloTerminateNotification)
     [0x000e] CreateCallback  Procedure: 0xFFFFF80669C367A0 (dfsc!DfscpContainerCreateNotify)
     [0x000e] DestroyCallback Procedure: 0xFFFFF80669C36C10 (dfsc!DfscpContainerTerminateNotify)
     [0x0013] CreateCallback  Procedure: 0xFFFFF80660172240 (HTTP!UxPodSiloCreateCallback)
     [0x0013] DestroyCallback Procedure: 0xFFFFF806601B4E90 (HTTP!UxPodSiloTerminateCallback)
```

7. There’s yet another command to list drivers:

```
0: kd> !ms_drivers
    | \Driver\fvevol                   | 0xffff80668100000 | 0x000D0000 | \SystemRoot\System32\DRIVERS\fvevol.sys
    | \Driver\vdrvroot                 | 0xfffff80667220000 | 0x00017000 | \SystemRoot\System32\drivers\vdrvroot.sys
    | \Driver\PptpMiniport             | 0xfffff8066afc0000 | 0x00021000 | \SystemRoot\System32\drivers\raspptp.sys
    | \Driver\usbuhci                  | 0xfffff80669ec0000 | 0x00011000 | \SystemRoot\System32\drivers\usbuhci.sys
    | \Driver\GpuEnergyDrv             | 0xfffff80669c00000 | 0x0000A000 | \SystemRoot\System32\drivers\gpuenergydrv.sys
    | \Driver\NetBT                    | 0xfffff806694a0000 | 0x0005A000 | \SystemRoot\System32\DRIVERS\netbt.sys
    | \Driver\acpiex                   | 0xfffff80666ec0000 | 0x00026000 | \SystemRoot\System32\Drivers\acpiex.sys
    | \Driver\Wdf01000                 | 0xfffff80666db0000 | 0x000D3000 | \SystemRoot\system32\drivers\Wdf01000.sys
    | \Driver\MYFAULT                  | 0xfffff80660570000 | 0x00008000 | \??\C:\WINDOWS\system32\drivers\myfault.sys
    | \Driver\WdNisDrv                 | 0xfffff8066b1e0000 | 0x0001A000 | \SystemRoot\system32\drivers\wd\WdNisDrv.sys
    | \Driver\mpsdrv                   | 0xfffff80660250000 | 0x0001B000 | \SystemRoot\System32\drivers\mpsdrv.sys
    | \Driver\storahci                 | 0xfffff80667620000 | 0x00031000 | \SystemRoot\System32\drivers\storahci.sys
    | \Driver\ndproxy                  | 0xfffff8066af10000 | 0x0001D000 | \SystemRoot\System32\DRIVERS\NDProxy.sys
    | \Driver\MMCSS                    | 0xfffff80660270000 | 0x00014000 | \SystemRoot\system32\drivers\mmcss.sys
    | \Driver\lltdio                   | 0xfffff8065ff90000 | 0x00018000 | \SystemRoot\system32\drivers\lltdio.sys
    | \Driver\BthEnum                  | 0xfffff806604c0000 | 0x00022000 | \SystemRoot\System32\drivers\BthEnum.sys
    | \Driver\bam                      | 0xfffff80669ce0000 | 0x00018000 | \SystemRoot\system32\drivers\bam.sys
    | \Driver\Psched                   | 0xfffff8066a7d0000 | 0x0002B000 | \SystemRoot\System32\drivers\pacer.sys
    | \Driver\BasicRender              | 0xfffff806699c0000 | 0x00011000 |
\SystemRoot\System32\DriverStore\FileRepository\basicrender.inf_amd64_e1a5502a3a50be4e\BasicRender.sys
    | \Driver\disk                     | 0xfffff80668330000 | 0x0001C000 | \SystemRoot\System32\drivers\disk.sys
    | \Driver\HTTP                     | 0xfffff80660080000 | 0x0019E000 | \SystemRoot\system32\drivers\HTTP.sys
    | \Driver\WscVReg                  | 0x0000000000000000 | 0x00000000 |
    | \Driver\monitor                  | 0xfffff8065fcb0000 | 0x0001C000 | \SystemRoot\System32\drivers\monitor.sys
    | \Driver\usbehci                  | 0xfffff8066a0d0000 | 0x0001A000 | \SystemRoot\System32\drivers\usbehci.sys
    | \Driver\ahcache                  | 0xfffff80669d00000 | 0x00053000 | \SystemRoot\System32\DRIVERS\ahcache.sys
    | \Driver\VMRawDsk                 | 0xfffff80668d60000 | 0x00010000 | \SystemRoot\system32\DRIVERS\vmrawdsk.sys
    | \Driver\iorate                   | 0xfffff806682f0000 | 0x00012000 | \SystemRoot\system32\drivers\iorate.sys
    | \Driver\pcw                      | 0xfffff80667200000 | 0x00014000 | \SystemRoot\System32\drivers\pcw.sys
    | \Driver\Ucx01000                 | 0xfffff8066a230000 | 0x00046000 | \SystemRoot\system32\drivers\ucx01000.sys
    | \Driver\USBXHCI                  | 0xfffff8066a190000 | 0x0009E000 | \SystemRoot\System32\drivers\USBXHCI.SYS
    | \Driver\partmgr                  | 0xfffff80667290000 | 0x00032000 | \SystemRoot\System32\drivers\partmgr.sys
    | \Driver\PEAUTH                   | 0xfffff8066ae00000 | 0x000CE000 | \SystemRoot\system32\drivers\peauth.sys
    | \Driver\MsLldp                   | 0xfffff8065ffb0000 | 0x00018000 | \SystemRoot\system32\drivers\mslldp.sys
    | \Driver\e1i68x64                 | 0xfffff8066a0f0000 | 0x00093000 | \SystemRoot\System32\drivers\e1i68x64.sys
    | \Driver\Vid                      | 0xfffff80669a40000 | 0x000B5000 | \SystemRoot\System32\drivers\Vid.sys
    | \Driver\ACPI_HAL                 | 0x0000000000000000 | 0x00000000 |
    | \Driver\spaceport                | 0xfffff806672d0000 | 0x000CF000 | \SystemRoot\System32\drivers\spaceport.sys
    | \Driver\Rasl2tp                  | 0xfffff8066af90000 | 0x00020000 | \SystemRoot\System32\drivers\rasl2tp.sys
    | \Driver\HidUsb                   | 0xfffff8066a570000 | 0x00012000 | \SystemRoot\System32\drivers\hidusb.sys
    | \Driver\vwififlt                 | 0xfffff8066a7b0000 | 0x0001A000 | \SystemRoot\System32\drivers\vwififlt.sys
    | \Driver\condrv                   | 0xfffff8066b1c0000 | 0x00013000 | \SystemRoot\System32\drivers\condrv.sys
    | \Driver\DXGKrnl                  | 0xfffff80669510000 | 0x0046E000 | \SystemRoot\System32\drivers\dxgkrnl.sys
    | \Driver\PnpManager               | 0x0000000000000000 | 0x00000000 |
    | \Driver\Null                     | 0xfffff80668d40000 | 0x0000A000 | \SystemRoot\System32\Drivers\Null.SYS
    | \Driver\vsock                    | 0xfffff80667460000 | 0x00018000 | \SystemRoot\system32\DRIVERS\vsock.sys
    | \Driver\intelpep                 | 0xfffff80667130000 | 0x00073000 | \SystemRoot\System32\drivers\intelpep.sys
    | \Driver\PRM                      | 0xfffff80666eb0000 | 0x0000D000 |
\SystemRoot\System32\DriverStore\FileRepository\prm.inf_amd64_7fc9bb8ba2b73803\PRM.sys
    | \Driver\RasAgileVpn              | 0xfffff8066af60000 | 0x00027000 | \SystemRoot\System32\drivers\AgileVpn.sys
    | \Driver\wanarp                   | 0xfffff8065fff0000 | 0x0001D000 | \SystemRoot\System32\DRIVERS\wanarp.sys
    | \Driver\SoftwareDevice           | 0x0000000000000000 | 0x00000000 |
```

```
    | \Driver\RFCOMM                | 0xfffff80660480000 | 0x0003C000 | \SystemRoot\System32\drivers\rfcomm.sys
    | \Driver\Serenum               | 0xfffff80669e50000 | 0x0000F000 | \SystemRoot\System32\drivers\serenum.sys
    | \Driver\CLFS                  | 0xfffff806614e0000 | 0x0006A000 | \SystemRoot\System32\drivers\CLFS.SYS
    | \Driver\WindowsTrustedRTProxy | 0xfffff806671f0000 | 0x0000B000 | \SystemRoot\System32\drivers\WindowsTrustedRTProxy.sys
    | \Driver\Serial                | 0xfffff80669e30000 | 0x0001D000 | \SystemRoot\System32\drivers\serial.sys
    | \Driver\NdisCap               | 0xfffff80669a00000 | 0x00013000 | \SystemRoot\System32\drivers\ndiscap.sys
    | \Driver\KSecDD                | 0xfffff80666b20000 | 0x00029000 | \SystemRoot\System32\drivers\ksecdd.sys
    | \Driver\volmgr                | 0xfffff806673a0000 | 0x0001B000 | \SystemRoot\System32\drivers\volmgr.sys
    | \Driver\DeviceApi             | 0x0000000000000000 | 0x00000000 |
    | \Driver\VMMemCtl              | 0xfffff80660290000 | 0x0000A000 | \SystemRoot\system32\DRIVERS\vmmemctl.sys
    | \Driver\umbus                 | 0xfffff80669d90000 | 0x00016000 |
\SystemRoot\System32\DriverStore\FileRepository\umbus.inf_amd64_0a89aff902a5c3a9\umbus.sys
    | \Driver\CNG                   | 0xfffff80666cf0000 | 0x000BC000 | \SystemRoot\System32\drivers\cng.sys
    | \Driver\Win32k                | 0x0000000000000000 | 0x00000000 |
    | \Driver\i8042prt              | 0xfffff80669db0000 | 0x00026000 | \SystemRoot\System32\drivers\i8042prt.sys
    | \Driver\npsvctrig             | 0xfffff80669bd0000 | 0x0000F000 | \SystemRoot\System32\drivers\npsvctrig.sys
    | \Driver\volume                | 0xfffff806681e0000 | 0x0000B000 | \SystemRoot\System32\drivers\volume.sys
    | \Driver\KSecPkg               | 0xfffff80667cd0000 | 0x00033000 | \SystemRoot\System32\Drivers\ksecpkg.sys
    | \Driver\TPM                   | 0xfffff806670b0000 | 0x00052000 | \SystemRoot\System32\drivers\tpm.sys
    | \Driver\mouclass              | 0xfffff80669e10000 | 0x00014000 | \SystemRoot\System32\drivers\mouclass.sys
    | \Driver\msisadrv              | 0xfffff80667010000 | 0x0000B000 | \SystemRoot\System32\drivers\msisadrv.sys
    | \Driver\IntelPMT              | 0xfffff806671d0000 | 0x00010000 | \SystemRoot\System32\drivers\IntelPMT.sys
    | \Driver\Ndu                   | 0xfffff8066b190000 | 0x00028000 | \SystemRoot\system32\drivers\Ndu.sys
    | \Driver\kbdclass              | 0xfffff80669de0000 | 0x00014000 | \SystemRoot\System32\drivers\kbdclass.sys
    | \Driver\mouhid                | 0xfffff8066a600000 | 0x00010000 | \SystemRoot\System32\drivers\mouhid.sys
    | \Driver\volsnap               | 0xfffff806681f0000 | 0x00073000 | \SystemRoot\System32\drivers\volsnap.sys
    | \Driver\nsiproxy              | 0xfffff80669bb0000 | 0x00012000 | \SystemRoot\system32\drivers\nsiproxy.sys
    | \Driver\WMIxWDM               | 0x0000000000000000 | 0x00000000 |
    | \Driver\RasSstp               | 0xfffff8066aef0000 | 0x0001D000 | \SystemRoot\System32\drivers\rassstp.sys
    | \Driver\MsQuic                | 0xfffff80660010000 | 0x00063000 | \SystemRoot\system32\drivers\msquic.sys
    | \Driver\BthPan                | 0xfffff806604f0000 | 0x00026000 | \SystemRoot\System32\drivers\bthpan.sys
    | \Driver\tdx                   | 0xfffff80669450000 | 0x00023000 | \SystemRoot\system32\DRIVERS\tdx.sys
    | \Driver\vmci                  | 0xfffff80667480000 | 0x0001C000 | \SystemRoot\System32\drivers\vmci.sys
    | \Driver\BTHUSB                | 0xfffff8066a630000 | 0x0001D000 | \SystemRoot\System32\drivers\BTHUSB.sys
    | \Driver\WindowsTrustedRT      | 0xfffff806671b0000 | 0x00017000 | \SystemRoot\system32\drivers\WindowsTrustedRT.sys
    | \Driver\RasPppoe              | 0xfffff8066aff0000 | 0x0001C000 | \SystemRoot\System32\DRIVERS\raspppoe.sys
    | \Driver\HDAudBus              | 0xfffff80669f60000 | 0x0002C000 | \SystemRoot\System32\drivers\HDAudBus.sys
    | \Driver\BasicDisplay          | 0xfffff806699a0000 | 0x00015000 |
\SystemRoot\System32\DriverStore\FileRepository\basicdisplay.inf_amd64_a3f9d7c24b3377b3\BasicDisplay.sys
    | \Driver\rdpbus                | 0xfffff8066a340000 | 0x0000F000 | \SystemRoot\System32\drivers\rdpbus.sys
    | \Driver\pdc                   | 0xfffff80667240000 | 0x0002F000 | \SystemRoot\system32\drivers\pdc.sys
    | \Driver\rspndr                | 0xfffff8065ffd0000 | 0x0001B000 | \SystemRoot\system32\drivers\rspndr.sys
    | \Driver\vmusbmouse            | 0xfffff8066a620000 | 0x00009000 | \SystemRoot\System32\drivers\vmusbmouse.sys
    | \Driver\HdAudAddService       | 0xfffff8066a3f0000 | 0x0007F000 | \SystemRoot\System32\drivers\HdAudio.sys
    | \Driver\mssmbios              | 0xfffff80669be0000 | 0x00010000 | \SystemRoot\System32\drivers\mssmbios.sys
    | \Driver\volmgrx               | 0xfffff806673f0000 | 0x00063000 | \SystemRoot\System32\drivers\volmgrx.sys
    | \Driver\pci                   | 0xfffff80667020000 | 0x00081000 | \SystemRoot\System32\drivers\pci.sys
    | \Driver\NdisVirtualBus        | 0xfffff8066a320000 | 0x0000D000 | \SystemRoot\System32\drivers\NdisVirtualBus.sys
    | \Driver\CmBatt                | 0xfffff8066a290000 | 0x00011000 | \SystemRoot\System32\drivers\CmBatt.sys
    | \Driver\vm3dmp_loader         | 0xfffff80669e60000 | 0x0000A000 | \SystemRoot\system32\DRIVERS\vm3dmp_loader.sys
    | \Driver\kdnic                 | 0xfffff80669d80000 | 0x0000E000 | \SystemRoot\System32\drivers\kdnic.sys
    | \Driver\cdrom                 | 0xfffff80668cd0000 | 0x00030000 | \SystemRoot\System32\drivers\cdrom.sys
    | \Driver\NDIS                  | 0xfffff80667aa0000 | 0x00180000 | \SystemRoot\system32\drivers\ndis.sys
    | \Driver\swenum                | 0xfffff8066a330000 | 0x0000C000 |
\SystemRoot\System32\DriverStore\FileRepository\swenum.inf_amd64_3bf6c0d173eb26c6\swenum.sys
    | \Driver\usbhub                | 0xfffff8066a350000 | 0x00084000 | \SystemRoot\System32\drivers\usbhub.sys
    | \Driver\rdyboost              | 0xfffff80668270000 | 0x0004F000 | \SystemRoot\System32\drivers\rdyboost.sys
    | \Driver\WFPLWFS               | 0xfffff806680c0000 | 0x00030000 | \SystemRoot\System32\drivers\wfplwfs.sys
    | \Driver\Tcpip                 | 0xfffff80667d10000 | 0x00316000 | \SystemRoot\System32\drivers\tcpip.sys
    | \Driver\SgrmAgent             | 0xfffff80666f10000 | 0x0001B000 | \SystemRoot\system32\drivers\SgrmAgent.sys
    | \Driver\USBHUB3               | 0xfffff8066a480000 | 0x000A8000 | \SystemRoot\System32\drivers\UsbHub3.sys
    | \Driver\intelppm              | 0xfffff8066a2d0000 | 0x0004C000 | \SystemRoot\System32\drivers\intelppm.sys
    | \Driver\gencounter            | 0xfffff8066a280000 | 0x0000B000 | \SystemRoot\System32\drivers\vmgencounter.sys
    | \Driver\Beep                  | 0xfffff80668d50000 | 0x0000A000 | \SystemRoot\System32\Drivers\Beep.SYS
    | \Driver\atapi                 | 0xfffff806675d0000 | 0x0000D000 | \SystemRoot\System32\drivers\atapi.sys
    | \Driver\NdisTapi              | 0xfffff8066b010000 | 0x0000F000 | \SystemRoot\System32\DRIVERS\ndistapi.sys
    | \Driver\usbccgp               | 0xfffff8066a530000 | 0x00034000 | \SystemRoot\System32\drivers\usbccgp.sys
    | \Driver\AFD                   | 0xfffff8066a700000 | 0x000A4000 | \SystemRoot\system32\drivers\afd.sys
    | \Driver\mountmgr              | 0xfffff806674a0000 | 0x0001E000 | \SystemRoot\System32\drivers\mountmgr.sys
    | \Driver\intelide              | 0xfffff806673c0000 | 0x0000B000 | \SystemRoot\System32\drivers\intelide.sys
    | \Driver\tcpipreg              | 0xfffff8066aed0000 | 0x00014000 | \SystemRoot\System32\drivers\tcpipreg.sys
    | \Driver\BTHPORT               | 0xfffff806602a0000 | 0x001D6000 | \SystemRoot\System32\drivers\BTHport.sys
    | \Driver\ksthunk               | 0xfffff8066a470000 | 0x0000F000 | \SystemRoot\system32\drivers\ksthunk.sys
    | \Driver\vmmouse               | 0xfffff80669e00000 | 0x00009000 | \SystemRoot\System32\drivers\vmmouse.sys
    | \Driver\afunix                | 0xfffff80668d80000 | 0x00013000 | \SystemRoot\system32\drivers\afunix.sys
    | \Driver\NdisWan               | 0xfffff8066b020000 | 0x0003A000 | \SystemRoot\System32\drivers\ndiswan.sys
    | \Driver\WudfRd                | 0xfffff8065fde0000 | 0x00054000 | \SystemRoot\System32\drivers\WUDFRd.sys
    | \Driver\vm3dmp                | 0xfffff80669e70000 | 0x0004B000 | \SystemRoot\system32\DRIVERS\vm3dmp.sys
    | \Driver\CompositeBus          | 0xfffff80669d60000 | 0x00013000 |
\SystemRoot\System32\DriverStore\FileRepository\compositebus.inf_amd64_ab6e2caeac172387\CompositeBus.sys
    | \Driver\EhStorClass           | 0xfffff80667660000 | 0x00022000 | \SystemRoot\System32\drivers\EhStorClass.sys
    | \Driver\LSI_SAS               | 0xfffff806674c0000 | 0x0001F000 | \SystemRoot\System32\drivers\lsi_sas.sys
    | \Driver\ACPI                  | 0xfffff80666f30000 | 0x000CC000 | \SystemRoot\System32\drivers\ACPI.sys
    | \FileSystem\mrxsmb10          | 0xfffff8066b060000 | 0x00053000 | \SystemRoot\system32\DRIVERS\mrxsmb10.sys
```

```
| \FileSystem\mrxsmb              | 0xfffff8066a650000 | 0x00097000 | \SystemRoot\system32\DRIVERS\mrxsmb.sys
| \FileSystem\mrxsmb20            | 0xfffff80660520000 | 0x00049000 | \SystemRoot\system32\DRIVERS\mrxsmb20.sys
| \FileSystem\storqosflt          | 0xfffff8065ff40000 | 0x0001A000 | \SystemRoot\system32\drivers\storqosflt.sys
| \FileSystem\bindflt             | 0xfffff8065ff60000 | 0x0002A000 | \SystemRoot\system32\drivers\bindflt.sys
| \FileSystem\luafv               | 0xfffff8065fe40000 | 0x0002B000 | \SystemRoot\system32\drivers\luafv.sys
| \FileSystem\CimFS               | 0xfffff80669420000 | 0x00025000 | \SystemRoot\System32\Drivers\CimFS.SYS
| \FileSystem\Wof                 | 0xfffff806676b0000 | 0x00043000 | \SystemRoot\System32\Drivers\Wof.sys
| \FileSystem\vmhgfs              | 0xfffff8066af30000 | 0x0002B000 | \SystemRoot\system32\DRIVERS\vmhgfs.sys
| \FileSystem\rdbss               | 0xfffff80669b30000 | 0x0007A000 | \SystemRoot\system32\DRIVERS\rdbss.sys
| \FileSystem\Fs_Rec              | 0xfffff80667a90000 | 0x0000D000 | \SystemRoot\System32\Drivers\Fs_Rec.sys
| \FileSystem\Msfs                | 0xfffff80669400000 | 0x00011000 | \SystemRoot\System32\Drivers\Msfs.SYS
| \FileSystem\Dfsc                | 0xfffff80669c10000 | 0x0002C000 | \SystemRoot\System32\Drivers\dfsc.sys
| \FileSystem\srvnet              | 0xfffff80668c30000 | 0x00057000 | \SystemRoot\System32\DRIVERS\srvnet.sys
| \FileSystem\wcifs               | 0xfffff8065fe70000 | 0x00038000 | \SystemRoot\system32\drivers\wcifs.sys
| \FileSystem\bowser              | 0xfffff80660220000 | 0x00024000 | \SystemRoot\system32\DRIVERS\bowser.sys
| \FileSystem\FltMgr              | 0xfffff80661580000 | 0x00073000 | \SystemRoot\System32\drivers\FLTMGR.SYS
| \FileSystem\Ntfs                | 0xfffff80667770000 | 0x00315000 | \SystemRoot\System32\Drivers\Ntfs.sys
| \FileSystem\CldFlt              | 0xfffff8065feb0000 | 0x00085000 | \SystemRoot\system32\drivers\cldflt.sys
| \FileSystem\Npfs                | 0xfffff806699e0000 | 0x0001C000 | \SystemRoot\System32\Drivers\Npfs.SYS
| \FileSystem\Mup                 | 0xfffff806682c0000 | 0x00026000 | \SystemRoot\System32\Drivers\mup.sys
| \FileSystem\RAW                 | 0x0000000000000000 | 0x00000000 |
| \FileSystem\WdFilter            | 0xfffff80667700000 | 0x0006C000 | \SystemRoot\system32\drivers\wd\WdFilter.sys
| \FileSystem\fastfat             | 0xfffff80669c70000 | 0x0006C000 | \SystemRoot\System32\Drivers\fastfat.SYS
| \FileSystem\FileInfo            | 0xfffff80667690000 | 0x0001B000 | \SystemRoot\System32\drivers\fileinfo.sys
| \FileSystem\srv2                | 0xfffff8066b0c0000 | 0x000CE000 | \SystemRoot\System32\DRIVERS\srv2.sys
| \FileSystem\NetBIOS             | 0xfffff80669a20000 | 0x00014000 | \SystemRoot\system32\drivers\netbios.sys
| \FileSystem\FileCrypt           | 0xfffff80668d10000 | 0x00015000 | \SystemRoot\system32\drivers\filecrypt.sys
```

When you click on a driver address link, it outputs further information:

```
0: kd> !ms_drivers /object 0xFFFFC38C2E6F9E00
 | \Driver\Beep                   | 0xfffff80668d50000 | 0x0000A000 | \SystemRoot\System32\Drivers\Beep.SYS
PDB:          beep.pdb
\---| IRP_MJ_CREATE                   | 0xFFFFF80668D51510 |    | Beep!BeepOpen
\---| IRP_MJ_CREATE_NAMED_PIPE        | 0xFFFFF80662033C40 |    | nt!IopInvalidDeviceRequest
\---| IRP_MJ_CLOSE                    | 0xFFFFF80668D511B0 |    | Beep!BeepClose
\---| IRP_MJ_READ                     | 0xFFFFF80662033C40 |    | nt!IopInvalidDeviceRequest
\---| IRP_MJ_WRITE                    | 0xFFFFF80662033C40 |    | nt!IopInvalidDeviceRequest
\---| IRP_MJ_QUERY_INFORMATION        | 0xFFFFF80662033C40 |    | nt!IopInvalidDeviceRequest
\---| IRP_MJ_SET_INFORMATION          | 0xFFFFF80662033C40 |    | nt!IopInvalidDeviceRequest
\---| IRP_MJ_QUERY_EA                 | 0xFFFFF80662033C40 |    | nt!IopInvalidDeviceRequest
\---| IRP_MJ_SET_EA                   | 0xFFFFF80662033C40 |    | nt!IopInvalidDeviceRequest
\---| IRP_MJ_FLUSH_BUFFERS            | 0xFFFFF80662033C40 |    | nt!IopInvalidDeviceRequest
\---| IRP_MJ_QUERY_VOLUME_INFORMATION | 0xFFFFF80662033C40 |    | nt!IopInvalidDeviceRequest
\---| IRP_MJ_SET_VOLUME_INFORMATION   | 0xFFFFF80662033C40 |    | nt!IopInvalidDeviceRequest
\---| IRP_MJ_DIRECTORY_CONTROL        | 0xFFFFF80662033C40 |    | nt!IopInvalidDeviceRequest
\---| IRP_MJ_FILE_SYSTEM_CONTROL      | 0xFFFFF80662033C40 |    | nt!IopInvalidDeviceRequest
\---| IRP_MJ_DEVICE_CONTROL           | 0xFFFFF80668D51290 |    | Beep!BeepDeviceControl
\---| IRP_MJ_INTERNAL_DEVICE_CONTROL  | 0xFFFFF80662033C40 |    | nt!IopInvalidDeviceRequest
\---| IRP_MJ_SHUTDOWN                 | 0xFFFFF80662033C40 |    | nt!IopInvalidDeviceRequest
\---| IRP_MJ_LOCK_CONTROL             | 0xFFFFF80662033C40 |    | nt!IopInvalidDeviceRequest
\---| IRP_MJ_CLEANUP                  | 0xFFFFF80668D51070 |    | Beep!BeepCleanup
\---| IRP_MJ_CREATE_MAILSLOT          | 0xFFFFF80662033C40 |    | nt!IopInvalidDeviceRequest
\---| IRP_MJ_QUERY_SECURITY           | 0xFFFFF80662033C40 |    | nt!IopInvalidDeviceRequest
\---| IRP_MJ_SET_SECURITY             | 0xFFFFF80662033C40 |    | nt!IopInvalidDeviceRequest
\---| IRP_MJ_POWER                    | 0xFFFFF80662033C40 |    | nt!IopInvalidDeviceRequest
\---| IRP_MJ_SYSTEM_CONTROL           | 0xFFFFF80662033C40 |    | nt!IopInvalidDeviceRequest
\---| IRP_MJ_DEVICE_CHANGE            | 0xFFFFF80662033C40 |    | nt!IopInvalidDeviceRequest
\---| IRP_MJ_QUERY_QUOTA              | 0xFFFFF80662033C40 |    | nt!IopInvalidDeviceRequest
\---| IRP_MJ_SET_QUOTA                | 0xFFFFF80662033C40 |    | nt!IopInvalidDeviceRequest
\---| IRP_MJ_PNP                      | 0xFFFFF80662033C40 |    | nt!IopInvalidDeviceRequest
```

8. There's also a possibility to navigate registry hives (whatever is accessible in the saved memory dump):

```
0: kd> !ms_hivelist

 |-----------------------|-------------------|----------------------------------------------------------|----------------------------------------------------------
 | Hive ('U' = Untrusted) | Key Node          | Hive Root Path                                           | File User Name
 |-----------------------|-------------------|----------------------------------------------------------|----------------------------------------------------------
 | 0xFFFFAC8A04296000 (T) | 0xFFFFAC8A042CA024 |                                                         |
 | 0xFFFFAC8A0427D000 (T) | 0xFFFFAC8A04DFF024 | \REGISTRY\MACHINE\SYSTEM                                |
 | 0xFFFFAC8A042F3000 (T) | 0xFFFFAC8A04323024 | \REGISTRY\MACHINE\HARDWARE                              |
 | 0xFFFFAC8A04E99000 (T) | 0x1CECAFD1024 | \REGISTRY\MACHINE\SOFTWARE                                   | \SystemRoot\System32\Config\SOFTWARE
 | 0xFFFFAC8A07D4F000 (U) | 0x1CECFDD1024 | \REGISTRY\MACHINE\BCD00000000                                | \Device\HarddiskVolume2\EFI\Microsoft\Boot\BCD
 | 0xFFFFAC8A043C6000 (U) | 0x1CECFDE1024 | \REGISTRY\USER\.DEFAULT                                      | \SystemRoot\System32\Config\DEFAULT
 | 0xFFFFAC8A07F23000 (T) | 0x1CECFE21024 | \REGISTRY\MACHINE\SECURITY                                   | \SystemRoot\System32\Config\SECURITY
 | 0xFFFFAC8A07FA8000 (T) | 0x1CECFE31024 | \REGISTRY\MACHINE\SAM                                        | \SystemRoot\System32\Config\SAM
 | 0xFFFFAC8A0805D000 (U) | 0x1CECFE41024 | \REGISTRY\USER\S-1-5-19                                      | \??\C:\WINDOWS\ServiceProfiles\LocalService\NTUSER.DAT
 | 0xFFFFAC8A080EF000 (U) | 0x1CECFE81024 | \REGISTRY\USER\S-1-5-20                                      | \??\C:\WINDOWS\ServiceProfiles\NetworkService\NTUSER.DAT
 | 0xFFFFAC8A082F0000 (U) | 0x1CECFEC1024 | \REGISTRY\A\{58b9ca97-8c6a-4d3f-b2a3-094dc2a5ef22}          | \SystemRoot\System32\Config\BBI
 | 0xFFFFAC8A09C93000 (U) | 0x1CECFF41024 | \REGISTRY\A\{5df3caa2-bec8-3361-e266-b8431f2000aa}          | \??\C:\WINDOWS\AppCompat\Programs\Amcache.hve
```

```
    | 0xFFFFAC8A09D28000 (U) | 0x1CED01C1024 | \REGISTRY\USER\S-1-5-21-3407489871-1359576761-456439074-1001          | \??\C:\Users\dumpa\ntuser.dat
    | 0xFFFFAC8A09CBF000 (U) | 0x1CED03C1024 | \REGISTRY\USER\S-1-5-21-3407489871-1359576761-456439074-1001_Classes  | \??\C:\Users\dumpa\AppData\Local\Microsoft\Windows\UsrClass.dat
    | 0xFFFFAC8A0A08A000 (U) | 0x1CED0AD1024 | \REGISTRY\MACHINE\DRIVERS                                             | \SystemRoot\System32\config\DRIVERS
    | 0xFFFFAC8A0A572000 (U) | 0x1CED0ED1024 | \REGISTRY\A\{755A1558-926B-47B2-942C-1FEAB054C3F6}                    |
\??\C:\ProgramData\Microsoft\Windows\AppRepository\Packages\MicrosoftWindows.Client.CBS_1000.22000.318.0_x64__cw5n1h2txyewy\ActivationStore.dat
    | 0xFFFFAC8A0A76B000 (U) | 0x1CED0F51024 | \REGISTRY\A\{05A54F95-D223-4331-92DC-E6C4B7680B91}                    |
\??\C:\ProgramData\Microsoft\Windows\AppRepository\Packages\Microsoft.UI.Xaml.CBS_2.62107.16001.0_x64__8wekyb3d8bbwe\ActivationStore.dat
    | 0xFFFFAC8A0AD9D000 (U) | 0x1CED0F71024 | \REGISTRY\A\{70876E76-6001-47B1-9DAD-0CA5C029FA64}                    |
\??\C:\ProgramData\Microsoft\Windows\AppRepository\Packages\Microsoft.Windows.StartMenuExperienceHost_10.0.22000.37_neutral_neutral_cw5n1h2txyewy\ActivationStore.dat
    | 0xFFFFAC8A0AD6D000 (U) | 0x1CED0F81024 | \REGISTRY\A\{025b49a0-05be-bbd8-8415-1c3d25581023}                    |
\??\C:\Users\dumpa\AppData\Local\Packages\MicrosoftWindows.Client.CBS_cw5n1h2txyewy\Settings\settings.dat
    | 0xFFFFAC8A0B2F3000 (U) | 0x1CED0F91024 | \REGISTRY\A\{63c66628-2adb-67b5-7980-54dc022f0877}                    |
\??\C:\Users\dumpa\AppData\Local\Packages\Microsoft.Windows.StartMenuExperienceHost_cw5n1h2txyewy\Settings\settings.dat
    | 0xFFFFAC8A0BC19000 (U) | 0x1CED0FA1024 | \REGISTRY\A\{85ED0ABD-CE0E-40E4-B36B-5E5E48841A3B}                    |
\??\C:\ProgramData\Microsoft\Windows\AppRepository\Packages\Microsoft.YourPhone_1.21092.149.0_x64__8wekyb3d8bbwe\ActivationStore.dat
    | 0xFFFFAC8A0BC1B000 (U) | 0x1CED1021024 | \REGISTRY\A\{59f1955c-8769-ab06-f595-896286b3611a}                    |
\??\C:\Users\dumpa\AppData\Local\Packages\Microsoft.YourPhone_8wekyb3d8bbwe\Settings\settings.dat
    | 0xFFFFAC8A0C2D4000 (U) | 0x1CED1071024 | \REGISTRY\A\{7AA29EF5-CE3B-4739-A0F3-D335F3524EAE}                    |
\??\C:\ProgramData\Microsoft\Windows\AppRepository\Packages\Microsoft.549981C3F5F10_3.2109.6305.0_x64__8wekyb3d8bbwe\ActivationStore.dat
    | 0xFFFFAC8A0C58E000 (U) | 0x1CED1091024 | \REGISTRY\A\{67f029a6-96bb-adaa-c0f6-6674aa081624}                    |
\??\C:\Users\dumpa\AppData\Local\Packages\Microsoft.549981C3F5F10_8wekyb3d8bbwe\Settings\settings.dat
    | 0xFFFFAC8A0C4CB000 (U) | 0x1CED10A1024 | \REGISTRY\A\{24A27D02-F79D-468A-AAA6-4691C9476502}                    |
\??\C:\ProgramData\Microsoft\Windows\AppRepository\Packages\Microsoft.UI.Xaml.2.4_2.42007.9001.0_x64__8wekyb3d8bbwe\ActivationStore.dat
    | 0xFFFFAC8A0B903000 (U) | 0x1CED1121024 | \REGISTRY\A\{542ec78d-f0de-892c-e096-46cc8228986d}                    |
\??\C:\WINDOWS\ServiceProfiles\NetworkService\AppData\Local\Microsoft\Windows\DeliveryOptimization\State\dosvcState.dat
```

```
0: kd> !ms_readknode 0xFFFFAC8A0427D000 0xFFFFAC8A04DFF024
 Key node ROOT contains 0 key values and 18 subkeys.

 [*] Subkeys (18):
   [ 0] 0xFFFFAC8A07072C1C | ActivationBroker          | LastWriteTime: 06/05/2021  13:11 UTC
   [ 1] 0xFFFFAC8A04DFF174 | ControlSet001             | LastWriteTime: 06/05/2021  13:11 UTC
   [ 2] 0xFFFFAC8A04F5A984 | DriverDatabase            | LastWriteTime: 11/12/2021  22:55 UTC
   [ 3] 0xFFFFAC8A07814654 |  Ê                        | LastWriteTime: 07/03/17948  02:38 UTC
   [ 4] 0xFFFFAC8A07073D74 | Input                     | LastWriteTime: 06/05/2021  13:11 UTC
   [ 5] 0xFFFFAC8A0707417C | Keyboard Layout           | LastWriteTime: 06/05/2021  18:09 UTC
   [ 6] 0xFFFFAC8A070743F4 | Maps                      | LastWriteTime: 11/12/2021  22:51 UTC
   [ 7] 0xFFFFAC8A0704890C | MountedDevices            | LastWriteTime: 11/12/2021  22:35 UTC
   [ 8] 0xFFFFAC8A070748E4 | ResourceManager           | LastWriteTime: 06/05/2021  13:11 UTC
   [ 9] 0xFFFFAC8A07074A2C | ResourcePolicyStore       | LastWriteTime: 06/05/2021  13:11 UTC
   [10] 0xFFFFAC8A07089B3C | RNG                       | LastWriteTime: 11/13/2021  22:14 UTC
   [11] 0xFFFFAC8A0707204C | Select                    | LastWriteTime: 06/05/2021  13:11 UTC
   [12] 0xFFFFAC8A07072124 | Setup                     | LastWriteTime: 11/13/2021  22:07 UTC
   [13] 0xFFFFAC8A07072534 | Software                  | LastWriteTime: 06/05/2021  13:11 UTC
   [14] 0xFFFFAC8A07089C3C | State                     | LastWriteTime: 06/05/2021  13:11 UTC
   [15] 0xFFFFAC8A0781CD7C | df8f5037}                 | LastWriteTime: 10/17/24018  00:22 UTC
   [16] 0xFFFFAC8A07089D8C | WPA                       | LastWriteTime: 11/12/2021  22:48 UTC
   [ 0] 0xFFFFAC8A04319024 | CurrentControlSet
```

```
0: kd> !ms_readknode 0xFFFFAC8A0427D000 0xFFFFAC8A07072534
 Key node Software contains 0 key values and 1 subkeys.

 [*] Subkeys (1):
   [ 0] 0xFFFFAC8A0707258C | Microsoft                 | LastWriteTime: 06/05/2021  18:09 UTC
```

```
0: kd> !ms_readknode 0xFFFFAC8A0427D000 0xFFFFAC8A0707258C
 Key node Microsoft contains 2 key values and 4 subkeys.

 [*] Subkeys (4):
   [ 0] 0xFFFFAC8A070726EC | BuildLayers               | LastWriteTime: 06/05/2021  13:11 UTC
   [ 1] 0xFFFFAC8A07089F5C | CTF                       | LastWriteTime: 06/05/2021  18:09 UTC
   [ 2] 0xFFFFAC8A07072ACC | ServicingLayers           | LastWriteTime: 06/05/2021  13:11 UTC
   [ 3] 0xFFFFAC8A0708A334 | TIP                       | LastWriteTime: 11/12/2021  22:56 UTC

 [*] Values (2):
   [ 0] 0xFFFFAC8A070725EC | BuildLab          |       22000.co_release.210604-1628 (REG_SZ)
   [ 1] 0xFFFFAC8A0707265C | BuildLabEx        |       22000.1.amd64fre.co_release.210604-1628 (REG_SZ)
```

9. There's a faster alternative to the **!object ** command:

```
0: kd> !ms_object

Object: \ (Directory)
|------|----------------------|-------------------|------------------------------------------------|
| Hdle | Object Type          | Addr              | Name                                           |
|------|----------------------|-------------------|------------------------------------------------|
| 0000 | Mutant               | 0xFFFFC38C2E5BD510 | PendingRenameMutex
| 0000 | Directory            | 0xFFFFAC8A0421C200 | ObjectTypes
| 0000 | FilterConnectionPort | 0xFFFFC38C317F2D10 | storqosfltport
| 0000 | FilterConnectionPort | 0xFFFFC38C2CD41B00 | MicrosoftMalwareProtectionRemoteIoPortWD
| 0000 | SymbolicLink         | 0xFFFFAC8A04273D40 | SystemRoot
| 0000 | Directory            | 0xFFFFAC8A048A3560 | Sessions
| 0000 | FilterConnectionPort | 0xFFFFC38C2CD41A50 | MicrosoftMalwareProtectionVeryLowIoPortWD
| 0000 | ALPC Port            | 0xFFFFC38C2C5DFB40 | SleepstudyControlPort
| 0000 | Directory            | 0xFFFFAC8A04256C80 | ArcName
| 0000 | FilterConnectionPort | 0xFFFFC38C31637EC0 | WcifsPort
| 0000 | Directory            | 0xFFFFAC8A0433B5E0 | NLS
| 0000 | Event                | 0xFFFFC38C318055E0 | LanmanServerAnnounceEvent
| 0000 | ALPC Port            | 0xFFFFC38C3190DBB0 | ThemeApiPort
| 0000 | Directory            | 0xFFFFAC8A049FDCE0 | Windows
| 0000 | Directory            | 0xFFFFAC8A04230060 | GLOBAL??
| 0000 | Directory            | 0xFFFFAC8A049FC0C0 | RPC Control
| 0000 | ALPC Port            | 0xFFFFC38C2CDC89F0 | PdcPort
| 0000 | Event                | 0xFFFFC38C2E8D6260 | EFSInitEvent
| 0000 | SymbolicLink         | 0xFFFFAC8A04A39310 | Dfs
| 0000 | Device               | 0xFFFFC38C2C56CC90 | clfs
| 0000 | Event                | 0xFFFFC38C2CC80530 | CsrSbSyncEvent
| 0000 | ALPC Port            | 0xFFFFC38C2E00DC60 | SeRmCommandPort
| 0000 | SymbolicLink         | 0xFFFFAC8A0421C060 | DosDevices
| 0000 | Directory            | 0xFFFFAC8A048A2660 | KnownDlls32
| 0000 | Key                  | 0xFFFFAC8A04248CC0 | \REGISTRY
| 0000 | Directory            | 0xFFFFAC8A04392A20 | BaseNamedObjects
| 0000 | Section              | 0xFFFFAC8A07DCC130 | Win32kCrossSessionGlobals
| 0000 | ALPC Port            | 0xFFFFC38C2C5DFDA0 | PowerPort
| 0000 | ALPC Port            | 0xFFFFC38C30577B20 | SmSsWinStationApiPort
| 0000 | Event                | 0xFFFFC38C2CC7C4D0 | UniqueInteractiveSessionIdEvent
| 0000 | Directory            | 0xFFFFAC8A0433CE60 | UMDFCommunicationPorts
```

```
| 0000 | Directory            | 0xFFFFAC8A04BA22A0 | KnownDlls
| 0000 | Device               | 0xFFFFC38C2EFB22D0 | FatCdrom
| 0000 | Device               | 0xFFFFC38C2EFB2500 | Fat
| 0000 | ALPC Port            | 0xFFFFC38C2C602B40 | PowerMonitorPort
| 0000 | Event                | 0xFFFFC38C2CC8EDB0 | DSYSDBG.Debug.Trace.Memory.298
| 0000 | Device               | 0xFFFFC38C2CDCA060 | Ntfs
| 0000 | Directory            | 0xFFFFAC8A0433C920 | FileSystem
| 0000 | Directory            | 0xFFFFAC8A0424ADA0 | KernelObjects
| 0000 | FilterConnectionPort | 0xFFFFC38C2CD414D0 | MicrosoftMalwareProtectionControlPortWD
| 0000 | ALPC Port            | 0xFFFFC38C3042CDD0 | SeLsaCommandPort
| 0000 | Directory            | 0xFFFFAC8A0423BB50 | Callback
| 0000 | FilterConnectionPort | 0xFFFFC38C317F34A0 | BindFltPort
| 0000 | Directory            | 0xFFFFAC8A042F88D0 | DriverStore
| 0000 | Directory            | 0xFFFFAC8A042134B0 | Security
| 0000 | FilterConnectionPort | 0xFFFFC38C2CD42340 | MicrosoftMalwareProtectionAsyncPortWD
| 0000 | Directory            | 0xFFFFAC8A04273430 | Device
| 0000 | SymbolicLink         | 0xFFFFAC8A046BCD10 | DriverData
| 0000 | ALPC Port            | 0xFFFFC38C2EA7BB70 | SmApiPort
| 0000 | FilterConnectionPort | 0xFFFFC38C317F2160 | CLDMSGPORT
| 0000 | FilterConnectionPort | 0xFFFFC38C2CD42080 | MicrosoftMalwareProtectionPortWD
| 0000 | SymbolicLink         | 0xFFFFAC8A04273AE0 | OSDataRoot
| 0000 | Event                | 0xFFFFC38C2CC91510 | SAM_SERVICE_STARTED
| 0000 | Directory            | 0xFFFFAC8A0433B7A0 | Driver
| 0000 | SymbolicLink         | 0xFFFFAC8A042B77B0 | DriverStores
|------|----------------------|--------------------|------------------------------------------------------------------------|
```

10. Yet another SSDT listing command but with the ability to disassemble the first instruction when DML is enabled:

```
0: kd> !ms_ssdt
    |-------|--------------------|-------------------------------------------------------|---------|--------|
    | Index | Address            | Name                                                  | Patched | Hooked |
    |-------|--------------------|-------------------------------------------------------|---------|--------|
    |     0 | 0xFFFFF8066209DEA0 | nt!NtAccessCheck                                      |         |        |
    |     1 | 0xFFFFF80662035150 | nt!NtWorkerFactoryWorkerReady                         |         |        |
    |     2 | 0xFFFFF806624B4DF0 | nt!NtAcceptConnectPort                                |         |        |
    |     3 | 0xFFFFF8066277BAE0 | nt!NtMapUserPhysicalPagesScatter                      |         |        |
    |     4 | 0xFFFFF8066256A4B0 | nt!NtWaitForSingleObject                              |         |        |
    |     5 | 0xFFFFF80662219260 | nt!NtCallbackReturn                                   |         |        |
    |     6 | 0xFFFFF80662580090 | nt!NtReadFile                                         |         |        |
    |     7 | 0xFFFFF8066256A670 | nt!NtDeviceIoControlFile                              |         |        |
    |     8 | 0xFFFFF806624EE280 | nt!NtWriteFile                                        |         |        |
    |     9 | 0xFFFFF8066257FE30 | nt!NtRemoveIoCompletion                               |         |        |
    |    10 | 0xFFFFF806624ED0D0 | nt!NtReleaseSemaphore                                 |         |        |
    |    11 | 0xFFFFF8066254B5B0 | nt!NtReplyWaitReceivePort                             |         |        |
    |    12 | 0xFFFFF80662524710 | nt!NtReplyPort                                        |         |        |
    |    13 | 0xFFFFF8066256FF60 | nt!NtSetInformationThread                             |         |        |
    |    14 | 0xFFFFF8066246FF60 | nt!NtSetEvent                                         |         |        |
    |    15 | 0xFFFFF8066256B880 | nt!NtClose                                            |         |        |
    |    16 | 0xFFFFF806625225F0 | nt!NtQueryObject                                      |         |        |
    |    17 | 0xFFFFF806624F6520 | nt!NtQueryInformationFile                             |         |        |
    |    18 | 0xFFFFF806624762E0 | nt!NtOpenKey                                          |         |        |
    |    19 | 0xFFFFF80662472F50 | nt!NtEnumerateValueKey                                |         |        |
    |    20 | 0xFFFFF8066258A1B0 | nt!NtFindAtom                                         |         |        |
    |    21 | 0xFFFFF806624E7C50 | nt!NtQueryDefaultLocale                               |         |        |
    |    22 | 0xFFFFF8066257AA80 | nt!NtQueryKey                                         |         |        |
    |    23 | 0xFFFFF80662554C40 | nt!NtQueryValueKey                                    |         |        |
    |    24 | 0xFFFFF806624E2C90 | nt!NtAllocateVirtualMemory                            |         |        |
    |    25 | 0xFFFFF806625825E0 | nt!NtQueryInformationProcess                          |         |        |
    |    26 | 0xFFFFF80662486720 | nt!NtWaitForMultipleObjects32                         |         |        |
    |    27 | 0xFFFFF806624BF2C0 | nt!NtWriteFileGather                                  |         |        |
    |    28 | 0xFFFFF806624E0280 | nt!NtSetInformationProcess                            |         |        |
    |    29 | 0xFFFFF8066251A6E0 | nt!NtCreateKey                                        |         |        |
    |    30 | 0xFFFFF80662575C80 | nt!NtFreeVirtualMemory                                |         |        |
    |    31 | 0xFFFFF80662763940 | nt!NtImpersonateClientOfPort                          |         |        |
    |    32 | 0xFFFFF806624FABE0 | nt!NtReleaseMutant                                    |         |        |
    |    33 | 0xFFFFF806624F8570 | nt!NtQueryInformationToken                            |         |        |
    |    34 | 0xFFFFF8066248D660 | nt!NtRequestWaitReplyPort                             |         |        |
    |    35 | 0xFFFFF80662576AA0 | nt!NtQueryVirtualMemory                               |         |        |
    |    36 | 0xFFFFF806624F56B0 | nt!NtOpenThreadToken                                  |         |        |
    |    37 | 0xFFFFF8066255E8C0 | nt!NtQueryInformationThread                           |         |        |
    |    38 | 0xFFFFF8066255F3D0 | nt!NtOpenProcess                                      |         |        |
    |    39 | 0xFFFFF806620981F0 | nt!NtSetInformationFile                               |         |        |
    |    40 | 0xFFFFF806625633A0 | nt!NtMapViewOfSection                                 |         |        |
    |    41 | 0xFFFFF806624F0050 | nt!NtAccessCheckAndAuditAlarm                         |         |        |
    |    42 | 0xFFFFF80662589660 | nt!NtUnmapViewOfSection                               |         |        |
    |    43 | 0xFFFFF8066254B5D0 | nt!NtReplyWaitReceivePortEx                           |         |        |
    |    44 | 0xFFFFF80662599A80 | nt!NtTerminateProcess                                 |         |        |
    |    45 | 0xFFFFF806627F8A20 | nt!NtSetEventBoostPriority                            |         |        |
    |    46 | 0xFFFFF8066249FFF0 | nt!NtReadFileScatter                                  |         |        |
    |    47 | 0xFFFFF806624F56D0 | nt!NtOpenThreadTokenEx                                |         |        |
    |    48 | 0xFFFFF8066255F9F0 | nt!NtOpenProcessTokenEx                               |         |        |
    |    49 | 0xFFFFF8066248A940 | nt!NtQueryPerformanceCounter                          |         |        |
    |    50 | 0xFFFFF8066255B890 | nt!NtEnumerateKey                                     |         |        |
    |    51 | 0xFFFFF806625055E0 | nt!NtOpenFile                                         |         |        |
    |    52 | 0xFFFFF8066257FD50 | nt!NtDelayExecution                                   |         |        |
    |    53 | 0xFFFFF806624E5A80 | nt!NtQueryDirectoryFile                               |         |        |
```

54	0xFFFFF80662582440	nt!NtQuerySystemInformation		
55	0xFFFFF806625D4540	nt!NtOpenSection		
56	0xFFFFF806627F8810	nt!NtQueryTimer		
57	0xFFFFF80662486870	nt!NtFsControlFile		
58	0xFFFFF80662546A40	nt!NtWriteVirtualMemory		
59	0xFFFFF80662495710	nt!NtCloseObjectAuditAlarm		
60	0xFFFFF8066258B020	nt!NtDuplicateObject		
61	0xFFFFF806625061F0	nt!NtQueryAttributesFile		
62	0xFFFFF80662476B90	nt!NtClearEvent		
63	0xFFFFF80662546A70	nt!NtReadVirtualMemory		
64	0xFFFFF806625D4470	nt!NtOpenEvent		
65	0xFFFFF80662542A10	nt!NtAdjustPrivilegesToken		
66	0xFFFFF80662560310	nt!NtDuplicateToken		
67	0xFFFFF80662215CC0	nt!NtContinue		
68	0xFFFFF806625DCFE0	nt!NtQueryDefaultUILanguage		
69	0xFFFFF806624C4410	nt!NtQueueApcThread		
70	0xFFFFF8066200C550	nt!NtYieldExecution		
71	0xFFFFF806627FF950	nt!NtAddAtom		
72	0xFFFFF806624D2170	nt!NtCreateEvent		
73	0xFFFFF806624F6E40	nt!NtQueryVolumeInformationFile		
74	0xFFFFF806625640D0	nt!NtCreateSection		
75	0xFFFFF80662497BE0	nt!NtFlushBuffersFile		
76	0xFFFFF806625B1180	nt!NtApphelpCacheControl		
77	0xFFFFF806627AA6C0	nt!NtCreateProcessEx		
78	0xFFFFF806627AA760	nt!NtCreateThread		
79	0xFFFFF80662596EC0	nt!NtIsProcessInJob		
80	0xFFFFF80662574E50	nt!NtProtectVirtualMemory		
81	0xFFFFF806624813F0	nt!NtQuerySection		
82	0xFFFFF806624928C0	nt!NtResumeThread		
83	0xFFFFF80662546720	nt!NtTerminateThread		
84	0xFFFFF80662763A40	nt!NtReadRequestData		
85	0xFFFFF80662505650	nt!NtCreateFile		
86	0xFFFFF806624AA5B0	nt!NtQueryEvent		
87	0xFFFFF80662763BC0	nt!NtWriteRequestData		
88	0xFFFFF80662477800	nt!NtOpenDirectoryObject		
89	0xFFFFF806624980F0	nt!NtAccessCheckByTypeAndAuditAlarm		
90	0xFFFFF806627F54E0	nt!NtQuerySystemTime		
91	0xFFFFF806624729C0	nt!NtWaitForMultipleObjects		
92	0xFFFFF80662465EF0	nt!NtSetInformationObject		
93	0xFFFFF80662479770	nt!NtCancelIoFile		
94	0xFFFFF8066209EC30	nt!NtTraceEvent		
95	0xFFFFF806625A34F0	nt!NtPowerInformation		
96	0xFFFFF806624F0440	nt!NtSetValueKey		
97	0xFFFFF806620C0050	nt!NtCancelTimer		
98	0xFFFFF8066216FD80	nt!NtSetTimer		
99	0xFFFFF80662036420	nt!NtAccessCheckByType		
100	0xFFFFF806623EF6B0	nt!NtAccessCheckByTypeResultList		
101	0xFFFFF806627C8430	nt!NtAccessCheckByTypeResultListAndAuditAlarm		
102	0xFFFFF806627C84E0	nt!NtAccessCheckByTypeResultListAndAuditAlarmByHandle		
103	0xFFFFF806627FFA70	nt!NtAcquireCrossVmMutant		
104	0xFFFFF806624BC070	nt!NtAcquireProcessActivityReference		
105	0xFFFFF80662497F70	nt!NtAddAtomEx		
106	0xFFFFF806627FC540	nt!NtAddBootEntry		
107	0xFFFFF806627FC570	nt!NtAddDriverEntry		
108	0xFFFFF80662499E50	nt!NtAdjustGroupsToken		
109	0xFFFFF806625DD710	nt!NT_DISK::GetPnpProperty		
110	0xFFFFF806627B0690	nt!NtAlertResumeThread		
111	0xFFFFF806627B07B0	nt!NtAlertThread		
112	0xFFFFF8066254BC30	nt!NtAlertThreadByThreadId		
113	0xFFFFF80662475120	nt!NtAllocateLocallyUniqueId		
114	0xFFFFF806624B4010	nt!NtAllocateReserveObject		
115	0xFFFFF8066277B210	nt!NtAllocateUserPhysicalPages		
116	0xFFFFF8066277B230	nt!NtAllocateUserPhysicalPagesEx		
117	0xFFFFF80662599F40	nt!NtAllocateUuids		
118	0xFFFFF806624E2920	nt!NtAllocateVirtualMemoryEx		
119	0xFFFFF806625271F0	nt!NtAlpcAcceptConnectPort		
120	0xFFFFF806624C07F0	nt!NtAlpcCancelMessage		
121	0xFFFFF80662524A90	nt!NtAlpcConnectPort		
122	0xFFFFF806625248B0	nt!NtAlpcConnectPortEx		
123	0xFFFFF8066249EA40	nt!NtAlpcCreatePort		
124	0xFFFFF8066252BF90	nt!NtAlpcCreatePortSection		
125	0xFFFFF806624A4DC0	nt!NtAlpcCreateResourceReserve		
126	0xFFFFF80662528CF0	nt!NtAlpcCreateSectionView		
127	0xFFFFF80662529900	nt!NtAlpcCreateSecurityContext		

128	0xFFFFF8066252BEA0	nt!NtAlpcDeletePortSection			
129	0xFFFFF8066266A690	nt!NtAlpcDeleteResourceReserve			
130	0xFFFFF8066252C870	nt!NtAlpcDeleteSectionView			
131	0xFFFFF80662529800	nt!NtAlpcDeleteSecurityContext			
132	0xFFFFF80662523A20	nt!NtAlpcDisconnectPort			
133	0xFFFFF80662763D10	nt!NtAlpcImpersonateClientContainerOfPort			
134	0xFFFFF806624F7BB0	nt!NtAlpcImpersonateClientOfPort			
135	0xFFFFF80662526EE0	nt!NtAlpcOpenSenderProcess			
136	0xFFFFF8066247F7E0	nt!NtAlpcOpenSenderThread			
137	0xFFFFF8066246EA40	nt!NtAlpcQueryInformation			
138	0xFFFFF8066252B9F0	nt!NtAlpcQueryInformationMessage			
139	0xFFFFF80662763F60	nt!NtAlpcRevokeSecurityContext			
140	0xFFFFF8066254C8B0	nt!NtAlpcSendWaitReceivePort			
141	0xFFFFF806625A28F0	nt!NtAlpcSetInformation			
142	0xFFFFF806625E36E0	nt!NtAreMappedFilesTheSame			
143	0xFFFFF80662596BE0	nt!NtAssignProcessToJobObject			
144	0xFFFFF806620D3DF0	nt!NtAssociateWaitCompletionPacket			
145	0xFFFFF8066221EAA0	nt!NtCallEnclave			
146	0xFFFFF806624A9E80	nt!NtCancelIoFileEx			
147	0xFFFFF80662734DB0	nt!NtCancelSynchronousIoFile			
148	0xFFFFF80662167900	nt!NtCancelTimer2			
149	0xFFFFF8066202F0A0	nt!NtCancelWaitCompletionPacket			
150	0xFFFFF806627AC670	nt!NtChangeProcessState			
151	0xFFFFF806627AC860	nt!NtChangeThreadState			
152	0xFFFFF806621D9280	nt!NtCommitComplete			
153	0xFFFFF806621D92A0	nt!NtCommitEnlistment			
154	0xFFFFF80662455EE0	nt!NtCommitRegistryTransaction			
155	0xFFFFF806621D92C0	nt!NtCommitTransaction			
156	0xFFFFF8066270B740	nt!NtCompactKeys			
157	0xFFFFF8066248BE50	nt!NtCompareObjects			
158	0xFFFFF806624C0EC0	nt!NtCompareSigningLevels			
159	0xFFFFF80662494E00	nt!NtCompareTokens			
160	0xFFFFF806624B6860	nt!ArbPreprocessEntry			
161	0xFFFFF8066270BA10	nt!NtCompressKey			
162	0xFFFFF80662523AC0	nt!NtConnectPort			
163	0xFFFFF80662215CD0	nt!NtContinueEx			
164	0xFFFFF80662803800	nt!NtConvertBetweenAuxiliaryCounterAndPerformanceCounter			
165	0xFFFFF806627F8970	nt!NtCreateCrossVmEvent			
166	0xFFFFF806627FFB40	nt!NtCreateCrossVmMutant			
167	0xFFFFF80662726760	nt!NtCreateDebugObject			
168	0xFFFFF8066247C040	nt!NtCreateDirectoryObject			
169	0xFFFFF8066247C020	nt!NtCreateDirectoryObjectEx			
170	0xFFFFF80662778590	nt!NtCreateEnclave			
171	0xFFFFF806621D92E0	nt!NtCreateEnlistment			
172	0xFFFFF806625DD710	nt!NT_DISK::GetPnpProperty			
173	0xFFFFF806624C6AE0	nt!NtCreateIRTimer			
174	0xFFFFF80662492D10	nt!NtCreateIoCompletion			
175	0xFFFFF806627368C0	nt!NtCreateIoRing			
176	0xFFFFF806625966C0	nt!NtCreateJobObject			
177	0xFFFFF806625DD640	nt!ArbAddReserved			
178	0xFFFFF80662519E50	nt!NtCreateKeyTransacted			
179	0xFFFFF8066263C0F0	nt!NtCreateKeyedEvent			
180	0xFFFFF806624D9F00	nt!NtCreateLowBoxToken			
181	0xFFFFF8066245A9F0	nt!NtCreateMailslotFile			
182	0xFFFFF8066247EB70	nt!NtCreateMutant			
183	0xFFFFF806624A90D0	nt!NtCreateNamedPipeFile			
184	0xFFFFF80662631D00	nt!NtCreatePagingFile			
185	0xFFFFF806627B0D50	nt!NtCreatePartition			
186	0xFFFFF8066249E9F0	nt!NtCreatePort			
187	0xFFFFF806624D7400	nt!NtCreatePrivateNamespace			
188	0xFFFFF806627AA630	nt!NtCreateProcess			
189	0xFFFFF806627ACA50	nt!NtCreateProcessStateChange			
190	0xFFFFF80662803930	nt!NtCreateProfile			
191	0xFFFFF80662803A10	nt!NtCreateProfileEx			
192	0xFFFFF806624BDCF0	nt!NtCreateRegistryTransaction			
193	0xFFFFF806621D9300	nt!NtCreateResourceManager			
194	0xFFFFF80662769980	nt!NtCreateSectionEx			
195	0xFFFFF8066258DEF0	nt!NtCreateSemaphore			
196	0xFFFFF8066247C390	nt!NtCreateSymbolicLinkObject			
197	0xFFFFF806624EAA10	nt!NtCreateThreadEx			
198	0xFFFFF806627ACC60	nt!NtCreateThreadStateChange			
199	0xFFFFF8066258FA80	nt!NtCreateTimer			
200	0xFFFFF806625A31A0	nt!NtCreateTimer2			
201	0xFFFFF806627C9AB0	nt!NtCreateToken			

202	0xFFFFF80662541580	nt!NtCreateTokenEx			
203	0xFFFFF806621D9320	nt!NtCreateTransaction			
204	0xFFFFF806621D9340	nt!NtCreateTransactionManager			
205	0xFFFFF80662504340	nt!NtCreateUserProcess			
206	0xFFFFF806624847D0	nt!NtCreateWaitCompletionPacket			
207	0xFFFFF8066249E9A0	nt!NtCreateWaitablePort			
208	0xFFFFF806625077F0	nt!NtCreateWnfStateName			
209	0xFFFFF806625A2E20	nt!NtCreateWorkerFactory			
210	0xFFFFF80662726970	nt!NtDebugActiveProcess			
211	0xFFFFF80662726B90	nt!NtDebugContinue			
212	0xFFFFF80662469310	nt!NtDeleteAtom			
213	0xFFFFF806627FC5A0	nt!NtDeleteBootEntry			
214	0xFFFFF806627FC730	nt!NtDeleteDriverEntry			
215	0xFFFFF806625F9700	nt!NtDeleteFile			
216	0xFFFFF80662517B70	nt!NtDeleteKey			
217	0xFFFFF806627C85A0	nt!NtDeleteObjectAuditAlarm			
218	0xFFFFF806625E1390	nt!NtDeletePrivateNamespace			
219	0xFFFFF8066250DA20	nt!NtDeleteValueKey			
220	0xFFFFF80662646940	nt!NtDeleteWnfStateData			
221	0xFFFFF80662507230	nt!NtDeleteWnfStateName			
222	0xFFFFF806625DD710	nt!NT_DISK::GetPnpProperty			
223	0xFFFFF806625F45C0	nt!NtDisableLastKnownGood			
224	0xFFFFF806627F5D40	nt!NtDisplayString			
225	0xFFFFF80662434E10	nt!NtDrawText			
226	0xFFFFF806625F3440	nt!NtEnableLastKnownGood			
227	0xFFFFF806627FC8C0	nt!NtEnumerateBootEntries			
228	0xFFFFF806627FCF20	nt!NtEnumerateDriverEntries			
229	0xFFFFF806627FD3E0	nt!NtEnumerateSystemEnvironmentValuesEx			
230	0xFFFFF806621D9360	nt!NtEnumerateTransactionObject			
231	0xFFFFF806624789B0	nt!NtExtendSection			
232	0xFFFFF806627CB210	nt!NtFilterBootOption			
233	0xFFFFF806624A9A00	nt!NtFilterToken			
234	0xFFFFF806625DD710	nt!NT_DISK::GetPnpProperty			
235	0xFFFFF80662497C10	nt!NtFlushBuffersFileEx			
236	0xFFFFF806626473D0	nt!NtFlushInstallUILanguage			
237	0xFFFFF806624B6860	nt!ArbPreprocessEntry			
238	0xFFFFF80662476350	nt!NtFlushKey			
239	0xFFFFF8066215E6A0	nt!NtFlushProcessWriteBuffers			
240	0xFFFFF8066259E360	nt!NtFlushVirtualMemory			
241	0xFFFFF806624B6860	nt!ArbPreprocessEntry			
242	0xFFFFF8066277B250	nt!NtFreeUserPhysicalPages			
243	0xFFFFF8066270BBD0	nt!NtFreezeRegistry			
244	0xFFFFF806621D9380	nt!NtFreezeTransactions			
245	0xFFFFF80662496270	nt!NtGetCachedSigningLevel			
246	0xFFFFF80662507FC0	nt!NtGetCompleteWnfStateSubscription			
247	0xFFFFF806624C1C00	nt!NtGetContextThread			
248	0xFFFFF806627AAF80	nt!NtGetCurrentProcessorNumber			
249	0xFFFFF806627AAFE0	nt!NtGetCurrentProcessorNumberEx			
250	0xFFFFF80662794D50	nt!NtGetDevicePowerState			
251	0xFFFFF80662496580	nt!NtGetMUIRegistryInfo			
252	0xFFFFF806624ACC10	nt!NtGetNextProcess			
253	0xFFFFF806624B1670	nt!NtGetNextThread			
254	0xFFFFF806625B50F0	nt!NtGetNlsSectionPtr			
255	0xFFFFF806621D93A0	nt!NtGetNotificationResourceManager			
256	0xFFFFF8066214D9F0	nt!NtGetWriteWatch			
257	0xFFFFF8066246A630	nt!NtImpersonateAnonymousToken			
258	0xFFFFF806624909D0	nt!NtImpersonateThread			
259	0xFFFFF80662778A90	nt!NtInitializeEnclave			
260	0xFFFFF8066249CFB0	nt!NtInitializeNlsFiles			
261	0xFFFFF806624C5470	nt!NtInitializeRegistry			
262	0xFFFFF806625E7180	nt!NtInitiatePowerAction			
263	0xFFFFF806625F0F50	nt!NtIsSystemResumeAutomatic			
264	0xFFFFF806624C3820	nt!NtIsUILanguageComitted			
265	0xFFFFF8066264BFF0	nt!NtListenPort			
266	0xFFFFF806624A63E0	nt!NtLoadDriver			
267	0xFFFFF80662778D70	nt!NtLoadEnclaveData			
268	0xFFFFF8066264C790	nt!NtLoadKey			
269	0xFFFFF806625F9D80	nt!NtLoadKey2			
270	0xFFFFF806624C4D10	nt!NtLoadKey3			
271	0xFFFFF8066251BF10	nt!NtLoadKeyEx			
272	0xFFFFF806624EDD70	nt!NtLockFile			
273	0xFFFFF806625F4E70	nt!NtLockProductActivationKeys			
274	0xFFFFF806625F6FC0	nt!NtLockRegistryKey			
275	0xFFFFF8066206B380	nt!NtLockVirtualMemory			

276	0xFFFFF806624C5BA0	nt!NtMakePermanentObject			
277	0xFFFFF806624BC550	nt!NtMakeTemporaryObject			
278	0xFFFFF806624A2630	nt!NtManageHotPatch			
279	0xFFFFF806624D0AF0	nt!NtManagePartition			
280	0xFFFFF806628027D0	nt!NtMapCMFModule			
281	0xFFFFF8066277B810	nt!NtMapUserPhysicalPages			
282	0xFFFFF806624B8DD0	nt!NtMapViewOfSectionEx			
283	0xFFFFF806627FD6A0	nt!NtModifyBootEntry			
284	0xFFFFF806627FD6D0	nt!NtModifyDriverEntry			
285	0xFFFFF8066249FCC0	nt!NtNotifyChangeDirectoryFile			
286	0xFFFFF8066249FD20	nt!NtNotifyChangeDirectoryFileEx			
287	0xFFFFF80662533AB0	nt!NtNotifyChangeKey			
288	0xFFFFF80662533B20	nt!NtNotifyChangeMultipleKeys			
289	0xFFFFF8066247B2F0	nt!NtNotifyChangeSession			
290	0xFFFFF806621D93C0	nt!NtOpenEnlistment			
291	0xFFFFF806625DD710	nt!NT_DISK::GetPnpProperty			
292	0xFFFFF80662734B00	nt!NtOpenIoCompletion			
293	0xFFFFF806625D37D0	nt!NtOpenJobObject			
294	0xFFFFF80662574050	nt!NtOpenKeyEx			
295	0xFFFFF8066270BC90	nt!NtOpenKeyTransacted			
296	0xFFFFF80662519FB0	nt!NtOpenKeyTransactedEx			
297	0xFFFFF80662803E60	nt!NtOpenKeyedEvent			
298	0xFFFFF806625D42F0	nt!NtOpenMutant			
299	0xFFFFF8066249F330	nt!NtOpenObjectAuditAlarm			
300	0xFFFFF80662649930	nt!NtOpenPartition			
301	0xFFFFF806624D6D90	nt!NtOpenPrivateNamespace			
302	0xFFFFF8066255F3B0	nt!NtOpenProcessToken			
303	0xFFFFF8066270BCB0	nt!NtOpenRegistryTransaction			
304	0xFFFFF806621D93E0	nt!NtOpenResourceManager			
305	0xFFFFF806625D43C0	nt!NtOpenSemaphore			
306	0xFFFFF806624BFA40	nt!NtOpenSession			
307	0xFFFFF80662472B10	nt!NtOpenSymbolicLinkObject			
308	0xFFFFF8066247FA10	nt!NtOpenThread			
309	0xFFFFF806627F8760	nt!NtOpenTimer			
310	0xFFFFF806621D9400	nt!NtOpenTransaction			
311	0xFFFFF806621D9420	nt!NtOpenTransactionManager			
312	0xFFFFF806625ACBE0	nt!NtPlugPlayControl			
313	0xFFFFF806621D9440	nt!NtPrePrepareComplete			
314	0xFFFFF806621D9460	nt!NtPrePrepareEnlistment			
315	0xFFFFF806621D9480	nt!NtPrepareComplete			
316	0xFFFFF806621D94A0	nt!NtPrepareEnlistment			
317	0xFFFFF80662543250	nt!NtPrivilegeCheck			
318	0xFFFFF80662602270	nt!NtPrivilegeObjectAuditAlarm			
319	0xFFFFF806624B1CB0	nt!NtPrivilegedServiceAuditAlarm			
320	0xFFFFF806621D94C0	nt!NtPropagationComplete			
321	0xFFFFF806621D94E0	nt!NtPropagationFailed			
322	0xFFFFF806628046F0	nt!NtPssCaptureVaSpaceBulk			
323	0xFFFFF806624ED010	nt!NtPulseEvent			
324	0xFFFFF80662803A80	nt!NtQueryAuxiliaryCounterFrequency			
325	0xFFFFF806627FD700	nt!NtQueryBootEntryOrder			
326	0xFFFFF806627FD980	nt!NtQueryBootOptions			
327	0xFFFFF80662165220	nt!NtQueryDebugFilterState			
328	0xFFFFF806624E5B10	nt!NtQueryDirectoryFileEx			
329	0xFFFFF8066252CCB0	nt!NtQueryDirectoryObject			
330	0xFFFFF806627FDC90	nt!NtQueryDriverEntryOrder			
331	0xFFFFF80662490E20	nt!NtQueryEaFile			
332	0xFFFFF80662505200	nt!NtQueryFullAttributesFile			
333	0xFFFFF8066249D4A0	nt!NtQueryInformationAtom			
334	0xFFFFF80662734EA0	nt!NtQueryInformationByName			
335	0xFFFFF806621D9500	nt!NtQueryInformationEnlistment			
336	0xFFFFF80662591710	nt!NtQueryInformationJobObject			
337	0xFFFFF80662763970	nt!NtQueryInformationPort			
338	0xFFFFF806621D9520	nt!NtQueryInformationResourceManager			
339	0xFFFFF806621D9540	nt!NtQueryInformationTransaction			
340	0xFFFFF806621D9560	nt!NtQueryInformationTransactionManager			
341	0xFFFFF8066243D250	nt!NtQueryInformationWorkerFactory			
342	0xFFFFF806625DD000	nt!NtQueryInstallUILanguage			
343	0xFFFFF806625E1020	nt!NtQueryIntervalProfile			
344	0xFFFFF80662734C20	nt!NtQueryIoCompletion			
345	0xFFFFF80662736E00	nt!NtQueryIoRingCapabilities			
346	0xFFFFF80662472420	nt!NtQueryLicenseValue			
347	0xFFFFF8066250CAE0	nt!NtQueryMultipleValueKey			
348	0xFFFFF806627FFBF0	nt!NtQueryMutant			
349	0xFFFFF8066270BDF0	nt!NtQueryOpenSubKeys			

350	0xFFFFF8066270C030	nt!NtQueryOpenSubKeysEx			
351	0xFFFFF806625DD650	nt!CmpCleanUpHigherLayerKcbCachesPreCallback			
352	0xFFFFF806627376B0	nt!NtQueryQuotaInformationFile			
353	0xFFFFF806624E39E0	nt!NtQuerySecurityAttributesToken			
354	0xFFFFF80662476660	nt!NtQuerySecurityObject			
355	0xFFFFF806624B25E0	nt!NtQuerySecurityPolicy			
356	0xFFFFF806627FF7C0	nt!NtQuerySemaphore			
357	0xFFFFF806624F8170	nt!NtQuerySymbolicLinkObject			
358	0xFFFFF806627FDFC0	nt!NtQuerySystemEnvironmentValue			
359	0xFFFFF806624B83F0	nt!NtQuerySystemEnvironmentValueEx			
360	0xFFFFF8066248CE80	nt!NtQuerySystemInformationEx			
361	0xFFFFF806624B5170	nt!NtQueryTimerResolution			
362	0xFFFFF80662509090	nt!NtQueryWnfStateData			
363	0xFFFFF8066249D980	nt!NtQueryWnfStateNameInformation			
364	0xFFFFF806624C5070	nt!NtQueueApcThreadEx			
365	0xFFFFF80662547170	nt!NtQueueApcThreadEx2			
366	0xFFFFF80662215FD0	nt!NtRaiseException			
367	0xFFFFF806624A8390	nt!NtRaiseHardError			
368	0xFFFFF806621D9580	nt!NtReadOnlyEnlistment			
369	0xFFFFF806623882E0	nt!NtReadVirtualMemoryEx			
370	0xFFFFF806621D95A0	nt!NtRecoverEnlistment			
371	0xFFFFF806621D95C0	nt!NtRecoverResourceManager			
372	0xFFFFF806621D95E0	nt!NtRecoverTransactionManager			
373	0xFFFFF806621D9B00	nt!NtRegisterProtocolAddressInformation			
374	0xFFFFF806624BC880	nt!NtRegisterThreadTerminatePort			
375	0xFFFFF80662803F60	nt!NtReleaseKeyedEvent			
376	0xFFFFF806620C3AD0	nt!NtReleaseWorkerFactoryWorker			
377	0xFFFFF806624736C0	nt!NtRemoveIoCompletionEx			
378	0xFFFFF80662726D90	nt!NtRemoveProcessDebug			
379	0xFFFFF8066270C390	nt!NtRenameKey			
380	0xFFFFF806621D9B20	nt!NtRenameTransactionManager			
381	0xFFFFF8066270C810	nt!NtReplaceKey			
382	0xFFFFF8066244FCC0	nt!NtReplacePartitionUnit			
383	0xFFFFF80662763AA0	nt!NtReplyWaitReplyPort			
384	0xFFFFF806624A3990	nt!NtRequestPort			
385	0xFFFFF806624D27B0	nt!NtResetEvent			
386	0xFFFFF806624CA730	nt!NtResetWriteWatch			
387	0xFFFFF8066270CB70	nt!NtRestoreKey			
388	0xFFFFF806627B0830	nt!NtResumeProcess			
389	0xFFFFF806621688F0	nt!NtRevertContainerImpersonation			
390	0xFFFFF806621D9600	nt!NtRollbackComplete			
391	0xFFFFF806621D9620	nt!NtRollbackEnlistment			
392	0xFFFFF8066245A080	nt!NtRollbackRegistryTransaction			
393	0xFFFFF806621D9640	nt!NtRollbackTransaction			
394	0xFFFFF806621D9B80	nt!NtRollforwardTransactionManager			
395	0xFFFFF806624533E0	nt!NtSaveKey			
396	0xFFFFF80662453400	nt!NtSaveKeyEx			
397	0xFFFFF8066270CDD0	nt!NtSaveMergedKeys			
398	0xFFFFF80662523B10	nt!NtSecureConnectPort			
399	0xFFFFF806626499F0	nt!NtSerializeBoot			
400	0xFFFFF806627FE2E0	nt!NtSetBootEntryOrder			
401	0xFFFFF806627FE4F0	nt!NtSetBootOptions			
402	0xFFFFF806624C3F50	nt!NtSetCachedSigningLevel			
403	0xFFFFF806624C3F80	nt!NtSetCachedSigningLevel2			
404	0xFFFFF806627AF460	nt!NtSetContextThread			
405	0xFFFFF80662626300	nt!NtSetDebugFilterState			
406	0xFFFFF8066264A5D0	nt!NtSetDefaultHardErrorPort			
407	0xFFFFF806625DC8C0	nt!NtSetDefaultLocale			
408	0xFFFFF806625DC8A0	nt!NtSetDefaultUILanguage			
409	0xFFFFF806627FE700	nt!NtSetDriverEntryOrder			
410	0xFFFFF806627370D0	nt!NtSetEaFile			
411	0xFFFFF806625DD710	nt!NT_DISK::GetPnpProperty			
412	0xFFFFF806625DD710	nt!NT_DISK::GetPnpProperty			
413	0xFFFFF80662052A10	nt!NtSetIRTimer			
414	0xFFFFF80662726F00	nt!NtSetInformationDebugObject			
415	0xFFFFF806621D9660	nt!NtSetInformationEnlistment			
416	0xFFFFF80662736EA0	nt!NtSetInformationIoRing			
417	0xFFFFF80662592BD0	nt!NtSetInformationJobObject			
418	0xFFFFF8066255E480	nt!NtSetInformationKey			
419	0xFFFFF806621D9680	nt!NtSetInformationResourceManager			
420	0xFFFFF80662781D70	nt!NtSetInformationSymbolicLink			
421	0xFFFFF80662467300	nt!NtSetInformationToken			
422	0xFFFFF806621D96A0	nt!NtSetInformationTransaction			
423	0xFFFFF806621D9B40	nt!NtSetInformationTransactionManager			

```
|    424 | 0xFFFFF8066253CCE0 | nt!NtSetInformationVirtualMemory                          |         |        |
|    425 | 0xFFFFF806620A3CD0 | nt!NtSetInformationWorkerFactory                          |         |        |
|    426 | 0xFFFFF806625E10F0 | nt!NtSetIntervalProfile                                   |         |        |
|    427 | 0xFFFFF8066254BE00 | nt!NtSetIoCompletion                                      |         |        |
|    428 | 0xFFFFF80662474090 | nt!NtSetIoCompletionEx                                    |         |        |
|    429 | 0xFFFFF806621D8FC0 | nt!BvgaSetVirtualFrameBuffer                              |         |        |
|    430 | 0xFFFFF806625DD710 | nt!NT_DISK::GetPnpProperty                                |         |        |
|    431 | 0xFFFFF806625DD710 | nt!NT_DISK::GetPnpProperty                                |         |        |
|    432 | 0xFFFFF80662737DC0 | nt!NtSetQuotaInformationFile                              |         |        |
|    433 | 0xFFFFF8066248C0D0 | nt!NtSetSecurityObject                                    |         |        |
|    434 | 0xFFFFF806627FE910 | nt!NtSetSystemEnvironmentValue                            |         |        |
|    435 | 0xFFFFF806624B8510 | nt!NtSetSystemEnvironmentValueEx                          |         |        |
|    436 | 0xFFFFF80662538B70 | nt!NtSetSystemInformation                                 |         |        |
|    437 | 0xFFFFF8066284F7E0 | nt!NtSetSystemPowerState                                  |         |        |
|    438 | 0xFFFFF806627F5560 | nt!NtSetSystemTime                                        |         |        |
|    439 | 0xFFFFF8066259C1A0 | nt!NtSetThreadExecutionState                              |         |        |
|    440 | 0xFFFFF80662167ED0 | nt!NtSetTimer2                                            |         |        |
|    441 | 0xFFFFF806620CF470 | nt!NtSetTimerEx                                           |         |        |
|    442 | 0xFFFFF80662539730 | nt!NtSetTimerResolution                                   |         |        |
|    443 | 0xFFFFF8066263DDB0 | nt!NtSetUuidSeed                                          |         |        |
|    444 | 0xFFFFF806625E3BA0 | nt!NtSetVolumeInformationFile                             |         |        |
|    445 | 0xFFFFF8066249DCF0 | nt!NtSetWnfProcessNotificationEvent                       |         |        |
|    446 | 0xFFFFF80662434F90 | nt!NtShutdownSystem                                       |         |        |
|    447 | 0xFFFFF80662046FE0 | nt!NtShutdownWorkerFactory                                |         |        |
|    448 | 0xFFFFF80662045160 | nt!NtSignalAndWaitForSingleObject                         |         |        |
|    449 | 0xFFFFF806621D9B60 | nt!NtSinglePhaseReject                                    |         |        |
|    450 | 0xFFFFF80662803AF0 | nt!NtStartProfile                                         |         |        |
|    451 | 0xFFFFF80662803D60 | nt!NtStopProfile                                          |         |        |
|    452 | 0xFFFFF806623559A0 | nt!NtSubmitIoRing                                         |         |        |
|    453 | 0xFFFFF80662508C30 | nt!NtSubscribeWnfStateChange                              |         |        |
|    454 | 0xFFFFF806627B08B0 | nt!NtSuspendProcess                                       |         |        |
|    455 | 0xFFFFF806624BD100 | nt!NtSuspendThread                                        |         |        |
|    456 | 0xFFFFF806624B7F10 | nt!NtSystemDebugControl                                   |         |        |
|    457 | 0xFFFFF806627793A0 | nt!NtTerminateEnclave                                     |         |        |
|    458 | 0xFFFFF806625997A0 | nt!NtTerminateJobObject                                   |         |        |
|    459 | 0xFFFFF806624A1880 | nt!NtTestAlert                                            |         |        |
|    460 | 0xFFFFF8066270D070 | nt!NtThawRegistry                                         |         |        |
|    461 | 0xFFFFF806621D96C0 | nt!NtThawTransactions                                     |         |        |
|    462 | 0xFFFFF806624FDA40 | nt!NtTraceControl                                         |         |        |
|    463 | 0xFFFFF806627FEC30 | nt!NtTranslateFilePath                                    |         |        |
|    464 | 0xFFFFF8066216DCF0 | nt!DefaultAddProfileSource                                |         |        |
|    465 | 0xFFFFF8066273DB40 | nt!NtUnloadDriver                                         |         |        |
|    466 | 0xFFFFF80662470160 | nt!NtUnloadKey                                            |         |        |
|    467 | 0xFFFFF80662470070 | nt!NtUnloadKey2                                           |         |        |
|    468 | 0xFFFFF806624701B0 | nt!NtUnloadKeyEx                                          |         |        |
|    469 | 0xFFFFF806624ED9C0 | nt!NtUnlockFile                                           |         |        |
|    470 | 0xFFFFF8066214BD80 | nt!NtUnlockVirtualMemory                                  |         |        |
|    471 | 0xFFFFF806625896D0 | nt!NtUnmapViewOfSectionEx                                 |         |        |
|    472 | 0xFFFFF80662507650 | nt!NtUnsubscribeWnfStateChange                            |         |        |
|    473 | 0xFFFFF80662508690 | nt!NtUpdateWnfStateData                                   |         |        |
|    474 | 0xFFFFF806625DD710 | nt!NT_DISK::GetPnpProperty                                |         |        |
|    475 | 0xFFFFF806624C6F20 | nt!NtWaitForAlertByThreadId                               |         |        |
|    476 | 0xFFFFF80662727090 | nt!NtWaitForDebugEvent                                    |         |        |
|    477 | 0xFFFFF80662804330 | nt!NtWaitForKeyedEvent                                    |         |        |
|    478 | 0xFFFFF80662138C40 | nt!NtWaitForWorkViaWorkerFactory                          |         |        |
|    479 | 0xFFFFF806625DD710 | nt!NT_DISK::GetPnpProperty                                |         |        |
|    480 | 0xFFFFF806625DD710 | nt!NT_DISK::GetPnpProperty                                |         |        |
```

11. There's a fast process list command that also shows terminated threads and combines some info from the PE header we usually get from the **!dh** command. We can also get the list of exported functions from modules and an indicator if they are hooked (however, to see imported functions, you need to dump IAT for modules of interest).

```
0: kd> !ms_process
```

```
Process:       System               (PID=0x0004 [4]) | [+Dlls] [+Exports] [+Handles] [+Threads] [+VADs] [+Scan]
[+Select context]
    ImageBase: 0xFFFFF80661E00000 ImageSize: 0x1047000 (IsPagedOut = False, IsSigned = -888430464)
    PDB:           ntkrnlmp.pdb
    Sections:      .rdata, .pdata, .idata, .edata, PROTDATA, GFIDS, Pad1, .text, PAGE, PAGELK, POOLCODE, PAGEKD,
PAGEVRFY, PAGEHDLS, PAGEBGFX, TRACESUP, PAGECMRC, KVASCODE, RETPOL, INITKDBG, MINIEX, INIT, Pad2, .data, ALMOSTRO,
CACHEALI, PAGEDATA, PAGEVRFD, INITDATA, Pad3, CFGRO, Pad4, .rsrc, .reloc,
```

```
Process:       Registry            (PID=0x0064 [100]) | [+Dlls] [+Exports] [+Handles] [+Threads] [+VADs] [+Scan]
[+Select context]
    ImageBase: 0x0 ImageSize: 0x0 (IsPagedOut = False, IsSigned = -888430456)
    Path:           Registry
    Sections:

Process:       smss.exe            (PID=0x0178 [376]) | [+Dlls] [+Exports] [+Handles] [+Threads] [+VADs] [+Scan]
[+Select context]
    ImageBase: 0x7FF6BC6A0000 ImageSize: 0x29000 (IsPagedOut = True, IsSigned = -888430464)
    Path:           \Device\HarddiskVolume4\Windows\System32\smss.exe
    Vendor:         Microsoft Corporation
    Version:        10.0.22000.1 (WinBuild.160101.0800)
    Description:    Windows Session Manager
    Commandline:    \SystemRoot\System32\smss.exe
    Sections:      .text, .rdata, .data, .pdata, .rsrc, .reloc,

Process:       csrss.exe           (PID=0x0200 [512]) | [+Dlls] [+Exports] [+Handles] [+Threads] [+VADs] [+Scan]
[+Select context]
    ImageBase: 0x7FF667950000 ImageSize: 0x7000 (IsPagedOut = False, IsSigned = -888430464)
    Path:           \Device\HarddiskVolume4\Windows\System32\csrss.exe
    PDB:            csrss.pdb
    Vendor:         Microsoft Corporation
    Version:        10.0.22000.1 (WinBuild.160101.0800)
    Description:    Client Server Runtime Process
    Commandline:    %SystemRoot%\system32\csrss.exe ObjectDirectory=\Windows SharedSection=1024,20480,768 Windows=On
SubSystemType=Windows ServerDll=basesrv,1 ServerDll=winsrv:UserServerDllInitialization,3 ServerDll=sxssrv,4
ProfileControl=Off MaxRequestThreads=16
    Sections:      .text, .rdata, .data, .pdata, .rsrc, .reloc,

Process:       wininit.exe         (PID=0x0248 [584]) | [+Dlls] [+Exports] [+Handles] [+Threads] [+VADs] [+Scan]
[+Select context]
    ImageBase: 0x7FF776170000 ImageSize: 0x85000 (IsPagedOut = True, IsSigned = -888430464)
    Path:           \Device\HarddiskVolume4\Windows\System32\wininit.exe
    Vendor:         Microsoft Corporation
    Version:        10.0.22000.1 (WinBuild.160101.0800)
    Description:    Windows Start-Up Application
    Commandline:    wininit.exe
    Sections:      .text, .rdata, .data, .pdata, .didat, .rsrc, .reloc,

Process:       csrss.exe           (PID=0x0250 [592]) | [+Dlls] [+Exports] [+Handles] [+Threads] [+VADs] [+Scan]
[+Select context]
    ImageBase: 0x7FF667950000 ImageSize: 0x7000 (IsPagedOut = False, IsSigned = -888430464)
    Path:           \Device\HarddiskVolume4\Windows\System32\csrss.exe
    PDB:            csrss.pdb
    Vendor:         Microsoft Corporation
    Version:        10.0.22000.1 (WinBuild.160101.0800)
    Description:    Client Server Runtime Process
    Commandline:    %SystemRoot%\system32\csrss.exe ObjectDirectory=\Windows SharedSection=1024,20480,768 Windows=On
SubSystemType=Windows ServerDll=basesrv,1 ServerDll=winsrv:UserServerDllInitialization,3 ServerDll=sxssrv,4
ProfileControl=Off MaxRequestThreads=16
    Sections:      .text, .rdata, .data, .pdata, .rsrc, .reloc,

Process:       services.exe        (PID=0x0290 [656]) | [+Dlls] [+Exports] [+Handles] [+Threads] [+VADs] [+Scan]
[+Select context]
    ImageBase: 0x7FF6D7A50000 ImageSize: 0xB5000 (IsPagedOut = True, IsSigned = -888430464)
    Path:           \Device\HarddiskVolume4\Windows\System32\services.exe
    PDB:            services.pdb
    Vendor:         Microsoft Corporation
    Version:        10.0.22000.51 (WinBuild.160101.0800)
    Description:    Services and Controller app
    Commandline:    C:\WINDOWS\system32\services.exe
    Sections:      .text, .rdata, .data, .pdata, .didat, .rsrc, .reloc,

Process:       lsass.exe           (PID=0x0298 [664]) | [+Dlls] [+Exports] [+Handles] [+Threads] [+VADs] [+Scan]
[+Select context]
    ImageBase: 0x7FF60B710000 ImageSize: 0x12000 (IsPagedOut = True, IsSigned = -888430464)
    Path:           \Device\HarddiskVolume4\Windows\System32\lsass.exe
    PDB:            lsass.pdb
    Vendor:         Microsoft Corporation
    Version:        10.0.22000.282 (WinBuild.160101.0800)
    Description:    Local Security Authority Process
    Commandline:    C:\WINDOWS\system32\lsass.exe
    Sections:      .text, .rdata, .data, .pdata, .didat, .rsrc, .reloc,
```

```
Process:       winlogon.exe        (PID=0x02b8 [696]) | [+Dlls] [+Exports] [+Handles] [+Threads] [+VADs] [+Scan]
[+Select context]
    ImageBase: 0x7FF75F330000 ImageSize: 0xDB000 (IsPagedOut = True, IsSigned = -888430456)
    Path:           \Device\HarddiskVolume4\Windows\System32\winlogon.exe
    PDB:            winlogon.pdb
    Vendor:         Microsoft Corporation
    Version:        10.0.22000.282 (WinBuild.160101.0800)
    Description:    Windows Logon Application
    Commandline:    winlogon.exe
    Sections:      .text, .rdata, .data, .pdata, .didat, .rsrc, .reloc,

[...]
```

```
0: kd> !ms_process /pid 0x250 /handles
```

```
Process:       csrss.exe           (PID=0x0250 [592]) | [+Dlls] [+Exports] [+Handles] [+Threads] [+VADs] [+Scan] [+Select context]
    ImageBase: 0x7FF667950000 ImageSize: 0x7000 (IsPagedOut = False, IsSigned = 1433968768)
    Path:           \Device\HarddiskVolume4\Windows\System32\csrss.exe
    PDB:            csrss.pdb
    Vendor:         Microsoft Corporation
    Version:        10.0.22000.1 (WinBuild.160101.0800)
    Description:    Client Server Runtime Process
    Commandline:    %SystemRoot%\system32\csrss.exe ObjectDirectory=\Windows SharedSection=1024,20480,768 Windows=On SubSystemType=Windows ServerDll=basesrv,1
ServerDll=winsrv:UserServerDllInitialization,3 ServerDll=sxssrv,4 ProfileControl=Off MaxRequestThreads=16
    Sections:      .text, .rdata, .data, .pdata, .rsrc, .reloc,

|------|----------------------|--------------------|------------------------------------------------------------------|
| Hdle | Object Type          | Addr               | Name                                                             |
|------|----------------------|--------------------|------------------------------------------------------------------|
| 0004 | Event                | 0xFFFFC38C306D6DE0 |
| 0008 | Event                | 0xFFFFC38C306D64E0 |
| 000c | Event                | 0xFFFFC38C306D6E60 |
| 0010 | WaitCompletionPacket | 0xFFFFC38C2EA44BB0 |
| 0014 | IoCompletion         | 0xFFFFC38C2ED58440 |
| 0018 | TpWorkerFactory      | 0xFFFFC38C30883B30 |
| 001c | IRTimer              | 0xFFFFC38C2E48E3C0 |
| 0020 | WaitCompletionPacket | 0xFFFFC38C2EA44460 |
| 0024 | IRTimer              | 0xFFFFC38C2E48D2C0 |
| 0028 | WaitCompletionPacket | 0xFFFFC38C2EA43900 |
| 002c | EtwRegistration      | 0xFFFFC38C2ED58520 |
| 0030 | EtwRegistration      | 0xFFFFC38C2ED58600 |
| 0034 | EtwRegistration      | 0xFFFFC38C2ED58980 |
| 0038 | EtwRegistration      | 0xFFFFC38C2ED58B40 |
| 003c | Directory            | 0xFFFFAC8A04BA22A0 | KnownDlls
| 0040 | Event                | 0xFFFFC38C306D65E0 |
| 0044 | Event                | 0xFFFFC38C306D61E0 |
| 0048 | File                 | 0xFFFFC38C3069D1B0 | \Windows\System32
| 004c | IoCompletion         | 0xFFFFC38C2EDF9E80 |
| 0050 | TpWorkerFactory      | 0xFFFFC38C30884AF0 |
| 0054 | IRTimer              | 0xFFFFC38C2E48E5E0 |
| 0058 | WaitCompletionPacket | 0xFFFFC38C2EA44E20 |
| 005c | IRTimer              | 0xFFFFC38C2E48D4E0 |
| 0060 | WaitCompletionPacket | 0xFFFFC38C2EA43B70 |
| 0064 | EtwRegistration      | 0xFFFFC38C2E7D9860 |
| 0068 | EtwRegistration      | 0xFFFFC38C2E7D9160 |
| 006c | Directory            | 0xFFFFAC8A043920C0 | BNOLINKS
| 0070 | SymbolicLink         | 0xFFFFAC8A07E6D7D0 | 1
| 0074 | Directory            | 0xFFFFAC8A043931A0 | 1
| 0078 | Directory            | 0xFFFFAC8A043922A0 | DosDevices
| 007c | Directory            | 0xFFFFAC8A04393B00 | Windows
| 0080 | ALPC Port            | 0xFFFFC38C2E757070 |
| 0084 | ALPC Port            | 0xFFFFC38C2E3ADB20 | ApiPort
| 0088 | Thread               | 0xFFFFC38C30887080 |
| 008c | Key                  | 0xFFFFAC8A04DF8F50 | \REGISTRY\MACHINE\SYSTEM\SYSTEM\CONTROLSET001\CONTROL\SESSION MANAGER
| 0090 | Section              | 0xFFFFAC8A07DCDB70 | SharedSection
| 0094 | Directory            | 0xFFFFAC8A04392840 | BaseNamedObjects
| 0098 | Directory            | 0xFFFFAC8A04392C00 | AppContainerNamedObjects
| 009c | SymbolicLink         | 0xFFFFAC8A07E6D250 | Global
| 00a0 | SymbolicLink         | 0xFFFFAC8A07E6D930 | Local
| 00a4 | SymbolicLink         | 0xFFFFAC8A07E6DEB0 | AppContainerNamedObjects
| 00a8 | SymbolicLink         | 0xFFFFAC8A07E6F820 | Session
| 00ac | Directory            | 0xFFFFAC8A04393380 | Restricted
| 00b0 | File                 | 0xFFFFC38C3069C9E0 | \Sessions\1\AppContainerNamedObjects
| 00b4 | EtwRegistration      | 0xFFFFC38C2E7D88A0 |
| 00b8 | EtwRegistration      | 0xFFFFC38C2E7D81A0 |
| 00bc | EtwRegistration      | 0xFFFFC38C2E7D9940 |
| 00c0 | EtwRegistration      | 0xFFFFC38C2E7D87C0 |
| 00c4 | Event                | 0xFFFFC38C306D63E0 |
| 00c8 | Event                | 0xFFFFC38C306D6F60 |
| 00cc | Event                | 0xFFFFC38C2CC85170 | EventRitExited
| 00d0 | Directory            | 0xFFFFAC8A04392840 | BaseNamedObjects
| 00d4 | Event                | 0xFFFFC38C306D66E0 |
| 00d8 | Event                | 0xFFFFC38C306D6760 |
| 00dc | Event                | 0xFFFFC38C306D6FE0 |
| 00e0 | Key                  | 0xFFFFAC8A04DF98E0 | \REGISTRY\MACHINE\SYSTEM\SYSTEM\CONTROLSET001\CONTROL\NLS\SORTING\VERSIONS
| 00e4 | EtwRegistration      | 0xFFFFC38C2E7D8980 |
| 00e8 | EtwRegistration      | 0xFFFFC38C2E7D8A60 |
| 00ec | EtwRegistration      | 0xFFFFC38C2E7D9240 |
| 00f0 | Key                  | 0xFFFFAC8A04DF99F0 | \REGISTRY\MACHINE\SOFTWARE\SOFTWARE\MICROSOFT\WINDOWS NT\CURRENTVERSION\IMAGE FILE EXECUTION OPTIONS
| 00f4 | Key                  | 0xFFFFAC8A09DB5550 | \REGISTRY\USER\S-1-5-21-3407489871-1359576761-456439074-1001\S-1-5-21-3407489871-1359576761-456439074-1001\SOFTWARE\MICROSOFT\WINDOWS NT\CURRENTVERSION\FONTS
| 00f8 | Event                | 0xFFFFC38C306D67E0 |
| 00fc | Key                  | 0xFFFFAC8A04DF9C10 | \REGISTRY\MACHINE\SOFTWARE\SOFTWARE\MICROSOFT\WINDOWS NT\CURRENTVERSION\FONTS
| 0100 | Event                | 0xFFFFC38C306D6960 |
| 0104 | Key                  | 0xFFFFAC8A04DF9E30 | \REGISTRY\MACHINE\SOFTWARE\SOFTWARE\MICROSOFT\WINDOWS NT\CURRENTVERSION\FONTLINK
| 0108 | Key                  | 0xFFFFAC8A09DB5DD0 | \REGISTRY\USER\S-1-5-21-3407489871-1359576761-456439074-1001\S-1-5-21-3407489871-1359576761-456439074-1001\CONTROL PANEL\INTERNATIONAL
| 010c | Event                | 0xFFFFC38C2CC8C5B0 | ScNetDrvMsg
| 0110 | Process              | 0xFFFFC38C32413080 | svchost.exe
| 0114 | Key                  | 0xFFFFAC8A07E961D0 | \REGISTRY\MACHINE\SYSTEM\SYSTEM\CONTROLSET001\CONTROL\PRIORITYCONTROL
| 0118 | Event                | 0xFFFFC38C2CC811B0 | TermSrvReadyEvent
| 011c | Thread               | 0xFFFFC38C3040C080 |
| 0120 | Thread               | 0xFFFFC38C3040E080 |
| 0124 | Event                | 0xFFFFC38C306A4260 |
| 0128 | WaitCompletionPacket | 0xFFFFC38C2EA49F60 |
| 012c | Thread               | 0xFFFFC38C3040F080 |
| 0130 | Thread               | 0xFFFFC38C30410080 |
| 0134 | Key                  | 0xFFFFAC8A07E95510 | \REGISTRY\MACHINE\SOFTWARE\SOFTWARE\MICROSOFT\WINDOWS\CURRENTVERSION\SIDEBYSIDE
| 0138 | ALPC Port            | 0xFFFFC38C3089ED20 | SbApiPort
| 013c | Thread               | 0xFFFFC38C30411080 |
| 0140 | ALPC Port            | 0xFFFFC38C3081FB00 |
| 0144 | Process              | 0xFFFFC38C33231080 | TabTip.exe
| 0148 | ALPC Port            | 0xFFFFC38C305DDD60 |
| 014c | Event                | 0xFFFFC38C306A4B60 |
| 0150 | IoCompletion         | 0xFFFFC38C2EDF4500 |
| 0154 | Event                | 0xFFFFC38C306A6EE0 |
| 0158 | IoCompletion         | 0xFFFFC38C308AD380 |
| 015c | ALPC Port            | 0xFFFFC38C30676C80 |
| 0160 | Process              | 0xFFFFC38C3041E080 | winlogon.exe
| 0164 | Thread               | 0xFFFFC38C3041F080 |
| 0168 | Thread               | 0xFFFFC38C3041D080 |
| 016c | Thread               | 0xFFFFC38C30440080 |
| 0170 | Event                | 0xFFFFC38C2CC8F490 | {773F1B9A-35B9-4E95-83A0-A210F2DE3B37}-running
| 0174 | Event                | 0xFFFFC38C2CC8E590 | {773F1B9A-35B9-4E95-83A0-A210F2DE3B37}-request
| 0178 | Thread               | 0xFFFFC38C30441080 |
| 017c | Event                | 0xFFFFC38C306A6960 |
| 0180 | IoCompletion         | 0xFFFFC38C308AD980 |
| 0184 | Event                | 0xFFFFC38C2CC8E6D0 | WinSta0_DesktopSwitch
| 0188 | WindowStation        | 0xFFFFC38C2EDAA2C0 | WinSta0
| 018c | Event                | 0xFFFFC38C306A6860 |
| 0190 | Semaphore            | 0xFFFFC38C306A7D60 |
| 0194 | Event                | 0xFFFFC38C306A7160 |
| 0198 | Timer                | 0xFFFFC38C2E79F6A0 |
| 019c | Event                | 0xFFFFC38C306A7560 |
| 01a0 | Event                | 0xFFFFC38C306A8060 |
| 01a4 | Event                | 0xFFFFC38C306A7E60 |
| 01a8 | RawInputManager      | 0xFFFFC38C308B5070 |
| 01ac | RawInputManager      | 0xFFFFC38C30442070 |
| 01b0 | Thread               | 0xFFFFC38C3043F080 |
| 01b4 | Process              | 0xFFFFC38C334020C0 | AppA.exe
| 01b8 | Thread               | 0xFFFFC38C3050B080 |
| 01bc | Section              | 0xFFFFAC8A09591EA0 |
| 01c0 | Section              | 0xFFFFAC8A0958EA20 |
| 01c4 | Section              | 0xFFFFAC8A08DBDEC0 |
| 01c8 | Section              | 0xFFFFAC8A09119620 |
| 01cc | Section              | 0xFFFFAC8A0958EAC0 |
| 01d0 | Thread               | 0xFFFFC38C31F8B080 |
| 01d4 | Section              | 0xFFFFAC8A0B5BAA30 |
| 01d8 | Process              | 0xFFFFC38C332CE080 | MiniSearchHost
| 01dc | Thread               | 0xFFFFC38C3300D080 |
| 01e0 | Section              | 0xFFFFAC8A08302800 |
| 01e4 | Thread               | 0xFFFFC38C3310A080 |
| 01e8 | Section              | 0xFFFFAC8A095997E0 |
| 01ec | ALPC Port            | 0xFFFFC38C30452070 |
| 01f0 | Thread               | 0xFFFFC38C308C2080 |
| 01f4 | Process              | 0xFFFFC38C304A61C0 | fontdrvhost.ex
| 01f8 | Thread               | 0xFFFFC38C3049F080 |
| 01fc | EtwRegistration      | 0xFFFFC38C307F97C0 |
| 0200 | EtwRegistration      | 0xFFFFC38C307F9DE0 |
| 0204 | EtwRegistration      | 0xFFFFC38C307F9B40 |
| 0208 | EtwRegistration      | 0xFFFFC38C307F9EC0 |
```

```
| 020c | EtwRegistration      | 0xFFFFC38C307FA080 |
| 0210 | EtwRegistration      | 0xFFFFC38C307FA160 |
| 0214 | EtwRegistration      | 0xFFFFC38C307FA320 |
| 0218 | Key                  | 0xFFFFAC8A07FF2610 | \REGISTRY\MACHINE
| 021c | Event                | 0xFFFFC38C304868E0 |
| 0220 | Mutant               | 0xFFFFC38C2CC928F0 |
| 0224 | Thread               | 0xFFFFC38C3056F040 |
| 0228 | Event                | 0xFFFFC38C3052B1E0 |
| 022c | IoCompletion         | 0xFFFFC38C305D9900 |
| 0230 | Event                | 0xFFFFC38C3211CB60 |
| 0234 | EtwRegistration      | 0xFFFFC38C307FBC80 |
| 0238 | EtwRegistration      | 0xFFFFC38C307FC7E0 |
| 023c | IoCompletion         | 0xFFFFC38C307FB140 |
| 0240 | File                 | 0xFFFFC38C304E9220 |
| 0244 | Event                | 0xFFFFC38C30532AE0 |
| 0248 | IoCompletion         | 0xFFFFC38C305F5DC0 |
| 024c | ALPC Port            | 0xFFFFC38C30575DA0 | AutoRotationApiPort
| 0250 | Thread               | 0xFFFFC38C30327080 |
| 0254 | ALPC Port            | 0xFFFFC38C32234D60 |
| 0258 | ALPC Port            | 0xFFFFC38C30326B00 |
| 025c | Event                | 0xFFFFC38C303545E0 |
| 0260 | IoCompletion         | 0xFFFFC38C3037EBC0 |
| 0264 | File                 | 0xFFFFC38C321532A0 | \Program Files\WindowsApps\Microsoft.LanguageExperiencePacken-GB_21388.1.1.0_neutral__8wekyb3d8bbwe\Windows\System32\en-GB\a57f412cdf7987b44743de05f94f48a7\winsrv.dll.mui
| 0268 | Section              | 0xFFFFAC8A0823A2A0 |
| 026c | ALPC Port            | 0xFFFFC38C309D0D60 |
| 0270 | Thread               | 0xFFFFC38C330B3080 |
| 0274 | Thread               | 0xFFFFC38C308BF080 |
| 0278 | Process              | 0xFFFFC38C30331080 | dwm.exe
| 027c | Thread               | 0xFFFFC38C2EBCD080 |
| 0280 | Thread               | 0xFFFFC38C331EA080 |
| 0284 | Thread               | 0xFFFFC38C3231C080 |
| 0288 | Section              | 0xFFFFAC8A08239B20 |
| 028c | Event                | 0xFFFFC38C30945F60 |
| 0290 | IoCompletion         | 0xFFFFC38C3092F580 |
| 0294 | Process              | 0xFFFFC38C32414080 | sihost.exe
| 0298 | ALPC Port            | 0xFFFFC38C317E2D60 |
| 029c | Event                | 0xFFFFC38C31750C60 |
| 02a0 | IoCompletion         | 0xFFFFC38C317D15C0 |
| 02a4 | Process              | 0xFFFFC38C324020C0 | RuntimeBroker.
| 02a8 | Thread               | 0xFFFFC38C32319080 |
| 02ac | ALPC Port            | 0xFFFFC38C32409530 |
| 02b0 | ALPC Port            | 0xFFFFC38C3178DD60 |
| 02b4 | Event                | 0xFFFFC38C32333560 |
| 02b8 | IoCompletion         | 0xFFFFC38C322D3700 |
| 02bc | ALPC Port            | 0xFFFFC38C327C29F0 |
| 02c0 | Process              | 0xFFFFC38C32455080 | svchost.exe
| 02c4 | Thread               | 0xFFFFC38C323F9080 |
| 02c8 | ALPC Port            | 0xFFFFC38C31E7D860 |
| 02cc | Thread               | 0xFFFFC38C326F9080 |
| 02d0 | Thread               | 0xFFFFC38C32CA9080 |
| 02d4 | Process              | 0xFFFFC38C324A4080 | taskhostw.exe
| 02d8 | Thread               | 0xFFFFC38C32417080 |
| 02dc | ALPC Port            | 0xFFFFC38C32450C00 |
| 02e0 | Process              | 0xFFFFC38C32B62080 | StartMenuExper
| 02e4 | Process              | 0xFFFFC38C32C98080 | RuntimeBroker.
| 02e8 | Thread               | 0xFFFFC38C32AAD080 |
| 02ec | Process              | 0xFFFFC38C326E2080 | explorer.exe
| 02f0 | Thread               | 0xFFFFC38C32621080 |
| 02f4 | Process              | 0xFFFFC38C32B5C080 | SearchHost.exe
| 02f8 | Thread               | 0xFFFFC38C3247D080 |
| 02fc | Section              | 0xFFFFAC8A09F1EC30 |
| 0300 | Section              | 0xFFFFAC8A0D362AD0 |
| 0304 | Section              | 0xFFFFAC8A09F08430 |
| 0308 | Section              | 0xFFFFAC8A09F0E5B0 |
| 030c | Section              | 0xFFFFAC8A0BBB1CD0 |
| 0310 | Section              | 0xFFFFAC8A0CA68E70 |
| 0314 | Section              | 0xFFFFAC8A09F1EA50 |
| 0318 | ALPC Port            | 0xFFFFC38C326922D0 |
| 031c | Section              | 0xFFFFAC8A09F1C390 |
| 0320 | Section              | 0xFFFFAC8A09F269D0 |
| 0324 | Thread               | 0xFFFFC38C32AA7380 |
| 0328 | Section              | 0xFFFFAC8A0959E5E0 |
| 032c | Section              | 0xFFFFAC8A09F27330 |
| 0330 | Process              | 0xFFFFC38C32691080 | svchost.exe
| 0334 | Thread               | 0xFFFFC38C32CA7080 |
| 0338 | Section              | 0xFFFFAC8A09F30890 |
| 033c | Section              | 0xFFFFAC8A09F2A710 |
| 0340 | Thread               | 0xFFFFC38C326DE080 |
| 0344 | Section              | 0xFFFFAC8A09F2A7B0 |
| 0348 | ALPC Port            | 0xFFFFC38C327CB790 |
| 034c | Thread               | 0xFFFFC38C324C7040 |
| 0350 | Thread               | 0xFFFFC38C32CA4080 |
| 0354 | ALPC Port            | 0xFFFFC38C32C6CD60 |
| 0358 | Section              | 0xFFFFAC8A09F35CF0 |
| 035c | Process              | 0xFFFFC38C32C6D080 | svchost.exe
| 0360 | Thread               | 0xFFFFC38C32C70080 |
| 0364 | ALPC Port            | 0xFFFFC38C32CA6D60 |
| 0368 | Thread               | 0xFFFFC38C31809080 |
...
...
...|
| 0508 | Section              | 0xFFFFAC8A0883C9A0 |
| 050c | Process              | 0xFFFFC38C3329B080 | svchost.exe
| 0510 | Thread               | 0xFFFFC38C3343A080 |
| 0514 | ALPC Port            | 0xFFFFC38C3371FD60 |
| 0518 | Thread               | 0xFFFFC38C31F85080 |
| 051c | Section              | 0xFFFFAC8A0CA3D810 |
| 0520 | Section              | 0xFFFFAC8A0CA3D8B0 |
| 0524 | ALPC Port            | 0xFFFFC38C2E5E6B00 |
| 0528 | ALPC Port            | 0xFFFFC38C2C538B00 |
| 052c | Thread               | 0xFFFFC38C32245080 |
| 0530 | Thread               | 0xFFFFC38C3270B080 |
| 0534 | Thread               | 0xFFFFC38C3270C080 |
| 0538 | Thread               | 0xFFFFC38C32704080 |
| 053c | Thread               | 0xFFFFC38C32817040 |
| 0540 | Thread               | 0xFFFFC38C324CC080 |
| 0544 | Process              | 0xFFFFC38C3010B0C0 | conhost.exe
| 0548 | Section              | 0xFFFFAC8A0CA69550 |
| 054c | Thread               | 0xFFFFC38C2ECD4080 |
| 0550 | Thread               | 0xFFFFC38C3340B080 |
| 0554 | ALPC Port            | 0xFFFFC38C2E89BDD0 |
| 055c | Section              | 0xFFFFAC8A0D3622B0 |
| 0560 | Section              | 0xFFFFAC8A0D35A510 |
| 0574 | Thread               | 0xFFFFC38C330E3080 |
| 0578 | Thread               | 0xFFFFC38C33AC3080 |
| 057c | Process              | 0xFFFFC38C2E16B080 | notmyfault64.e
| 0580 | Section              | 0xFFFFAC8A0D380210 |
| 0588 | Section              | 0xFFFFAC8A0D37FA90 |
| 058c | Thread               | 0xFFFFC38C33ABD080 |
| 059c | Section              | 0xFFFFAC8A095A50C0 |
| 05a0 | Section              | 0xFFFFAC8A0B050C30 |
| 05ac | Section              | 0xFFFFAC8A0D377A70 |
| 05b0 | Section              | 0xFFFFAC8A0D3768F0 |
```

```
0: kd> !ms_process /pid 0x250 /threads
```

```
Process:        csrss.exe           (PID=0x0250 [592]) | [+Dlls] [+Exports] [+Handles] [+Threads] [+VADs] [+Scan] [+Select context]
    ImageBase: 0x7FF667950000 ImageSize: 0x7000 (IsPagedOut = False, IsSigned = -888430464)
    Path:           \Device\HarddiskVolume4\Windows\System32\csrss.exe
    PDB:            csrss.pdb
    Vendor:         Microsoft Corporation
    Version:        10.0.22000.1 (WinBuild.160101.0800)
    Description:    Client Server Runtime Process
    Commandline:    %SystemRoot%\system32\csrss.exe ObjectDirectory=\Windows SharedSection=1024,20480,768 Windows=On SubSystemType=Windows ServerDll=basesrv,1 ServerDll=winsrv:UserServerDllInitialization,3 ServerDll=sxssrv,4 ProfileControl=Off MaxRequestThreads=16
    Sections:       .text, .rdata, .data, .pdata, .rsrc, .reloc,
    |--------|--------|--------------------|------------------------------------------------|--------------------|--------------------|
    | Proc   | Thrd   | Addr               | Name                                           | Create time        | Exit time          |
    |--------|--------|--------------------|------------------------------------------------|--------------------|--------------------|
    | 0x0250 | 0x0264 | 0x00007FFC884B6870 | ntdll!TppWorkerThread                          | 13/11/2021 22:14:27 | 00/00/   0 00:00:00 |
    | 0x0250 | 0x0268 | 0x00007FFC85961820 | CSRSRV!CsrApiRequestThread                     | 13/11/2021 22:14:27 | 00/00/   0 00:00:00 |
    | 0x0250 | 0x02a0 | 0x00007FFC858FE680 | winsrvext!TerminalServerRequestThread          | 13/11/2021 22:14:28 | 00/00/   0 00:00:00 |
    | 0x0250 | 0x02a4 | 0x00007FFC858F2710 | winsrvext!GdiAddInitialFontsThread             | 13/11/2021 22:14:28 | 13/11/2021 22:14:29 |
    | 0x0250 | 0x02a8 | 0x00007FFC858F3430 | winsrvext!NotificationThread                   | 13/11/2021 22:14:28 | 00/00/   0 00:00:00 |
    | 0x0250 | 0x02ac | 0x00007FFC858F3950 | winsrvext!PowerNotificationThread              | 13/11/2021 22:14:28 | 00/00/   0 00:00:00 |
    | 0x0250 | 0x02b0 | 0x00007FFC859674B0 | CSRSRV!CsrSbApiRequestThread                   | 13/11/2021 22:14:28 | 00/00/   0 00:00:00 |
    | 0x0250 | 0x02f0 | 0x00007FFC85961820 | CSRSRV!CsrApiRequestThread                     | 13/11/2021 22:14:28 | 00/00/   0 00:00:00 |
    | 0x0250 | 0x02fc | 0x00007FFC858F3FC0 | winsrvext!StartCreateSystemThreads             | 13/11/2021 22:14:28 | 00/00/   0 00:00:00 |
    | 0x0250 | 0x0300 | 0x00007FFC858F3FC0 | winsrvext!StartCreateSystemThreads             | 13/11/2021 22:14:28 | 00/00/   0 00:00:00 |
    | 0x0250 | 0x01bc | 0x00007FFC884B6870 | ntdll!TppWorkerThread                          | 13/11/2021 22:14:29 | 00/00/   0 00:00:00 |
    | 0x0250 | 0x0318 | 0x00007FFC858FCB30 | winsrvext!AutoRotationRequestThread            | 13/11/2021 22:14:30 | 00/00/   0 00:00:00 |
    | 0x0250 | 0x039c | 0x00007FFC85961820 | CSRSRV!CsrApiRequestThread                     | 13/11/2021 22:14:30 | 00/00/   0 00:00:00 |
    | 0x0250 | 0x1204 | 0xFFFFBD43FB968DB0 | cdd!PresentWorkerThread                        | 13/11/2021 22:14:47 | 00/00/   0 00:00:00 |
```

```
0: kd> !ms_process /pid 0x250 /dlls /exports

Process:       csrss.exe          (PID=0x0250 [592]) | [+Dlls] [+Exports] [+Handles] [+Threads] [+VADs] [+Scan]
[+Select context]
    ImageBase: 0x7FF667950000 ImageSize: 0x7000 (IsPagedOut = False, IsSigned = -888430464)
    Path:           \Device\HarddiskVolume4\Windows\System32\csrss.exe
    PDB:            csrss.pdb
    Vendor:         Microsoft Corporation
    Version:        10.0.22000.1 (WinBuild.160101.0800)
    Description:    Client Server Runtime Process
    Commandline:    %SystemRoot%\system32\csrss.exe ObjectDirectory=\Windows SharedSection=1024,20480,768 Windows=On
SubSystemType=Windows ServerDll=basesrv,1 ServerDll=winsrv:UserServerDllInitialization,3 ServerDll=sxssrv,4
ProfileControl=Off MaxRequestThreads=16
    Sections:      .text, .rdata, .data, .pdata, .rsrc, .reloc,
    -> [  0]: (     ) C:\WINDOWS\system32\csrss.exe (ImageBase: 0x7FF667950000, ImageSize: 0x7000)
    -> [  1]: (     ) C:\WINDOWS\SYSTEM32\ntdll.dll (ImageBase: 0x7FFC884A0000, ImageSize: 0x207000)
    |------|------|--------------------|----------------------------------------------------|---------|
    | Indx | Ord  | Addr               | Name                                               | Patched | Hooked |
    |------|------|--------------------|----------------------------------------------------|---------|
    |    0 |    1 | 0x00007FFC884B2A50 | A_SHAFinal                                         |         |
    |    1 |    2 | 0x00007FFC884B2B80 | A_SHAInit                                          |         |
    |    2 |    3 | 0x00007FFC884B2BC0 | A_SHAUpdate                                        |         |
    |    3 |    4 | 0x00007FFC8858BAB0 | AlpcAdjustCompletionListConcurrencyCount           |         |
    |    4 |    5 | 0x00007FFC88514790 | AlpcFreeCompletionListMessage                      |         |
    |    5 |    6 | 0x00007FFC8858BAE0 | AlpcGetCompletionListLastMessageInformation        |         |
    |    6 |    7 | 0x00007FFC8858BB00 | AlpcGetCompletionListMessageAttributes             |         |
    |    7 |    8 | 0x00007FFC88518A00 | AlpcGetHeaderSize                                  |         |
    |    8 |    9 | 0x00007FFC885189C0 | AlpcGetMessageAttribute                            |         |
    |    9 |   10 | 0x00007FFC884BDE70 | AlpcGetMessageFromCompletionList                   |         |
    |   10 |   11 | 0x00007FFC8852D6B0 | AlpcGetOutstandingCompletionListMessageCount       |         |
    |   11 |   12 | 0x00007FFC88518960 | AlpcInitializeMessageAttribute                     |         |
    |   12 |   13 | 0x00007FFC8852BCF0 | AlpcMaxAllowedMessageLength                        |         |
    |   13 |   14 | 0x00007FFC8852D660 | AlpcRegisterCompletionList                         |         |
    |   14 |   15 | 0x00007FFC88519F90 | AlpcRegisterCompletionListWorkerThread             |         |
    |   15 |   16 | 0x00007FFC8852D8D0 | AlpcRundownCompletionList                          |         |
    |   16 |   17 | 0x00007FFC8852D8F0 | AlpcUnregisterCompletionList                       |         |
    |   17 |   18 | 0x00007FFC88519F30 | AlpcUnregisterCompletionListWorkerThread           |         |
    |   18 |   19 | 0x00007FFC8851D7D0 | ApiSetQueryApiSetPresence                          |         |
    |   19 |   20 | 0x00007FFC8852D770 | ApiSetQueryApiSetPresenceEx                        |         |
    |   20 |   21 | 0x00007FFC885194F0 | CsrAllocateCaptureBuffer                           |         |
    |   21 |   22 | 0x00007FFC885194A0 | CsrAllocateMessagePointer                          |         |
    |   22 |   23 | 0x00007FFC88518A60 | CsrCaptureMessageBuffer                            |         |
    |   23 |   24 | 0x00007FFC885192F0 | CsrCaptureMessageMultiUnicodeStringsInPlace        |         |
    |   24 |   25 | 0x00007FFC885193F0 | CsrCaptureMessageString                            |         |
    |   25 |   26 | 0x00007FFC88576440 | CsrCaptureTimeout                                  |         |
    |   26 |   27 | 0x00007FFC88519140 | CsrClientCallServer                                |         |
    |   27 |   28 | 0x00007FFC88518AC0 | CsrClientConnectToServer                           |         |
    |   28 |   29 | 0x00007FFC88519110 | CsrFreeCaptureBuffer                               |         |
    |   29 |   30 | 0x00007FFC88576470 | CsrGetProcessId                                    |         |
    |   30 |   31 | 0x00007FFC88532A60 | CsrIdentifyAlertableThread                         |         |
    |   31 |   32 | 0x00007FFC88581CA0 | CsrSetPriorityClass                                |         |
    |   32 |   33 | 0x00007FFC88576490 | CsrVerifyRegion                                    |         |
    |   33 |   34 | 0x00007FFC88546F70 | DbgBreakPoint                                      |         |
    |   34 |   35 | 0x00007FFC884A6930 | DbgPrint                                           |         |
    |   35 |   36 | 0x00007FFC884A5C50 | DbgPrintEx                                         |         |
    |   36 |   37 | 0x00007FFC8858BB40 | DbgPrintReturnControlC                             |         |
    |   37 |   38 | 0x00007FFC8858BB90 | DbgPrompt                                          |         |
    |   38 |   39 | 0x00007FFC8858BBE0 | DbgQueryDebugFilterState                           |         |
    |   39 |   40 | 0x00007FFC8858BBF0 | DbgSetDebugFilterState                             |         |
    |   40 |   41 | 0x00007FFC88577C50 | DbgUiConnectToDbg                                  |         |
    |   41 |   42 | 0x00007FFC88577CC0 | DbgUiContinue                                      |         |
    |   42 |   43 | 0x00007FFC88577CF0 | DbgUiConvertStateChangeStructure                   |         |
    |   43 |   44 | 0x00007FFC88577D00 | DbgUiConvertStateChangeStructureEx                 |         |
    |   44 |   45 | 0x00007FFC88577FB0 | DbgUiDebugActiveProcess                            |         |
    |   45 |   46 | 0x00007FFC88578020 | DbgUiGetThreadDebugObject                          |         |
    |   46 |   47 | 0x00007FFC88578040 | DbgUiIssueRemoteBreakin                            |         |
    |   47 |   48 | 0x00007FFC885780B0 | DbgUiRemoteBreakin                                 |         |
    |   48 |   49 | 0x00007FFC88578110 | DbgUiSetThreadDebugObject                          |         |
    |   49 |   50 | 0x00007FFC88578130 | DbgUiStopDebugging                                 |         |
    |   50 |   51 | 0x00007FFC88578150 | DbgUiWaitStateChange                               |         |
    |   51 |   52 | 0x00007FFC88546F80 | DbgUserBreakPoint                                  |         |
    |   52 |   53 | 0x00007FFC8852CA70 | EtwCheckCoverage                                   |         |
    |   53 |   54 | 0x00007FFC885C1DD0 | EtwCreateTraceInstanceId                           |         |
```

```
     |  54 |  55 | 0x00007FFC884A7460 | EtwDeliverDataBlock                     |         |
     |  55 |  56 | 0x00007FFC885C19B0 | EtwEnumerateProcessRegGuids             |         |
     |  56 |  57 | 0x00007FFC884FE160 | EtwEventActivityIdControl               |         |
     |  57 |  58 | 0x00007FFC884A4AD0 | EtwEventEnabled                         |         |
     |  58 |  59 | 0x00007FFC8851A6B0 | EtwEventProviderEnabled                 |         |
     |  59 |  60 | 0x00007FFC884B5920 | EtwEventRegister                        |         |
     |  60 |  61 | 0x00007FFC884B54D0 | EtwEventSetInformation                  |         |
     |  61 |  62 | 0x00007FFC884A6560 | EtwEventUnregister                      |         |
     |  62 |  63 | 0x00007FFC884A6180 | EtwEventWrite                           |         |
     |  63 |  64 | 0x00007FFC884A49E0 | EtwEventWriteEndScenario                |         |
     |  64 |  65 | 0x00007FFC884A6120 | EtwEventWriteEx                         |         |
     |  65 |  66 | 0x00007FFC884A60D0 | EtwEventWriteFull                       |         |
     |  66 |  67 | 0x00007FFC8852A460 | EtwEventWriteNoRegistration             |         |
     |  67 |  68 | 0x00007FFC884A2EC0 | EtwEventWriteStartScenario              |         |
     |  68 |  69 | 0x00007FFC885C1AB0 | EtwEventWriteString                     |         |
     |  69 |  70 | 0x00007FFC884A4EC0 | EtwEventWriteTransfer                   |         |
     |  70 |  71 | 0x00007FFC885270F0 | EtwGetTraceEnableFlags                  |         |
     |  71 |  72 | 0x00007FFC885270B0 | EtwGetTraceEnableLevel                  |         |
     |  72 |  73 | 0x00007FFC88527070 | EtwGetTraceLoggerHandle                 |         |
     |  73 |  74 | 0x00007FFC8852DF80 | EtwLogTraceEvent                        |         |
     |  74 |  75 | 0x00007FFC884B65B0 | EtwNotificationRegister                 |         |
     |  75 |  76 | 0x00007FFC884A6570 | EtwNotificationUnregister               |         |
     |  76 |  77 | 0x00007FFC884A6BF0 | EtwProcessPrivateLoggerRequest          |         |
     |  77 |  78 | 0x00007FFC88532950 | EtwRegisterSecurityProvider             |         |
     |  78 |  79 | 0x00007FFC8852BC20 | EtwRegisterTraceGuidsA                  |         |
     |  79 |  80 | 0x00007FFC884B5310 | EtwRegisterTraceGuidsW                  |         |
     |  80 |  81 | 0x00007FFC884A7CA0 | EtwReplyNotification                    |         |
     |  81 |  82 | 0x00007FFC884A4B60 | EtwSendNotification                     |         |
     |  82 |  83 | 0x00007FFC88531380 | EtwSetMark                              |         |
     |  83 |  84 | 0x00007FFC885C1E30 | EtwTraceEventInstance                   |         |
     |  84 |  85 | 0x00007FFC884A6410 | EtwTraceMessage                         |         |
     |  85 |  86 | 0x00007FFC884A6440 | EtwTraceMessageVa                       |         |
     |  86 |  87 | 0x00007FFC884A6510 | EtwUnregisterTraceGuids                 |         |
     |  87 |  88 | 0x00007FFC88521C60 | EtwWriteUMSecurityEvent                 |         |
     |  88 |  89 | 0x00007FFC884A7F80 | EtwpCreateEtwThread                     |         |
     |  89 |  90 | 0x00007FFC884A8470 | EtwpGetCpuSpeed                         |         | Yes
     |  90 |  91 | 0x00007FFC885C2F70 | EvtIntReportAuthzEventAndSourceAsync    |         |
     |  91 |  92 | 0x00007FFC884A5C90 | EvtIntReportEventAndSourceAsync         |         |
     |  92 |  93 | 0x00007FFC88547020 | ExpInterlockedPopEntrySListEnd          |         |
     |  93 |  94 | 0x00007FFC88547017 | ExpInterlockedPopEntrySListFault        |         |
     |  94 |  95 | 0x00007FFC88547007 | ExpInterlockedPopEntrySListResume       |         |
     |  95 |  96 | 0x00007FFC88547350 | KiRaiseUserExceptionDispatcher          |         |
     |  96 |  97 | 0x00007FFC88547180 | KiUserApcDispatcher                     |         |
     |  97 |  98 | 0x00007FFC88547290 | KiUserCallbackDispatcher                |         |
     |  98 |  99 | 0x00007FFC885472E0 | KiUserExceptionDispatcher               |         |
     |  99 | 100 | 0x00007FFC8862D500 | KiUserInvertedFunctionTable             |         |
     | 100 | 101 | 0x00007FFC884D83D0 | LdrAccessResource                       |         | Yes
     | 101 | 102 | 0x00007FFC884FFC40 | LdrAddDllDirectory                      |         |
     | 102 | 103 | 0x00007FFC88507280 | LdrAddLoadAsDataTable                   |         |
     | 103 | 104 | 0x00007FFC884D4F00 | LdrAddRefDll                            |         |
[...]
```

```
0: kd> u 0x00007FFC85A34A70 L1
gdi32full!NtGdiCombineRgn:
00007ffc`85a34a70 ff2552a30700    jmp     qword ptr [gdi32full!_imp_NtGdiCombineRgn (00007ffc`85aaedc8)]
```

```
0: kd> u 0x00007FFC884A7F80 L1
ntdll!EtwpCreateEtwThread:
00007ffc`884a7f80 4c8bdc          mov     r11,rsp
```

Note: Hooking can be normal in most cases.

12. We close logging before exiting WinDbg:

```
0: kd> .logclose
Closing open log file C:\EWMDA-Dumps\Complete\x64\ES5.log
```

Exercise ES6

- **Goal:** Explore 0cchext WinDbg extension
- **Memory Analysis Patterns:** Execution Residue (Unmanaged Space); Namespace; Context Pointer; Rough Stack Trace (Unmanaged Space); Step Dumps; Evental Dumps
- \EWMDA\Exercise-ES6.pdf

0cchext
https://github.com/0cch/0cchext

Exercise ES6: Explore Occhext WinDbg Extension

Goal: Explore the Occhext[10] WinDbg extension.

Memory Analysis Patterns: Execution Residue (Unmanaged Space); Namespace; Context Pointer; Rough Stack Trace (Unmanaged Space); Step Dumps; Evental Dumps.

1. Launch WinDbg.

2. Open \EWMDA-Dumps\Complete\x64\MEMORY-W11.DMP.

3. We get the dump file loaded:

```
Microsoft (R) Windows Debugger Version 10.0.27668.1000 AMD64
Copyright (c) Microsoft Corporation. All rights reserved.


Loading Dump File [C:\EWMDA-Dumps\Complete\x64\MEMORY-W11.DMP]
Kernel Bitmap Dump File: Full address space is available


************* Path validation summary **************
Response                         Time (ms)     Location
Deferred                                       srv*
Symbol search path is: srv*
Executable search path is:
Windows 10 Kernel Version 22000 MP (2 procs) Free x64
Product: WinNt, suite: TerminalServer SingleUserTS Personal
Edition build lab: 22000.1.amd64fre.co_release.210604-1628
Kernel base = 0xfffff806`61e00000 PsLoadedModuleList = 0xfffff806`62a296b0
Debug session time: Sat Nov 13 23:17:16.607 2021 (UTC + 1:00)
System Uptime: 0 days 0:03:06.813
Loading Kernel Symbols
...............................................................
................................................................
................................................................
..
Loading User Symbols
...................................
Loading unloaded module list
........
For analysis of this file, run !analyze -v
nt!KeBugCheckEx:
fffff806`62215590 mov     qword ptr [rsp+8],rcx ss:0018:ffffbe82`96f64670=000000000000000a
```

4. We open a log file:

```
0: kd> .logopen C:\EWMDA-Dumps\Complete\x64\ES6.log
Opened log file 'C:\EWMDA-Dumps\Complete\x64\ES6.log'
```

[10] https://github.com/Occh/Occhext

5. We downloaded the latest release at the time of this writing[11] and included it in the dump archive. We can load it now:

```
0: kd> .load C:\EWMDA-Dumps\0cchext\x64\0cchext

0: kd> !0cchext.help
Commands for C:\EWMDA-Dumps\0cchext\x64\0cchext.dll:
  !a                 - Assembles instruction mnemonics and puts the resulting
                       instruction codes into memory.
  !a64               - Input x64 asm code.
  !accessmask        - Interpret ACCESS MASK value
  !addmodule         - Adds a synthetic module to the module list the debugger
                       maintains for the current process.
  !addsymbol         - Adds a synthetic symbol to a module in the current
                       process.
  !autocmd           - Execute the debugger commands.(The config file is
                       autocmd.ini)
  !bing              - Use bing to search.
  !carray            - Show data in C array style.
  !cppexcrname       - Print cpp exception name.
  !dlsym             - Download symbol by path.
  !dpx               - Display the contents of memory in the given range.
  !dttoc             - Translate 'dt' command output text to C struct.
  !dtx               - Displays information about structures. (The config file is
                       struct.ini)
  !du8               - Display UTF-8 string.
  !err               - Decodes and displays information about an error value.
  !favcmd            - Display the favorite debugger commands.(The config file is
                       favcmd.ini)
  !filepath          - Show file path by handle.
  !google            - Use google to search.
  !grep              - Search plain-text data sets for lines matching a regular
                       expression.
  !gt                - Go and interrupted after a period of time (ms).
  !help              - Displays information on available extension commands
  !hwnd              - Show window information by handle.
  !import_vs_bps     - Import visual studio breakpoints.
  !init_script_env   - Initialize script environment.
  !listmodule        - List the synthetic modules.
  !listsymbol        - List the synthetic symbols.
  !logcmd            - Log command line to log file
  !memstat           - Statistics virtual memory allocation.
  !oledata           - Print tagSOleTlsData.
  !pe_export         - Dump PE export functions
  !pe_import         - Dump PE import modules and functions
  !rawpcap_start     - Start to capture IP packet. (requires administrative
                       privileges)
  !rawpcap_stop      - Stop capturing. (requires administrative privileges)
  !removemodule      - removes a synthetic module from the module list the
                       debugger maintains for the current process.
  !removesymbol      - Specifies the synthetic symbol to remove.
  !rr                - Read registers and show the information.
  !setdlsympath      - Set download symbol path.
  !setvprot          - Set the protection on a region of committed pages in the
                       virtual address space of the debuggee process.
  !stackstat         - Statistics duplicate stack data.
```

[11] https://github.com/0cch/0cchext/releases/tag/1.20.2.111

```
  !threadname       - List thread name.
  !traceclear       - Clear trace event.
  !traceclose       - Close a trace event.
  !tracecreate      - Create a trace event.
  !tracedisplay     - Display trace event.
  !url              - Open a URL in a default browser.
  !version          - Displays the version information for 0cchext.dll
  !wql              - Query system information with WMI.
!help <cmd> will give more information for a particular command
```

We now show examples of commands we found useful.

6. The **!dpx** command is a combined version of **dps**, **du**, and **da** commands (some UNICODE noise is removed):

```
0: kd> !dpx @rsp 50
ffffbe8296f64668  fffff806622281a9  [S] nt!KiBugCheckDispatch+0x69 (fffff806`622281a9)  [U] ""
ffffbe8296f64670  000000000000000a  [D] ........
ffffbe8296f64678  ffffac8a0d8ea010  [D] ........
ffffbe8296f64680  0000000000000002  [D] ........
ffffbe8296f64688  0000000000000000  [D] ........
ffffbe8296f64690  fffff80660571981  [S] myfault+0x1981 (fffff806`60571981)
ffffbe8296f64698  0000000000000000  [D] ........
ffffbe8296f646a0  0000000000000000  [D] ........
ffffbe8296f646a8  0000000000000000  [D] ........
ffffbe8296f646b0  0000000000000000  [D] ........
ffffbe8296f646b8  0000000000000000  [D] ........
ffffbe8296f646c0  0000000000000000  [D] ........
ffffbe8296f646c8  0000000000000000  [D] ........
ffffbe8296f646d0  0000000000000000  [D] ........
ffffbe8296f646d8  0000000000000000  [D] ........
ffffbe8296f646e0  0000000000000000  [D] ........
ffffbe8296f646e8  0000000000000000  [D] ........
ffffbe8296f646f0  0000000000000000  [D] ........
ffffbe8296f646f8  0000000000000000  [D] ........
ffffbe8296f64700  0000000000000000  [D] ........
ffffbe8296f64708  0000000000000000  [D] ........
ffffbe8296f64710  0000000000000000  [D] ........
ffffbe8296f64718  0000000000000000  [D] ........
ffffbe8296f64720  0000000000000000  [D] ........
ffffbe8296f64728  0000000000000000  [D] ........
ffffbe8296f64730  0000000000000000  [D] ........
ffffbe8296f64738  0000000000000000  [D] ........
ffffbe8296f64740  0000000000000000  [D] ........
ffffbe8296f64748  0000000000000000  [D] ........
ffffbe8296f64750  0000000000000000  [D] ........
ffffbe8296f64758  ffffbd43fa8b2468  [S] win32kbase!gDomainHookLock (ffffbd43`fa8b2468)
ffffbe8296f64760  fffffc571d9ef0d5  [D] ....W...
ffffbe8296f64768  ffffbd43fa619191  [S] win32kbase!ThreadUnlock1+0x71 (ffffbd43`fa619191)
ffffbe8296f64770  ffffac8a0d8ea010  [D] ........
ffffbe8296f64778  ffffc38c31efb390  [D] ...1....
ffffbe8296f64780  ffffc38c31efb360  [U] ".Ę"  [A] "."
ffffbe8296f64788  ffffc38c31efb370  [D] p..1....
ffffbe8296f64790  ffffc38c2c4792d0  [U] ".Ő."  [A] "."
ffffbe8296f64798  0000000000000001  [D] ........
ffffbe8296f647a0  ffffc38c34dd8690  [U] ".Ø"  [A] "."
ffffbe8296f647a8  fffff80662224300  [S] nt!KiPageFault+0x440 (fffff806`62224300)
ffffbe8296f647b0  0000000000000000  [D] ........
ffffbe8296f647b8  ffffbd11c0e0c2b8  [D] ........
ffffbe8296f647c0  ffff2703d5aecdf2  [D] .....'..
ffffbe8296f647c8  ffffbd11c253e710  [U] "."  [A] "..."
ffffbe8296f647d0  0000000000000f4d  [D] M.......
ffffbe8296f647d8  00001f8001000000  [D] ........
```

```
ffffbe8296f647e0  0000000000001000  [D] ........
ffffbe8296f647e8  ffffac8a0d8e7000  [D] .p......
ffffbe8296f647f0  ffffac8a0d480000  [D] ..H.....
ffffbe8296f647f8  ffffac8a0d480000  [D] ..H.....
ffffbe8296f64800  ffffc38c2c402000  [U] ""  [A] "UMDu"
ffffbe8296f64808  fffff80662a5f540  [S] nt!ExPoolState+0x4580 (fffff806`62a5f540)  [U] ".."  [A] "."
ffffbe8296f64810  ffffac8a0d8e7000  [D] .p......
ffffbe8296f64818  fffff8066258de9e  [S] nt!KeUserModeCallback+0x27e (fffff806`6258de9e)
ffffbe8296f64820  0000000000000000  [D] ........
ffffbe8296f64828  0000000000000000  [D] ........
ffffbe8296f64830  0000000000000000  [D] ........
ffffbe8296f64838  0000000000000000  [D] ........
ffffbe8296f64840  0000000000000000  [D] ........
ffffbe8296f64848  0000000000000000  [D] ........
ffffbe8296f64850  0000000000000000  [D] ........
ffffbe8296f64858  0000000000000000  [D] ........
ffffbe8296f64860  0000000000000000  [D] ........
ffffbe8296f64868  0000000000000000  [D] ........
ffffbe8296f64870  0000000000000000  [D] ........
ffffbe8296f64878  0000000000000000  [D] ........
ffffbe8296f64880  ffffac8a0d8ea010  [D] ........
ffffbe8296f64888  0000000000000000  [D] ........
ffffbe8296f64890  0000000000000103  [D] ........
ffffbe8296f64898  0000000000000000  [D] ........
ffffbe8296f648a0  0000000000000001  [D] ........
ffffbe8296f648a8  0000000000000000  [D] ........
ffffbe8296f648b0  0000000000000800  [D] ........
ffffbe8296f648b8  fffff8066286b964  [S] nt!ExAllocatePoolWithTag+0x64 (fffff806`6286b964)
ffffbe8296f648c0  0000000000000000  [D] ........
ffffbe8296f648c8  0000000000000000  [D] ........
ffffbe8296f648d0  0000000000000001  [D] ........
ffffbe8296f648d8  ffffc38c31efb370  [D] p..1....
ffffbe8296f648e0  ffffc38c34dd8690  [U] ".Ø"  [A] "."
```

7. A useful alternative to the **dt** command is **!dttoc**:

```
0: kd> !dttoc _KPROCESS
struct _KPROCESS {
	_DISPATCHER_HEADER Header;
	_LIST_ENTRY ProfileListHead;
	QWORD DirectoryTableBase;
	_LIST_ENTRY ThreadListHead;
	DWORD ProcessLock;
	DWORD ProcessTimerDelay;
	QWORD DeepFreezeStartTime;
	_KAFFINITY_EX Affinity;
	_LIST_ENTRY ReadyListHead;
	_SINGLE_LIST_ENTRY SwapListEntry;
	_KAFFINITY_EX ActiveProcessors;
	union {
		Int4B ProcessFlags;
		struct {
			DWORD AutoAlignment:1;
			DWORD DisableBoost:1;
			DWORD DisableQuantum:1;
			DWORD DeepFreeze:1;
			DWORD TimerVirtualization:1;
			DWORD CheckStackExtents:1;
			DWORD CacheIsolationEnabled:1;
			DWORD PpmPolicy:4;
			DWORD VaSpaceDeleted:1;
```

```
                DWORD MultiGroup:1;
                DWORD ReservedFlags:19;
            };
        };
        DWORD ActiveGroupsMask;
        Char BasePriority;
        Char QuantumReset;
        Char Visited;
        _KEXECUTE_OPTIONS Flags;
        WORD ThreadSeed[32];
        WORD IdealProcessor[32];
        WORD IdealNode[32];
        WORD IdealGlobalNode;
        WORD Spare1;
        _KSTACK_COUNT StackCount;
        _LIST_ENTRY ProcessListEntry;
        QWORD CycleTime;
        QWORD ContextSwitches;
        _KSCHEDULING_GROUP* SchedulingGroup;
        DWORD FreezeCount;
        DWORD KernelTime;
        DWORD UserTime;
        DWORD ReadyTime;
        QWORD UserDirectoryTableBase;
        BYTE AddressPolicy;
        BYTE Spare2[71];
        VOID* InstrumentationCallback;
        <unnamed-tag> SecureState;
        QWORD KernelWaitTime;
        QWORD UserWaitTime;
        QWORD LastRebalanceQpc;
        VOID* PerProcessorCycleTimes;
        QWORD ExtendedFeatureDisableMask;
        WORD PrimaryGroup;
        WORD Spare3[3];
        VOID* UserCetLogging;
        QWORD EndPadding[3];
};
```

8. If we need to see imported and exported functions for a module with a possible filter, we can use **!pe_import** and **!pe_export** commands:

```
0: kd> !pe_export USER32.dll *Create*
ID   Address     Export Name     Symbol Name
0064 00007ffc8800f6d0  CreateAcceleratorTableA  USER32!CreateAcceleratorTableA (00007ffc`8800f6d0)
0065 00007ffc87ff1f30  CreateAcceleratorTableW  USER32!NtUserCreateAcceleratorTable (00007ffc`87ff1f30)
0066 00007ffc87fc28c0  CreateCaret  USER32!CreateCaretStub (00007ffc`87fc28c0)
0067 00007ffc87ff0450  CreateCursor  USER32!CreateCursor (00007ffc`87ff0450)
0068 00007ffc87ff1f50  CreateDCompositionHwndTarget  USER32!NtUserCreateDCompositionHwndTarget (00007ffc`87ff1f50)
0069 00007ffc8804b100  CreateDesktopA  USER32!CreateDesktopA (00007ffc`8804b100)
006A 00007ffc8804b140  CreateDesktopExA  USER32!CreateDesktopExA (00007ffc`8804b140)
006B 00007ffc87feadd0  CreateDesktopExW  USER32!CreateDesktopExW (00007ffc`87feadd0)
006C 00007ffc87fead90  CreateDesktopW  USER32!CreateDesktopW (00007ffc`87fead90)
006D 00007ffc8800f760  CreateDialogIndirectParamA  USER32!CreateDialogIndirectParamA (00007ffc`8800f760)
006E 00007ffc87fc32c0  CreateDialogIndirectParamAorW  USER32!CreateDialogIndirectParamAorW (00007ffc`87fc32c0)
006F 00007ffc87fc2b30  CreateDialogIndirectParamW  USER32!CreateDialogIndirectParamW (00007ffc`87fc2b30)
0070 00007ffc8800f790  CreateDialogParamA  USER32!CreateDialogParamA (00007ffc`8800f790)
0071 00007ffc87fc2f60  CreateDialogParamW  USER32!CreateDialogParamW (00007ffc`87fc2f60)
0072 00007ffc8800f8b0  CreateIcon  USER32!CreateIcon (00007ffc`8800f8b0)
0073 00007ffc8800f990  CreateIconFromResource  USER32!CreateIconFromResource (00007ffc`8800f990)
0074 00007ffc87fc7850  CreateIconFromResourceEx  USER32!CreateIconFromResourceEx (00007ffc`87fc7850)
```

```
0075 00007ffc87fcc160  CreateIconIndirect  USER32!CreateIconIndirect (00007ffc`87fcc160)
0076 00007ffc88039130  CreateMDIWindowA  USER32!CreateMDIWindowA (00007ffc`88039130)
0077 00007ffc880391b0  CreateMDIWindowW  USER32!CreateMDIWindowW (00007ffc`880391b0)
0078 00007ffc87ff09c0  CreateMenu  USER32!CreateMenu (00007ffc`87ff09c0)
0079 00007ffc87fec4e0  CreatePopupMenu  USER32!CreatePopupMenu (00007ffc`87fec4e0)
007A 00007ffc8803fc80  CreateSyntheticPointerDevice  USER32!CreateSyntheticPointerDevice (00007ffc`8803fc80)
007B 00007ffc8804cc70  CreateSystemThreads  USER32!CreateSystemThreads (00007ffc`8804cc70)
007C 00007ffc87feb9a0  CreateWindowExA  USER32!CreateWindowExA (00007ffc`87feb9a0)
007D 00007ffc87fc8030  CreateWindowExW  USER32!CreateWindowExW (00007ffc`87fc8030)
007E 00007ffc87fc46e0  CreateWindowInBand  USER32!CreateWindowInBand (00007ffc`87fc46e0)
007F 00007ffc87fc5ad0  CreateWindowInBandEx  USER32!CreateWindowInBandEx (00007ffc`87fc5ad0)
0080 00007ffc88045b40  CreateWindowIndirect  USER32!CreateWindowIndirect (00007ffc`88045b40)
0081 00007ffc8804b580  CreateWindowStationA  USER32!CreateWindowStationA (00007ffc`8804b580)
0082 00007ffc87fdf250  CreateWindowStationW  USER32!CreateWindowStationW (00007ffc`87fdf250)
008C 00007ffc8802af20  DdeCreateDataHandle  USER32!DdeCreateDataHandle (00007ffc`8802af20)
008D 00007ffc8802c1c0  DdeCreateStringHandleA  USER32!DdeCreateStringHandleA (00007ffc`8802c1c0)
008E 00007ffc87fd7400  DdeCreateStringHandleW  USER32!DdeCreateStringHandleW (00007ffc`87fd7400)
0394 00007ffc87fea0c0  ShutdownBlockReasonCreate  USER32!ShutdownBlockReasonCreate (00007ffc`87fea0c0)
```

```
0: kd> !pe_import USER32.dll *Create*
GDI32.dll  (detail)
001A 00007ffc86c91b50  ExtCreateRegion  GDI32!ExtCreateRegion (00007ffc`86c91b50)
0024 00007ffc86c92b20  CreateRectRgnIndirect  GDI32!CreateRectRgnIndirect (00007ffc`86c92b20)
0027 00007ffc86c92b40  CreateRectRgn  GDI32!CreateRectRgn (00007ffc`86c92b40)
002E 00007ffc86c987d0  CreateEllipticRgn  GDI32!CreateEllipticRgn (00007ffc`86c987d0)
0033 00007ffc86c95210  CreatePen  GDI32!CreatePenStub (00007ffc`86c95210)
0034 00007ffc86c94fc0  CreateBrushIndirect  GDI32!CreateBrushIndirectStub (00007ffc`86c94fc0)
003E 00007ffc86c94c50  CreateSolidBrush  GDI32!CreateSolidBrushStub (00007ffc`86c94c50)
0044 00007ffc86c95420  CreatePalette  GDI32!CreatePaletteStub (00007ffc`86c95420)
0056 00007ffc86c91350  CreateFontIndirectW  GDI32!CreateFontIndirectW (00007ffc`86c91350)
0058 00007ffc86c996f0  GdiCreateLocalEnhMetaFile  GDI32!GdiCreateLocalEnhMetaFile (00007ffc`86c996f0)
0059 00007ffc86c99710  GdiCreateLocalMetaFilePict  GDI32!GdiCreateLocalMetaFilePict (00007ffc`86c99710)
006E 00007ffc86c92a40  CreateDIBSection  GDI32!CreateDIBSectionStub (00007ffc`86c92a40)
006F 00007ffc86c946b0  CreateBitmap  GDI32!CreateBitmapStub (00007ffc`86c946b0)
0070 00007ffc86c94b00  CreateCompatibleBitmap  GDI32!CreateCompatibleBitmapStub (00007ffc`86c94b00)
0071 00007ffc86c94870  CreateDIBitmap  GDI32!CreateDIBitmapStub (00007ffc`86c94870)
0072 00007ffc86c913a0  CreateDCW  GDI32!CreateDCW (00007ffc`86c913a0)
0073 00007ffc86c99f90  GdiTrackHCreate  GDI32!GdiTrackHCreate (00007ffc`86c99f90)
0076 00007ffc86c93eb0  CreateCompatibleDC  GDI32!CreateCompatibleDCStub (00007ffc`86c93eb0)

KERNELBASE.dll  (detail)

api-ms-win-core-apiquery-l1-1-0.dll  (detail)

api-ms-win-core-apiquery-l2-1-0.dll  (detail)

api-ms-win-core-appinit-l1-1-0.dll  (detail)

api-ms-win-core-atoms-l1-1-0.dll  (detail)

api-ms-win-core-debug-l1-1-0.dll  (detail)

api-ms-win-core-delayload-l1-1-0.dll  (detail)

api-ms-win-core-delayload-l1-1-1.dll  (detail)

api-ms-win-core-errorhandling-l1-1-0.dll  (detail)

api-ms-win-core-errorhandling-l1-1-2.dll  (detail)

api-ms-win-core-file-l1-1-0.dll  (detail)
0004 00007ffc85c227b0  CreateFileW  KERNELBASE!CreateFileW (00007ffc`85c227b0)

api-ms-win-core-handle-l1-1-0.dll  (detail)

api-ms-win-core-heap-l1-1-0.dll  (detail)

api-ms-win-core-heap-l2-1-0.dll  (detail)

api-ms-win-core-heap-obsolete-l1-1-0.dll  (detail)

api-ms-win-core-kernel32-legacy-l1-1-0.dll  (detail)
```

```
api-ms-win-core-kernel32-legacy-l1-1-1.dll  (detail)

api-ms-win-core-kernel32-private-l1-1-0.dll  (detail)

api-ms-win-core-libraryloader-l1-2-0.dll  (detail)

api-ms-win-core-localization-l1-2-0.dll  (detail)

api-ms-win-core-localization-obsolete-l1-2-0.dll  (detail)

api-ms-win-core-memory-l1-1-0.dll  (detail)
0000 00007ffc85c33c70  CreateFileMappingW  KERNELBASE!CreateFileMappingW (00007ffc`85c33c70)

api-ms-win-core-memory-l1-1-3.dll  (detail)

api-ms-win-core-privateprofile-l1-1-0.dll  (detail)

api-ms-win-core-processenvironment-l1-1-0.dll  (detail)

api-ms-win-core-processthreads-l1-1-0.dll  (detail)
0003 00007ffc876baab0  CreateProcessW  KERNEL32!CreateProcessWStub (00007ffc`876baab0)
0004 00007ffc876b9e40  CreateThread  KERNEL32!CreateThreadStub (00007ffc`876b9e40)

api-ms-win-core-processthreads-l1-1-1.dll  (detail)

api-ms-win-core-profile-l1-1-0.dll  (detail)

api-ms-win-core-registry-l1-1-0.dll  (detail)
0000 00007ffc85c23b00  RegCreateKeyExW  KERNELBASE!RegCreateKeyExW (00007ffc`85c23b00)

api-ms-win-core-sidebyside-l1-1-0.dll  (detail)

api-ms-win-core-string-l1-1-0.dll  (detail)

api-ms-win-core-string-l2-1-0.dll  (detail)

api-ms-win-core-string-obsolete-l1-1-0.dll  (detail)

api-ms-win-core-stringansi-l1-1-0.dll  (detail)

api-ms-win-core-synch-l1-1-0.dll  (detail)
0003 00007ffc85c33e00  CreateSemaphoreExW  KERNELBASE!CreateSemaphoreExW (00007ffc`85c33e00)
000A 00007ffc85c33cd0  CreateMutexExW  KERNELBASE!CreateMutexExW (00007ffc`85c33cd0)

api-ms-win-core-synch-l1-2-0.dll  (detail)

api-ms-win-core-sysinfo-l1-1-0.dll  (detail)

api-ms-win-core-threadpool-l1-2-0.dll  (detail)
0001 00007ffc85c506a0  CreateThreadpoolTimer  KERNELBASE!CreateThreadpoolTimer (00007ffc`85c506a0)

api-ms-win-eventing-provider-l1-1-0.dll  (detail)

api-ms-win-security-base-l1-1-0.dll  (detail)

api-ms-win-stateseparation-helpers-l1-1-0.dll  (detail)

ntdll.dll  (detail)
000E 00007ffc885436f0  NtCreateKey  ntdll!NtCreateKey (00007ffc`885436f0)
0012 00007ffc885137c0  RtlCreateUnicodeStringFromAsciiz  ntdll!RtlCreateUnicodeStringFromAsciiz (00007ffc`885137c0)
0025 00007ffc8851e0d0  RtlCreateHashTable  ntdll!RtlCreateHashTable (00007ffc`8851e0d0)

win32u.dll  (detail)
0001 00007ffc85b22e80  NtUserCreateLocalMemHandle  win32u!NtUserCreateLocalMemHandle (00007ffc`85b22e80)
0067 00007ffc85b28ce0  NtUserCreateWindowStation  win32u!NtUserCreateWindowStation (00007ffc`85b28ce0)
0069 00007ffc85b28c00  NtUserCreateDesktopEx  win32u!NtUserCreateDesktopEx (00007ffc`85b28c00)
006E 00007ffc85b28ca0  NtUserCreatePopupMenu  win32u!NtUserCreatePopupMenu (00007ffc`85b28ca0)
008F 00007ffc85b22160  NtUserCreateWindowEx  win32u!NtUserCreateWindowEx (00007ffc`85b22160)
0096 00007ffc85b2c2e0  NtUserShutdownBlockReasonCreate  win32u!NtUserShutdownBlockReasonCreate (00007ffc`85b2c2e0)
00A6 00007ffc85b235a0  NtCreateCompositionInputSink  win32u!NtCreateCompositionInputSink (00007ffc`85b235a0)
00A7 00007ffc85b28c80  NtUserCreatePalmRejectionDelayZone  win32u!NtUserCreatePalmRejectionDelayZone
(00007ffc`85b28c80)
00AE 00007ffc85b28cc0  NtUserCreateSystemThreads  win32u!NtUserCreateSystemThreads (00007ffc`85b28cc0)
00EB 00007ffc85b21920  NtUserCreateCaret  win32u!NtUserCreateCaret (00007ffc`85b21920)
```

```
0120 00007ffc85b28c60  NtUserCreateMenu  win32u!NtUserCreateMenu (00007ffc`85b28c60)
0139 00007ffc85b28c20  NtUserCreateEmptyCursorObject  win32u!NtUserCreateEmptyCursorObject (00007ffc`85b28c20)
0276 00007ffc85b28be0  NtUserCreateDCompositionHwndTarget  win32u!NtUserCreateDCompositionHwndTarget
(00007ffc`85b28be0)
0277 00007ffc85b28ba0  NtUserCreateActivationObject  win32u!NtUserCreateActivationObject (00007ffc`85b28ba0)
0278 00007ffc85b22f40  NtUserCreateAcceleratorTable  win32u!NtUserCreateAcceleratorTable (00007ffc`85b22f40)

0: kd> !pe_import Beep.sys *
ntoskrnl.exe  (detail)
0000 fffff8066204d550  IoStartNextPacket  nt!IoStartNextPacket (fffff806`6204d550)
0001 fffff8066204d830  KeRemoveDeviceQueue  nt!KeRemoveDeviceQueue (fffff806`6204d830)
0002 fffff8066209e1f0  MmUnlockPagableImageSection  nt!MmUnlockPagableImageSection (fffff806`6209e1f0)
0003 fffff8066248a840  MmLockPagableDataSection  nt!MmLockPagableDataSection (fffff806`6248a840)
0004 fffff8066212e920  ExReleaseFastMutex  nt!ExReleaseFastMutex (fffff806`6212e920)
0005 fffff806621d82d0  IoSetStartIoAttributes  nt!IoSetStartIoAttributes (fffff806`621d82d0)
0006 fffff806620c5f40  RtlInitUnicodeString  nt!RtlInitUnicodeString (fffff806`620c5f40)
0007 fffff80662020710  KeInitializeSpinLock  nt!KzInitializeSpinLock (fffff806`62020710)
0008 fffff806620a38d0  IoDeleteDevice  nt!IoDeleteDevice (fffff806`620a38d0)
0009 fffff8066204d470  IoStartPacket  nt!IoStartPacket (fffff806`6204d470)
000A fffff80662130d80  KeLowerIrql  nt!KzLowerIrql (fffff806`62130d80)
000B fffff80662048720  IoCsqInitialize  nt!IoCsqInitialize (fffff806`62048720)
000C fffff806620e5e70  ExAcquireFastMutex  nt!ExAcquireFastMutex (fffff806`620e5e70)
000D fffff8066236c200  KeRemoveEntryDeviceQueue  nt!KeRemoveEntryDeviceQueue (fffff806`6236c200)
000E fffff806625210d0  IoCreateDevice  nt!IoCreateDevice (fffff806`625210d0)
000F fffff8066201b570  IoAcquireCancelSpinLock  nt!IoAcquireCancelSpinLock (fffff806`6201b570)
0010 fffff806620c56a0  KeInitializeEvent  nt!KeInitializeEvent (fffff806`620c56a0)
0011 fffff80662098030  KfRaiseIrql  nt!KzRaiseIrql (fffff806`62098030)
0012 fffff80662134910  IofCompleteRequest  nt!IofCompleteRequest (fffff806`62134910)
0013 fffff8066201dc70  IoReleaseCancelSpinLock  nt!IoReleaseCancelSpinLock (fffff806`6201dc70)
0014 fffff80662053d70  IoGetRequestorSessionId  nt!IoGetRequestorSessionId (fffff806`62053d70)
0015 fffff80662095c70  KeAcquireSpinLockRaiseToDpc  nt!KeAcquireSpinLockRaiseToDpc (fffff806`62095c70)
0016 fffff80662130c20  KeReleaseSpinLock  nt!KeReleaseSpinLock (fffff806`62130c20)
0017 fffff80662020840  IoCsqRemoveNextIrp  nt!IoCsqRemoveNextIrp (fffff806`62020840)
0018 fffff80662020740  IoCsqInsertIrp  nt!IoCsqInsertIrp (fffff806`62020740)

0: kd> .process /r /p
Implicit process is now ffffc38c`2e16b080
Loading User Symbols
..................................

************* Symbol Loading Error Summary **************
Module name            Error
SharedUserData         No error - symbol load deferred
WdFilter               The system cannot find the file specified
vm3dmp                 The system cannot find the file specified
peauth                 The system cannot find the file specified
myfault                The system cannot find the file specified

You can troubleshoot most symbol related issues by turning on symbol loading diagnostics (!sym noisy) and repeating
the command that caused symbols to be loaded.
You should also verify that your symbol search path (.sympath) is correct.

0: kd> !pe_import notmyfault64.exe *Create*
ADVAPI32.dll  (detail)
0000 00007ffc874ed710  CreateServiceA  ADVAPI32!CreateServiceAStub (00007ffc`874ed710)
0012 00007ffc875036a0  RegCreateKeyA  ADVAPI32!RegCreateKeyA (00007ffc`875036a0)

COMCTL32.dll  (detail)

COMDLG32.dll  (detail)

GDI32.dll  (detail)
0005 00007ffc86c94c50  CreateSolidBrush  GDI32!CreateSolidBrushStub (00007ffc`86c94c50)
0006 00007ffc86c9bb60  CreateFontIndirectA  GDI32!CreateFontIndirectAStub (00007ffc`86c9bb60)
0007 00007ffc86c93eb0  CreateCompatibleDC  GDI32!CreateCompatibleDCStub (00007ffc`86c93eb0)
0008 00007ffc86c94b00  CreateCompatibleBitmap  GDI32!CreateCompatibleBitmapStub (00007ffc`86c94b00)

KERNEL32.dll  (detail)
000F 00007ffc876c2ed0  CreateFileW  KERNEL32!CreateFileW (00007ffc`876c2ed0)
002E 00007ffc876c2ec0  CreateFileA  KERNEL32!CreateFileA (00007ffc`876c2ec0)
006F 00007ffc876b9e40  CreateThread  KERNEL32!CreateThreadStub (00007ffc`876b9e40)

SHELL32.dll  (detail)
```

```
SHLWAPI.dll  (detail)

USER32.dll  (detail)

VERSION.dll  (detail)
```

9. The **!rr** command is similar to the **!for_each_register** script in the Context Pointer analysis pattern:

```
0: kd> !rr
rax  ffffbe8296f64770  [D] pG......
rbx  ffffac8a0d8ea010  [D] ........
rcx  000000000000000a  [D] ........
rdx  ffffac8a0d8ea010  [D] ........
rsi  ffffc38c31efb360  [D] `..1....  [U] ".Ę"  [A] "."
rdi  ffffc38c31efb390  [D] ...1....
rip  fffff80662215590  [D] .U!b....  [S] nt!KeBugCheckEx (fffff806`62215590)
rsp  ffffbe8296f64668  [D] hF......
rbp  ffffbe8296f64830  [D] 0H......
 r8  0000000000000002  [D] ........
 r9  0000000000000000  [D] ........
r10  fffff80660571981  [D] ..W`....  [S] myfault+0x1981 (fffff806`60571981)
r11  ffffac8a0d8e7000  [D] .p......
r12  ffffc38c31efb370  [D] p..1....
r13  ffffc38c2c4792d0  [D] ..G,....  [U] ".Ő."  [A] "."
r14  0000000000000001  [D] ........
r15  ffffc38c34dd8690  [D] ...4....  [U] ".Ø"  [A] "."
```

10. The **!dpx** command is similar to a combination of **dpS**, **dpp**, and **da**, **du**:

```
0: kd> ~1s

1: kd> !thread
THREAD ffffc38c3038d080  Cid 0acc.1f80  Teb: 000000abfee90000 Win32Thread: 0000000000000000 RUNNING on processor 1
Not impersonating
DeviceMap                 ffffac8a0423d290
Owning Process            ffffc38c31ae00c0       Image:         svchost.exe
Attached Process          ffffc38c2c515080       Image:         Registry
Wait Start TickCount      11956         Ticks: 0
Context Switch Count      1321          IdealProcessor: 0
UserTime                  00:00:00.234
KernelTime                00:00:00.062
Win32 Start Address ntdll!TppWorkerThread (0x00007ffc884b6870)
Stack Init ffffbe82956a7c70 Current ffffbe82956a6a70
Base ffffbe82956a8000 Limit ffffbe82956a2000 Call 0000000000000000
Priority 10  BasePriority 10  Priority Floor 7  IoPriority 3  PagePriority 5
Child-SP          RetAddr           : Args to Child                                                           : Call Site
ffffbe82`956a6cb0 fffff806`624f1f3d : ffffac8a`0cabecf0 00000000`00000001 00000000`00000000 ffffac8a`0cabecf0 : nt!CmpReportNotifyHelper+0xf4
ffffbe82`956a6d30 fffff806`62512c54 : ffffac8a`04e99048 ffffbe82`956a6f90 ffffbe82`956a7870 00000000`00000000 : nt!CmpReportNotifyForKcbStack+0x45
ffffbe82`956a6d70 fffff806`6257dbc3 : ffffbe82`956a7090 ffffbe82`956a0000 ffffc38c`332c4aa0 ffffbe82`956a7190 : nt!CmpCreateChild+0x66c
ffffbe82`956a6e90 fffff806`6257b4ef : 00000000`0000001a ffffbe82`956a73c0 ffffbe82`956a7348 00000000`00000000 : nt!CmpDoParseKey+0x22b3
ffffbe82`956a72d0 fffff806`62572562 : fffff806`6257b201 ffffc38c`00000000 ffffc38c`332c4aa0 00000000`00000001 : nt!CmpParseKey+0x2df
ffffbe82`956a74c0 fffff806`625719d1 : 00000000`00000000 ffffbe82`956a76f0 00000000`00000040 ffffc38c`2c4ff140 : nt!ObpLookupObjectName+0x652
ffffbe82`956a7660 fffff806`6251abd0 : 00000000`00000000 000000ab`ffcfcbe8 00000000`00000000 ffffc38c`2c4ff140 : nt!ObOpenObjectByNameEx+0x1f1
ffffbe82`956a7790 fffff806`6251a732 : 00000000`00000000 00000000`00000000 ffffc57`1e02ced5 00000000`00000000 : nt!CmCreateKey+0x480
ffffbe82`956a7a10 fffff806`62227b75 : 00000000`00000000 00000000`00000008 ffffffff`ffffffff 000000ab`ffcfd9a0 : nt!NtCreateKey+0x52
ffffbe82`956a7a70 00007ffc`88543704 : 00000000`00000000 00000000`00000000 00000000`00000000 00000000`00000000 : nt!KiSystemServiceCopyEnd+0x25 (TrapFrame
@ ffffbe82`956a7ae0)
000000ab`ffcfcb98 00000000`00000000 : 00000000`00000000 00000000`00000000 00000000`00000000 00000000`00000000 : ntdll!NtCreateKey+0x14

1: kd> !dpx ffffbe82956a2000 ffffbe82956a8000
Start memory scan  : 0xffffbe82956a2000
End memory scan    : 0xffffbe82956a8000

               r11 : 0xffffbe82956a6d28 : 0xfffff806624f1f3d : nt!CmpReportNotifyForKcbStack+0x45
0xffffbe82956a5388 : 0xfffff80662195c79 : nt!HalpHvCounterQueryCounter+0x19
0xffffbe82956a53b8 : 0xfffff806621a6329 : nt!EtwpCCSwapTrace+0x1a9
0xffffbe82956a5428 : 0xfffff806621a6127 : nt!EtwpLogContextSwapEvent+0x107
0xffffbe82956a5458 : 0xfffff8066212ea65 : nt!ExReleaseAutoExpandPushLockShared+0x85
```

```
0xffffbe82956a54b8 : 0xfffff806621a5fd3 : nt!EtwTraceContextSwap+0x83
0xffffbe82956a5538 : 0xfffff8066212ed7f : nt!KeSetEvent+0xdf
0xffffbe82956a55c8 : 0xfffff8066158c008 : FLTMGR!FltpFsControlCompletion+0x18
0xffffbe82956a55f8 : 0xfffff80662134a67 : nt!IopfCompleteRequest+0x127
0xffffbe82956a5678 : 0xfffff80662132955 : nt!KiSwapThread+0x8a5
0xffffbe82956a56a8 : 0xfffff806677e26c0 : Ntfs!NtfsCompareValues
0xffffbe82956a56c8 : 0xfffff8066789e8a6 : Ntfs!BinarySearchIndex+0x176
0xffffbe82956a5728 : 0xfffff80662a54e00 : nt!MiSystemPartition
0xffffbe82956a58c0 : 0xfffff80662a54e00 : nt!MiSystemPartition
0xffffbe82956a58f8 : 0xfffff80662a55940 : nt!MiSystemPartition+0xb40
0xffffbe82956a5900 : 0xfffff80662a54e00 : nt!MiSystemPartition
0xffffbe82956a5928 : 0xfffff8066210c6e2 : nt!MiUnlinkPageFromListEx+0x882
0xffffbe82956a5930 : 0xfffff80662a55940 : nt!MiSystemPartition+0xb40
0xffffbe82956a5938 : 0xfffff80662a55960 : nt!MiSystemPartition+0xb60
0xffffbe82956a5978 : 0xfffff80662a54e00 : nt!MiSystemPartition
0xffffbe82956a59d0 : 0xfffff80662a54e00 : nt!MiSystemPartition
0xffffbe82956a5a08 : 0xfffff806621090b1 : nt!MiAddWorkingSetEntries+0x451
0xffffbe82956a5ac8 : 0xfffff80662108965 : nt!MiAllocateWsle+0x295
0xffffbe82956a5ad8 : 0xfffff806620b3013 : nt!MiReleasePageFileInfo+0xf3
0xffffbe82956a5b88 : 0xfffff8066210b817 : nt!MiResolveTransitionFault+0x6f7
0xffffbe82956a5bf8 : 0xfffff80662a54e00 : nt!MiSystemPartition
0xffffbe82956a5c18 : 0xfffff806620e8fda : nt!MiSynchronizeSystemVa+0xfa
0xffffbe82956a5c58 : 0xfffff806621290cc : nt!MiDispatchFault+0x2ac
0xffffbe82956a5ca8 : 0xfffff8066200fa78 : nt!HalpApicRequestInterrupt+0xd8
0xffffbe82956a5cf0 : 0xffffc38c2ceb41b0 : 0xffffc38c2c5ac1f0 : 0xfffff80662a23c48 : nt!PopFxSystemWorkPool+0x48
0xffffbe82956a5d18 : 0xfffff8066212ae7d : nt!HalpInterruptSendIpi+0xfd
0xffffbe82956a5e28 : 0xfffff806620ad92e : nt!RtlpHpAcquireLockExclusive+0x2a
0xffffbe82956a5e58 : 0xfffff80662101412 : nt!RtlpHpLfhSlotAllocate+0x2b2
0xffffbe82956a5ef8 : 0xffffac8a0d78a030 :  !da "UUUUUUUUUUUUUUUUUUUUUUUUUUUUUUUUUUUUUUUUUUUUUUUUU"
0xffffbe82956a5f08 : 0xffffac8a0b297030 :  !da "UUUUUUUUUUUUQUUUUEUUUUU"
0xffffbe82956a5f58 : 0xfffff80662100733 : nt!ExAllocateHeapPool+0x2a3
0xffffbe82956a5fa8 : 0xfffff8066209a480 : nt!SeAccessCheckWithHint+0x640
0xffffbe82956a6018 : 0xfffff806620c669c : nt!KiSetAddressPolicy+0xc
0xffffbe82956a6038 : 0xfffff8066212f98d : nt!KiExitDispatcher+0x1fd
0xffffbe82956a6048 : 0xfffff806620c69bd : nt!KiStackAttachProcess+0x24d
0xffffbe82956a6058 : 0xfffff8066212ca87 : nt!wil_details_FeatureReporting_ReportUsageToServiceDirect+0xd7
0xffffbe82956a6088 : 0xfffff80662557981 : nt!HvpGetCellContextInitialize+0x15
0xffffbe82956a60b8 : 0xfffff8066255795f : nt!HvpReleaseCellPaged+0x2f
0xffffbe82956a6118 : 0xfffff806620c669c : nt!KiSetAddressPolicy+0xc
0xffffbe82956a6128 : 0xfffff80662084277 : nt!wil_details_FeatureReporting_ReportUsageToService+0x37
0xffffbe82956a6148 : 0xfffff806620c6c35 : nt!KiSwapProcess+0x75
0xffffbe82956a6178 : 0xfffff806620c6dfa : nt!KiUnstackDetachProcess+0x17a
0xffffbe82956a61d8 : 0xfffff806628b132b : nt!CmpDetachFromRegistryProcess+0xb
0xffffbe82956a64c8 : 0xfffff8066212ca87 : nt!wil_details_FeatureReporting_ReportUsageToServiceDirect+0xd7
0xffffbe82956a64d8 : 0xfffff806625b13f1 : nt!VrpRegistryCallback+0xc1
0xffffbe82956a6538 : 0xfffff8066257f305 : nt!CmpCallCallBacksEx+0x3f5
0xffffbe82956a6570 : 0xffffac8a0991b810 : 0xfffff80662a49700 : nt!CallbackListHead
0xffffbe82956a65f8 : 0xfffff8066212cb4f : nt!CmpIsRegistryLockAcquired+0x2f
0xffffbe82956a6608 : 0xfffff8066247b748 : nt!RtlEqualPrefixSid+0x58
0xffffbe82956a6628 : 0xfffff80662566829 : nt!RtlpCopyEffectiveAce+0x159
0xffffbe82956a6648 : 0xfffff8066257b655 : nt!CmpParseKey+0x445
0xffffbe82956a66b8 : 0xfffff806620c4d50 : nt!RtlEqualSid+0x20
0xffffbe82956a66e8 : 0xfffff8066246e781 : nt!RtlpIsDuplicateAce+0xf1
0xffffbe82956a6758 : 0xfffff806621012db : nt!RtlpHpLfhSlotAllocate+0x17b
0xffffbe82956a6848 : 0xfffff806620ad92e : nt!RtlpHpAcquireLockExclusive+0x2a
0xffffbe82956a6878 : 0xfffff806620acafc : nt!RtlpHpLfhSubsegmentFreeBlock+0x25c
0xffffbe82956a68f8 : 0xfffff80662103bb0 : nt!ExFreeHeapPool+0x340
0xffffbe82956a6978 : 0xfffff806621012db : nt!RtlpHpLfhSlotAllocate+0x17b
0xffffbe82956a69a8 : 0xfffff8066286b019 : nt!ExFreePool+0x9
0xffffbe82956a6a78 : 0xfffff80662100733 : nt!ExAllocateHeapPool+0x2a3
0xffffbe82956a6b18 : 0xfffff80662103bb0 : nt!ExFreeHeapPool+0x340
0xffffbe82956a6b28 : 0xfffff806625579ff : nt!HvpGetCellPaged+0x6f
0xffffbe82956a6b48 : 0xfffff80662515f2e : nt!HvpAddFreeCellHint+0x82
0xffffbe82956a6b98 : 0xffffac8a0c7d2370 :  !du "1675f55f"
0xffffbe82956a6bb8 : 0xfffff80662557981 : nt!HvpGetCellContextInitialize+0x15
0xffffbe82956a6bc0 : 0xffffac8a0c7d2370 :  !du "1675f55f"
0xffffbe82956a6bc8 : 0xfffff8066286b019 : nt!ExFreePool+0x9
0xffffbe82956a6be8 : 0xfffff8066255795f : nt!HvpReleaseCellPaged+0x2f
0xffffbe82956a6bf8 : 0xfffff8066251d4ea : nt!CmpFree+0x1a
0xffffbe82956a6c18 : 0xffffac8a0c7d2370 :  !du "1675f55f"
0xffffbe82956a6c28 : 0xfffff80662512178 : nt!CmpAddSubKeyToList+0x174
0xffffbe82956a6c50 : 0xffffbe82956a6ce8 : 0xfffff806628b13f6 : nt!CmUnlockHiveSecurity+0x12
0xffffbe82956a6c58 : 0xfffff80662557981 : nt!HvpGetCellContextInitialize+0x15
0xffffbe82956a6c80 : 0xffffac8a0c7d2370 :  !du "1675f55f"
```

```
0xffffbe82956a6c88 : 0xfffff80662557981 : nt!HvpGetCellContextInitialize+0x15
0xffffbe82956a6ca8 : 0xfffff806624f1fda : nt!CmpReportNotifyHelper+0x5a
0xffffbe82956a6cc8 : 0xfffff80662557981 : nt!HvpGetCellContextInitialize+0x15
0xffffbe82956a6cd8 : 0xfffff80662557a3a : nt!HvpMapEntryGetBlockAddress+0xe
0xffffbe82956a6ce8 : 0xfffff806628b13f6 : nt!CmUnlockHiveSecurity+0x12
0xffffbe82956a6d28 : 0xfffff806624f1f3d : nt!CmpReportNotifyForKcbStack+0x45
0xffffbe82956a6d68 : 0xfffff80662512c54 : nt!CmpCreateChild+0x66c
0xffffbe82956a6ee8 : 0xfffff80662573ccc : nt!RtlEqualUnicodeString+0x1c
0xffffbe82956a7068 : 0xfffff80662a54e00 : nt!MiSystemPartition
0xffffbe82956a7278 : 0xfffff8066212cb4f : nt!CmpIsRegistryLockAcquired+0x2f
0xffffbe82956a72c8 : 0xfffff8066257b4ef : nt!CmpParseKey+0x2df
0xffffbe82956a73a8 : 0xfffff8066201b528 : nt!RtlpOwnerAcesPresent+0xa8
0xffffbe82956a74a8 : 0xfffff8066257b210 : nt!CmpParseKey
0xffffbe82956a74b8 : 0xfffff80662572562 : nt!ObpLookupObjectName+0x652
0xffffbe82956a74c0 : 0xfffff8066257b201 : nt!NtQueryKey+0x781
0xffffbe82956a7518 : 0xfffff80662103bb0 : nt!ExFreeHeapPool+0x340
0xffffbe82956a7658 : 0xfffff806625719d1 : nt!ObOpenObjectByNameEx+0x1f1
0xffffbe82956a76e8 : 0xffffac8a04864120 : 0xffffac8a0991b810 : 0xfffff80662a49700 : nt!CallbackListHead
0xffffbe82956a7710 : 0xffffac8a08cb9080 :  !da ""Advapi  k""
0xffffbe82956a7788 : 0xfffff8066251abd0 : nt!CmCreateKey+0x480
0xffffbe82956a7a08 : 0xfffff8066251a732 : nt!NtCreateKey+0x52
0xffffbe82956a7a68 : 0xfffff80662227b75 : nt!KiSystemServiceCopyEnd+0x25
0xffffbe82956a7aa8 : 0xfffff8066256b8b9 : nt!NtClose+0x39
0xffffbe82956a7ad8 : 0xfffff80662227b75 : nt!KiSystemServiceCopyEnd+0x25
0xffffbe82956a7ae0 : 0xffffc38c3038d080 :  Trap @ ffffbe82956a7ae0
0xffffbe82956a7c48 : 0x00007ffc88543704 : ntdll!NtCreateKey+0x14
```

11. Finally, we look at a useful command for memory dump collections: **!autocmd**. It can be used as a script to replay against particular memory dump types and filenames. We already created an example *autocmd.ini* in the extension folder:

```
[all]
!analyze -v

[kernel dump]
!process 0 0

[WordPad.exe dump]
~*k
```

For our dump this command will replay **!analyze -v** and **!process 0 0**. For *wordpad.DMP*, it replays **!analyze -v** and **~*k** commands. This functionality can also be useful for enforcing checklists.

12. We close logging before exiting WinDbg:

```
1: kd> .logclose
Closing open log file C:\EWMDA-Dumps\Complete\x64\ES6.log
```

Exercise ES7

- **Goal:** Explore pykd WinDbg extension
- **Memory Analysis Patterns:** Execution Residue (Unmanaged Space)
- \EWMDA\Exercise-ES7.pdf

Exercise ES7: Explore pykd WinDbg Extension

Goal: Explore the pykd[12] WinDbg extension.

Memory Analysis Patterns: Execution Residue (Unmanaged Space).

1. Launch WinDbg.

2. Open \EWMDA-Dumps\Complete\x64\MEMORY-W11.DMP

3. We get the dump file loaded:

```
Microsoft (R) Windows Debugger Version 10.0.27668.1000 AMD64
Copyright (c) Microsoft Corporation. All rights reserved.


Loading Dump File [C:\EWMDA-Dumps\Complete\x64\MEMORY-W11.DMP]
Kernel Bitmap Dump File: Full address space is available


************* Path validation summary **************
Response                         Time (ms)     Location
Deferred                                       srv*
Symbol search path is: srv*
Executable search path is:
Windows 10 Kernel Version 22000 MP (2 procs) Free x64
Product: WinNt, suite: TerminalServer SingleUserTS Personal
Edition build lab: 22000.1.amd64fre.co_release.210604-1628
Kernel base = 0xfffff806`61e00000 PsLoadedModuleList = 0xfffff806`62a296b0
Debug session time: Sat Nov 13 23:17:16.607 2021 (UTC + 1:00)
System Uptime: 0 days 0:03:06.813
Loading Kernel Symbols
...............................................................
................................................................
................................................................
..
Loading User Symbols
...................................
Loading unloaded module list
........
For analysis of this file, run !analyze -v
nt!KeBugCheckEx:
fffff806`62215590 mov     qword ptr [rsp+8],rcx ss:0018:ffffbe82`96f64670=000000000000000a
```

4. We open a log file:

```
0: kd> .logopen C:\EWMDA-Dumps\Complete\x64\ES10.log
Opened log file 'C:\EWMDA-Dumps\Complete\x64\ES10.log'
```

[12] https://github.com/ivellioscolin/pykd

5. The necessary WinDbg extension is already included in the memory dumps archive you downloaded in Exercise E0. Load the pykd bootstrap extension and verify that it shows help:

```
0: kd> .load C:\EWMDA-Dumps\pykd\pykd

0: kd> !help

usage:

!help
	print this text

!info
	list installed python interpreters

!select version
	change default version of a python interpreter

!py [version] [options] [file]
	run python script or REPL

	Version:
	-2           : use Python2
	-2.x         : use Python2.x
	-3           : use Python3
	-3.x         : use Python3.x

	Options:
	-g --global  : run code in the common namespace
	-l --local   : run code in the isolated namespace
	-m --module  : run module as the __main__ module ( see the python command line option -m
)

	command samples:
	"!py"                          : run REPL
	"!py --local"                  : run REPL in the isolated namespace
	"!py -g script.py 10 "string"" : run a script file with an argument in the commom
namespace
	"!py -m module_name" : run a named module as the __main__

0: kd> !info
failed to find python interpreter
```

Note: On our training machine, we don't have any Python version installed. We recommend installing version 3.11.x and not upgrading pip when seeing this warning in the shell or WinDbg:

```
[notice] A new release of pip is available: 24.0 -> 24.2
[notice] To update, run: EngHost.exe -m pip install --upgrade pip
```

or

```
[notice] A new release of pip is available: 24.0 -> 24.2
[notice] To update, run: python.exe -m pip install --upgrade pip
```

6. Install Python version 3.11.9 from https://www.python.org/downloads/release/python-3119/. We used a custom *python-3.11.9-amd64.exe* install to the *C:\Python311* folder for all users:

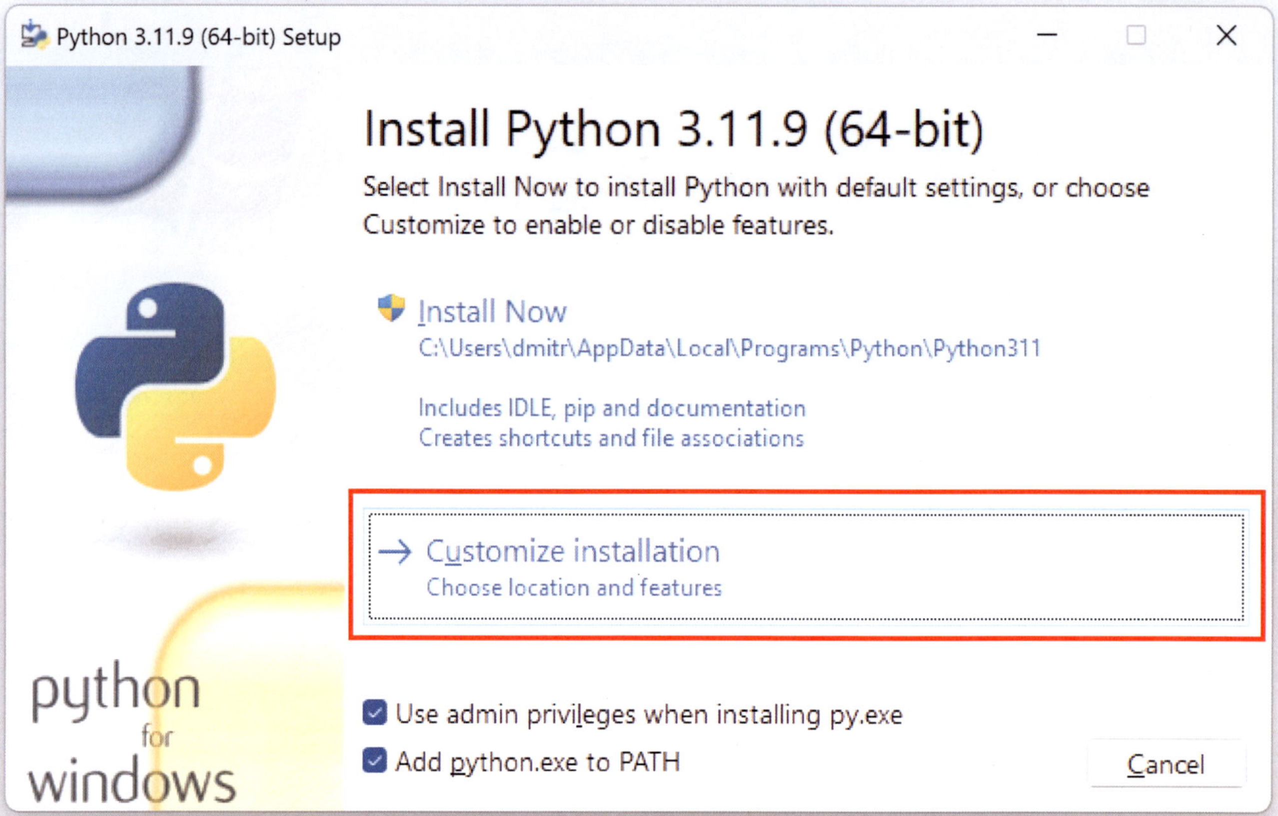
Python 3.11.9 (64-bit) Setup
Install Python 3.11.9 (64-bit)
Select Install Now to install Python with default settings, or choose Customize to enable or disable features.
Install Now
C:\Users\dmitr\AppData\Local\Programs\Python\Python311
Includes IDLE, pip and documentation
Creates shortcuts and file associations
Customize installation
Choose location and features
Use admin privileges when installing py.exe
Add python.exe to PATH
Cancel
python
for
windows

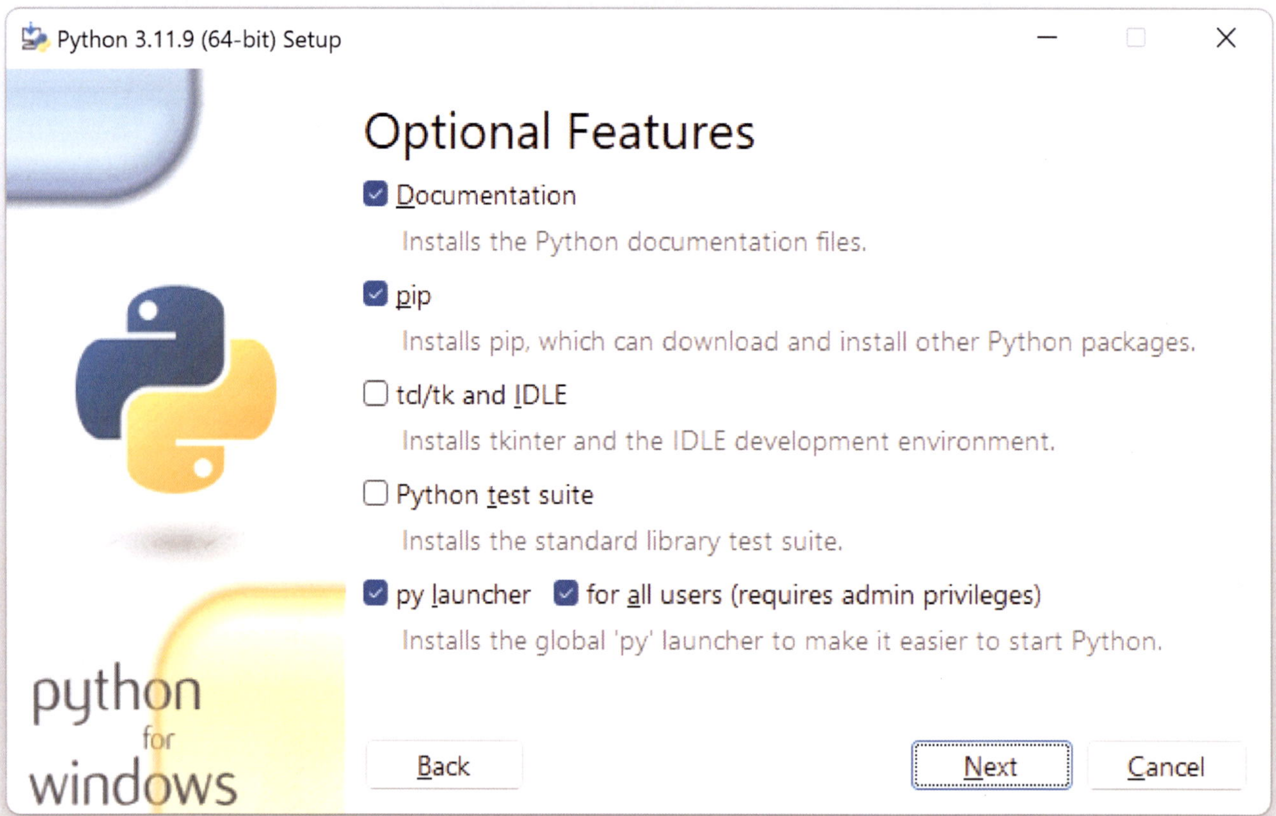
Python 3.11.9 (64-bit) Setup
Optional Features
Documentation
Installs the Python documentation files.
pip
Installs pip, which can download and install other Python packages.
tcl/tk and IDLE
Installs tkinter and the IDLE development environment.
Python test suite
Installs the standard library test suite.
py launcher
for all users (requires admin privileges)
Installs the global 'py' launcher to make it easier to start Python.
Back
Next
Cancel
python
for
windows

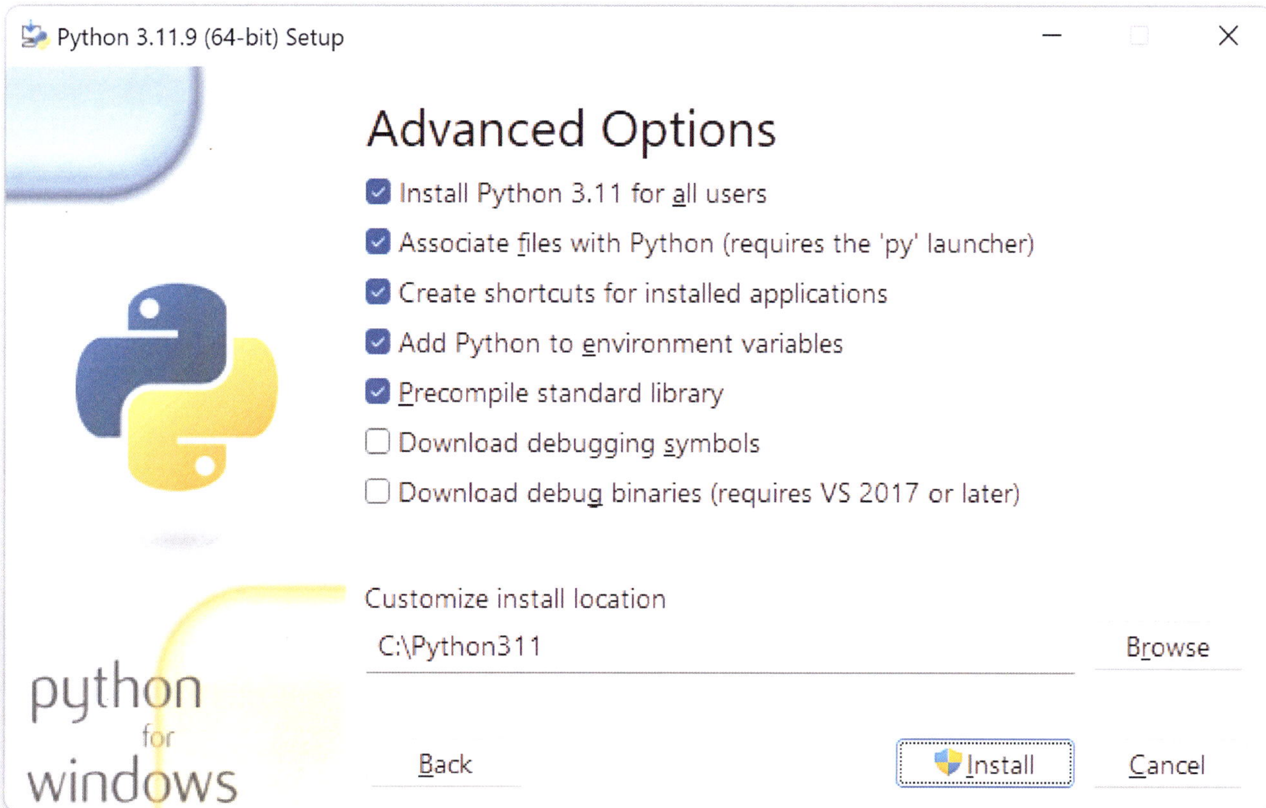

7. Check that the required Python version is installed:

```
0: kd> !info

pykd bootstrapper version: 2.0.0.25

Installed python:

Version:        Status:     Image:
------------------------------------------------------------------------------
* 3.11 x86-64   Unloaded    C:\Python311\python311.dll
```

Note: If your current selected version is different from 3.11 (in case there are several installed versions) use this command:

```
0: kd> !select -3.11
```

8. Install pykd inside WinDbg using the *pykd-0.3.4.15-cp311-none-win_amd64.whl* file included in the memory dumps archive you downloaded in Exercise E0 (also check for any updates in the maintenance repo[13]):

```
C:\EWMDA-Dumps>pip install C:\EWMDA-Dumps\pykd\pykd-0.3.4.15-cp311-none-win_amd64.whl
Processing c:\ewmda-dumps\pykd\pykd-0.3.4.15-cp311-none-win_amd64.whl
Installing collected packages: pykd
Successfully installed pykd-0.3.4.15
```

[13] https://github.com/ivellioscolin/pykd

or

```
0: kd> !pip install C:\EWMDA-Dumps\pykd\pykd-0.3.4.15-cp311-none-win_amd64.whl
Processing c:\ewmda-dumps\pykd\pykd-0.3.4.15-cp311-none-win_amd64.whl
Installing collected packages: pykd
Successfully installed pykd-0.3.4.15
```

```
0: kd> !pip list
Package    Version
---------- --------
pip        24.0
pykd       0.3.4.15
setuptools 65.5.0
```

```
0: kd> !pip show pykd
Name: pykd
Version: 0.3.4.15
Summary: python windbg extension
Home-page:
Author:
Author-email:
License:
Location: C:\Python311\Lib\site-packages
Requires:
Required-by:
```

9. Check that we can launch REPL:

```
0: kd> !py
Python 3.11.9 (tags/v3.11.9:de54cf5, Apr  2 2024, 10:12:12) [MSC v.1938 64 bit (AMD64)] on
win32
Type "help", "copyright", "credits" or "license" for more information.
(InteractiveConsole)
>>>
```

10. Now we walk through pykd functions exposed to REPL/scripts. We can execute WinDbg commands, including other extensions with suppressed output, and results are stored in the variable that we can print/process later:

```
>>> s = dbgCommand("!thread -1 3f", True)
```

```
>>> print (s)
THREAD ffffc38c33ac3080  Cid 09d4.2038  Teb: 0000003f07458000 Win32Thread: ffffc38c34d480b0 RUNNING on processor 0
IRP List:
    ffffc38c31efb360: (0006,0118) Flags: 00060000  Mdl: 00000000
Not impersonating
DeviceMap                 ffffac8a09519830
Owning Process            ffffc38c2e16b080       Image:         notmyfault64.exe
Attached Process          N/A            Image:         N/A
Wait Start TickCount      11956          Ticks: 0
Context Switch Count      1135           IdealProcessor: 1
UserTime                  00:00:00.015
KernelTime                00:00:00.093
Win32 Start Address notmyfault64 (0x00007ff7be365384)
Stack Init ffffbe8296f64fb0 Current ffffbe82968923a0
Base ffffbe8296f65000 Limit ffffbe8296f5f000 Call 0000000000000000
Priority 12 BasePriority 8 PriorityDecrement 2 IoPriority 2 PagePriority 5
```

```
Child-SP          RetAddr           Call Site
ffffbe82`96f64668 fffff806`622281a9 nt!KeBugCheckEx
ffffbe82`96f64670 fffff806`62224300 nt!KiBugCheckDispatch+0x69
ffffbe82`96f647b0 fffff806`60571981 nt!KiPageFault+0x440 (TrapFrame @ ffffbe82`96f647b0)
ffffbe82`96f64940 fffff806`60571d3d myfault+0x1981
ffffbe82`96f64970 fffff806`60571ea1 myfault+0x1d3d
ffffbe82`96f64ab0 fffff806`62102f65 myfault+0x1ea1
ffffbe82`96f64b10 fffff806`6256b532 nt!IofCallDriver+0x55
ffffbe82`96f64b50 fffff806`6256acbf nt!IopSynchronousServiceTail+0x1d2
ffffbe82`96f64c00 fffff806`6256a6c6 nt!IopXxxControlFile+0x5df
ffffbe82`96f64d40 fffff806`62227b75 nt!NtDeviceIoControlFile+0x56
ffffbe82`96f64db0 00007ffc`88543444 nt!KiSystemServiceCopyEnd+0x25 (TrapFrame @ ffffbe82`96f64e20)
0000003f`0731ec08 00007ffc`85c23edb ntdll!NtDeviceIoControlFile+0x14
0000003f`0731ec10 00007ffc`876b5f91 KERNELBASE!DeviceIoControl+0x6b
0000003f`0731ec80 00007ff7`be36342f KERNEL32!DeviceIoControlImplementation+0x81
0000003f`0731ecd0 00007ffc`87fd484b notmyfault64+0x342f
0000003f`0731edd0 00007ffc`87fd409b USER32!UserCallDlgProcCheckWow+0x14b
0000003f`0731eeb0 00007ffc`880197c9 USER32!DefDlgProcWorker+0xcb
0000003f`0731ef70 00007ffc`87fd1c4c USER32!DefDlgProcA+0x39
0000003f`0731efb0 00007ffc`87fd179c USER32!UserCallWinProcCheckWow+0x33c
0000003f`0731f120 00007ffc`87fe4b4d USER32!DispatchClientMessage+0x9c
0000003f`0731f180 00007ffc`885472b4 USER32!_fnDWORD+0x3d
0000003f`0731f1e0 00007ffc`85b21434 ntdll!KiUserCallbackDispatcherContinue (TrapFrame @ 0000003f`0731f0a8)
0000003f`0731f268 00007ffc`87fd08cf win32u!NtUserMessageCall+0x14
0000003f`0731f270 00007ffc`87fd0737 USER32!SendMessageWorker+0x12f
0000003f`0731f310 00007ffc`73c550bf USER32!SendMessageW+0x137
0000003f`0731f370 00007ffc`73c88822 COMCTL32!Button_ReleaseCapture+0xbb
0000003f`0731f3a0 00007ffc`87fd1c4c COMCTL32!Button_WndProc+0x802
0000003f`0731f4b0 00007ffc`87fd0ea6 USER32!UserCallWinProcCheckWow+0x33c
0000003f`0731f620 00007ffc`87fd6084 USER32!DispatchMessageWorker+0x2a6
0000003f`0731f6a0 00007ffc`73c35f9f USER32!IsDialogMessageW+0x104
0000003f`0731f700 00007ffc`73c35e48 COMCTL32!Prop_IsDialogMessage+0x4b
0000003f`0731f740 00007ffc`73c35abd COMCTL32!_RealPropertySheet+0x2c0
0000003f`0731f810 00007ffc`73d00953 COMCTL32!_PropertySheet+0x49
0000003f`0731f840 00007ff7`be364cd0 COMCTL32!PropertySheetA+0x53
0000003f`0731f8e0 00007ff7`be365292 notmyfault64+0x4cd0
0000003f`0731fbb0 00007ffc`876b54e0 notmyfault64+0x5292
0000003f`0731fbf0 00007ffc`884a485b KERNEL32!BaseThreadInitThunk+0x10
0000003f`0731fc20 00000000`00000000 ntdll!RtlUserThreadStart+0x2b
```

11. We can evaluate expressions:

```
>>> e = expr("@rsp + 10")

>>> print ("%x" % e)
ffffbe8296f64678

>>> print (f"{e:0x}")
ffffbe8296f64678
```

12. Register values can be accessed via the **reg** function, and the corresponding symbol (if available) can be found via the **findSymbol** function:

```
>>> print (f'{reg("rbx"):0x}')
ffffac8a0d8ea010

>>> print (f'{findSymbol(reg("rip"))}')
nt!KeBugCheckEx
```

13. Memory values can be accessed via **ptrByte**[**Word** | **DWord** | **QWord** | **Ptr**] functions. We can also read a list of values using **loadBytes**[**Words** | **DWords** | **QWords** | **Ptrs**] functions:

```
>>> print (f"{ptrQWord(0xffffbe8296f65000-0x80):0x}")
7ffc82cd9040
```

```
>>> stack_region = loadPtrs( 0xffffbe8296f5f000, int((0xffffbe8296f65000 -
0xffffbe8296f5f000)/0x8) )

>>> import string

>>> for val in stack_region: sym = findSymbol(val); print (f'{val:016x} {sym if not (sym[0] in
string.hexdigits) or "!" in sym or "+" in sym else ""}')
...<Enter>
0000f0da00000010
0000f0da00000010
[...]
0000f0da00000010
0000f0da00000010
fffff80662af2490 nt!KiAbTreeArray+cdd0
fffff806620faf7b nt!KiAbEntryGetLockedHeadEntry+2cb
0000000000000000
0000f0da00000010
0000f0da00000010
0000f0da00000010
7fffac8a04297378
00000000ffffffff
7fffac8a04297378
00000000ffffffff
0000000000000000
0000000000000000
0000000000000000
0000f0da00000010
ffffac8a042c96e0
0000000000000000
0000000000000000
ffffc38c326f9720
fffff80660cddcf0
0000000000000000
0000000000000000
fffff80662133ff7 nt!KiAbProcessContextSwitch+1c7
ffffc38c326f9080
ffffc38c326f9080
00000000ffffffff
0000f0da00000010
00000048041102f6
0000000000000004
0000000000000000
0000000000000000
3333333333333333
0000000000000494
ffffc38c33751080
ffffc38c326f9080
ffffd480dbb00180
fffff8066221d507 nt!SwapContext+1c7
004fa46fb19bbdff
ffffac8a00400000
ffffbe8200000000
ffffc38c326f9080
fffffb6a406e1cd0
fffffb7db5203708
fffffb7dbeda9018
fffffb7dbedf6d48
0000000000000138
```

```
fffff806620f5b0e nt!MiGetPhysicalAddress+da
0000f0da0000000a
0000f0da00000000
0000f0da00000010
fffff8066221d0cf nt!KiDispatchInterrupt+f
fffffb6a406e1cd0
fffffb7db5203708
fffffb7dbeda9018
fffffb7dbedf6d48
ffffbe8296f62f20
0000000000000000
0000000000000000
ffffc38c2cd881a0
00000000fffffff8
fffff806620f5a1d nt!MmGetPhysicalAddress+1d
0000000000000138
fffff806674c36cc lsi_sas!BuildScatterGather+d0
00000000bfdee588
0000000000000000
0000000000040282
fffff806674f0c38 storport!StorPortGetPhysicalAddress+1c8
0000000000000001
0000000000000000
ffffd480dc39a588
ffffd480dc39a5b8
0000000000003000
ffffd480dc39a450
ffffd480dc39a588
0000000040200342
0000000000000001
ffffc38c32a50960
ffffc38c2cd80010
0000000000000028
00000000bfdee588
fffff806674c3046 lsi_sas!LSImpiBuildIo+176
000000000000001e
0000000000282001
0000000000000000
ffffbe820000000f
fffffc57bfdee588
ffffac8a00000000
0000000000000000
ffffd480dc39a128
ffffc38c32a50960
ffffd480dc39a030
01d7d8dc35cb4a1f
fffff806674e55de storport!RaidAdapterPostScatterGatherExecute+4fe
ffffd480dc39a030
01d7d8dc35cb4a1f
0000000000000000
ffffd480dc39a030
00000000002820f2
0000000000000000
ffffc38c2cd88470
0000000000000002
0000000000000000
ffffc38c2cd881a0
ffffd480dc39a118
ffffd480dc39a128
```

```
ffffc38c32f11690
ffffc38c2cd813d0
ffffd480dc39a030
ffffc38c32f116d8
0000000000000000
fffff806674e4152 storport!RaidpAdapterContinueScatterGather+42
ffffac8a00003000
ffffd480dc39a118
ffffc38c32262dd0
ffffc38c32a50960
0000000000000000
fffff8066201256b nt!HalBuildScatterGatherListV2+25b
ffffc38c32f116d8
0000000000000018
0000000000000000
0000000000000000
ffffbe8296f63080
ffffbe8296f63028
ffffbe8296f63020
0000000000000000
0000000000000000
ffffd480dc39a118
ffffc38c2cd88480
0000000000804000
ffffc38c32262dd0
0000000000003000
ffffc38c2cd8d1a0
fffff806699a251f BasicDisplay!CopyBitsTo_4+3af
ffffc38c2cd881a0
fffff806674e44aa storport!RaUnitStartIo+32a
ffffd480dc39a030
ffffc38c2cd88050
00000009000000e0
0000001a00000001
000000170000003f
000000010000001a
ffffd480dba650fa
ffffbe8296f63210
ffffbe8296f63238
fffff806000001a8
ffffc38c32262e48
0000000000000300
0000000000000000
fffff80662a54e00 nt!MiSystemPartition
ffffbe8296f63230
ffffbe8296f63870
ffffc38c306b5ac0
0000000696f60005
0000000000000001
0000000000000000
0000000000000000
0000000000000000
ffff94d7d0ddb592
0000000000000001
ffffbe8296f63210
0000000000000009
ffffbe8296f63238
ffffd480dba65078
00000000ffffff0f
```

```
fffff806699a1146 BasicDisplay!BltBits+136
00000000ffffff46
ffffbe8296f63271
ffffc38c3020f010
0000000040200342
ffffbe8296f63201
ffffac8a03a03cc0
ffffac8a0d78a000
fffff806621a4a19 nt!FioFwReadBytesAtOffset+1d
ffffffffffffffff
000000000000001e
000000000000001a
0000000000000009
0000000000000000
ffffd480dba65078
00000000ffffff0f
ffffc38c3020f010
00000000ffffff46
fffff806699a1d7e BasicDisplay!BASIC_DISPLAY_DRIVER::SystemDisplayWrite+116
ffffbe8296f63238
ffffbe8296f63210
ffffd48000000001
ffffbe8296f63260
ffffd480dba65078
0000000400000005
ffffff0ffffff f46
0000000900000001
000000000000001a
ffffd480dd1c0000
0000000400000050
0000000000000000
0000028000000001
00000000000001e0
000000f1000000ba
0000010b000000c3
ffff94d7d0ddb402
00000000ffffff90
0000000000000020
ffffbe8296f635e8
0000000000000001
ffffd480dba65030
ffffbe8296f63440
00000000000000f1
ffffbe8296f63460
fffff806699a1df4 BasicDisplay!BddDdiSystemDisplayWrite+24
ffffbe8296f63360
fffff80662a0de40 nt!BcpWorkspace
ffffd4807fffffff
ffffd48000000240
0000002c00000005
ffffd480000000ba
ffffd480000000f1
0000002cff000000
000000f100000000
fffff80669570728 dxgkrnl!DpiSystemDisplayWrite+d8
0000000000000004
ffffd480dba5b200
0000000000000020
ffffbe8296f635e8
```

```
0000000000000005
00000000000000ba
ffffd480000000f1
0000000000000000
0000000000000000
fffff806621a2da9 nt!GxpWriteFrameBufferPixels+1f9
ffffd480dba65030
ffffd480dba65030
ffffbe8296f63390
ffffd480dba65001
ffffbe8296f633c8
ffffbe8296f63401
ffffbe8296f63440
0000000000000000
0000000000000000
fffff80600000000
000001e000000280
fffff80600000280
ffffbe8296f634c0
000000f1000000ba
0000001a00000009
000000000000041c
ffffd480dba65030
ffffbe8296f63440
ffffbe8296f635e8
ffffbe8296f63410
000000090000001a
0001b58800000001
ffffd480dba65078
0000000000000000
ffffc38c2c4b99b8
ffffd480dba5bb50
0000000000000000
0000000000000000
000000090000001a
0001b58800000004
0000000000000000
ffffd480dba65078
0000000000000000
0000000000000000
0000000000000000
0000000000000000
0000000000000000
ffffbe8296f634a0
fffffc571d9e85a5
0000000000000000
0000000000000000
ffffc38c2c4b9900
0000000000000009
0000000000000000
0000000000000000
0000000000000000
ffffbe8296f635e8
fffff806621a2b96 nt!BgpGxDrawRectangle+76
000000090000000b
0001b58800000020
ffffd480dba65030
ffffd480dba651e0
0000000000000000
```

```
0000000000000000
0000000000000000
0000000000000000
0000000000000000
0000000000000000
0000000000000000
0000000000000000
0000000000000000
0000000000000000
000000000000000a
fffff806621a7261 nt!KeFlushCurrentTbOnly+61
ffffc38c2e6313e8
0000000000000002
ffffc38c2e6314b0
0000000000000008
ffffbe8200001000
0000000000000000
0000000000000000
0000000000000000
0000000000000000
0000000000000000
0000000000000000
0000000000000000
0000000000000000
0000000000000000
0000000000000000
0000000000000000
0000000000000000
0000000000000000
0000000000000000
0000000000000000
0000000000000000
0000000000000000
0000000000000000
0000000000000000
0000000000000000
0000000000000000
0000000000000000
0000000000000000
0000000000000000
0000000000000000
0000000000000000
0000000000000000
0000000000000000
0000000000000000
0000000000000000
0000000000000000
0000000000000000
0000000000000000
0000000000000000
0000000000000008
fffffc571d9e83a5
fffff806605c36cc dump_lsi_sas!BuildScatterGather+d0
ffffc38c2e6310d0
fffff8066218c2ea nt!IoMapTransfer+6a
0000000000000000
ffffc38c2cd813d0
0000000000000001
0000000000000000
```

```
ffffd480dd280138
ffffd480dd280168
ffffbe8296f63800
ffffd480dd280000
ffffd480dd280138
00000000000000ac
0000000000000000
ffffc38c2e6313e8
ffffc38c2e6314b0
ffffc38c2e63132a
00000000bf9d8138
fffff806605c3046 dump_lsi_sas!LSImpiBuildIo+176
ffffc38c2e63101e
0000000000010001
0000000000000000
000000000000000f
ffffc38cbf9d8138
ffffbe8296f63901
ffffbe8296f638f8
0000000000010000
0000000000010000
000000000000000a
ffffc38c2e631018
fffff806605941cd dump_diskdump!StartIo+a5
ffffc38c0000fec8
ffffc38c2e6313e8
ffffc38c2e6313e8
ffffc38c2e631018
ffffc38c2e6313e8
fffff80660591f33 dump_diskdump!ExecuteSrb+1f
ffffbe8296f63940
0000000000000000
0000000000000000
fffff80668c0d489 crashdmp!IsBufferValid+29
0000000000010000
0000000000000000
ffffc38c2e631018
fffff806605917d4 dump_diskdump!DiskDumpWrite+1d4
ffffbe8296f63900
ffffbe8296f63940
ffffc38c2e6313e8
0000000000000000
00000000000000ac
0000000000000000
0000000000000000
0000000000010000
ffffbe8296f6380a
0000000000010000
0000000000010000
0000000000010000
0000000043f25000
fffff80668c0b3fd crashdmp!CrashdmpWriteRoutine+9d
ffffc38c308efcf0
ffffbe8296f638f8
ffffbe8296f63940
ffffbe8296f63940
0000000043f25000
fffff80668c13c50 crashdmp!Context+50
0000000043f25000
```

```
fffff80668c0ae9c crashdmp!WritePageSpanToDisk+318
00000000cc0db000
ffffbe8296f639c0
0000000000000000
fffff80668c13c50 crashdmp!Context+50
0000000000000000
ffffbe8296f639a0
0000000000000001
0000000b07de7000
fffff80668c0b360 crashdmp!CrashdmpWriteRoutine
fffff80668c0b1b0 crashdmp!CrashdmpWritePendingRoutine
0000000000030000
0000000000044027
fffff80668c13c50 crashdmp!Context+50
00000000000a0000
ffffbe8296f63a98
00000000000400d7
0000000000000000
0000000000110000
0000000000000000
ffffd480db780000
ffffd480db780000
0000000000010000
0000000000044027
0000000000044028
0000000000044029
000000000004402a
000000000004402b
000000000004402c
000000000004402d
000000000004402e
000000000004402f
0000000000044030
0000000000044031
0000000000044032
0000000000044033
0000000000044034
0000000000044035
0000000000044036
0000000000000000
0000000000000000
ffff9b9b49acde4e
000000000000fee7
fffff80668c13c50 crashdmp!Context+50
00000000000000a0
0000000000000000
0000000000043ff7
0000000000000000
0000000000000000
ffffbe8296f63ca9
fffff80668c09686 crashdmp!WriteBitmapDump+486
0000000000000000
0000000000000000
0000000000000000
0000000000000000
ffffbe8296f63ab0
ffffbe8296f63a94
0000000000000000
0000000000000000
```

```
0000000000000000
000000000043ff7
0000000000000000
000000000007c009
0000000000000000
0000000000000000
0000000000000000
0000000000000000
00000000000000a0
000000000043eca
0000000000140000
0000000000000000
fffff80662346490 nt!HvlGetEncryptedData
0000000000000000
0000000000000000
0000000000000000
000000000043eca
00000000000ffea8
0000000000000010
0000000000140000
ffffc38c2e363038
fffff80668c13c50 crashdmp!Context+50
00000000000ffea8
fffff80662346490 nt!HvlGetEncryptedData
000000000000ef31
000000000000ef32
000000000000ef33
000000000000ef34
000000000000ef35
000000000000ef5e
000000000000ef5f
000000000000ef60
000000000000ef61
000000000000ef62
000000000000ef63
000000000000ef64
000000000000ef65
000000000000ef66
000000000000ef67
000000000000ef68
ffff9b9b49acdcde
0000000000000000
0000000000000000
0000000000000002
0000000000000000
fffff80668c13c50 crashdmp!Context+50
0000000000002000
0000000000031f45
0000000000000004
fffff80668c082be crashdmp!DumpWrite+57e
ffffc38c2e361000
fffff80662362bb0 nt!KiBugCheckProgress
00000000756be768
0000000000000000
0000000000031f00
0000000000000000
0000000000000000
0000000000000000
0000000000000000
```

```
0000000000000000
0000000000000000
0000000000000000
0000000000000000
0000000000000000
0000000000000000
fffff80662362bb0 nt!KiBugCheckProgress
fffff80662346490 nt!HvlGetEncryptedData
0000000000000004
ffff9b9b49acde7e
00000000c0000001
0000000000000000
ffff9b9b49acdaae
00000000000000d1
0000000000000002
ffffac8a0d8ea010
fffff80662362bb0 nt!KiBugCheckProgress
0000000000000000
fffff80662362bb0 nt!KiBugCheckProgress
ffffbe8296f63e11
fffff80668c062dd crashdmp!CrashdmpWrite+23d
0000000000000000
ffffbe8296f63e11
fffff80662362bb0 nt!KiBugCheckProgress
0000000000000000
0000000000000000
fffff8066234f01e nt!IoWriteCrashDump+52a
0000000000000000
ffffbe8296f63e11
ffffc38c2e363000
0000000000000000
0000000000000000
fffff7cf40001618
ffffbe8296f63fc0
fffff806623197e9 nt!HalpApicHvUpdateCallback+9
0056004900520001
0049005f00520000
0000000000510001
ffffbe8296f640a0
ffffc38c33ac3080
0000000000000000
0000000000000002
fffff8066234e810 nt!IoSetDumpRange
fffff8066234e0b0 nt!IoFreeDumpRange
ffffbe8296f63de8
ffffc38c2e363000
0000000000000000
0000000000000000
0000000000140000
ffffc38c2e363038
0000000000000000
fffff80660571981 myfault+1981
fffffc571d9e8b85
ffffbe8296f63fc0
fffff80662362bb0 nt!KiBugCheckProgress
0000000000000001
ffffc38c2c479200
0000000000000003
0000000000000001
```

```
0000000000000000
fffff80660cd5180
ffffbe8296f63fc0
fffff80662362df9 nt!KiBugCheckWriteCrashDump+51
0000000000000008
fffff80662a2b650 nt!KeBugCheckReasonCallbackListHead
0000000000000000
0000000000000000
fffff80660571981 myfault+1981
ffffbe8296f640a0
ffffc38c33ac3080
fffff80662362bb0 nt!KiBugCheckProgress
0000000000000000
0000000000000000
fffff80660cd5180
fffff8066236257a nt!KeBugCheck2+cba
fffff80600000008
0000000000000000
0000000000000000
ffffc38c2e436000
fffff80660571981 myfault+1981
ffffc38c00000000
0000000000000000
fffff8066201256b nt!HalBuildScatterGatherListV2+25b
ffffc30032000101
0000000000000101
0000000000000000
0000000000000000
ffffbe820000000a
ffffbe8200000000
0000000000000000
0000000000000004
ffffc38c334f0590
ffffc38c33ac3080
fffff80660cd5180
fffff80662362bb0 nt!KiBugCheckProgress
ffffc38c00000000
ffffbe8296f65000
ffffbe8296f5f000
0000000000000000
0000000000000000
fffff806674e44aa storport!RaUnitStartIo+32a
0000000000200001
0000000000000002
0000000000000000
0000000000000000
0000000000000000
0000000000000000
0000000000000000
0000000000000000
0000000000000000
0000000000000000
0000000000000000
0000000000000000
0000000000000000
0000000000000000
0000000000000000
0000000000000000
0000000000000000
```

```
0000000000000000
0000000000000000
0000000000000000
0000000000000000
0000000000000000
0000000000000000
0000000000000000
0000000000000000
0000000000000000
0000000000000000
0000000000000000
0000000000000000
0000000000000000
0000000000000000
0000000000000000
0000000000000000
0000000040200382
0000000000000000
0000000000000000
0000000000000000
0000000000000000
0000000000000000
0000000000000000
00001f800010000f
0053002b002b0010
000402820018002b
0000000000000000
0000000000000000
0000000000000000
0000000000000000
0000000000000000
0000000000000000
ffffbe8296f64770
000000000000000a
ffffac8a0d8ea010
ffffac8a0d8ea010
ffffbe8296f64668
ffffbe8296f64830
ffffc38c31efb360
ffffc38c31efb390
0000000000000002
0000000000000000
fffff80660571981 myfault+1981
ffffac8a0d8e7000
ffffc38c31efb370
ffffc38c2c4792d0
0000000000000001
ffffc38c34dd8690
fffff80662215590 nt!KeBugCheckEx
000000000000027f
0000000000000000
0000000000000000
0000000000001f80
0000000000000000
0000000000000000
0000000000000000
0000000000000000
0000000000000000
0000000000000000
```

0000000000000000
0000000000000000
0000000000000000
0000000000000000
0000000000000000
0000000000000000
0000000000000000
0000000000000000
0000000000000000
0000000000000000
0000000000000000
0000000000000000
0000000000000000
0000000000000000
0000000000000000
0000000000000000
0000000000000000
0000000000000000
0000000000000000
0000000000000000
0000000000000000
0000000000000000
0000000000000000
0000000000000000
0000000000000000
0000000000000000
0000000000000000
0000000000000000
0000000000000000
0000000000000000
0000000000000000
0000000000000000
0000000000000000
0000000000000000
0000000000000000
0000000000000000
0000000000000000
0000000000000000
0000000000000000
0000000000000000
0000000000000000
0000000000000000
0000000000000000
0000000000000000
0000000000000000
0000000000000000
0000000000000000
0000000000000000
0000000000000000
0000000000000000
0000000000000000
0000000000000000
0000000000000000
0000000000000000
0000000000000000
0000000000000000
0000000000000000
0000000000000000
0000000000000000

0000000000000000
0000000000000000
0000000000000000
0000000000000000
0000000000000000
0000000000000000
0000000000000000
0000000000000000
0000000000000000
0000000000000000
0000000000000000
0000000000000000
0000000000000000
0000000000000000
0000000000000000
0000000000000000
0000000000000000
0000000000000000
0000000000000000
0000000000000000
0000000000000000
0000000000000000
0000000000000000
0000000000000000
0000000000000000
0000000000000000
0000000000000000
0000000000000000
0000000000000000
0000000000000000
0000000000000000
0000000000000000
0000000000000000
0000000000000000
0000000000000000
0000000000000000
0000000000000000
0000000000000000
0000000000000000
0000000000000000
0000000000000000
0000000000000000
0000000000000000
0000000000000000
0000000000000000
0000000000000000
0000000000000000
0000000000000000
0000000000000000
0000000000000000
0000000000000000
0000000000000000
0000000000000000
0000000000000000
0000000000000000
0000000000000000
0000000000000000
0000000000000000
ffffac8a0d8ea010

```
ffffac8a0d8ea010
0000000000000000
ffffbe8296f647b0
fffff80662021ef6 nt!MiRaisedIrqlFault+1ae
0000000000000000
0000000000000003
0000000000000000
ffffbe8296f646d0
ffffc38c306d4f10
0000000000000000
ffffc38c34dd8690
0000000000000001
ffffc38c2c4792d0
ffffc38c31efb370
ffffc38c31efb390
ffffc38c31efb360
ffffbe8296f64830
fffff80662215697 nt!KeBugCheckEx+107
0000000000000000
0000000000020454
ffffac8a0d8ea010
ffffbd43fb6ebd5a
win32kfull!SharedUserCritOnly::UnlockDomainShared<DLT_HOOK>::UnlockDomainExclusive<>::UnlockObj
ectLock<>::~UnlockObjectLock<>+3e
fffff80660571981 myfault+1981
0000000000000000
0000000000040282
fffff806622281a9 nt!KiBugCheckDispatch+69
000000000000000a
ffffac8a0d8ea010
0000000000000002
0000000000000000
fffff80660571981 myfault+1981
0000000000000000
0000000000000000
0000000000000000
0000000000000000
0000000000000000
0000000000000000
0000000000000000
0000000000000000
0000000000000000
0000000000000000
0000000000000000
0000000000000000
0000000000000000
0000000000000000
0000000000000000
0000000000000000
0000000000000000
0000000000000000
0000000000000000
0000000000000000
0000000000000000
0000000000000000
0000000000000000
ffffbd43fa8b2468 win32kbase!gDomainHookLock
fffffc571d9ef0d5
```

```
ffffbd43fa619191 win32kbase!ThreadUnlock1+71
ffffac8a0d8ea010
ffffc38c31efb390
ffffc38c31efb360
ffffc38c31efb370
ffffc38c2c4792d0
0000000000000001
ffffc38c34dd8690
fffff80662224300 nt!KiPageFault+440
0000000000000000
ffffbd11c0e0c2b8
ffff2703d5aecdf2
ffffbd11c253e710
0000000000000f4d
00001f8001000000
0000000000001000
ffffac8a0d8e7000
ffffac8a0d480000
ffffac8a0d480000
ffffc38c2c402000
fffff80662a5f540 nt!ExPoolState+4580
ffffac8a0d8e7000
fffff8066258de9e nt!KeUserModeCallback+27e
0000000000000000
0000000000000000
0000000000000000
0000000000000000
0000000000000000
0000000000000000
0000000000000000
0000000000000000
0000000000000000
0000000000000000
0000000000000000
0000000000000000
ffffac8a0d8ea010
0000000000000000
0000000000000103
0000000000000000
0000000000000001
0000000000000000
0000000000000800
fffff8066286b964 nt!ExAllocatePoolWithTag+64
0000000000000000
0000000000000000
0000000000000001
ffffc38c31efb370
ffffc38c34dd8690
ffffc38c2c4792d0
ffffc38c31efb390
ffffc38c31efb360
ffffac8a0d8e7010
ffffbe8296f64bb1
0000000000000000
fffff80660571981 myfault+1981
0000000000000010
0000000000050282
ffffbe8296f64940
0000000000000018
```

```
ffffbe8296f64d10
fffff8066d8cee70
0000000000000000
ffffc38c306d4f70
0000000000000000
fffff80660571d3d myfault+1d3d
0000000000001000
0000000000000000
ffffc38c33ac3080
ffffbd11c0e0c010
0000000000000000
0000000000000000
ffffc38c306d4f10
fffff8066212df2c nt!ExReleaseResourceAndLeaveCriticalRegion+7c
ffffc38c306d4f10
fffff8066d8cee70
fffff8066d8cee70
fffff80600000000
ffffbd43fa8b2468 win32kbase!gDomainHookLock
ffffbd11c0e0c010
0000000000000000
ffffc38c306d4f70
0000000000000000
0000000000000000
ffffbd11c0e0c010
ffffbd43fa6a305e win32kbase!tagDomLock::UnLockExclusive+e
0000000000000001
ffffbe8296f64b18
0000000000000000
ffffc38c306d4f70
ffffbe8296f64a78
ffffbd43fb5dfa63 win32kfull!FreeDelayedHooks+e3
ffffbe8296f64bb0
00000000cd56fd8b
0000000000000001
fffff806621036ea nt!RtlHashBytes2+1a
ffffbd43fa8b2468 win32kbase!gDomainHookLock
ffffbd43fb5cec01 win32kfull!GetJournallingQueue+51
ffffbd43fa8af108 win32kbase!gDomainDummyLock
9948a42f5fd49696
0000000000000000
fffff806624a42fd nt!AstGetHashedBitNumbers+c1
ffff6a98d8ef3384
ffffbd11c0e0c000
0000000000000001
fffff80660571ea1 myfault+1ea1
ffffc38c31efb360
fffff806624a4204 nt!AstAddBloomFilter+1c
ffffc38c2c4792d0
0000000000005fd4
0000000000000000
fffff80600000000
00005fd483360018
ffffc38c31efb390
ffffc38c2c4792d0
fffff8066256df14 nt!AstLogIoctl+1d4
0000000000000001
fffff80662102f65 nt!IofCallDriver+55
ffffc38c31efb360
```

```
0000000000000002
0000000000000000
0000000000000000
0000000000000000
ffffc38c34dd8690
0000000083360018
fffff8066256b532 nt!IopSynchronousServiceTail+1d2
0000000000000001
ffffc38c31efb360
ffffbe8296f64bb1
fffff80662102d23 nt!IopAllocateIrpPrivate+183
ffffc38c2e16b080
ffffbd4300000000
ffffc30000000000
ffffc38c34dd8690
0000000000000000
0000000000000001
0000000000000000
0000000000000001
ffffc38c34dd8690
fffffc571d9efd95
0000000000000000
0000000000000001
0000000000000000
0000000000000001
ffffc38c34dd8690
ffffc38c31efb360
ffffbe8296f64ea0
fffff8066256acbf nt!IopXxxControlFile+5df
ffffc38c00000000
ffffbe8296f64ea0
0000000083360018
0000000083360018
ffffbe8296f64c01
ffffbd43fb690901 win32kfull!ClientImmProcessKey+c5
fffff80600000002
ffffbd43fa643fb8 win32kbase!UserSessionSwitchLeaveCrit+f8
0000000000000000
0000000000000001
0000000000000000
00000000fa619100
0000000000000100
ffffc38c34dd8690
0000000000000000
ffffc38c2c4792d0
00000000000002b1
0000000000000000
0000000000000000
0000000000000000
0000000000000000
ffffc38c34dd8690
ffffc38c31efb360
ffffbd1183360018
0012019f00000000
ffffbd43fb67b3a8 win32kfull!NtUserMessageCall+1d8
ffffc38c33ac3080
fffff8066d8cee70
ffffbd11c0e0c010
fffff8066d8cfd20
```

```
0000000000000000
fffff806000002b1
0000000000000001
0000000000000111
0000000000020454
0000000000020454
ffffbe8296f64dc8
0000003f0731ec28
ffffc38c33ac3080
fffff8066256a6c6 nt!NtDeviceIoControlFile+56
0000000000000000
0000000000000000
0000000000000000
0000000000000000
0000003f0731ec60
0000000083360001
0000000000000000
ffffc38c00000000
0000000000000000
0000000000000000
ffffbe8200000001
fffff8066d8cfd20
0000000000000000
fffff80662227b75 nt!KiSystemServiceCopyEnd+25
0000000000000000
0000000000000000
ffff6a98d8ef3484
0000000000070000
0000003f0731ec60
0000000083360018
0000000000000000
0000000000000000
0000000000000000
000001e900000000
ffffc38c33ac3080
0000000000000000
0000000000000000
fffff80662227b75 nt!KiSystemServiceCopyEnd+25
0000000000000b1a
00001e95f25e0a40
0000000000000000
ffffbe8296892b60
0000003f00000000
00001f8002080000
0000000000000007
00000000000001fc
0000000000000000
000001e9be2c6fc0
0000000000000002
8b05075c38d18070
0000000000000246
0000003f07458000
0000000000000000
0000000000000000
0000000000000000
0000000000000000
0000000000000000
0000000000000000
0000000000000000
```

```
0000000000000000
0000000000000000
0000000000000000
0000000000000000
0000000000000000
00007ffc73cbf929 COMCTL32!Button_WndProc+37909
0000000000000000
0000000000000000
0000000000000000
0000000000000000
0000000000000000
0000000000000000
0000000000000000
0000000000000000
0000000000000000
0000000000000000
0000000000000000
0000000000000000
0000000000000000
0000000000000000
00000000000001fc
0000000000000000
00000000000001fc
00007ffc82cd9040 uxtheme!CPaintBufferAnimation::`vftable'
00007ffc88543444 ntdll!NtDeviceIoControlFile+14
0000000000000033
0000000000000246
0000003f0731ec08
000000000000002b
ffffbe8296f65000
ffffbe8296f5f000
ffffbe8296893000
ffffbe829688d000
ffffbe82968923a0
ffffbe8296892c70
0000000000000000
0000000000000000
0000000000000000
0000000000000000
```

14. Characters and wide characters can be read using **loadChars** and **loadWChars** functions. Zero-terminated strings can be read using **loadCStr** and **loadWStr** functions. _ANSI_STRING and _UNICODE_STRING structures can be read using **loadAnsiString** and **loadUnicodeString** functions.

```
>>> loadWStr(0x000001e9bdfcc4d0)
'ALLUSERSPROFILE=C:\\ProgramData'

>>> loadUnicodeString(0xfffff80662b3d700)
'\\REGISTRY\\MACHINE\\HARDWARE\\DESCRIPTION\\SYSTEM'
```

15. Invalid address access can be handled via exception processing or checks:

```
>>> try: print (ptrPtr(0))
... except MemoryException: print ("Invalid address")
...<Enter>
Invalid address
```

```
>>> addr = 0

>>> if isValid(addr): print (ptrPtr(addr))
... else: print ("Invalid address")
...<Enter>
Invalid address
```

16. Symbolic information can be accessed from the **module** class. For example:

```
>>> nt = module("nt")

>>> print (nt)
Module: nt
Start: fffff80661e00000 End: fffff80662e47000 Size: 1047000
Image: ntkrnlmp.exe
Symbols: C:\ProgramData\Dbg\sym\ntkrnlmp.pdb\32C1A669D5FFEFD41091F636CFDB6E991\ntkrnlmp.pdb
Timestamp: c16011b9 (10/21/72 18:04:41)
Check Sum: b33bc4

>>> loadUnicodeString(nt.CmRegistryMachineHardwareDescriptionSystemName)
'\\REGISTRY\\MACHINE\\HARDWARE\\DESCRIPTION\\SYSTEM'

>>> print (nt.type("_DRIVER_OBJECT"))
class/struct : _DRIVER_OBJECT Size: 0x150 (336)
   +0000 Type                       : Int2B
   +0002 Size                       : Int2B
   +0008 DeviceObject               : _DEVICE_OBJECT*
   +0010 Flags                      : UInt4B
   +0018 DriverStart                : Void*
   +0020 DriverSize                 : UInt4B
   +0028 DriverSection              : Void*
   +0030 DriverExtension            : _DRIVER_EXTENSION*
   +0038 DriverName                 : _UNICODE_STRING
   +0048 HardwareDatabase           : _UNICODE_STRING*
   +0050 FastIoDispatch             : _FAST_IO_DISPATCH*
   +0058 DriverInit                 : Int4B(__cdecl*)(_DRIVER_OBJECT*, _UNICODE_STRING*)
   +0060 DriverStartIo              : Void(__cdecl*)(_DEVICE_OBJECT*, _IRP*)
   +0068 DriverUnload               : Void(__cdecl*)(_DRIVER_OBJECT*)
   +0070 MajorFunction              : Int4B(__cdecl*[28])(_DEVICE_OBJECT*, _IRP*)

>>> print (nt.typedVar("_DRIVER_OBJECT", 0xffffc38c335386d0))
struct/class: _DRIVER_OBJECT at 0xffffc38c335386d0
   +0000 Type                       : Int2B   0x4 (4)
   +0002 Size                       : Int2B   0x150 (336)
   +0008 DeviceObject               : _DEVICE_OBJECT*   0xffffc38c2c4792d0 (18446677605538566864)
   +0010 Flags                      : UInt4B   0x12 (18)
   +0018 DriverStart                : Void*   0xfffff80660570000 (18446735305002647552)
   +0020 DriverSize                 : UInt4B   0x8000 (32768)
   +0028 DriverSection              : Void*   0xffffc38c334f0590 (18446677605656495504)
   +0030 DriverExtension            : _DRIVER_EXTENSION*   0xffffc38c33538820 (18446677605656791072)
   +0038 DriverName                 : _UNICODE_STRING
   +0048 HardwareDatabase           : _UNICODE_STRING*   0xfffff80662b3d700 (18446735305042286336)
   +0050 FastIoDispatch             : _FAST_IO_DISPATCH*   0 (0)
   +0058 DriverInit                 : Int4B(__cdecl*)(_DRIVER_OBJECT*, _UNICODE_STRING*)   0xfffff80660576058
(18446735305002672216)
   +0060 DriverStartIo              : Void(__cdecl*)(_DEVICE_OBJECT*, _IRP*)   0 (0)
   +0068 DriverUnload               : Void(__cdecl*)(_DRIVER_OBJECT*)   0xfffff80660571f40 (18446735305002655552)
   +0070 MajorFunction              : Int4B(__cdecl*[28])(_DEVICE_OBJECT*, _IRP*)
```

```
>>> print (typedVar("nt!_DRIVER_OBJECT", 0xffffc38c335386d0).field("DriverName"))
struct/class: _UNICODE_STRING at 0xffffc38c33538708
   +0000 Length                    : UInt2B   0x1e (30)
   +0002 MaximumLength             : UInt2B   0x1e (30)
   +0008 Buffer                    : WChar*   0xffffc38c33636cf0 (18446677605657832688)

>>> print (typedVar("nt!_DRIVER_OBJECT", 0xffffc38c335386d0).field("HardwareDatabase"))
Ptr _UNICODE_STRING* at 0xffffc38c33538718 Value: 0xfffff80662b3d700 (18446735305042286336)

>>> print (typedVar("nt!_DRIVER_OBJECT", 0xffffc38c335386d0).field("HardwareDatabase").deref())
struct/class: _UNICODE_STRING at 0xfffff80662b3d700
   +0000 Length                    : UInt2B   0x5a (90)
   +0002 MaximumLength             : UInt2B   0x5c (92)
   +0008 Buffer                    : WChar*   0xfffff8066283dce0 (18446735305039142112)
```

17. Now, we write a script to dump *stack_region* values to a CSV file for later offline analysis.

```
>>> stack_region_csv = open("C:\EWMDA-Dumps\scripts\stack_region.csv", "wt")

>>> _ = stack_region_csv.write("Value,Symbol\n")

>>> for val in stack_region: sym = findSymbol(val); sym = sym if not (sym[0] in
string.hexdigits) or "!" in sym or "+" in sym else ""; _ =
stack_region_csv.write(f"{val:016x},{sym}\n")
...<Enter>

>>> stack_region_csv.close()
```

The file should contain this output:

```
Value,Symbol
0000f0da00000010,
0000f0da00000010,
[...]
ffff9b9b49acdcde,
0000000000000000,
0000000000000000,
0000000000000002,
0000000000000000,
fffff80668c13c50,crashdmp!Context+50
0000000000002000,
0000000000031f45,
0000000000000004,
fffff80668c082be,crashdmp!DumpWrite+57e
ffffc38c2e361000,
fffff80662362bb0,nt!KiBugCheckProgress
00000000756be768,
0000000000000000,
0000000000031f00,
0000000000000000,
[...]
```

18. Unfortunately, we were not able to import packages like *Pandas* and *Matplotlib* because of their dependency on *NumPy,* which hangs due to the GIL lock. We recommend using Polars[14] for data exploration and manipulation:

```
>> quit()
```

```
0: kd> !pip install polars
Collecting polars
  Downloading polars-1.7.1-cp38-abi3-win_amd64.whl.metadata (14 kB)
Downloading polars-1.7.1-cp38-abi3-win_amd64.whl (32.1 MB)
   ---------------------------------------- 32.1/32.1 MB 28.5 MB/s eta 0:00:00
Installing collected packages: polars
Successfully installed polars-1.7.1
```

```
0: kd> !py
Python 3.11.9 (tags/v3.11.9:de54cf5, Apr  2 2024, 10:12:12) [MSC v.1938 64 bit (AMD64)] on win32
Type "help", "copyright", "credits" or "license" for more information.
(InteractiveConsole)
>>>
```

```
>>> import polars as pl
```

```
>>> df = pl.read_csv("C:\EWMDA-Dumps\scripts\stack_region.csv")
```

```
>>> print(df)
shape: (3_072, 2)
┌──────────────────┬────────┐
│ Value            ┆ Symbol │
│ ---              ┆ ---    │
│ str              ┆ str    │
╞══════════════════╪════════╡
│ 0000f0da00000010 ┆ null   │
│ 0000f0da00000010 ┆ null   │
│ 0000f0da00000010 ┆ null   │
│ 0000f0da00000010 ┆ null   │
│ 0000f0da00000010 ┆ null   │
│ …                ┆ …      │
│ ffffbe8296892c70 ┆ null   │
│ 0000000000000000 ┆ null   │
│ 0000000000000000 ┆ null   │
│ 0000000000000000 ┆ null   │
│ 0000000000000000 ┆ null   │
└──────────────────┴────────┘
```

19. We quit REPL and close logging before exiting WinDbg:

```
>>> quit()
```

```
0: kd> .logclose
Closing open log file C:\EWMDA-Dumps\Complete\x64\ES10.log
```

[14] https://www.pola.rs/

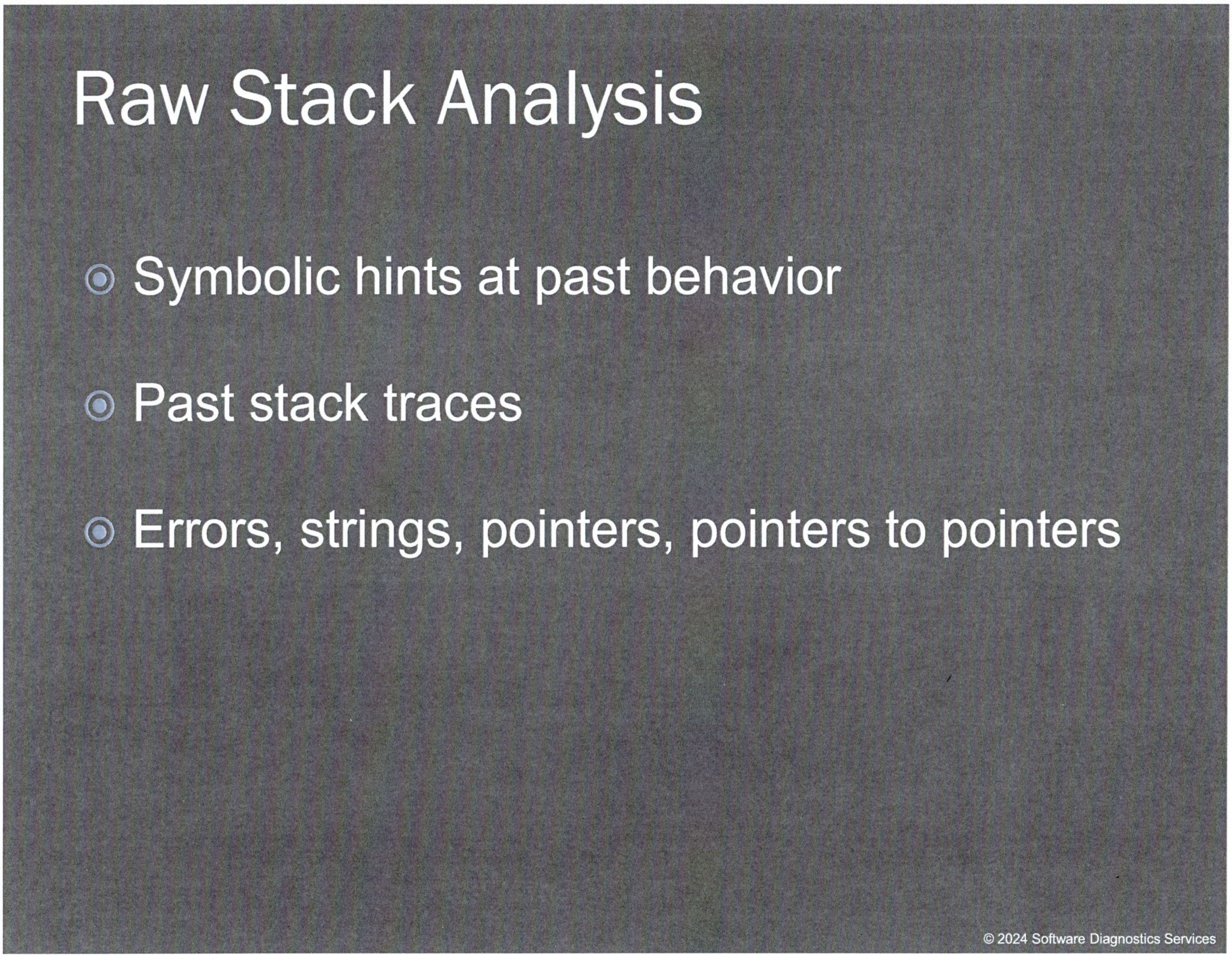

Raw Stack Analysis
Symbolic hints at past behavior
Past stack traces
Errors, strings, pointers, pointers to pointers
© 2024 Software Diagnostics Services

You may have noticed that I particularly emphasized the importance of raw stack data analysis. This is because a memory snapshot is static. But we can see symbolic hints of past dynamic execution. Despite parts of memory being overwritten by function calls and local variable allocations, there is some possibility to reconstruct past stack trace fragments, get errors, their distribution, string fragments, and follow pointer chains.

Exercise ES8

- **Goal:** Explore snapshot WinDbg extension
- **Memory Analysis Patterns:** Active Thread
- \EWMDA\Exercise-ES8.pdf

snapshot
https://github.com/0vercl0k/snapshot

Exercise ES8: Explore snapshot WinDbg Extension

Goal: Explore the snapshot[15] WinDbg extension.

Memory Analysis Patterns: Active Thread.

1. For this exercise we need a Hyper-V debugging environment:

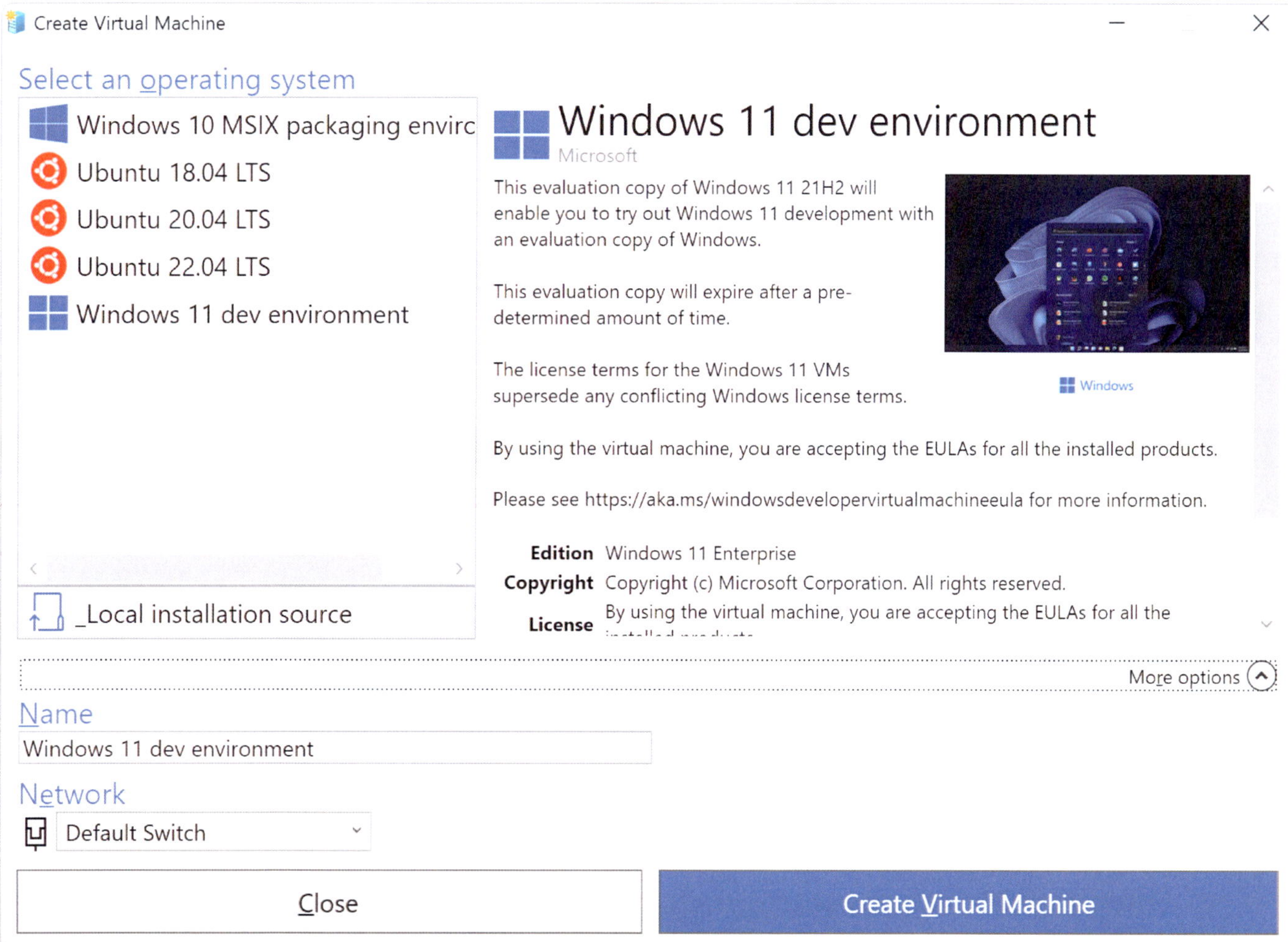

2. We use network debugging via KDNET[16]. For Windows 11 dev environment and Windows 11 Pro host, we found that with the *Default Switch* network, everything works fine with WinDbg. Below are the steps that were required on my Windows 11 laptop.

---

15 https://github.com/0vercl0k/snapshot

16 https://learn.microsoft.com/en-us/windows-hardware/drivers/debugger/setting-up-network-debugging-of-a-virtual-machine-host

3. After creating a Windows 11 dev environment VM, disable Secure Boot in Security Settings in VM properties:

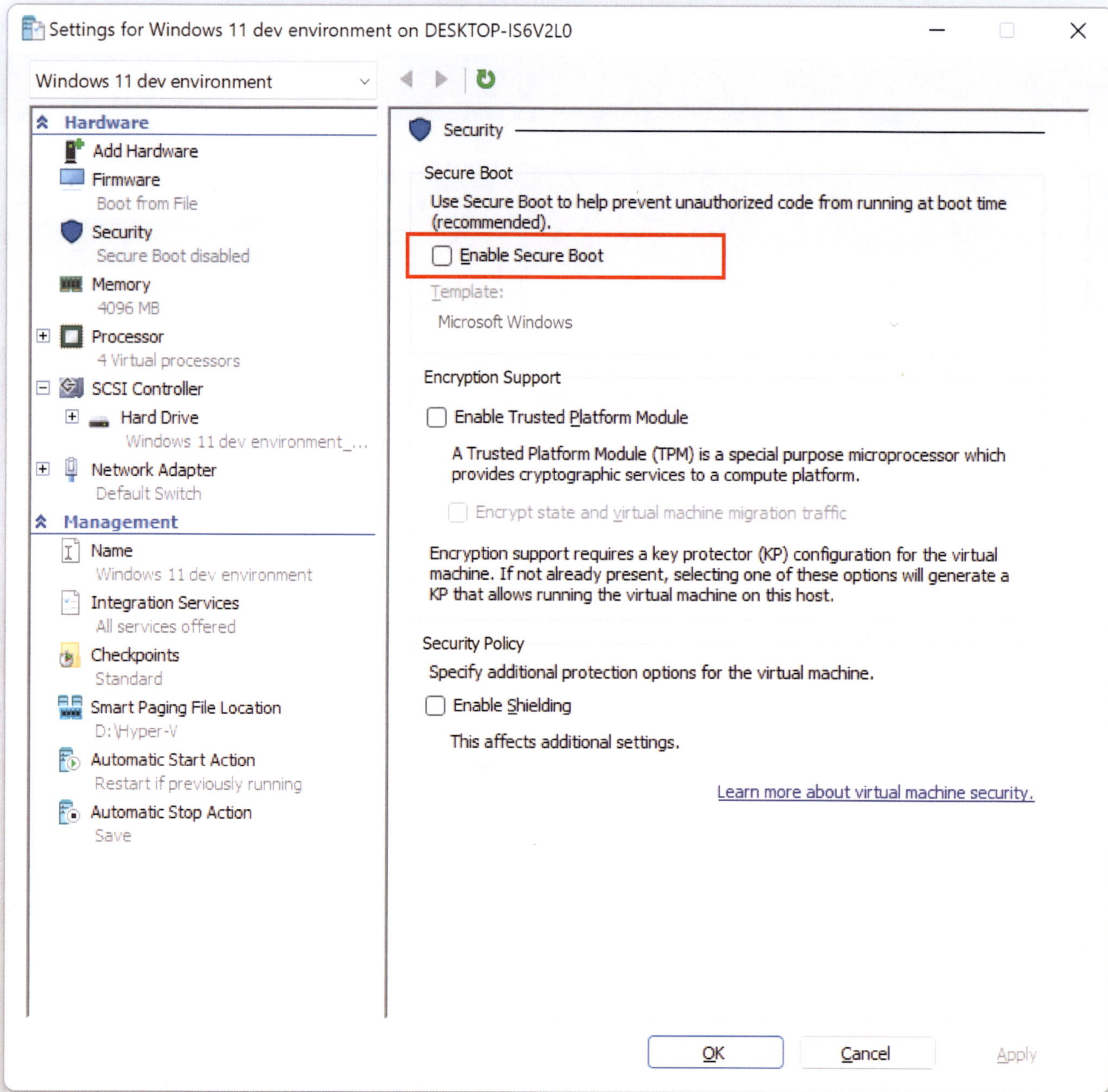

4. For this exercise you need to set the number of virtual processors to 1:

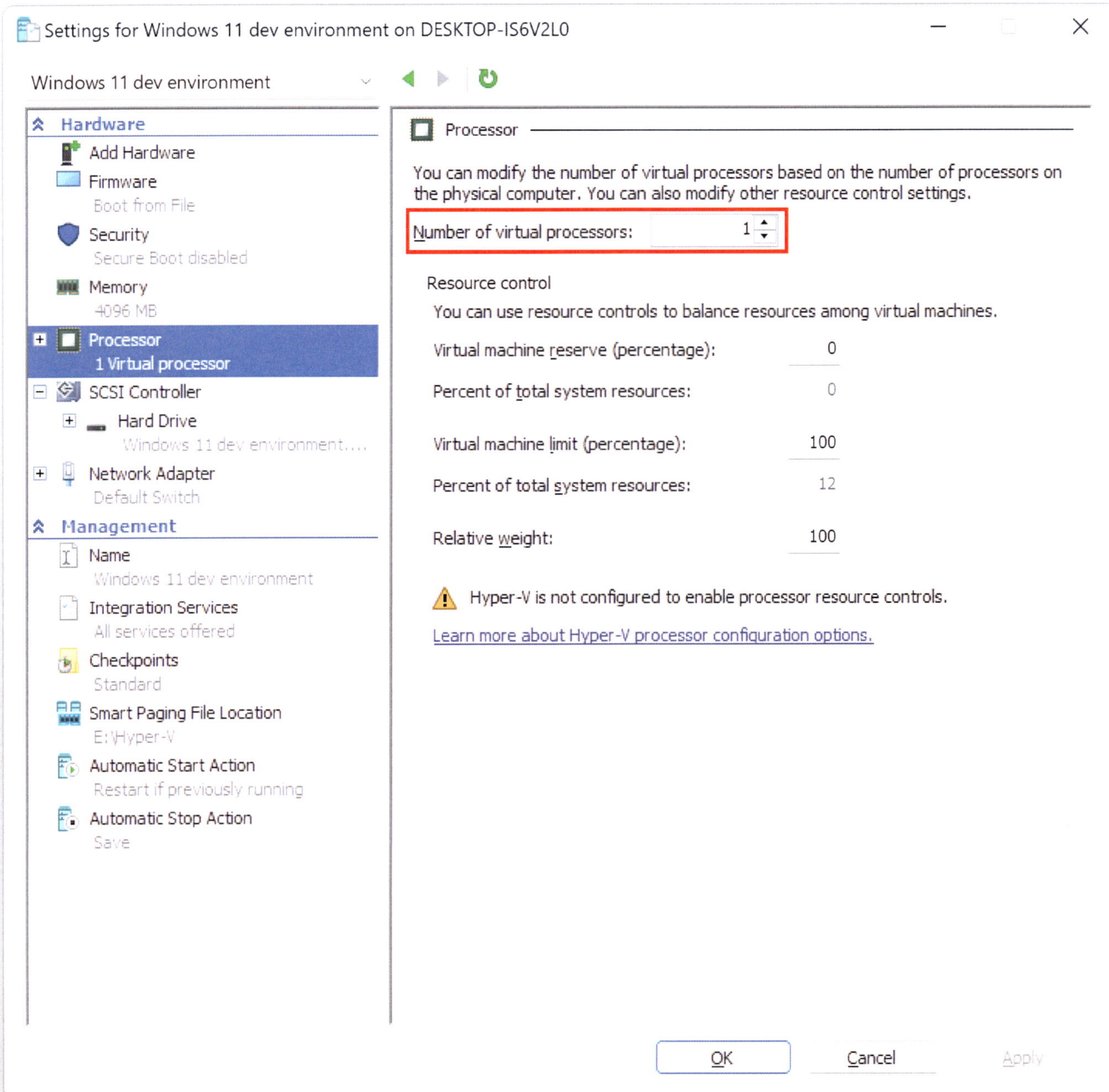

5. Install Debugging Tools for Windows as a standalone toolset on the Guest VM[17].

[17] https://learn.microsoft.com/en-gb/windows-hardware/drivers/debugger/debugger-download-tools

6. On the Host computer, run Command Prompt and note the IP4 address of the *Default Switch* (it may be different and change with every new Hyper-V start after the Host restart):

```
C:\Users\user>ipconfig
Windows IP Configuration
[...]
Ethernet adapter vEthernet (Default Switch):
   Connection-specific DNS Suffix  . :
   Link-local IPv6 Address . . . . . : [...]
   IPv4 Address. . . . . . . . . . . : 172.24.64.1
   Subnet Mask . . . . . . . . . . . : 255.255.240.0
   Default Gateway . . . . . . . . . :
[...]
```

7. On the Guest VM, create the *C:\KDNET* folder and copy *kdnet.exe* and *VerifiedNICList.xml* files from your Debugging Tools for Windows installation folder (for example, *C:\Program Files (x86)\Windows Kits\10\Debuggers\x64*) to it.

8. On the Guest VM, run Command Prompt as Administrator and get the debugging key after specifying the host address and port (your key should be different):

```
c:\KDNET>kdnet

Network debugging is supported by this Microsoft Hypervisor Virtual Machine


c:\KDNET>kdnet 172.24.64.1 50005

Enabling network debugging on Network debugging is supported by this Microsoft Hypervisor
Virtual Machine.

To debug this vm, run the following command on your debugger host machine.
windbg -k net:port=50005,key=32ukpvnlc4og1.pfmgb910kzwo.2tohb1pajmuis.1gt40au5vdzb3

Then restart this VM by running shutdown -r -t 0 from this command prompt.

c:\KDNET>shutdown -r -t 0
```

Note: We do not reconnect to the guest VM on the host when we see the Virtual Machine Connection message box:

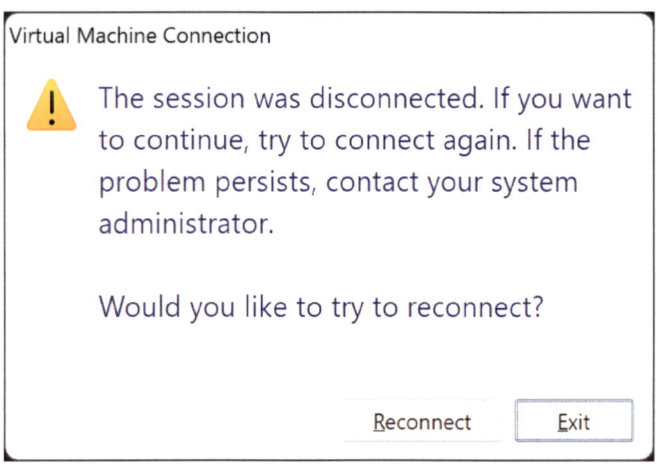

Virtual Machine Connection
The session was disconnected. If you want to continue, try to connect again. If the problem persists, contact your system administrator.
Would you like to try to reconnect?
Reconnect
Exit

9. On the Host computer, launch WinDbg and choose *File \ Attach to kernel* option. Specify the *Port number* and *Key* obtained from the Guest VM in the *Net* tab:

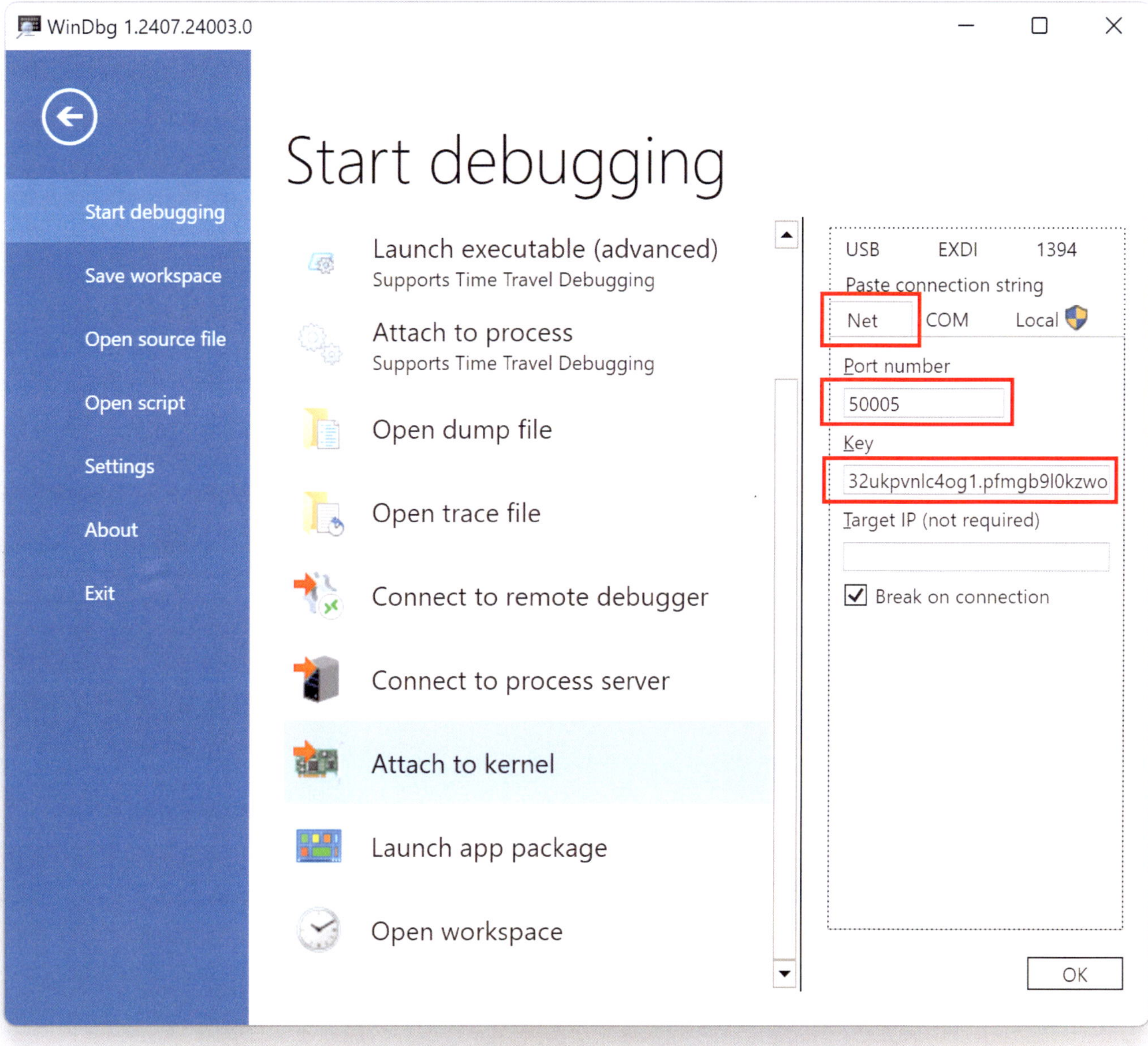

10. WinDbg is now connected to the Guest VM:

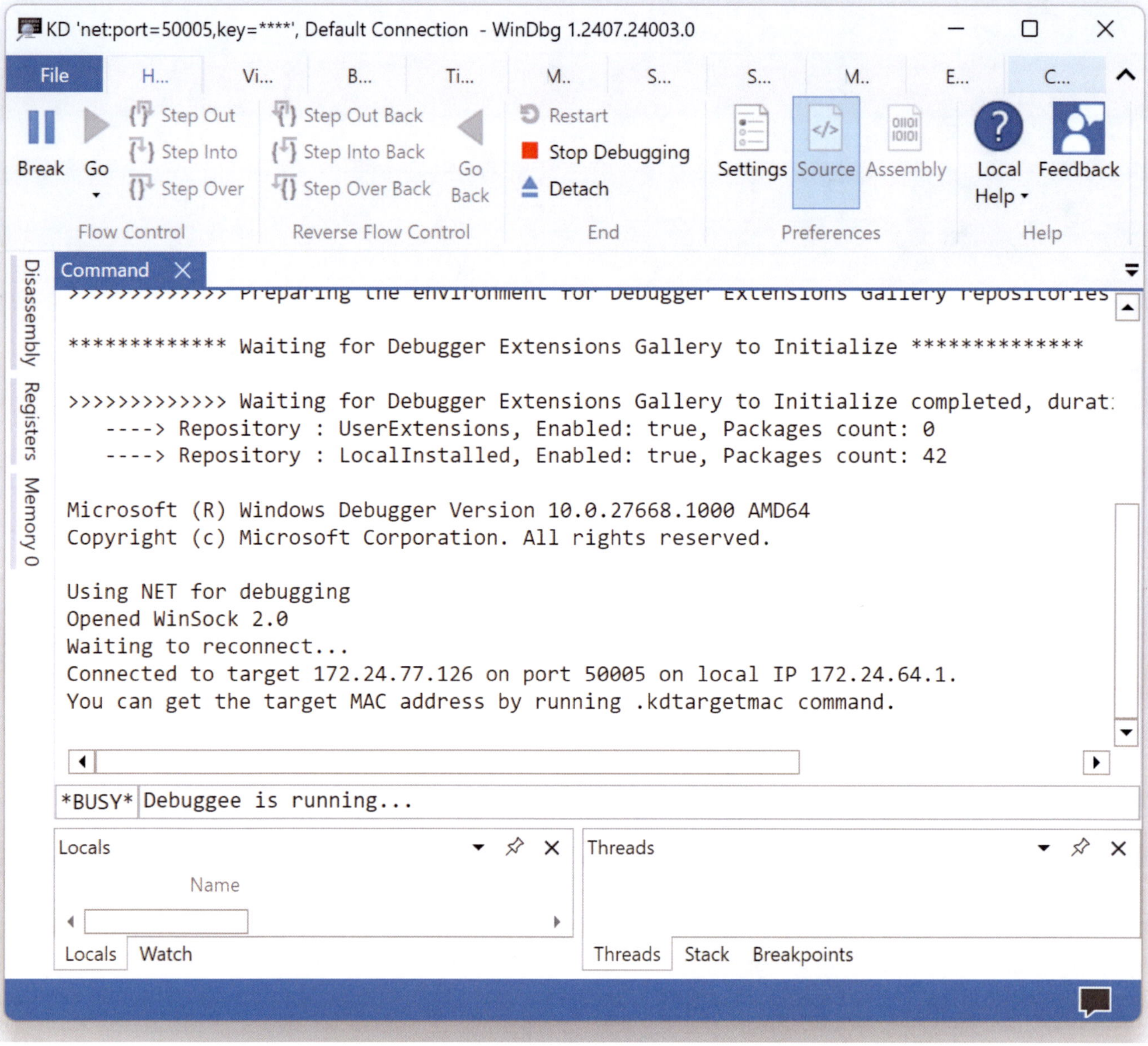

11. Use *the Break* button and wait. After some time, we get this output:

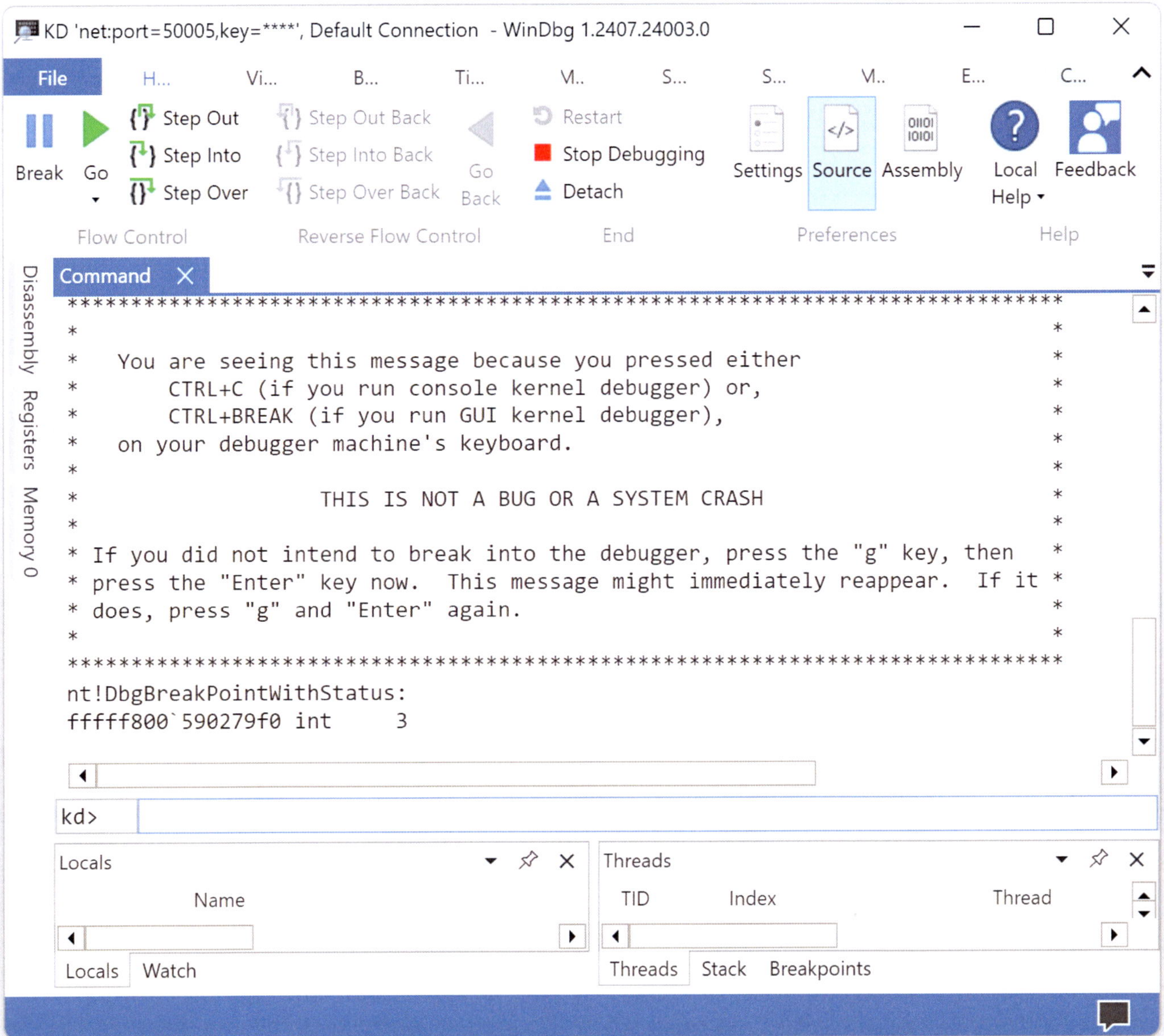

12. We now check the stack trace of the current thread using the **k** command (the output may vary depending on when you broke into the system):

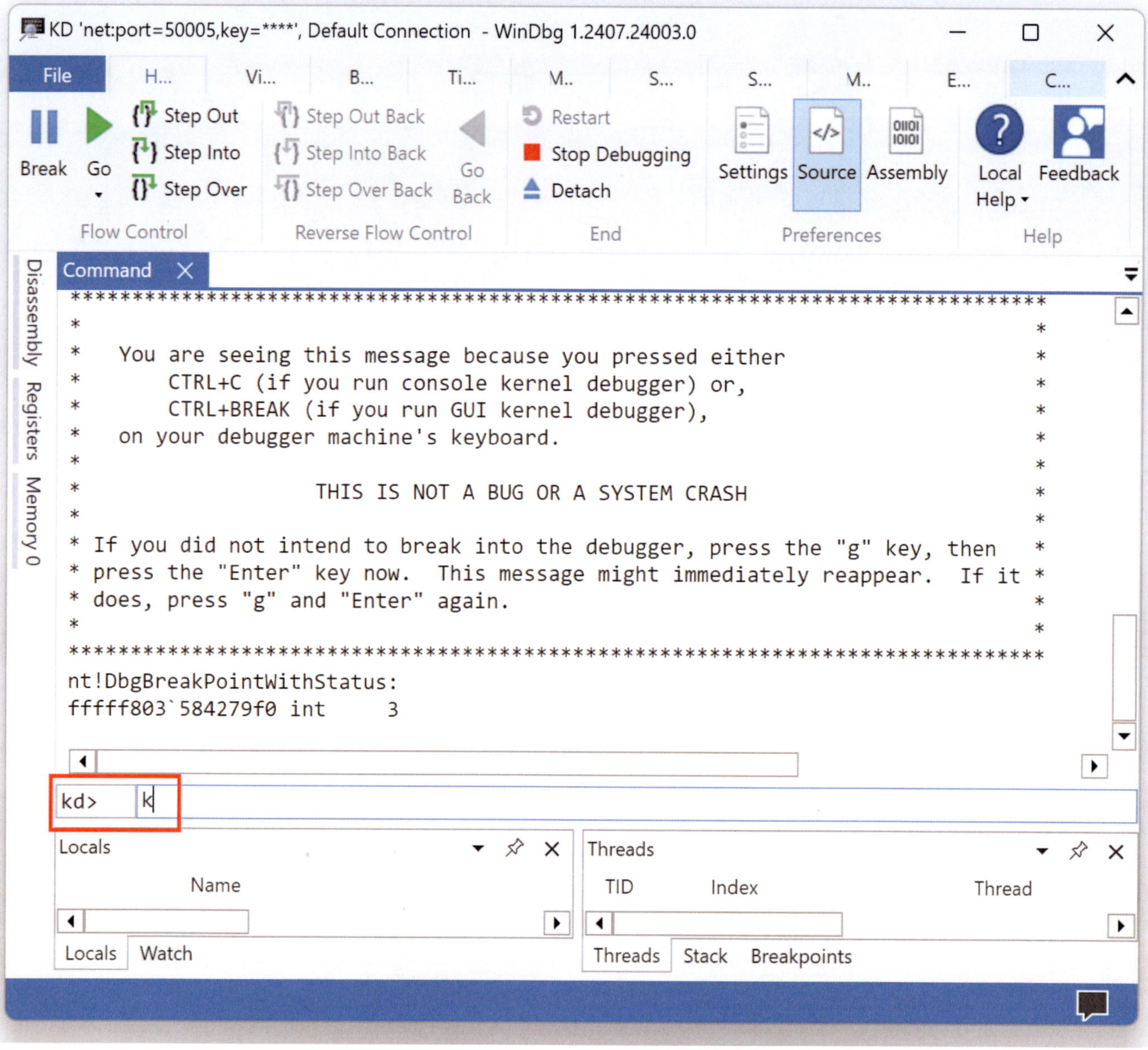

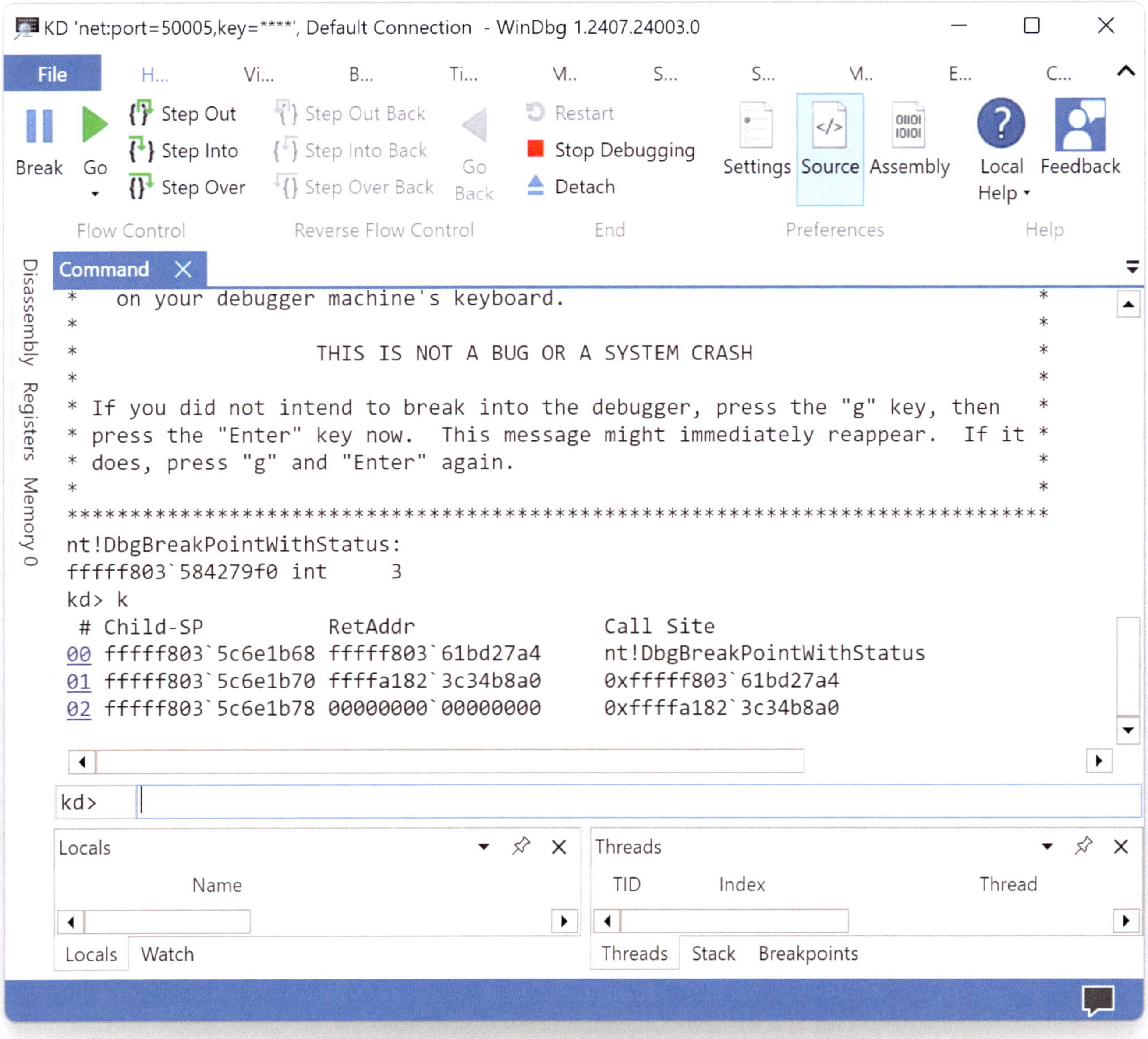

13. Here's the full command window content:

```
Microsoft (R) Windows Debugger Version 10.0.27668.1000 AMD64
Copyright (c) Microsoft Corporation. All rights reserved.

Using NET for debugging
Opened WinSock 2.0
Waiting to reconnect...
Connected to target 172.24.77.126 on port 50005 on local IP 172.24.64.1.
You can get the target MAC address by running .kdtargetmac command.
Connected to Windows 10 22000 x64 target at (Sun Sep 15 18:26:31.977 2024 (UTC + 1:00)), ptr64
TRUE
Kernel Debugger connection established.

************* Path validation summary **************
Response                         Time (ms)     Location
Deferred                                       srv*
Symbol search path is: srv*
```

```
Executable search path is:
Windows 10 Kernel Version 22000 MP (1 procs) Free x64
Product: WinNt, suite: TerminalServer SingleUserTS
Edition build lab: 22000.1.amd64fre.co_release.210604-1628
Kernel base = 0xfffff803`58000000 PsLoadedModuleList = 0xfffff803`58c297b0
Debug session time: Sun Sep 15 18:26:31.710 2024 (UTC + 1:00)
System Uptime: 0 days 0:01:06.441
Break instruction exception - code 80000003 (first chance)
*******************************************************************************
*                                                                             *
*   You are seeing this message because you pressed either                    *
*       CTRL+C (if you run console kernel debugger) or,                       *
*       CTRL+BREAK (if you run GUI kernel debugger),                          *
*   on your debugger machine's keyboard.                                      *
*                                                                             *
*                   THIS IS NOT A BUG OR A SYSTEM CRASH                       *
*                                                                             *
* If you did not intend to break into the debugger, press the "g" key, then   *
* press the "Enter" key now.  This message might immediately reappear.  If it *
* does, press "g" and "Enter" again.                                          *
*                                                                             *
*******************************************************************************
nt!DbgBreakPointWithStatus:
fffff803`584279f0 int     3
```

```
kd> k
 # Child-SP          RetAddr               Call Site
00 fffff803`5c6e1b68 fffff803`61bd27a4     nt!DbgBreakPointWithStatus
01 fffff803`5c6e1b70 ffffa182`3c34b8a0     0xfffff803`61bd27a4
02 fffff803`5c6e1b78 00000000`00000000     0xffffa182`3c34b8a0
```

14. The stack trace doesn't have current symbols applied, so we load them using the **.reload** command:

```
kd> .reload
Connected to Windows 10 22000 x64 target at (Sun Sep 15 18:29:20.142 2024 (UTC + 1:00)), ptr64
TRUE
Loading Kernel Symbols
...............................................................
................................................................
.......................................
Loading User Symbols
.....
Loading unloaded module list
.........
```

15. Now the **k** command should produce the correct stack trace (the output may vary depending on when you broke into the system):

```
kd> k
# Child-SP          RetAddr               Call Site
00 fffff803`5c6e1b68 fffff803`61bd27a4      nt!DbgBreakPointWithStatus
01 fffff803`5c6e1b70 fffff803`5828d6f4      kdnic!RxReceiveIndicateDpc+0x74
02 fffff803`5c6e1bd0 fffff803`5828bce4      nt!KiProcessExpiredTimerList+0x204
03 fffff803`5c6e1d00 fffff803`58426f65      nt!KiRetireDpcList+0x714
04 fffff803`5c6e1fb0 fffff803`58426d40      nt!KxRetireDpcList+0x5
```

```
05 ffffed8a`5a484910 fffff803`58426415     nt!KiDispatchInterruptContinue
06 ffffed8a`5a484940 fffff803`584202f1     nt!KiDpcInterruptBypass+0x25
07 ffffed8a`5a484950 fffff803`584322e1     nt!KiInterruptDispatchNoLockNoEtw+0xb1
08 ffffed8a`5a484ae0 00007ffd`9fce4654     nt!KiSystemServiceUser+0xbb
09 0000008e`823ee768 00007ffd`9fc5c9ce     ntdll!NtProtectVirtualMemory+0x14
0a 0000008e`823ee770 00007ffd`9fc5c978     ntdll!LdrpChangeMrdataProtection+0x4e
0b 0000008e`823ee7b0 00007ffd`9fc744ef     ntdll!LdrProtectMrdata+0x74
0c 0000008e`823ee7e0 00007ffd`9fc74c41     ntdll!RtlInsertInvertedFunctionTable+0x53
0d 0000008e`823ee820 00007ffd`9fc8cdd2     ntdll!LdrpProcessMappedModule+0x155
0e 0000008e`823ee880 00007ffd`9fc8d41d     ntdll!LdrpMapDllWithSectionHandle+0x13e
0f 0000008e`823ee8e0 00007ffd`9fc7e504     ntdll!LdrpLoadKnownDll+0xe1
10 0000008e`823ee940 00007ffd`9fc7d55f     ntdll!LdrpLoadDependentModuleInternal+0xc14
11 0000008e`823eed90 00007ffd`9fc7d224     ntdll!LdrpLoadDependentModuleA+0x1ff
12 0000008e`823eef40 00007ffd`9fd1fc26     ntdll!LdrpMapAndSnapDependency+0x210
13 0000008e`823eefc0 00007ffd`9fd0d706     ntdll!LdrpInitializeProcess+0x1b3a
14 0000008e`823ef380 00007ffd`9fcbae53     ntdll!_LdrpInitialize+0x5287a
15 0000008e`823ef400 00007ffd`9fcbad7e     ntdll!LdrpInitializeInternal+0x6b
16 0000008e`823ef680 00000000`00000000     ntdll!LdrInitializeThunk+0xe
```

16. We open a log file:

```
kd> .logopen C:\EWMDA-Dumps\Complete\x64\ES8.log
Opened log file 'C:\EWMDA-Dumps\Complete\x64\ES8.log'
```

17. We cloned the latest repository at the time of this writing, built it, and included it in the dump archive (the extension is written in Rust). We can load it now:

```
kd> .load C:\EWMDA-Dumps\snapshot\snapshot

kd> !snapshot -h
[dbgeng-rs] Usage: snapshot [OPTIONS] [STATE_PATH]

Arguments:
  [STATE_PATH]  The path to save the snapshot to

Options:
  -k, --kind <KIND>  The kind of snapshot to take [default: full] [possible values: active-
kernel, full]
  -h, --help         Print help
```

18. We choose to save an active kernel snapshot (this may take some time):

```
kd> !snapshot -k active-kernel C:\EWMDA-Dumps
[dbgeng-rs] Dumping the CPU state into C:\EWMDA-Dumps\state.22000.1.amd64fre.co_release.210604-
1628.20240915_1837\regs.json..
[dbgeng-rs] Dumping the memory state into C:\EWMDA-
Dumps\state.22000.1.amd64fre.co_release.210604-1628.20240915_1837\mem.dmp..
Creating C:\\EWMDA-Dumps\\state.22000.1.amd64fre.co_release.210604-1628.20240915_1837\\mem.dmp
- Active kernel and user memory range dump
Collecting pages to write to the dump. This may take a while.
0% written.
5% written. 2 min 31 sec remaining.
10% written. 1 min 45 sec remaining.
15% written. 1 min 34 sec remaining.
20% written. 1 min 32 sec remaining.
25% written. 1 min 22 sec remaining.
30% written. 42 sec remaining.
```

```
ValidateSequenceNumber: Sequence number too far ahead for validation.
ValidateSequenceNumber: Sequence number too far ahead for validation.
ValidateSequenceNumber: Sequence number too far ahead for validation.
ValidateSequenceNumber: Sequence number too far ahead for validation.
35% written. 45 sec remaining.
ValidateSequenceNumber: Sequence number too far ahead for validation.
ValidateSequenceNumber: Sequence number too far ahead for validation.
ValidateSequenceNumber: Sequence number too far ahead for validation.
40% written. 44 sec remaining.
45% written. 37 sec remaining.
ValidateSequenceNumber: Sequence number too far ahead for validation.
50% written. 34 sec remaining.
ValidateSequenceNumber: Sequence number too far ahead for validation.
55% written. 27 sec remaining.
ValidateSequenceNumber: Sequence number too far ahead for validation.
ValidateSequenceNumber: Sequence number too far ahead for validation.
ValidateSequenceNumber: Sequence number too far ahead for validation.
ValidateSequenceNumber: Sequence number too far ahead for validation.
60% written. 27 sec remaining.
65% written. 22 sec remaining.
70% written. 17 sec remaining.
75% written. 14 sec remaining.
80% written. 17 sec remaining.
85% written. 18 sec remaining.
90% written. 12 sec remaining.
ValidateSequenceNumber: Sequence number too far ahead for validation.
95% written. 4 sec remaining.
Wrote 3.7 GB in 1 min 31 sec.
The average transfer rate was 41.2 MB/s.
Wrote 3717 pages of 0xdeadfeed into this dump file for memory that could not be
read successfully by the kernel memory manager.  The kernel memory manager can
not read pages that have a held page lock, are on the failed memory page list,
or which have been hot removed from the system.
Dump successfully written
[dbgeng-rs] Done!
```

19. We resume the guest VM and close logging before exiting WinDbg:

```
kd> g
```

```
kd> .logclose
Closing open log file C:\EWMDA-Dumps\Complete\x64\ES8.log
```

20. To verify the saved dump, we open it in another instance of WinDbg:

```
Microsoft (R) Windows Debugger Version 10.0.27668.1000 AMD64
Copyright (c) Microsoft Corporation. All rights reserved.

Loading Dump File [C:\EWMDA-Dumps\state.22000.1.amd64fre.co_release.210604-
1628.20240915_1837\mem.dmp]
Kernel Range Dump File: Active memory pages (user + kernel) are available

************* Path validation summary **************
Response                         Time (ms)     Location
Deferred                                       srv*
Symbol search path is: srv*
Executable search path is:
```

```
Windows 10 Kernel Version 22000 UP Free x64
Product: WinNt, suite: TerminalServer SingleUserTS
Edition build lab: 22000.1.amd64fre.co_release.210604-1628
Kernel base = 0xfffff803`58000000 PsLoadedModuleList = 0xfffff803`58c297b0
Debug session time: Sun Sep 15 18:26:31.710 2024 (UTC + 1:00)
System Uptime: 0 days 0:01:06.441
Loading Kernel Symbols
...............................................................
Loading User Symbols
.....
Loading unloaded module list
.........
*******************************************************************************
*                                                                             *
*   You are seeing this message because you pressed either                    *
*       CTRL+C (if you run console kernel debugger) or,                       *
*       CTRL+BREAK (if you run GUI kernel debugger),                          *
*   on your debugger machine's keyboard.                                      *
*                                                                             *
*                   THIS IS NOT A BUG OR A SYSTEM CRASH                       *
*                                                                             *
* If you did not intend to break into the debugger, press the "g" key, then   *
* press the "Enter" key now.  This message might immediately reappear.  If it *
* does, press "g" and "Enter" again.                                          *
*                                                                             *
*******************************************************************************
For analysis of this file, run !analyze -v
nt!DbgBreakPointWithStatus:
fffff803`584279f0 int     3

kd> k
 # Child-SP          RetAddr               Call Site
00 fffff803`5c6e1b68 fffff803`61bd27a4     nt!DbgBreakPointWithStatus
01 fffff803`5c6e1b70 fffff803`5828d6f4     kdnic!RxReceiveIndicateDpc+0x74
02 fffff803`5c6e1bd0 fffff803`5828bce4     nt!KiProcessExpiredTimerList+0x204
03 fffff803`5c6e1d00 fffff803`58426f65     nt!KiRetireDpcList+0x714
04 fffff803`5c6e1fb0 fffff803`58426d40     nt!KxRetireDpcList+0x5
05 ffffed8a`5a484910 fffff803`58426415     nt!KiDispatchInterruptContinue
06 ffffed8a`5a484940 fffff803`584202f1     nt!KiDpcInterruptBypass+0x25
07 ffffed8a`5a484950 fffff803`584322e1     nt!KiInterruptDispatchNoLockNoEtw+0xb1
08 ffffed8a`5a484ae0 00007ffd`9fce4654     nt!KiSystemServiceUser+0xbb
09 0000008e`823ee768 00007ffd`9fc5c9ce     ntdll!NtProtectVirtualMemory+0x14
0a 0000008e`823ee770 00007ffd`9fc5c978     ntdll!LdrpChangeMrdataProtection+0x4e
0b 0000008e`823ee7b0 00007ffd`9fc744ef     ntdll!LdrProtectMrdata+0x74
0c 0000008e`823ee7e0 00007ffd`9fc74c41     ntdll!RtlInsertInvertedFunctionTable+0x53
0d 0000008e`823ee820 00007ffd`9fc8cdd2     ntdll!LdrpProcessMappedModule+0x155
0e 0000008e`823ee880 00007ffd`9fc8d41d     ntdll!LdrpMapDllWithSectionHandle+0x13e
0f 0000008e`823ee8e0 00007ffd`9fc7e504     ntdll!LdrpLoadKnownDll+0xe1
10 0000008e`823ee940 00007ffd`9fc7d55f     ntdll!LdrpLoadDependentModuleInternal+0xc14
11 0000008e`823eed90 00007ffd`9fc7d224     ntdll!LdrpLoadDependentModuleA+0x1ff
12 0000008e`823eef40 00007ffd`9fd1fc26     ntdll!LdrpMapAndSnapDependency+0x210
13 0000008e`823eefc0 00007ffd`9fd0d706     ntdll!LdrpInitializeProcess+0x1b3a
14 0000008e`823ef380 00007ffd`9fcbae53     ntdll!_LdrpInitialize+0x5287a
15 0000008e`823ef400 00007ffd`9fcbad7e     ntdll!LdrpInitializeInternal+0x6b
16 0000008e`823ef680 00000000`00000000     ntdll!LdrInitializeThunk+0xe
```

21. We exit WinDbg.

Exercise ES9

- **Goal:** Explore WinDbg Copilot
- **Memory Analysis Patterns:** Analysis Summary; Annotated Stack Trace; Disassembly Summary; Region Summary
- \EWMDA\Exercise-ES9.pdf

WinDbg Copilot (the original repo was not available at the time of this writing)
https://github.com/DumpAnalysis/WinDbg_Copilot

Exercise ES9: Explore WinDbg Copilot

Goal: Explore WinDbg Copilot[18].

Memory Analysis Patterns: Analysis Summary; Annotated Stack Trace; Disassembly Summary; Region Summary.

1. We use Python 3.11 for this exercise. WinDbg Classic is also required.

2. Install WinDbg-Copilot *pykd-0.3.4.15-cp311-none-win_amd64.whl* file included in the memory dumps archive you downloaded in Exercise E0 (also check for any updates in the previously forked repo):

```
C:\EWMDA-Dumps>pip install C:\EWMDA-Dumps\WinDbg_Copilot\ WinDbg_Copilot-1.0.51-py3-none-any.whl
Processing c:\ewmda-dumps\windbg_copilot\windbg_copilot-1.0.51-py3-none-any.whl
Collecting openai>=0.27.2 (from WinDbg-Copilot==1.0.51)
  Downloading openai-1.47.0-py3-none-any.whl.metadata (24 kB)
Collecting tiktoken>=0.4.0 (from WinDbg-Copilot==1.0.51)
  Downloading tiktoken-0.7.0-cp311-cp311-win_amd64.whl.metadata (6.8 kB)
Collecting anyio<5,>=3.5.0 (from openai>=0.27.2->WinDbg-Copilot==1.0.51)
  Downloading anyio-4.6.0-py3-none-any.whl.metadata (4.6 kB)
Collecting distro<2,>=1.7.0 (from openai>=0.27.2->WinDbg-Copilot==1.0.51)
  Downloading distro-1.9.0-py3-none-any.whl.metadata (6.8 kB)
Collecting httpx<1,>=0.23.0 (from openai>=0.27.2->WinDbg-Copilot==1.0.51)
  Downloading httpx-0.27.2-py3-none-any.whl.metadata (7.1 kB)
Collecting jiter<1,>=0.4.0 (from openai>=0.27.2->WinDbg-Copilot==1.0.51)
  Downloading jiter-0.5.0-cp311-none-win_amd64.whl.metadata (3.7 kB)
Collecting pydantic<3,>=1.9.0 (from openai>=0.27.2->WinDbg-Copilot==1.0.51)
  Downloading pydantic-2.9.2-py3-none-any.whl.metadata (149 kB)
     ---------------------------------------- 149.4/149.4 kB 1.8 MB/s eta 0:00:00
Collecting sniffio (from openai>=0.27.2->WinDbg-Copilot==1.0.51)
  Downloading sniffio-1.3.1-py3-none-any.whl.metadata (3.9 kB)
Collecting tqdm>4 (from openai>=0.27.2->WinDbg-Copilot==1.0.51)
  Downloading tqdm-4.66.5-py3-none-any.whl.metadata (57 kB)
     ---------------------------------------- 57.6/57.6 kB 3.0 MB/s eta 0:00:00
Collecting typing-extensions<5,>=4.11 (from openai>=0.27.2->WinDbg-Copilot==1.0.51)
  Downloading typing_extensions-4.12.2-py3-none-any.whl.metadata (3.0 kB)
Collecting regex>=2022.1.18 (from tiktoken>=0.4.0->WinDbg-Copilot==1.0.51)
  Downloading regex-2024.9.11-cp311-cp311-win_amd64.whl.metadata (41 kB)
     ---------------------------------------- 41.5/41.5 kB 1.0 MB/s eta 0:00:00
Collecting requests>=2.26.0 (from tiktoken>=0.4.0->WinDbg-Copilot==1.0.51)
  Downloading requests-2.32.3-py3-none-any.whl.metadata (4.6 kB)
Collecting idna>=2.8 (from anyio<5,>=3.5.0->openai>=0.27.2->WinDbg-Copilot==1.0.51)
  Downloading idna-3.10-py3-none-any.whl.metadata (10 kB)
Collecting certifi (from httpx<1,>=0.23.0->openai>=0.27.2->WinDbg-Copilot==1.0.51)
  Downloading certifi-2024.8.30-py3-none-any.whl.metadata (2.2 kB)
Collecting httpcore==1.* (from httpx<1,>=0.23.0->openai>=0.27.2->WinDbg-Copilot==1.0.51)
  Downloading httpcore-1.0.5-py3-none-any.whl.metadata (20 kB)
Collecting h11<0.15,>=0.13 (from httpcore==1.*->httpx<1,>=0.23.0->openai>=0.27.2->WinDbg-Copilot==1.0.51)
  Downloading h11-0.14.0-py3-none-any.whl.metadata (8.2 kB)
Collecting annotated-types>=0.6.0 (from pydantic<3,>=1.9.0->openai>=0.27.2->WinDbg-Copilot==1.0.51)
  Downloading annotated_types-0.7.0-py3-none-any.whl.metadata (15 kB)
```

[18] The original repo was not available at the time of this writing: https://github.com/DumpAnalysis/WinDbg_Copilot

```
Collecting pydantic-core==2.23.4 (from pydantic<3,>=1.9.0->openai>=0.27.2->WinDbg-
Copilot==1.0.51)
  Downloading pydantic_core-2.23.4-cp311-none-win_amd64.whl.metadata (6.7 kB)
Collecting charset-normalizer<4,>=2 (from requests>=2.26.0->tiktoken>=0.4.0->WinDbg-
Copilot==1.0.51)
  Downloading charset_normalizer-3.3.2-cp311-cp311-win_amd64.whl.metadata (34 kB)
Collecting urllib3<3,>=1.21.1 (from requests>=2.26.0->tiktoken>=0.4.0->WinDbg-Copilot==1.0.51)
  Downloading urllib3-2.2.3-py3-none-any.whl.metadata (6.5 kB)
Collecting colorama (from tqdm>4->openai>=0.27.2->WinDbg-Copilot==1.0.51)
  Downloading colorama-0.4.6-py2.py3-none-any.whl.metadata (17 kB)
Downloading openai-1.47.0-py3-none-any.whl (375 kB)
   ━━━━━━━━━━━━━━━━━━━━━━━━━━━━━━━━━━━━━━━━ 375.6/375.6 kB 5.8 MB/s eta 0:00:00
Downloading tiktoken-0.7.0-cp311-cp311-win_amd64.whl (799 kB)
   ━━━━━━━━━━━━━━━━━━━━━━━━━━━━━━━━━━━━━━━━ 799.0/799.0 kB 3.9 MB/s eta 0:00:00
Downloading anyio-4.6.0-py3-none-any.whl (89 kB)
   ━━━━━━━━━━━━━━━━━━━━━━━━━━━━━━━━━━━━━━━━ 89.6/89.6 kB 2.6 MB/s eta 0:00:00
Downloading distro-1.9.0-py3-none-any.whl (20 kB)
Downloading httpx-0.27.2-py3-none-any.whl (76 kB)
   ━━━━━━━━━━━━━━━━━━━━━━━━━━━━━━━━━━━━━━━━ 76.4/76.4 kB 2.1 MB/s eta 0:00:00
Downloading httpcore-1.0.5-py3-none-any.whl (77 kB)
   ━━━━━━━━━━━━━━━━━━━━━━━━━━━━━━━━━━━━━━━━ 77.9/77.9 kB 4.5 MB/s eta 0:00:00
Downloading jiter-0.5.0-cp311-none-win_amd64.whl (191 kB)
   ━━━━━━━━━━━━━━━━━━━━━━━━━━━━━━━━━━━━━━━━ 191.0/191.0 kB 2.9 MB/s eta 0:00:00
Downloading pydantic-2.9.2-py3-none-any.whl (434 kB)
   ━━━━━━━━━━━━━━━━━━━━━━━━━━━━━━━━━━━━━━━━ 434.9/434.9 kB 3.9 MB/s eta 0:00:00
Downloading pydantic_core-2.23.4-cp311-none-win_amd64.whl (1.9 MB)
   ━━━━━━━━━━━━━━━━━━━━━━━━━━━━━━━━━━━━━━━━ 1.9/1.9 MB 4.2 MB/s eta 0:00:00
Downloading regex-2024.9.11-cp311-cp311-win_amd64.whl (274 kB)
   ━━━━━━━━━━━━━━━━━━━━━━━━━━━━━━━━━━━━━━━━ 274.0/274.0 kB 4.3 MB/s eta 0:00:00
Downloading requests-2.32.3-py3-none-any.whl (64 kB)
   ━━━━━━━━━━━━━━━━━━━━━━━━━━━━━━━━━━━━━━━━ 64.9/64.9 kB 1.2 MB/s eta 0:00:00
Downloading sniffio-1.3.1-py3-none-any.whl (10 kB)
Downloading tqdm-4.66.5-py3-none-any.whl (78 kB)
   ━━━━━━━━━━━━━━━━━━━━━━━━━━━━━━━━━━━━━━━━ 78.4/78.4 kB 4.5 MB/s eta 0:00:00
Downloading typing_extensions-4.12.2-py3-none-any.whl (37 kB)
Downloading annotated_types-0.7.0-py3-none-any.whl (13 kB)
Downloading certifi-2024.8.30-py3-none-any.whl (167 kB)
   ━━━━━━━━━━━━━━━━━━━━━━━━━━━━━━━━━━━━━━━━ 167.3/167.3 kB 3.3 MB/s eta 0:00:00
Downloading charset_normalizer-3.3.2-cp311-cp311-win_amd64.whl (99 kB)
   ━━━━━━━━━━━━━━━━━━━━━━━━━━━━━━━━━━━━━━━━ 99.9/99.9 kB 2.9 MB/s eta 0:00:00
Downloading idna-3.10-py3-none-any.whl (70 kB)
   ━━━━━━━━━━━━━━━━━━━━━━━━━━━━━━━━━━━━━━━━ 70.4/70.4 kB 1.9 MB/s eta 0:00:00
Downloading urllib3-2.2.3-py3-none-any.whl (126 kB)
   ━━━━━━━━━━━━━━━━━━━━━━━━━━━━━━━━━━━━━━━━ 126.3/126.3 kB 3.6 MB/s eta 0:00:00
Downloading colorama-0.4.6-py2.py3-none-any.whl (25 kB)
Downloading h11-0.14.0-py3-none-any.whl (58 kB)
   ━━━━━━━━━━━━━━━━━━━━━━━━━━━━━━━━━━━━━━━━ 58.3/58.3 kB 3.0 MB/s eta 0:00:00
Installing collected packages: urllib3, typing-extensions, sniffio, regex, jiter, idna, h11,
distro, colorama, charset-normalizer, certifi, annotated-types, tqdm, requests, pydantic-core,
httpcore, anyio, tiktoken, pydantic, httpx, openai, WinDbg-Copilot
Successfully installed WinDbg-Copilot-1.0.51 annotated-types-0.7.0 anyio-4.6.0 certifi-
2024.8.30 charset-normalizer-3.3.2 colorama-0.4.6 distro-1.9.0 h11-0.14.0 httpcore-1.0.5 httpx-
0.27.2 idna-3.10 jiter-0.5.0 openai-1.47.0 pydantic-2.9.2 pydantic-core-2.23.4 regex-2024.9.11
requests-2.32.3 sniffio-1.3.1 tiktoken-0.7.0 tqdm-4.66.5 typing-extensions-4.12.2 urllib3-2.2.3
```

Note: You may want this additional requirement:

```
C:\EWMDA-Dumps>pip install openai==0.28
Collecting openai==0.28
  Downloading openai-0.28.0-py3-none-any.whl.metadata (13 kB)
Requirement already satisfied: requests>=2.20 in c:\python311\lib\site-packages (from
openai==0.28) (2.32.3)
Requirement already satisfied: tqdm in c:\python311\lib\site-packages (from openai==0.28)
(4.66.5)
Collecting aiohttp (from openai==0.28)
  Downloading aiohttp-3.10.5-cp311-cp311-win_amd64.whl.metadata (7.8 kB)
Requirement already satisfied: charset-normalizer<4,>=2 in c:\python311\lib\site-packages (from
requests>=2.20->openai==0.28) (3.3.2)
Requirement already satisfied: idna<4,>=2.5 in c:\python311\lib\site-packages (from
requests>=2.20->openai==0.28) (3.10)
Requirement already satisfied: urllib3<3,>=1.21.1 in c:\python311\lib\site-packages (from
requests>=2.20->openai==0.28) (2.2.3)
Requirement already satisfied: certifi>=2017.4.17 in c:\python311\lib\site-packages (from
requests>=2.20->openai==0.28) (2024.8.30)
Collecting aiohappyeyeballs>=2.3.0 (from aiohttp->openai==0.28)
  Downloading aiohappyeyeballs-2.4.0-py3-none-any.whl.metadata (5.9 kB)
Collecting aiosignal>=1.1.2 (from aiohttp->openai==0.28)
  Downloading aiosignal-1.3.1-py3-none-any.whl.metadata (4.0 kB)
Collecting attrs>=17.3.0 (from aiohttp->openai==0.28)
  Downloading attrs-24.2.0-py3-none-any.whl.metadata (11 kB)
Collecting frozenlist>=1.1.1 (from aiohttp->openai==0.28)
  Downloading frozenlist-1.4.1-cp311-cp311-win_amd64.whl.metadata (12 kB)
Collecting multidict<7.0,>=4.5 (from aiohttp->openai==0.28)
  Downloading multidict-6.1.0-cp311-cp311-win_amd64.whl.metadata (5.1 kB)
Collecting yarl<2.0,>=1.0 (from aiohttp->openai==0.28)
  Downloading yarl-1.11.1-cp311-cp311-win_amd64.whl.metadata (49 kB)
     ---------------------------------------- 49.8/49.8 kB 840.8 kB/s eta 0:00:00
Requirement already satisfied: colorama in c:\python311\lib\site-packages (from tqdm-
>openai==0.28) (0.4.6)
Downloading openai-0.28.0-py3-none-any.whl (76 kB)
   ---------------------------------------- 76.5/76.5 kB 2.1 MB/s eta 0:00:00
Downloading aiohttp-3.10.5-cp311-cp311-win_amd64.whl (379 kB)
   ---------------------------------------- 379.1/379.1 kB 6.0 MB/s eta 0:00:00
Downloading aiohappyeyeballs-2.4.0-py3-none-any.whl (12 kB)
Downloading aiosignal-1.3.1-py3-none-any.whl (7.6 kB)
Downloading attrs-24.2.0-py3-none-any.whl (63 kB)
   ---------------------------------------- 63.0/63.0 kB 3.3 MB/s eta 0:00:00
Downloading frozenlist-1.4.1-cp311-cp311-win_amd64.whl (50 kB)
   ---------------------------------------- 50.5/50.5 kB 2.5 MB/s eta 0:00:00
Downloading multidict-6.1.0-cp311-cp311-win_amd64.whl (28 kB)
Downloading yarl-1.11.1-cp311-cp311-win_amd64.whl (110 kB)
   ---------------------------------------- 110.5/110.5 kB 6.7 MB/s eta 0:00:00
Installing collected packages: multidict, frozenlist, attrs, aiohappyeyeballs, yarl, aiosignal,
aiohttp, openai
  Attempting uninstall: openai
    Found existing installation: openai 1.47.0
    Uninstalling openai-1.47.0:
      Successfully uninstalled openai-1.47.0
Successfully installed aiohappyeyeballs-2.4.0 aiohttp-3.10.5 aiosignal-1.3.1 attrs-24.2.0
frozenlist-1.4.1 multidict-6.1.0 openai-0.28.0 yarl-1.11.1
```

3. Set the OPENAI_API_KEY environment variable with your Project API secret key value. If you are new to OpenAI API check this page[19]. If you don't set this variable, you will be asked for the key value later.

4. Start Python and execute the following commands:

```
C:\EWMDA-Dumps>python
Python 3.11.9 (tags/v3.11.9:de54cf5, Apr  2 2024, 10:12:12) [MSC v.1938 64 bit (AMD64)] on win32
Type "help", "copyright", "credits" or "license" for more information.
>>> import WinDbg_Copilot as Copilot

>>> Copilot.start()

Do you want to use OpenAI API or Azure OpenAI? 1 for OpenAI API, 2 for Azure OpenAI: 1

Do you want to use model gpt-3.5-turbo-16k-0613 or model gpt-4? 1 for gpt-3.5-turbo-16k-0613, 2 for gpt-4: 2

Environment variable WinDbg_PATH is not found on your machine, please input WinDbg installation path which contains WinDbg.exe: C:\Program Files (x86)\Windows Kits\10\Debuggers\x64

This software is used for debugging learning purpose, please do not load any customer data.

Do you want to open dump/trace file or connect to remote debugger? 1 for dump/trace file, 2 for remote debugger: 1

Please enter your memory dump file path, only *.dmp or *.run files are supported. Memory dump file path: c:\ewmda-dumps\complete\x64\memory-w11.dmp

Environment variable _NT_SYMBOL_PATH is not found on your machine, set default symbol path to srv*C:\symbols*https://msdl.microsoft.com/download/symbols

************* Preparing the environment for Debugger Extensions Gallery repositories **************
   ExtensionRepository : Implicit
   UseExperimentalFeatureForNugetShare : true
   AllowNugetExeUpdate : true
   NonInteractiveNuget : true
   AllowNugetMSCredentialProviderInstall : true
   AllowParallelInitializationOfLocalRepositories : true

   EnableRedirectToV8JsProvider : false

   -- Configuring repositories
      ----> Repository : LocalInstalled, Enabled: true
      ----> Repository : UserExtensions, Enabled: true

>>>>>>>>>>>>> Preparing the environment for Debugger Extensions Gallery repositories completed, duration 0.000 seconds

************* Waiting for Debugger Extensions Gallery to Initialize **************

>>>>>>>>>>>>> Waiting for Debugger Extensions Gallery to Initialize completed, duration 0.016 seconds
   ----> Repository : UserExtensions, Enabled: true, Packages count: 0
```

[19] https://platform.openai.com/settings/organization/billing/overview

```
   ----> Repository : LocalInstalled, Enabled: true, Packages count: 29

Microsoft (R) Windows Debugger Version 10.0.26100.1 AMD64
Copyright (c) Microsoft Corporation. All rights reserved.


Loading Dump File [c:\ewmda-dumps\complete\x64\memory-w11.dmp]
Kernel Bitmap Dump File: Full address space is available


************* Path validation summary **************
Response                         Time (ms)     Location
Deferred
srv*C:\symbols*https://msdl.microsoft.com/download/symbols
Symbol search path is: srv*C:\symbols*https://msdl.microsoft.com/download/symbols
Executable search path is:
Windows 10 Kernel Version 22000 MP (2 procs) Free x64
Product: WinNt, suite: TerminalServer SingleUserTS Personal
Edition build lab: 22000.1.amd64fre.co_release.210604-1628
Kernel base = 0xfffff806`61e00000 PsLoadedModuleList = 0xfffff806`62a296b0
Debug session time: Sat Nov 13 23:17:16.607 2021 (UTC + 1:00)
System Uptime: 0 days 0:03:06.813
Loading Kernel Symbols
..............................................................
...............................................................
...............................................................
..
Loading User Symbols
..................................
Loading unloaded module list
........
For analysis of this file, run !analyze -v
0: kd> cdb: Reading initial command '.echo Command Completed'
Command Completed
0: kd> .  0 64-bit Kernel bitmap dump: c:\ewmda-dumps\complete\x64\memory-w11.dmp
0: kd> Command Completed

Do you want to load any debug extensions? Debug extension dll path:<Enter>


0: kd> No extension DLL name provided
0: kd> Command Completed

Do you want to add any symbol file path? Symbol file path:<Enter>


0: kd> Symbol search path is: srv*C:\symbols*https://msdl.microsoft.com/download/symbols
Expanded Symbol search path is: srv*c:\symbols*https://msdl.microsoft.com/download/symbols

************* Path validation summary **************
Response                         Time (ms)     Location
Deferred
srv*C:\symbols*https://msdl.microsoft.com/download/symbols
0: kd> Command Completed

Hello, I am WinDbg Copilot, I'm here to assist you.

The given commands are used to interact with WinDbg Copilot, a tool that utilizes the OpenAI
model for assistance with debugging. The commands include:
```

```
    !chat: Chat mode, conversation will be sent to OpenAI ChatGPT model, ChatGPT can reply with
simple explanations or suggest a single command to execute to further analyze the problem. User
will decide to execute the suggested command or not.
    !command: Command mode, user inputs are sent to debugger and debugger outputs will be sent
to OpenAI ChatGPT model, ChatGPT can reply with simple explanations or suggest a single command
to execute to further analyze the problem.
    !problem <problem statement>: Updates the problem description by providing a new problem
statement.
    !quit or !q or q or qq: Terminates the debugger session.
    !help or !h: Provides help information.

Note: WinDbg Copilot requires an active Internet connection to function properly, as it relies
on Openai API.

Problem description: I want to explore this dump.

Thinking...

Sure, to start exploring the dump, you can use the command `!analyze -v` to perform an
automatic debug analysis.

<exec>!analyze -v</exec>

Do you want to execute command: !analyze -v? Y or N: Y


0: kd> *******************************************************************************
*                                                                             *
*                        Bugcheck Analysis                                    *
*                                                                             *
*******************************************************************************

DRIVER_IRQL_NOT_LESS_OR_EQUAL (d1)
An attempt was made to access a pageable (or completely invalid) address at an
interrupt request level (IRQL) that is too high.  This is usually
caused by drivers using improper addresses.
If kernel debugger is available get stack backtrace.
Arguments:
Arg1: ffffac8a0d8ea010, memory referenced
Arg2: 0000000000000002, IRQL
Arg3: 0000000000000000, value 0 = read operation, 1 = write operation
Arg4: fffff80660571981, address which referenced memory

Debugging Details:
------------------

Unable to load image \??\C:\WINDOWS\system32\drivers\myfault.sys, Win32 error 0n2

KEY_VALUES_STRING: 1

    Key  : Analysis.CPU.mSec
    Value: 1905

    Key  : Analysis.DebugAnalysisManager
    Value: Create

    Key  : Analysis.Elapsed.mSec
    Value: 24128
```

```
    Key  : Analysis.Init.CPU.mSec
    Value: 249

    Key  : Analysis.Init.Elapsed.mSec
    Value: 28656

    Key  : Analysis.Memory.CommitPeak.Mb
    Value: 136

    Key  : WER.OS.Branch
    Value: co_release

    Key  : WER.OS.Timestamp
    Value: 2021-06-04T16:28:00Z

    Key  : WER.OS.Version
    Value: 10.0.22000.1


FILE_IN_CAB:  memory-w11.dmp

VIRTUAL_MACHINE:  VMware

BUGCHECK_CODE:  d1

BUGCHECK_P1: ffffac8a0d8ea010

BUGCHECK_P2: 2

BUGCHECK_P3: 0

BUGCHECK_P4: fffff80660571981

READ_ADDRESS: unable to get nt!PspSessionIdBitmap
 ffffac8a0d8ea010 Paged pool

BLACKBOXBSD: 1 (!blackboxbsd)


BLACKBOXNTFS: 1 (!blackboxntfs)


BLACKBOXWINLOGON: 1

PROCESS_NAME:  notmyfault64.exe

TRAP_FRAME:  ffffbe8296f647b0 -- (.trap 0xffffbe8296f647b0)
NOTE: The trap frame does not contain all registers.
Some register values may be zeroed or incorrect.
rax=0000000000001000 rbx=0000000000000000 rcx=ffffac8a0d8e7000
rdx=ffffac8a0d480000 rsi=0000000000000000 rdi=0000000000000000
rip=fffff80660571981 rsp=ffffbe8296f64940 rbp=ffffbe8296f64bb1
 r8=ffffac8a0d480000  r9=ffffc38c2c402000 r10=fffff80662a5f540
r11=ffffac8a0d8e7000 r12=0000000000000000 r13=0000000000000000
r14=0000000000000000 r15=0000000000000000
iopl=0         nv up ei ng nz na pe nc
myfault+0x1981:
fffff806`60571981 8b03            mov     eax,dword ptr [rbx] ds:00000000`00000000=????????
```

```
Resetting default scope

STACK_TEXT:
ffffbe82`96f64668 fffff806`622281a9     : 00000000`0000000a ffffac8a`0d8ea010 00000000`00000002
00000000`00000000 : nt!KeBugCheckEx
ffffbe82`96f64670 fffff806`62224300     : 00000000`00000000 ffffbd11`c0e0c2b8 ffff2703`d5aecdf2
ffffbd11`c253e710 : nt!KiBugCheckDispatch+0x69
ffffbe82`96f647b0 fffff806`60571981     : ffffbe82`96f64d10 fffff806`6d8cee70 00000000`00000000
ffffc38c`306d4f70 : nt!KiPageFault+0x440
ffffbe82`96f64940 fffff806`60571d3d     : 00000000`00001000 00000000`00000000 ffffc38c`33ac3080
ffffbd11`c0e0c010 : myfault+0x1981
ffffbe82`96f64970 fffff806`60571ea1     : ffffc38c`31efb360 fffff806`624a4204 ffffc38c`2c4792d0
00000000`00005fd4 : myfault+0x1d3d
ffffbe82`96f64ab0 fffff806`62102f65     : ffffc38c`31efb360 00000000`00000002 00000000`00000000
00000000`00000000 : myfault+0x1ea1
ffffbe82`96f64b10 fffff806`6256b532     : 00000000`00000001 ffffc38c`31efb360 ffffbe82`96f64bb1
fffff806`62102d23 : nt!IofCallDriver+0x55
ffffbe82`96f64b50 fffff806`6256acbf     : ffffc38c`00000000 ffffbe82`96f64ea0 00000000`83360018
00000000`83360018 : nt!IopSynchronousServiceTail+0x1d2
ffffbe82`96f64c00 fffff806`6256a6c6     : 00000000`00000000 00000000`00000000 00000000`00000000
00000000`00000000 : nt!IopXxxControlFile+0x5df
ffffbe82`96f64d40 fffff806`62227b75     : 00000000`00000000 00000000`00000000 ffff6a98`d8ef3484
00000000`00070000 : nt!NtDeviceIoControlFile+0x56
ffffbe82`96f64db0 00007ffc`88543444     : 00007ffc`85c23edb 00000000`0002043c 0000003f`0731ef49
000001e9`bdfc0000 : nt!KiSystemServiceCopyEnd+0x25
0000003f`0731ec08 00007ffc`85c23edb     : 00000000`0002043c 0000003f`0731ef49 000001e9`bdfc0000
00000000`00000000 : ntdll!NtDeviceIoControlFile+0x14
0000003f`0731ec10 00007ffc`876b5f91     : 00000000`83360018 00000000`00000000 00000000`00000000
00007ffc`880199f9 : KERNELBASE!DeviceIoControl+0x6b
0000003f`0731ec80 00007ff7`be36342f     : 00000000`00020454 0000003f`0731ed69 0000003f`0731ed69
00000000`00000000 : KERNEL32!DeviceIoControlImplementation+0x81
0000003f`0731ecd0 00007ffc`87fd484b     : 00000000`00000001 00000000`00000001 00000000`00000001
00000000`00000002 : notmyfault64+0x342f
0000003f`0731edd0 00007ffc`87fd409b     : 00000000`00000000 00007ff7`be3632d0 00000000`00000111
000001e9`be6d6f60 : USER32!UserCallDlgProcCheckWow+0x14b
0000003f`0731eeb0 00007ffc`880197c9     : 00000000`0004046e 00000000`000000f3 00000000`0004046e
00000000`00000000 : USER32!DefDlgProcWorker+0xcb
0000003f`0731ef70 00007ffc`87fd1c4c     : 00000000`00000001 00000000`00000000 00000000`00000001
00000000`00000000 : USER32!DefDlgProcA+0x39
0000003f`0731efb0 00007ffc`87fd179c     : 00003130`08652f97 00007ffc`885430e0 00000000`00020454
00007ffc`00000111 : USER32!UserCallWinProcCheckWow+0x33c
0000003f`0731f120 00007ffc`87fe4b4d     : 00000000`00000000 00000000`00000000 00000000`000003f9
00000000`000c0000 : USER32!DispatchClientMessage+0x9c
0000003f`0731f180 00007ffc`885472b4     : 00000000`00000000 00000000`00000000 00000000`00000000
00000000`00000000 : USER32!_fnDWORD+0x3d
0000003f`0731f1e0 00007ffc`85b21434     : 00007ffc`87fd08cf 00000000`00000000 00007ffc`87fe4b65
00000000`00000000 : ntdll!KiUserCallbackDispatcherContinue
0000003f`0731f268 00007ffc`87fd08cf     : 00000000`00000000 00007ffc`87fe4b65 00000000`00000000
00000000`00000000 : win32u!NtUserMessageCall+0x14
0000003f`0731f270 00007ffc`87fd0737     : 00007ffc`85b2b2d4 00000000`00000000 00000000`000003f9
00000000`0004046e : USER32!SendMessageWorker+0x12f
0000003f`0731f310 00007ffc`73c550bf     : 000001e9`be027260 00000000`00000001 00000000`50010001
00000000`00000001 : USER32!SendMessageW+0x137
0000003f`0731f370 00007ffc`73c88822     : 00000000`00000202 0000003f`0731f449 00000000`00000000
00000000`00000000 : COMCTL32!Button_ReleaseCapture+0xbb
0000003f`0731f3a0 00007ffc`87fd1c4c     : 00000000`00000000 00000000`80000000 00000000`00000001
00000000`00000000 : COMCTL32!Button_WndProc+0x802
0000003f`0731f4b0 00007ffc`87fd0ea6     : 00000000`00000000 00007ffc`73c88020 00000000`0004046e
00007ffc`00000202 : USER32!UserCallWinProcCheckWow+0x33c
```

```
0000003f`0731f620 00007ffc`87fd6084     : 00007ffc`73c88020 00000000`00000000 000001e9`be6d3570
00000000`0004046e : USER32!DispatchMessageWorker+0x2a6
0000003f`0731f6a0 00007ffc`73c35f9f     : 000001e9`bdfe6080 0000003f`0731f7a9 00000000`00000100
00000000`00020450 : USER32!IsDialogMessageW+0x104
0000003f`0731f700 00007ffc`73c35e48     : 000001e9`bdfd09e0 0000003f`0731f7a9 00000000`00000000
1002ccdb`00000001 : COMCTL32!Prop_IsDialogMessage+0x4b
0000003f`0731f740 00007ffc`73c35abd     : 0000003f`0731f860 0000003f`0731f860 00000000`83360018
000001e9`bdfe6080 : COMCTL32!_RealPropertySheet+0x2c0
0000003f`0731f810 00007ffc`73d00953     : 000001e9`bdfe6080 0000003f`0731f940 00007ffc`87f9d130
00000000`00000000 : COMCTL32!_PropertySheet+0x49
0000003f`0731f840 00007ff7`be364cd0     : 0000003f`0731f9e0 00000000`83360018 00000000`00000000
0000003f`0731f9e0 : COMCTL32!PropertySheetA+0x53
0000003f`0731f8e0 00007ff7`be365292     : 00000000`00000001 00000000`00000001 00000000`00000000
00000000`00000000 : notmyfault64+0x4cd0
0000003f`0731fbb0 00007ffc`876b54e0     : 00000000`00000000 00000000`00000000 00000000`00000000
00000000`00000000 : notmyfault64+0x5292
0000003f`0731fbf0 00007ffc`884a485b     : 00000000`00000000 00000000`00000000 00000000`00000000
00000000`00000000 : KERNEL32!BaseThreadInitThunk+0x10
0000003f`0731fc20 00000000`00000000     : 00000000`00000000 00000000`00000000 00000000`00000000
00000000`00000000 : ntdll!RtlUserThreadStart+0x2b


SYMBOL_NAME:  myfault+1981

MODULE_NAME: myfault

IMAGE_NAME:  myfault.sys

STACK_COMMAND:  .cxr; .ecxr ; kb

BUCKET_ID_FUNC_OFFSET:  1981

FAILURE_BUCKET_ID:  AV_myfault!unknown_function

OS_VERSION:  10.0.22000.1

BUILDLAB_STR:  co_release

OSPLATFORM_TYPE:  x64

OSNAME:  Windows 10

FAILURE_ID_HASH:  {9745090a-9bce-ccba-c096-ca6e9ca04c64}

Followup:     MachineOwner
---------

0: kd> Command Completed

Thinking...

The error `DRIVER_IRQL_NOT_LESS_OR_EQUAL` typically indicates a driver attempted to access
pageable memory at a process IRQL that was too high. It seems like the driver `myfault.sys` is
causing the issue.

To get more information about this driver, you can use the `lmv` command.

<exec>lmv m myfault</exec>
```

```
Do you want to execute command: lmv m myfault? Y or N: Y


0: kd> Browse full module list
start             end                 module name
fffff806`60570000 fffff806`60578000   myfault    (no symbols)
    Loaded symbol image file: myfault.sys
    Image path: \??\C:\WINDOWS\system32\drivers\myfault.sys
    Image name: myfault.sys
    Browse all global symbols  functions  data
    Timestamp:        Wed Jun 12 19:36:53 2019 (5D014645)
    CheckSum:         0000953A
    ImageSize:        00008000
    Translations:     0000.04b0 0000.04e4 0409.04b0 0409.04e4
    Information from resource tables:
0: kd> Command Completed

Thinking...

The `myfault.sys` driver seems to be causing the issue. This driver is often used for testing
and intentionally causing crashes. If you're not currently testing, it's possible that this
driver was left over from previous testing or it's being used by a malicious program.

You might want to consider removing or disabling this driver. If you're not sure how to do
this, you might want to consult with a system administrator or another expert.

No command suggested.

Chat> What commands do you suggest to explore this complete memory dump?

Thinking...

To further explore the memory dump, you can use the `!process` command to display information
about the current process.


<exec>!process 0 0</exec>

Do you want to execute command: !process 0 0? Y or N: N
```

5. We switch to the command mode:

```
Chat> !command
Command mode, user inputs are sent to debugger and debugger outputs will be sent to OpenAI
ChatGPT model, ChatGPT can reply with simple explanations or suggest a single command to
execute to further analyze the problem.

Command> !analyze -v
0: kd> *******************************************************************************
*                                                                             *
*                        Bugcheck Analysis                                    *
*                                                                             *
*******************************************************************************

DRIVER_IRQL_NOT_LESS_OR_EQUAL (d1)
An attempt was made to access a pageable (or completely invalid) address at an
interrupt request level (IRQL) that is too high.  This is usually
caused by drivers using improper addresses.
If kernel debugger is available get stack backtrace.
```

```
Arguments:
Arg1: ffffac8a0d8ea010, memory referenced
Arg2: 0000000000000002, IRQL
Arg3: 0000000000000000, value 0 = read operation, 1 = write operation
Arg4: fffff80660571981, address which referenced memory

Debugging Details:
------------------

Unable to load image \??\C:\WINDOWS\system32\drivers\myfault.sys, Win32 error 0n2

KEY_VALUES_STRING: 1

    Key  : Analysis.CPU.mSec
    Value: 2734

    Key  : Analysis.DebugAnalysisManager
    Value: Create

    Key  : Analysis.Elapsed.mSec
    Value: 6532

    Key  : Analysis.Init.CPU.mSec
    Value: 421

    Key  : Analysis.Init.Elapsed.mSec
    Value: 68852

    Key  : Analysis.Memory.CommitPeak.Mb
    Value: 135

    Key  : WER.OS.Branch
    Value: co_release

    Key  : WER.OS.Timestamp
    Value: 2021-06-04T16:28:00Z

    Key  : WER.OS.Version
    Value: 10.0.22000.1


FILE_IN_CAB:  memory-w11.dmp

VIRTUAL_MACHINE:  VMware

BUGCHECK_CODE:  d1

BUGCHECK_P1: ffffac8a0d8ea010

BUGCHECK_P2: 2

BUGCHECK_P3: 0

BUGCHECK_P4: fffff80660571981

READ_ADDRESS: unable to get nt!PspSessionIdBitmap
 ffffac8a0d8ea010 Paged pool

BLACKBOXBSD: 1 (!blackboxbsd)
```

```
BLACKBOXNTFS: 1 (!blackboxntfs)


BLACKBOXWINLOGON: 1

PROCESS_NAME:  notmyfault64.exe

TRAP_FRAME:  ffffbe8296f647b0 -- (.trap 0xffffbe8296f647b0)
NOTE: The trap frame does not contain all registers.
Some register values may be zeroed or incorrect.
rax=0000000000001000 rbx=0000000000000000 rcx=ffffac8a0d8e7000
rdx=ffffac8a0d480000 rsi=0000000000000000 rdi=0000000000000000
rip=fffff80660571981 rsp=ffffbe8296f64940 rbp=ffffbe8296f64bb1
 r8=ffffac8a0d480000  r9=ffffc38c2c402000 r10=fffff80662a5f540
r11=ffffac8a0d8e7000 r12=0000000000000000 r13=0000000000000000
r14=0000000000000000 r15=0000000000000000
iopl=0         nv up ei ng nz na pe nc
myfault+0x1981:
fffff806`60571981 8b03            mov     eax,dword ptr [rbx] ds:00000000`00000000=????????
Resetting default scope

STACK_TEXT:
ffffbe82`96f64668 fffff806`622281a9     : 00000000`0000000a ffffac8a`0d8ea010 00000000`00000002
00000000`00000000 : nt!KeBugCheckEx
ffffbe82`96f64670 fffff806`62224300     : 00000000`00000000 ffffbd11`c0e0c2b8 ffff2703`d5aecdf2
ffffbd11`c253e710 : nt!KiBugCheckDispatch+0x69
ffffbe82`96f647b0 fffff806`60571981     : ffffbe82`96f64d10 fffff806`6d8cee70 00000000`00000000
ffffc38c`306d4f70 : nt!KiPageFault+0x440
ffffbe82`96f64940 fffff806`60571d3d     : 00000000`00001000 00000000`00000000 ffffc38c`33ac3080
ffffbd11`c0e0c010 : myfault+0x1981
ffffbe82`96f64970 fffff806`60571ea1     : ffffc38c`31efb360 fffff806`624a4204 ffffc38c`2c4792d0
00000000`00005fd4 : myfault+0x1d3d
ffffbe82`96f64ab0 fffff806`62102f65     : ffffc38c`31efb360 00000000`00000002 00000000`00000000
00000000`00000000 : myfault+0x1ea1
ffffbe82`96f64b10 fffff806`6256b532     : 00000000`00000001 ffffc38c`31efb360 ffffbe82`96f64bb1
fffff806`62102d23 : nt!IofCallDriver+0x55
ffffbe82`96f64b50 fffff806`6256acbf     : ffffc38c`00000000 ffffbe82`96f64ea0 00000000`83360018
00000000`83360018 : nt!IopSynchronousServiceTail+0x1d2
ffffbe82`96f64c00 fffff806`6256a6c6     : 00000000`00000000 00000000`00000000 00000000`00000000
00000000`00000000 : nt!IopXxxControlFile+0x5df
ffffbe82`96f64d40 fffff806`62227b75     : 00000000`00000000 00000000`00000000 ffff6a98`d8ef3484
00000000`00070000 : nt!NtDeviceIoControlFile+0x56
ffffbe82`96f64db0 00007ffc`88543444     : 00007ffc`85c23edb 00000000`0002043c 0000003f`0731ef49
000001e9`bdfc0000 : nt!KiSystemServiceCopyEnd+0x25
0000003f`0731ec08 00007ffc`85c23edb     : 00000000`0002043c 0000003f`0731ef49 000001e9`bdfc0000
00000000`00000000 : ntdll!NtDeviceIoControlFile+0x14
0000003f`0731ec10 00007ffc`876b5f91     : 00000000`83360018 00000000`00000000 00000000`00000000
00007ffc`880199f9 : KERNELBASE!DeviceIoControl+0x6b
0000003f`0731ec80 00007ff7`be36342f     : 00000000`00020454 0000003f`0731ed69 0000003f`0731ed69
00000000`00000000 : KERNEL32!DeviceIoControlImplementation+0x81
0000003f`0731ecd0 00007ffc`87fd484b     : 00000000`00000001 00000000`00000001 00000000`00000001
00000000`00000002 : notmyfault64+0x342f
0000003f`0731edd0 00007ffc`87fd409b     : 00000000`00000000 00007ff7`be3632d0 00000000`00000111
000001e9`be6d6f60 : USER32!UserCallDlgProcCheckWow+0x14b
0000003f`0731eeb0 00007ffc`880197c9     : 00000000`0004046e 00000000`000000f3 00000000`0004046e
00000000`00000000 : USER32!DefDlgProcWorker+0xcb
```

```
0000003f`0731ef70 00007ffc`87fd1c4c     : 00000000`00000001 00000000`00000000 00000000`00000001
00000000`00000000 : USER32!DefDlgProcA+0x39
0000003f`0731efb0 00007ffc`87fd179c     : 00003130`08652f97 00007ffc`885430e0 00000000`00020454
00007ffc`00000111 : USER32!UserCallWinProcCheckWow+0x33c
0000003f`0731f120 00007ffc`87fe4b4d     : 00000000`00000000 00000000`00000000 00000000`000003f9
00000000`000c0000 : USER32!DispatchClientMessage+0x9c
0000003f`0731f180 00007ffc`885472b4     : 00000000`00000000 00000000`00000000 00000000`00000000
00000000`00000000 : USER32!_fnDWORD+0x3d
0000003f`0731f1e0 00007ffc`85b21434     : 00007ffc`87fd08cf 00000000`00000000 00007ffc`87fe4b65
00000000`00000000 : ntdll!KiUserCallbackDispatcherContinue
0000003f`0731f268 00007ffc`87fd08cf     : 00000000`00000000 00007ffc`87fe4b65 00000000`00000000
00000000`00000000 : win32u!NtUserMessageCall+0x14
0000003f`0731f270 00007ffc`87fd0737     : 00007ffc`85b2b2d4 00000000`00000000 00000000`000003f9
00000000`0004046e : USER32!SendMessageWorker+0x12f
0000003f`0731f310 00007ffc`73c550bf     : 000001e9`be027260 00000000`00000001 00000000`50010001
00000000`00000001 : USER32!SendMessageW+0x137
0000003f`0731f370 00007ffc`73c88822     : 00000000`00000202 0000003f`0731f449 00000000`00000000
00000000`00000000 : COMCTL32!Button_ReleaseCapture+0xbb
0000003f`0731f3a0 00007ffc`87fd1c4c     : 00000000`00000000 00000000`80000000 00000000`00000001
00000000`00000000 : COMCTL32!Button_WndProc+0x802
0000003f`0731f4b0 00007ffc`87fd0ea6     : 00000000`00000000 00007ffc`73c88020 00000000`0004046e
00007ffc`00000202 : USER32!UserCallWinProcCheckWow+0x33c
0000003f`0731f620 00007ffc`87fd6084     : 00007ffc`73c88020 00000000`00000000 000001e9`be6d3570
00000000`0004046e : USER32!DispatchMessageWorker+0x2a6
0000003f`0731f6a0 00007ffc`73c35f9f     : 000001e9`bdfe6080 0000003f`0731f7a9 00000000`00000100
00000000`00020450 : USER32!IsDialogMessageW+0x104
0000003f`0731f700 00007ffc`73c35e48     : 000001e9`bdfd09e0 0000003f`0731f7a9 00000000`00000000
1002ccdb`00000001 : COMCTL32!Prop_IsDialogMessage+0x4b
0000003f`0731f740 00007ffc`73c35abd     : 0000003f`0731f860 0000003f`0731f860 00000000`83360018
000001e9`bdfe6080 : COMCTL32!_RealPropertySheet+0x2c0
0000003f`0731f810 00007ffc`73d00953     : 000001e9`bdfe6080 0000003f`0731f940 00007ffc`87f9d130
00000000`00000000 : COMCTL32!_PropertySheet+0x49
0000003f`0731f840 00007ff7`be364cd0     : 0000003f`0731f9e0 00000000`83360018 00000000`00000000
0000003f`0731f9e0 : COMCTL32!PropertySheetA+0x53
0000003f`0731f8e0 00007ff7`be365292     : 00000000`00000001 00000000`00000001 00000000`00000000
00000000`00000000 : notmyfault64+0x4cd0
0000003f`0731fbb0 00007ffc`876b54e0     : 00000000`00000000 00000000`00000000 00000000`00000000
00000000`00000000 : notmyfault64+0x5292
0000003f`0731fbf0 00007ffc`884a485b     : 00000000`00000000 00000000`00000000 00000000`00000000
00000000`00000000 : KERNEL32!BaseThreadInitThunk+0x10
0000003f`0731fc20 00000000`00000000     : 00000000`00000000 00000000`00000000 00000000`00000000
00000000`00000000 : ntdll!RtlUserThreadStart+0x2b


SYMBOL_NAME:  myfault+1981

MODULE_NAME: myfault

IMAGE_NAME:  myfault.sys

STACK_COMMAND:  .cxr; .ecxr ; kb

BUCKET_ID_FUNC_OFFSET:  1981

FAILURE_BUCKET_ID:  AV_myfault!unknown_function

OS_VERSION:  10.0.22000.1

BUILDLAB_STR:  co_release
```

```
OSPLATFORM_TYPE:  x64

OSNAME:  Windows 10

FAILURE_ID_HASH:  {9745090a-9bce-ccba-c096-ca6e9ca04c64}

Followup:     MachineOwner
---------

0: kd> Command Completed

Thinking...

The output indicates that a DRIVER_IRQL_NOT_LESS_OR_EQUAL error occurred, which is typically
caused by a driver attempting to access pageable memory at a process IRQL that was too high.

The driver in question is `myfault.sys` and the process name is `notmyfault64.exe`. This
suggests that the crash was intentionally caused for debugging or demonstration purposes, as
these names are associated with a tool used to intentionally crash a system for such reasons.

The error occurred when trying to read the memory address `ffffac8a0d8ea010` at IRQL 2. The
faulting instruction is at `fffff80660571981` in `myfault.sys`.

The stack trace shows the sequence of function calls leading up to the crash, starting with
`nt!KeBugCheckEx`, which is the function that Windows uses to stop the system and display the
bug check (also known as a "blue screen" error).

The `FAILURE_BUCKET_ID` is `AV_myfault!unknown_function`, which indicates that the crash
occurred in the `myfault.sys` driver, but the specific function within the driver where the
crash occurred could not be determined.

To further investigate, you might want to look at the source code

Command> !thread
0: kd> THREAD ffffc38c33ac3080  Cid 09d4.2038  Teb: 0000003f07458000 Win32Thread:
ffffc38c34d480b0 RUNNING on processor 0
IRP List:
    ffffc38c31efb360: (0006,0118) Flags: 00060000  Mdl: 00000000
Not impersonating
DeviceMap                 ffffac8a09519830
Owning Process            ffffc38c2e16b080       Image:         notmyfault64.exe
Attached Process          N/A            Image:         N/A
Wait Start TickCount      11956          Ticks: 0
Context Switch Count      1135           IdealProcessor: 1
UserTime                  00:00:00.015
KernelTime                00:00:00.093
Win32 Start Address notmyfault64 (0x00007ff7be365384)
Stack Init ffffbe8296f64fb0 Current ffffbe82968923a0
Base ffffbe8296f65000 Limit ffffbe8296f5f000 Call 0000000000000000
Priority 12  BasePriority 8  Foreground Boost 2  IoPriority 2  PagePriority 5
Part of process with FOREGROUND Priority
Child-SP          RetAddr               : Args to Child
: Call Site
ffffbe82`96f64668 fffff806`622281a9     : 00000000`0000000a ffffac8a`0d8ea010 00000000`00000002
00000000`00000000 : nt!KeBugCheckEx
ffffbe82`96f64670 fffff806`62224300     : 00000000`00000000 ffffbd11`c0e0c2b8 ffff2703`d5aecdf2
ffffbd11`c253e710 : nt!KiBugCheckDispatch+0x69
```

```
ffffbe82`96f647b0 fffff806`60571981     : ffffbe82`96f64d10 fffff806`6d8cee70 00000000`00000000
ffffc38c`306d4f70 : nt!KiPageFault+0x440 (TrapFrame @ ffffbe82`96f647b0)
ffffbe82`96f64940 fffff806`60571d3d     : 00000000`00001000 00000000`00000000 ffffc38c`33ac3080
ffffbd11`c0e0c010 : myfault+0x1981
ffffbe82`96f64970 fffff806`60571ea1     : ffffc38c`31efb360 fffff806`624a4204 ffffc38c`2c4792d0
00000000`00005fd4 : myfault+0x1d3d
ffffbe82`96f64ab0 fffff806`62102f65     : ffffc38c`31efb360 00000000`00000002 00000000`00000000
00000000`00000000 : myfault+0x1ea1
ffffbe82`96f64b10 fffff806`6256b532     : 00000000`00000001 ffffc38c`31efb360 ffffbe82`96f64bb1
fffff806`62102d23 : nt!IofCallDriver+0x55
ffffbe82`96f64b50 fffff806`6256acbf     : ffffc38c`00000000 ffffbe82`96f64ea0 00000000`83360018
00000000`83360018 : nt!IopSynchronousServiceTail+0x1d2
ffffbe82`96f64c00 fffff806`6256a6c6     : 00000000`00000000 00000000`00000000 00000000`00000000
00000000`00000000 : nt!IopXxxControlFile+0x5df
ffffbe82`96f64d40 fffff806`62227b75     : 00000000`00000000 00000000`00000000 ffff6a98`d8ef3484
00000000`00070000 : nt!NtDeviceIoControlFile+0x56
ffffbe82`96f64db0 00007ffc`88543444     : 00007ffc`85c23edb 00000000`0002043c 0000003f`0731ef49
000001e9`bdfc0000 : nt!KiSystemServiceCopyEnd+0x25 (TrapFrame @ ffffbe82`96f64e20)
0000003f`0731ec08 00007ffc`85c23edb     : 00000000`0002043c 0000003f`0731ef49 000001e9`bdfc0000
00000000`00000000 : ntdll!NtDeviceIoControlFile+0x14
0000003f`0731ec10 00007ffc`876b5f91     : 00000000`83360018 00000000`00000000 00000000`00000000
00007ffc`880199f9 : KERNELBASE!DeviceIoControl+0x6b
0000003f`0731ec80 00007ff7`be36342f     : 00000000`00020454 0000003f`0731ed69 0000003f`0731ed69
00000000`00000000 : KERNEL32!DeviceIoControlImplementation+0x81
0000003f`0731ecd0 00007ffc`87fd484b     : 00000000`00000001 00000000`00000001 00000000`00000001
00000000`00000002 : notmyfault64+0x342f
0000003f`0731edd0 00007ffc`87fd409b     : 00000000`00000000 00007ff7`be3632d0 00000000`00000111
000001e9`be6d6f60 : USER32!UserCallDlgProcCheckWow+0x14b
0000003f`0731eeb0 00007ffc`880197c9     : 00000000`0004046e 00000000`000000f3 00000000`0004046e
00000000`00000000 : USER32!DefDlgProcWorker+0xcb
0000003f`0731ef70 00007ffc`87fd1c4c     : 00000000`00000001 00000000`00000000 00000000`00000001
00000000`00000000 : USER32!DefDlgProcA+0x39
0000003f`0731efb0 00007ffc`87fd179c     : 00003130`08652f97 00007ffc`885430e0 00000000`00020454
00007ffc`00000111 : USER32!UserCallWinProcCheckWow+0x33c
0000003f`0731f120 00007ffc`87fe4b4d     : 00000000`00000000 00000000`00000000 00000000`000003f9
00000000`000c0000 : USER32!DispatchClientMessage+0x9c
0000003f`0731f180 00007ffc`885472b4     : 00000000`00000000 00000000`00000000 00000000`00000000
00000000`00000000 : USER32!_fnDWORD+0x3d
0000003f`0731f1e0 00007ffc`85b21434     : 00007ffc`87fd08cf 00000000`00000000 00007ffc`87fe4b65
00000000`00000000 : ntdll!KiUserCallbackDispatcherContinue (TrapFrame @ 0000003f`0731f0a8)
0000003f`0731f268 00007ffc`87fd08cf     : 00000000`00000000 00007ffc`87fe4b65 00000000`00000000
00000000`00000000 : win32u!NtUserMessageCall+0x14
0000003f`0731f270 00007ffc`87fd0737     : 00007ffc`85b2b2d4 00000000`00000000 00000000`000003f9
00000000`0004046e : USER32!SendMessageWorker+0x12f
0000003f`0731f310 00007ffc`73c550bf     : 000001e9`be027260 00000000`00000001 00000000`50010001
00000000`00000001 : USER32!SendMessageW+0x137
0000003f`0731f370 00007ffc`73c88822     : 00000000`00000202 0000003f`0731f449 00000000`00000000
00000000`00000000 : COMCTL32!Button_ReleaseCapture+0xbb
0000003f`0731f3a0 00007ffc`87fd1c4c     : 00000000`00000000 00000000`80000000 00000000`00000001
00000000`00000000 : COMCTL32!Button_WndProc+0x802
0000003f`0731f4b0 00007ffc`87fd0ea6     : 00000000`00000000 00007ffc`73c88020 00000000`0004046e
00007ffc`00000202 : USER32!UserCallWinProcCheckWow+0x33c
0000003f`0731f620 00007ffc`87fd6084     : 00007ffc`73c88020 00000000`00000000 000001e9`be6d3570
00000000`0004046e : USER32!DispatchMessageWorker+0x2a6
0000003f`0731f6a0 00007ffc`73c35f9f     : 000001e9`bdfe6080 0000003f`0731f7a9 00000000`00000100
00000000`00020450 : USER32!IsDialogMessageW+0x104
0000003f`0731f700 00007ffc`73c35e48     : 000001e9`bdfd09e0 0000003f`0731f7a9 00000000`00000000
1002ccdb`00000001 : COMCTL32!Prop_IsDialogMessage+0x4b
```

```
0000003f`0731f740 00007ffc`73c35abd     : 0000003f`0731f860 0000003f`0731f860 00000000`83360018
000001e9`bdfe6080 : COMCTL32!_RealPropertySheet+0x2c0
0000003f`0731f810 00007ffc`73d00953     : 000001e9`bdfe6080 0000003f`0731f940 00007ffc`87f9d130
00000000`00000000 : COMCTL32!_PropertySheet+0x49
0000003f`0731f840 00007ff7`be364cd0     : 0000003f`0731f9e0 00000000`83360018 00000000`00000000
0000003f`0731f9e0 : COMCTL32!PropertySheetA+0x53
0000003f`0731f8e0 00007ff7`be365292     : 00000000`00000001 00000000`00000001 00000000`00000000
00000000`00000000 : notmyfault64+0x4cd0
0000003f`0731fbb0 00007ffc`876b54e0     : 00000000`00000000 00000000`00000000 00000000`00000000
00000000`00000000 : notmyfault64+0x5292
0000003f`0731fbf0 00007ffc`884a485b     : 00000000`00000000 00000000`00000000 00000000`00000000
00000000`00000000 : KERNEL32!BaseThreadInitThunk+0x10
0000003f`0731fc20 00000000`00000000     : 00000000`00000000 00000000`00000000 00000000`00000000
00000000`00000000 : ntdll!RtlUserThreadStart+0x2b

0: kd> Command Completed

Thinking...

The output shows the thread stack of the process `notmyfault64.exe` which caused the crash. The
stack trace shows the sequence of function calls leading up to the crash, starting with
`nt!KeBugCheckEx`, which is the function that Windows uses to stop the system and display the
bug check (also known as a "blue screen" error).

The `myfault.sys` driver is involved in the crash, as indicated by the calls to
`myfault+0x1981`, `myfault+0x1d3d`, and `myfault+0x1ea1`. This driver is associated with the
NotMyFault tool, which is used to intentionally cause system crashes for debugging and learning
purposes.

The crash occurred during a Device I/O Control operation, as indicated by the call to
`nt!NtDeviceIoControlFile`.

To further investigate, you might want to look at the source code of the `myfault.sys` driver,
if it's available. You could also analyze the memory dump file (`memory-w11.dmp`) that was
likely created when the crash occurred.

Command> !quit
Goodbye, have a nice day!
>>> exit()

C:\EWMDA-Dumps>
```

Exercise ES10

- **Goal:** Explore ChatDBG WinDbg extension
- **Memory Analysis Patterns:** Frame Trace
- \EWMDA\Exercise-ES10.pdf

ChatDBG

https://github.com/plasma-umass/ChatDBG

Exercise ES10: Explore ChatDBG WinDbg Extension

Goal: Explore ChatDBG[20] WinDbg extension.

Memory Analysis Patterns: Frame Trace.

1. We use Python 3.11 for this exercise. WinDbg Classic is also required if you want to build the extension from the source.

2. Install ChatDBG python module:

```
C:\EWMDA-Dumps>pip install chatdbg
Collecting chatgpt
  Downloading chatgpt-2.2212.0-py3-none-any.whl.metadata (804 bytes)
Collecting tls-client (from chatgpt)
  Downloading tls_client-1.0.1-py3-none-any.whl.metadata (5.0 kB)
Collecting rich (from chatgpt)
  Downloading rich-13.8.1-py3-none-any.whl.metadata (18 kB)
Collecting markdown-it-py>=2.2.0 (from rich->chatgpt)
  Downloading markdown_it_py-3.0.0-py3-none-any.whl.metadata (6.9 kB)
Collecting pygments<3.0.0,>=2.13.0 (from rich->chatgpt)
  Downloading pygments-2.18.0-py3-none-any.whl.metadata (2.5 kB)
Collecting mdurl~=0.1 (from markdown-it-py>=2.2.0->rich->chatgpt)
  Downloading mdurl-0.1.2-py3-none-any.whl.metadata (1.6 kB)
Downloading chatgpt-2.2212.0-py3-none-any.whl (24 kB)
Downloading rich-13.8.1-py3-none-any.whl (241 kB)
   ---------------------------------------- 241.6/241.6 kB 2.5 MB/s eta 0:00:00
Downloading tls_client-1.0.1-py3-none-any.whl (41.3 MB)
   ---------------------------------------- 41.3/41.3 MB 16.0 MB/s eta 0:00:00
Downloading markdown_it_py-3.0.0-py3-none-any.whl (87 kB)
   ---------------------------------------- 87.5/87.5 kB 1.2 MB/s eta 0:00:00
Downloading pygments-2.18.0-py3-none-any.whl (1.2 MB)
   ---------------------------------------- 1.2/1.2 MB 38.6 MB/s eta 0:00:00
Downloading mdurl-0.1.2-py3-none-any.whl (10.0 kB)
Installing collected packages: tls-client, pygments, mdurl, markdown-it-py, rich, chatgpt
Successfully installed chatgpt-2.2212.0 markdown-it-py-3.0.0 mdurl-0.1.2 pygments-2.18.0 rich-
13.8.1 tls-client-1.0.1
```

3. Set the OPENAI_API_KEY environment variable with your Project API secret key value. If you are new to OpenAI API check this page[21].

4. Launch WinDbg.

5. Open \EWMDA-Dumps\Process\x64\AppD1A.DMP.

[20] https://github.com/plasma-umass/ChatDBG

[21] https://platform.openai.com/settings/organization/billing/overview

6. We get the dump file loaded:

```
Loading Dump File [C:\EWMDA-Dumps\Process\x64\AppD1A.DMP]
User Mini Dump File with Full Memory: Only application data is available


************* Path validation summary **************
Response                         Time (ms)     Location
Deferred                                       srv*
Symbol search path is: srv*
Executable search path is:
Windows 10 Version 22631 MP (8 procs) Free x64
Product: WinNt, suite: SingleUserTS
Edition build lab: 22621.1.amd64fre.ni_release.220506-1250
Debug session time: Sun Sep 29 12:03:57.000 2024 (UTC + 1:00)
System Uptime: 3 days 0:04:15.925
Process Uptime: 0 days 0:00:32.000
.............................
For analysis of this file, run !analyze -v
win32u!NtUserWaitMessage+0x14:
00007ffa`9f3415f4 ret
```

7. We open a log file:

```
0:000> .logopen C:\EWMDA-Dumps\Process\x64\ES10.log
Opened log file 'C:\EWMDA-Dumps\Process\x64\ES10.log'
```

8. We cloned the repo at the time of this writing[22], built, and included the extension DLL in the dump archive. We can load it now:

```
0:000> .load C:\EWMDA-Dumps\ChatDBG\chatdbg
```

9. There is no help, and the only command is **!why**:

```
0:000> !why
ChatDBG needs debug information to work properly. Recompile your code with the /Zi flag.
```

Note: The command required debugging symbols for frames in the current stack trace.

```
0:000> .sympath+ C:\EWMDA-Dumps\Process\x64\
Symbol search path is: srv*;C:\EWMDA-Dumps\Process\x64\
Expanded Symbol search path is:
cache*;SRV*https://msdl.microsoft.com/download/symbols;c:\ewmda-dumps\process\x64\

************* Path validation summary **************
Response                         Time (ms)     Location
Deferred                                       srv*
OK                                             C:\EWMDA-Dumps\Process\x64\

0:000> !why
Without any error message or traceback, it's really hard to point out the exact
problem in your code.

However, there are two potential points of failure in frame 1's function -
```

[22] https://github.com/plasma-umass/ChatDBG

```
`wWinMain()` at `C:\AWD4\AppD1A\AppD1A\AppD1A.cpp:44`.

1. `wchar_t* lpCmdLine = 0x0000024c`02d7810c ""`: Check if you're performing any
operation on `lpCmdLine`. As per the provided code, it seems to point to an
empty string. Any access beyond its memory space could cause error.

2. `HACCEL__* hAccelTable = 0x00000000`00000001 struct HACCEL__ *`: The
`hAccelTable` is assigned with what seems to be an address which might not be
valid. Make sure `hAccelTable` is properly initialized and the address it stores
is valid. Any access to an invalid memory address either for reading or writing
could likely cause a crash.

In frame 2, the function `__scrt_common_main_seh()` at
`D:\a\_work\1\s\src\vctools\crt\vcstartup\src\startup\exe_common.inl:288` is
part of the Visual Studio C++ runtime which handles startup and shutdown of the
program.

If the error is occurring here, the issue possibly lies in the setup or teardown
of your application, like improper initialization of global/static objects, not
closing a file, etc.

Again, without a specific error message or traceback, it is hard to diagnose the
exact issue.

As a fix, I would suggest to carefully review the initialization and termination
of your data, ensuring that memory pointers are valid before access and that
you're not causing a buffer overflow with your strings. Remember to always
handle exceptions and manage your memory carefully to prevent crashes and leaks.
```

```
0:000> k
 # Child-SP          RetAddr               Call Site
00 000000e8`fd59f498 00007ffa`9fc2170e     win32u!NtUserWaitMessage+0x14
01 000000e8`fd59f4a0 00007ffa`9fc2157c     user32!DialogBox2+0x172
02 000000e8`fd59f550 00007ffa`9fc9b266     user32!InternalDialogBox+0x178
03 000000e8`fd59f5b0 00007ffa`9fc99bc9     user32!SoftModalMessageBox+0x826
04 000000e8`fd59f6f0 00007ffa`9fc9a9a8     user32!MessageBoxWorker+0x341
05 000000e8`fd59f8a0 00007ffa`9fc9aa2e     user32!MessageBoxTimeoutW+0x198
06 000000e8`fd59f9a0 00007ff6`a1cb107f     user32!MessageBoxW+0x4e
07 000000e8`fd59f9e0 00007ff6`a1cb168a     AppD1A!wWinMain+0x7f
[C:\AWD4\AppD1A\AppD1A\AppD1A.cpp @ 44]
08 (Inline Function) --------`--------     AppD1A!invoke_main+0x21
[D:\a\_work\1\s\src\vctools\crt\vcstartup\src\startup\exe_common.inl @ 118]
09 000000e8`fd59fa40 00007ffa`a18e257d     AppD1A!__scrt_common_main_seh+0x106
[D:\a\_work\1\s\src\vctools\crt\vcstartup\src\startup\exe_common.inl @ 288]
0a 000000e8`fd59fa80 00007ffa`a1aeaf28     kernel32!BaseThreadInitThunk+0x1d
0b 000000e8`fd59fab0 00000000`00000000     ntdll!RtlUserThreadStart+0x28

0:000> kP
 # Child-SP          RetAddr               Call Site
00 000000e8`fd59f498 00007ffa`9fc2170e     win32u!NtUserWaitMessage+0x14
01 000000e8`fd59f4a0 00007ffa`9fc2157c     user32!DialogBox2+0x172
02 000000e8`fd59f550 00007ffa`9fc9b266     user32!InternalDialogBox+0x178
03 000000e8`fd59f5b0 00007ffa`9fc99bc9     user32!SoftModalMessageBox+0x826
04 000000e8`fd59f6f0 00007ffa`9fc9a9a8     user32!MessageBoxWorker+0x341
05 000000e8`fd59f8a0 00007ffa`9fc9aa2e     user32!MessageBoxTimeoutW+0x198
06 000000e8`fd59f9a0 00007ff6`a1cb107f     user32!MessageBoxW+0x4e
07 000000e8`fd59f9e0 00007ff6`a1cb168a     AppD1A!wWinMain(
                    struct HINSTANCE__ * hInstance = 0x00007ff6`a1cb0000,
                    struct HINSTANCE__ * hPrevInstance = 0x00000000`00000000,
```

```
                  wchar_t * lpCmdLine = 0x0000024c`02d7810c "",
                  int nCmdShow = 0n1)+0x7f [C:\AWD4\AppD1A\AppD1A\AppD1A.cpp @ 44]
08 (Inline Function) --------`--------     AppD1A!invoke_main(void)+0x21
[D:\a\_work\1\s\src\vctools\crt\vcstartup\src\startup\exe_common.inl @ 118]
09 000000e8`fd59fa40 00007ffa`a18e257d     AppD1A!__scrt_common_main_seh(void)+0x106
[D:\a\_work\1\s\src\vctools\crt\vcstartup\src\startup\exe_common.inl @ 288]
0a 000000e8`fd59fa80 00007ffa`a1aeaf28     kernel32!BaseThreadInitThunk+0x1d
0b 000000e8`fd59fab0 00000000`00000000     ntdll!RtlUserThreadStart+0x28

0:000> .srcpath C:\EWMDA-Dumps\Process\x64\
Source search path is: C:\EWMDA-Dumps\Process\x64\

************* Path validation summary **************
Response                         Time (ms)     Location
OK                                             C:\EWMDA-Dumps\Process\x64\

0:000> !why
The root cause of the error is not clearly indicated in the information
provided. Without an actual error message or traceback, it's not possible to
provide a specific, accurate answer.

However, looking at the content available we can suggest that there is an issue
with the wWinMain function at line 44 in the AppD1A.cpp file (from frame 1).
There could possibly be a misuse or wrong assignment of the HINSTANCE__ pointers
(hInstance and hPrevInstance), or the wchar_t pointer (lpCmdLine), or the
HACCEL__ pointer (hAccelTable), or the tagMSG structure (msg).

For a precise fix, we need additional information such as the nature of the
error, the execution context, meaning of the local variables, the application's
goal, and the source code surrounding line 44 of AppD1A.cpp. The breakpoint hit
message could mean that the program execution has reached a predefined pause
point for debugging, or it could refer to an exception thrown by the code.

Please provide additional details for more accurate help.

0:000> !why
The error is originating from the source file `C:\AWD4\AppD1A\AppD1A\AppD1A.cpp`
within the function `wWinMain()`. This happens at line 44, where the program is
likely trying to interact with an Accelerator table, with an invalid handle
pointing to it.

The variable `HACCEL__* hAccelTable` is given a value of `0x00000000`00000001,
which is most likely incorrect as this memory address doesn't seem to be valid
and could be pointing to a random or undefined location in memory. It's not the
null pointer either, which adds to the confusion.

The fix would be to ensure that `hAccelTable` is assigned an instance of a valid
Accelerator table. If you are trying to reference a null pointer, ensure that
`hAccelTable` is assigned NULL (0x0) directly. However, if this `HACCEL`
variable should be a valid instance of an Accelerator table, you would need to
ensure it is correctly initialized before being accessed at the line 44 in
`AppD1A.cpp`. Little can be said without seeing more context of the code, but
the error appears to be due to this uninitialized or incorrectly assigned
pointer to `HACCEL__* hAccelTable`.

0:000> .frame 7
07 000000e8`fd59f9e0 00007ff6`a1cb168a     AppD1A!wWinMain+0x7f
[C:\AWD4\AppD1A\AppD1A\AppD1A.cpp @ 44]
```

```
0:000> !why
Based on the provided information, we cannot see any particular line of code
where an error has occurred since no specific error message or offending line of
code is provided. However, we have a breakpoint hit and there is a suggestion
that the issue is occurring somewhere between lines 34 and 44 in AppD1A.cpp file
and lines 278 to 288 in the exe_common.inl file, possibly during the call to the
wWinMain function from the Microsoft's CRT startup code
"__scrt_common_main_seh".

Issues such as improper initialization, null pointer dereference, or memory leak
could very well be the root cause. But without additional information, such as
an explicit error message or a glimpse at the internals of the functions in
these given lines of code, it's impossible to propose an exact root cause or
fix.

Given the structure of the "wWinMain" function it could be related to the
initialization of the main window, the creation of a certain control or the
loading of certain application dependent resources.

A possible approach to help resolve this issue could include:

- Carefully inspecting the code between lines 34 and 44 in AppD1A.cpp file and
lines 278 to 288 in the exe_common.inl file for any suspicious activity, like
accessing uninitialized variables, possible null pointer dereference, or any
operation that might throw an exception.
- Using a debugger to step through the execution of the code while closely
monitoring the state of variables and program flow.
- Looking for updates or patches that may fix any known issues with the relevant
libraries or SDK.
- Consulting the documentation for any guidance on common pitfalls or required
initial configurations which might have been overlooked.

0:000> .frame /c 7
07 000000e8`fd59f9e0 00007ff6`a1cb168a     AppD1A!wWinMain+0x7f
[C:\AWD4\AppD1A\AppD1A\AppD1A.cpp @ 44]
rax=000000000000100a rbx=0000000000000001 rcx=0000024c02eb8e40
rdx=0000024c0344e8e0 rsi=0000000000000000 rdi=0000000000000000
rip=00007ff6a1cb107f rsp=000000e8fd59f9e0 rbp=0000000000000000
 r8=000000e8fd59f498  r9=0000000000000000 r10=0000000000000000
r11=0000000000000246 r12=0000000000000000 r13=0000000000000000
r14=0000000000000000 r15=0000000000000000
iopl=0         nv up ei pl zr na po nc
cs=0033  ss=002b  ds=002b  es=002b  fs=0053  gs=002b             efl=00000246
AppD1A!wWinMain+0x7f:
00007ff6`a1cb107f mov     edx,dword ptr [rsp+78h] ss:000000e8`fd59fa58=00000001

0:000> !why
The error gives no information as to the issue with the code. Errors can occur
when breakpoints are hit during execution. With breakpoints, the application
temporarily stops executing and allows developers to inspect the code at that
exact moment. It isn't necessarily a sign of a fault or bug in the code.

However, if there is indeed an error, we cannot ascertain it by the information
provided. Additional context such as error messages or which values didn't
behave as expected would be crucial in diagnosing the cause.

The source codes given don't suggest an apparent error as neither of the two
local variables in frame 2 in "exe_common.inl" nor the four local variables and
an object in frame 1 in "AppD1A.cpp" have problematic assigns or
```

initializations.

Without more information, suggestions for fixing potential, unseen problems could include:

- Checking the function calls made in the unidentified code areas in "AppD1A.cpp" and "exe_common.inl" since they're not presented in the question.
- Source code debugging, line by line, to see how values change.
- Using debugging tools to inspect variables and memory states at the breakpoint.

Please ensure that the breakpoint does not pause the program at normal behavior or recheck the implementation logic if this pause is unintended.

```
0:000> .cxr
Resetting default scope

0:000> .frame 7
07 000000e8`fd59f9e0 00007ff6`a1cb168a     AppD1A!wWinMain+0x7f
[C:\AWD4\AppD1A\AppD1A\AppD1A.cpp @ 44]

0:000> dv hAccelTable
    hAccelTable = 0x00000000`00000001

0:000> dv /i /V
prv param  000000e8`fd59fa40 @rsp+0x0060            hInstance = 0x00007ff6`a1cb0000
prv param  000000e8`fd59fa48 @rsp+0x0068        hPrevInstance = 0x00000000`00000000
prv param  000000e8`fd59fa50 @rsp+0x0070            lpCmdLine = 0x0000024c`02d7810c ""
prv param  000000e8`fd59fa58 @rsp+0x0078             nCmdShow = 0n1
prv local  000000e8`fd59fa08 @rsp+0x0028                  msg = {msg=0x0 wp=0x1000100000000
lp=0x0}
prv local  000000e8`fd59fa00 @rsp+0x0020          hAccelTable = 0x00000000`00000001

0:000> !why
```

The error originates from the source code in C:\AWD4\AppD1A\AppD1A\AppD1A.cpp at line 44. This is the location within the wWinMain function where the error occurs. From the description provided for each stack frame, we can see that this error is happening because the function wWinMain is attempting to access an invalid acceleration table. This is indicated by 'HACCEL__* hAccelTable = 0x00000000`00000001 struct HACCEL__ *'. This value suggests that the variable hAccelTable might have been incorrectly initialized or that the memory to which it is pointing was somehow modified or deleted.

As for a possible solution, the programmer should ensure the acceleration table that is being pointed to by hAccelTable is properly initialized and loaded before being used. This might mean checking if the file or resource from which the acceleration table is being loaded is valid.

Furthermore, they need to also confirm that the memory the hAccelTable is pointing to hasn't been unintentionally altered or deallocated prematurely at some point elsewhere in the program.

The second stack frame in D:\a_work\1\s\src\vctools\crt\vcstartup\src\startup\exe_common.inl would not be the cause of the error since this is the common MSVCRT startup code, which usually does not contain user-created runtime errors.

Please note that a deeper investigation with the complete source code and possibly a debugger might be required to fully understand and resolve the issue.

Note: Analyzing the output and source code, we see that the extension failed to notice that the error message was shown after executing *MyRegisterClass* and the value of not yet initialized *hAccelTable* is irrelevant:

```
int APIENTRY _tWinMain(_In_ HINSTANCE hInstance,
                     _In_opt_ HINSTANCE hPrevInstance,
                     _In_ LPTSTR    lpCmdLine,
                     _In_ int       nCmdShow)
{
      UNREFERENCED_PARAMETER(hPrevInstance);
      UNREFERENCED_PARAMETER(lpCmdLine);

      // TODO: Place code here.
      MSG msg;
      HACCEL hAccelTable;

      // Initialize global strings
      LoadString(hInstance, IDS_APP_TITLE, szTitle, MAX_LOADSTRING);
      LoadString(hInstance, IDC_APPD1A, szWindowClass, MAX_LOADSTRING);
      if (!MyRegisterClass(hInstance))
      {
            MessageBox(NULL, L"Cannot initialize the program", L"Error", MB_ICONERROR | MB_OK
| MB_SETFOREGROUND);
      }

      // Perform application initialization:
>>>   if (!InitInstance (hInstance, nCmdShow))
      {
            return FALSE;
      }

      hAccelTable = LoadAccelerators(hInstance, MAKEINTRESOURCE(IDC_APPD1A));

      // Main message loop:
      while (GetMessage(&msg, NULL, 0, 0))
      {
            if (!TranslateAccelerator(msg.hwnd, hAccelTable, &msg))
            {
                  TranslateMessage(&msg);
                  DispatchMessage(&msg);
            }
      }

      return (int) msg.wParam;
}
```

Note: We also see that the extension analyzes only stack frames for which we have debug symbols.

10. Launch another instance of WinDbg.

11. Open \EWMDA-Dumps\Process\x64\AppD3.exe.33748.dmp.

12. We get the dump file loaded:

```
Loading Dump File [C:\EWMDA-Dumps\Process\x64\AppD3.exe.33748.dmp]
User Mini Dump File with Full Memory: Only application data is available


************* Path validation summary **************
Response                         Time (ms)     Location
Deferred                                       srv*
Symbol search path is: srv*
Executable search path is:
Windows 10 Version 22631 MP (8 procs) Free x64
Product: WinNt, suite: SingleUserTS
Edition build lab: 22621.1.amd64fre.ni_release.220506-1250
Debug session time: Sun Sep 29 13:34:24.000 2024 (UTC + 1:00)
System Uptime: 3 days 1:34:40.257
Process Uptime: 0 days 0:00:13.000
....................................
This dump file has an exception of interest stored in it.
The stored exception information can be accessed via .ecxr
(83d4.1260): Stack overflow - code c00000fd (first/second chance not available)
For analysis of this file, run !analyze -v
*** WARNING: Unable to verify checksum for AppD3.exe
AppD3+0x2470:
00007ff7`27d52470 rep movs byte ptr [rdi],byte ptr [rsi]
```

13. We open a log file:

```
0:000> .logappend C:\EWMDA-Dumps\Process\x64\ES10.log
Opened log file 'C:\EWMDA-Dumps\Process\x64\ES10.log'
```

14. Load the extension, set the symbol path, and ask the why question:

```
0:000> .load C:\EWMDA-Dumps\ChatDBG\chatdbg

0:000> .sympath+ C:\EWMDA-Dumps\Process\x64\
Symbol search path is: srv*;C:\EWMDA-Dumps\Process\x64\
Expanded Symbol search path is:
cache*;SRV*https://msdl.microsoft.com/download/symbols;c:\ewmda-dumps\process\x64\

************* Path validation summary **************
Response                         Time (ms)     Location
Deferred                                       srv*
OK                                             C:\EWMDA-Dumps\Process\x64\

0:000> !why
The root cause of this error is a stack overflow in function `bar()` in
`AppD3.cpp`.

It happens because there seems to be a recursive call inside function `bar()`
that does not have a proper base case to end the recursion. The parameter
`param1` decreases from `0n484` in the first frame to `0n466` in the last frame,
which suggests that `param1` might be used to control the recursive depth.
However, the recursion does not stop even when `param1` goes down significantly,
leading to a stack overflow.

To fix the error, you need to review the recursive logic in function `bar()` at
line 351 in `AppD3.cpp`. A typical fix would involve setting a proper base case.
```

````
For example, if `param1` is indeed used to control the recursion depth, an `if`
condition might be added at the start of the function:

```cpp
if (param1 <= 0) {
    return;  // end the recursion when param1 is less than or equal to 0
}
```

The precise base case would of course depend on the details of the recursive
logic. Afterwards, you should test your code again to ensure no stack overflow
occurs.

0:000> k 10
 # Child-SP          RetAddr               Call Site
00 00000042`51ac3eb0 00007ff7`27d524b9     AppD3!bar+0x40 [C:\AWD3\AppD3\AppD3\AppD3.cpp @ 347]
01 00000042`51ac4700 00007ff7`27d524b9     AppD3!bar+0x89 [C:\AWD3\AppD3\AppD3\AppD3.cpp @ 351]
02 00000042`51ac4f50 00007ff7`27d524b9     AppD3!bar+0x89 [C:\AWD3\AppD3\AppD3\AppD3.cpp @ 351]
03 00000042`51ac57a0 00007ff7`27d524b9     AppD3!bar+0x89 [C:\AWD3\AppD3\AppD3\AppD3.cpp @ 351]
04 00000042`51ac5ff0 00007ff7`27d524b9     AppD3!bar+0x89 [C:\AWD3\AppD3\AppD3\AppD3.cpp @ 351]
05 00000042`51ac6840 00007ff7`27d524b9     AppD3!bar+0x89 [C:\AWD3\AppD3\AppD3\AppD3.cpp @ 351]
06 00000042`51ac7090 00007ff7`27d524b9     AppD3!bar+0x89 [C:\AWD3\AppD3\AppD3\AppD3.cpp @ 351]
07 00000042`51ac78e0 00007ff7`27d524b9     AppD3!bar+0x89 [C:\AWD3\AppD3\AppD3\AppD3.cpp @ 351]
08 00000042`51ac8130 00007ff7`27d524b9     AppD3!bar+0x89 [C:\AWD3\AppD3\AppD3\AppD3.cpp @ 351]
09 00000042`51ac8980 00007ff7`27d524b9     AppD3!bar+0x89 [C:\AWD3\AppD3\AppD3\AppD3.cpp @ 351]
0a 00000042`51ac91d0 00007ff7`27d524b9     AppD3!bar+0x89 [C:\AWD3\AppD3\AppD3\AppD3.cpp @ 351]
0b 00000042`51ac9a20 00007ff7`27d524b9     AppD3!bar+0x89 [C:\AWD3\AppD3\AppD3\AppD3.cpp @ 351]
0c 00000042`51aca270 00007ff7`27d524b9     AppD3!bar+0x89 [C:\AWD3\AppD3\AppD3\AppD3.cpp @ 351]
0d 00000042`51acaac0 00007ff7`27d524b9     AppD3!bar+0x89 [C:\AWD3\AppD3\AppD3\AppD3.cpp @ 351]
0e 00000042`51acb310 00007ff7`27d524b9     AppD3!bar+0x89 [C:\AWD3\AppD3\AppD3\AppD3.cpp @ 351]
0f 00000042`51acbb60 00007ff7`27d524b9     AppD3!bar+0x89 [C:\AWD3\AppD3\AppD3\AppD3.cpp @ 351]

0:000> .srcpath C:\EWMDA-Dumps\Process\x64\
Source search path is: C:\EWMDA-Dumps\Process\x64\

************* Path validation summary **************
Response                         Time (ms)     Location
OK                                             C:\EWMDA-Dumps\Process\x64\

0:000> !why
The error is due to a stack overflow, caused by the recursive calling of the
function 'bar' in the source code file at location
C:\AWD3\AppD3\AppD3\AppD3.cpp:351. In each frame from 1 to 20, the function
'bar' is continuously invoked without a proper base case to terminate the
recursion, which results in an exceeding of the call stack limit.

The root cause of the error is a logical issue pertaining to the recursive
control flow of the application. Without an appropriate base case to halt the
recursive calls, the maximum number of recursive function calls which the stack
can handle is quickly consumed, resulting in the stack overflow error.

A potential fix for this error would be to review the function 'bar' at
C:\AWD3\AppD3\AppD3\AppD3.cpp:351 and introduce a base case to halt the
recursion. The base case depends on the logic of the program. For instance, it
might be that when param1 reaches a certain value, the recursion should
terminate. Thus, one might add a condition like `if (param1 <= 0) return;` at
the start of the function to halt excessive recursive calls.
````

```
0:000> kP 10
 # Child-SP          RetAddr               Call Site
00 00000042`51ac3eb0 00007ff7`27d524b9     AppD3!bar(
                    int param1 = 0n484,
                    char * param2 = 0x00007ff7`27d6d9d8 "Hello World!",
                    wchar_t * param3 = 0x00007ff7`27d6d9e8 "Hello World Wide!")+0x40
[C:\AWD3\AppD3\AppD3\AppD3.cpp @ 347]
01 00000042`51ac4700 00007ff7`27d524b9     AppD3!bar(
                    int param1 = 0n484,
                    char * param2 = 0x00007ff7`27d6d9d8 "Hello World!",
                    wchar_t * param3 = 0x00007ff7`27d6d9e8 "Hello World Wide!")+0x89
[C:\AWD3\AppD3\AppD3\AppD3.cpp @ 351]
02 00000042`51ac4f50 00007ff7`27d524b9     AppD3!bar(
                    int param1 = 0n483,
                    char * param2 = 0x00007ff7`27d6d9d8 "Hello World!",
                    wchar_t * param3 = 0x00007ff7`27d6d9e8 "Hello World Wide!")+0x89
[C:\AWD3\AppD3\AppD3\AppD3.cpp @ 351]
03 00000042`51ac57a0 00007ff7`27d524b9     AppD3!bar(
                    int param1 = 0n482,
                    char * param2 = 0x00007ff7`27d6d9d8 "Hello World!",
                    wchar_t * param3 = 0x00007ff7`27d6d9e8 "Hello World Wide!")+0x89
[C:\AWD3\AppD3\AppD3\AppD3.cpp @ 351]
04 00000042`51ac5ff0 00007ff7`27d524b9     AppD3!bar(
                    int param1 = 0n481,
                    char * param2 = 0x00007ff7`27d6d9d8 "Hello World!",
                    wchar_t * param3 = 0x00007ff7`27d6d9e8 "Hello World Wide!")+0x89
[C:\AWD3\AppD3\AppD3\AppD3.cpp @ 351]
05 00000042`51ac6840 00007ff7`27d524b9     AppD3!bar(
                    int param1 = 0n480,
                    char * param2 = 0x00007ff7`27d6d9d8 "Hello World!",
                    wchar_t * param3 = 0x00007ff7`27d6d9e8 "Hello World Wide!")+0x89
[C:\AWD3\AppD3\AppD3\AppD3.cpp @ 351]
06 00000042`51ac7090 00007ff7`27d524b9     AppD3!bar(
                    int param1 = 0n479,
                    char * param2 = 0x00007ff7`27d6d9d8 "Hello World!",
                    wchar_t * param3 = 0x00007ff7`27d6d9e8 "Hello World Wide!")+0x89
[C:\AWD3\AppD3\AppD3\AppD3.cpp @ 351]
07 00000042`51ac78e0 00007ff7`27d524b9     AppD3!bar(
                    int param1 = 0n478,
                    char * param2 = 0x00007ff7`27d6d9d8 "Hello World!",
                    wchar_t * param3 = 0x00007ff7`27d6d9e8 "Hello World Wide!")+0x89
[C:\AWD3\AppD3\AppD3\AppD3.cpp @ 351]
08 00000042`51ac8130 00007ff7`27d524b9     AppD3!bar(
                    int param1 = 0n477,
                    char * param2 = 0x00007ff7`27d6d9d8 "Hello World!",
                    wchar_t * param3 = 0x00007ff7`27d6d9e8 "Hello World Wide!")+0x89
[C:\AWD3\AppD3\AppD3\AppD3.cpp @ 351]
09 00000042`51ac8980 00007ff7`27d524b9     AppD3!bar(
                    int param1 = 0n476,
                    char * param2 = 0x00007ff7`27d6d9d8 "Hello World!",
                    wchar_t * param3 = 0x00007ff7`27d6d9e8 "Hello World Wide!")+0x89
[C:\AWD3\AppD3\AppD3\AppD3.cpp @ 351]
0a 00000042`51ac91d0 00007ff7`27d524b9     AppD3!bar(
                    int param1 = 0n475,
                    char * param2 = 0x00007ff7`27d6d9d8 "Hello World!",
                    wchar_t * param3 = 0x00007ff7`27d6d9e8 "Hello World Wide!")+0x89
[C:\AWD3\AppD3\AppD3\AppD3.cpp @ 351]
0b 00000042`51ac9a20 00007ff7`27d524b9     AppD3!bar(
                    int param1 = 0n474,
```

```
                    char * param2 = 0x00007ff7`27d6d9d8 "Hello World!",
                    wchar_t * param3 = 0x00007ff7`27d6d9e8 "Hello World Wide!")+0x89
[C:\AWD3\AppD3\AppD3\AppD3.cpp @ 351]
0c 00000042`51aca270 00007ff7`27d524b9     AppD3!bar(
                    int param1 = 0n473,
                    char * param2 = 0x00007ff7`27d6d9d8 "Hello World!",
                    wchar_t * param3 = 0x00007ff7`27d6d9e8 "Hello World Wide!")+0x89
[C:\AWD3\AppD3\AppD3\AppD3.cpp @ 351]
0d 00000042`51acaac0 00007ff7`27d524b9     AppD3!bar(
                    int param1 = 0n472,
                    char * param2 = 0x00007ff7`27d6d9d8 "Hello World!",
                    wchar_t * param3 = 0x00007ff7`27d6d9e8 "Hello World Wide!")+0x89
[C:\AWD3\AppD3\AppD3\AppD3.cpp @ 351]
0e 00000042`51acb310 00007ff7`27d524b9     AppD3!bar(
                    int param1 = 0n471,
                    char * param2 = 0x00007ff7`27d6d9d8 "Hello World!",
                    wchar_t * param3 = 0x00007ff7`27d6d9e8 "Hello World Wide!")+0x89
[C:\AWD3\AppD3\AppD3\AppD3.cpp @ 351]
0f 00000042`51acbb60 00007ff7`27d524b9     AppD3!bar(
                    int param1 = 0n470,
                    char * param2 = 0x00007ff7`27d6d9d8 "Hello World!",
                    wchar_t * param3 = 0x00007ff7`27d6d9e8 "Hello World Wide!")+0x89
[C:\AWD3\AppD3\AppD3\AppD3.cpp @ 351]
```

Note: The extension correctly identified the stack overflow but incorrectly identified that the *param1* value is decreasing with each call. We can also see that symbol files are necessary for stack frames:

```
0:000> ~9s
win32u!NtUserMessageCall+0x14:
00007ffa`9f341554 ret

0:009> k
 # Child-SP          RetAddr               Call Site
00 00000042`526ff528 00007ffa`9fc37918     win32u!NtUserMessageCall+0x14
01 00000042`526ff530 00007ffa`9fc3a375     user32!SendMessageWorker+0x2e8
02 00000042`526ff5e0 00007ffa`9fc3bbd5     user32!SendOrCallDefWindowProc+0x4d
03 00000042`526ff620 00007ffa`6294b977     user32!GetWindowTextW+0x25
04 00000042`526ff670 00007ffa`629396d7     UIAutomationCore!BasicHwndUtils::IsRemoteAppMarkerWindow+0x2b
05 00000042`526ff8c0 00007ffa`6294bf5d     UIAutomationCore!InProcProxyEventListener::OnWinEvent+0x67
06 00000042`526ff950 00007ffa`6294c860     UIAutomationCore!WinEventsManager::ThreadState::HandleWinEvent+0x7b
07 00000042`526ff9a0 00007ffa`6294cac1     UIAutomationCore!WinEventsManager::WindowsAppMessageCallback+0x40
08 00000042`526ff9f0 00007ffa`6294c13c     UIAutomationCore!std::_Func_impl_no_alloc<void (__cdecl*)(tagMSG const &
__ptr64,WinEventsManager::ThreadState & __ptr64) noexcept,void,tagMSG const & __ptr64,WinEventsManager::ThreadState &
__ptr64>::_Do_call+0x21
09 00000042`526ffa20 00007ffa`6294c5fb
UIAutomationCore!WorkerThread<WinEventsManager::ThreadState>::ProcessOne+0x3c
0a 00000042`526ffa50 00007ffa`62b354a1
UIAutomationCore!WorkerThread<WinEventsManager::ThreadState>::ThreadProc+0x137
0b 00000042`526ffbc0 00007ffa`9f469333
UIAutomationCore!std::thread::_Invoke<std::tuple<<lambda_d869f02c39f35682526e1a41b8686bac> >,0>+0x11
0c 00000042`526ffbf0 00007ffa`a18e257d     ucrtbase!thread_start<unsigned int (__cdecl*)(void *),1>+0x93
0d 00000042`526ffc20 00007ffa`a1aeaf28     kernel32!BaseThreadInitThunk+0x1d
0e 00000042`526ffc50 00000000`00000000     ntdll!RtlUserThreadStart+0x28

0:009> !why
ChatDBG needs debug information to work properly. Recompile your code with the /Zi flag.
```

15. Launch yet another instance of WinDbg.

16. Open \EWMDA-Dumps\Process\x64\AppD3.DMP.

17. We get the dump file loaded:

```
Microsoft (R) Windows Debugger Version 10.0.27704.1001 AMD64
Copyright (c) Microsoft Corporation. All rights reserved.


Loading Dump File [C:\EWMDA-Dumps\Process\x64\AppD3.DMP]
User Mini Dump File with Full Memory: Only application data is available


************* Path validation summary **************
Response                         Time (ms)     Location
Deferred                                       srv*
Symbol search path is: srv*
Executable search path is:
Windows 10 Version 22631 MP (8 procs) Free x64
Product: WinNt, suite: SingleUserTS
Edition build lab: 22621.1.amd64fre.ni_release.220506-1250
Debug session time: Sun Sep 29 13:40:21.000 2024 (UTC + 1:00)
System Uptime: 3 days 1:40:37.828
Process Uptime: 0 days 0:00:24.000
..................................
For analysis of this file, run !analyze -v
win32u!NtUserGetMessage+0x14:
00007ffa`9f341534 ret
```

18. We open a log file:

```
0:000> .logappend C:\EWMDA-Dumps\Process\x64\ES10.log
Opened log file 'C:\EWMDA-Dumps\Process\x64\ES10.log'
```

19. Load the extension, set the symbol path, and ask the why question:

```
0:000> .load C:\EWMDA-Dumps\ChatDBG\chatdbg

0:000> .sympath+ C:\EWMDA-Dumps\Process\x64\
Symbol search path is: srv*;C:\EWMDA-Dumps\Process\x64\
Expanded Symbol search path is:
cache*;SRV*https://msdl.microsoft.com/download/symbols;c:\ewmda-dumps\process\x64\

************* Path validation summary **************
Response                         Time (ms)     Location
Deferred                                       srv*
OK                                             C:\EWMDA-Dumps\Process\x64\

0:000> !why
The error appears to occur in the `AppD3.cpp` file but without the error message
or more context about the code itself, it's difficult to pinpoint the cause of
the error and propose a fix. Still, by looking at the provided frames we notice
that `hAccelTable` in frame 1 has been assigned a value which possibly can't be
interpreted as a valid `HACCEL` instance pointer. This could be causing the
application to crash when it attempts to use `hAccelTable`.

To fix the problem, you need to initialize `hAccelTable` properly. This
initialization usually happens with the `LoadAccelerators` function, so check if
you are calling this function correctly and it returns a valid handle. Here is a
basic usage of `LoadAccelerators`:
```

```
```C++
hAccelTable = LoadAccelerators(hInstance, MAKEINTRESOURCE(IDC_NAME));
```

where `IDC_NAME` is a placeholder for your application's specific name
identifier. If you use a wrong identifier or `LoadAccelerators` fails for some
reason (missing resource, for example), `hAccelTable` could be invalid causing a
crash.

Remember to always check that `LoadAccelerators` returns a valid handle before
using the `hAccelTable`.

There could be other potential issues in your code causing the crash, but
without the actual source code or error output, this is one of the best guesses
that can be made with the provided information.
```

```
0:000> k
 # Child-SP          RetAddr               Call Site
00 000000b1`868ffbe8 00007ffa`9fc453fa     win32u!NtUserGetMessage+0x14
01 000000b1`868ffbf0 00007ff6`6e8e15ed     user32!GetMessageW+0x2a
02 000000b1`868ffc50 00007ff6`6e8e6552     AppD3!wWinMain+0x9d [C:\AWD3\AppD3\AppD3\AppD3.cpp @ 57]
03 (Inline Function) --------`--------     AppD3!invoke_main+0x21
[d:\a01\_work\43\s\src\vctools\crt\vcstartup\src\startup\exe_common.inl @ 118]
04 000000b1`868ffcc0 00007ffa`a18e257d     AppD3!__scrt_common_main_seh+0x106
[d:\a01\_work\43\s\src\vctools\crt\vcstartup\src\startup\exe_common.inl @ 288]
05 000000b1`868ffd00 00007ffa`a1aeaf28     kernel32!BaseThreadInitThunk+0x1d
06 000000b1`868ffd30 00000000`00000000     ntdll!RtlUserThreadStart+0x28
```

Note: This is the normal dump and the reasoning about a possible error is unnecessary.

20. Close all instances of WinDbg.

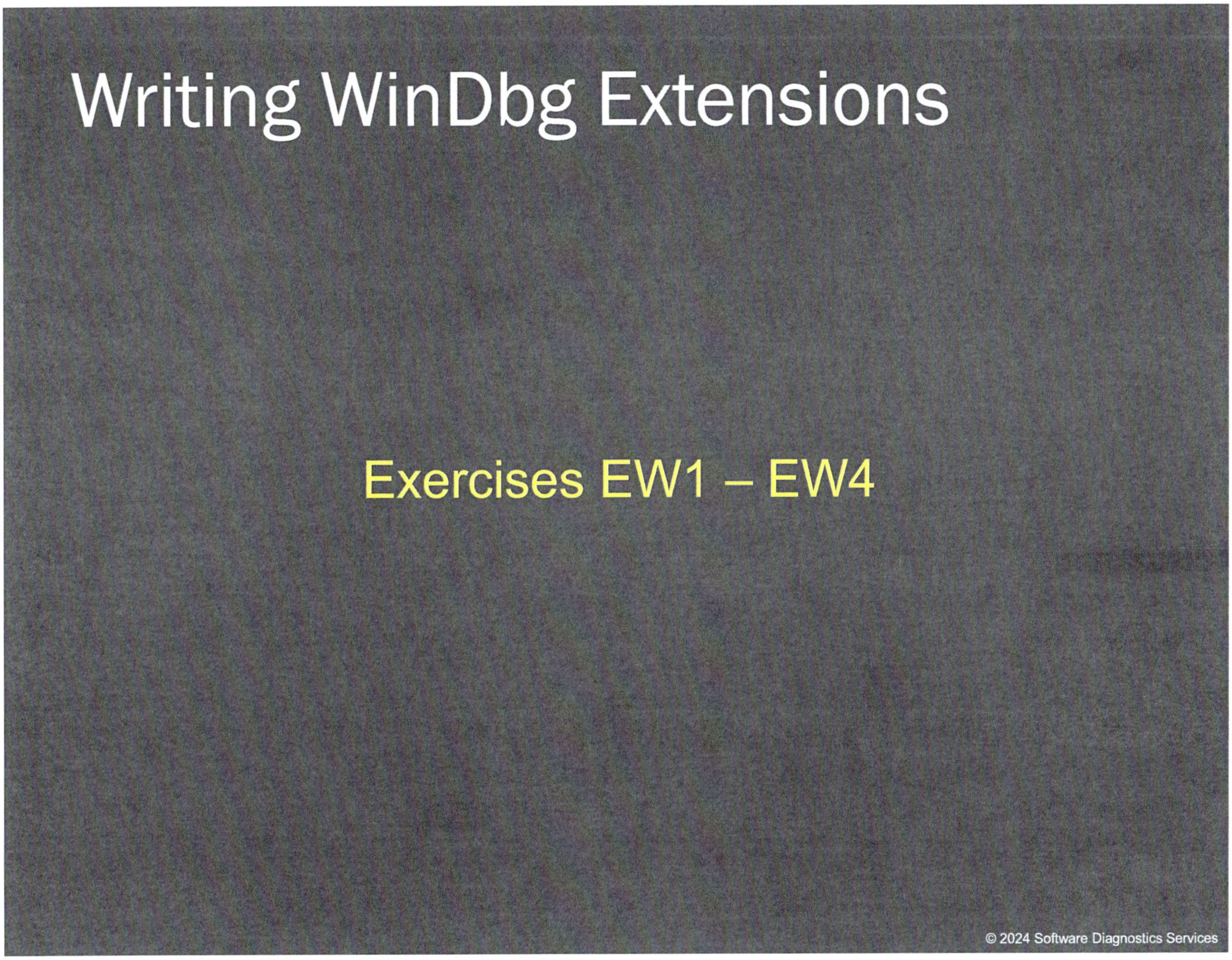

Writing WinDbg Extensions
Exercises EW1 – EW4
© 2024 Software Diagnostics Services

For this part, I created four exercises.

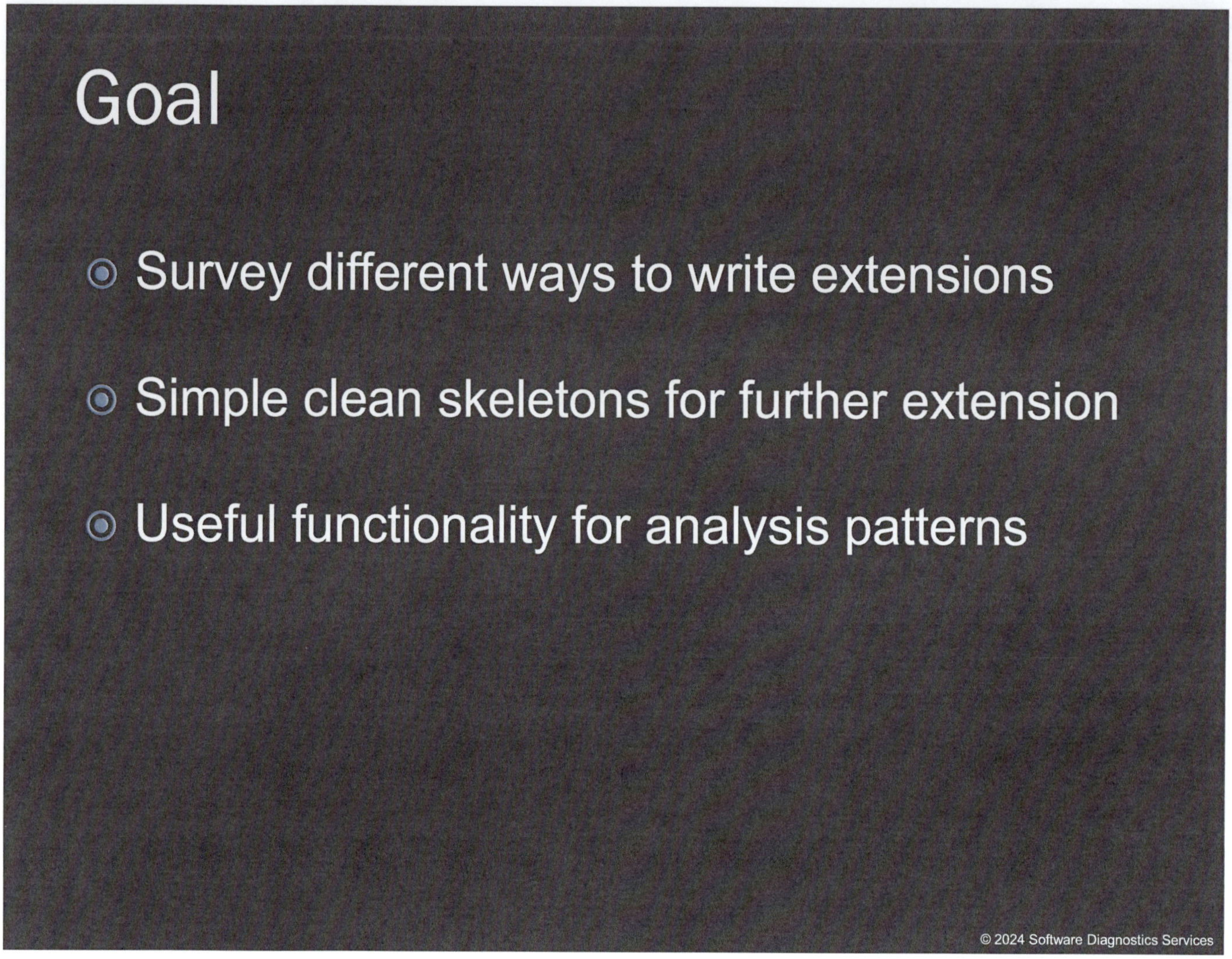

Goal
Survey different ways to write extensions
Simple clean skeletons for further extension
Useful functionality for analysis patterns
© 2024 Software Diagnostics Services

We have three goals to meet during this part of writing our own WinDbg extensions. First, try different ways to see what way does suit our needs the best. Create simple, minimal, and clean template skeletons. And finally, add some useful functionality.

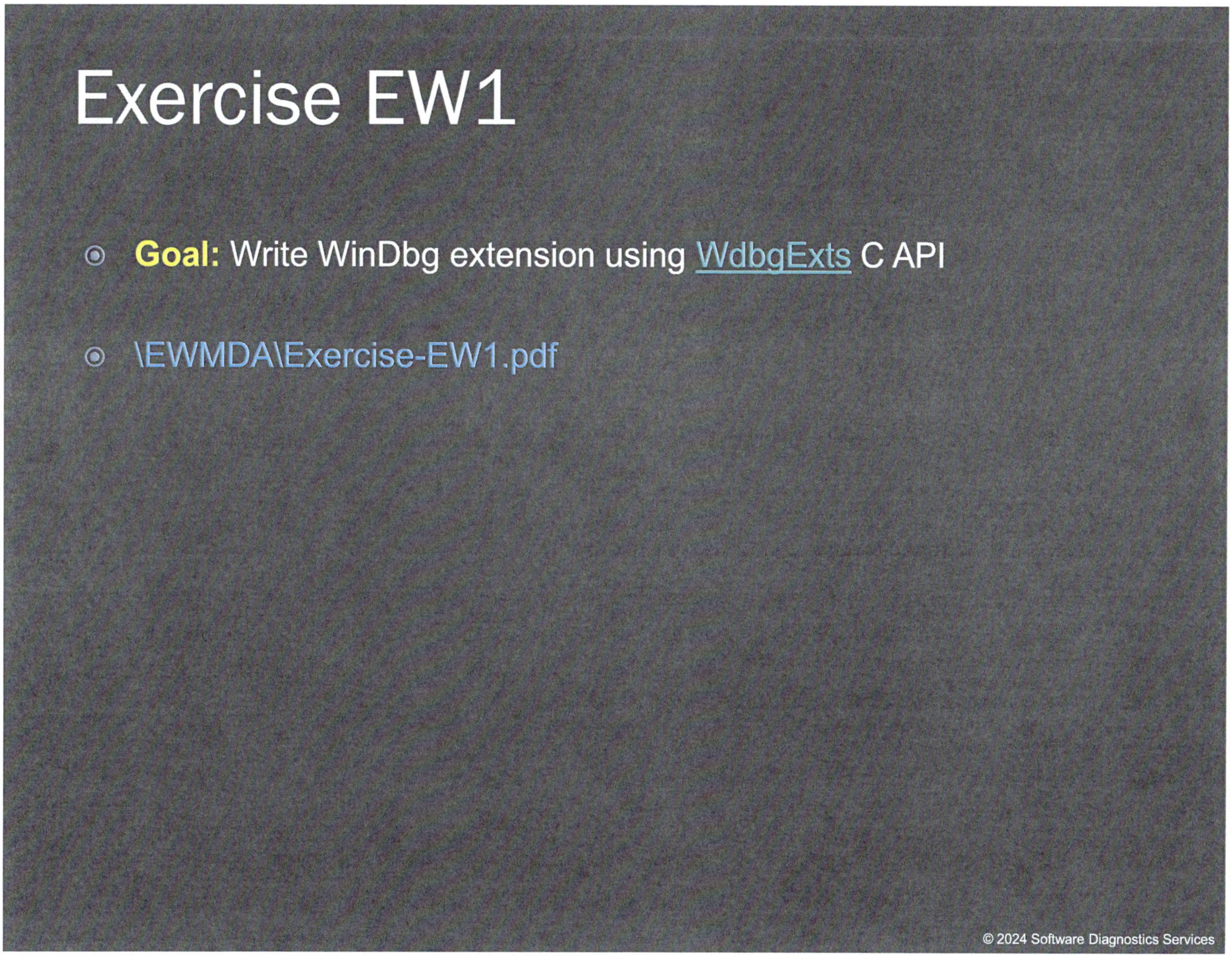
Exercise EW1
Goal: Write WinDbg extension using WdbgExts C API
\EWMDA\Exercise-EW1.pdf
© 2024 Software Diagnostics Services

WdbgExts
https://learn.microsoft.com/en-us/windows-hardware/drivers/debugger/wdbgexts-functions

Exercise EW1: Writing WinDbg Extension (WdbgExts C API)

Goal: Write WinDbg extension using WdbgExts[23] C API.

Prerequisites: Visual Studio Community 2022 with Desktop Development with C++ and Windows SDK version 10.0.22621.0.

1. Launch Visual Studio 2022.

2. Choose Create New Project:

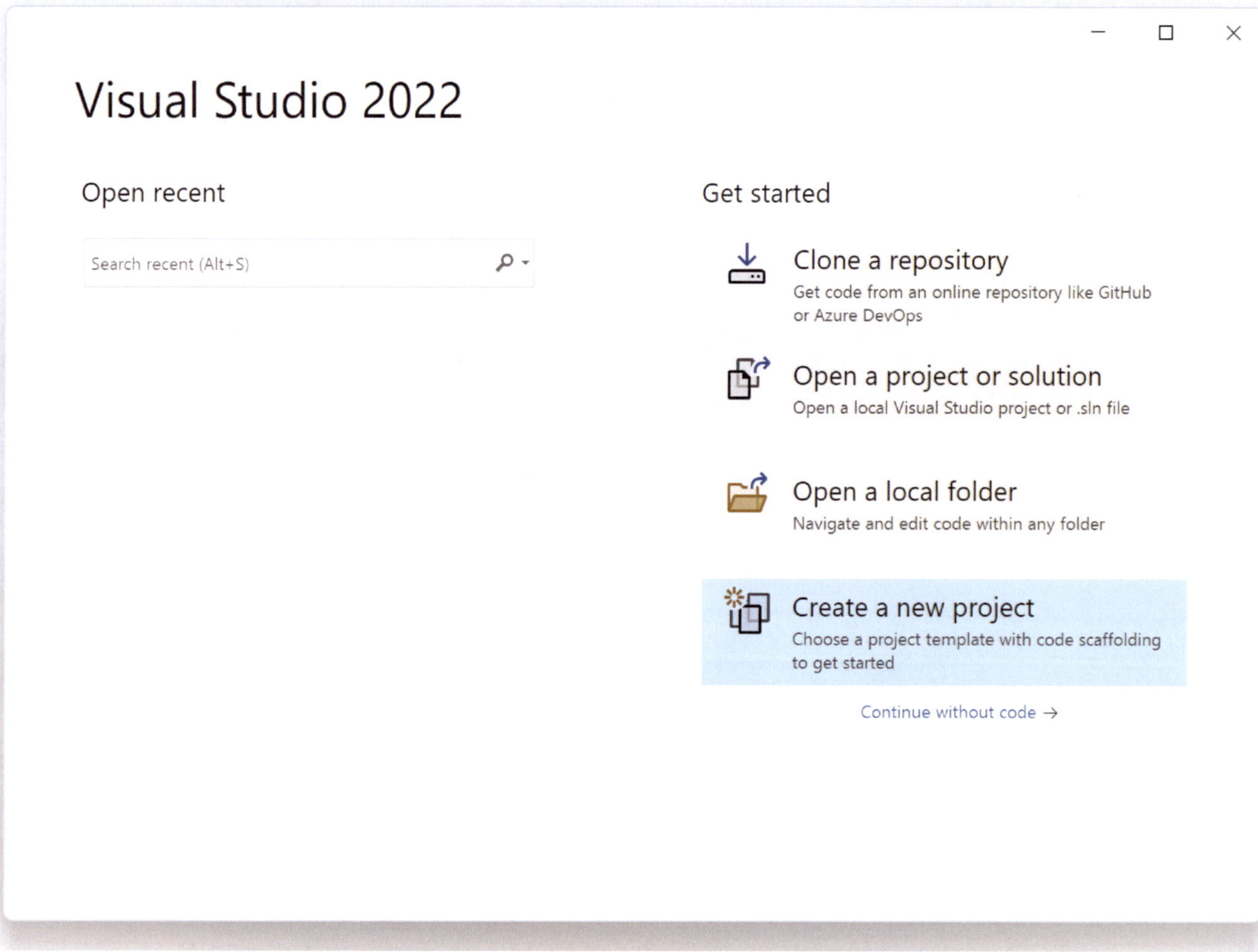

[23] https://learn.microsoft.com/en-us/windows-hardware/drivers/debugger/wdbgexts-functions

3. Select Empty Project type:

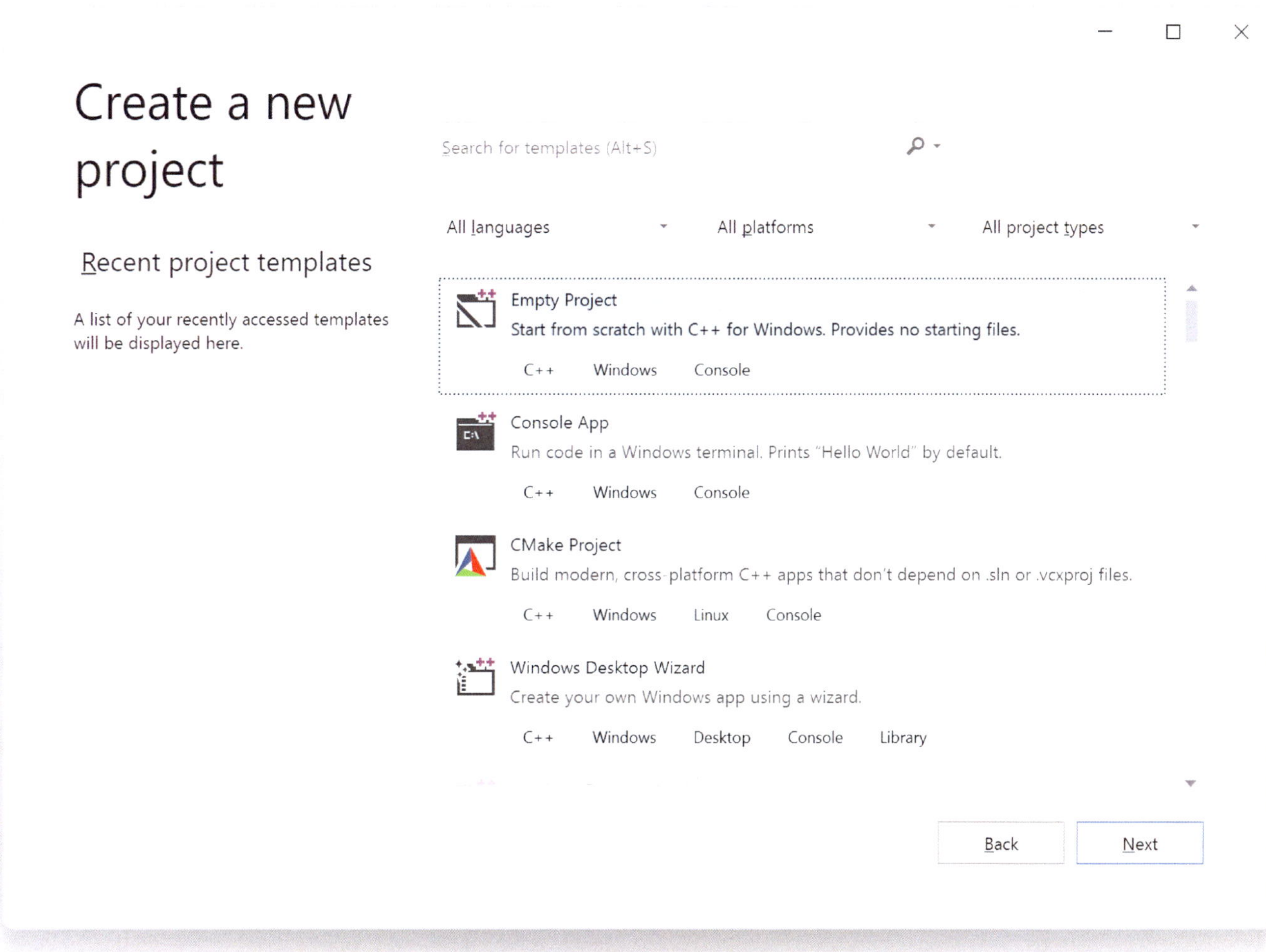

Create a new project
Search for templates (Alt+S)
All languages
All platforms
All project types
Recent project templates
A list of your recently accessed templates will be displayed here.
Empty Project
Start from scratch with C++ for Windows. Provides no starting files.
C++ Windows Console
Console App
Run code in a Windows terminal. Prints "Hello World" by default.
C++ Windows Console
CMake Project
Build modern, cross-platform C++ apps that don't depend on .sln or .vcxproj files.
C++ Windows Linux Console
Windows Desktop Wizard
Create your own Windows app using a wizard.
C++ Windows Desktop Console Library
Back
Next

4. Name the solution and project **checklist**:

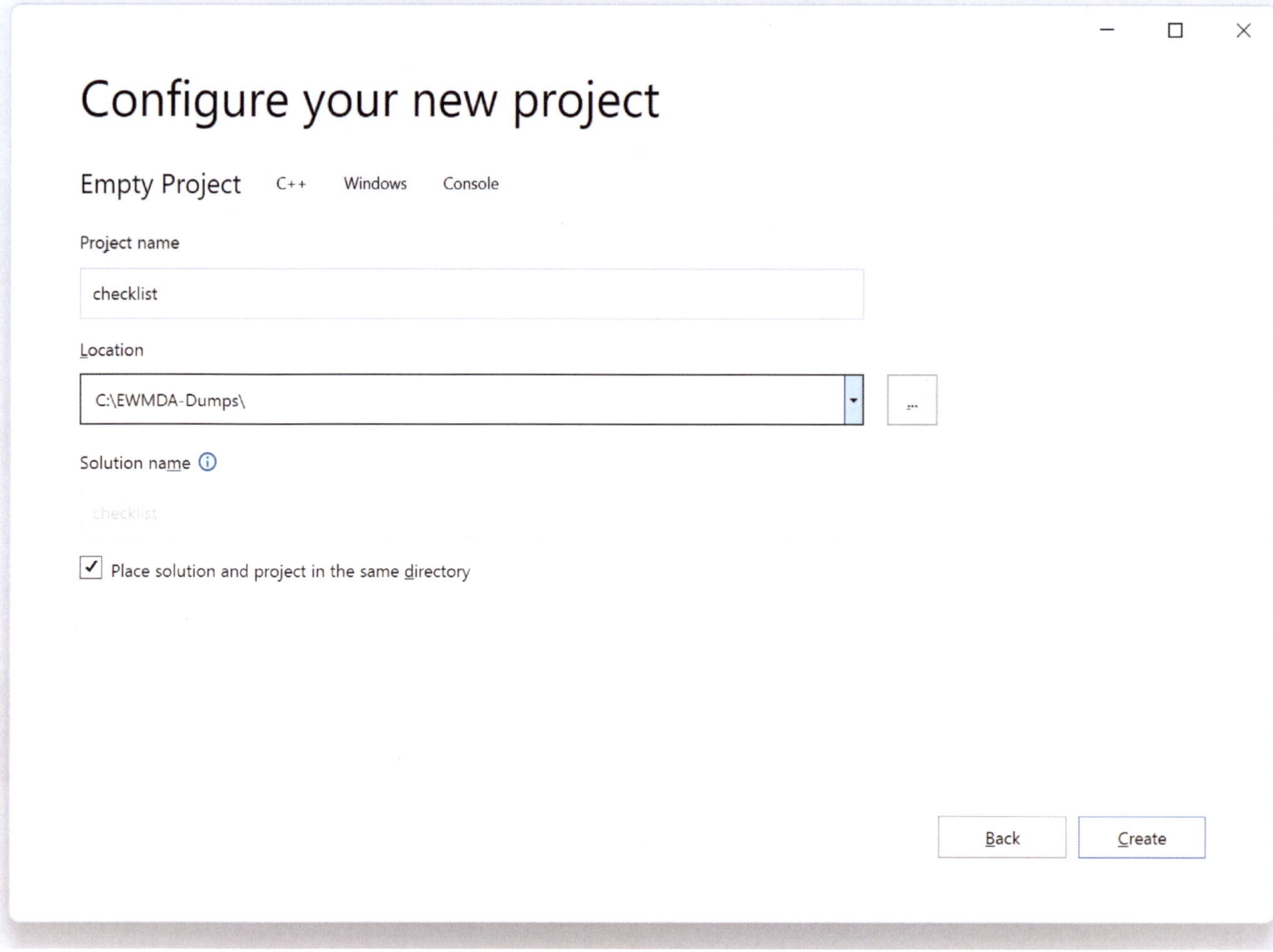

5. Create the project, and you get this initial Solution Explorer list (we also changed the current Solution Configuration to Release):

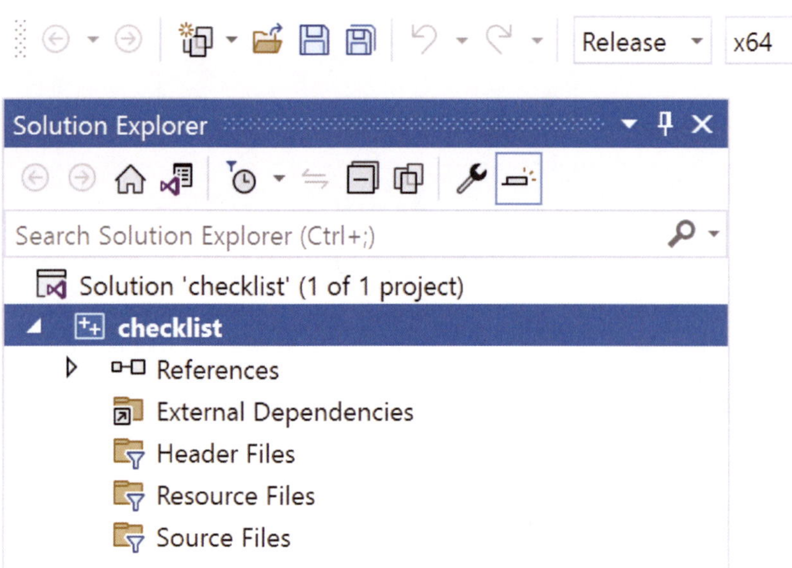

6. Right-click on checklist project and choose Add \ New Item...:

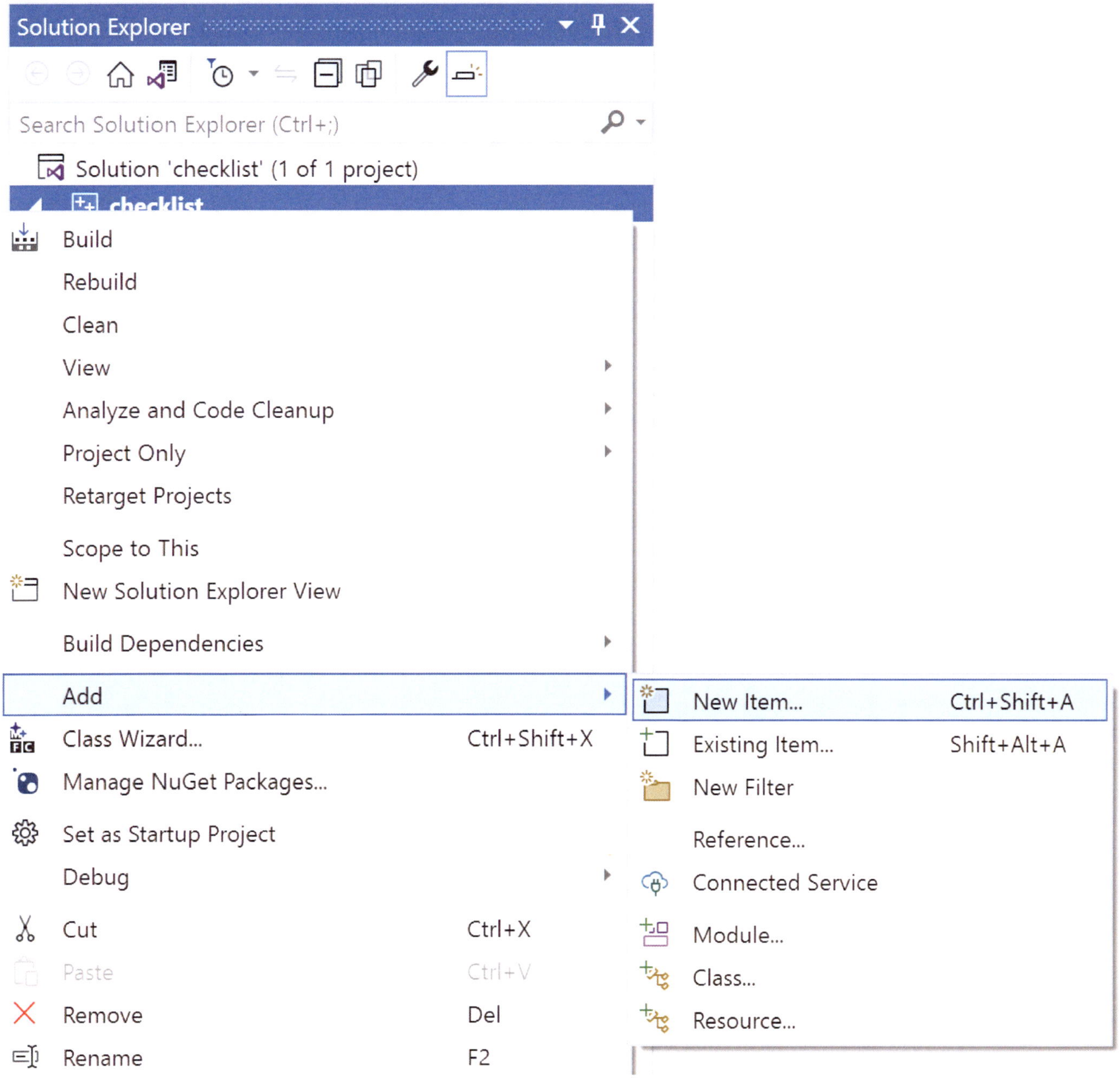

7. Add Module-Definition File (*.def) and name it *checklist.def*:

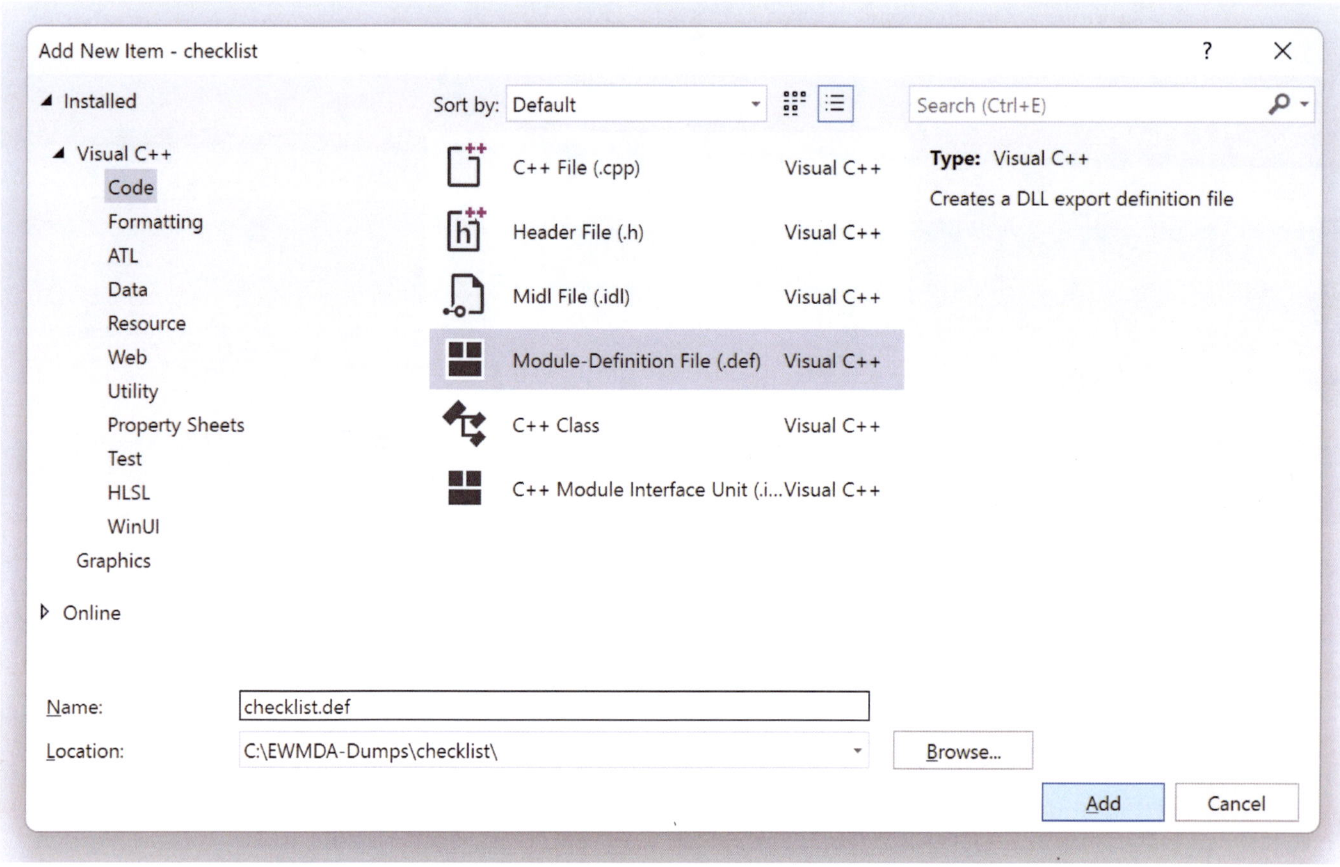

8. Add the following code to the *checklist.def* file.

```
EXPORTS

; exported functions implement !help and !checklist WinDbg extension commands

help
checklist

; exported service functions provided for WinDbg

WinDbgExtensionDllInit
ExtensionApiVersion
```

9. Add *checklist.cpp* to Source files. We intend to use C++ internally.

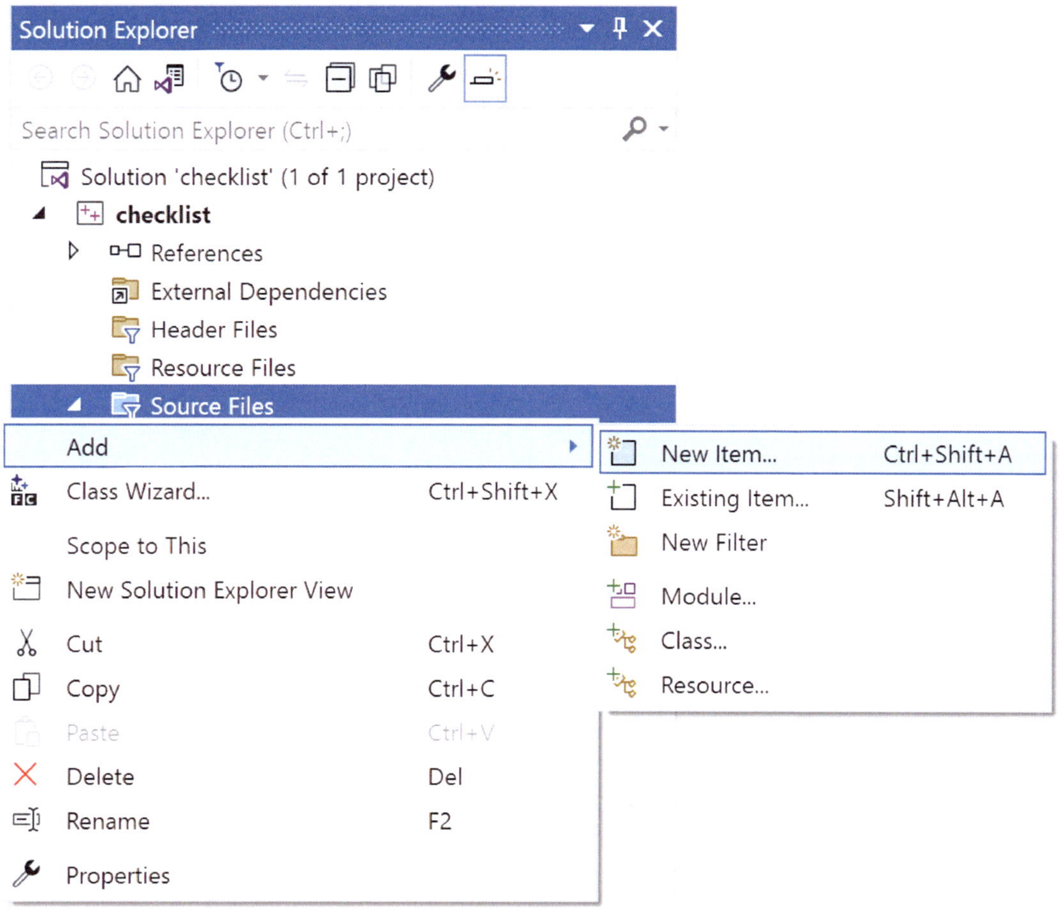
Solution Explorer
Search Solution Explorer (Ctrl+;)
Solution 'checklist' (1 of 1 project)
checklist
References
External Dependencies
Header Files
Resource Files
Source Files
Add
Class Wizard... Ctrl+Shift+X
Scope to This
New Solution Explorer View
Cut Ctrl+X
Copy Ctrl+C
Paste Ctrl+V
Delete Del
Rename F2
Properties
New Item... Ctrl+Shift+A
Existing Item... Shift+Alt+A
New Filter
Module...
Class...
Resource...

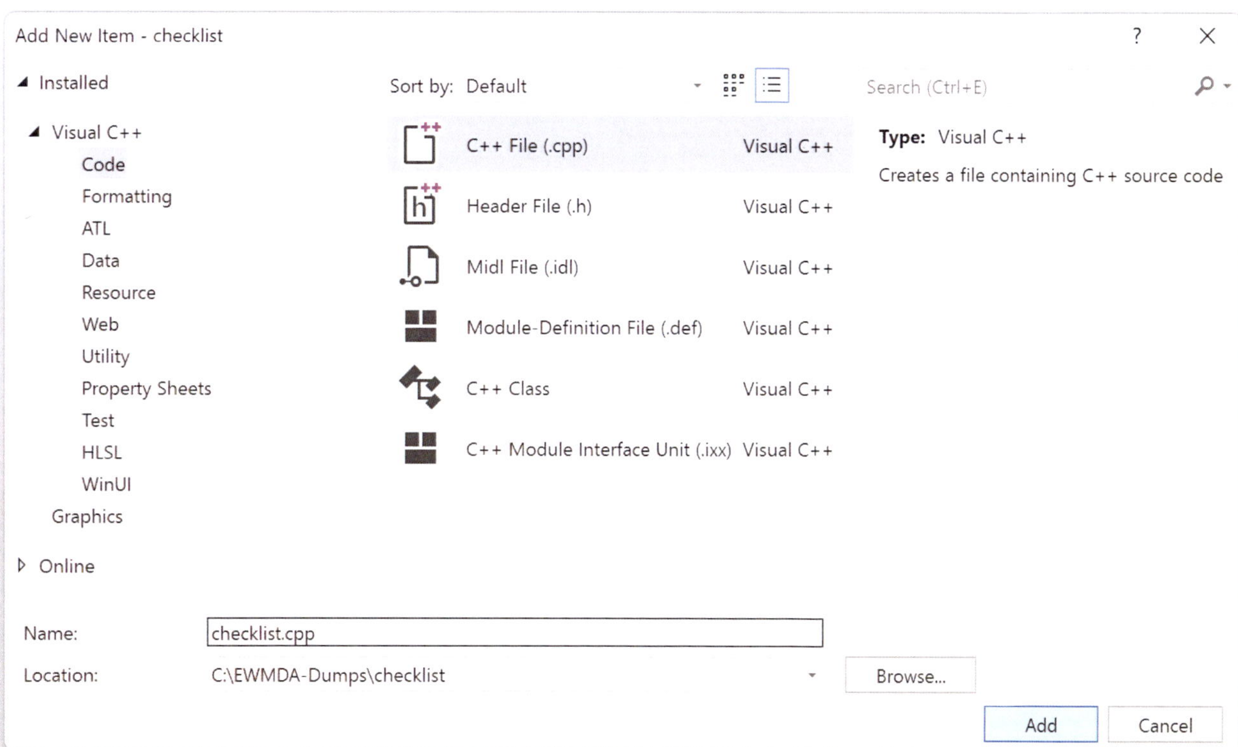
Add New Item - checklist
Installed
Visual C++
Code
Formatting
ATL
Data
Resource
Web
Utility
Property Sheets
Test
HLSL
WinUI
Graphics
Online
Sort by: Default
C++ File (.cpp) Visual C++
Header File (.h) Visual C++
Midl File (.idl) Visual C++
Module-Definition File (.def) Visual C++
C++ Class Visual C++
C++ Module Interface Unit (.ixx) Visual C++
Search (Ctrl+E)
Type: Visual C++
Creates a file containing C++ source code
Name: checklist.cpp
Location: C:\EWMDA-Dumps\checklist
Browse...
Add
Cancel

10. Add the following code to *checklist.cpp*.

```
#include <windows.h>
```

Define `KDEXT_64BIT` to have 64-bit pointers automatically cast to 32-bit pointers on 32-bit platforms.

```
#define KDEXT_64BIT
#include <wdbgexts.h>
#include <ntverp.h>
```

We are required to return the address of the `EXT_API_VERSION` structure from this exported function: `ExtensionApiVersion`.

```
EXT_API_VERSION ApiVersion = {   (VER_PRODUCTVERSION_W >> 8),
                                 (VER_PRODUCTVERSION_W & 0xff),
                                 EXT_API_VERSION_NUMBER64, 0 };

extern "C" LPEXT_API_VERSION ExtensionApiVersion(VOID)
{
    return &ApiVersion;
}
```

`WINDBG_EXTENSION_APIS` structure contains function pointers to read memory, get symbols, print to command window, etc. We get the address of this structure when the exported function `WinDbgExtensionDllInit` is called by WinDbg.

```
WINDBG_EXTENSION_APIS ExtensionApis;

extern "C" VOID WinDbgExtensionDllInit(PWINDBG_EXTENSION_APIS lpExtensionApis, USHORT MajorVersion, USHORT
MinorVersion)
{
    ExtensionApis = *lpExtensionApis;
    return;
}
```

We use the `DECLARE_API` macro to define our extension commands. `args` contains command parameters as a string. `dprintf` is a macro that expands to `WINDBG_EXTENSION_APIS` member function pointer to output routine.

```
extern "C" DECLARE_API(help)
{
        dprintf("Checklist Debugger Extension DLL (Version 1.0.0.0).\nOutputs checklist from
https://www.dumpanalysis.org/windows-memory-analysis-checklist.\n\n"
                "Commands:\n"
                "    checklist          - Shows the current memory analysis checklist categories.\n"
                "    checklist category - Shows the current memory analysis checklist for the specified category.\n");
}

DECLARE_API(checklist)
{
        switch (toupper(args[0]))
        {
        case 'G':
                dprintf("General Memory Analysis Checklist:\n\n"
                        "Symbol servers (.symfix)\n"
                        "Internal database(s) search\n"
                        "Google or Microsoft search for suspected components as this could be a known issue. Sometimes
a simple search immediately points to the fix on a vendor’s site\n"
                        "The tool used to save a dump (to flag false positive, incomplete or inconsistent dumps)\n"
                        "OS/SP version (version)\n"
                        "Language\n"
                        "Debug time\n"
                        "System uptime\n"
                        "Computer name (dS srv!srvcomputername or !envvar COMPUTERNAME)\n"
```

```
                "List of loaded and unloaded modules (lmv or !dlls)\n"
                "Hardware configuration (!sysinfo)\n"
                ".kframes 1000\n");
            break;
        case 'A':
            dprintf("Memory Analysis Checklist for Application or Service:\n\n"
                "Default analysis (!analyze -v or !analyze -v -hang for hangs)\n"
                "Critical sections (!cs -s -l -o, !locks) for both crashes and hangs\n"
                "Component timestamps, duplication and paths. DLL Hell? (lmv and !dlls)\n"
                "Do any newer components exist?\n"
                "Process threads (~*kv or !uniqstack) for multiple exceptions and blocking functions\n"
                "Process uptime\n"
                "Your components on the full raw stack of the problem thread\n"
                "Your components on the full raw stack of the main application thread\n"
                "Process size\n"
                "Number of threads\n"
                "Gflags value (!gflag)\n"
                "Time consumed by threads (!runaway)\n"
                "Environment (!peb)\n"
                "Import table (!dh)\n"
                "Hooked functions (!chkimg)\n"
                "Exception handlers (!exchain)\n"
                "Computer name (!envvar COMPUTERNAME)\n"
                "Process heap stats and validation (!heap -s, !heap -s -v)\n"
                "CLR threads? (mscorwks or clr modules on stack traces) Yes: use .NET checklist\n"
                "Hidden (unhandled and handled) exceptions on thread raw stacks\n");
            break;
        case 'S':
            dprintf("Memory Analysis Checklist for System Hang:\n\n"
                "Default analysis (!analyze -v -hang)\n"
                "ERESOURCE contention (!locks)\n"
                "Processes and virtual memory including session space (!vm 4)\n"
                "Important services are present and not hanging (for example, terminal or IMA services for
Citrix environments)\n"
                "Pools (!poolused)\n"
                "Waiting threads (!stacks)\n"
                "Critical system queues (!exqueue f)\n"
                "I/O (!irpfind)\n"
                "The list of all thread stack traces (!process 0 3f)\n"
                "LPC/ALPC chain for suspected threads (!lpc message or !alpc /m after search for \"Waiting for
reply to LPC\" or \"Waiting for reply to ALPC\" in !process 0 3f output)\n"
                "Mutants (search for \"Mutants - owning thread\" in !process 0 3f output)\n"
                "Critical sections for suspected processes (!cs -l -o -s)\n"
                "Sessions, session processes (!session, !sprocess)\n"
                "Processes (size, handle table size) (!process 0 0)\n"
                "Running threads (!running)\n"
                "Ready threads (!ready)\n"
                "DPC queues (!dpcs)\n"
                "The list of APCs (!apc)\n"
                "Internal queued spinlocks (!qlocks)\n"
                "Computer name (dS srv!srvcomputername)\n"
                "File cache, VACB (!filecache)\n"
                "File objects for blocked thread IRPs (!irp -> !fileobj)\n"
                "Network (!ndiskd.miniports and !ndiskd.pktpools)\n"
                "Disk (!scsikd.classext -> !scsikd.classext class_device 2)\n"
                "Modules rdbss, mrxdav, mup, mrxsmb in stack traces\n"
                "Functions Ntfs!Ntfs* and nt!Fs* in stack traces\n");
            break;
        case 'B':
            dprintf("Memory Analysis Checklist for BSOD:\n\n"
                "Default analysis (!analyze -v)\n"
                "Pool address (!pool)\n"
                "Component timestamps (lmv)\n"
                "Processes and virtual memory (!vm 4)\n"
                "Current threads on other processors\n"
                "Raw stack\n"
                "Bugcheck description (including ln exception address for corrupt or truncated dumps)\n"
                "Bugcheck callback data (!bugdump for systems prior to Windows XP SP1)\n"
                "Bugcheck secondary callback data (.enumtag)\n"
                "Computer name (dS srv!srvcomputername)\n"
                "Hardware configuration (!sysinfo)\n");
            break;
        case '.':
        case 'N':
```

```
                dprintf("Memory Analysis Checklist for .NET Application or Service:\n\n"
                        "CLR module and SOS extension versions (lmv and .chain)\n"
                        "Managed exceptions (~*e !pe)\n"
                        "Nested managed exceptions (!pe -nested)\n"
                        "Managed threads (!Threads -special)\n"
                        "Managed stack traces (~*e !CLRStack)\n"
                        "Managed execution residue (~*e !DumpStackObjects and !DumpRuntimeTypes)\n"
                        "Managed heap (!VerifyHeap, !DumpHeap -stat and !eeheap -gc)\n"
                        "GC handles (!GCHandles, !GCHandleLeaks)\n"
                        "Finalizer queue (!FinalizeQueue)\n"
                        "Sync blocks (!syncblk)\n");
                break;
        default:
                dprintf("The following memory analysis checklist categories are available:\n\n"
                        "    G(eneral)\n"
                        "    A(pplication)\n"
                        "    S(ystem)\n"
                        "    B(SOD)\n"
                        "    .(NET)\n");
        }
}
```

11. Now we configure our project settings.

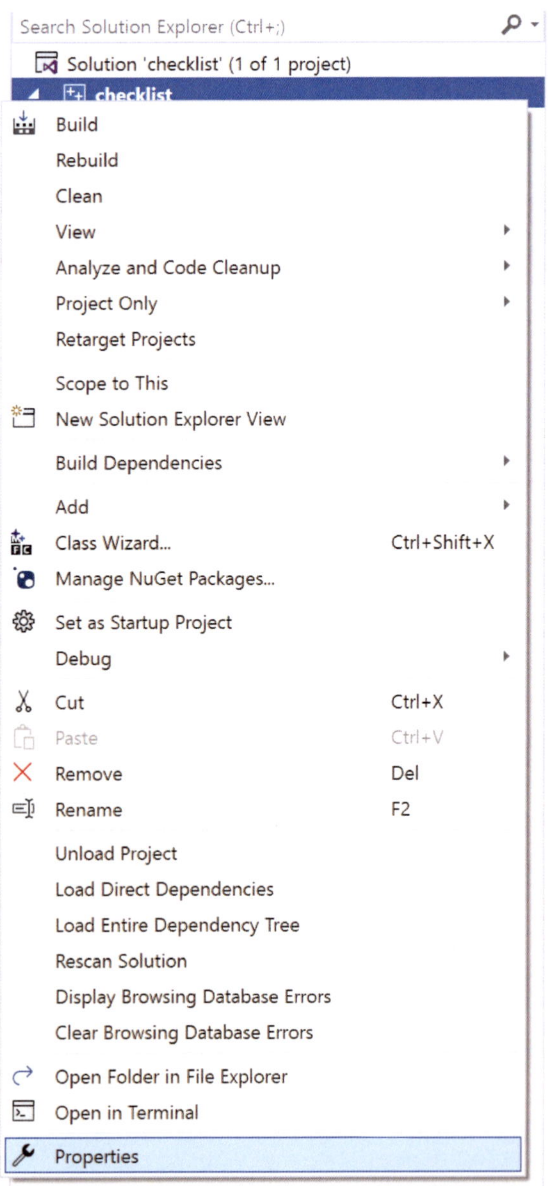

12. Set Configuration Type to Dynamic Library (.dll):

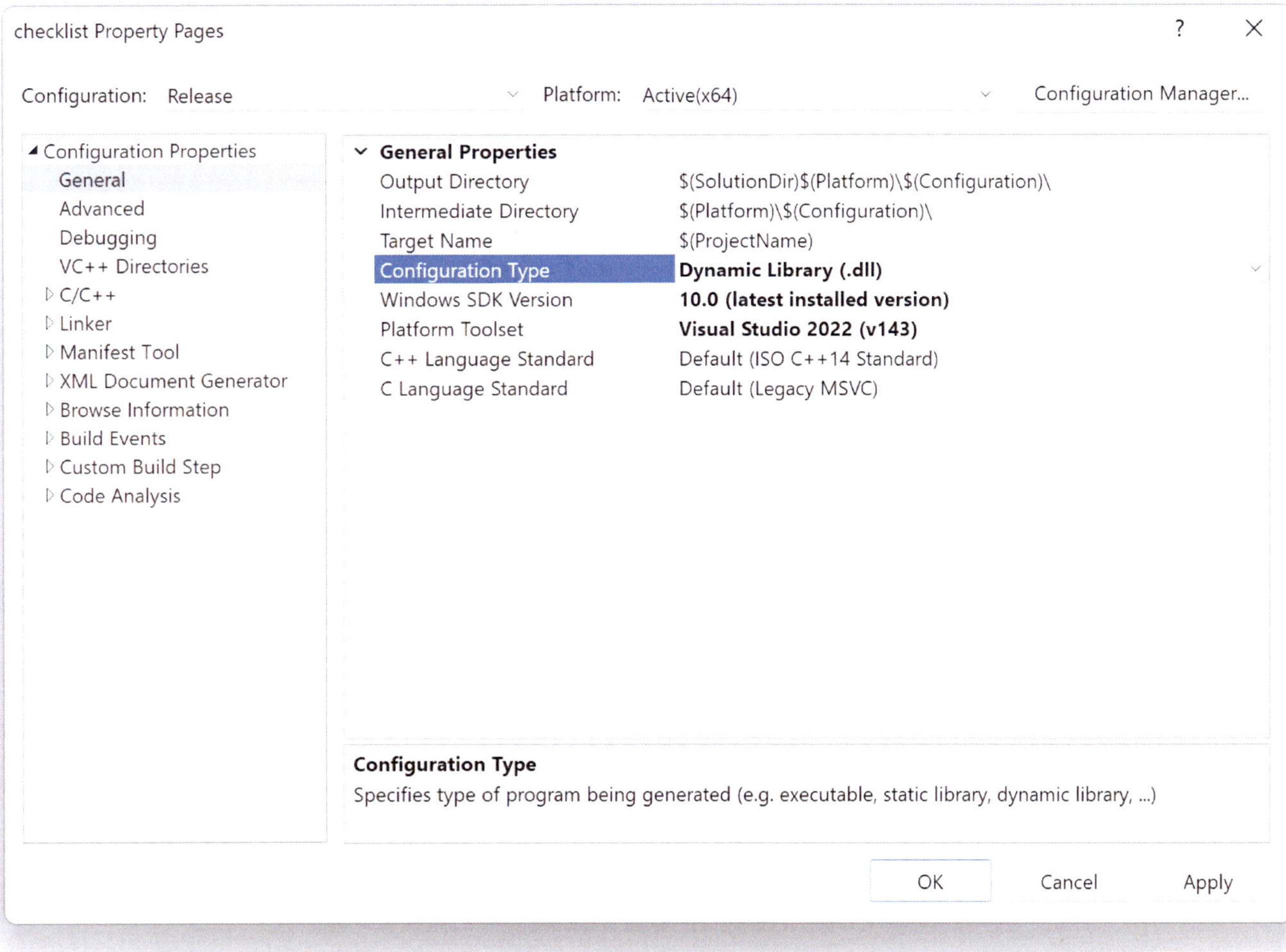

13. Do not set Character Set and Whole Program Optimization properties:

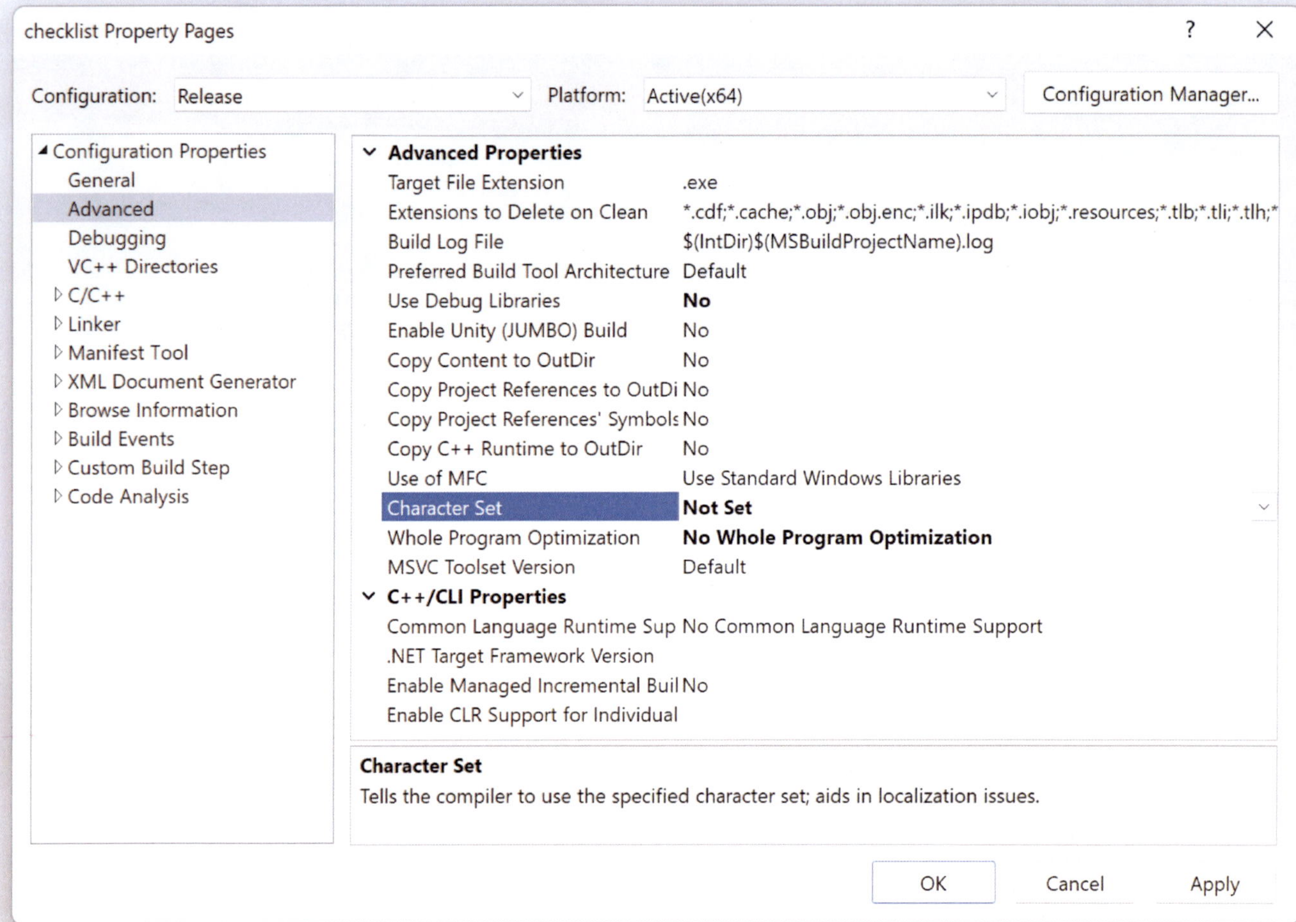

14. Set Runtime Library to Multi-threaded (/MT):

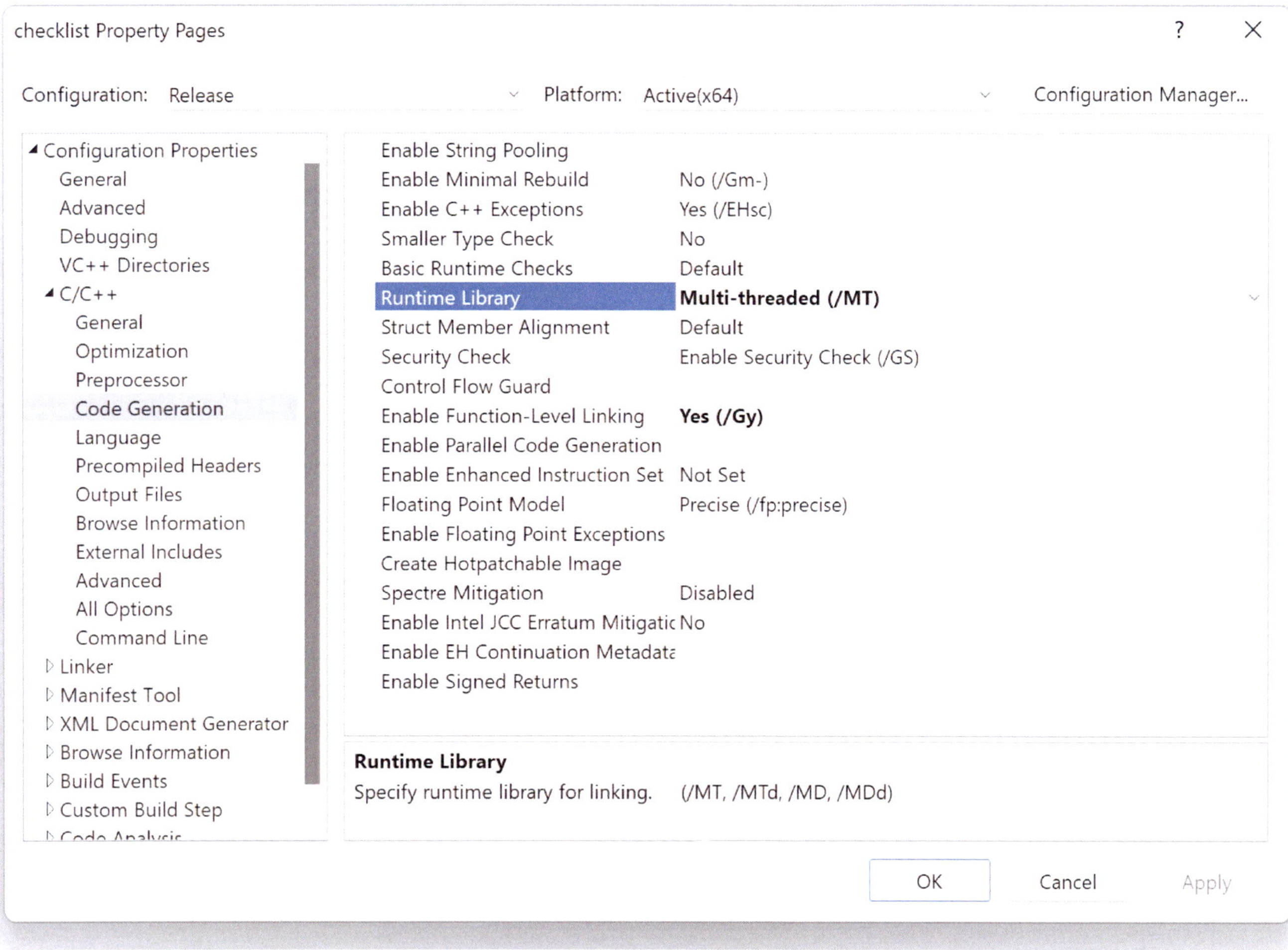
checklist Property Pages
Configuration: Release
Platform: Active(x64)
Configuration Manager...
Configuration Properties
General
Advanced
Debugging
VC++ Directories
C/C++
General
Optimization
Preprocessor
Code Generation
Language
Precompiled Headers
Output Files
Browse Information
External Includes
Advanced
All Options
Command Line
Linker
Manifest Tool
XML Document Generator
Browse Information
Build Events
Custom Build Step
Enable String Pooling
Enable Minimal Rebuild No (/Gm-)
Enable C++ Exceptions Yes (/EHsc)
Smaller Type Check No
Basic Runtime Checks Default
Runtime Library Multi-threaded (/MT)
Struct Member Alignment Default
Security Check Enable Security Check (/GS)
Control Flow Guard
Enable Function-Level Linking Yes (/Gy)
Enable Parallel Code Generation
Enable Enhanced Instruction Set Not Set
Floating Point Model Precise (/fp:precise)
Enable Floating Point Exceptions
Create Hotpatchable Image
Spectre Mitigation Disabled
Enable Intel JCC Erratum Mitigatic No
Enable EH Continuation Metadata
Enable Signed Returns
Runtime Library
Specify runtime library for linking. (/MT, /MTd, /MD, /MDd)
OK
Cancel
Apply

15. We now build Release x64 configuration:

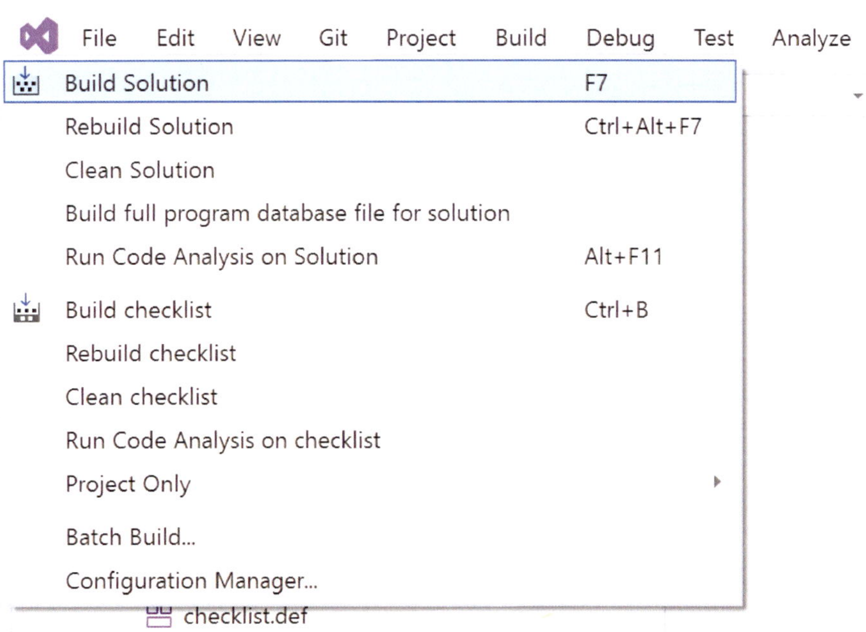
File
Edit
View
Git
Project
Build
Debug
Test
Analyze
Build Solution F7
Rebuild Solution Ctrl+Alt+F7
Clean Solution
Build full program database file for solution
Run Code Analysis on Solution Alt+F11
Build checklist Ctrl+B
Rebuild checklist
Clean checklist
Run Code Analysis on checklist
Project Only
Batch Build...
Configuration Manager...
checklist.def

16. If everything was done correctly, we should have no errors:

```
Build started...
1>------ Build started: Project: checklist, Configuration: Release x64 ------
1>checklist.cpp
1>   Creating library C:\EWMDA-Dumps\checklist\x64\Release\checklist.lib and object C:\EWMDA-Dumps\checklist\x64\Release\checklist.exp
1>checklist.vcxproj -> C:\EWMDA-Dumps\checklist\x64\Release\checklist.dll
========== Build: 1 succeeded, 0 failed, 0 up-to-date, 0 skipped ==========
```

Note: If you want the pure C extension, you can rename *checklist.cpp* as *checklist.c* and make the following changes:

```
extern VOID WinDbgExtensionDllInit(PWINDBG_EXTENSION_APIS lpExtensionApis, USHORT MajorVersion, USHORT
...

extern DECLARE_API(help)
...
```

17. Open \EWMDA-Dumps\Complete\x64\MEMORY-W11.DMP.

```
Microsoft (R) Windows Debugger Version 10.0.27704.1001 AMD64
Copyright (c) Microsoft Corporation. All rights reserved.


Loading Dump File [C:\EWMDA-Dumps\Complete\x64\MEMORY-W11.DMP]
Kernel Bitmap Dump File: Full address space is available


************* Path validation summary **************
Response                         Time (ms)     Location
Deferred                                       srv*
Symbol search path is: srv*
Executable search path is:
Windows 10 Kernel Version 22000 MP (2 procs) Free x64
Product: WinNt, suite: TerminalServer SingleUserTS Personal
Edition build lab: 22000.1.amd64fre.co_release.210604-1628
Kernel base = 0xfffff806`61e00000 PsLoadedModuleList = 0xfffff806`62a296b0
Debug session time: Sat Nov 13 23:17:16.607 2021 (UTC + 1:00)
System Uptime: 0 days 0:03:06.813
Loading Kernel Symbols
..............................................................
...............................................................
...............................................................
..
Loading User Symbols
..................................
Loading unloaded module list
........
For analysis of this file, run !analyze -v
nt!KeBugCheckEx:
fffff806`62215590 mov     qword ptr [rsp+8],rcx ss:0018:ffffbe82`96f64670=000000000000000a
```

18. Load the built checklist extension and execute some commands:

```
0: kd> .load C:\EWMDA-Dumps\checklist\x64\Release\checklist
```

```
0: kd> !help
Checklist Debugger Extension DLL (Version 1.0.0.0).
Outputs checklist from https://www.dumpanalysis.org/windows-memory-analysis-checklist.

Commands:
    checklist          - Shows the current memory analysis checklist categories.
    checklist category - Shows the current memory analysis checklist for the specified
category.

0: kd> !checklist
The following memory analysis checklist categories are available:

    G(eneral)
    A(pplication)
    S(ystem)
    B(SOD)
    .(NET)

0: kd> !checklist b
Memory Analysis Checklist for BSOD:

Default analysis (!analyze -v)
Pool address (!pool)
Component timestamps (lmv)
Processes and virtual memory (!vm 4)
Current threads on other processors
Raw stack
Bugcheck description (including ln exception address for corrupt or truncated dumps)
Bugcheck callback data (!bugdump for systems prior to Windows XP SP1)
Bugcheck secondary callback data (.enumtag)
Computer name (dS srv!srvcomputername)
Hardware configuration (!sysinfo)
```

19. We exit WinDbg.

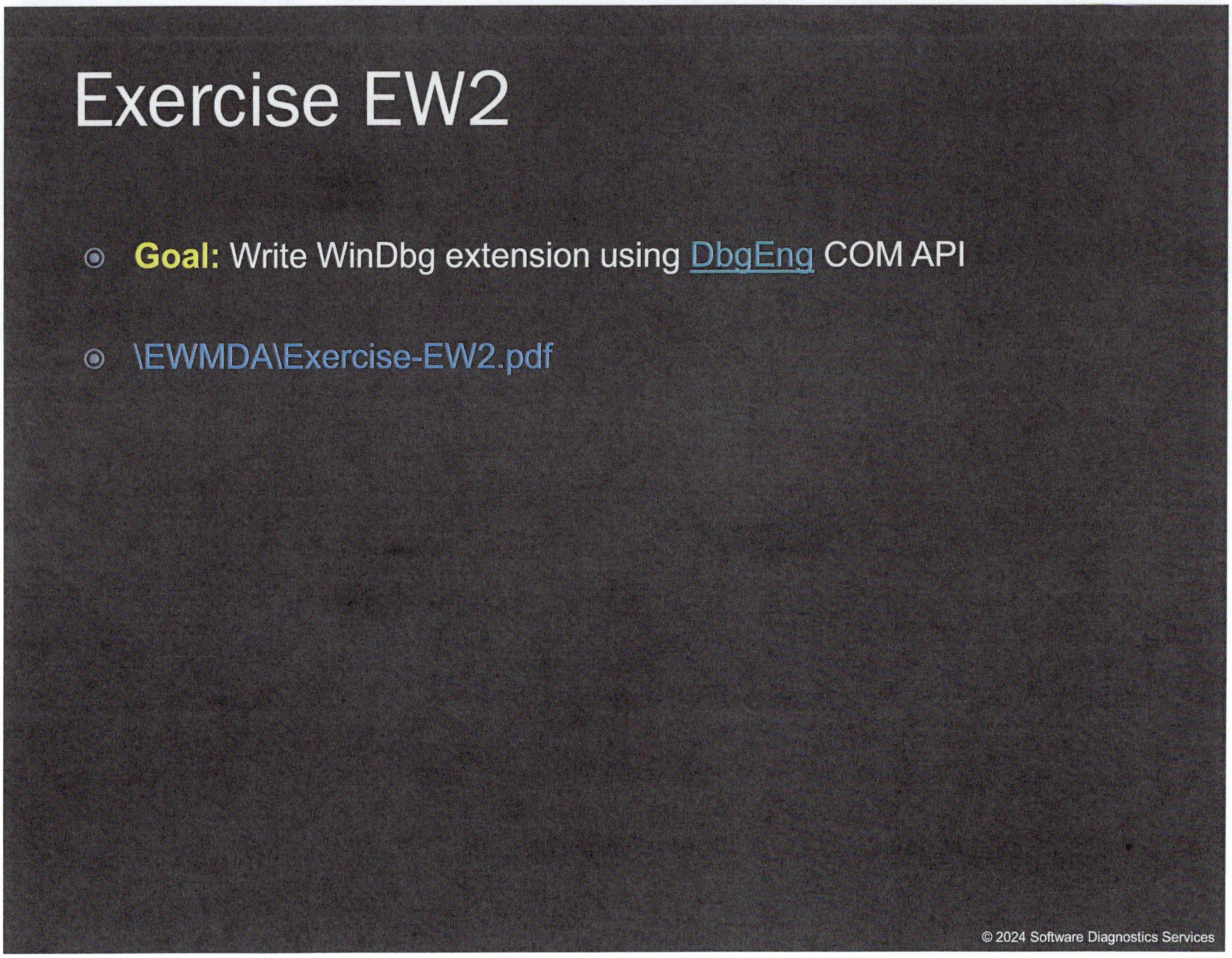
Exercise EW2
Goal: Write WinDbg extension using DbgEng COM API
\EWMDA\Exercise-EW2.pdf
© 2024 Software Diagnostics Services

DbgEng
https://learn.microsoft.com/en-us/windows-hardware/drivers/debugger/debugger-engine-reference

Exercise EW2: Writing WinDbg Extension (DbgEng COM API)

Goal: Write WinDbg extension using DbgEng[24] COM API.

Prerequisites: Visual Studio Community 2022 with Desktop Development with C++ and Windows 11 SDK version 10.0.22621.0.

1. Launch Visual Studio 2022.

2. Choose Create New Project:

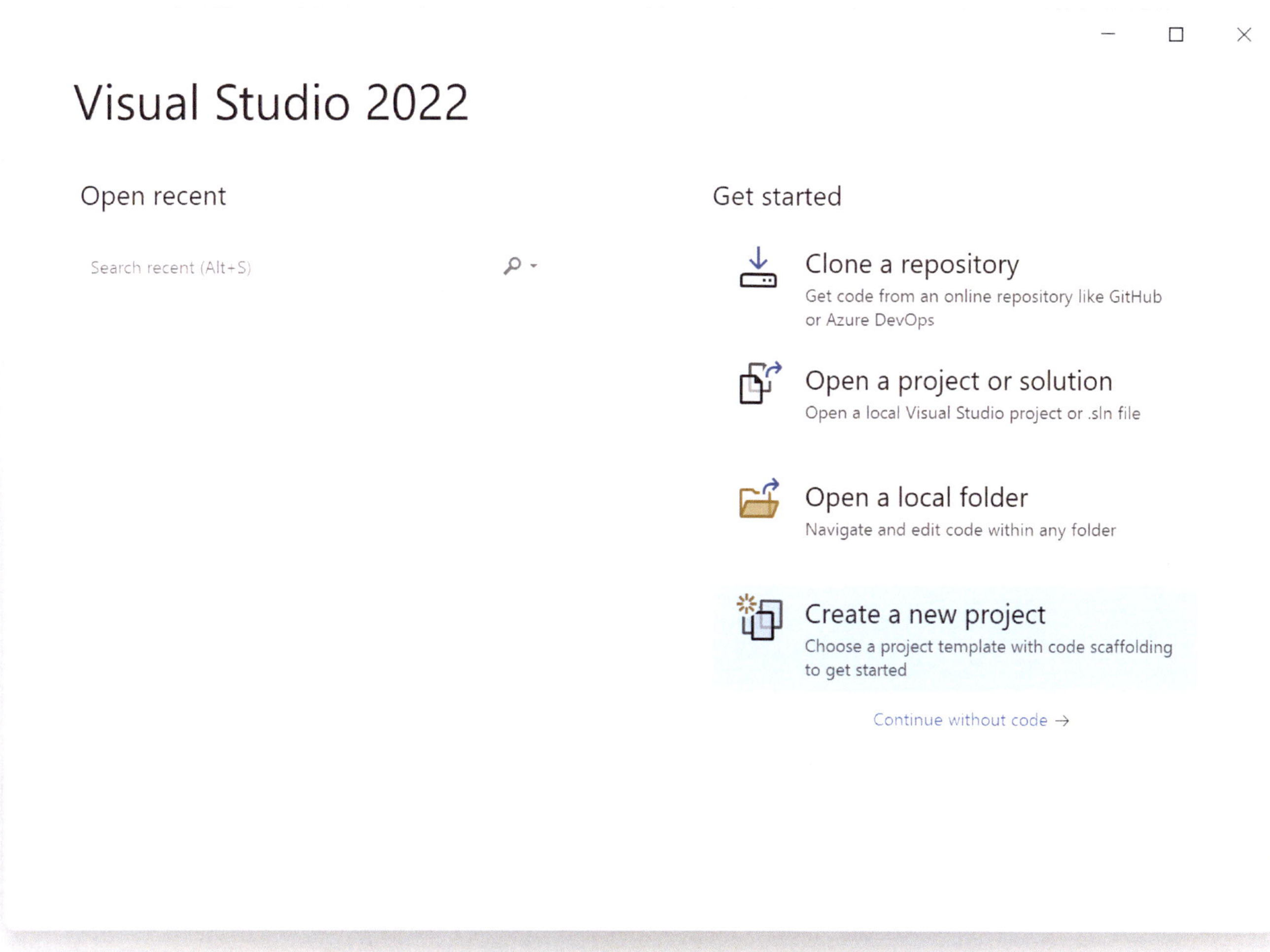

[24] https://learn.microsoft.com/en-us/windows-hardware/drivers/debugger/debugger-engine-reference

3. Select Empty Project type:

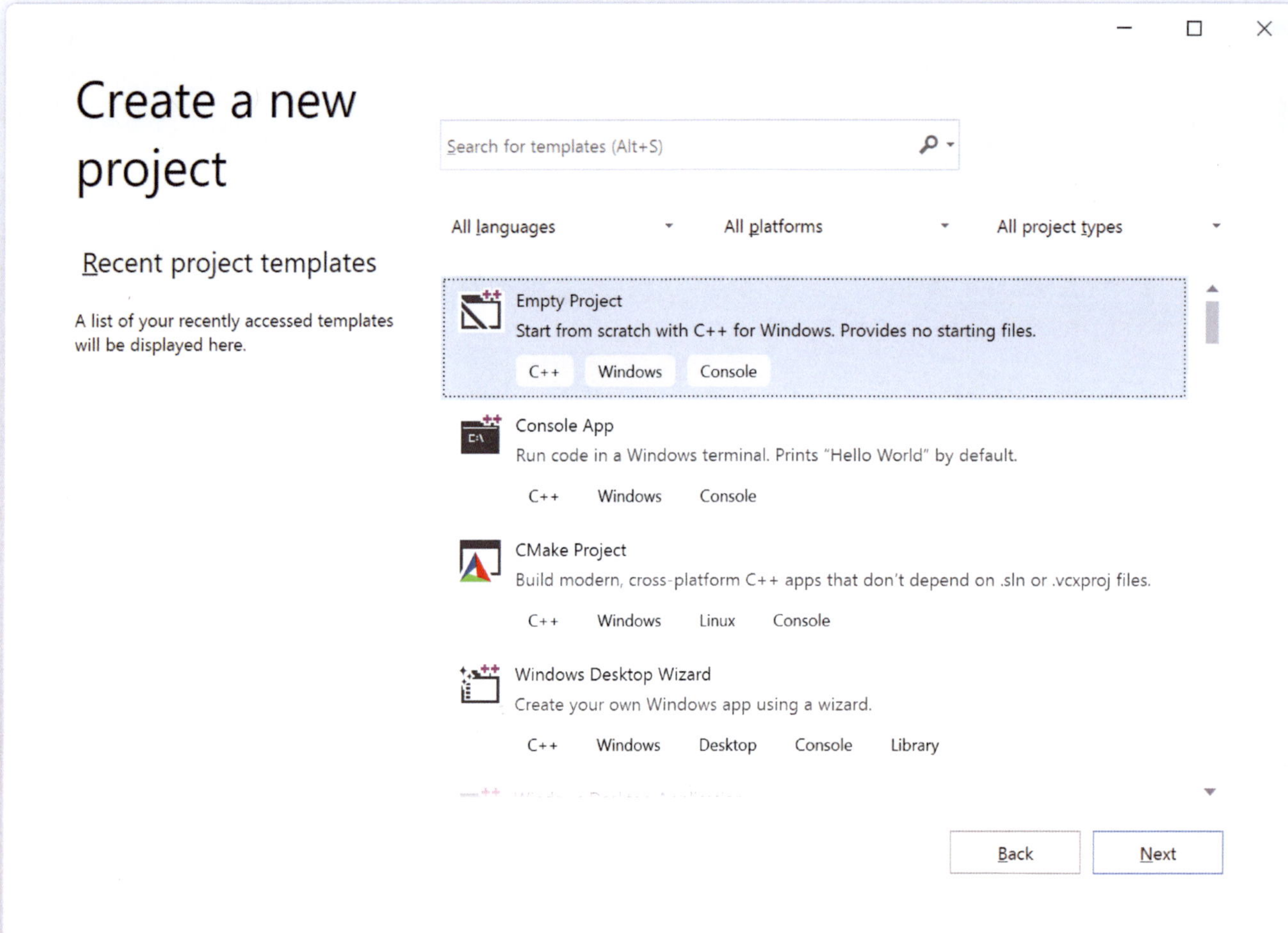

4. Name the solution and project **residue**:

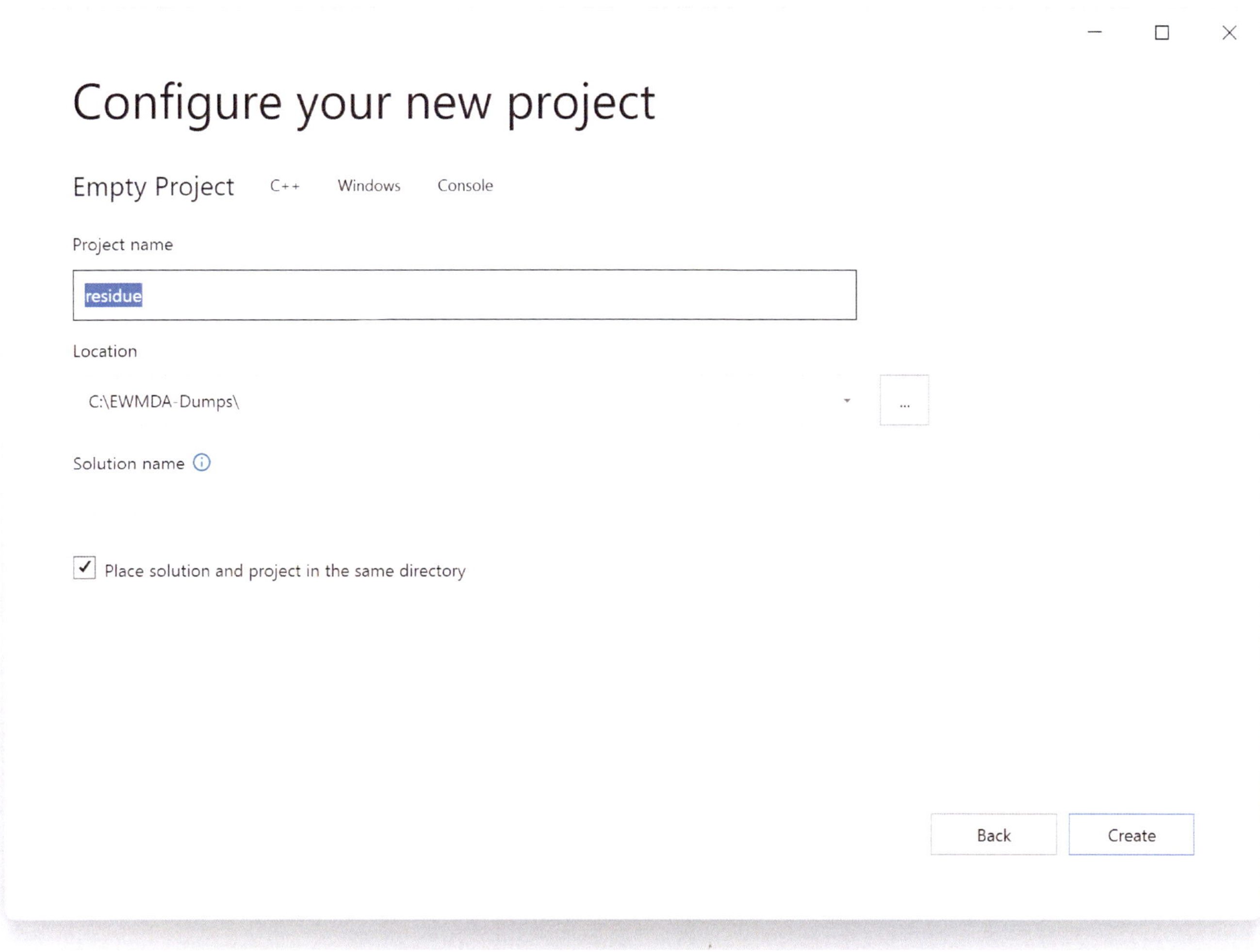

5. Create the project and change the current Solution Configuration to Release.

6. Add Module-Definition File (*.def) *residue.def* to the list of project files.

7. Add the following code to the *residue.def* file.

```
EXPORTS

; exported functions implement !help and !search WinDbg extension commands

    help
    search

; exported service functions provided for WinDbg

    DebugExtensionInitialize
    DebugExtensionUninitialize
```

8. Add *residues.cpp* to to Source files. We intend to use C++ internally.

9. Add the following code to *residue.cpp*.

```
#include <windows.h>
#include <dbgeng.h>

#include <string>
#include <format>
#include <ranges>
#include <vector>
#include <string_view>
```

We are required to link `dbgeng.lib` to use `DebugCreate` to create various interfaces:

```
#pragma comment(lib, "dbgeng.lib")
```

Through `DebugClient` interface, we can get other interfaces required for our extension functionality: control the debugger, read memory, and get symbolic information. We decided to get these interfaces upfront globally and not inside extension commands to simplify interface lifetime management (you can try this as a homework exercise: you also don't need to include `dbgeng.lib`);

```
PDEBUG_CLIENT DebugClient{};
PDEBUG_CONTROL5 DebugControl{};
PDEBUG_DATA_SPACES4 MemorySpace{};
PDEBUG_SYMBOLS5 Symbols{};

extern "C" HRESULT CALLBACK DebugExtensionInitialize(OUT PULONG Version, OUT PULONG Flags)
{
	*Version = DEBUG_EXTENSION_VERSION(0, 1);
	*Flags = 0;

	if (HRESULT hr = DebugCreate(__uuidof(IDebugClient), (void**)&DebugClient); hr != S_OK)
	{
		return hr;
	}

	if (HRESULT hr = DebugClient->QueryInterface(__uuidof(IDebugControl5), (void**)&DebugControl); hr != S_OK)
	{
		return hr;
	}

	if (HRESULT hr = DebugClient->QueryInterface(__uuidof(IDebugDataSpaces4), (void**)&MemorySpace); hr != S_OK)
	{
		return hr;
	}

	return DebugClient->QueryInterface(__uuidof(IDebugSymbols5), (void**)&Symbols);
}
```

We need to release all queried interfaces (COM object lifetime management).

```
extern "C" void CALLBACK DebugExtensionUninitialize(void)
{
	if (Symbols)
	{
		Symbols->Release();
	}

	if (MemorySpace)
	{
		MemorySpace->Release();
	}

	if (DebugControl)
	{
```

```
		DebugControl->Release();
	}

	if (DebugClient)
	{
		DebugClient->Release();
	}

	return;
}
```

Functions implementing extension commands get the client interface to obtain additional interfaces (we already got what we need in `DebugExtensionInitialize`) and an argument string to parse.

```
extern "C" HRESULT CALLBACK help(PDEBUG_CLIENT5 Client, PCSTR args)
{
	return DebugControl->ControlledOutput(DEBUG_OUTCTL_AMBIENT_DML, DEBUG_OUTPUT_NORMAL, "%s",
		"<b>Residue</b> Debugger Extension DLL (Version 1.0.0.0)\n"
		"Commands:\n"
		"    search address size value [level] [0]       - Deep search of pointer-sized values with level of
dereferences and optional symbols.\n");
	return S_OK;
}

extern "C" HRESULT CALLBACK search(PDEBUG_CLIENT5 Client, PCSTR args)
{
```

First, we need to split the argument string into individual arguments and convert them to `ULONG64` values, which we make accessible in the `params` vector through `param_idx` indices. We use the new C++20 Standard Library technique.

```
	const enum param_idx { ADDRESS, SIZE, VALUE, LEVEL, SYMBOLS };
	std::vector<ULONG64> params;

	std::string_view params_view{ args };
	std::string_view delim{ " " };
	for (const auto word : std::views::split(params_view, delim))
	{
		try
		{
			params.push_back(std::stoull(std::string(word.begin(), word.end()), nullptr, 16));
		}
		catch (...)
		{
			return E_FAIL;
		}
	}
```

The first 3 parameters are required.

```
	if (params.size() < 3)
	{
		return E_FAIL;
	}
```

The default value of the 4th optional parameter is 1.

```
	if (params.size() < 4)
	{
		params.push_back(1);
	}
```

The default value of the 5th optional parameter is 0.

```
if (params.size() < 5)
{
        params.push_back(0);
}

if (!params[SIZE] || !params[LEVEL])
{
        return S_OK;
}
```

We limit the search only to 10 levels of indirection.

```
if (params[LEVEL] > 10)
{
        params[LEVEL] = 10;
}
```

For each address, we get its value, interpret it as an address, and get its value too (similar to the **dpp** command), and continue the same up to LEVEL times while printing values as a line highlighting the value we search for in bold. If an address is invalid, set the dereferenced value to `0xbad`. If showing symbols is specified in command arguments, we show a symbolic value beside each address. We use new C++20 formatting.

```
std::size_t region_size = params[SIZE];
std::size_t levels = params[LEVEL];

for (std::size_t loc{ 0 }; loc < region_size; ++loc)
{
        std::string line;
        ULONG64 value{};

        for (std::size_t level{ 0 }; level <= levels; ++level)
        {
                PVOID buffer{};

                if (!level)
                {
                        value = params[ADDRESS] + loc * sizeof(PVOID);
                }
                else if (value != 0xbad)
                {
                        if (HRESULT hr = MemorySpace->ReadVirtual(value, &buffer, sizeof(buffer),
                              nullptr); hr == S_OK)
                        {
                                value = reinterpret_cast<ULONG64>(buffer);
                        }
                        else
                        {
                                value = 0xbad;
                        }

                }

                auto match = value == params[VALUE];
                line += ((match) ? "<b>" : "") + std::format("{:016x} ", value) + ((match) ? "</b>" : "");

                if (params[SYMBOLS])
                {
                        CHAR symbol[_MAX_PATH]{ 0 };
                        ULONG64 offset{};

                        if (HRESULT hr = Symbols->GetNameByOffset(value, symbol, sizeof(symbol),
                              nullptr, &offset); hr == S_OK)
                        {
                                line += symbol + std::format("+0x{:x} ", offset);
```

```
                }
            }
        }

        line += "\n";

        DebugControl->ControlledOutput(DEBUG_OUTCTL_AMBIENT_DML, DEBUG_OUTPUT_NORMAL, "%s", line.c_str());
    }

    return S_OK;
}
```

10. Now we configure our project settings.

11. Set Configuration Type to Dynamic Library (.dll) and C++ Language Standard to ISO C++20 Standard:

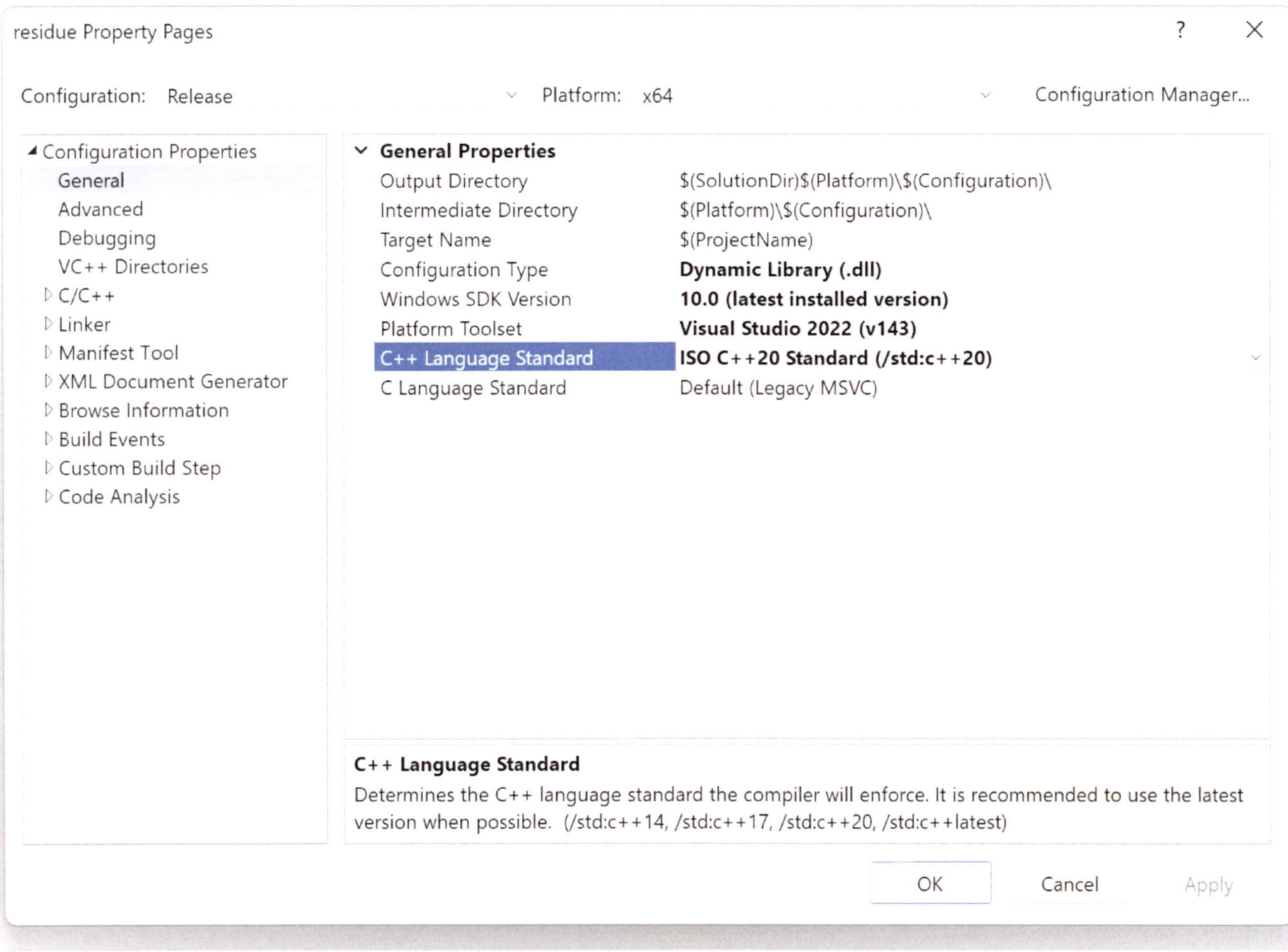

12. Set Use Unicode Character Set and Use Link Time Code Generation properties:

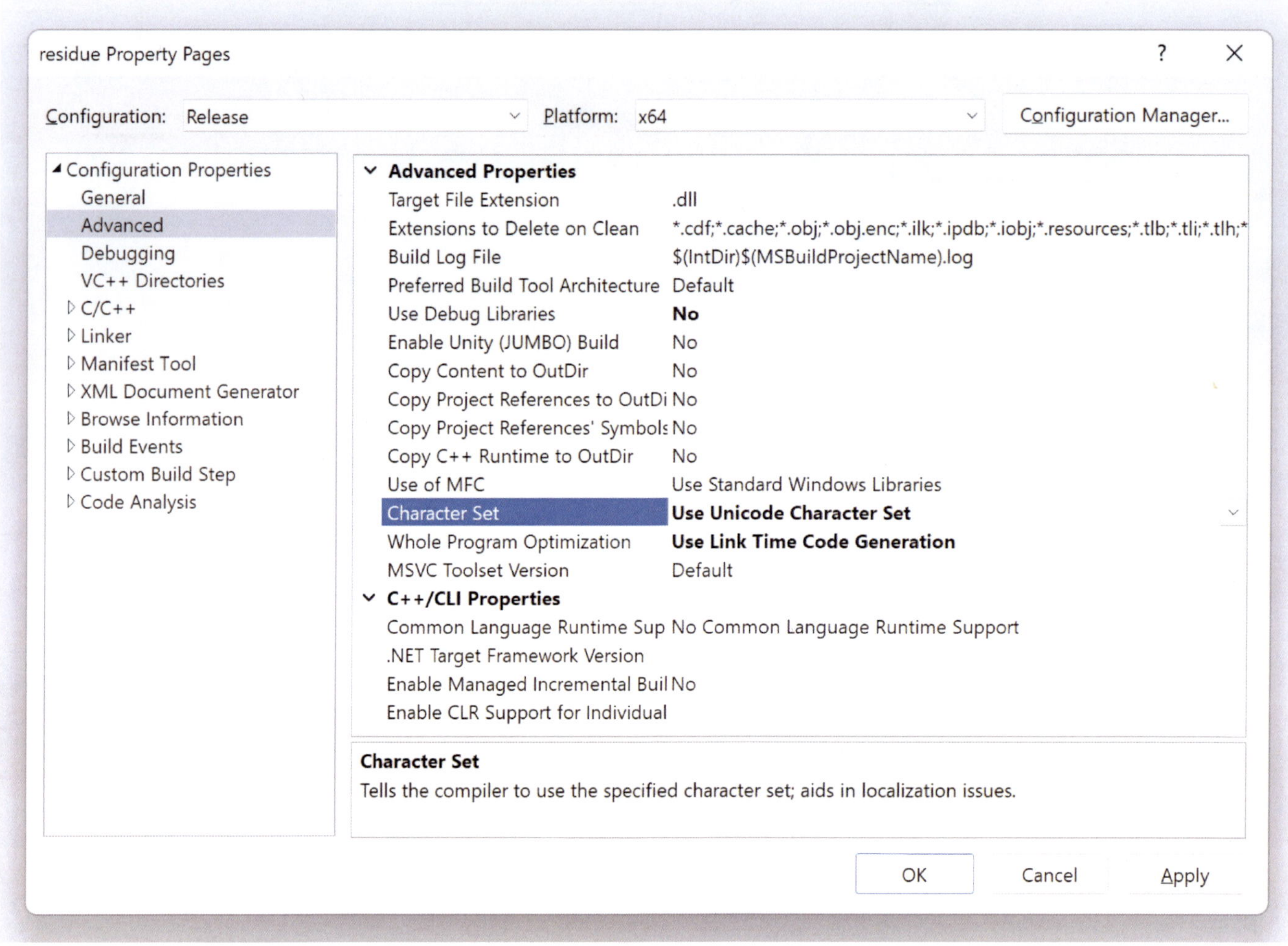

13. Set Runtime Library to Multi-threaded (/MT):

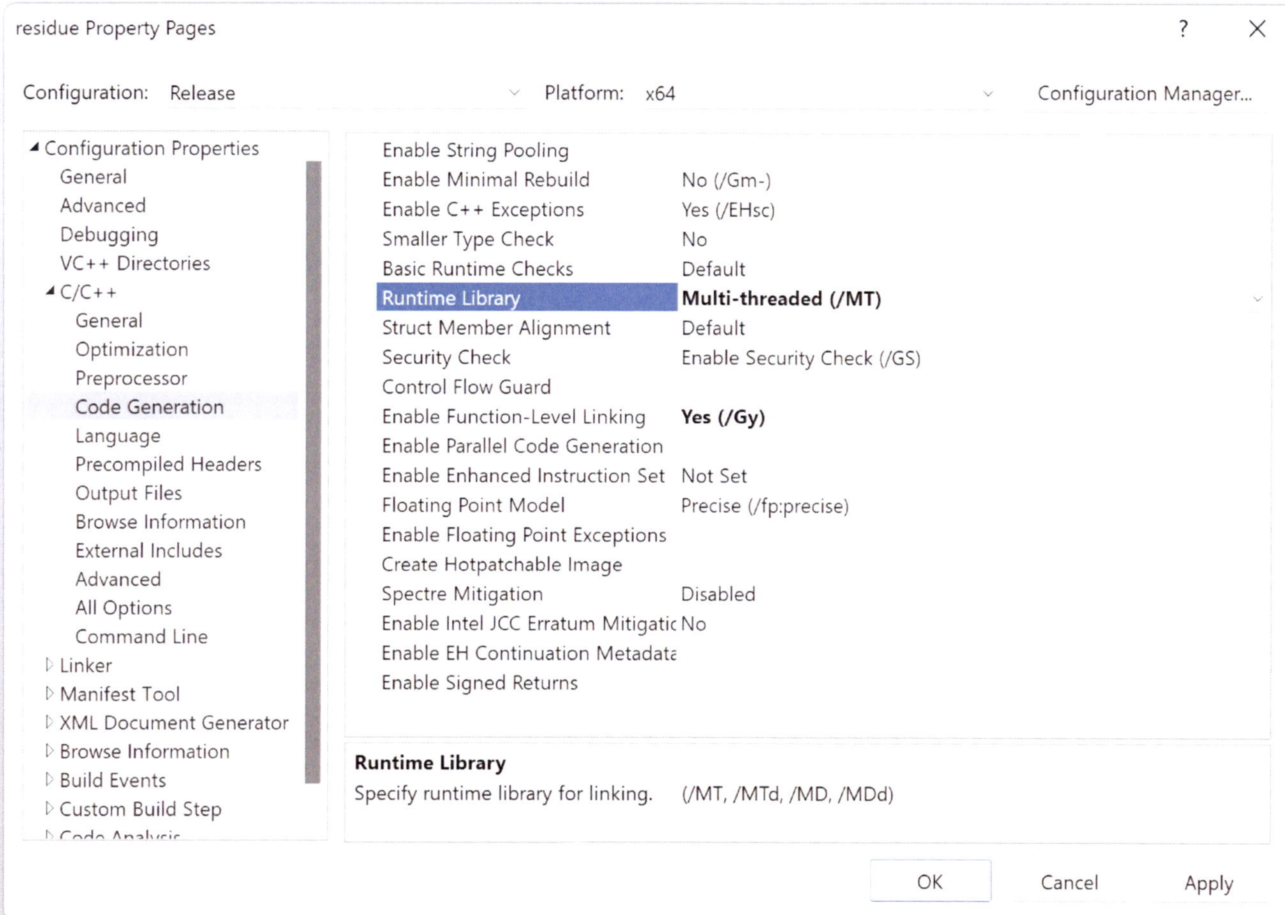

14. We now build the Release x64 configuration. If everything was done correctly, we should have no errors:

```
Rebuild started...
1>------ Rebuild All started: Project: residue, Configuration: Release x64 ------
1>residue.cpp
1>   Creating library C:\EWMDA-Dumps\residue\x64\Release\residue.lib and object C:\EWMDA-Dumps\residue\x64\Release\residue.exp
1>Generating code
1>Previous IPDB not found, fall back to full compilation.
1>All 985 functions were compiled because no usable IPDB/IOBJ from previous compilation was found.
1>Finished generating code
1>residue.vcxproj -> C:\EWMDA-Dumps\residue\x64\Release\residue.dll
========== Rebuild All: 1 succeeded, 0 failed, 0 skipped ==========
```

15. Open \EWMDA-Dumps\Complete\x64\MEMORY-W11.DMP.

```
Microsoft (R) Windows Debugger Version 10.0.27704.1001 AMD64
Copyright (c) Microsoft Corporation. All rights reserved.


Loading Dump File [C:\EWMDA-Dumps\Complete\x64\MEMORY-W11.DMP]
```

```
Kernel Bitmap Dump File: Full address space is available


************* Path validation summary **************
Response                         Time (ms)     Location
Deferred                                       srv*
Symbol search path is: srv*
Executable search path is:
Windows 10 Kernel Version 22000 MP (2 procs) Free x64
Product: WinNt, suite: TerminalServer SingleUserTS Personal
Edition build lab: 22000.1.amd64fre.co_release.210604-1628
Kernel base = 0xfffff806`61e00000 PsLoadedModuleList = 0xfffff806`62a296b0
Debug session time: Sat Nov 13 23:17:16.607 2021 (UTC + 1:00)
System Uptime: 0 days 0:03:06.813
Loading Kernel Symbols
..............................................................
...............................................................
...............................................................
..
Loading User Symbols
..................................
Loading unloaded module list
........
For analysis of this file, run !analyze -v
nt!KeBugCheckEx:
fffff806`62215590 mov     qword ptr [rsp+8],rcx ss:0018:ffffbe82`96f64670=000000000000000a
```

16. We open a log file since we have some real memory output from the extension:

```
0: kd> .logopen C:\EWMDA-Dumps\Complete\x64\EW2.log
Opened log file 'C:\EWMDA-Dumps\Complete\x64\EW2.log'
```

17. Load the built residue extension and execute some commands:

```
0: kd> .load C:\EWMDA-Dumps\residue\x64\Release\residue
```

```
0: kd> !help
Residue Debugger Extension DLL (Version 1.0.0.0)
Commands:
    search address size value [level] [0]     - Deep search of pointer-sized values with level
of dereferences.
```

```
0: kd> ? @rsp
Evaluate expression: -72006888962456 = ffffbe82`96f64668
```

```
0: kd> !search ffffbe8296f64668 1 0
ffffbe8296f64668 fffff806622281a9
```

```
0: kd> !search ffffbe8296f64668 10 0
ffffbe8296f64668 fffff806622281a9
ffffbe8296f64670 000000000000000a
ffffbe8296f64678 ffffac8a0d8ea010
ffffbe8296f64680 0000000000000002
ffffbe8296f64688 0000000000000000
ffffbe8296f64690 fffff80660571981
ffffbe8296f64698 0000000000000000
ffffbe8296f646a0 0000000000000000
ffffbe8296f646a8 0000000000000000
```

```
ffffbe8296f646b0 0000000000000000
ffffbe8296f646b8 0000000000000000
ffffbe8296f646c0 0000000000000000
ffffbe8296f646c8 0000000000000000
ffffbe8296f646d0 0000000000000000
ffffbe8296f646d8 0000000000000000
ffffbe8296f646e0 0000000000000000

0: kd> !search ffffbe8296f64668 10 0 1 1
ffffbe8296f64668 fffff806622281a9 nt!KiBugCheckDispatch
ffffbe8296f64670 000000000000000a
ffffbe8296f64678 ffffac8a0d8ea010
ffffbe8296f64680 0000000000000002
ffffbe8296f64688 0000000000000000
ffffbe8296f64690 fffff80660571981 myfault
ffffbe8296f64698 0000000000000000
ffffbe8296f646a0 0000000000000000
ffffbe8296f646a8 0000000000000000
ffffbe8296f646b0 0000000000000000
ffffbe8296f646b8 0000000000000000
ffffbe8296f646c0 0000000000000000
ffffbe8296f646c8 0000000000000000
ffffbe8296f646d0 0000000000000000
ffffbe8296f646d8 0000000000000000
ffffbe8296f646e0 0000000000000000

0: kd> !search ffffbe8296f64668 10 0 2
ffffbe8296f64668 fffff806622281a9 666666666666c390
ffffbe8296f64670 000000000000000a 0000000000000bad
ffffbe8296f64678 ffffac8a0d8ea010 0000000000000bad
ffffbe8296f64680 0000000000000002 0000000000000bad
ffffbe8296f64688 0000000000000000 0000000000000bad
ffffbe8296f64690 fffff80660571981 0010009b8d48038b
ffffbe8296f64698 0000000000000000 0000000000000bad
ffffbe8296f646a0 0000000000000000 0000000000000bad
ffffbe8296f646a8 0000000000000000 0000000000000bad
ffffbe8296f646b0 0000000000000000 0000000000000bad
ffffbe8296f646b8 0000000000000000 0000000000000bad
ffffbe8296f646c0 0000000000000000 0000000000000bad
ffffbe8296f646c8 0000000000000000 0000000000000bad
ffffbe8296f646d0 0000000000000000 0000000000000bad
ffffbe8296f646d8 0000000000000000 0000000000000bad
ffffbe8296f646e0 0000000000000000 0000000000000bad

0: kd> !search ffffbe8296f64668 10 0 3
ffffbe8296f64668 fffff806622281a9 666666666666c390 0000000000000bad
ffffbe8296f64670 000000000000000a 0000000000000bad 0000000000000bad
ffffbe8296f64678 ffffac8a0d8ea010 0000000000000bad 0000000000000bad
ffffbe8296f64680 0000000000000002 0000000000000bad 0000000000000bad
ffffbe8296f64688 0000000000000000 0000000000000bad 0000000000000bad
ffffbe8296f64690 fffff80660571981 0010009b8d48038b 0000000000000bad
ffffbe8296f64698 0000000000000000 0000000000000bad 0000000000000bad
ffffbe8296f646a0 0000000000000000 0000000000000bad 0000000000000bad
ffffbe8296f646a8 0000000000000000 0000000000000bad 0000000000000bad
ffffbe8296f646b0 0000000000000000 0000000000000bad 0000000000000bad
ffffbe8296f646b8 0000000000000000 0000000000000bad 0000000000000bad
ffffbe8296f646c0 0000000000000000 0000000000000bad 0000000000000bad
ffffbe8296f646c8 0000000000000000 0000000000000bad 0000000000000bad
ffffbe8296f646d0 0000000000000000 0000000000000bad 0000000000000bad
```

```
ffffbe8296f646d8 0000000000000000 0000000000000bad 0000000000000bad
ffffbe8296f646e0 0000000000000000 0000000000000bad 0000000000000bad

0: kd> !search ffffbe8296f64668 30 0 3
ffffbe8296f64668 fffff806622281a9 666666666666c390 0000000000000bad
ffffbe8296f64670 000000000000000a 0000000000000bad 0000000000000bad
ffffbe8296f64678 ffffac8a0d8ea010 0000000000000bad 0000000000000bad
ffffbe8296f64680 0000000000000002 0000000000000bad 0000000000000bad
ffffbe8296f64688 0000000000000000 0000000000000bad 0000000000000bad
ffffbe8296f64690 fffff80660571981 0010009b8d48038b 0000000000000bad
ffffbe8296f64698 0000000000000000 0000000000000bad 0000000000000bad
ffffbe8296f646a0 0000000000000000 0000000000000bad 0000000000000bad
ffffbe8296f646a8 0000000000000000 0000000000000bad 0000000000000bad
ffffbe8296f646b0 0000000000000000 0000000000000bad 0000000000000bad
ffffbe8296f646b8 0000000000000000 0000000000000bad 0000000000000bad
ffffbe8296f646c0 0000000000000000 0000000000000bad 0000000000000bad
ffffbe8296f646c8 0000000000000000 0000000000000bad 0000000000000bad
ffffbe8296f646d0 0000000000000000 0000000000000bad 0000000000000bad
ffffbe8296f646d8 0000000000000000 0000000000000bad 0000000000000bad
ffffbe8296f646e0 0000000000000000 0000000000000bad 0000000000000bad
ffffbe8296f646e8 0000000000000000 0000000000000bad 0000000000000bad
ffffbe8296f646f0 0000000000000000 0000000000000bad 0000000000000bad
ffffbe8296f646f8 0000000000000000 0000000000000bad 0000000000000bad
ffffbe8296f64700 0000000000000000 0000000000000bad 0000000000000bad
ffffbe8296f64708 0000000000000000 0000000000000bad 0000000000000bad
ffffbe8296f64710 0000000000000000 0000000000000bad 0000000000000bad
ffffbe8296f64718 0000000000000000 0000000000000bad 0000000000000bad
ffffbe8296f64720 0000000000000000 0000000000000bad 0000000000000bad
ffffbe8296f64728 0000000000000000 0000000000000bad 0000000000000bad
ffffbe8296f64730 0000000000000000 0000000000000bad 0000000000000bad
ffffbe8296f64738 0000000000000000 0000000000000bad 0000000000000bad
ffffbe8296f64740 0000000000000000 0000000000000bad 0000000000000bad
ffffbe8296f64748 0000000000000000 0000000000000bad 0000000000000bad
ffffbe8296f64750 0000000000000000 0000000000000bad 0000000000000bad
ffffbe8296f64758 ffffbd43fa8b2468 ffffc38c306d4f10 ffffc38c306d4910
ffffbe8296f64760 fffffc571d9ef0d5 0000000000000bad 0000000000000bad
ffffbe8296f64768 ffffbd43fa619191 c4834878245c8b48 0000000000000bad
ffffbe8296f64770 ffffac8a0d8ea010 0000000000000bad 0000000000000bad
ffffbe8296f64778 ffffc38c31efb390 0000000000000000 0000000000000bad
ffffbe8296f64780 ffffc38c31efb360 0000000001180006 0000000000000bad
ffffbe8296f64788 ffffc38c31efb370 0000000000060000 0000000000000bad
ffffbe8296f64790 ffffc38c2c4792d0 0000000101500003 0000000000000bad
ffffbe8296f64798 0000000000000001 0000000000000bad 0000000000000bad
ffffbe8296f647a0 ffffc38c34dd8690 0000000000d80005 0000000000000bad
ffffbe8296f647a8 fffff80662224300 0f44d8ebffb0c033 0000000000000bad
ffffbe8296f647b0 0000000000000000 0000000000000bad 0000000000000bad
ffffbe8296f647b8 ffffbd11c0e0c2b8 0000000000000000 0000000000000bad
ffffbe8296f647c0 ffff2703d5aecdf2 0000000000000bad 0000000000000bad
ffffbe8296f647c8 ffffbd11c253e710 000000000002047f 0000000000000bad
ffffbe8296f647d0 0000000000000f4d 0000000000000bad 0000000000000bad
ffffbe8296f647d8 00001f8001000000 0000000000000bad 0000000000000bad
ffffbe8296f647e0 0000000000001000 0000000000000bad 0000000000000bad
```

```
0: kd> !search ffffbe8296f64668 30 0 3 1
ffffbe8296f64668 fffff806622281a9 nt!KiBugCheckDispatch+0x69 666666666666c390 0000000000000bad
ffffbe8296f64670 000000000000000a 0000000000000bad 0000000000000bad
ffffbe8296f64678 ffffac8a0d8ea010 0000000000000bad 0000000000000bad
ffffbe8296f64680 0000000000000002 0000000000000bad 0000000000000bad
ffffbe8296f64688 0000000000000000 0000000000000bad 0000000000000bad
ffffbe8296f64690 fffff80660571981 myfault+0x1981 0010009b8d48038b 0000000000000bad
ffffbe8296f64698 0000000000000000 0000000000000bad 0000000000000bad
ffffbe8296f646a0 0000000000000000 0000000000000bad 0000000000000bad
ffffbe8296f646a8 0000000000000000 0000000000000bad 0000000000000bad
ffffbe8296f646b0 0000000000000000 0000000000000bad 0000000000000bad
ffffbe8296f646b8 0000000000000000 0000000000000bad 0000000000000bad
ffffbe8296f646c0 0000000000000000 0000000000000bad 0000000000000bad
ffffbe8296f646c8 0000000000000000 0000000000000bad 0000000000000bad
ffffbe8296f646d0 0000000000000000 0000000000000bad 0000000000000bad
ffffbe8296f646d8 0000000000000000 0000000000000bad 0000000000000bad
ffffbe8296f646e0 0000000000000000 0000000000000bad 0000000000000bad
ffffbe8296f646e8 0000000000000000 0000000000000bad 0000000000000bad
ffffbe8296f646f0 0000000000000000 0000000000000bad 0000000000000bad
ffffbe8296f646f8 0000000000000000 0000000000000bad 0000000000000bad
ffffbe8296f64700 0000000000000000 0000000000000bad 0000000000000bad
ffffbe8296f64708 0000000000000000 0000000000000bad 0000000000000bad
ffffbe8296f64710 0000000000000000 0000000000000bad 0000000000000bad
ffffbe8296f64718 0000000000000000 0000000000000bad 0000000000000bad
ffffbe8296f64720 0000000000000000 0000000000000bad 0000000000000bad
ffffbe8296f64728 0000000000000000 0000000000000bad 0000000000000bad
ffffbe8296f64730 0000000000000000 0000000000000bad 0000000000000bad
ffffbe8296f64738 0000000000000000 0000000000000bad 0000000000000bad
ffffbe8296f64740 0000000000000000 0000000000000bad 0000000000000bad
ffffbe8296f64748 0000000000000000 0000000000000bad 0000000000000bad
ffffbe8296f64750 0000000000000000 0000000000000bad 0000000000000bad
ffffbe8296f64758 ffffbd43fa8b2468 win32kbase!gDomainHookLock+0x0 ffffc38c306d4f10 ffffc38c306d4910
ffffbe8296f64760 fffffc571d9ef0d5 0000000000000bad 0000000000000bad
ffffbe8296f64768 ffffbd43fa619191 win32kbase!ThreadUnlock1+0x71 c4834878245c8b48 0000000000000bad
ffffbe8296f64770 ffffac8a0d8ea010 0000000000000bad 0000000000000bad
ffffbe8296f64778 ffffc38c31efb390 0000000000000000 0000000000000bad
ffffbe8296f64780 ffffc38c31efb360 0000000001180006 0000000000000bad
ffffbe8296f64788 ffffc38c31efb370 0000000000060000 0000000000000bad
ffffbe8296f64790 ffffc38c2c4792d0 0000000101500003 0000000000000bad
ffffbe8296f64798 0000000000000001 0000000000000bad 0000000000000bad
ffffbe8296f647a0 ffffc38c34dd8690 0000000000d80005 0000000000000bad
ffffbe8296f647a8 fffff80662224300 nt!KiPageFault0x440 0f44d8ebffb0c033 0000000000000bad
ffffbe8296f647b0 0000000000000000 0000000000000bad 0000000000000bad
ffffbe8296f647b8 ffffbd11c0e0c2b8 0000000000000000 0000000000000bad
ffffbe8296f647c0 ffff2703d5aecdf2 0000000000000bad 0000000000000bad
ffffbe8296f647c8 ffffbd11c253e710 000000000002047f 0000000000000bad
ffffbe8296f647d0 0000000000000f4d 0000000000000bad 0000000000000bad
ffffbe8296f647d8 00001f8001000000 0000000000000bad 0000000000000bad
ffffbe8296f647e0 0000000000001000 0000000000000bad 0000000000000bad
```

18. We close logging before exiting WinDbg:

```
0: kd> .logclose
Closing open log file C:\EWMDA-Dumps\Complete\x64\EW2.log
```

19. We exit WinDbg.

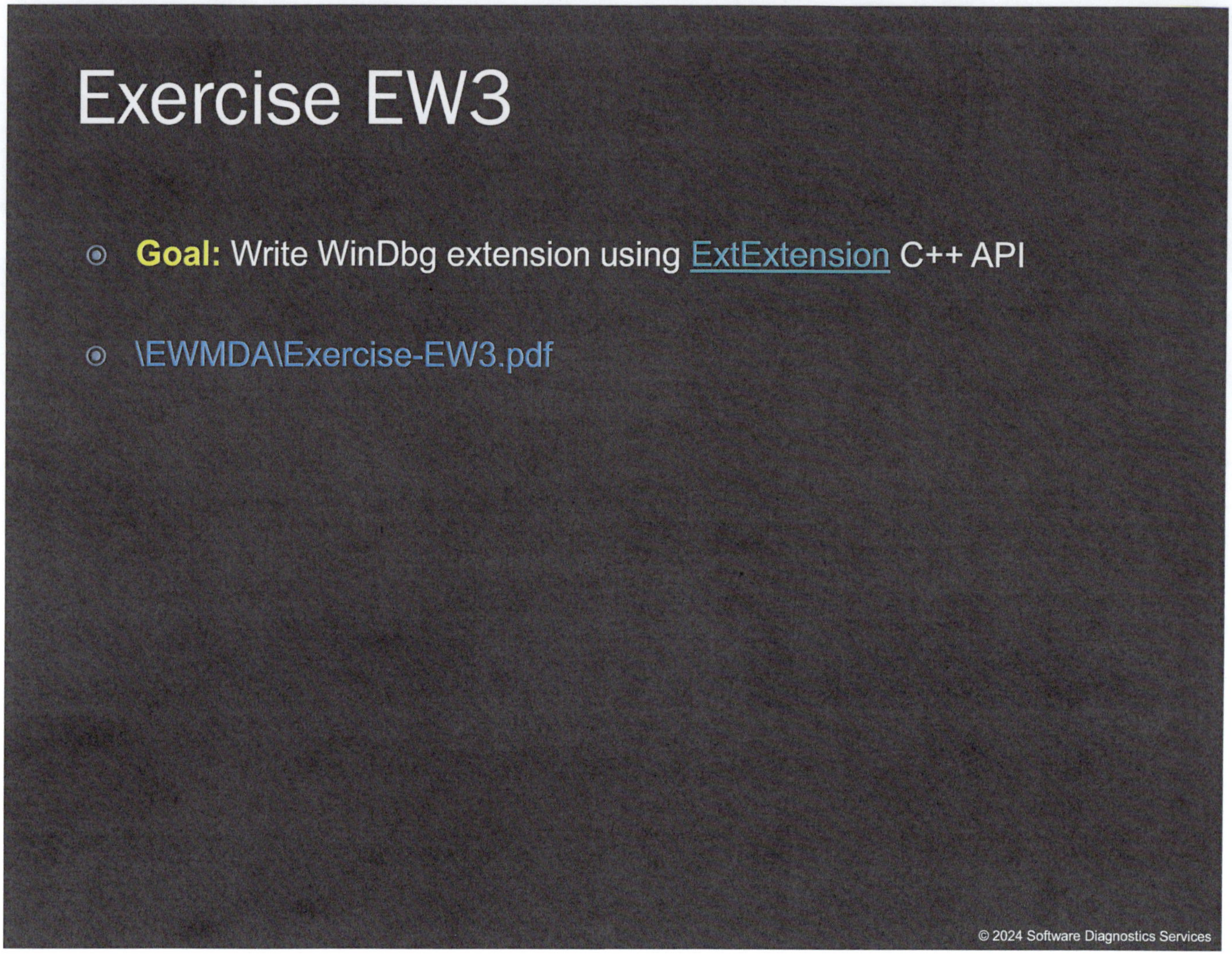
Exercise EW3
Goal: Write WinDbg extension using ExtExtension C++ API
\EWMDA\Exercise-EW3.pdf
© 2024 Software Diagnostics Services

ExtExtension
https://learn.microsoft.com/en-us/windows-hardware/drivers/debugger/extextension

Exercise EW3: Writing WinDbg Extension (ExtExtension C++ API)

Goal: Write WinDbg extension using ExtExtension[25] C++ API.

Prerequisites: Visual Studio Community 2022 with Desktop Development with C++ and Windows 11 SDK version 10.0.22621.0. Debugging Tools for Windows (see Exercise E0).

1. Launch Visual Studio 2022.

2. Choose Create New Project:

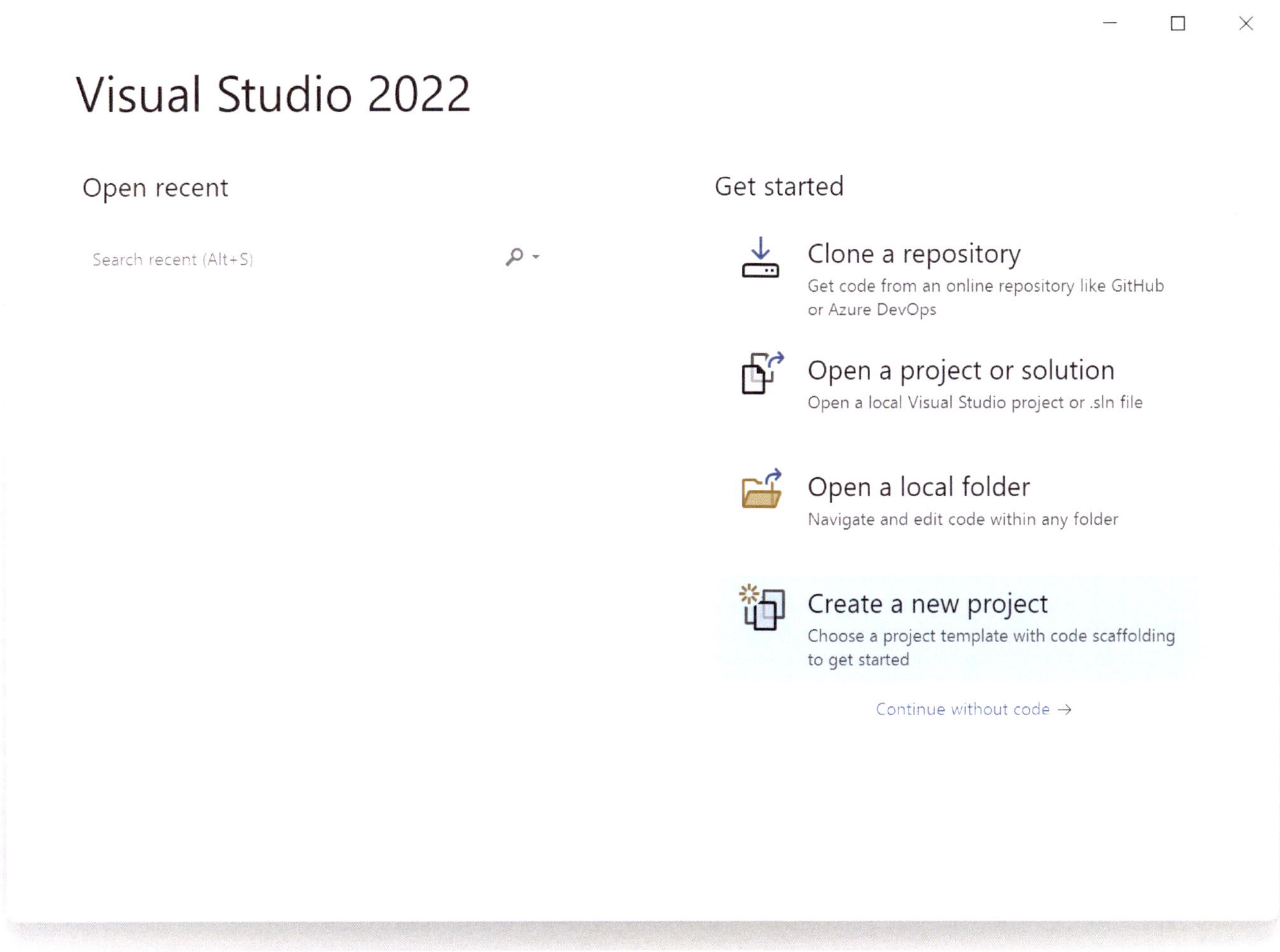

[25] https://learn.microsoft.com/en-us/windows-hardware/drivers/debugger/extextension

3. Select Empty Project type:

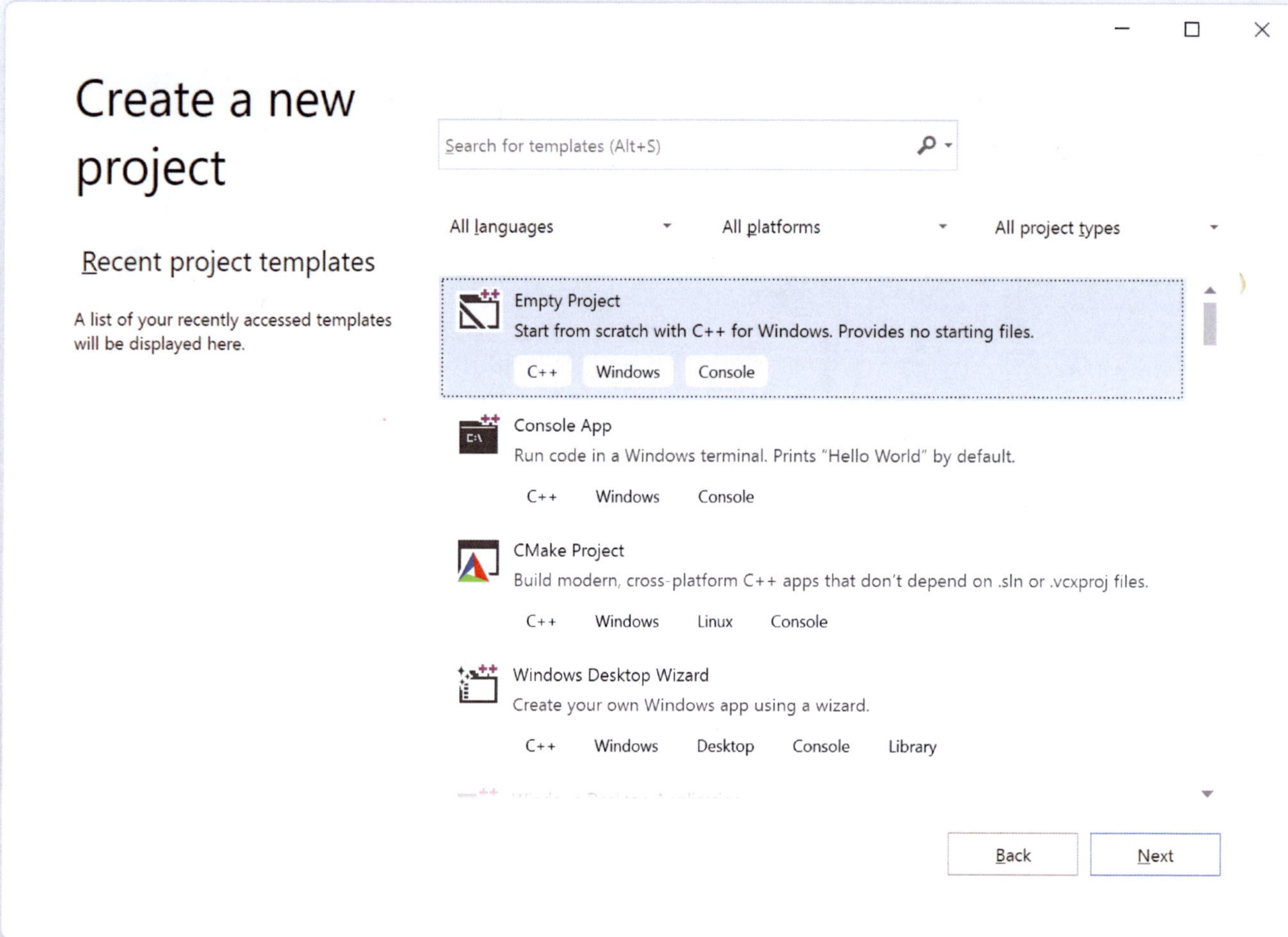

4.	Name the solution and project **checklist2**. We are going to reimplement the **checklist** extension and add DML support to it.

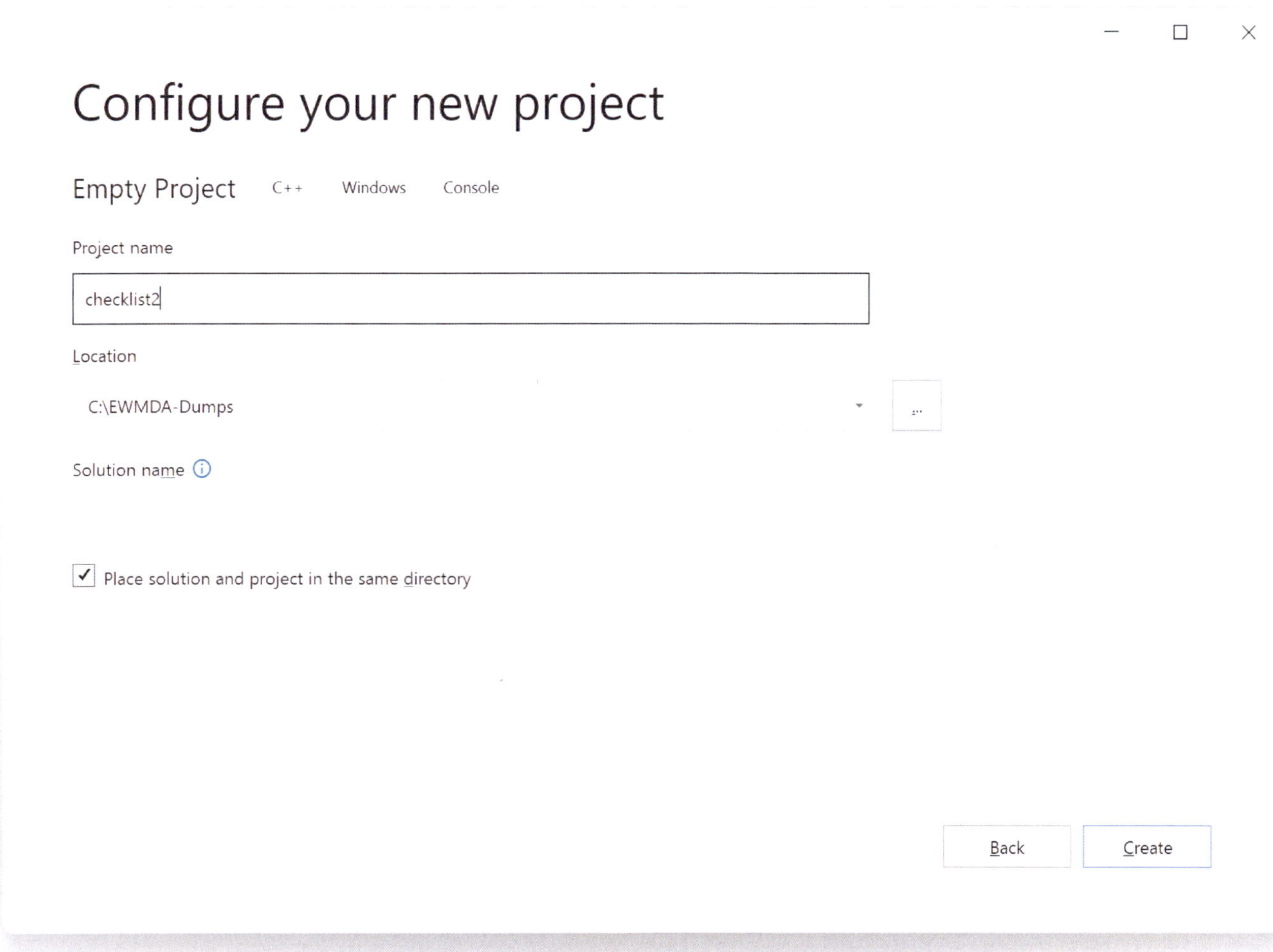

5.	Create the project and change the current Solution Configuration to Release.

6.	Add Module-Definition File (*.def) *checklist2.def* to the list of project files.

7.	Add the following code to *checklist2.def*.

```
EXPORTS

; exported functions implement !help and !checklist WinDbg extension commands

    help
    checklist

; exported service functions provided for WinDbg

    DebugExtensionNotify
    DebugExtensionInitialize
    DebugExtensionUninitialize
```

8. Add *checklist2.cpp* to Source files.

9. Add the following code to *checklist2.cpp*.

```
#include <windows.h>
#include <engextcpp.hpp>

class EXT_CLASS : public ExtExtension
{
public:
```

There is no need to declare and define the **!help** command as its output is generated automatically from command definitions.

```
        EXT_COMMAND_METHOD(checklist);
};

EXT_DECLARE_GLOBALS();
```

The definition of the extension command includes the specification for the help string.

```
EXT_COMMAND(checklist,
        "Shows the current memory analysis checklist.",
        "{;s,o,d="";category;Shows the current memory analysis checklist for the specified category.}")
{
        PCSTR args = GetUnnamedArgStr(0);

        switch (toupper(args[0]))
        {
        case 'G':
                Dml(
                        "General Memory Analysis Checklist:\n\n"
                        "Symbol servers (.symfix)\n"
                        "Internal database(s) search\n"
                        "Google or Microsoft search for suspected components as this could be a known issue. Sometimes
a simple search immediately points to the fix on a vendor's site\n"
                        "The tool used to save a dump (to flag false positive, incomplete or inconsistent dumps)\n"
                        "OS/SP version (version)\n"
                        "Language\n"
                        "Debug time\n"
                        "System uptime\n"
                        "Computer name (dS srv!srvcomputername or !envvar COMPUTERNAME)\n"
                        "List of loaded and unloaded modules (lmv or !dlls)\n"
                        "Hardware configuration (!sysinfo)\n"
                        ".kframes 1000\n"
                        "\n"
                        "<link cmd=\"!checklist\">Back</link>\n");
                break;
        case 'A':
                Dml(
                        "Memory Analysis Checklist for Application or Service:\n\n"
                        "Default analysis (!analyze -v or !analyze -v -hang for hangs)\n"
                        "Critical sections (!cs -s -l -o, !locks) for both crashes and hangs\n"
                        "Component timestamps, duplication and paths. DLL Hell? (lmv and !dlls)\n"
                        "Do any newer components exist?\n"
                        "Process threads (~*kv or !uniqstack) for multiple exceptions and blocking functions\n"
                        "Process uptime\n"
                        "Your components on the full raw stack of the problem thread\n"
                        "Your components on the full raw stack of the main application thread\n"
                        "Process size\n"
                        "Number of threads\n"
                        "Gflags value (!gflag)\n"
                        "Time consumed by threads (!runaway)\n"
                        "Environment (!peb)\n"
                        "Import table (!dh)\n"
                        "Hooked functions (!chkimg)\n"
```

```
                    "Exception handlers (!exchain)\n"
                    "Computer name (!envvar COMPUTERNAME)\n"
                    "Process heap stats and validation (!heap -s, !heap -s -v)\n"
                    "CLR threads? (mscorwks or clr modules on stack traces) Yes: use .NET checklist\n"
                    "Hidden (unhandled and handled) exceptions on thread raw stacks\n"
                    "\n"
                    "<link cmd=\"!checklist\">Back</link>\n");
            break;
        case 'S':
            Dml(
                    "Memory Analysis Checklist for System Hang:\n\n"
                    "Default analysis (!analyze -v -hang)\n"
                    "ERESOURCE contention (!locks)\n"
                    "Processes and virtual memory including session space (!vm 4)\n"
                    "Important services are present and not hanging (for example, terminal or IMA services for
Citrix environments)\n"
                    "Pools (!poolused)\n"
                    "Waiting threads (!stacks)\n"
                    "Critical system queues (!exqueue f)\n"
                    "I/O (!irpfind)\n"
                    "The list of all thread stack traces (!process 0 3f)\n"
                    "LPC/ALPC chain for suspected threads (!lpc message or !alpc /m after search for \"Waiting for
reply to LPC\" or \"Waiting for reply to ALPC\" in !process 0 3f output)\n"
                    "Mutants (search for \"Mutants - owning thread\" in !process 0 3f output)\n"
                    "Critical sections for suspected processes (!cs -l -o -s)\n"
                    "Sessions, session processes (!session, !sprocess)\n"
                    "Processes (size, handle table size) (!process 0 0)\n"
                    "Running threads (!running)\n"
                    "Ready threads (!ready)\n"
                    "DPC queues (!dpcs)\n"
                    "The list of APCs (!apc)\n"
                    "Internal queued spinlocks (!qlocks)\n"
                    "Computer name (dS srv!srvcomputername)\n"
                    "File cache, VACB (!filecache)\n"
                    "File objects for blocked thread IRPs (!irp -> !fileobj)\n"
                    "Network (!ndiskd.miniports and !ndiskd.pktpools)\n"
                    "Disk (!scsikd.classext -> !scsikd.classext class_device 2)\n"
                    "Modules rdbss, mrxdav, mup, mrxsmb in stack traces\n"
                    "Functions Ntfs!Ntfs* and nt!Fs* in stack traces\n"
                    "\n"
                    "<link cmd=\"!checklist\">Back</link>\n");
            break;
        case 'B':
            Dml(
                    "Memory Analysis Checklist for BSOD:\n\n"
                    "Default analysis (!analyze -v)\n"
                    "Pool address (!pool)\n"
                    "Component timestamps (lmv)\n"
                    "Processes and virtual memory (!vm 4)\n"
                    "Current threads on other processors\n"
                    "Raw stack\n"
                    "Bugcheck description (including ln exception address for corrupt or truncated dumps)\n"
                    "Bugcheck callback data (!bugdump for systems prior to Windows XP SP1)\n"
                    "Bugcheck secondary callback data (.enumtag)\n"
                    "Computer name (dS srv!srvcomputername)\n"
                    "Hardware configuration (!sysinfo)\n"
                    "\n"
                    "<link cmd=\"!checklist\">Back</link>\n");
            break;
        case '.':
        case 'N':
            Dml(
                    "Memory Analysis Checklist for .NET Application or Service:\n\n"
                    "CLR module and SOS extension versions (lmv and .chain)\n"
                    "Managed exceptions (~*e !pe)\n"
                    "Nested managed exceptions (!pe -nested)\n"
                    "Managed threads (!Threads -special)\n"
                    "Managed stack traces (~*e !CLRStack)\n"
                    "Managed execution residue (~*e !DumpStackObjects and !DumpRuntimeTypes)\n"
                    "Managed heap (!VerifyHeap, !DumpHeap -stat and !eeheap -gc)\n"
                    "GC handles (!GCHandles, !GCHandleLeaks)\n"
                    "Finalizer queue (!FinalizeQueue)\n"
                    "Sync blocks (!syncblk)\n"
                    "\n"
```

```
                    "<link cmd=\"!checklist\">Back</link>\n");
            break;
        default:
            Dml(
                    "The following memory analysis checklist categories are available:\n\n"
                    "<link cmd=\"!checklist G\">General [G]</link>\n"
                    "<link cmd=\"!checklist A\">Application [A]</link>\n"
                    "<link cmd=\"!checklist S\">System [S]</link>\n"
                    "<link cmd=\"!checklist B\">BSOD [B]</link>\n"
                    "<link cmd=\"!checklist .\">.NET [.]</link>\n");
    }
}
```

10. Copy *engextcpp.cpp* and *engextcpp.hpp* from the Debugging Tools for Windows installation folder (for example, C:\Program Files (x86)\Windows Kits\10\Debuggers\inc) to the project directory (for example, C:\EWMDA-Dumps\checklist2) and add them to the project (Existing Item...).

11. Now, we will configure our project settings.

12. Set Configuration Type to Dynamic Library (.dll):

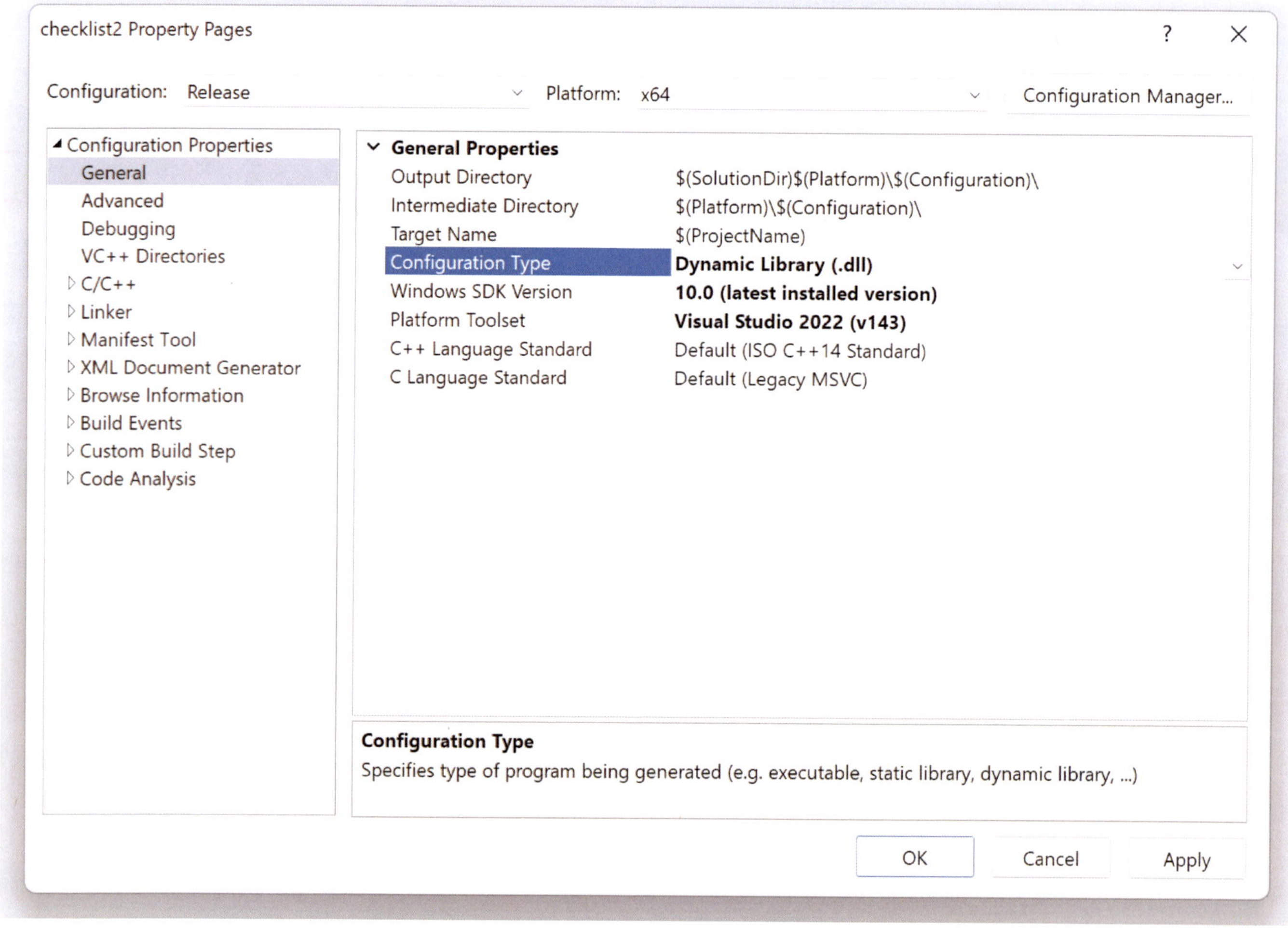

13. Set Use Unicode Character Set and Use Link Time Code Generation properties:

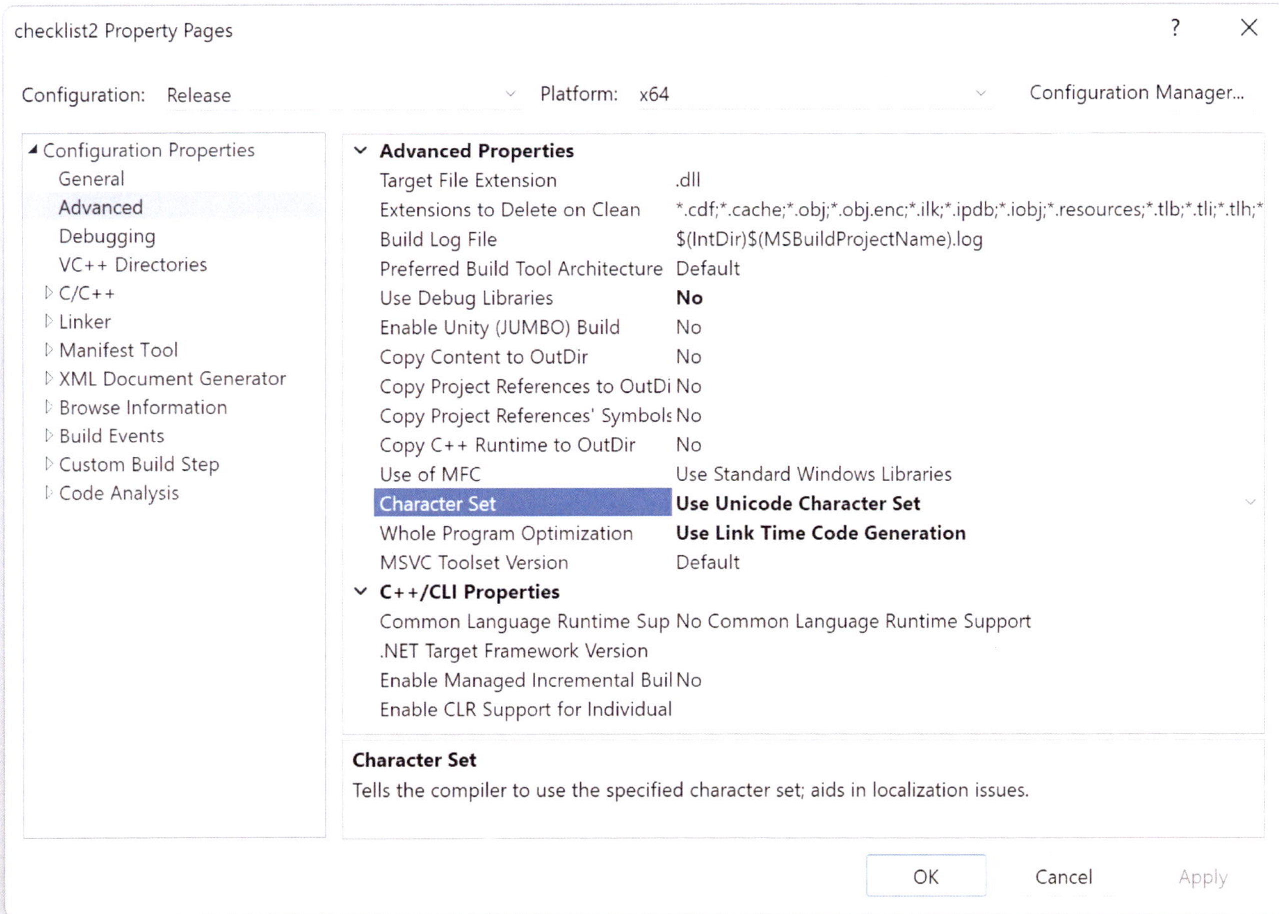

14. Add **.** to Additional Include Directories:

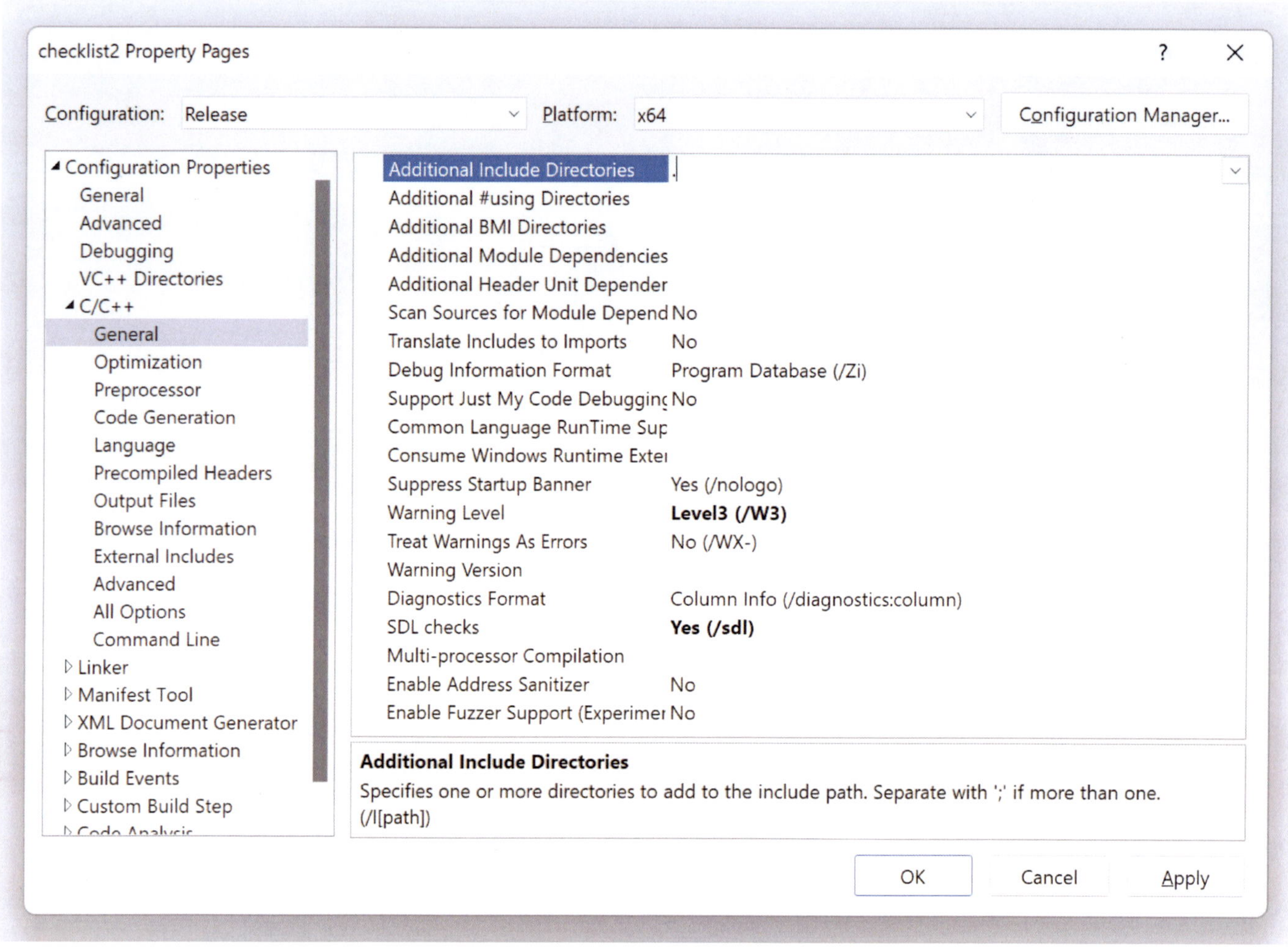

15. Set Runtime Library to Multi-threaded (/MT):

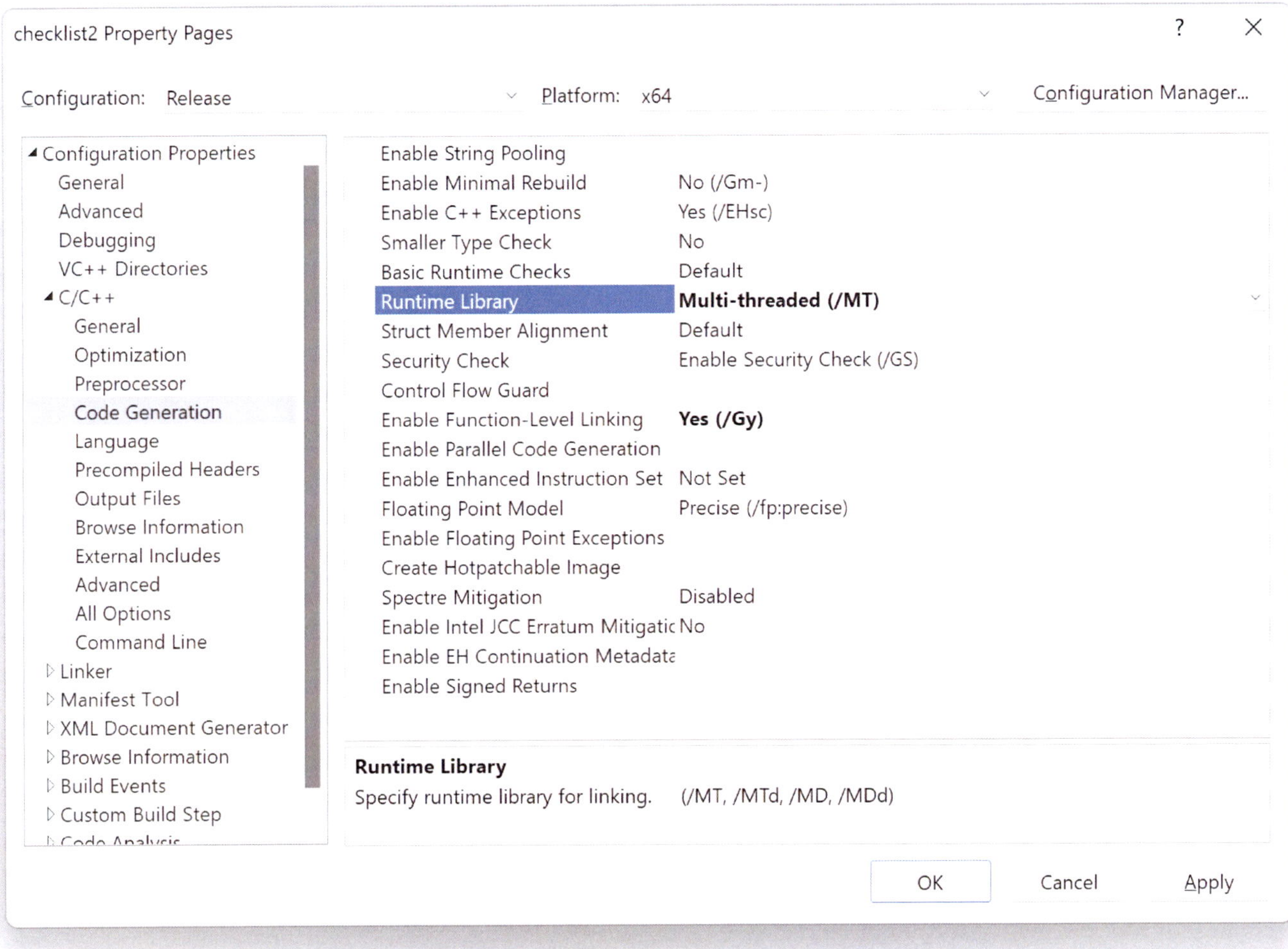

16. Set Conformance mode to Default:

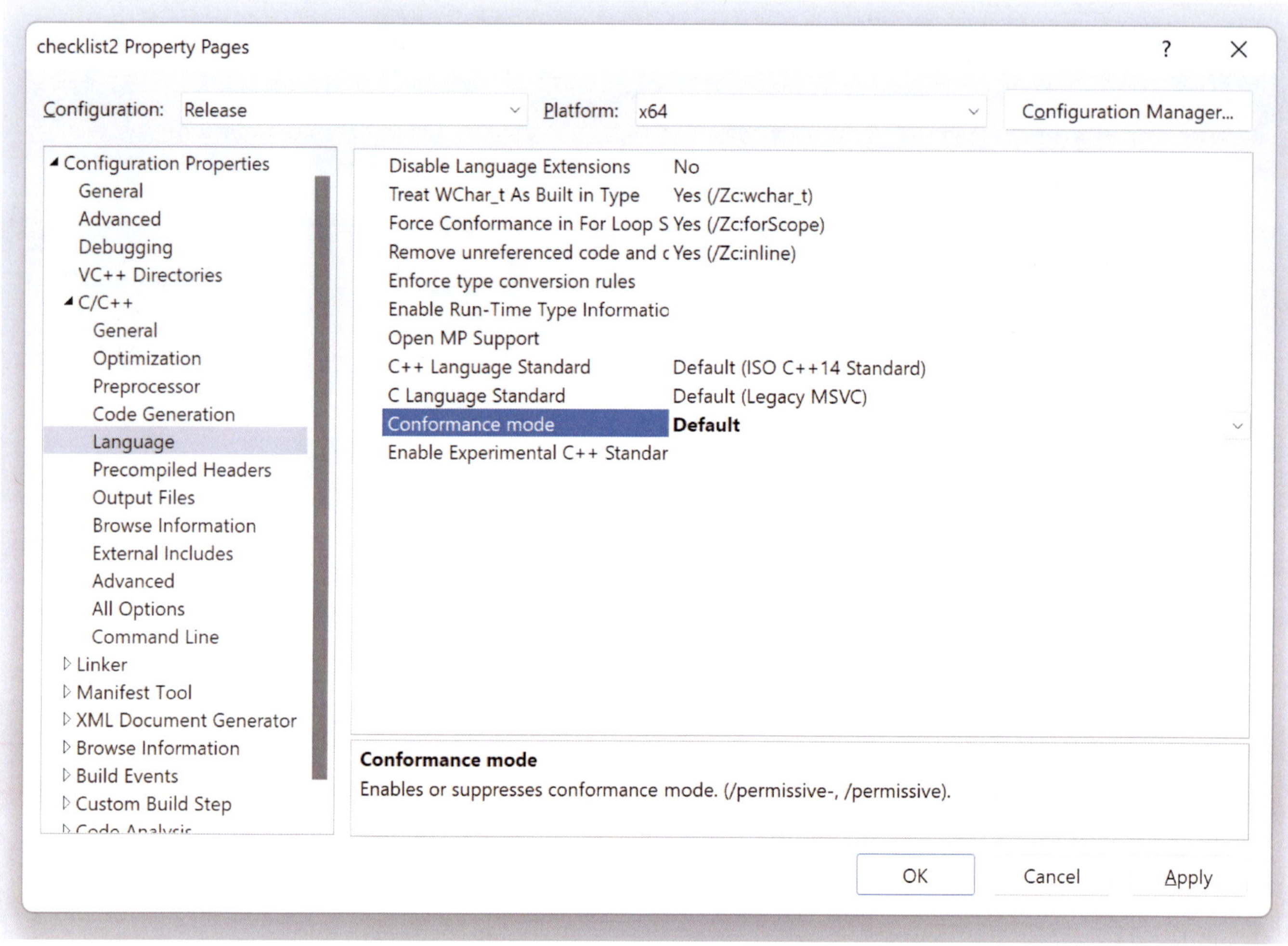

17. We now build the Release x64 configuration. If everything was done correctly, we should have no errors:

```
Build started...
1>------ Build started: Project: checklist2, Configuration: Release x64 ------
1>checklist2.cpp
1>engextcpp.cpp
1>   Creating library C:\EWMDA-Dumps\checklist2\x64\Release\checklist2.lib and object C:\EWMDA-
Dumps\checklist2\x64\Release\checklist2.exp
1>Generating code
1>Previous IPDB not found, fall back to full compilation.
1>All 349 functions were compiled because no usable IPDB/IOBJ from previous compilation was
found.
1>Finished generating code
1>checklist2.vcxproj -> C:\EWMDA-Dumps\checklist2\x64\Release\checklist2.dll
========== Build: 1 succeeded, 0 failed, 0 up-to-date, 0 skipped ==========
```

18. Open \EWMDA-Dumps\Complete\x64\MEMORY-W11.DMP.

```
Microsoft (R) Windows Debugger Version 10.0.27704.1001 AMD64
Copyright (c) Microsoft Corporation. All rights reserved.


Loading Dump File [C:\EWMDA-Dumps\Complete\x64\MEMORY-W11.DMP]
Kernel Bitmap Dump File: Full address space is available


************* Path validation summary **************
Response                         Time (ms)     Location
Deferred                                       srv*
Symbol search path is: srv*
Executable search path is:
Windows 10 Kernel Version 22000 MP (2 procs) Free x64
Product: WinNt, suite: TerminalServer SingleUserTS Personal
Edition build lab: 22000.1.amd64fre.co_release.210604-1628
Kernel base = 0xfffff806`61e00000 PsLoadedModuleList = 0xfffff806`62a296b0
Debug session time: Sat Nov 13 23:17:16.607 2021 (UTC + 1:00)
System Uptime: 0 days 0:03:06.813
Loading Kernel Symbols
...............................................................
................................................................
................................................................
..
Loading User Symbols
...................................
Loading unloaded module list
........
For analysis of this file, run !analyze -v
nt!KeBugCheckEx:
fffff806`62215590 mov     qword ptr [rsp+8],rcx ss:0018:ffffbe82`96f64670=000000000000000a
```

19. Load the built *checklist2* extension and execute some commands:

```
0: kd> .load C:\EWMDA-Dumps\checklist2\x64\Release\checklist2

0: kd> !checklist2.help
Commands for C:\EWMDA-Dumps\checklist2\x64\Release\checklist2.dll:
  !checklist - Shows the current memory analysis checklist.
  !help      - Displays information on available extension commands
!help <cmd> will give more information for a particular command

0: kd> !checklist
The following memory analysis checklist categories are available:

General [G]
Application [A]
System [S]
BSOD [B]
.NET [.]
```

```
0: kd> !checklist B
Memory Analysis Checklist for BSOD:

Default analysis (!analyze -v)
Pool address (!pool)
Component timestamps (lmv)
Processes and virtual memory (!vm 4)
Current threads on other processors
Raw stack
Bugcheck description (including ln exception address for corrupt or truncated dumps)
Bugcheck callback data (!bugdump for systems prior to Windows XP SP1)
Bugcheck secondary callback data (.enumtag)
Computer name (dS srv!srvcomputername)
Hardware configuration (!sysinfo)

Back
```

```
0: kd> !checklist
The following memory analysis checklist categories are available:

General [G]
Application [A]
System [S]
BSOD [B]
.NET [.]
```

20. We exit WinDbg.

Exercise EW4

- **Goal:** Write WinDbg extension using Rust
- \EWMDA\Exercise-EW4.pdf

Exercise EW4: Writing WinDbg Extension (Rust)

Goal: Write WinDbg extension using Rust.

Prerequisites: VS Code and Rust development environment.

1. Create a new Rust library project *checklist-rs*.

```
C:\EWMDA-Dumps>cargo new --lib checklist-rs
     Created library `checklist-rs` package
```

2. Open the checklist-rs folder in VS Code.

3. Open the *Cargo.toml* file and add the following keys and dependencies:

```
[lib]
crate-type = ["cdylib"]

[dependencies]
dbgeng = "0.2"
windows = { version = "0.52", features = ["Win32_Foundation"] }
```

4. Open the *src\lib.rs* file and delete all content.

5. Add the following content:

```
use dbgeng::{client::DebugClient, dlogln};
use windows::core::{IUnknown, Interface, HRESULT, PCSTR};
use windows::Win32::Foundation::{E_ABORT, S_OK};

#[no_mangle]
extern "C" fn help(raw_client: *mut std::ffi::c_void, _args: PCSTR) -> HRESULT {

    let Some(client) = (unsafe { IUnknown::from_raw_borrowed(&raw_client) }) else {
        return E_ABORT;
    };

    let Ok(dbg) = DebugClient::new(client) else {
        return E_ABORT;
    };

    let _ = dlogln!(dbg,
r"Checklist Debugger Extension DLL (Version 1.0.0.0).
Outputs checklist from https://www.dumpanalysis.org/windows-memory-analysis-checklist.

Commands:
    checklist          - Shows the current memory analysis checklist categories.
    checklist category - Shows the current memory analysis checklist for the specified
category.");
```

```
    S_OK
}

#[no_mangle]
extern "C" fn checklist(raw_client: *mut std::ffi::c_void, args: PCSTR) -> HRESULT {

    let Some(client) = (unsafe { IUnknown::from_raw_borrowed(&raw_client) }) else {
        return E_ABORT;
    };

    let Ok(dbg) = DebugClient::new(client) else {
        return E_ABORT;
    };

    let Ok(args) = (unsafe { args.to_string() }) else {
        return E_ABORT;
    };

    let _ = match args.to_uppercase().chars().next() {
        Some('G') => dlogln!(dbg,
r"General Memory Analysis Checklist:

Symbol servers (.symfix)
Internal database(s) search
Google or Microsoft search for suspected components as this could be a known issue. Sometimes a
simple search immediately points to the fix on a vendor's site
The tool used to save a dump (to flag false positive, incomplete or inconsistent dumps)
OS/SP version (version)
Language
Debug time
System uptime
Computer name (dS srv!srvcomputername or !envvar COMPUTERNAME)
List of loaded and unloaded modules (lmv or !dlls)
Hardware configuration (!sysinfo)
.kframes 1000"),

        Some('A') => dlogln!(dbg,
r"Memory Analysis Checklist for Application or Service:

Default analysis (!analyze -v or !analyze -v -hang for hangs)
Critical sections (!cs -s -l -o, !locks) for both crashes and hangs
Component timestamps, duplication and paths. DLL Hell? (lmv and !dlls)
Do any newer components exist?
Process threads (~*kv or !uniqstack) for multiple exceptions and blocking functions
Process uptime
Your components on the full raw stack of the problem thread
Your components on the full raw stack of the main application thread
```

```
Process size
Number of threads
Gflags value (!gflag)
Time consumed by threads (!runaway)
Environment (!peb)
Import table (!dh)
Hooked functions (!chkimg)
Exception handlers (!exchain)
Computer name (!envvar COMPUTERNAME)
Process heap stats and validation (!heap -s, !heap -s -v)
CLR threads? (mscorwks or clr modules on stack traces) Yes: use .NET checklist below
Hidden (unhandled and handled) exceptions on thread raw stacks"),

        Some('S') => dlogln!(dbg,
r#"Memory Analysis Checklist for System Hang:

Default analysis (!analyze -v -hang)
ERESOURCE contention (!locks)
Processes and virtual memory including session space (!vm 4)
Important services are present and not hanging
Pools (!poolused)
Waiting threads (!stacks)
Critical system queues (!exqueue f)
I/O (!irpfind)
The list of all thread stack traces (!process 0 3f)
LPC/ALPC chain for suspected threads (!lpc message or !alpc /m after search for "Waiting for
reply to LPC" or "Waiting for reply to ALPC" in !process 0 3f output)
RPC threads (search for "RPCRT4!OSF" in !process 0 3f output)
Mutants (search for "Mutant - owning thread" in !process 0 3f output)
Critical sections for suspected processes (!cs -l -o -s)
Sessions, session processes (!session, !sprocess)
Processes (size, handle table size) (!process 0 0)
Running threads (!running)
Ready threads (!ready)
DPC queues (!dpcs)
The list of APCs (!apc)
Internal queued spinlocks (!qlocks)
Computer name (dS srv!srvcomputername)
File cache, VACB (!filecache)
File objects for blocked thread IRPs (!irp -> !fileobj)
Network (!ndiskd.miniports and !ndiskd.pktpools)
Disk (!scsikd.classext -> !scsikd.classext class_device 2)
Modules rdbss, mrxdav, mup, mrxsmb in stack traces
Functions Ntfs!Ntfs*, nt!Fs* and fltmgr!Flt* in stack traces"#),

        Some('B') => dlogln!(dbg,
r"Memory Analysis Checklist for BSOD:
```

```
Default analysis (!analyze -v)
Pool address (!pool)
Component timestamps (lmv)
Processes and virtual memory (!vm 4)
Current threads on other processors
Raw stack
Bugcheck description (including ln exception address for corrupt or truncated dumps)
Bugcheck callback data (!bugdump for systems prior to Windows XP SP1)
Bugcheck secondary callback data (.enumtag)
Computer name (dS srv!srvcomputername)
Hardware configuration (!sysinfo)"),

        Some('.') | Some('N') => dlogln!(dbg,
r"Memory Analysis Checklist for .NET Application or Service:

CLR module and SOS extension versions (lmv and .chain)
Managed exceptions (~*e !pe)
Nested managed exceptions (!pe -nested)
Managed threads (!Threads -special)
Managed stack traces (~*e !CLRStack)
Managed execution residue (~*e !DumpStackObjects and !DumpRuntimeTypes)
Managed heap (!VerifyHeap, !DumpHeap -stat and !eeheap -gc)
GC handles (!GCHandles, !GCHandleLeaks)
Finalizer queue (!FinalizeQueue)
Sync blocks (!syncblk)"),

        _ => dlogln!(dbg,
r"The following memory analysis checklist categories are available:

    G(eneral)
    A(pplication)
    S(ystem)
    B(SOD)
    .(NET)")

    };

    S_OK
}

#[no_mangle]
extern "C" fn DebugExtensionInitialize(_version: *mut u32, _flags: *mut u32) -> HRESULT {
    S_OK
}

#[no_mangle]
extern "C" fn DebugExtensionUninitialize() {
}
```

Note: The code is a fusion of Exercise EW1 *checklist* extension, Exercise EW2 *DbgEng* logic, and Exercise ES8 *snapshot* Rust extension source code.

6. Build the extension.

```
C:\EWMDA-Dumps\checklist-rs> cargo build --release
   Compiling windows_x86_64_msvc v0.52.6
   Compiling anyhow v1.0.89
   Compiling bitflags v2.6.0
   Compiling windows-targets v0.52.6
   Compiling windows-core v0.52.0
   Compiling windows v0.52.0
   Compiling dbgeng v0.2.0
   Compiling checklist-rs v0.1.0 (C:\EWMDA-Dumps\checklist-rs)
    Finished `release` profile [optimized] target(s) in 33.11s
```

7. Open \EWMDA-Dumps\Complete\x64\MEMORY-W11.DMP.

```
Microsoft (R) Windows Debugger Version 10.0.27704.1001 AMD64
Copyright (c) Microsoft Corporation. All rights reserved.


Loading Dump File [C:\EWMDA-Dumps\Complete\x64\MEMORY-W11.DMP]
Kernel Bitmap Dump File: Full address space is available


************* Path validation summary **************
Response                         Time (ms)     Location
Deferred                                       srv*
Symbol search path is: srv*
Executable search path is:
Windows 10 Kernel Version 22000 MP (2 procs) Free x64
Product: WinNt, suite: TerminalServer SingleUserTS Personal
Edition build lab: 22000.1.amd64fre.co_release.210604-1628
Kernel base = 0xfffff806`61e00000 PsLoadedModuleList = 0xfffff806`62a296b0
Debug session time: Sat Nov 13 23:17:16.607 2021 (UTC + 1:00)
System Uptime: 0 days 0:03:06.813
Loading Kernel Symbols
...............................................................
................................................................
................................................................
..
Loading User Symbols
...................................
Loading unloaded module list
........
For analysis of this file, run !analyze -v
nt!KeBugCheckEx:
fffff806`62215590 mov     qword ptr [rsp+8],rcx ss:0018:ffffbe82`96f64670=000000000000000a
```

8. Load the built checklist extension and execute some commands:

```
0: kd> .load C:\EWMDA-Dumps\checklist-rs\target\release\checklist_rs.dll
```

```
0: kd> !help
[dbgeng-rs] Checklist Debugger Extension DLL (Version 1.0.0.0).\nOutputs checklist from
https://www.dumpanalysis.org/windows-memory-analysis-checklist.

Commands:
    checklist          - Shows the current memory analysis checklist categories.
    checklist category - Shows the current memory analysis checklist for the specified
category.
0: kd> !checklist
[dbgeng-rs] The following memory analysis checklist categories are available:

    G(eneral)
    A(pplication)
    S(ystem)
    B(SOD)
    .(NET)

0: kd> !checklist b
[dbgeng-rs] Memory Analysis Checklist for BSOD:

Default analysis (!analyze -v)
Pool address (!pool)
Component timestamps (lmv)
Processes and virtual memory (!vm 4)
Current threads on other processors
Raw stack
Bugcheck description (including ln exception address for corrupt or truncated dumps)
Bugcheck callback data (!bugdump for systems prior to Windows XP SP1)
Bugcheck secondary callback data (.enumtag)
Computer name (dS srv!srvcomputername)
Hardware configuration (!sysinfo)
```

9. We exit WinDbg.

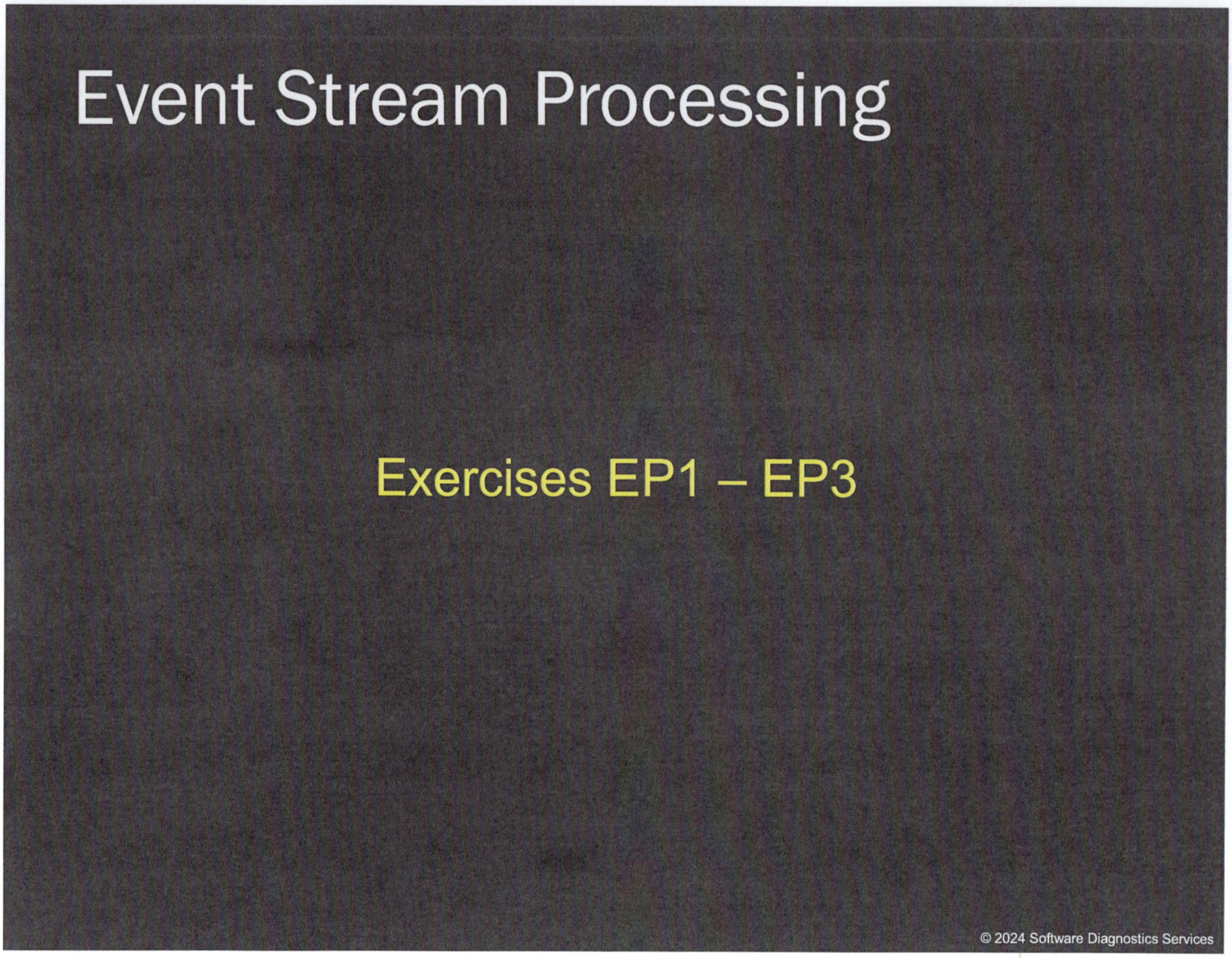
Event Stream Processing
Exercises EP1 – EP3
© 2024 Software Diagnostics Services

In this part, we look at one solution to store and process WinDbg logs: Apache Kafka. I chose it because of my own experience with it. However, there are many other products and platforms, and I may cover some of them in the next edition of this course.

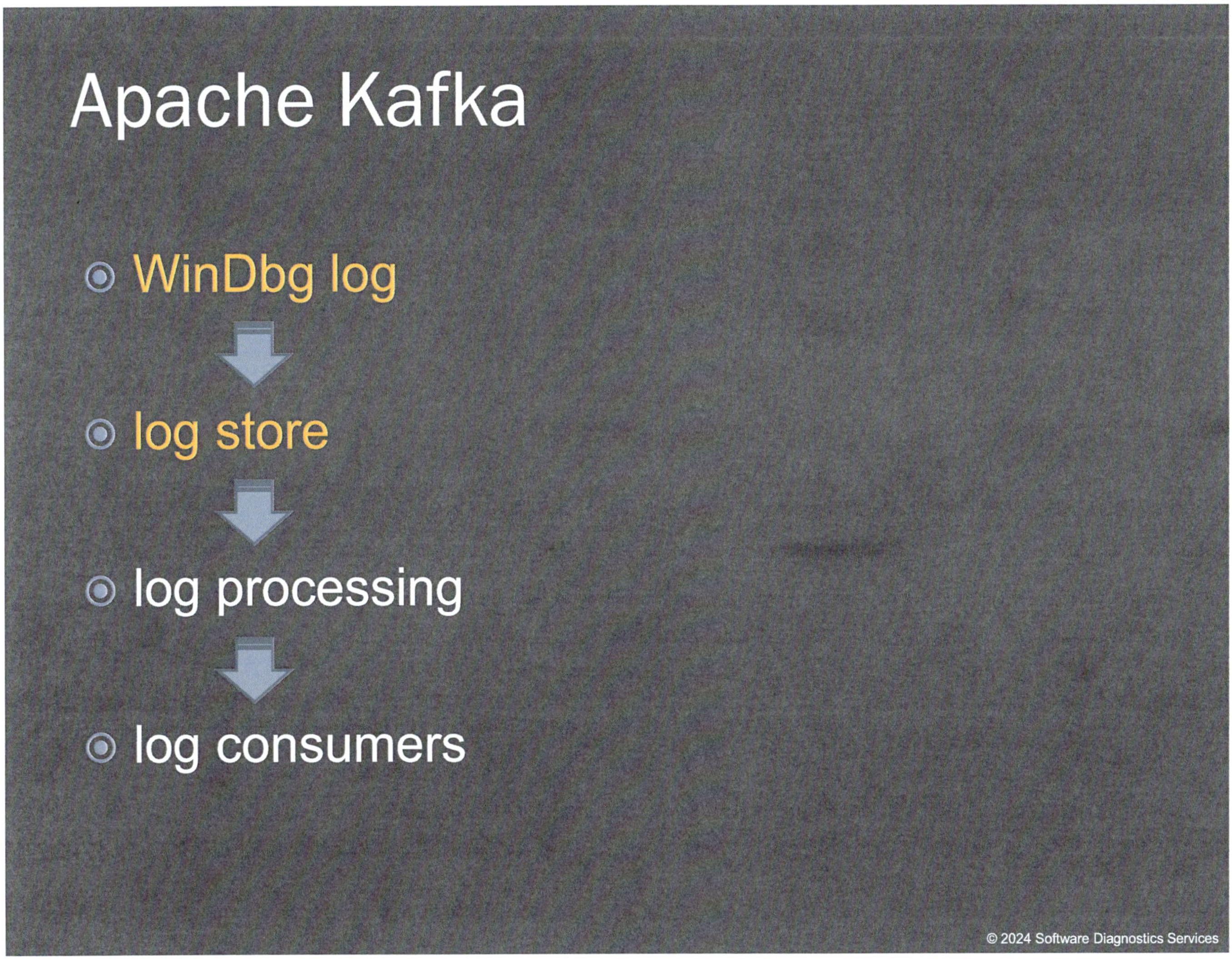

If you have never heard of Kafka, it is a distributed log store and stream processing platform. It is also scalable and has real-time processing capabilities. For our learning purposes, we ignore all these enterprise-level features and use just a single computer installation without any replication. We also cover only storing logs via a simple technique. Writing code using Kafka API is outside the scope of this short training. Please refer to Apache Kafka's official site, which has tutorials, and two books are also mentioned in the References slide.

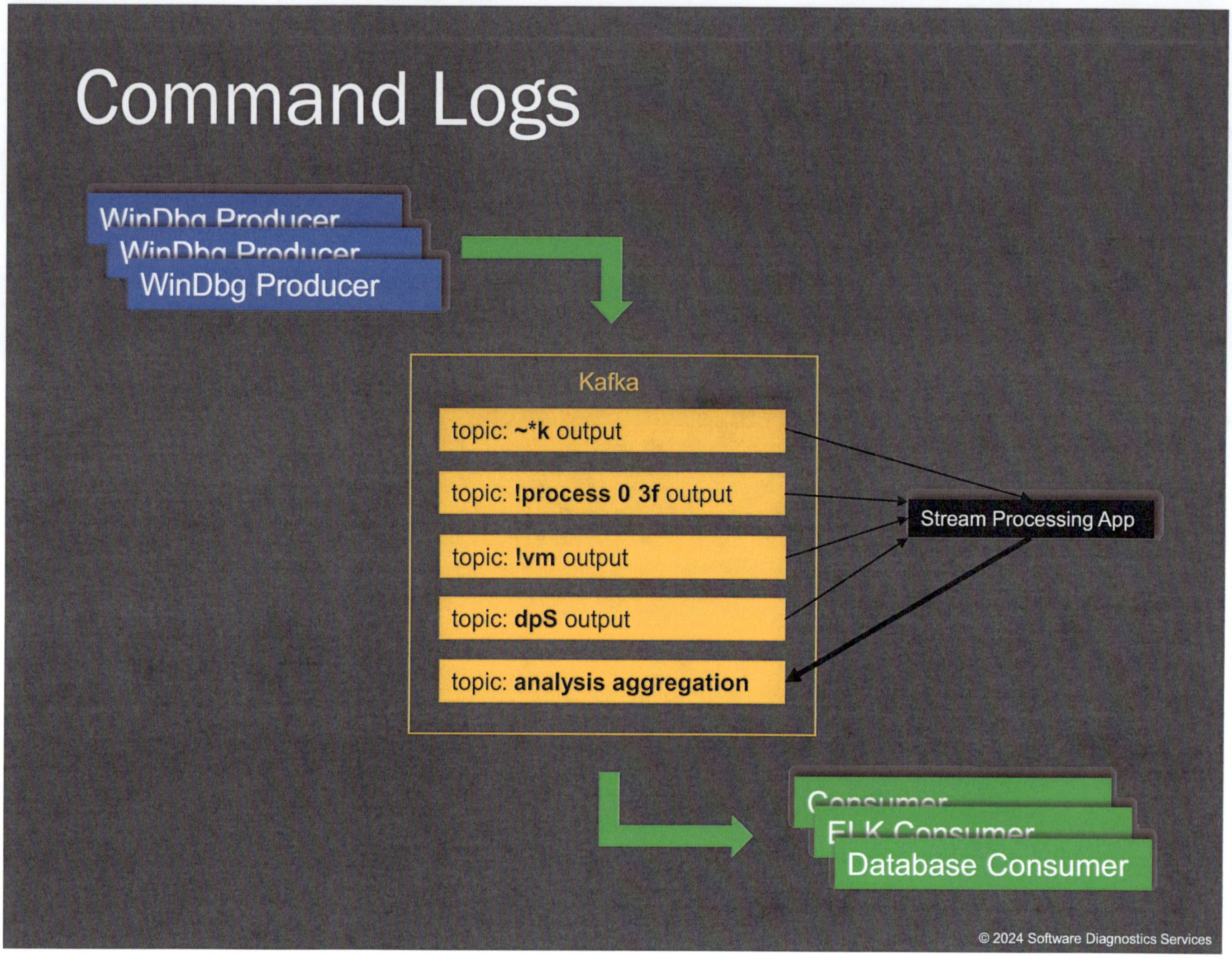

This diagram illustrates a typical architecture involving Kafka. There are producers that emit events of different complexity and in different formats (text, JSON, binary) to named Kafka topics. Optionally, there are applications that read such events in FIFO order, process them, and store results as events in other named Kafka topics. Then, there are consumers that can process events from any topic and, for example, forward them to other platforms for further processing.

Exercise EP1

- **Goal:** Install Apache Kafka and verify that it works correctly
- \EWMDA\Exercise-EP1.pdf

Exercise EP1: Install Kafka Environment

Goal: Install Apache Kafka[26] and verify that it works correctly.

1. Launch WSL2 Debian or Ubuntu.

2. Install JDK:

```
$ sudo apt update
...

$ sudo apt install openjdk-11-jre-headless
...

$ java --version
openjdk 11.0.16 2022-07-19
OpenJDK Runtime Environment (build 11.0.16+8-post-Debian-1deb10u1)
OpenJDK 64-Bit Server VM (build 11.0.16+8-post-Debian-1deb10u1, mixed mode, sharing)
```

3. Download and extract the latest Kafka release (we use version 3.2.1 for Scala 2.13).

```
$ tar -xzf kafka_2.13-3.8.0.tgz

$ cd kafka_2.13-3.8.0
```

4. Start services:

```
~/kafka_2.13-3.8.0$ bin/zookeeper-server-start.sh config/zookeeper.properties &
...

~/kafka_2.13-3.8.0$ bin/kafka-server-start.sh config/server.properties &
...
```

5. Create the *windbg-log* topic and list available topics:

```
~/kafka_2.13-3.8.0$ bin/kafka-topics.sh --create --topic windbg-log --bootstrap-server
localhost:9092
...
Created topic windbg-log.

~/kafka_2.13-3.8.0$ bin/kafka-topics.sh --list --bootstrap-server localhost:9092
windbg-log
```

6. Write a test event:

```
~/kafka_2.13-3.8.0$ echo "Test log event" | bin/kafka-console-producer.sh --topic windbg-log --
bootstrap-server localhost:9092
...
```

[26] https://kafka.apache.org/

7. Read a test event from the beginning:

```
~/kafka_2.13-3.8.0$ bin/kafka-console-consumer.sh --topic windbg-log --from-beginning --
bootstrap-server localhost:9092
...
Test log event
^C
Processed a total of 1 messages
```

8. Describe the *windbg-log* topic:

```
~/kafka_2.13-3.8.0$ bin/kafka-topics.sh --bootstrap-server localhost:9092 --describe --topic
windbg-log
...
Topic: windbg-log       TopicId: Qc8MuODzQ-KAC80rULqIPw PartitionCount: 1
ReplicationFactor: 1    Configs:
        Topic: windbg-log       Partition: 0    Leader: 0       Replicas: 0     Isr: 0  Elr:
N/A          LastKnownElr: N/A
```

9. Shutdown services in reverse order:

```
~/kafka_2.13-3.8.0$ ps
  PID TTY          TIME CMD
   10 pts/0    00:00:00 bash
 2430 pts/0    00:00:03 java
 2865 pts/0    00:00:18 java
 6973 pts/0    00:00:00 ps

~/kafka_2.13-3.8.0$ kill -SIGINT 2865
~/kafka_2.13-3.8.0$ [2024-10-13 07:52:56,572] INFO Terminating process due to signal SIGINT
(org.apache.kafka.common.utils.LoggingSignalHandler)
[2024-10-13 07:52:56,574] INFO [KafkaServer id=0] shutting down (kafka.server.KafkaServer)
[2024-10-13 07:52:56,575] INFO [KafkaServer id=0] Starting controlled shutdown
(kafka.server.KafkaServer)
...
[2024-10-13 07:52:57,535] INFO [KafkaServer id=0] shut down completed
(kafka.server.KafkaServer)

[2]+  Exit 130                bin/kafka-server-start.sh config/server.properties

~/kafka_2.13-3.8.0$ kill -SIGINT 2430
[1]+  Exit 130                bin/zookeeper-server-start.sh config/zookeeper.properties
```

10. Check where our topic is stored:

```
~/kafka_2.13-3.8.0$ ls -l /tmp/kafka-logs/windbg-log-0/
total 20
-rw-r--r-- 1 coredump coredump  0 Oct 13 07:52 00000000000000000000.index
-rw-r--r-- 1 coredump coredump 82 Oct 13 07:50 00000000000000000000.log
-rw-r--r-- 1 coredump coredump 12 Oct 13 07:52 00000000000000000000.timeindex
-rw-r--r-- 1 coredump coredump 56 Oct 13 07:52 00000000000000000001.snapshot
-rw-r--r-- 1 coredump coredump  8 Oct 13 07:50 leader-epoch-checkpoint
-rw-r--r-- 1 coredump coredump 43 Oct 13 07:50 partition.metadata
```

Exercise EP2

- **Goal:** Connect WinDbg to Kafka for logging to various topics
- **Memory Analysis Patterns:** Structure Sheaf; Stack Trace (Command); Stack Trace Collection (Commands)
- \EWMDA\Exercise-EP2.pdf

Exercise EP2: Connect WinDbg to Kafka

Goal: Connect WinDbg to Kafka for logging into various topics.

Memory Analysis Patterns: Structure Sheaf; Stack Trace (Command); Stack Trace Collection (Commands).

1. Launch WSL2 Debian or Ubuntu.

2. Start services:

```
$ cd kafka_2.13-3.8.0

~/kafka_2.13-3.8.0$ bin/zookeeper-server-start.sh config/zookeeper.properties &
...

~/kafka_2.13-3.8.0$ bin/kafka-server-start.sh config/server.properties &
...
```

3. Start producing log lines from /EWMDA-Dumps/windbg.log:

```
~/kafka_2.13-3.8.0$ touch /mnt/c/EWMDA-Dumps/windbg.log

~/kafka_2.13-3.8.0$ tail -n +1 -f ---disable-inotify /mnt/c/EWMDA-Dumps/windbg.log | bin/kafka-
console-producer.sh --topic windbg-log --bootstrap-server localhost:9092 &
...
```

4. Start consuming new log lines from the *windbg-log* topic (already existing events are not shown because we do not specify **--from-beginning**):

```
~/kafka_2.13-3.8.0$ bin/kafka-console-consumer.sh --topic windbg-log --bootstrap-server
localhost:9092
```

5. Launch WinDbg and open \EWMDA-Dumps\Complete\x64\MEMORY-W11.DMP.

```
Microsoft (R) Windows Debugger Version 10.0.27704.1001 AMD64
Copyright (c) Microsoft Corporation. All rights reserved.


Loading Dump File [C:\EWMDA-Dumps\Complete\x64\MEMORY-W11.DMP]
Kernel Bitmap Dump File: Full address space is available


************* Path validation summary **************
Response                         Time (ms)     Location
Deferred                                       srv*
Symbol search path is: srv*
Executable search path is:
Windows 10 Kernel Version 22000 MP (2 procs) Free x64
Product: WinNt, suite: TerminalServer SingleUserTS Personal
Edition build lab: 22000.1.amd64fre.co_release.210604-1628
Kernel base = 0xfffff806`61e00000 PsLoadedModuleList = 0xfffff806`62a296b0
Debug session time: Sat Nov 13 23:17:16.607 2021 (UTC + 1:00)
System Uptime: 0 days 0:03:06.813
Loading Kernel Symbols
```

```
................................................................
.................................................................
.................................................................
..
Loading User Symbols
...............................
Loading unloaded module list
.......
For analysis of this file, run !analyze -v
nt!KeBugCheckEx:
fffff806`62215590 mov     qword ptr [rsp+8],rcx ss:0018:ffffbe82`96f64670=000000000000000a
```

6. Specify log file *C:\EWMDA-Dumps\windbg.log* in append mode:

```
0: kd> .logappend C:\EWMDA-Dumps\windbg.log
Opened log file 'C:\EWMDA-Dumps\windbg.log'
```

Note: In the terminal window, we see the same command output from the consumer.

7. Run a few commands. We see their output in the consumer. Then we stop the consumer via ^C:

```
Opened log file 'C:\EWMDA-Dumps\windbg.log'
0: kd> k
k
 # Child-SP          RetAddr               Call Site
00 ffffbe82`96f64668 fffff806`622281a9     nt!KeBugCheckEx
01 ffffbe82`96f64670 fffff806`62224300     nt!KiBugCheckDispatch+0x69
02 ffffbe82`96f647b0 fffff806`60571981     nt!KiPageFault+0x440
03 ffffbe82`96f64940 fffff806`60571d3d     myfault+0x1981
04 ffffbe82`96f64970 fffff806`60571ea1     myfault+0x1d3d
05 ffffbe82`96f64ab0 fffff806`62102f65     myfault+0x1ea1
06 ffffbe82`96f64b10 fffff806`6256b532     nt!IofCallDriver+0x55
07 ffffbe82`96f64b50 fffff806`6256acbf     nt!IopSynchronousServiceTail+0x1d2
08 ffffbe82`96f64c00 fffff806`6256a6c6     nt!IopXxxControlFile+0x5df
09 ffffbe82`96f64d40 fffff806`62227b75     nt!NtDeviceIoControlFile+0x56
0a ffffbe82`96f64db0 00007ffc`88543444     nt!KiSystemServiceCopyEnd+0x25
0b 0000003f`0731ec08 00007ffc`85c23edb     ntdll!NtDeviceIoControlFile+0x14
0c 0000003f`0731ec10 00007ffc`876b5f91     KERNELBASE!DeviceIoControl+0x6b
0d 0000003f`0731ec80 00007ff7`be36342f     KERNEL32!DeviceIoControlImplementation+0x81
0e 0000003f`0731ecd0 00007ffc`87fd484b     notmyfault64+0x342f
0f 0000003f`0731edd0 00007ffc`87fd409b     USER32!UserCallDlgProcCheckWow+0x14b
10 0000003f`0731eeb0 00007ffc`880197c9     USER32!DefDlgProcWorker+0xcb
11 0000003f`0731ef70 00007ffc`87fd1c4c     USER32!DefDlgProcA+0x39
12 0000003f`0731efb0 00007ffc`87fd179c     USER32!UserCallWinProcCheckWow+0x33c
13 0000003f`0731f120 00007ffc`87fe4b4d     USER32!DispatchClientMessage+0x9c
14 0000003f`0731f180 00007ffc`885472b4     USER32!_fnDWORD+0x3d
15 0000003f`0731f1e0 00007ffc`85b21434     ntdll!KiUserCallbackDispatcherContinue
16 0000003f`0731f268 00007ffc`87fd08cf     win32u!NtUserMessageCall+0x14
17 0000003f`0731f270 00007ffc`87fd0737     USER32!SendMessageWorker+0x12f
18 0000003f`0731f310 00007ffc`73c550bf     USER32!SendMessageW+0x137
19 0000003f`0731f370 00007ffc`73c88822     COMCTL32!Button_ReleaseCapture+0xbb
1a 0000003f`0731f3a0 00007ffc`87fd1c4c     COMCTL32!Button_WndProc+0x802
1b 0000003f`0731f4b0 00007ffc`87fd0ea6     USER32!UserCallWinProcCheckWow+0x33c
1c 0000003f`0731f620 00007ffc`87fd6084     USER32!DispatchMessageWorker+0x2a6
1d 0000003f`0731f6a0 00007ffc`73c35f9f     USER32!IsDialogMessageW+0x104
1e 0000003f`0731f700 00007ffc`73c35e48     COMCTL32!Prop_IsDialogMessage+0x4b
1f 0000003f`0731f740 00007ffc`73c35abd     COMCTL32!_RealPropertySheet+0x2c0
```

```
20 0000003f`0731f810 00007ffc`73d00953     COMCTL32!_PropertySheet+0x49
21 0000003f`0731f840 00007ff7`be364cd0     COMCTL32!PropertySheetA+0x53
22 0000003f`0731f8e0 00007ff7`be365292     notmyfault64+0x4cd0
23 0000003f`0731fbb0 00007ffc`876b54e0     notmyfault64+0x5292
24 0000003f`0731fbf0 00007ffc`884a485b     KERNEL32!BaseThreadInitThunk+0x10
25 0000003f`0731fc20 00000000`00000000     ntdll!RtlUserThreadStart+0x2b

^C
...
Processed a total of 42 messages
~/kafka_2.13-3.8.0$
```

8. Shutdown producer and services in reverse order:

```
~/kafka_2.13-3.8.0$ ps
  PID TTY          TIME CMD
   10 pts/0    00:00:00 bash
 7815 pts/0    00:00:03 java
 8246 pts/0    00:00:15 java
 8741 pts/0    00:00:00 tail
 8742 pts/0    00:00:03 java
 9546 pts/0    00:00:00 ps

~/kafka_2.13-3.8.0$ kill -SIGINT 8741
[3]+  Exit 130                tail -n +1 -f ---disable-inotify /mnt/c/EWMDA-Dumps/windbg.log |
bin/kafka-console-producer.sh --topic windbg-log --broker-list localhost:9092

~/kafka_2.13-3.8.0$ kill -SIGINT 8246
...
[2]+  Exit 130                bin/kafka-server-start.sh config/server.properties

~/kafka_2.13-3.8.0$ kill -SIGINT 7815
[1]+  Exit 130                bin/zookeeper-server-start.sh config/zookeeper.properties
```

9. In WinDbg, there's a possibility to redirect individual commands to specific files for later processing (these can be forwarded to per-command topics in Kafka):

```
0: kd> .shell -ci "!vm" more >C:\EWMDA-Dumps\vm.log
.shell: Process exited
```

10. If we had installed Kafka on Windows directly, we could have used Kafka scripts from WinDbg commands directly.

11. We close logging before exiting WinDbg:

```
0: kd> .logclose
Closing open log file C:\EWMDA-Dumps\windbg.log
```

Exercise EP3

- **Goal:** Configure Kafka Connect to send WinDbg output
- \EWMDA\Exercise-EP3.pdf

Exercise EP3: Configure Kafka Connect to Send WinDbg Output

Goal: Configure Kafka Connect to send WinDbg output.

1. Launch WSL2 Debian or Ubuntu.

2. Start services:

```
$ cd kafka_2.13-3.8.0

~/kafka_2.13-3.8.0$ bin/zookeeper-server-start.sh config/zookeeper.properties &
...

~/kafka_2.13-3.8.0$ bin/kafka-server-start.sh config/server.properties &
...
```

3. Create the connector configuration and save it in *~/windbg-source.properties*:

```
name=windbg-source-connector
connector.class=FileStreamSource
tasks.max=1
file=/mnt/c/EWMDA-Dumps/windbg.log
topic=windbg-log
```

4. Add the following line to the *config/connect-standalone.properties* file:

```
plugin.path=libs/connect-file-3.8.0.jar
```

5. Comment out the following lines in the *config/connect-standalone.properties* file:

```
# key.converter.schemas.enable=true
# value.converter.schemas.enable=true
```

6. Change key and value converters in the *config/connect-standalone.properties* file from JSON to String converters:

```
key.converter=org.apache.kafka.connect.storage.StringConverter
value.converter=org.apache.kafka.connect.storage.StringConverter
```

7. Create the *windbg.log* file if not done before and Run Kafka Connect:

```
~/kafka_2.13-3.8.0$ touch /mnt/c/EWMDA-Dumps/windbg.log

~/kafka_2.13-3.8.0$ bin/connect-standalone.sh config/connect-standalone.properties windbg-
source.properties &
```

8. Start consuming new log lines from the *windbg-log* topic (already existing events are not shown because we do not specify **--from-beginning**):

```
~/kafka_2.13-3.8.0$ bin/kafka-console-consumer.sh --topic windbg-log --bootstrap-server
localhost:9092
```

9. Launch WinDbg and open \EWMDA-Dumps\Complete\x64\MEMORY-W11.DMP.

```
Microsoft (R) Windows Debugger Version 10.0.27704.1001 AMD64
Copyright (c) Microsoft Corporation. All rights reserved.


Loading Dump File [C:\EWMDA-Dumps\Complete\x64\MEMORY-W11.DMP]
Kernel Bitmap Dump File: Full address space is available


************* Path validation summary **************
Response                         Time (ms)     Location
Deferred                                       srv*
Symbol search path is: srv*
Executable search path is:
Windows 10 Kernel Version 22000 MP (2 procs) Free x64
Product: WinNt, suite: TerminalServer SingleUserTS Personal
Edition build lab: 22000.1.amd64fre.co_release.210604-1628
Kernel base = 0xfffff806`61e00000 PsLoadedModuleList = 0xfffff806`62a296b0
Debug session time: Sat Nov 13 23:17:16.607 2021 (UTC + 1:00)
System Uptime: 0 days 0:03:06.813
Loading Kernel Symbols
..............................................................
...............................................................
...............................................................
..
Loading User Symbols
..................................
Loading unloaded module list
........
For analysis of this file, run !analyze -v
nt!KeBugCheckEx:
fffff806`62215590 mov     qword ptr [rsp+8],rcx ss:0018:ffffbe82`96f64670=000000000000000a
```

10. Specify log file *C:\EWMDA-Dumps\windbg.log* in append mode:

```
0: kd> .logappend C:\EWMDA-Dumps\windbg.log
Opened log file 'C:\EWMDA-Dumps\windbg.log'
```

Note: In the terminal window, we see the same command output from the consumer.

11. Run a few commands. We see their output in the consumer. Then we stop the consumer via ^C:

```
0: kd> !kdexts.vm
!kdexts.vm
Page File: \??\C:\pagefile.sys
  Current:   4456448 Kb  Free Space:   4456440 Kb
  Minimum:   4456448 Kb  Maximum:      7704060 Kb
Page File: \??\C:\swapfile.sys
  Current:    262144 Kb  Free Space:    262136 Kb
  Minimum:    262144 Kb  Maximum:      6163248 Kb
No Name for Paging File
  Current:  11897160 Kb  Free Space:  11804392 Kb
  Minimum:  11897160 Kb  Maximum:     11897160 Kb

Physical Memory:           1048275 (    4193100 Kb)
Available Pages:            481556 (    1926224 Kb)
```

```
ResAvail Pages:            904345 (    3617380 Kb)
Locked IO Pages:                0 (          0 Kb)
Free System PTEs:      4294976237 (17179904948 Kb)

******* 420544 kernel stack PTE allocations have failed ******


******* 1 kernel stack growth attempts have failed ******

Modified Pages:             12613 (      50452 Kb)
Modified PF Pages:          12417 (      49668 Kb)
Modified No Write Pages:       26 (        104 Kb)
NonPagedPool Usage:           211 (        844 Kb)
NonPagedPoolNx Usage:       19388 (      77552 Kb)
NonPagedPool Max:      4294967296 (17179869184 Kb)
PagedPool Usage:            30455 (     121820 Kb)
PagedPool Maximum:     4294967296 (17179869184 Kb)
Processor Commit:             398 (       1592 Kb)
Unable to read nt!_LIST_ENTRY.Flink at 0000000000000000
Shared Commit:              37525 (     150100 Kb)
Special Pool:                   0 (          0 Kb)
Kernel Stacks:              11736 (      46944 Kb)
Pages For MDLs:              1925 (       7700 Kb)
ContigMem Pages:             1887 (       7548 Kb)
Partition Pages:                0 (          0 Kb)
Pages For AWE:                  0 (          0 Kb)
NonPagedPool Commit:        21511 (      86044 Kb)
PagedPool Commit:           30455 (     121820 Kb)
Driver Commit:              13439 (      53756 Kb)
Boot Commit:                 4777 (      19108 Kb)
PFN Array Commit:           13317 (      53268 Kb)
SmallNonPagedPtesCommit:      158 (        632 Kb)
SlabAllocatorPages:          4608 (      18432 Kb)
SkPagesInUnchargedSlabs:        0 (          0 Kb)
CrossPartitionCommit:           0 (          0 Kb)
System PageTables:            800 (       3200 Kb)
ProcessLockedFilePages:        14 (         56 Kb)
Pagefile Hash Pages:            0 (          0 Kb)
Sum System Commit:         137942 (     551768 Kb)
Total Private:             370651 (    1482604 Kb)
Misc/Transient Commit:       6500 (      26000 Kb)
Committed pages:           515093 (    2060372 Kb)
Commit limit:             2162387 (    8649548 Kb)

  Pid ImageName                     Commit   SharedCommit        Debt

  288 dwm.exe                    205364 Kb       89620 Kb        0 Kb
  c98 MsMpEng.exe                183928 Kb        2220 Kb        0 Kb
 1838 MsMpEngCP.exe              162084 Kb         244 Kb        0 Kb
  fcc explorer.exe               110120 Kb       69404 Kb        0 Kb
 153c SearchHost.exe              83208 Kb       12780 Kb        0 Kb
 117c svchost.exe                 41824 Kb        1912 Kb        0 Kb
  8b0 svchost.exe                 37168 Kb        1840 Kb        0 Kb
 1e74 Cortana.exe                 29144 Kb        2952 Kb        0 Kb
 16c0 WmiPrvSE.exe                27888 Kb        4324 Kb        0 Kb
 14d0 StartMenuExperienceHost.    26140 Kb        8892 Kb        0 Kb
 1b14 YourPhone.exe               24784 Kb        3020 Kb        0 Kb
 1f9c vmtoolsd.exe                23512 Kb        3788 Kb        0 Kb
  840 svchost.exe                 19140 Kb        1816 Kb        0 Kb
```

```
1cf8 MiniSearchHost.exe           18436 Kb         8352 Kb          0 Kb
1df4 TextInputHost.exe            15636 Kb         7472 Kb          0 Kb
177c SearchIndexer.exe            15600 Kb         2688 Kb          0 Kb
 a34 svchost.exe                  13984 Kb         2132 Kb          0 Kb
 cd4 svchost.exe                  12728 Kb         1888 Kb          0 Kb
 500 svchost.exe                  12208 Kb         2852 Kb          0 Kb
 350 svchost.exe                  10476 Kb         2224 Kb          0 Kb
1fe0 OneDrive.exe                 10068 Kb         3608 Kb          0 Kb
 b44 svchost.exe                   9692 Kb         1820 Kb          0 Kb
1784 svchost.exe                   9224 Kb         2860 Kb          0 Kb
1268 svchost.exe                   9196 Kb         2464 Kb          0 Kb
 acc svchost.exe                   8564 Kb         1836 Kb          0 Kb
1ea0 smartscreen.exe               8136 Kb         2472 Kb          0 Kb
 c8c vmtoolsd.exe                  8000 Kb         1880 Kb          0 Kb
 ca4 svchost.exe                   7932 Kb         1840 Kb          0 Kb
 b58 svchost.exe                   7876 Kb         1828 Kb          0 Kb
  64 Registry                      7368 Kb            0 Kb          0 Kb
 59c svchost.exe                   6728 Kb         1836 Kb          0 Kb
 6e0 svchost.exe                   6720 Kb         2232 Kb          0 Kb
1300 MoUsoCoreWorker.exe           6716 Kb         1844 Kb          0 Kb
1214 sihost.exe                    6576 Kb         2460 Kb          0 Kb
1868 dllhost.exe                   6552 Kb         2296 Kb          0 Kb
11d0 RuntimeBroker.exe             6500 Kb         2688 Kb          0 Kb
 298 lsass.exe                     6496 Kb         2116 Kb          0 Kb
13a8 RuntimeBroker.exe             6400 Kb         3680 Kb          0 Kb
 3cc svchost.exe                   6304 Kb          564 Kb          0 Kb
1224 conhost.exe                   6284 Kb        10768 Kb          0 Kb
 af8 audiodg.exe                   6280 Kb         1820 Kb          0 Kb
2088 svchost.exe                   5964 Kb         2588 Kb          0 Kb
 b14 spoolsv.exe                   5936 Kb         1840 Kb          0 Kb
1228 svchost.exe                   5924 Kb         2464 Kb          0 Kb
 c64 WmiPrvSE.exe                  5596 Kb         1824 Kb          0 Kb
 69c svchost.exe                   5416 Kb         1840 Kb          0 Kb
1f2c RuntimeBroker.exe             5164 Kb         2496 Kb          0 Kb
 290 services.exe                  5076 Kb          236 Kb          0 Kb
11b4 svchost.exe                   5040 Kb         2116 Kb          0 Kb
12d8 taskhostw.exe                 4744 Kb         3536 Kb          0 Kb
23b4 SgrmBroker.exe                4448 Kb          216 Kb          0 Kb
 63c svchost.exe                   4288 Kb         1816 Kb          0 Kb
1e34 svchost.exe                   4116 Kb         1836 Kb          0 Kb
 f94 dllhost.exe                   4104 Kb         1832 Kb          0 Kb
 cb4 svchost.exe                   3864 Kb         2124 Kb          0 Kb
12e0 svchost.exe                   3804 Kb         1844 Kb          0 Kb
23dc sppsvc.exe                    3744 Kb         1796 Kb          0 Kb
 e34 dllhost.exe                   3740 Kb         1864 Kb          0 Kb
1a2c TabTip.exe                    3660 Kb         2200 Kb          0 Kb
 e18 svchost.exe                   3584 Kb         1836 Kb          0 Kb
1d40 NisSrv.exe                    3564 Kb         1820 Kb          0 Kb
2258 RuntimeBroker.exe             3444 Kb         2472 Kb          0 Kb
 a18 svchost.exe                   3420 Kb         1888 Kb          0 Kb
1a14 ctfmon.exe                    3368 Kb         3268 Kb          0 Kb
1514 svchost.exe                   3352 Kb         2456 Kb          0 Kb
1f58 SecurityHealthService.ex      3328 Kb         1848 Kb          0 Kb
107c svchost.exe                   3292 Kb         2188 Kb          0 Kb
 7b0 svchost.exe                   3236 Kb         2124 Kb          0 Kb
 c80 VGAuthService.exe             3220 Kb         1848 Kb          0 Kb
 c1c svchost.exe                   3168 Kb         1840 Kb          0 Kb
1a70 svchost.exe                   3164 Kb         1832 Kb          0 Kb
 8a8 svchost.exe                   3148 Kb         1820 Kb          0 Kb
```

```
  a60 svchost.exe                     3068 Kb         1824 Kb          0 Kb
  fb0 svchost.exe                     2976 Kb         2128 Kb          0 Kb
  614 svchost.exe                     2852 Kb         2124 Kb          0 Kb
 10a0 msdtc.exe                       2840 Kb         1824 Kb          0 Kb
  dd8 svchost.exe                     2840 Kb         1820 Kb          0 Kb
  2b8 winlogon.exe                    2800 Kb         6708 Kb          0 Kb
  81c svchost.exe                     2780 Kb         1816 Kb          0 Kb
  9f0 svchost.exe                     2760 Kb         1948 Kb          0 Kb
 1c30 svchost.exe                     2700 Kb         1844 Kb          0 Kb
  648 svchost.exe                     2676 Kb         1836 Kb          0 Kb
 19ac svchost.exe                     2580 Kb         1820 Kb          0 Kb
 1e98 UsoClient.exe                   2464 Kb         2120 Kb          0 Kb
  1c8 svchost.exe                     2396 Kb         1836 Kb          0 Kb
  4b4 svchost.exe                     2392 Kb         1828 Kb          0 Kb
 23fc svchost.exe                     2380 Kb         1836 Kb          0 Kb
  a84 svchost.exe                     2376 Kb         1836 Kb          0 Kb
  3b0 WUDFHost.exe                    2356 Kb         1816 Kb          0 Kb
  948 svchost.exe                     2328 Kb         1816 Kb          0 Kb
  c68 svchost.exe                     2320 Kb         1836 Kb          0 Kb
  5dc svchost.exe                     2316 Kb         1840 Kb          0 Kb
  4ec svchost.exe                     2296 Kb         1840 Kb          0 Kb
  e88 svchost.exe                     2280 Kb         1820 Kb          0 Kb
 1568 svchost.exe                     2244 Kb         1840 Kb          0 Kb
  708 svchost.exe                     2220 Kb         1824 Kb          0 Kb
  4cc svchost.exe                     2200 Kb         2168 Kb          0 Kb
  9cc svchost.exe                     2160 Kb         1820 Kb          0 Kb
  6cc svchost.exe                     2120 Kb         1836 Kb          0 Kb
  470 svchost.exe                     2072 Kb         1820 Kb          0 Kb
 17d0 svchost.exe                     2048 Kb         1816 Kb          0 Kb
 1284 AppA.exe                        2032 Kb         3328 Kb          0 Kb
  958 svchost.exe                     2012 Kb         1840 Kb          0 Kb
  9d4 notmyfault64.exe                1920 Kb         3896 Kb          0 Kb
  4f8 svchost.exe                     1904 Kb         1824 Kb          0 Kb
  b8c svchost.exe                     1900 Kb         1820 Kb          0 Kb
  200 csrss.exe                       1880 Kb         8268 Kb          0 Kb
  c2c VSSVC.exe                       1860 Kb         1836 Kb          0 Kb
  250 csrss.exe                       1860 Kb         4896 Kb          0 Kb
  450 svchost.exe                     1852 Kb         1844 Kb          0 Kb
  780 svchost.exe                     1840 Kb         2240 Kb          0 Kb
 1f4c SecurityHealthSystray.ex        1816 Kb         2172 Kb          0 Kb
  97c svchost.exe                     1812 Kb         1836 Kb          0 Kb
  348 fontdrvhost.exe                 1812 Kb          228 Kb          0 Kb
  498 svchost.exe                     1804 Kb         1820 Kb          0 Kb
  c4c svchost.exe                     1736 Kb         1816 Kb          0 Kb
 2048 svchost.exe                     1712 Kb         1816 Kb          0 Kb
  a50 svchost.exe                     1708 Kb         1816 Kb          0 Kb
  670 svchost.exe                     1620 Kb         1836 Kb          0 Kb
  248 wininit.exe                     1604 Kb         1796 Kb          0 Kb
 1638 svchost.exe                     1568 Kb         2168 Kb          0 Kb
  458 svchost.exe                     1532 Kb         1816 Kb          0 Kb
 1db4 svchost.exe                     1504 Kb         1832 Kb          0 Kb
  758 svchost.exe                     1484 Kb         1832 Kb          0 Kb
 1fcc vm3dservice.exe                 1400 Kb         3252 Kb          0 Kb
  5bc svchost.exe                     1388 Kb         1820 Kb          0 Kb
  468 svchost.exe                     1364 Kb         1816 Kb          0 Kb
  340 fontdrvhost.exe                 1360 Kb          228 Kb          0 Kb
  8c0 svchost.exe                     1316 Kb         1832 Kb          0 Kb
  c78 svchost.exe                     1292 Kb         1832 Kb          0 Kb
  178 smss.exe                        1144 Kb          132 Kb          0 Kb
```

```
  cf4 AggregatorHost.exe                1056 Kb          236 Kb          0 Kb
  8f8 MemCompression                     172 Kb            0 Kb          0 Kb
 219c MoNotificationUx.exe                80 Kb            0 Kb          0 Kb
 2110 MoNotificationUx.exe                80 Kb            0 Kb          0 Kb
 14e0 MoNotificationUx.exe                80 Kb            0 Kb          0 Kb
 13ac userinit.exe                        80 Kb            0 Kb          0 Kb
 12bc taskhostw.exe                       80 Kb            0 Kb          0 Kb
 12b0 MoNotificationUx.exe                80 Kb            0 Kb          0 Kb
  540 TabTip.exe                          80 Kb            0 Kb          0 Kb
    4 System                              40 Kb          296 Kb          0 Kb

^C
...
Processed a total of 201 messages
~/kafka_2.13-3.8.0$
```

Note: If you ran this exercise before and now the connector stopped producing output remove the */tmp/connect.offsets* file and restart the connector.

12. Shutdown connector and services in reverse order:

```
~/kafka_2.13-3.8.0$ ps
  PID TTY          TIME CMD
   10 pts/0    00:00:00 bash
 9593 pts/0    00:00:08 java
10026 pts/0    00:00:36 java
12699 pts/0    00:00:28 java
13541 pts/0    00:00:00 ps

~/kafka_2.13-3.8.0$ kill -SIGINT 12699
[3]+  Exit 130                bin/connect-standalone.sh config/connect-standalone.properties
windbg-source.properties

~/kafka_2.13-3.8.0$ kill -SIGINT 10026
...
[2]+  Exit 130                bin/kafka-server-start.sh config/server.properties

~/kafka_2.13-3.8.0$ kill -SIGINT 9593
[1]+  Exit 130                bin/zookeeper-server-start.sh config/zookeeper.properties
```

13. We close logging before exiting WinDbg:

```
0: kd> .logclose
Closing open log file C:\EWMDA-Dumps\windbg.log
```

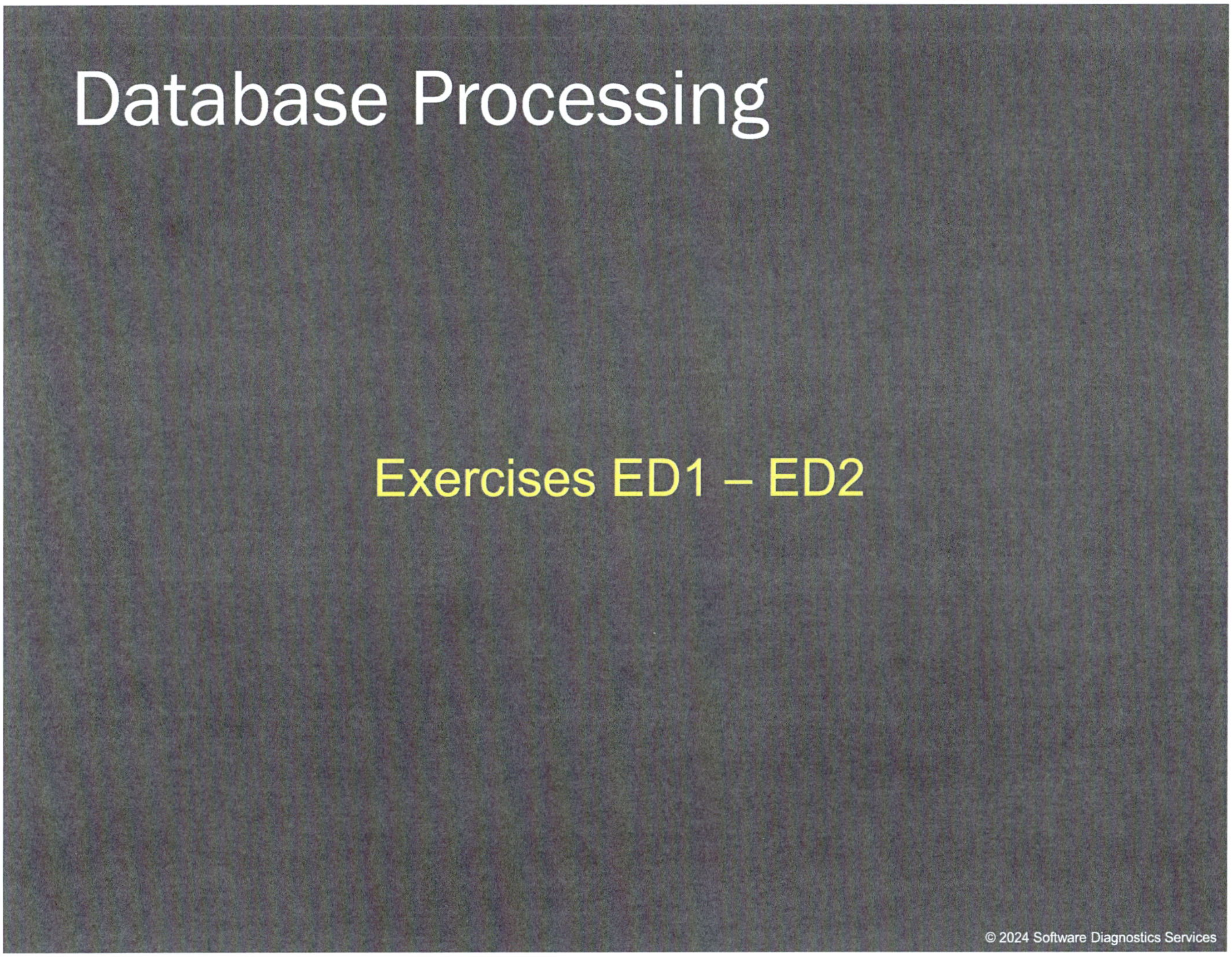
Database Processing
Exercises ED1 – ED2
© 2024 Software Diagnostics Services

In this part, we look at another solution to store WinDbg logs: MongoDB. I chose it because of my own experience with JSON data processing. However, there are many other products and platforms, and I may cover some of them in the next edition of this course.

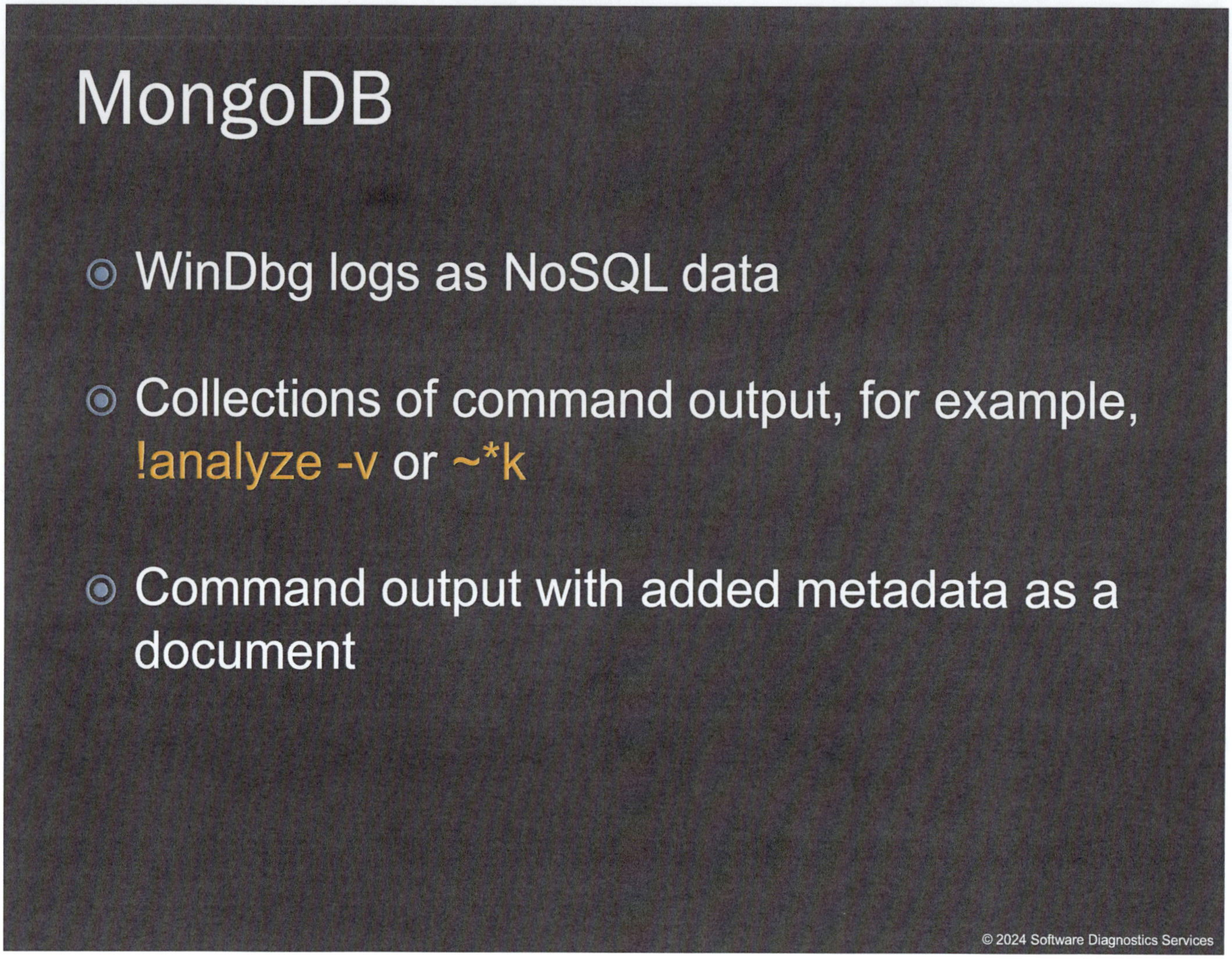

MongoDB
WinDbg logs as NoSQL data
Collections of command output, for example, !analyze -v or ~*k
Command output with added metadata as a document
© 2024 Software Diagnostics Services

Because of different output formats, WinDbg commands are best described as NoSQL documents instead of tabular data. Some command output is in a tabular format, and their analysis is the subject of the next part. We can store the output of particular commands as documents in the appropriate document collections with added metadata, for example, the dump file name, date, and problem description. Then, we can search documents for similar diagnostic indicators.

Exercise ED1

- **Goal:** Install MongoDB and verify that it works correctly
- \EWMDA\Exercise-ED1.pdf

Exercise ED1: Install MongoDB Environment

Goal: Install MongoDB[27] and verify that it works correctly.

1. Go to the MongoDB site and choose the Community edition.

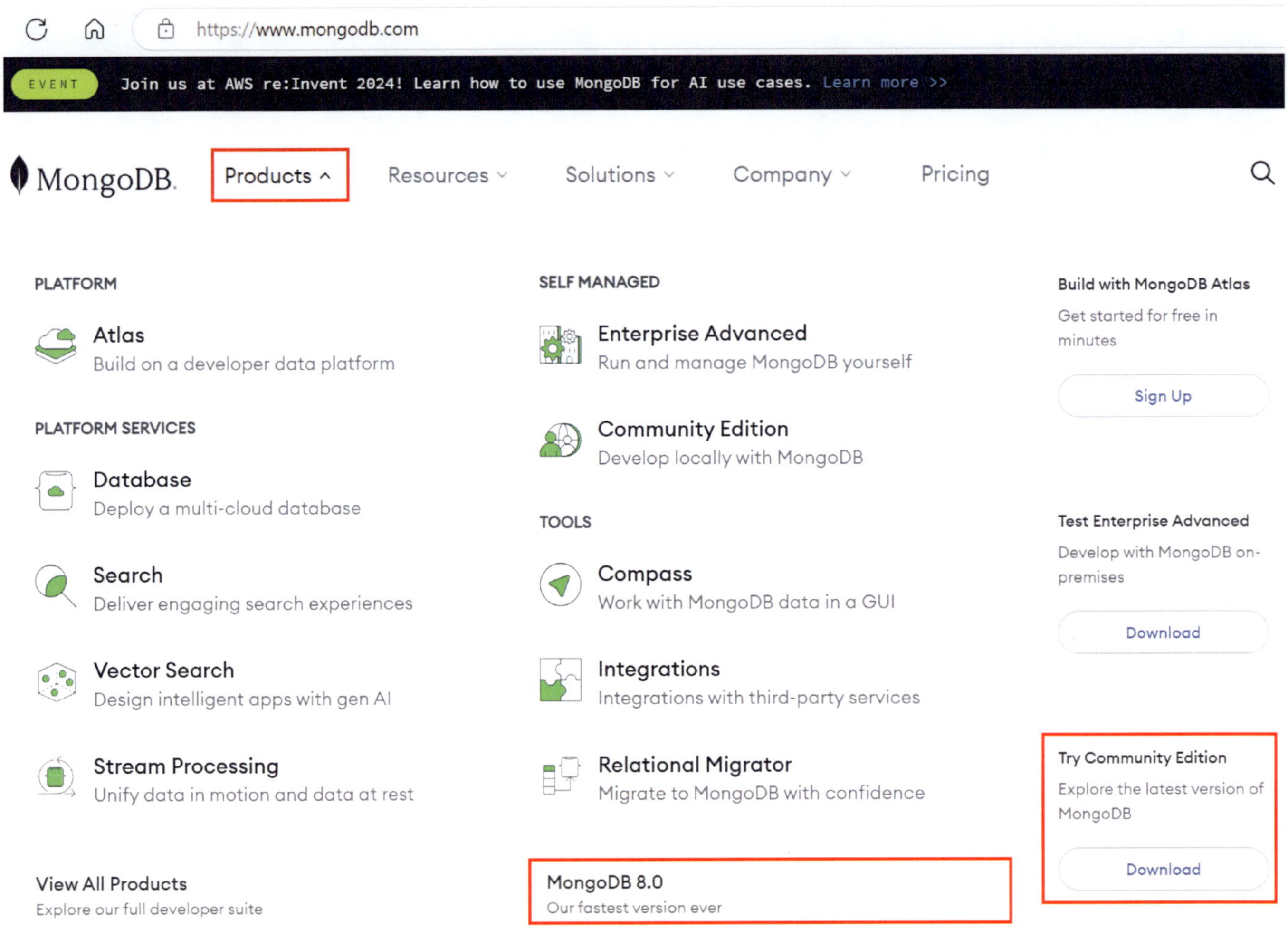

[27] https://www.mongodb.com/

2. Download the latest Windows MSI.

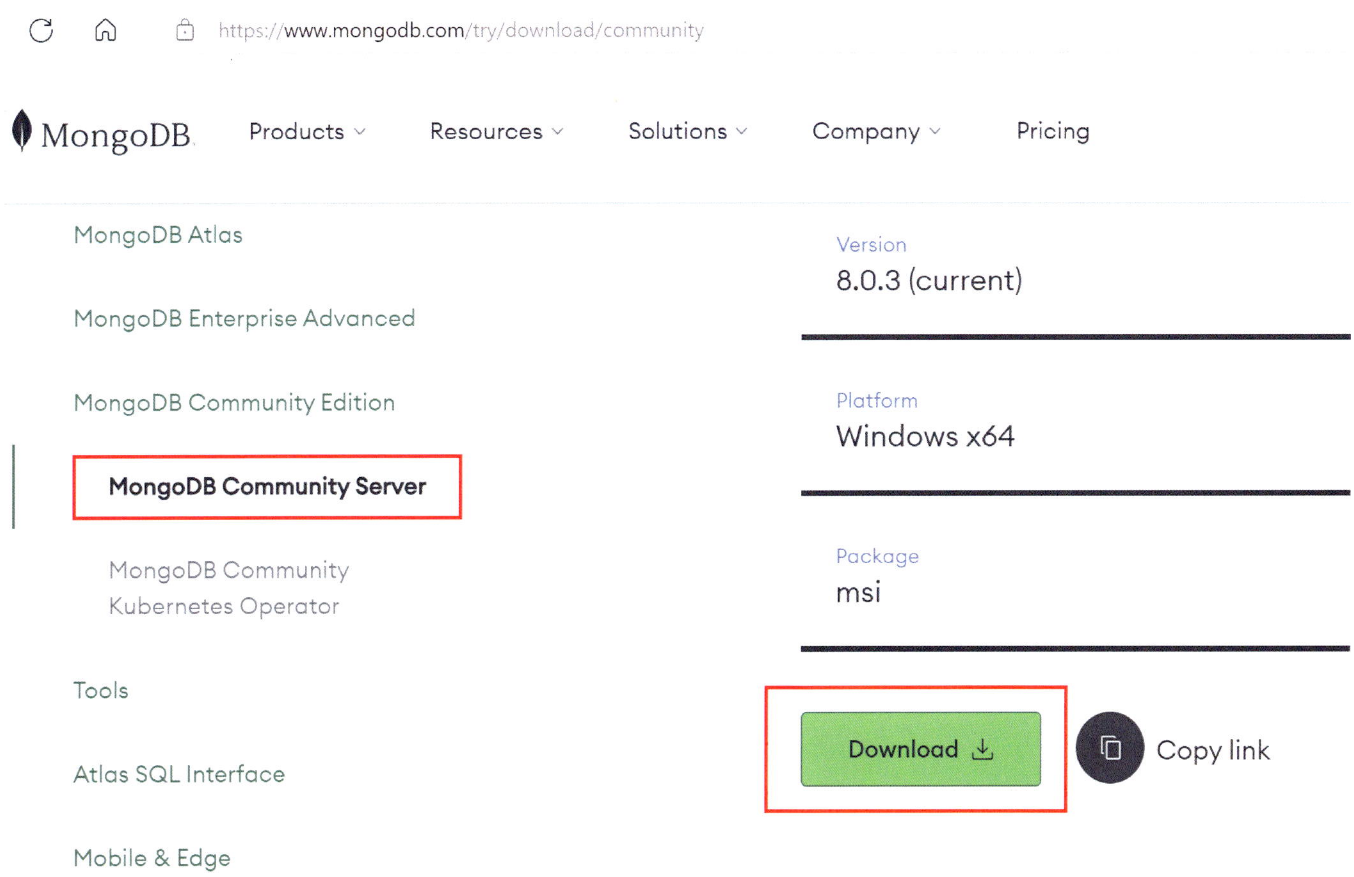

3. Install and choose all default options for the Complete type of installation.

4. After the installtion, MongoDB Compass should start.

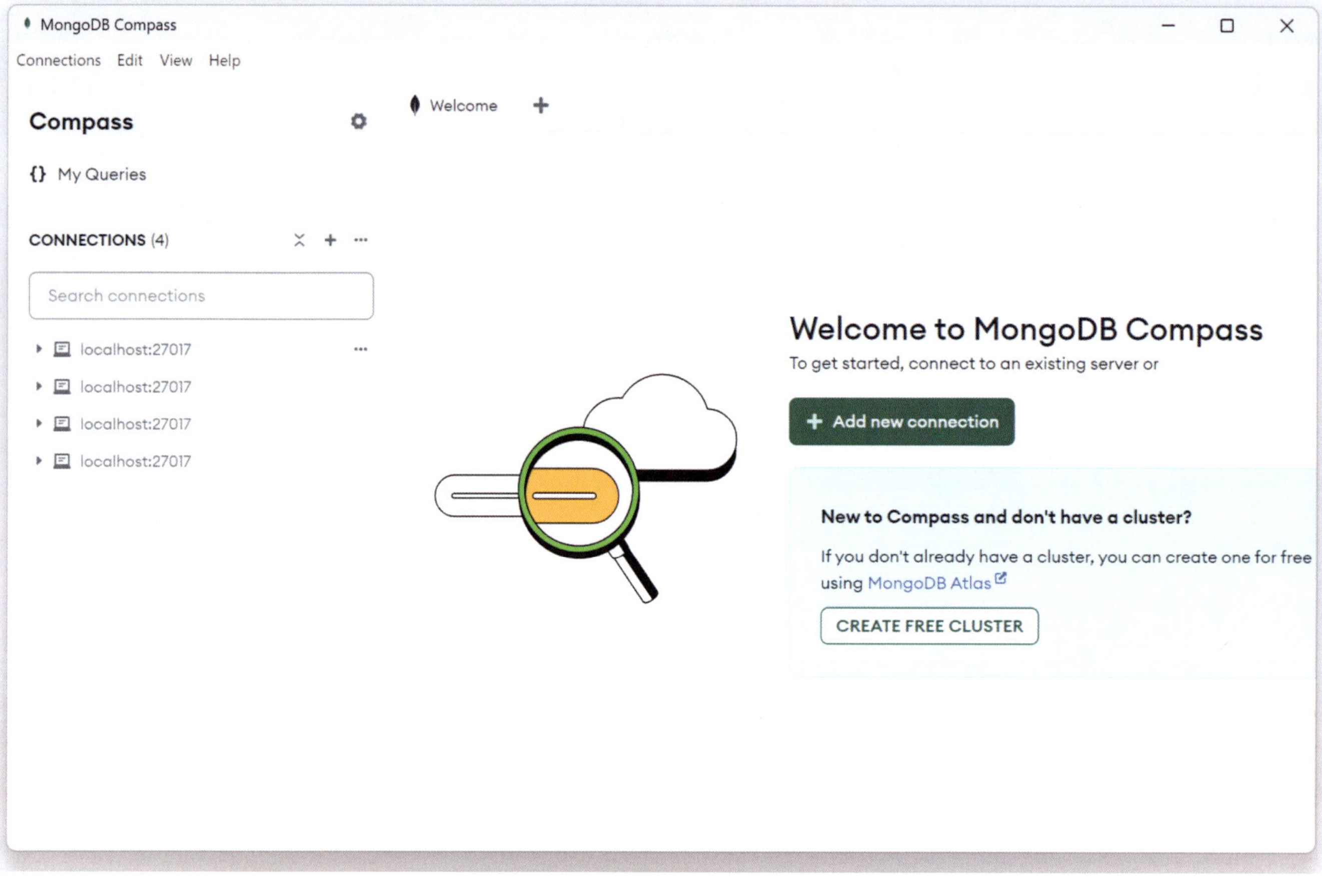

5. Exit MongoDB Compass.

6. Now select Tools. Choose and download MongoDB Database Tools Windows MSI.

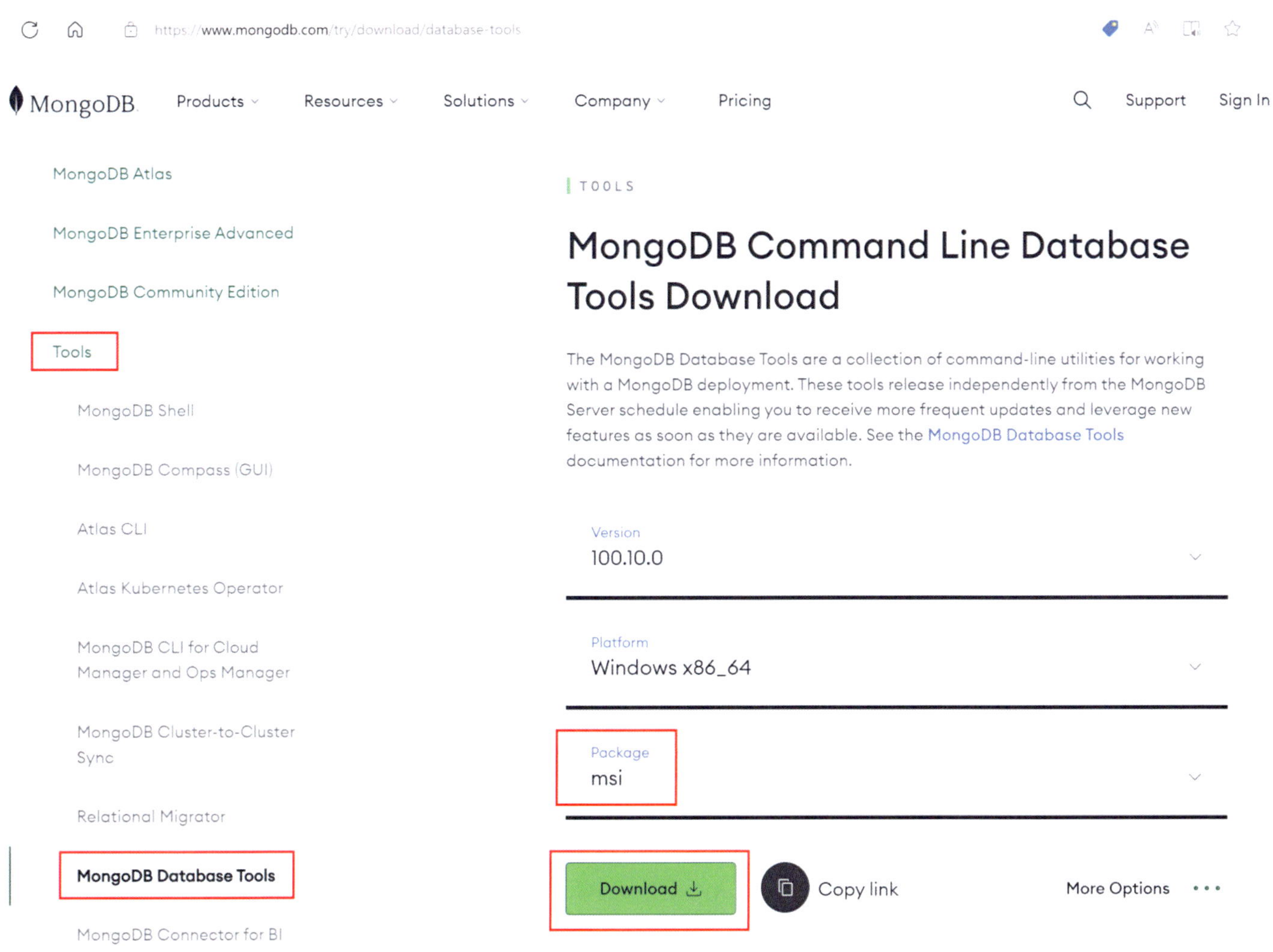

7. Install and choose all default options.

8. In Tools, select MongoDB Shell and download the Windows zip file:

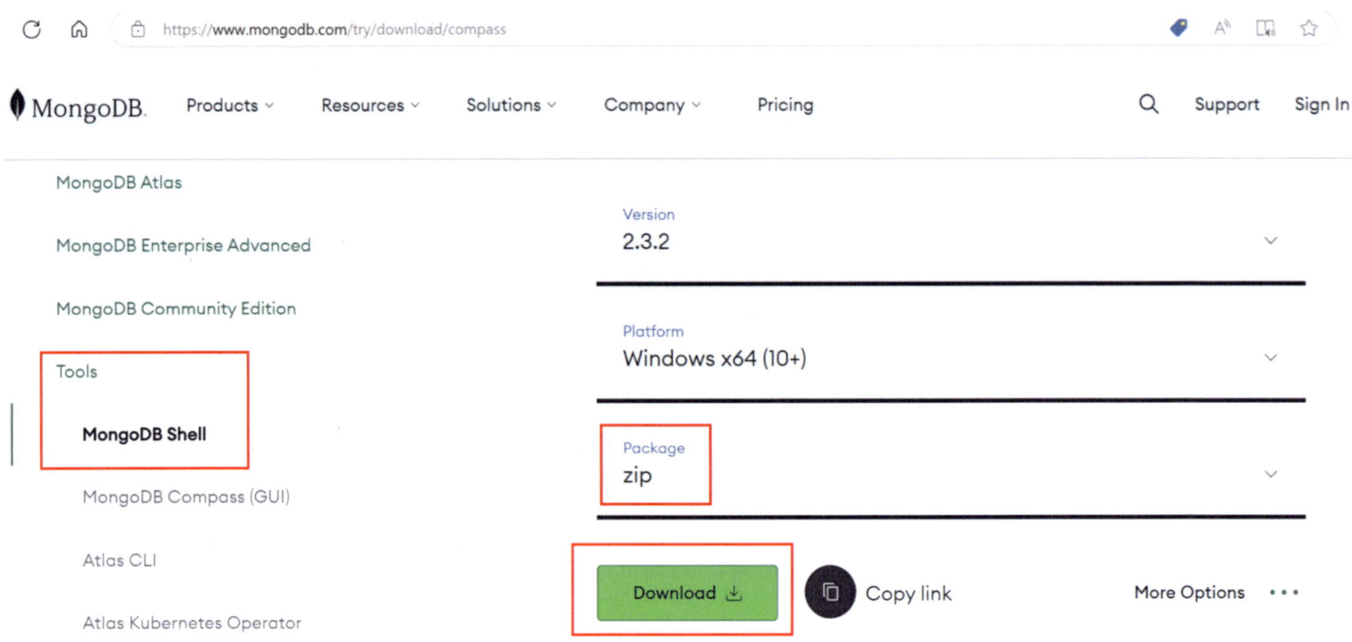

9. Copy files from the archive bin folder to C:\Program Files\MongoDB\Server\8.0\bin.

10. Start *mongosh.exe* from C:\Program Files\MongoDB\Server\8.0\bin and choose default localhost connection when prompted.

```
Please enter a MongoDB connection string (Default: mongodb://localhost/):

Current Mongosh Log ID: 671df1330366e5f1fe86b01c
Connecting to:
mongodb://127.0.0.1:27017/?directConnection=true&serverSelectionTimeoutMS=2000&appName=mongosh+
2.3.2
Using MongoDB:          8.0.3
Using Mongosh:          2.3.2

For mongosh info see: https://www.mongodb.com/docs/mongodb-shell/

------
   The server generated these startup warnings when booting
   2024-10-27T07:26:02.397+00:00: Access control is not enabled for the database. Read and
write access to data and configuration is unrestricted
------

Warning: Found ~/.mongorc.js, but not ~/.mongoshrc.js. ~/.mongorc.js will not be loaded.
  You may want to copy or rename ~/.mongorc.js to ~/.mongoshrc.js.
test>
```

11. Verify that the database connection is working by using this command:

```
test> show dbs
admin   40.00 KiB
config  48.00 KiB
local   40.00 KiB
test>
```

12. Quit the shell.

```
test> quit
```

Exercise ED2

- **Goal:** Connect WinDbg to MongoDB for storing analysis documents
- \EWMDA\Exercise-ED2.pdf

Exercise ED2: Connect WinDbg to MongoDB

Goal: Connect WinDbg to MongoDB for storing analysis documents.

1. Launch WinDbg.

2. Open \EWMDA-Dumps\Complete\x64\MEMORY-W11.DMP

3. We get the dump file loaded:

```
Loading Dump File [C:\EWMDA-Dumps\Complete\x64\MEMORY-W11.DMP]
Kernel Bitmap Dump File: Full address space is available


************* Path validation summary **************
Response                         Time (ms)     Location
Deferred                                       srv*
Symbol search path is: srv*
Executable search path is:
Windows 10 Kernel Version 22000 MP (2 procs) Free x64
Product: WinNt, suite: TerminalServer SingleUserTS Personal
Edition build lab: 22000.1.amd64fre.co_release.210604-1628
Kernel base = 0xfffff806`61e00000 PsLoadedModuleList = 0xfffff806`62a296b0
Debug session time: Sat Nov 13 22:17:16.607 2021 (UTC + 0:00)
System Uptime: 0 days 0:03:06.813
Loading Kernel Symbols
..............................................................
...............................................................
...............................................................
..
Loading User Symbols
..................................
Loading unloaded module list
........
For analysis of this file, run !analyze -v
nt!KeBugCheckEx:
fffff806`62215590 mov     qword ptr [rsp+8],rcx ss:0018:ffffbe82`96f64670=000000000000000a
```

4. Load *pykd* bootstrap extension:

```
0: kd> .load C:\EWMDA-Dumps\pykd\pykd
```

5. Install *pymongo* libraries:

```
0: kd> !pip install pymongo
Collecting pymongo
  Downloading pymongo-4.10.1-cp311-cp311-win_amd64.whl.metadata (22 kB)
Collecting dnspython<3.0.0,>=1.16.0 (from pymongo)
  Downloading dnspython-2.7.0-py3-none-any.whl.metadata (5.8 kB)
Downloading pymongo-4.10.1-cp311-cp311-win_amd64.whl (876 kB)
   ---------------------------------------- 876.5/876.5 kB 3.5 MB/s eta 0:00:00
Downloading dnspython-2.7.0-py3-none-any.whl (313 kB)
   ---------------------------------------- 313.6/313.6 kB 4.9 MB/s eta 0:00:00
Installing collected packages: dnspython, pymongo
```

```
Successfully installed dnspython-2.7.0 pymongo-4.10.1
```

6. Launch REPL:

```
0: kd> !py
Python 3.11.9 (tags/v3.11.9:de54cf5, Apr  2 2024, 10:12:12) [MSC v.1938 64 bit (AMD64)] on
win32
Type "help", "copyright", "credits" or "license" for more information.
(InteractiveConsole)
>>>
```

7. Create an **analyses** database (plural of analysis):

```
>>> import pymongo

>>> client = pymongo.MongoClient()

>>> client
MongoClient(host=['localhost:27017'], document_class=dict, tz_aware=False, connect=True)

>>> analyses_db = client["analyses"]
```

8. Create a **stack_traces** collection in the **analyses** database:

```
>>> stack_traces_collection = analyses_db["stack_traces"]
```

9. Get a stack trace using one of the WinDbg commands:

```
>>> s = dbgCommand("k", True)

>>> print (s)
 # Child-SP          RetAddr               Call Site
00 ffffbe82`96f64668 fffff806`622281a9     nt!KeBugCheckEx
01 ffffbe82`96f64670 fffff806`62224300     nt!KiBugCheckDispatch+0x69
02 ffffbe82`96f647b0 fffff806`60571981     nt!KiPageFault+0x440
03 ffffbe82`96f64940 fffff806`60571d3d     myfault+0x1981
04 ffffbe82`96f64970 fffff806`60571ea1     myfault+0x1d3d
05 ffffbe82`96f64ab0 fffff806`62102f65     myfault+0x1ea1
06 ffffbe82`96f64b10 fffff806`6256b532     nt!IofCallDriver+0x55
07 ffffbe82`96f64b50 fffff806`6256acbf     nt!IopSynchronousServiceTail+0x1d2
08 ffffbe82`96f64c00 fffff806`6256a6c6     nt!IopXxxControlFile+0x5df
09 ffffbe82`96f64d40 fffff806`62227b75     nt!NtDeviceIoControlFile+0x56
0a ffffbe82`96f64db0 00007ffc`88543444     nt!KiSystemServiceCopyEnd+0x25
0b 0000003f`0731ec08 00007ffc`85c23edb     ntdll!NtDeviceIoControlFile+0x14
0c 0000003f`0731ec10 00007ffc`876b5f91     KERNELBASE!DeviceIoControl+0x6b
0d 0000003f`0731ec80 00007ff7`be36342f     KERNEL32!DeviceIoControlImplementation+0x81
0e 0000003f`0731ecd0 00007ffc`87fd484b     notmyfault64+0x342f
0f 0000003f`0731edd0 00007ffc`87fd409b     USER32!UserCallDlgProcCheckWow+0x14b
10 0000003f`0731eeb0 00007ffc`880197c9     USER32!DefDlgProcWorker+0xcb
11 0000003f`0731ef70 00007ffc`87fd1c4c     USER32!DefDlgProcA+0x39
12 0000003f`0731efb0 00007ffc`87fd179c     USER32!UserCallWinProcCheckWow+0x33c
13 0000003f`0731f120 00007ffc`87fe4b4d     USER32!DispatchClientMessage+0x9c
14 0000003f`0731f180 00007ffc`885472b4     USER32!_fnDWORD+0x3d
15 0000003f`0731f1e0 00007ffc`85b21434     ntdll!KiUserCallbackDispatcherContinue
16 0000003f`0731f268 00007ffc`87fd08cf     win32u!NtUserMessageCall+0x14
```

```
17 0000003f`0731f270 00007ffc`87fd0737     USER32!SendMessageWorker+0x12f
18 0000003f`0731f310 00007ffc`73c550bf     USER32!SendMessageW+0x137
19 0000003f`0731f370 00007ffc`73c88822     COMCTL32!Button_ReleaseCapture+0xbb
1a 0000003f`0731f3a0 00007ffc`87fd1c4c     COMCTL32!Button_WndProc+0x802
1b 0000003f`0731f4b0 00007ffc`87fd0ea6     USER32!UserCallWinProcCheckWow+0x33c
1c 0000003f`0731f620 00007ffc`87fd6084     USER32!DispatchMessageWorker+0x2a6
1d 0000003f`0731f6a0 00007ffc`73c35f9f     USER32!IsDialogMessageW+0x104
1e 0000003f`0731f700 00007ffc`73c35e48     COMCTL32!Prop_IsDialogMessage+0x4b
1f 0000003f`0731f740 00007ffc`73c35abd     COMCTL32!_RealPropertySheet+0x2c0
20 0000003f`0731f810 00007ffc`73d00953     COMCTL32!_PropertySheet+0x49
21 0000003f`0731f840 00007ff7`be364cd0     COMCTL32!PropertySheetA+0x53
22 0000003f`0731f8e0 00007ff7`be365292     notmyfault64+0x4cd0
23 0000003f`0731fbb0 00007ffc`876b54e0     notmyfault64+0x5292
24 0000003f`0731fbf0 00007ffc`884a485b     KERNEL32!BaseThreadInitThunk+0x10
25 0000003f`0731fc20 00000000`00000000     ntdll!RtlUserThreadStart+0x2b
```

10. Create a **stack_trace** document and insert it into the **stack_traces** collection:

```
>>> stack_trace = { "dump_name": "MEMORY-W11.DMP", "stack_trace": s }

>>> stack_trace
{'dump_name': 'MEMORY-W11.DMP', 'stack_trace': ' # Child-SP          RetAddr               Call
Site\n00 ffffbe82`96f64668 fffff806`622281a9     nt!KeBugCheckEx\n01 ffffbe82`96f64670
fffff806`62224300     nt!KiBugCheckDispatch+0x69\n02 ffffbe82`96f647b0 fffff806`60571981
nt!KiPageFault+0x440\n03 ffffbe82`96f64940 fffff806`60571d3d     myfault+0x1981\n04
ffffbe82`96f64970 fffff806`60571ea1     myfault+0x1d3d\n05 ffffbe82`96f64ab0 fffff806`62102f65
myfault+0x1ea1\n06 ffffbe82`96f64b10 fffff806`6256b532     nt!IofCallDriver+0x55\n07
ffffbe82`96f64b50 fffff806`6256acbf     nt!IopSynchronousServiceTail+0x1d2\n08
ffffbe82`96f64c00 fffff806`6256a6c6     nt!IopXxxControlFile+0x5df\n09 ffffbe82`96f64d40
fffff806`62227b75     nt!NtDeviceIoControlFile+0x56\n0a ffffbe82`96f64db0 00007ffc`88543444
nt!KiSystemServiceCopyEnd+0x25\n0b 0000003f`0731ec08 00007ffc`85c23edb
ntdll!NtDeviceIoControlFile+0x14\n0c 0000003f`0731ec10 00007ffc`876b5f91
KERNELBASE!DeviceIoControl+0x6b\n0d 0000003f`0731ec80 00007ff7`be36342f
KERNEL32!DeviceIoControlImplementation+0x81\n0e 0000003f`0731ecd0 00007ffc`87fd484b
notmyfault64+0x342f\n0f 0000003f`0731edd0 00007ffc`87fd409b
USER32!UserCallDlgProcCheckWow+0x14b\n10 0000003f`0731eeb0 00007ffc`880197c9
USER32!DefDlgProcWorker+0xcb\n11 0000003f`0731ef70 00007ffc`87fd1c4c
USER32!DefDlgProcA+0x39\n12 0000003f`0731efb0 00007ffc`87fd179c
USER32!UserCallWinProcCheckWow+0x33c\n13 0000003f`0731f120 00007ffc`87fe4b4d
USER32!DispatchClientMessage+0x9c\n14 0000003f`0731f180 00007ffc`885472b4
USER32!_fnDWORD+0x3d\n15 0000003f`0731f1e0 00007ffc`85b21434
ntdll!KiUserCallbackDispatcherContinue\n16 0000003f`0731f268 00007ffc`87fd08cf
win32u!NtUserMessageCall+0x14\n17 0000003f`0731f270 00007ffc`87fd0737
USER32!SendMessageWorker+0x12f\n18 0000003f`0731f310 00007ffc`73c550bf
USER32!SendMessageW+0x137\n19 0000003f`0731f370 00007ffc`73c88822
COMCTL32!Button_ReleaseCapture+0xbb\n1a 0000003f`0731f3a0 00007ffc`87fd1c4c
COMCTL32!Button_WndProc+0x802\n1b 0000003f`0731f4b0 00007ffc`87fd0ea6
USER32!UserCallWinProcCheckWow+0x33c\n1c 0000003f`0731f620 00007ffc`87fd6084
USER32!DispatchMessageWorker+0x2a6\n1d 0000003f`0731f6a0 00007ffc`73c35f9f
USER32!IsDialogMessageW+0x104\n1e 0000003f`0731f700 00007ffc`73c35e48
COMCTL32!Prop_IsDialogMessage+0x4b\n1f 0000003f`0731f740 00007ffc`73c35abd
COMCTL32!_RealPropertySheet+0x2c0\n20 0000003f`0731f810 00007ffc`73d00953
COMCTL32!_PropertySheet+0x49\n21 0000003f`0731f840 00007ff7`be364cd0
COMCTL32!PropertySheetA+0x53\n22 0000003f`0731f8e0 00007ff7`be365292
notmyfault64+0x4cd0\n23 0000003f`0731fbb0 00007ffc`876b54e0     notmyfault64+0x5292\n24
0000003f`0731fbf0 00007ffc`884a485b     KERNEL32!BaseThreadInitThunk+0x10\n25 0000003f`0731fc20
00000000`00000000     ntdll!RtlUserThreadStart+0x2b\n'}
```

```
>>> stack_traces_collection.insert_one(stack_trace)
InsertOneResult(ObjectId('671e0776d18d633ce2a2cf8e'), acknowledged=True)
```

11. Print all documents from the **stack_traces** collection:

```
>>> for st in analyses_db.stack_traces.find(): print(st)
...
{'_id': ObjectId('671e0776d18d633ce2a2cf8e'), 'dump_name': 'MEMORY-W11.DMP', 'stack_trace': ' #
Child-SP          RetAddr               Call Site\n00 ffffbe82`96f64668 fffff806`622281a9
nt!KeBugCheckEx\n01 ffffbe82`96f64670 fffff806`62224300     nt!KiBugCheckDispatch+0x69\n02
ffffbe82`96f647b0 fffff806`60571981     nt!KiPageFault+0x440\n03 ffffbe82`96f64940
fffff806`60571d3d     myfault+0x1981\n04 ffffbe82`96f64970 fffff806`60571ea1
myfault+0x1d3d\n05 ffffbe82`96f64ab0 fffff806`62102f65     myfault+0x1ea1\n06 ffffbe82`96f64b10
fffff806`6256b532     nt!IofCallDriver+0x55\n07 ffffbe82`96f64b50 fffff806`6256acbf
nt!IopSynchronousServiceTail+0x1d2\n08 ffffbe82`96f64c00 fffff806`6256a6c6
nt!IopXxxControlFile+0x5df\n09 ffffbe82`96f64d40 fffff806`62227b75
nt!NtDeviceIoControlFile+0x56\n0a ffffbe82`96f64db0 00007ffc`88543444
nt!KiSystemServiceCopyEnd+0x25\n0b 0000003f`0731ec08 00007ffc`85c23edb
ntdll!NtDeviceIoControlFile+0x14\n0c 0000003f`0731ec10 00007ffc`876b5f91
KERNELBASE!DeviceIoControl+0x6b\n0d 0000003f`0731ec80 00007ff7`be36342f
KERNEL32!DeviceIoControlImplementation+0x81\n0e 0000003f`0731ecd0 00007ffc`87fd484b
notmyfault64+0x342f\n0f 0000003f`0731edd0 00007ffc`87fd409b
USER32!UserCallDlgProcCheckWow+0x14b\n10 0000003f`0731eeb0 00007ffc`880197c9
USER32!DefDlgProcWorker+0xcb\n11 0000003f`0731ef70 00007ffc`87fd1c4c
USER32!DefDlgProcA+0x39\n12 0000003f`0731efb0 00007ffc`87fd179c
USER32!UserCallWinProcCheckWow+0x33c\n13 0000003f`0731f120 00007ffc`87fe4b4d
USER32!DispatchClientMessage+0x9c\n14 0000003f`0731f180 00007ffc`885472b4
USER32!_fnDWORD+0x3d\n15 0000003f`0731f1e0 00007ffc`85b21434
ntdll!KiUserCallbackDispatcherContinue\n16 0000003f`0731f268 00007ffc`87fd08cf
win32u!NtUserMessageCall+0x14\n17 0000003f`0731f270 00007ffc`87fd0737
USER32!SendMessageWorker+0x12f\n18 0000003f`0731f310 00007ffc`73c550bf
USER32!SendMessageW+0x137\n19 0000003f`0731f370 00007ffc`73c88822
COMCTL32!Button_ReleaseCapture+0xbb\n1a 0000003f`0731f3a0 00007ffc`87fd1c4c
COMCTL32!Button_WndProc+0x802\n1b 0000003f`0731f4b0 00007ffc`87fd0ea6
USER32!UserCallWinProcCheckWow+0x33c\n1c 0000003f`0731f620 00007ffc`87fd6084
USER32!DispatchMessageWorker+0x2a6\n1d 0000003f`0731f6a0 00007ffc`73c35f9f
USER32!IsDialogMessageW+0x104\n1e 0000003f`0731f700 00007ffc`73c35e48
COMCTL32!Prop_IsDialogMessage+0x4b\n1f 0000003f`0731f740 00007ffc`73c35abd
COMCTL32!_RealPropertySheet+0x2c0\n20 0000003f`0731f810 00007ffc`73d00953
COMCTL32!_PropertySheet+0x49\n21 0000003f`0731f840 00007ff7`be364cd0
COMCTL32!PropertySheetA+0x53\n22 0000003f`0731f8e0 00007ff7`be365292
notmyfault64+0x4cd0\n23 0000003f`0731fbb0 00007ffc`876b54e0     notmyfault64+0x5292\n24
0000003f`0731fbf0 00007ffc`884a485b     KERNEL32!BaseThreadInitThunk+0x10\n25 0000003f`0731fc20
00000000`00000000     ntdll!RtlUserThreadStart+0x2b\n'}
```

12. Print all stack traces from the **stack_traces** collection documents:

```
>>> for st in analyses_db.stack_traces.find(): print(st["stack_trace"])
...
 # Child-SP          RetAddr               Call Site
00 ffffbe82`96f64668 fffff806`622281a9     nt!KeBugCheckEx
01 ffffbe82`96f64670 fffff806`62224300     nt!KiBugCheckDispatch+0x69
02 ffffbe82`96f647b0 fffff806`60571981     nt!KiPageFault+0x440
03 ffffbe82`96f64940 fffff806`60571d3d     myfault+0x1981
04 ffffbe82`96f64970 fffff806`60571ea1     myfault+0x1d3d
05 ffffbe82`96f64ab0 fffff806`62102f65     myfault+0x1ea1
06 ffffbe82`96f64b10 fffff806`6256b532     nt!IofCallDriver+0x55
07 ffffbe82`96f64b50 fffff806`6256acbf     nt!IopSynchronousServiceTail+0x1d2
```

```
08 ffffbe82`96f64c00 fffff806`6256a6c6     nt!IopXxxControlFile+0x5df
09 ffffbe82`96f64d40 fffff806`62227b75     nt!NtDeviceIoControlFile+0x56
0a ffffbe82`96f64db0 00007ffc`88543444     nt!KiSystemServiceCopyEnd+0x25
0b 0000003f`0731ec08 00007ffc`85c23edb     ntdll!NtDeviceIoControlFile+0x14
0c 0000003f`0731ec10 00007ffc`876b5f91     KERNELBASE!DeviceIoControl+0x6b
0d 0000003f`0731ec80 00007ff7`be36342f     KERNEL32!DeviceIoControlImplementation+0x81
0e 0000003f`0731ecd0 00007ffc`87fd484b     notmyfault64+0x342f
0f 0000003f`0731edd0 00007ffc`87fd409b     USER32!UserCallDlgProcCheckWow+0x14b
10 0000003f`0731eeb0 00007ffc`880197c9     USER32!DefDlgProcWorker+0xcb
11 0000003f`0731ef70 00007ffc`87fd1c4c     USER32!DefDlgProcA+0x39
12 0000003f`0731efb0 00007ffc`87fd179c     USER32!UserCallWinProcCheckWow+0x33c
13 0000003f`0731f120 00007ffc`87fe4b4d     USER32!DispatchClientMessage+0x9c
14 0000003f`0731f180 00007ffc`885472b4     USER32!_fnDWORD+0x3d
15 0000003f`0731f1e0 00007ffc`85b21434     ntdll!KiUserCallbackDispatcherContinue
16 0000003f`0731f268 00007ffc`87fd08cf     win32u!NtUserMessageCall+0x14
17 0000003f`0731f270 00007ffc`87fd0737     USER32!SendMessageWorker+0x12f
18 0000003f`0731f310 00007ffc`73c550bf     USER32!SendMessageW+0x137
19 0000003f`0731f370 00007ffc`73c88822     COMCTL32!Button_ReleaseCapture+0xbb
1a 0000003f`0731f3a0 00007ffc`87fd1c4c     COMCTL32!Button_WndProc+0x802
1b 0000003f`0731f4b0 00007ffc`87fd0ea6     USER32!UserCallWinProcCheckWow+0x33c
1c 0000003f`0731f620 00007ffc`87fd6084     USER32!DispatchMessageWorker+0x2a6
1d 0000003f`0731f6a0 00007ffc`73c35f9f     USER32!IsDialogMessageW+0x104
1e 0000003f`0731f700 00007ffc`73c35e48     COMCTL32!Prop_IsDialogMessage+0x4b
1f 0000003f`0731f740 00007ffc`73c35abd     COMCTL32!_RealPropertySheet+0x2c0
20 0000003f`0731f810 00007ffc`73d00953     COMCTL32!_PropertySheet+0x49
21 0000003f`0731f840 00007ff7`be364cd0     COMCTL32!PropertySheetA+0x53
22 0000003f`0731f8e0 00007ff7`be365292     notmyfault64+0x4cd0
23 0000003f`0731fbb0 00007ffc`876b54e0     notmyfault64+0x5292
24 0000003f`0731fbf0 00007ffc`884a485b     KERNEL32!BaseThreadInitThunk+0x10
25 0000003f`0731fc20 00000000`00000000     ntdll!RtlUserThreadStart+0x2b
```

13. Search for **Exception** stack trace pattern in the **stack_traces** collection:

```
>>> pattern = { "stack_trace": { "$regex": "Exception" } }

>>> for st in analyses_db.stack_traces.find(pattern): print(st["stack_trace"])
...
```

14. Search for **DeviceIo** stack trace pattern in the **stack_traces** collection:

```
>>> pattern = { "stack_trace": { "$regex": "DeviceIo" } }

>>> for st in analyses_db.stack_traces.find(pattern): print(st["stack_trace"])
...
# Child-SP          RetAddr               Call Site
00 ffffbe82`96f64668 fffff806`622281a9     nt!KeBugCheckEx
01 ffffbe82`96f64670 fffff806`62224300     nt!KiBugCheckDispatch+0x69
02 ffffbe82`96f647b0 fffff806`60571981     nt!KiPageFault+0x440
03 ffffbe82`96f64940 fffff806`60571d3d     myfault+0x1981
04 ffffbe82`96f64970 fffff806`60571ea1     myfault+0x1d3d
05 ffffbe82`96f64ab0 fffff806`62102f65     myfault+0x1ea1
06 ffffbe82`96f64b10 fffff806`6256b532     nt!IofCallDriver+0x55
07 ffffbe82`96f64b50 fffff806`6256acbf     nt!IopSynchronousServiceTail+0x1d2
08 ffffbe82`96f64c00 fffff806`6256a6c6     nt!IopXxxControlFile+0x5df
09 ffffbe82`96f64d40 fffff806`62227b75     nt!NtDeviceIoControlFile+0x56
0a ffffbe82`96f64db0 00007ffc`88543444     nt!KiSystemServiceCopyEnd+0x25
0b 0000003f`0731ec08 00007ffc`85c23edb     ntdll!NtDeviceIoControlFile+0x14
0c 0000003f`0731ec10 00007ffc`876b5f91     KERNELBASE!DeviceIoControl+0x6b
```

```
0d 0000003f`0731ec80 00007ff7`be36342f     KERNEL32!DeviceIoControlImplementation+0x81
0e 0000003f`0731ecd0 00007ffc`87fd484b     notmyfault64+0x342f
0f 0000003f`0731edd0 00007ffc`87fd409b     USER32!UserCallDlgProcCheckWow+0x14b
10 0000003f`0731eeb0 00007ffc`880197c9     USER32!DefDlgProcWorker+0xcb
11 0000003f`0731ef70 00007ffc`87fd1c4c     USER32!DefDlgProcA+0x39
12 0000003f`0731efb0 00007ffc`87fd179c     USER32!UserCallWinProcCheckWow+0x33c
13 0000003f`0731f120 00007ffc`87fe4b4d     USER32!DispatchClientMessage+0x9c
14 0000003f`0731f180 00007ffc`885472b4     USER32!_fnDWORD+0x3d
15 0000003f`0731f1e0 00007ffc`85b21434     ntdll!KiUserCallbackDispatcherContinue
16 0000003f`0731f268 00007ffc`87fd08cf     win32u!NtUserMessageCall+0x14
17 0000003f`0731f270 00007ffc`87fd0737     USER32!SendMessageWorker+0x12f
18 0000003f`0731f310 00007ffc`73c550bf     USER32!SendMessageW+0x137
19 0000003f`0731f370 00007ffc`73c88822     COMCTL32!Button_ReleaseCapture+0xbb
1a 0000003f`0731f3a0 00007ffc`87fd1c4c     COMCTL32!Button_WndProc+0x802
1b 0000003f`0731f4b0 00007ffc`87fd0ea6     USER32!UserCallWinProcCheckWow+0x33c
1c 0000003f`0731f620 00007ffc`87fd6084     USER32!DispatchMessageWorker+0x2a6
1d 0000003f`0731f6a0 00007ffc`73c35f9f     USER32!IsDialogMessageW+0x104
1e 0000003f`0731f700 00007ffc`73c35e48     COMCTL32!Prop_IsDialogMessage+0x4b
1f 0000003f`0731f740 00007ffc`73c35abd     COMCTL32!_RealPropertySheet+0x2c0
20 0000003f`0731f810 00007ffc`73d00953     COMCTL32!_PropertySheet+0x49
21 0000003f`0731f840 00007ff7`be364cd0     COMCTL32!PropertySheetA+0x53
22 0000003f`0731f8e0 00007ff7`be365292     notmyfault64+0x4cd0
23 0000003f`0731fbb0 00007ffc`876b54e0     notmyfault64+0x5292
24 0000003f`0731fbf0 00007ffc`884a485b     KERNEL32!BaseThreadInitThunk+0x10
25 0000003f`0731fc20 00000000`00000000     ntdll!RtlUserThreadStart+0x2b
```

15. Quit WinDbg.

16. Run MongoDB Shell *C:\Program Files\MongoDB\Server\6.0\bin\mongosh.exe* and accept the default connection string. Execute the following command to explore our new database and its collections and do some queries:

```
test> show dbs
admin      40.00 KiB
analyses   40.00 KiB
config     48.00 KiB
local      40.00 KiB

test> use analyses
switched to db analyses

analyses> show collections
stack_traces

analyses> db.stack_traces.find()
[
  {
    _id: ObjectId('671e0776d18d633ce2a2cf8e'),
    dump_name: 'MEMORY-W11.DMP',
    stack_trace: ' # Child-SP          RetAddr               Call Site\n' +
      '00 ffffbe82`96f64668 fffff806`622281a9     nt!KeBugCheckEx\n' +
      '01 ffffbe82`96f64670 fffff806`62224300     nt!KiBugCheckDispatch+0x69\n' +
      '02 ffffbe82`96f647b0 fffff806`60571981     nt!KiPageFault+0x440\n' +
      '03 ffffbe82`96f64940 fffff806`60571d3d     myfault+0x1981\n' +
      '04 ffffbe82`96f64970 fffff806`60571ea1     myfault+0x1d3d\n' +
      '05 ffffbe82`96f64ab0 fffff806`62102f65     myfault+0x1ea1\n' +
      '06 ffffbe82`96f64b10 fffff806`6256b532     nt!IofCallDriver+0x55\n' +
      '07 ffffbe82`96f64b50 fffff806`6256acbf     nt!IopSynchronousServiceTail+0x1d2\n' +
```

```
    '08 ffffbe82`96f64c00 fffff806`6256a6c6     nt!IopXxxControlFile+0x5df\n' +
    '09 ffffbe82`96f64d40 fffff806`62227b75     nt!NtDeviceIoControlFile+0x56\n' +
    '0a ffffbe82`96f64db0 00007ffc`88543444     nt!KiSystemServiceCopyEnd+0x25\n' +
    '0b 0000003f`0731ec08 00007ffc`85c23edb     ntdll!NtDeviceIoControlFile+0x14\n' +
    '0c 0000003f`0731ec10 00007ffc`876b5f91     KERNELBASE!DeviceIoControl+0x6b\n' +
    '0d 0000003f`0731ec80 00007ff7`be36342f     KERNEL32!DeviceIoControlImplementation+0x81\n' +
    '0e 0000003f`0731ecd0 00007ffc`87fd484b     notmyfault64+0x342f\n' +
    '0f 0000003f`0731edd0 00007ffc`87fd409b     USER32!UserCallDlgProcCheckWow+0x14b\n' +
    '10 0000003f`0731eeb0 00007ffc`880197c9     USER32!DefDlgProcWorker+0xcb\n' +
    '11 0000003f`0731ef70 00007ffc`87fd1c4c     USER32!DefDlgProcA+0x39\n' +
    '12 0000003f`0731efb0 00007ffc`87fd179c     USER32!UserCallWinProcCheckWow+0x33c\n' +
    '13 0000003f`0731f120 00007ffc`87fe4b4d     USER32!DispatchClientMessage+0x9c\n' +
    '14 0000003f`0731f180 00007ffc`885472b4     USER32!_fnDWORD+0x3d\n' +
    '15 0000003f`0731f1e0 00007ffc`85b21434     ntdll!KiUserCallbackDispatcherContinue\n' +
    '16 0000003f`0731f268 00007ffc`87fd08cf     win32u!NtUserMessageCall+0x14\n' +
    '17 0000003f`0731f270 00007ffc`87fd0737     USER32!SendMessageWorker+0x12f\n' +
    '18 0000003f`0731f310 00007ffc`73c550bf     USER32!SendMessageW+0x137\n' +
    '19 0000003f`0731f370 00007ffc`73c88822     COMCTL32!Button_ReleaseCapture+0xbb\n' +
    '1a 0000003f`0731f3a0 00007ffc`87fd1c4c     COMCTL32!Button_WndProc+0x802\n' +
    '1b 0000003f`0731f4b0 00007ffc`87fd0ea6     USER32!UserCallWinProcCheckWow+0x33c\n' +
    '1c 0000003f`0731f620 00007ffc`87fd6084     USER32!DispatchMessageWorker+0x2a6\n' +
    '1d 0000003f`0731f6a0 00007ffc`73c35f9f     USER32!IsDialogMessageW+0x104\n' +
    '1e 0000003f`0731f700 00007ffc`73c35e48     COMCTL32!Prop_IsDialogMessage+0x4b\n' +
    '1f 0000003f`0731f740 00007ffc`73c35abd     COMCTL32!_RealPropertySheet+0x2c0\n' +
    '20 0000003f`0731f810 00007ffc`73d00953     COMCTL32!_PropertySheet+0x49\n' +
    '21 0000003f`0731f840 00007ff7`be364cd0     COMCTL32!PropertySheetA+0x53\n' +
    '22 0000003f`0731f8e0 00007ff7`be365292     notmyfault64+0x4cd0\n' +
    '23 0000003f`0731fbb0 00007ffc`876b54e0     notmyfault64+0x5292\n' +
    '24 0000003f`0731fbf0 00007ffc`884a485b     KERNEL32!BaseThreadInitThunk+0x10\n' +
    '25 0000003f`0731fc20 00000000`00000000     ntdll!RtlUserThreadStart+0x2b\n'
  }
]

analyses> quit
```

Note: It is also possible to explore our database in MongoDB Compass.

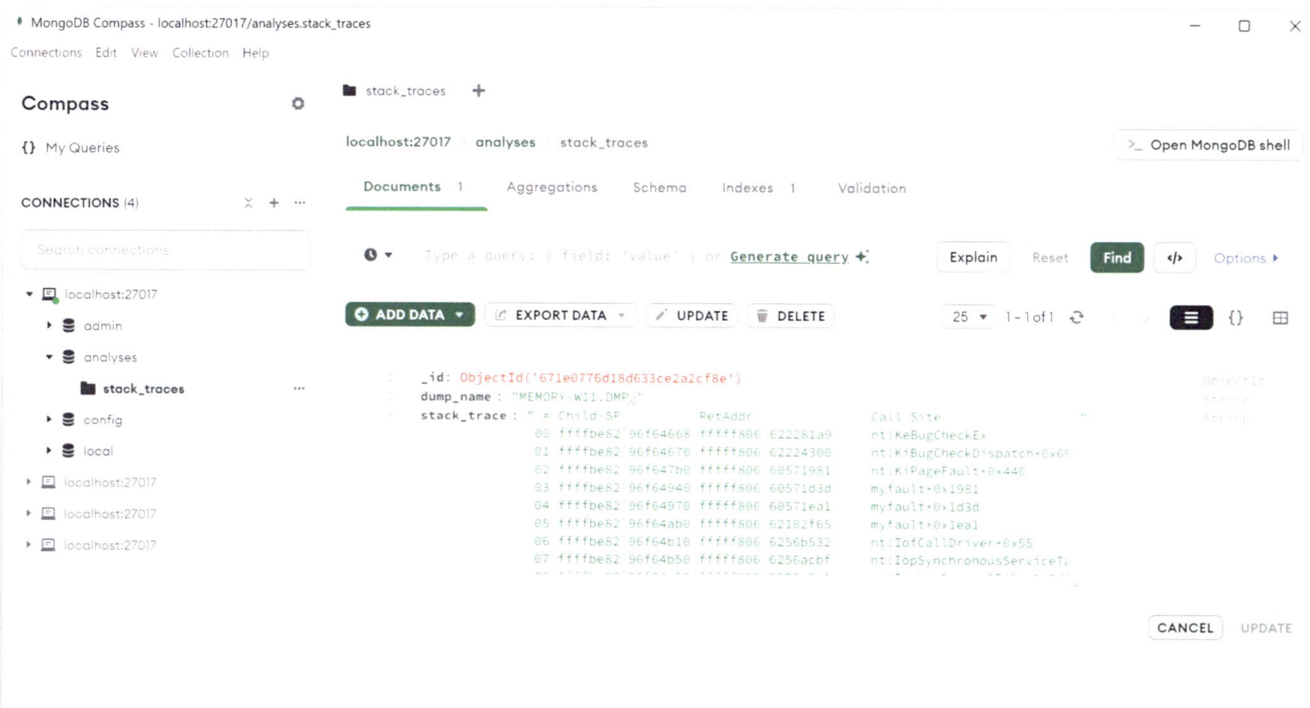

Data Science and Visualization

Exercises EV1 – EV3

Usually, execution residue from stack and heap regions is in a tabular format, and its analysis is the subject of this part.

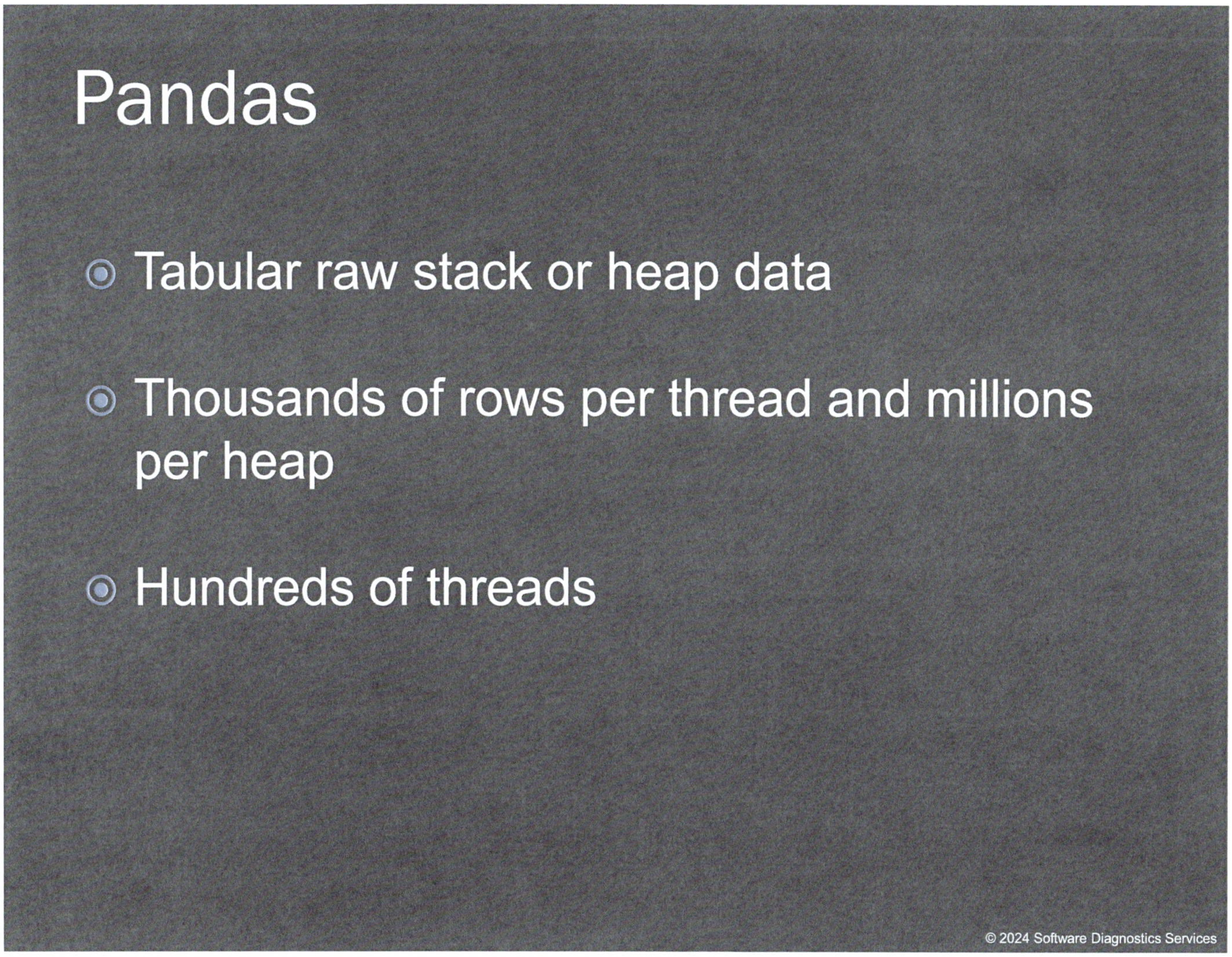

Pandas
Tabular raw stack or heap data
Thousands of rows per thread and millions per heap
Hundreds of threads
© 2024 Software Diagnostics Services

The amount of data in such WinDbg execution residue output is enormous, especially if all threads are considered. Such a data analysis requires additional processing, including data cleansing and visualization for insights. We chose Pandas and Matplotlib Python packages and Jupyter Notebook as data exploration platform for this purpose since they are widely used in data science.

Exercise EV1

- **Goal:** Install Jupyter Notebook and verify that it works correctly
- \EWMDA\Exercise-EV1.pdf

Exercise EV1: Install Jupyter Notebook Environment

Goal: Install Jupyter Notebook and verify that it works correctly.

1. We assume you have Python installed. We use Python 3.11 for this exercise.

2. Install notebook using Windows command prompt:

```
>cd C:\EWMDA-Dumps

C:\EWMDA-Dumps>pip install notebook
...
```

3. Launch notebook:

```
C:\EWMDA-Dumps>jupyter notebook
...
[I 2024-10-27 09:59:13.773 ServerApp] Serving notebooks from local directory: C:\EWMDA-Dumps
[I 2024-10-27 09:59:13.773 ServerApp] Jupyter Server 2.14.2 is running at:
[I 2024-10-27 09:59:13.774 ServerApp]
http://localhost:8888/tree?token=b6543efbd4fcbf1fd30988550cc11972aed57d00c31ab1dd
[I 2024-10-27 09:59:13.774 ServerApp]
http://127.0.0.1:8888/tree?token=b6543efbd4fcbf1fd30988550cc11972aed57d00c31ab1dd
[I 2024-10-27 09:59:13.774 ServerApp] Use Control-C to stop this server and shut down all
kernels (twice to skip confirmation).
...
```

Note: The browser window should open:

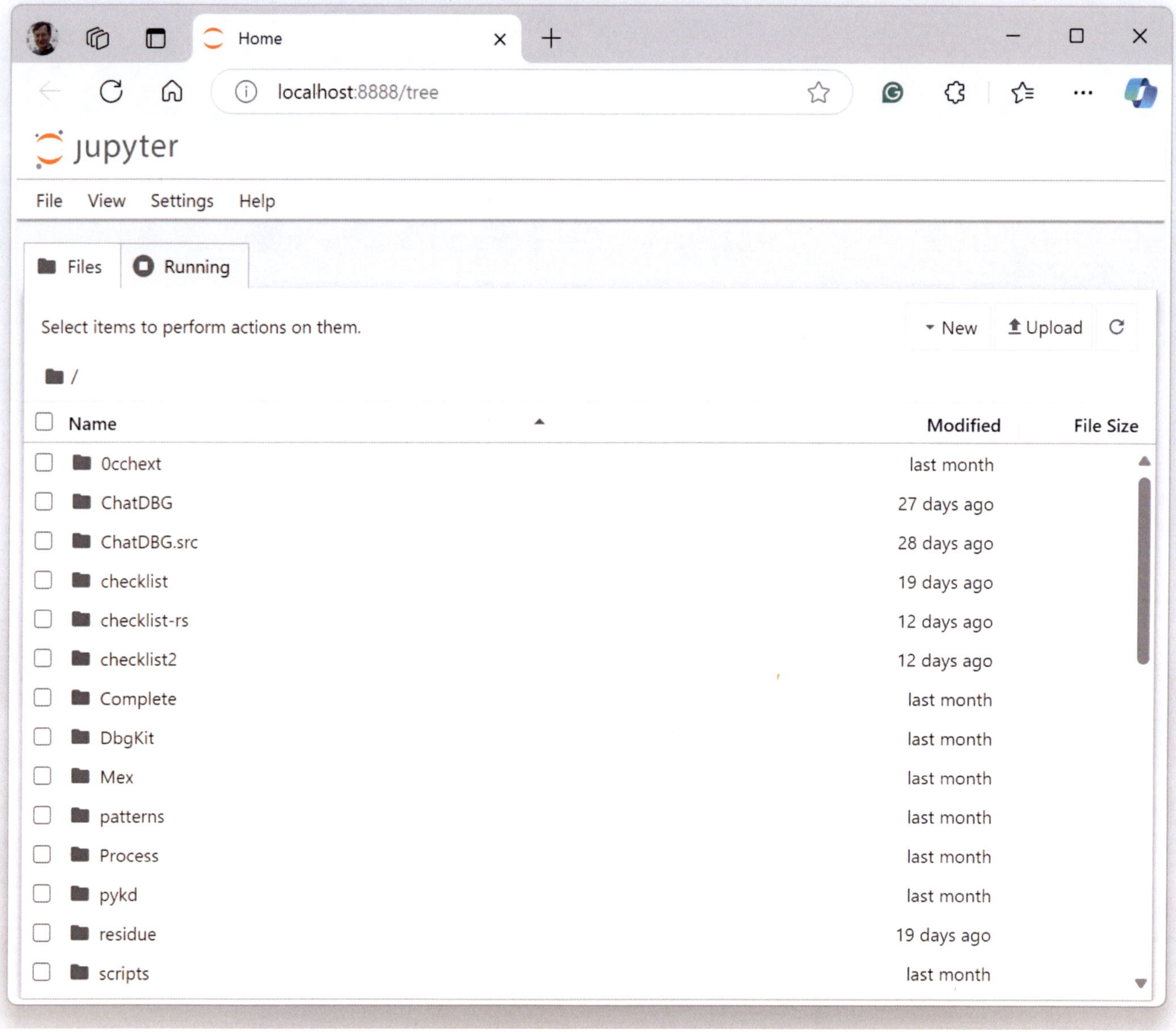

4. We create a new notebook:

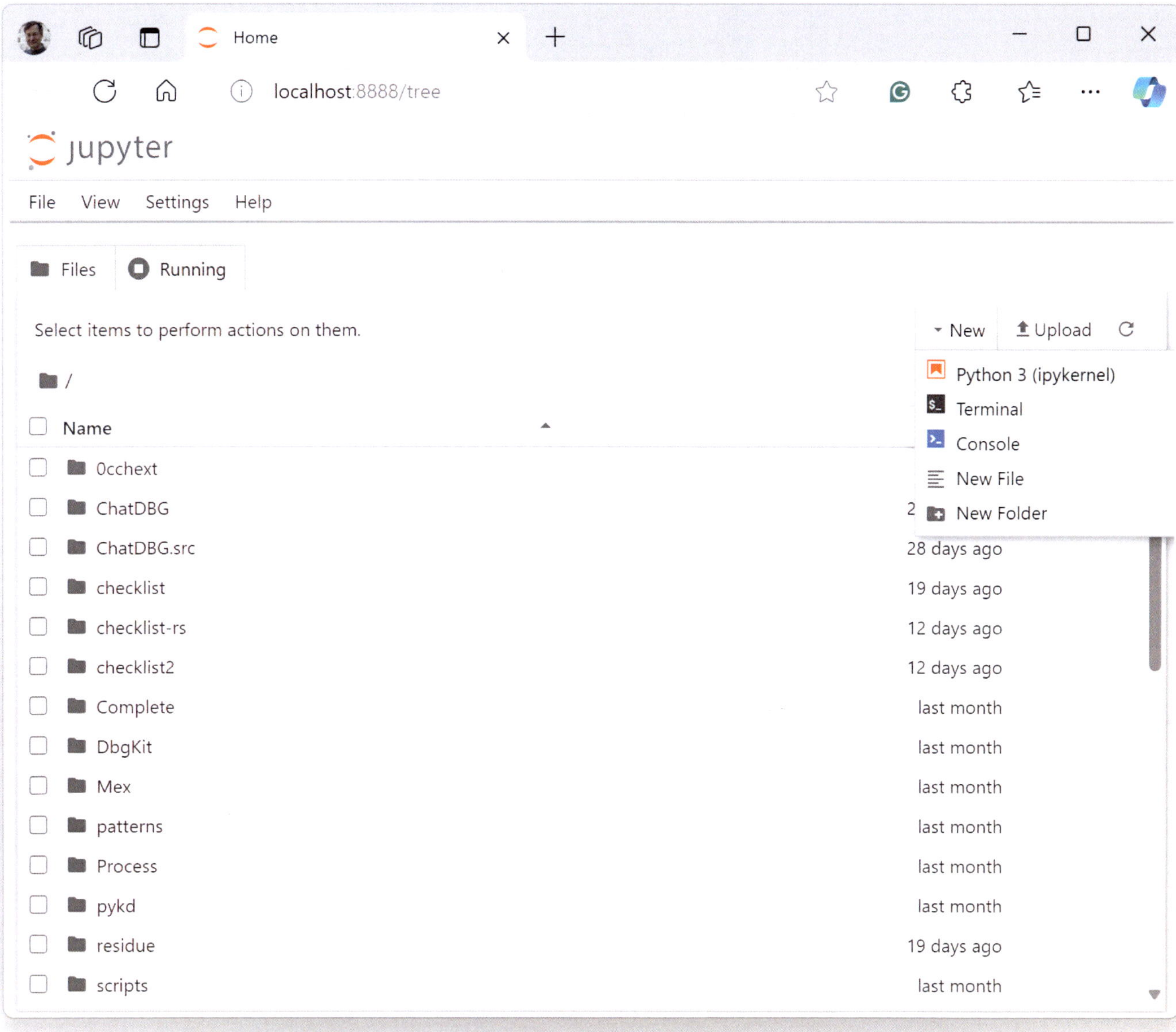

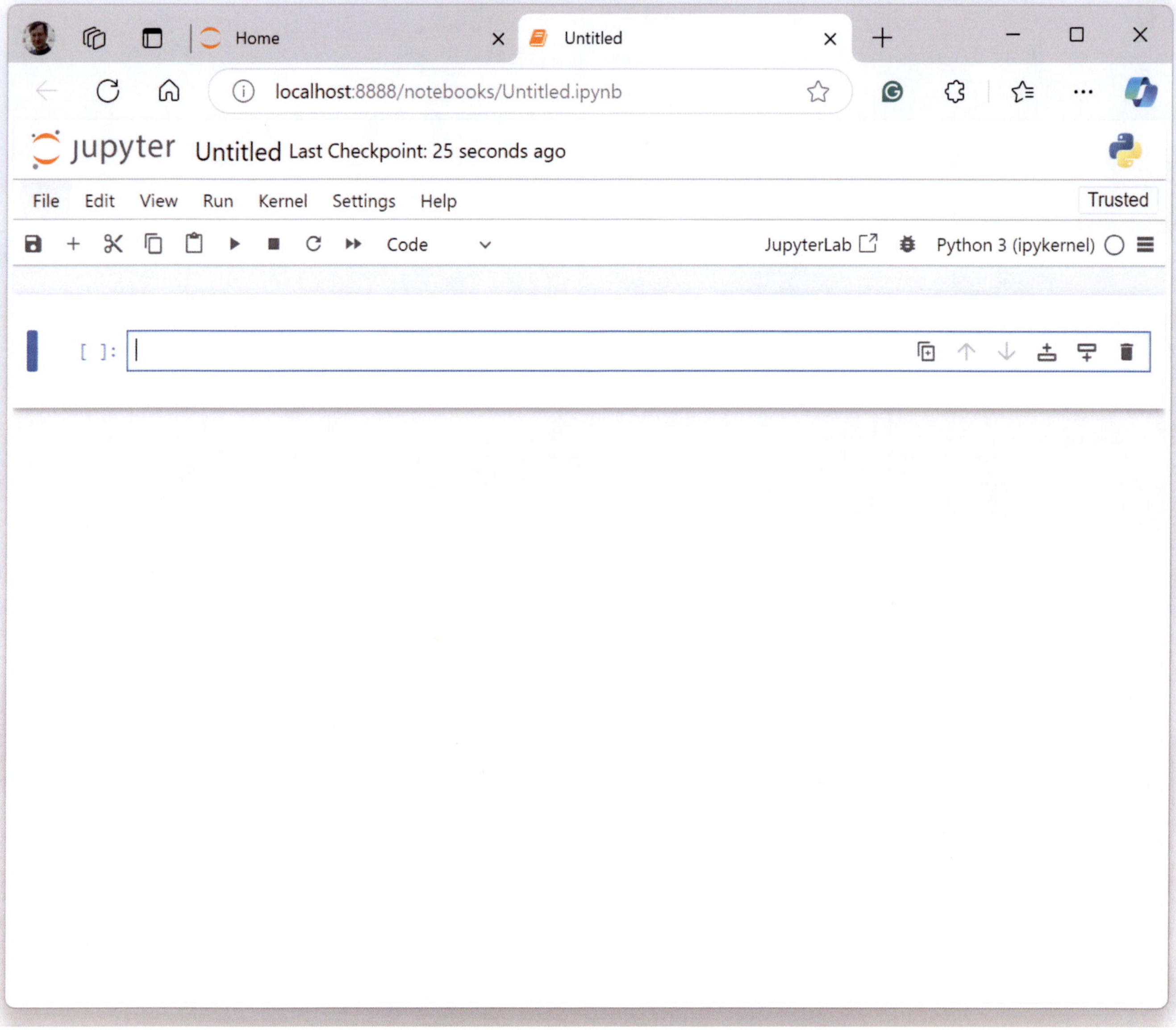
Home
Untitled
localhost:8888/notebooks/Untitled.ipynb
jupyter Untitled Last Checkpoint: 25 seconds ago
File Edit View Run Kernel Settings Help
Trusted
Code
JupyterLab
Python 3 (ipykernel)
[ ]:

5. Enter sample Python code in a notebook cell and execute via Shift-Enter:

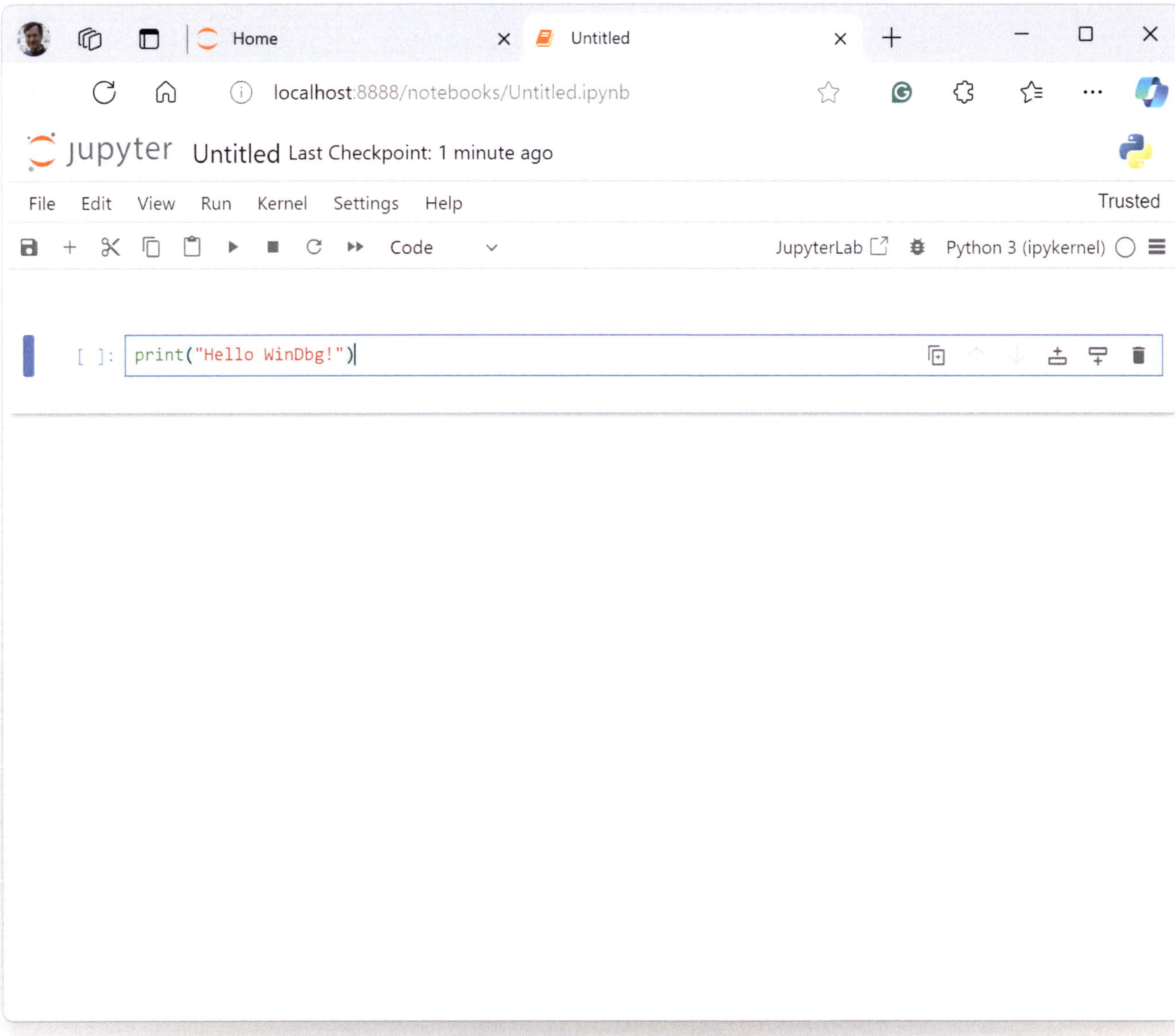

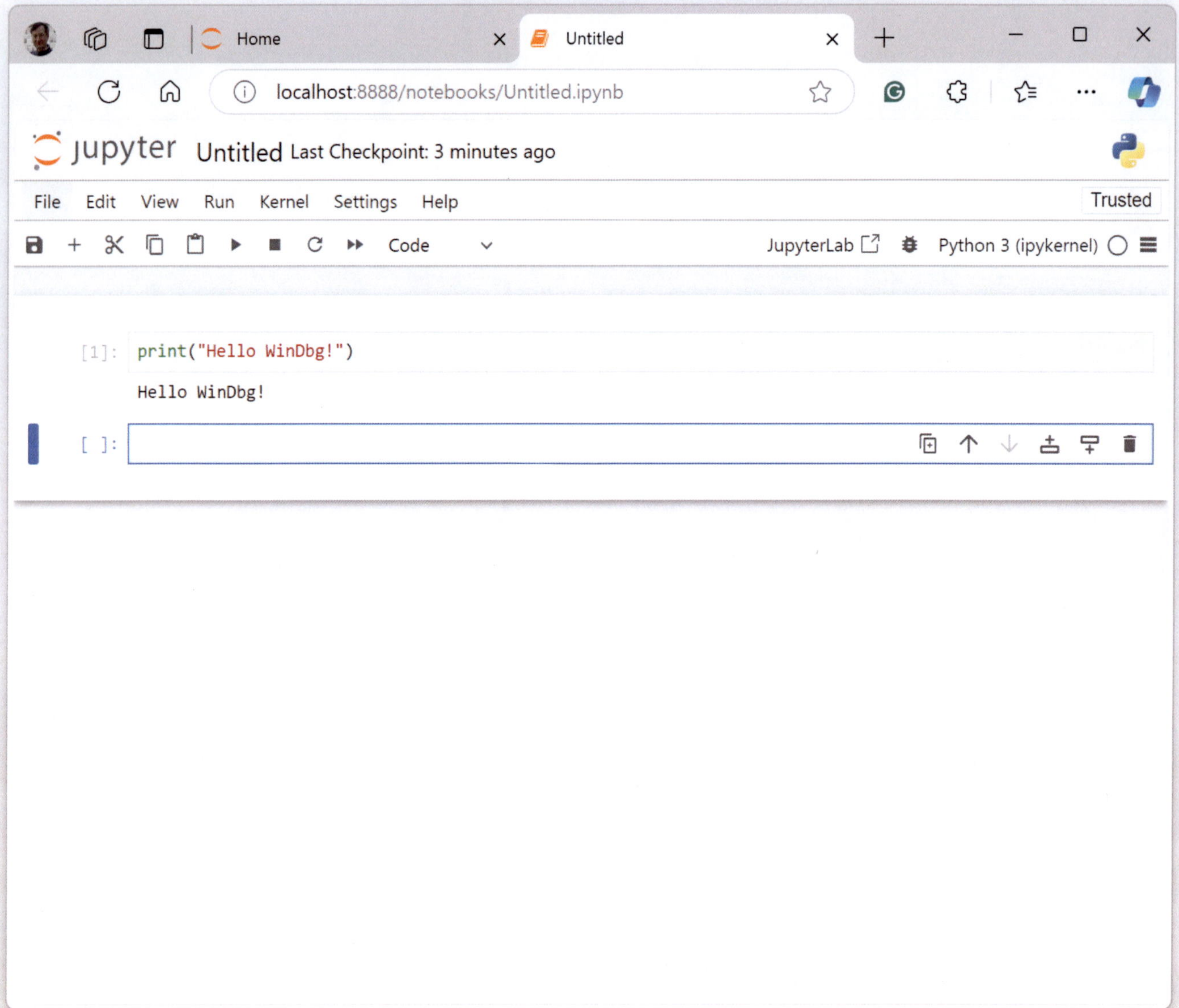
Home
Untitled
localhost:8888/notebooks/Untitled.ipynb
jupyter Untitled Last Checkpoint: 3 minutes ago
File Edit View Run Kernel Settings Help
Trusted
Code
JupyterLab
Python 3 (ipykernel)
[1]: print("Hello WinDbg!")
Hello WinDbg!
[ ]:

6. Save the current notebook to a file and exit the browser session:

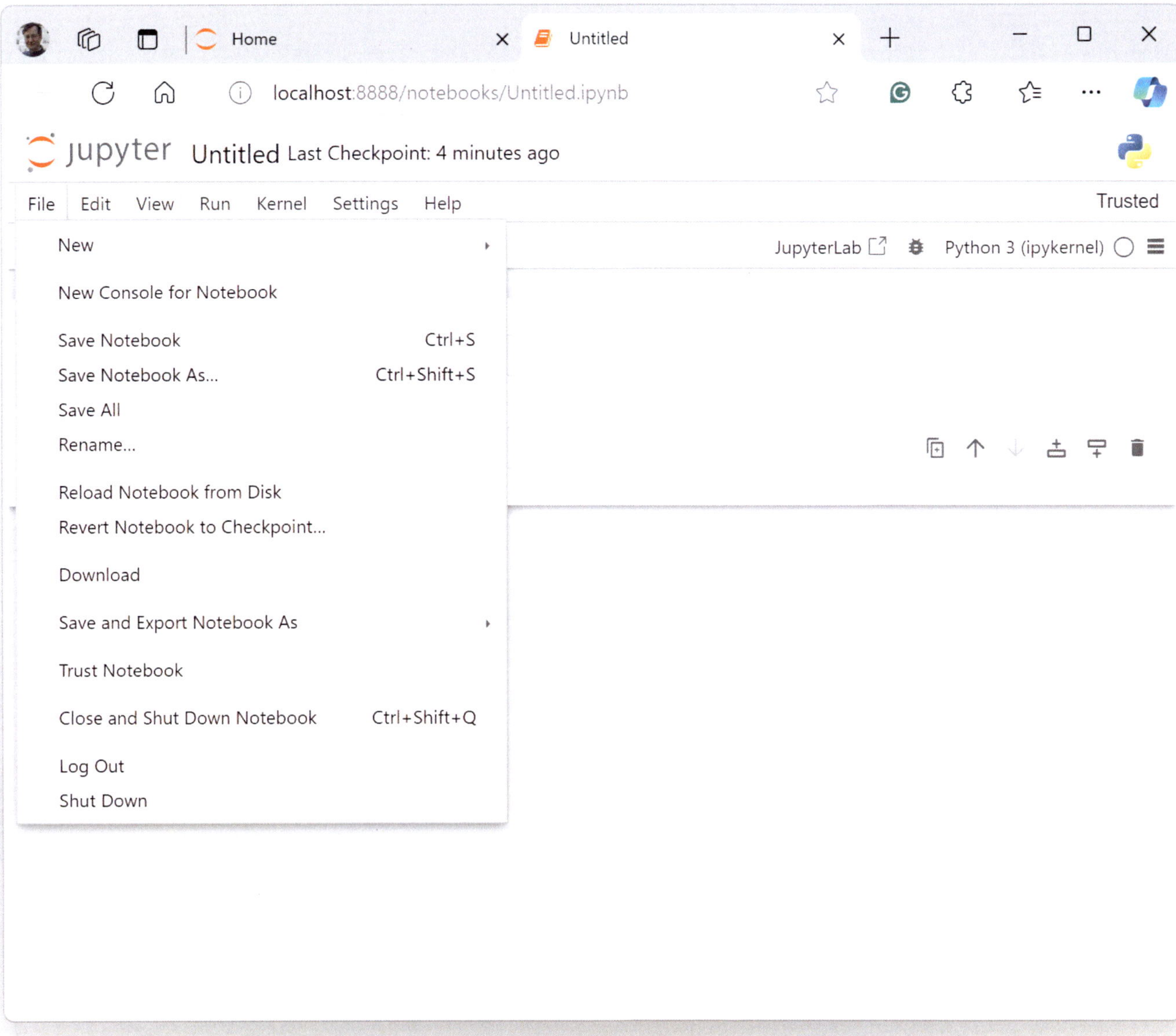

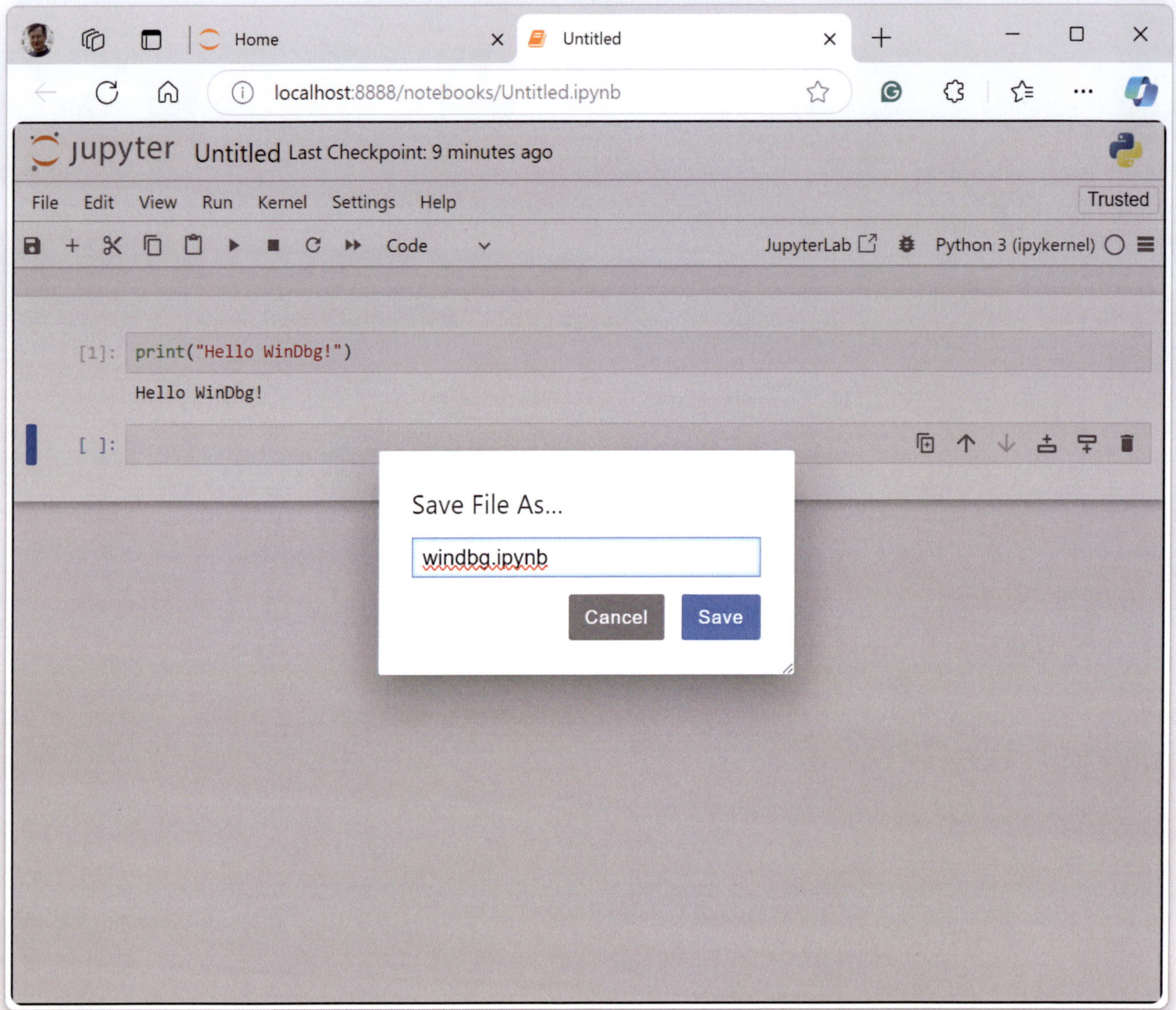

7. Switch to the command prompt window and send **^C**:

```
^C
[I 2024-10-27 10:38:35.048 ServerApp] Interrupted...

C:\EWMDA-Dumps>
```

Exercise EV2

- **Goal:** Explore various execution residue statistics and visualization opportunities using Pandas and Matplotlib
- **Memory Analysis Patterns:** Execution Residue (Unmanaged Space); Region Profile; Region Clusters; Namespace
- \EWMDA\Exercise-EV2.pdf

Exercise EV2: Execution Residue Visualization

Goal: Explore various execution residue visualization opportunities using Pandas[28] and Matplotlib[29].

Memory Analysis Patterns: Execution Residue (Unmanaged Space); Region Profile; Region Clusters; Namespace.

1. Install Pandas, Matplotlib, and ydata-profiling[30] if this was not done before:

```
>cd C:\EWMDA-Dumps

C:\EWMDA-Dumps>pip install pandas
...

C:\EWMDA-Dumps>pip install matplotlib
...

C:\EWMDA-Dumps>pip install ydata_profiling
...

C:\EWMDA-Dumps>pip install wordcloud
...

C:\EWMDA-Dumps>pip install ipywidgets
...
```

2. Launch Jupyter Notebook:

```
C:\EWMDA-Dumps>jupyter notebook
[I 2024-10-27 10:49:12.012 ServerApp] Serving notebooks from local directory: C:\EWMDA-Dumps
[I 2024-10-27 10:49:12.012 ServerApp] Jupyter Server 2.14.2 is running at:
[I 2024-10-27 10:49:12.012 ServerApp]
http://localhost:8888/tree?token=6aee6b21c3ca553789e496844017292bd4ef139f8eaa731e
[I 2024-10-27 10:49:12.013 ServerApp]
http://127.0.0.1:8888/tree?token=6aee6b21c3ca553789e496844017292bd4ef139f8eaa731e
[I 2024-10-27 10:49:12.013 ServerApp] Use Control-C to stop this server and shut down all
kernels (twice to skip confirmation).
[C 2024-10-27 10:49:12.181 ServerApp]

    To access the server, open this file in a browser:
        file:///C:/Users/dmitr/AppData/Roaming/jupyter/runtime/jpserver-2896-open.html
    Or copy and paste one of these URLs:
        http://localhost:8888/tree?token=6aee6b21c3ca553789e496844017292bd4ef139f8eaa731e
        http://127.0.0.1:8888/tree?token=6aee6b21c3ca553789e496844017292bd4ef139f8eaa731e
```

Note: The browser window should open.

[28] https://pandas.pydata.org/

[29] https://matplotlib.org/

[30] https://github.com/ydataai/ydata-profiling

3. Open *windbg.ipynb* file:

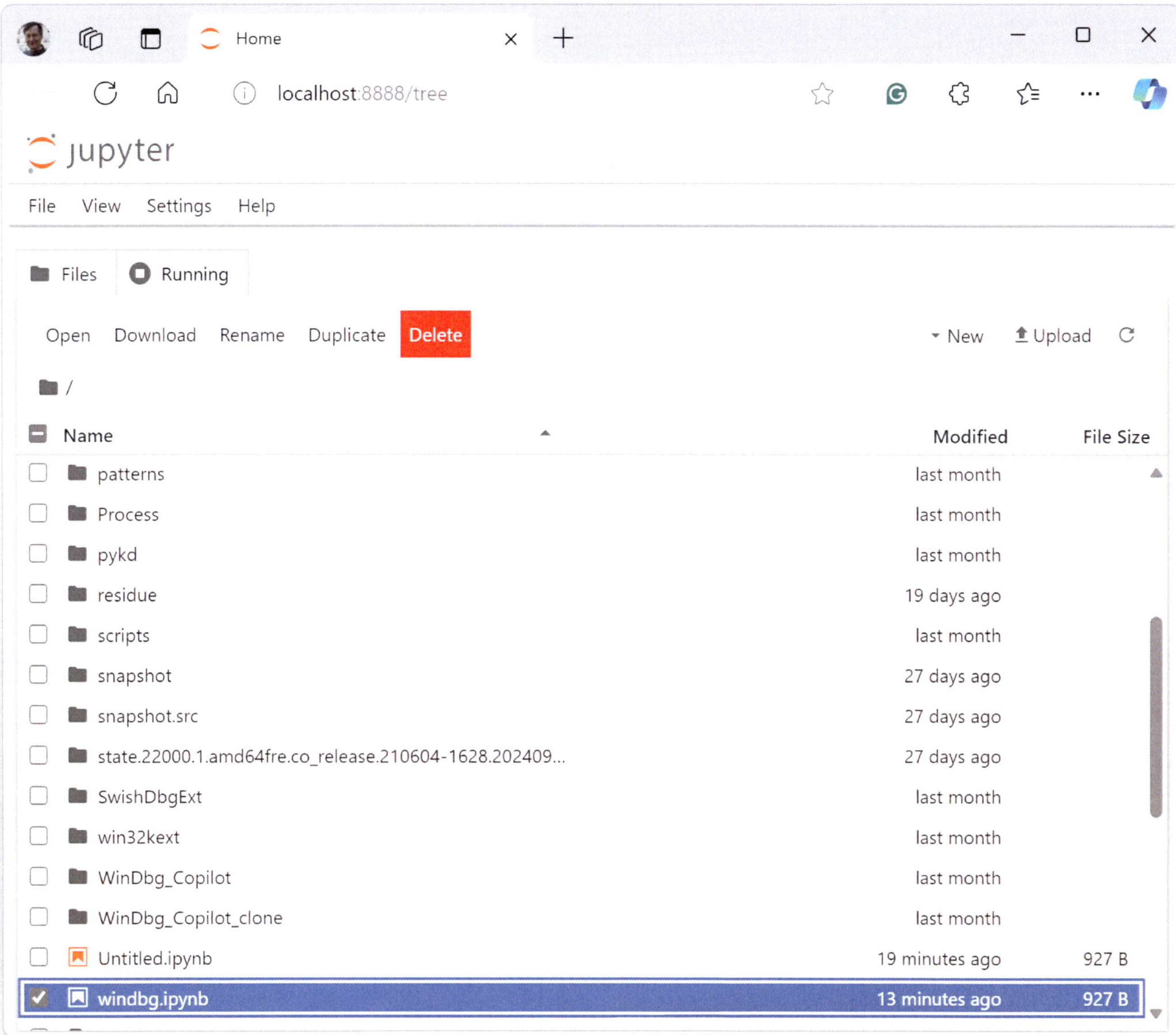

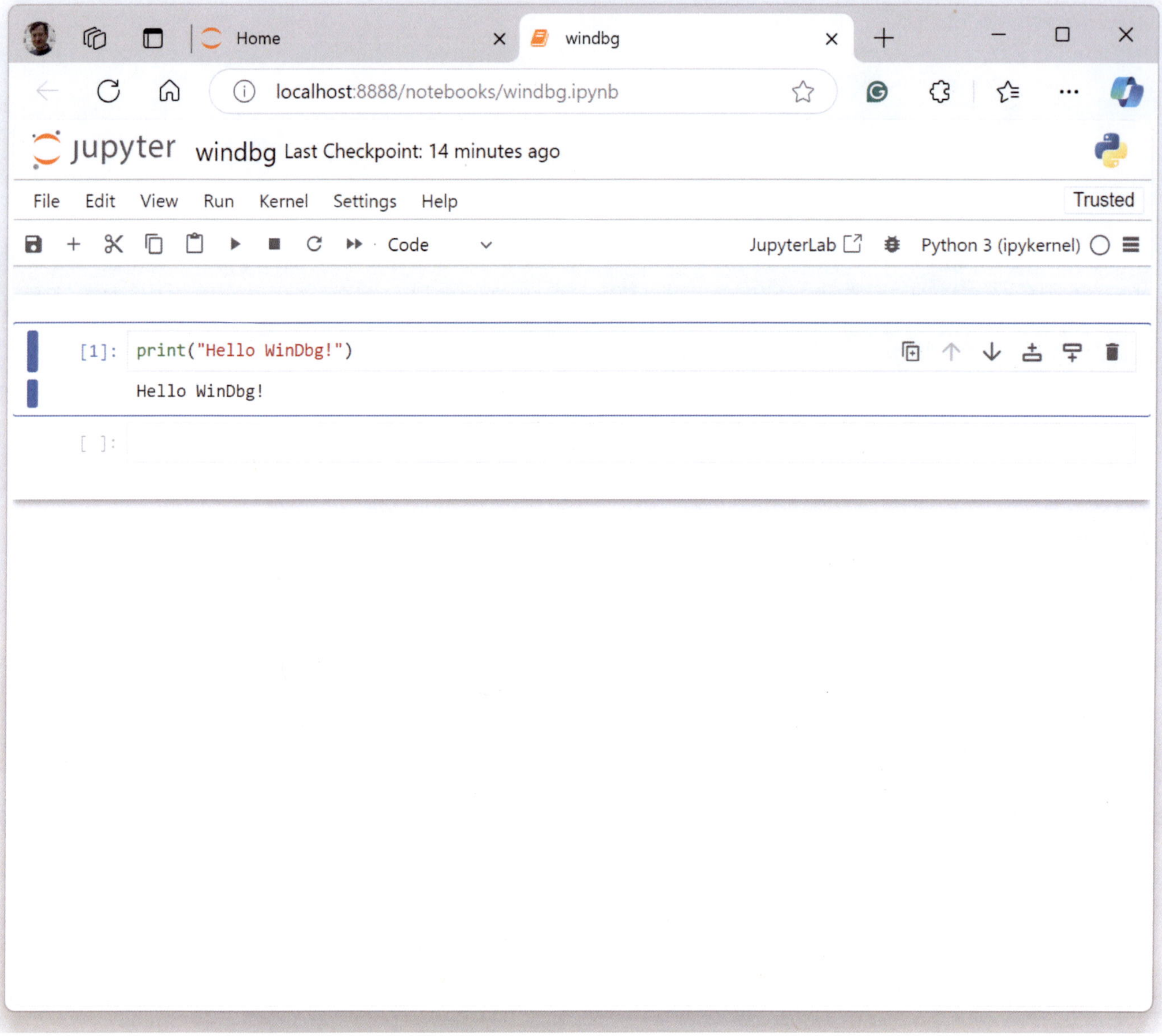

4. Enter this code and execute (Shift-Enter):

```
import pandas
import ydata_profiling

df = pandas.read_csv("scripts/stack_region.csv")
html_file = open("stack.html", "w")
html_file.write (ydata_profiling.ProfileReport(df).to_html())
html_file.close()
```

Open *C:\EWMDA-Dumps\stack.html* in a browser to see the region profile and various statistics such as most frequent values and symbols.

5. To view all data frame rows, you need to remove the maximum number:

```
pandas.set_option('display.max_rows', None)
df
```

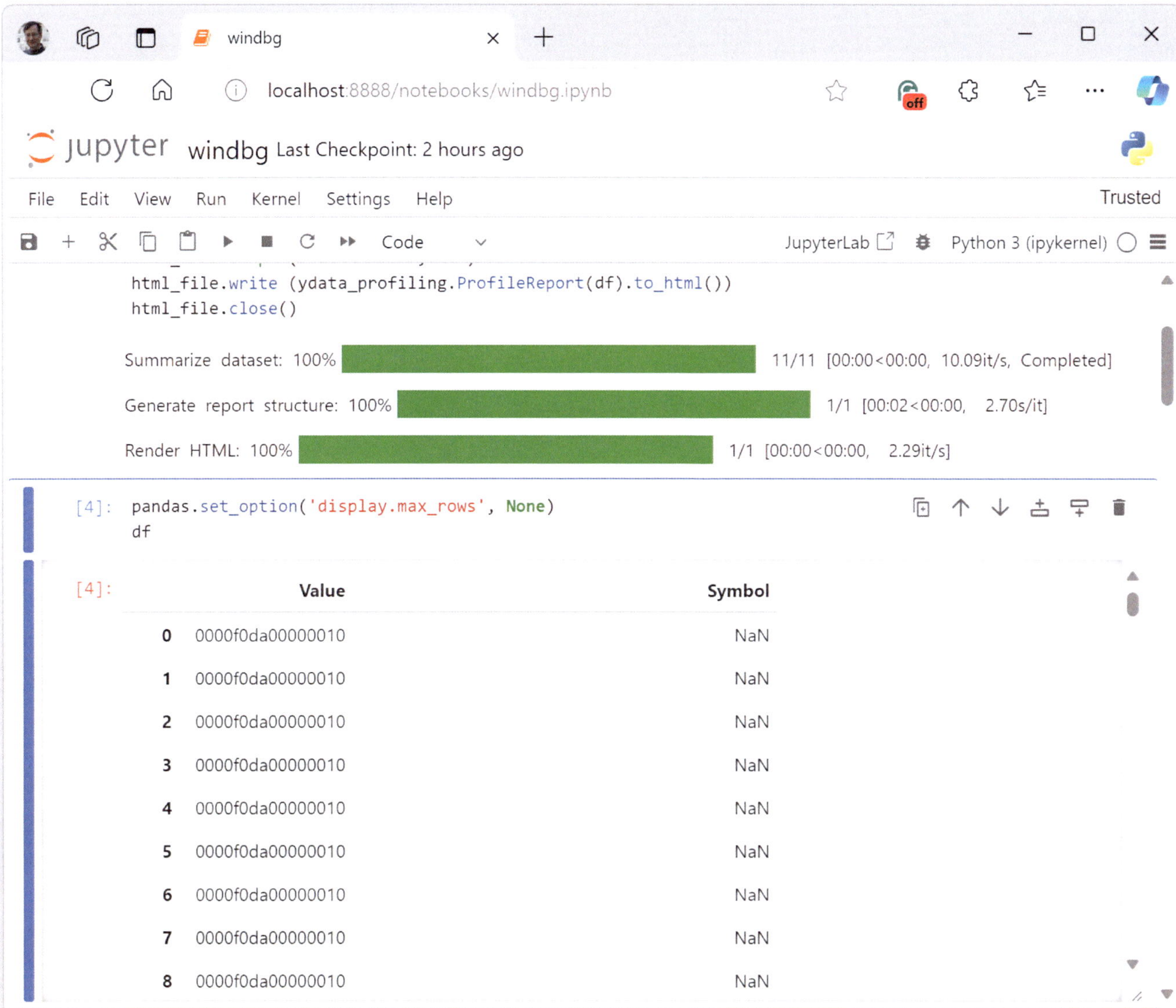

6. Get region clusters of values using this code:

```
df["Value"].value_counts().sort_index()
```

We should get the following output:

```
0000000000000000     556
0000000000000001      25
0000000000000002      10
0000000000000003       2
0000000000000004       5
0000000000000005       1
0000000000000007       1
0000000000000008       3
0000000000000009       3
000000000000000a       4
000000000000000f       1
```

0000000000000010	2
0000000000000018	2
000000000000001a	2
000000000000001e	2
0000000000000020	2
0000000000000028	1
000000000000002b	1
0000000000000033	1
00000000000000a0	2
00000000000000ac	2
00000000000000ba	1
00000000000000d1	1
00000000000000f1	1
0000000000000100	1
0000000000000101	1
0000000000000103	1
0000000000000111	1
0000000000000138	2
00000000000001e0	1
00000000000001fc	3
0000000000000246	2
000000000000027f	1
00000000000002b1	1
0000000000000300	1
000000000000041c	1
0000000000000494	1
0000000000000800	1
0000000000000b1a	1
0000000000000f4d	1
0000000000001000	2
0000000000001f80	1
0000000000002000	1
0000000000003000	2
0000000000005fd4	1
000000000000ef31	1
000000000000ef32	1
000000000000ef33	1
000000000000ef34	1
000000000000ef35	1
000000000000ef5e	1
000000000000ef5f	1
000000000000ef60	1
000000000000ef61	1
000000000000ef62	1
000000000000ef63	1
000000000000ef64	1
000000000000ef65	1
000000000000ef66	1
000000000000ef67	1
000000000000ef68	1
000000000000fee7	1
0000000000010000	8
0000000000010001	1
0000000000020454	3
0000000000030000	1
0000000000031f00	1
0000000000031f45	1
00000000000400d7	1
0000000000040282	2

0000000000043eca	2
0000000000043ff7	2
0000000000044027	2
0000000000044028	1
0000000000044029	1
000000000004402a	1
000000000004402b	1
000000000004402c	1
000000000004402d	1
000000000004402e	1
000000000004402f	1
0000000000044030	1
0000000000044031	1
0000000000044032	1
0000000000044033	1
0000000000044034	1
0000000000044035	1
0000000000044036	1
0000000000050282	1
0000000000070000	1
000000000007c009	1
00000000000a0000	1
00000000000ffea8	2
0000000000110000	1
0000000000140000	3
0000000000200001	1
0000000000282001	1
00000000002820f2	1
0000000000510001	1
0000000000804000	1
0000000040200342	2
0000000040200382	1
0000000043f25000	3
00000000756be768	1
0000000083360001	1
0000000083360018	4
00000000bf9d8138	1
00000000bfdee588	2
00000000c0000001	1
00000000cc0db000	1
00000000cd56fd8b	1
00000000fa619100	1
00000000ffffff0f	2
00000000ffffff46	2
00000000ffffff90	1
00000000fffffff8	1
00000000ffffffff	3
000000010000001a	1
0000000400000005	1
0000000400000050	1
0000000696f60005	1
0000000900000001	1
000000090000000b	1
000000090000001a	2
00000009000000e0	1
0000000b07de7000	1
000000170000003f	1
0000001a00000001	1
0000001a00000009	1

0000002c00000005	1
0000002cff000000	1
0000003f00000000	1
0000003f0731ec08	1
0000003f0731ec28	1
0000003f0731ec60	2
0000003f07458000	1
00000048041102f6	1
000000f100000000	1
000000f1000000ba	2
0000010b000000c3	1
000001e000000280	1
000001e900000000	1
000001e9be2c6fc0	1
0000028000000001	1
00001e95f25e0a40	1
00001f800010000f	1
00001f8001000000	1
00001f8002080000	1
00005fd483360018	1
00007ffc73cbf929	1
00007ffc82cd9040	1
00007ffc88543444	1
0000f0da00000000	1
0000f0da0000000a	1
0000f0da00000010	1838
0001b58800000001	1
0001b58800000004	1
0001b58800000020	1
000402820018002b	1
0012019f00000000	1
0049005f00520000	1
004fa46fb19bbdff	1
0053002b002b0010	1
0056004900520001	1
01d7d8dc35cb4a1f	2
3333333333333333	1
7fffac8a04297378	2
8b05075c38d18070	1
9948a42f5fd49696	1
ffff2703d5aecdf2	1
ffff6a98d8ef3384	1
ffff6a98d8ef3484	1
ffff94d7d0ddb402	1
ffff94d7d0ddb592	1
ffff9b9b49acdaae	1
ffff9b9b49acdcde	1
ffff9b9b49acde4e	1
ffff9b9b49acde7e	1
ffffac8a00000000	1
ffffac8a00003000	1
ffffac8a00400000	1
ffffac8a03a03cc0	1
ffffac8a042c96e0	1
ffffac8a0d480000	2
ffffac8a0d78a000	1
ffffac8a0d8e7000	3
ffffac8a0d8e7010	1
ffffac8a0d8ea010	9

ffffbd1183360018	1
ffffbd11c0e0c000	1
ffffbd11c0e0c010	4
ffffbd11c0e0c2b8	1
ffffbd11c253e710	1
ffffbd4300000000	1
ffffbd43fa619191	1
ffffbd43fa643fb8	1
ffffbd43fa6a305e	1
ffffbd43fa8af108	1
ffffbd43fa8b2468	3
ffffbd43fb5cec01	1
ffffbd43fb5dfa63	1
ffffbd43fb67b3a8	1
ffffbd43fb690901	1
ffffbd43fb6ebd5a	1
ffffbe8200000000	2
ffffbe8200000001	1
ffffbe820000000a	1
ffffbe820000000f	1
ffffbe8200001000	1
ffffbe829688d000	1
ffffbe82968923a0	1
ffffbe8296892b60	1
ffffbe8296892c70	1
ffffbe8296893000	1
ffffbe8296f5f000	2
ffffbe8296f62f20	1
ffffbe8296f63020	1
ffffbe8296f63028	1
ffffbe8296f63080	1
ffffbe8296f63201	1
ffffbe8296f63210	3
ffffbe8296f63230	1
ffffbe8296f63238	3
ffffbe8296f63260	1
ffffbe8296f63271	1
ffffbe8296f63360	1
ffffbe8296f63390	1
ffffbe8296f633c8	1
ffffbe8296f63401	1
ffffbe8296f63410	1
ffffbe8296f63440	3
ffffbe8296f63460	1
ffffbe8296f634a0	1
ffffbe8296f634c0	1
ffffbe8296f635e8	4
ffffbe8296f63800	1
ffffbe8296f6380a	1
ffffbe8296f63870	1
ffffbe8296f638f8	2
ffffbe8296f63900	1
ffffbe8296f63901	1
ffffbe8296f63940	4
ffffbe8296f639a0	1
ffffbe8296f639c0	1
ffffbe8296f63a94	1
ffffbe8296f63a98	1
ffffbe8296f63ab0	1

ffffbe8296f63ca9	1
ffffbe8296f63de8	1
ffffbe8296f63e11	3
ffffbe8296f63fc0	3
ffffbe8296f640a0	2
ffffbe8296f64668	1
ffffbe8296f646d0	1
ffffbe8296f64770	1
ffffbe8296f647b0	1
ffffbe8296f64830	2
ffffbe8296f64940	1
ffffbe8296f64a78	1
ffffbe8296f64b18	1
ffffbe8296f64bb0	1
ffffbe8296f64bb1	2
ffffbe8296f64c01	1
ffffbe8296f64d10	1
ffffbe8296f64dc8	1
ffffbe8296f64ea0	2
ffffbe8296f65000	2
ffffc30000000000	1
ffffc30032000101	1
ffffc38c00000000	4
ffffc38c0000fec8	1
ffffc38c2c402000	1
ffffc38c2c479200	1
ffffc38c2c4792d0	7
ffffc38c2c4b9900	1
ffffc38c2c4b99b8	1
ffffc38c2cd80010	1
ffffc38c2cd813d0	2
ffffc38c2cd88050	1
ffffc38c2cd881a0	3
ffffc38c2cd88470	1
ffffc38c2cd88480	1
ffffc38c2cd8d1a0	1
ffffc38c2e16b080	1
ffffc38c2e361000	1
ffffc38c2e363000	2
ffffc38c2e363038	2
ffffc38c2e436000	1
ffffc38c2e631018	3
ffffc38c2e63101e	1
ffffc38c2e6310d0	1
ffffc38c2e63132a	1
ffffc38c2e6313e8	6
ffffc38c2e6314b0	2
ffffc38c3020f010	2
ffffc38c306b5ac0	1
ffffc38c306d4f10	3
ffffc38c306d4f70	3
ffffc38c308efcf0	1
ffffc38c31efb360	9
ffffc38c31efb370	4
ffffc38c31efb390	5
ffffc38c32262dd0	2
ffffc38c32262e48	1
ffffc38c326f9080	4
ffffc38c326f9720	1

ffffc38c32a50960	3
ffffc38c32f11690	1
ffffc38c32f116d8	2
ffffc38c334f0590	1
ffffc38c33751080	1
ffffc38c33ac3080	7
ffffc38c34dd8690	10
ffffc38cbf9d8138	1
ffffd48000000001	1
ffffd480000000ba	1
ffffd480000000f1	2
ffffd48000000240	1
ffffd4807fffffff	1
ffffd480db780000	2
ffffd480dba5b200	1
ffffd480dba5bb50	1
ffffd480dba65001	1
ffffd480dba65030	5
ffffd480dba65078	5
ffffd480dba650fa	1
ffffd480dba651e0	1
ffffd480dbb00180	1
ffffd480dc39a030	5
ffffd480dc39a118	3
ffffd480dc39a128	2
ffffd480dc39a450	1
ffffd480dc39a588	2
ffffd480dc39a5b8	1
ffffd480dd1c0000	1
ffffd480dd280000	1
ffffd480dd280138	2
ffffd480dd280168	1
fffff7cf40001618	1
fffff80600000000	3
fffff80600000002	1
fffff80600000008	1
fffff806000001a8	1
fffff80600000280	1
fffff806000002b1	1
fffff80660571981	7
fffff80660571d3d	1
fffff80660571ea1	1
fffff806605917d4	1
fffff80660591f33	1
fffff806605941cd	1
fffff806605c3046	1
fffff806605c36cc	1
fffff80660cd5180	3
fffff80660cddcf0	1
fffff8066201256b	2
fffff80662021ef6	1
fffff806620f5a1d	1
fffff806620f5b0e	1
fffff806620faf7b	1
fffff80662102d23	1
fffff80662102f65	1
fffff806621036ea	1
fffff8066212df2c	1
fffff80662133ff7	1

fffff8066218c2ea	1
fffff806621a2b96	1
fffff806621a2da9	1
fffff806621a4a19	1
fffff806621a7261	1
fffff80662215590	1
fffff80662215697	1
fffff8066221d0cf	1
fffff8066221d507	1
fffff80662224300	1
fffff80662227b75	2
fffff806622281a9	1
fffff806623197e9	1
fffff80662346490	3
fffff8066234e0b0	1
fffff8066234e810	1
fffff8066234f01e	1
fffff8066236257a	1
fffff80662362bb0	8
fffff80662362df9	1
fffff806624a4204	1
fffff806624a42fd	1
fffff8066256a6c6	1
fffff8066256acbf	1
fffff8066256b532	1
fffff8066256df14	1
fffff8066258de9e	1
fffff8066286b964	1
fffff80662a0de40	1
fffff80662a2b650	1
fffff80662a54e00	1
fffff80662a5f540	1
fffff80662af2490	1
fffff806674c3046	1
fffff806674c36cc	1
fffff806674e4152	1
fffff806674e44aa	2
fffff806674e55de	1
fffff806674f0c38	1
fffff80668c062dd	1
fffff80668c082be	1
fffff80668c09686	1
fffff80668c0ae9c	1
fffff80668c0b1b0	1
fffff80668c0b360	1
fffff80668c0b3fd	1
fffff80668c0d489	1
fffff80668c13c50	6
fffff80669570728	1
fffff806699a1146	1
fffff806699a1d7e	1
fffff806699a1df4	1
fffff806699a251f	1
fffff8066d8cee70	4
fffff8066d8cfd20	2
fffffb6a406e1cd0	2
fffffb7db5203708	2
fffffb7dbeda9018	2
fffffb7dbedf6d48	2

```
fffffc571d9e83a5       1
fffffc571d9e85a5       1
fffffc571d9e8b85       1
fffffc571d9ef0d5       1
fffffc571d9efd95       1
fffffc57bfdee588       1
ffffff0ffffff46        1
ffffffffffffffff       1
```

7. Get region namespaces using this code:

```
df[["Symbol"]].drop_duplicates().sort_values(by="Symbol")[:-1].style.set_properties(**{'text-align': 'left'})
```

We should get the following output:

```
BasicDisplay!BASIC_DISPLAY_DRIVER::SystemDisplayWrite+116
BasicDisplay!BddDdiSystemDisplayWrite+24
BasicDisplay!BltBits+136
BasicDisplay!CopyBitsTo_4+3af
COMCTL32!Button_WndProc+37909
crashdmp!Context+50
crashdmp!CrashdmpWrite+23d
crashdmp!CrashdmpWritePendingRoutine
crashdmp!CrashdmpWriteRoutine
crashdmp!CrashdmpWriteRoutine+9d
crashdmp!DumpWrite+57e
crashdmp!IsBufferValid+29
crashdmp!WriteBitmapDump+486
crashdmp!WritePageSpanToDisk+318
dump_diskdump!DiskDumpWrite+1d4
dump_diskdump!ExecuteSrb+1f
dump_diskdump!StartIo+a5
dump_lsi_sas!BuildScatterGather+d0
dump_lsi_sas!LSImpiBuildIo+176
dxgkrnl!DpiSystemDisplayWrite+d8
lsi_sas!BuildScatterGather+d0
lsi_sas!LSImpiBuildIo+176
myfault+1981
myfault+1d3d
myfault+1ea1
nt!AstAddBloomFilter+1c
nt!AstGetHashedBitNumbers+c1
nt!AstLogIoctl+1d4
nt!BcpWorkspace
nt!BgpGxDrawRectangle+76
nt!ExAllocatePoolWithTag+64
nt!ExPoolState+4580
nt!ExReleaseResourceAndLeaveCriticalRegion+7c
nt!FioFwReadBytesAtOffset+1d
nt!GxpWriteFrameBufferPixels+1f9
nt!HalBuildScatterGatherListV2+25b
nt!HalpApicHvUpdateCallback+9
nt!HvlGetEncryptedData
nt!IoFreeDumpRange
nt!IoMapTransfer+6a
nt!IoSetDumpRange
nt!IoWriteCrashDump+52a
```

```
nt!IofCallDriver+55
nt!IopAllocateIrpPrivate+183
nt!IopSynchronousServiceTail+1d2
nt!IopXxxControlFile+5df
nt!KeBugCheck2+cba
nt!KeBugCheckEx
nt!KeBugCheckEx+107
nt!KeBugCheckReasonCallbackListHead
nt!KeFlushCurrentTbOnly+61
nt!KeUserModeCallback+27e
nt!KiAbEntryGetLockedHeadEntry+2cb
nt!KiAbProcessContextSwitch+1c7
nt!KiAbTreeArray+cdd0
nt!KiBugCheckDispatch+69
nt!KiBugCheckProgress
nt!KiBugCheckWriteCrashDump+51
nt!KiDispatchInterrupt+f
nt!KiPageFault+440
nt!KiSystemServiceCopyEnd+25
nt!MiGetPhysicalAddress+da
nt!MiRaisedIrqlFault+1ae
nt!MiSystemPartition
nt!MmGetPhysicalAddress+1d
nt!NtDeviceIoControlFile+56
nt!RtlHashBytes2+1a
nt!SwapContext+1c7
ntdll!NtDeviceIoControlFile+14
storport!RaUnitStartIo+32a
storport!RaidAdapterPostScatterGatherExecute+4fe
storport!RaidpAdapterContinueScatterGather+42
storport!StorPortGetPhysicalAddress+1c8
uxtheme!CPaintBufferAnimation::`vftable'
win32kbase!ThreadUnlock1+71
win32kbase!UserSessionSwitchLeaveCrit+f8
win32kbase!gDomainDummyLock
win32kbase!gDomainHookLock
win32kbase!tagDomLock::UnLockExclusive+e
win32kfull!ClientImmProcessKey+c5
win32kfull!FreeDelayedHooks+e3
win32kfull!GetJournallingQueue+51
win32kfull!NtUserMessageCall+1d8
win32kfull!SharedUserCritOnly::UnlockDomainShared::UnlockDomainExclusive<>::UnlockObjectLock<>:
:~UnlockObjectLock<>+3e
```

8. Get the word cloud of modules using this code:

```
import re

symbols = df.loc[:, "Symbol"].drop_duplicates().values[1:]
symbols = [re.split(r"[+!]", x)[0] for x in symbols]

import wordcloud

wc = wordcloud.WordCloud(background_color='white').generate(" ".join(symbols))

import matplotlib.pyplot as plt
%matplotlib inline
```

```
plt.figure(figsize=(10,10))
plt.imshow(wc)
plt.axis("off")
plt.show()
```

We should get a similar picture:

9. For anomaly detection, sometimes a word cloud where less frequent words are more prominent than common ones, based on their inverse frequency is useful:

```
from collections import Counter

symbol_counts = Counter(symbols)

inverse_frequencies = {symbol: 1 / count for symbol, count in symbol_counts.items()}

wc = wordcloud.WordCloud(background_color='white')
wc.generate_from_frequencies(inverse_frequencies)

plt.figure(figsize=(10,10))
plt.imshow(wc)
plt.axis("off")
plt.show()
```

We should get a similar picture:

10. Close the browser, switch to the command prompt window, and send **^C**:

```
^C
[I 2024-10-27 13:16:17.191 ServerApp] Interrupted...

C:\EWMDA-Dumps>
```

Exercise EV3

- **Goal:** Find anomalies in stack traces from different executions
- **Memory Analysis Patterns:** Rough Stack Trace Collection (Unmanaged Space); Namespace
- \EWMDA\Exercise-EV3.pdf

Exercise EV3: Find Anomalies in Stack Traces

Goal: Find anomalies in stack traces from different executions.

Memory Analysis Patterns: Rough Stack Trace Collection (Unmanaged Space); Namespace.

1. There was a problem when running Firefox: it hung after some time. Good (ok) and problem (fail) stack trace collections from process memory dumps were identical, and execution residues were collected from each memory dump using this WinDbg script and saved in log files (residues-ok.log and residues-fail.log):

```
~*e r? $t1 = ((ntdll!_NT_TIB *)@$teb)->StackLimit; r? $t2 = ((ntdll!_NT_TIB *)@$teb)-
>StackBase; !teb; dps @$t1 @$t2
```

Note: To avoid sharing potential sensitive stack region data, non-return address data was filtered out using the *\EWMDA-Dumps\ML\filter.py* Python program:

```
# Extended Windows Memory Dump Analysis, Version 2.0
# Exercise EV3

import re

# Read execution residue data from a text file for ok case
with open('residues-ok.log', 'r') as file:
    data_ok = file.read()

file = open('rough-trace-ok.log', 'w')

pattern = r"[0-9a-fA-F]{8}`[0-9a-fA-F]{8}  [0-9a-fA-F?]{8}`[0-9a-fA-F?]{8}$"

# filter and write only lines with symbols
filtered_output = [line for line in data_ok.splitlines() if not re.match(pattern, line)]
with open('rough-trace-ok.log', 'w') as file:
    file.write("\n".join(filtered_output))

# Read execution residue data from a text file for fail case
with open('residues-fail.log', 'r') as file:
    data_fail = file.read()

# filter and write only lines with symbols
filtered_output = [line for line in data_fail.splitlines() if not re.match(pattern, line)]
with open('rough-trace-fail.log', 'w') as file:
    file.write("\n".join(filtered_output))
```

Note: The produced rough stack trace collections separated by TEB output were saved in *\EWMDA-Dumps\ML\rough-trace-ok.log* and *\EWMDA-Dumps\ML\rough-trace-fail.log* files.

2. Our goal is to compare both rough stack trace collections and find symbolic and module references in the fail case that are not present in the ok case. It is done via the *\EWMDA-Dumps\ML\set-difference.py* Python program:

```
# Extended Windows Memory Dump Analysis, Version 2.0
# Exercise EV3

import re

# Regular expression pattern to match module and ignore the !function+offset
module_pattern = re.compile(r'(\w+)(?=!)')
# Regular expression pattern to match module!function and ignore the offset
symbol_pattern = re.compile(r'(\w+!\w+)(?:\+\w+)?')

# Read data from a text file for ok case
with open('rough-trace-ok.log', 'r') as file:
    data_ok = file.read()

# A set to store unique symbols for ok case
all_symbols_ok = set(symbol_pattern.findall(data_ok))

# A set to store unique modules for ok case
all_modules_ok = set(module_pattern.findall(data_ok))

# Read data from a text file for fail case
with open('rough-trace-fail.log', 'r') as file:
    data_fail = file.read()

# A set to store unique symbols for fail case
all_symbols_fail = set(symbol_pattern.findall(data_fail))

# A set to store unique modules for fail case
all_modules_fail = set(module_pattern.findall(data_fail))

# A set of symbols not found in ok case
symbol_difference_fail_ok = all_symbols_fail - all_symbols_ok
print("Symbols not found in ok case: ")
for s in sorted(symbol_difference_fail_ok):
    print(s)

# A set of modules not found in ok case
module_difference_fail_ok = all_modules_fail - all_modules_ok
print("\nModules not found in ok case: ")
for s in sorted(module_difference_fail_ok):
    print(s)
```

Note: We have the following output:

```
PS C:\EWMDA-Dumps\ML> & C:/Python311/python.exe c:/EWMDA-Dumps/ML/set-difference.py
Symbols not found in ok case:
KERNELBASE!BaseRegGetKeySemantics
KERNELBASE!BaseRegGetUserAndMachineClass
KERNELBASE!BaseRegOpenClassKey
KERNELBASE!BasepLoadLibraryAsDataFileInternal
KERNELBASE!CreateFileW
KERNELBASE!DestroyPrivateObjectSecurity
KERNELBASE!DeviceIoControl
KERNELBASE!NlsValidateLocale
KERNELBASE!VerpQueryValue
MMDevAPI!AudiosrvBinding
OneCoreUAPCommonProxyStub!CRT_INIT
OneCoreUAPCommonProxyStub!DllMainCRTStartup
OneCoreUAPCommonProxyStub!NdrOleAllocate
OneCoreUAPCommonProxyStub!NdrOleFree
OneCoreUAPCommonProxyStub!_NULL_IMPORT_DESCRIPTOR
OneCoreUAPCommonProxyStub!gPFactory
advapi32!GetAceStub
avrt!_AvrtDllInitialize
bcryptPrimitives!SymCryptRngAesGenerateSmall
bcryptPrimitives!SymCryptRngAesUpdate
cdp!dllmain_dispatch
clr!InitDefaultDomain_V1
combase!IOrCallback_DispatchTable
combase!IOrCallback_ServerInfo
combase!IOrCallback_ServerRoutineTable
combase!IUpdateResolverBindings
combase!_UpdateResolverBindings
combase!g_wszInprocHandler16
combase!orcb__MIDL_ProcFormatString
combase!orcb__MIDL_TypeFormatString
dsreg!tlgWriteTransfer_EventWriteTransfer
dwmapi!_tlgWriteTemplate
firefox!TargetNtOpenKeyEx
freebl3!FREEBL_GetVector
imm32!ImmGetIMEFileNameW
imm32!ImmGetImeInfoEx
kernel32!DeviceIoControlImplementation
kernel32!GetCurrentProcess
kernel32!SbSupportedOsList
kernel32!SbpCreateSwitchContext
kernel32!SbpIsTraceEnabled
kernel32!timeGetTime
mozglue!blink
mscoreei!_imp_GetProcAddress
mscoreei!try_get_function
msvcrt!wcstoxlX
netprofm!DllMainCRTStartup
nss3!CERT_DecodeAVAValue
nss3!CERT_GetOidString
nss3!PR_CreateFileMap
nss3!PR_NewCondVar
nss3!PR_SetFDInheritable
nss3!SECITEM_DupItem_Util
nss3!SECKEY_EncryptedPrivateKeyInfoTemplate
```

```
nss3!SEC_IA5StringTemplate_Util
nss3!SEC_QuickDERDecodeItem_Util
nss3!sqlite3_bind_text16
nss3!sqlite3_stmt_readonly
nss3!sqlite3_user_data
ntdll!ApiSetpSearchForApiSetHost
ntdll!EtwpEventWriteFull
ntdll!EtwpRegistrationCompare
ntdll!GetLCIDFromLangListNodeWithLICCheck
ntdll!LdrResGetRCConfig
ntdll!LdrpGetFromMUIMemCache
ntdll!LdrpResSearchResourceInsideDirectory
ntdll!LdrpResolveProcedureAddress
ntdll!NtCreateFile
ntdll!NtdllDispatchMessage_W
ntdll!RtlCapabilityCheck
ntdll!RtlDeleteSecurityObject
ntdll!RtlpDecRefWnfNameSubscription
ntdll!RtlpFreeDebugInfo
ntdll!RtlpImageDirectoryEntryToDataEx
ntdll!RtlpQueryEnvironmentCache
ntdll!RtlpWnfNotificationThread
ntdll!TppWaitCompletion
ntdll!setjmpexused
ntmarta!GetNamedSecurityInfoW
ntmarta!MartaAddRefFileContext
ntmarta!MartaCloseFileContext
ntmarta!MartaGetFileParentContext
ntmarta!MartaGetRightsFromContext
ntmarta!MartaOpenFileNamedObject
powrprof!CallNtPowerInformation
powrprof!PowerpSettingCallback
rpcrt4!DispatchToStubInCNoAvrf
rpcrt4!DuplicateString3
rpcrt4!I_RpcSend
rpcrt4!Invoke
rpcrt4!LRPC_ADDRESS
rpcrt4!LRPC_SASSOCIATION
rpcrt4!LRPC_SCALL
rpcrt4!MesDecodeBufferHandleCreate
rpcrt4!Ndr64pCompleteAsyncCall
rpcrt4!NdrAsyncServerCall
rpcrt4!NdrpCompleteAsyncServerCall
rpcrt4!NdrpFreeAsyncMsg
rpcrt4!NdrpServerUnMarshal
rpcrt4!RPC_INTERFACE
rpcrt4!RpcAsyncCompleteCall
ucrtbase!LangCountryEnumProcEx
ucrtbase!__acrt_AppPolicyGetThreadInitializationTypeInternal
ucrtbase!_free_base
ucrtbase!common_vsnprintf_s
ucrtbase!nstream
ucrtbase!wcsnicmp_l
ucrtbase_clr0400!_acrt_initial_locale_data
ucrtbase_clr0400!common_vsprintf
ucrtbase_clr0400!format_validation_lookup_table
user32!GetScreenRect
user32!GetSystemMetrics
user32!PowerNotificationCallback
```

```
user32!RealDefWindowProcWorker
user32!RealGetSystemMetrics
user32!__PchSym_
user32!_fnDWORD
user32!fnPOWERBROADCAST
vcruntime140_1_7ffffbd10000!CallSettingFrame
win32u!NtUserPeekMessage
ws2_32!WahRemoveHandleContext
xul!mozilla_dump_image

Modules not found in ok case:
CoreMessaging
cdp
dsreg
freebl3
imm32
ntmarta
powrprof
vcruntime140_1_7ffffbd10000
```

Note: Some symbols may be coincidental.

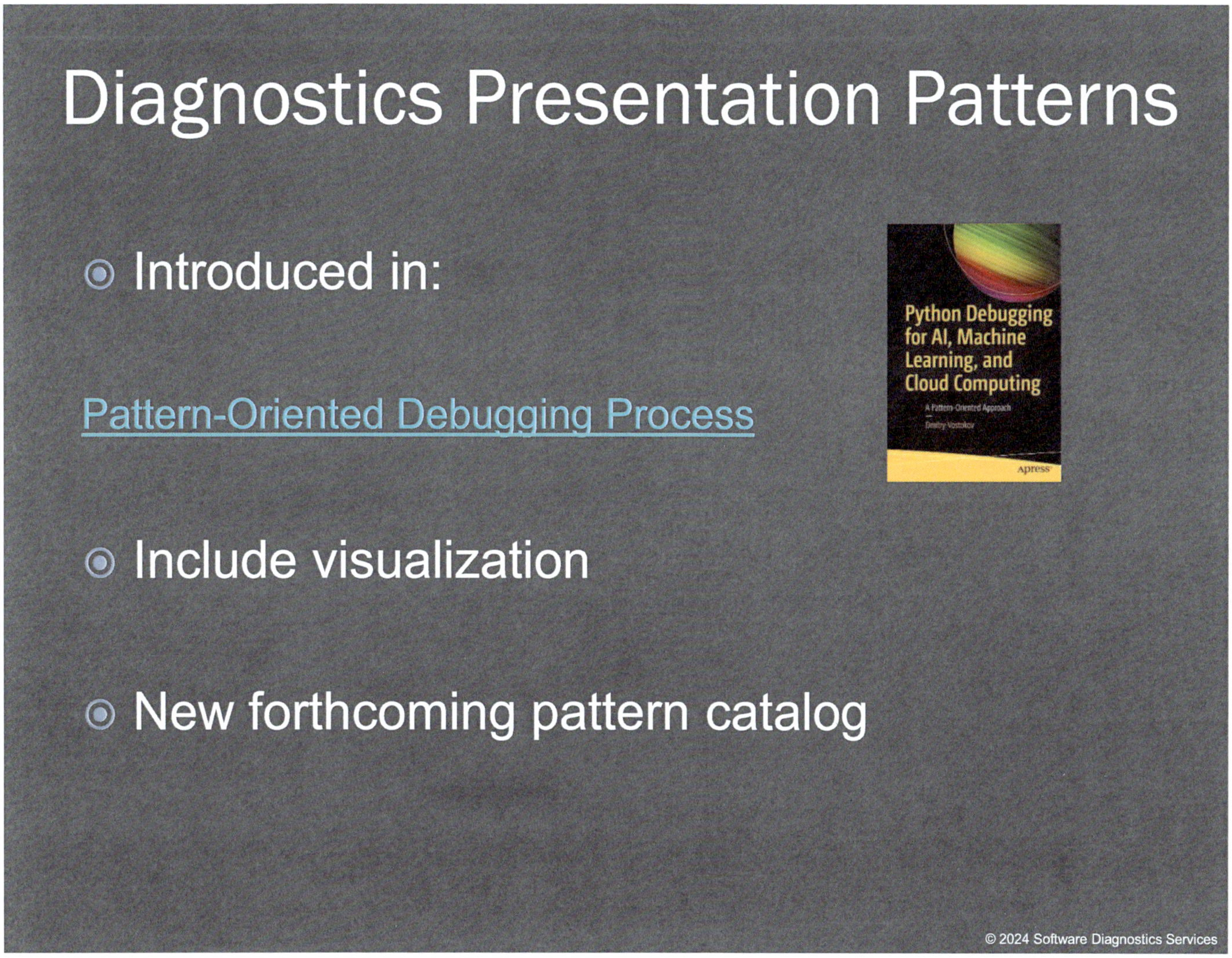

Some time ago, I felt a need to add software diagnostics presentation patterns in addition to debugging presentation patterns introduced earlier. These presentation patterns should include visualization, and I'm working on initial patterns to add to the new pattern catalog.

Pattern-Oriented Debugging Process
https://www.dumpanalysis.org/pattern-oriented-debugging-process

Machine Learning and AI

Exercises ML1 – ML3

Our last three exercises use various machine learning methods to compute similarities and anomalies between (rough) stack traces. We assume familiarity with the basics of traditional machine learning. Please consider the provided source code as a template for further exploration.

Exercise ML1

- **Goal:** Compute the similarity of stack traces from different executions
- **Memory Analysis Patterns:** Stack Trace Collection (Unmanaged Space); Rough Stack Trace Collection (Unmanaged Space)
- **Feature Extraction:** Function Call Frequencies; N-grams; TF-IDF
- **Comparison:** Cosine Similarity; Jaccard Similarity
- \EWMDA\Exercise-ML1.pdf

Exercise ML1: Compute Similarity of Stack Traces

Goal: Compute the similarity of stack traces from different executions.

Memory Analysis Patterns: Stack Trace Collection (Unmanaged Space); Rough Stack Trace Collection (Unmanaged Space).

Feature Extraction: Function Call Frequencies; N-grams; TF-IDF.

Comparison: Cosine Similarity; Jaccard Similarity.

1. We use the same set of log files from Exercise EV3: *\EWMDA-Dumps\ML\rough-trace-ok.log* and *\EWMDA-Dumps\ML\rough-trace-fail.log* for the Firefox problem. You may need to install the *scikit-learn* Python package.

2. Our goal is to compute the similarity of rough stack trace collections as a whole. It is done via the *\EWMDA-Dumps\ML\trace-similarity.py* Python program:

```
# Extended Windows Memory Dump Analysis, Version 2.0
# Exercise ML1

import re
import numpy as np

from sklearn.feature_extraction.text import CountVectorizer
from sklearn.feature_extraction.text import TfidfVectorizer
from sklearn.metrics.pairwise import cosine_similarity
from sklearn.metrics import jaccard_score

# Regular expression pattern to match module!function and ignore the offset
symbol_pattern = re.compile(r'(\w+!\w+)(?:\+\w+)?')

# Read data from a text file for ok case
with open('rough-trace-ok.log', 'r') as file:
    data_ok = file.read()

# A set to store unique symbols for ok case
all_symbols_ok = set(symbol_pattern.findall(data_ok))

# Read data from a text file for fail case
with open('rough-trace-fail.log', 'r') as file:
    data_fail = file.read()

# A set to store unique symbols for fail case
all_symbols_fail = set(symbol_pattern.findall(data_fail))

# Create textual documents representing stack traces
document_ok = "\n".join(all_symbols_ok)
document_fail = "\n".join(all_symbols_fail)
```

```python
# Symbol frequencies
vectorizer = CountVectorizer()
symbol_freq = vectorizer.fit_transform([document_ok, document_fail])
# Calculate cosine similarity
cosine_sim = cosine_similarity(symbol_freq[0:1], symbol_freq[1:2])
print("Cosine similarity (symbol frequencies):", cosine_sim[0][0])
# Calculate Jaccard similarity
symbol_freq = symbol_freq.toarray()
symbol_freq_binary = np.where(symbol_freq > 0, 1, 0)
jaccard_sim = jaccard_score(symbol_freq_binary[0], symbol_freq_binary[1])
print(f"Jaccard similarity (symbol frequencies): {jaccard_sim:.2f}")

# N-grams
vectorizer = CountVectorizer(ngram_range=(2, 2))  # Generate bigrams
ngrams = vectorizer.fit_transform([document_ok, document_fail])
# Calculate cosine similarity
cosine_sim = cosine_similarity(ngrams[0:1], ngrams[1:2])
print("Cosine similarity (bigrams):", cosine_sim[0][0])
# Calculate Jaccard similarity
ngrams = ngrams.toarray()
ngrams_binary = np.where(ngrams > 0, 1, 0)
jaccard_sim = jaccard_score(ngrams_binary[0], ngrams_binary[1])
print(f"Jaccard similarity (bigrams)): {jaccard_sim:.2f}")

# TF-IDF similarity with unigrams
vectorizer = TfidfVectorizer()
tfidf_matrix = vectorizer.fit_transform([document_ok, document_fail])
cosine_sim = cosine_similarity(tfidf_matrix[0:1], tfidf_matrix[1:2])
print("Cosine Similarity (TF-IDF, unigrams):", cosine_sim[0][0])
# Calculate Jaccard similarity
tfidf_matrix = tfidf_matrix.toarray()
tfidf_matrix_binary = np.where(tfidf_matrix > 0, 1, 0)
jaccard_sim = jaccard_score(tfidf_matrix_binary[0], tfidf_matrix_binary[1])
print(f"Jaccard similarity (TF-IDF, unigrams)): {jaccard_sim:.2f}")

# TF-IDF similarity with bigrams
vectorizer = TfidfVectorizer(ngram_range=(2, 2))
tfidf_matrix = vectorizer.fit_transform([document_ok, document_fail])
cosine_sim = cosine_similarity(tfidf_matrix[0:1], tfidf_matrix[1:2])
print("Cosine similarity (TF-IDF, bigrams):", cosine_sim[0][0])
# Calculate Jaccard similarity
tfidf_matrix = tfidf_matrix.toarray()
tfidf_matrix_binary = np.where(tfidf_matrix > 0, 1, 0)
jaccard_sim = jaccard_score(tfidf_matrix_binary[0], tfidf_matrix_binary[1])
print(f"Jaccard similarity (TF-IDF, bigrams): {jaccard_sim:.2f}")
```

Note: We have the following output:

```
PS C:\EWMDA-Dumps\ML> & C:/Python311/python.exe c:/EWMDA-Dumps/ML/trace-similarity.py
Cosine similarity (symbol frequencies): 0.9772467118236781
Jaccard similarity (symbol frequencies): 0.68
Cosine similarity (bigrams): 0.6456175755756943
Jaccard similarity (bigrams)): 0.47
Cosine Similarity (TF-IDF, unigrams): 0.9734470901659812
Jaccard similarity (TF-IDF, unigrams)): 0.68
Cosine similarity (TF-IDF, bigrams): 0.48173166577275617
Jaccard similarity (TF-IDF, bigrams): 0.47
```

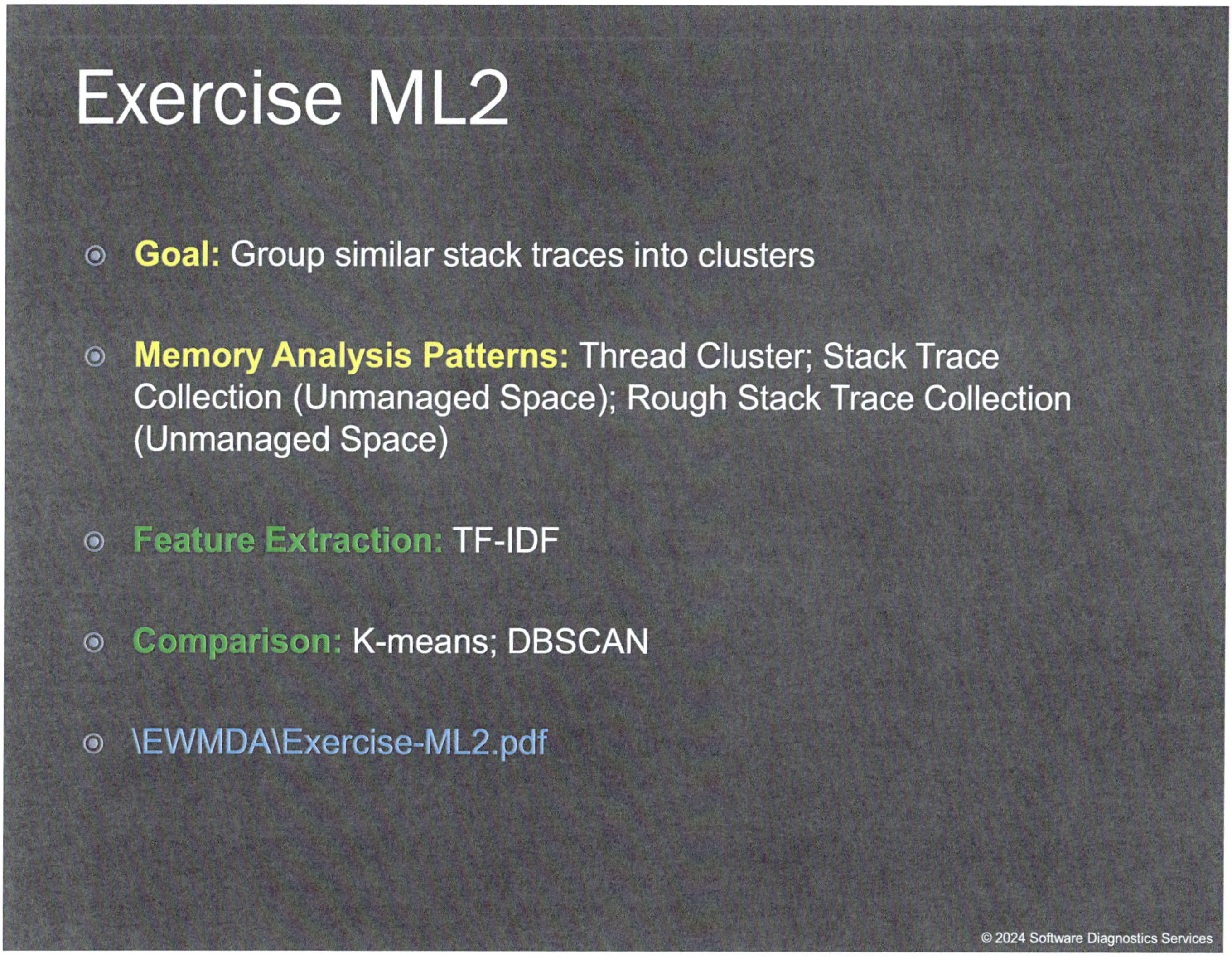
Exercise ML2
Goal: Group similar stack traces into clusters
Memory Analysis Patterns: Thread Cluster; Stack Trace Collection (Unmanaged Space); Rough Stack Trace Collection (Unmanaged Space)
Feature Extraction: TF-IDF
Comparison: K-means; DBSCAN
\EWMDA\Exercise-ML2.pdf
© 2024 Software Diagnostics Services

Exercise ML2: Group Stack Traces into Clusters

Goal: Group similar stack traces into clusters.

Memory Analysis Patterns: Thread Cluster; Stack Trace Collection (Unmanaged Space); Rough Stack Trace Collection (Unmanaged Space).

Feature Extraction: TF-IDF.

Comparison: K-means; DBSCAN.

1. We use the same set of log files from Exercise ML1: *\EWMDA-Dumps\ML\rough-trace-ok.log* and *\EWMDA-Dumps\ML\rough-trace-fail.log* for the Firefox problem.

2. Our goal is to group similar rough stack traces from both collections. It is done via the *\EWMDA-Dumps\ML\trace_clustering.py* Python program:

```
# Extended Windows Memory Dump Analysis, Version 2.0
# Exercise ML2

import re

from sklearn.feature_extraction.text import TfidfVectorizer
from sklearn.cluster import KMeans
from sklearn.cluster import DBSCAN

# Regular expression to split fragments by "TEB" markers
fragment_pattern = re.compile(r'(?:TEB at .+?)(?=\n\S|$)', re.DOTALL)

# Regular expression pattern to match module!function and ignore the offset
symbol_pattern = re.compile(r'(\w+!\w+)(?:\+\w+)?')

# Read data from a text file for ok case
with open('rough-trace-ok.log', 'r') as file:
    data_ok = file.read()

# Split data into fragments based on the TEB marker
fragments_ok = fragment_pattern.split(data_ok)
fragments_ok = fragments_ok[1:] # ignore the first empty fragment

# remove addresses from fragments
fragments_ok_filtered = []
for f in fragments_ok:
    fragments_ok_filtered.append("\n".join(symbol_pattern.findall(f)))

# Read data from a text file for fail case
with open('rough-trace-fail.log', 'r') as file:
    data_fail = file.read()
```

```
# Split data into fragments based on the TEB marker
fragments_fail = fragment_pattern.split(data_fail)
fragments_fail = fragments_fail[1:] # ignore the first empty fragment

# remove addresses from fragments
fragments_fail_filtered = []
for f in fragments_fail:
    fragments_fail_filtered.append("\n".join(symbol_pattern.findall(f)))

# TF-IDF Vectorization
vectorizer = TfidfVectorizer()
tfidf_matrix_ok = vectorizer.fit_transform(fragments_ok_filtered)
tfidf_matrix_fail = vectorizer.fit_transform(fragments_fail_filtered)

# K-means with the number of clusters
kmeans = KMeans(n_clusters=10, random_state=0)
kmeans.fit(tfidf_matrix_ok)
print("K-means cluster labels (ok case):", kmeans.labels_)
kmeans = KMeans(n_clusters=10, random_state=0)
kmeans.fit(tfidf_matrix_fail)
print("K-means cluster labels (fail case):", kmeans.labels_)

# DBSCAN with a distance threshold (eps) and minimum samples per cluster (min_samples)
dbscan = DBSCAN(eps=0.5, min_samples=1)
dbscan.fit(tfidf_matrix_ok)
print("DBSCAN cluster labels (ok case):", dbscan.labels_)
dbscan = DBSCAN(eps=0.5, min_samples=1)
dbscan.fit(tfidf_matrix_fail)
print("DBSCAN cluster labels (fail case):", dbscan.labels_)
```

Note: We have the following output:

```
PS C:\EWMDA-Dumps\ML> & C:/Python311/python.exe c:/EWMDA-Dumps/ML/trace-clustering.py
K-means cluster labels (ok case): [5 9 8 2 2 5 7 2 6 3 5 2 5 5 5 7 6 8 2 8 5 5 5 5 5 2 7 8 7 2
6 2 2 8 3 2 7
 3 2 3 2 2 2 9 9 0 2 2 7 2 5 1 3 3 2 8 5 5 4 7 3 3 2 1 1 1 1 1 1 1 1 1 1 1
 3 2 7 7 7 4 4 9 6]
K-means cluster labels (fail case): [3 4 4 1 6 3 0 0 7 5 3 0 3 3 3 4 7 0 7 4 3 3 3 3 3 0 0 4 6
3 7 0 1 8 5 0 3
 5 0 5 0 0 9 9 2 0 3 3 3 2 5 0 6 5 3 7 4 5 3 5 2 2 2 2 2 2 5 5 0 4 0 0 0 0
 0]
DBSCAN cluster labels (ok case): [ 0  1  2  3  4  5  6  7  8  9  7  7  0  0  0 10  8 11 12 13
14 14 14 14
 14 15 16 17 18 19 20  7 21 22 23  7 16 23  7 23  7  7  7 24 25 26 27  7
 28 29 30 31 23 23  7 32 14 14 33 34 23 23 35 31 31 31 31 31 31 31 31 31
 31 31 23  7 36 16 16 33 33 37  8]
DBSCAN cluster labels (fail case): [ 0  1  2  3  4  5  6  7  8  9  7  7  0  0  0 10  8  7 11 12
7  7  7  7
  7 13 14 15 16 17 18  7 19 20  9  7  7  9  7  9  7  7 21 22 23 24 25 26
 27 28  9  7 29  9  7 30 31  9  7  9 28 28 28 28 28 28  9  9 32 33  7 34
  7  7 35]
```

Exercise ML3

- **Goal:** Identify anomalous stack traces
- **Memory Analysis Patterns:** Stack Trace Collection (Unmanaged Space); Rough Stack Trace Collection (Unmanaged Space)
- **Feature Extraction:** TF-IDF
- **Comparison:** Isolation Forest; Autoencoders
- \EWMDA\Exercise-ML3.pdf

Exercise ML3: Identify Anomalous Stack Traces

Goal: Identify anomalous stack traces.

Memory Analysis Patterns: Stack Trace Collection (Unmanaged Space); Rough Stack Trace Collection (Unmanaged Space).

Feature Extraction: TF-IDF.

Comparison: Isolation Forest; Autoencoders.

1. We use the same set of log files from Exercise ML2: *\EWMDA-Dumps\ML\rough-trace-ok.log* and *\EWMDA-Dumps\ML\rough-trace-fail.log* for the Firefox problem. You may need to install the *tensorflow* Python package.

2. Our goal is to identify anomalous rough stack traces from both collections. It is done via the *\EWMDA-Dumps\ML\trace_anomalies.py* Python program:

```
# Extended Windows Memory Dump Analysis, Version 2.0
# Exercise ML3

import re
import numpy as np
import tensorflow as tf

from sklearn.feature_extraction.text import TfidfVectorizer
from sklearn.ensemble import IsolationForest

# Regular expression to split fragments by "TEB" markers
fragment_pattern = re.compile(r'(?:TEB at .+?)(?=\n\S|$)', re.DOTALL)

# Regular expression pattern to match module!function and ignore the offset
symbol_pattern = re.compile(r'(\w+!\w+)(?:\+\w+)?')

# Read data from a text file for ok case
with open('rough-trace-ok.log', 'r') as file:
    data_ok = file.read()

# Split data into fragments based on the TEB marker
fragments_ok = fragment_pattern.split(data_ok)
fragments_ok = fragments_ok[1:] # ignore the first empty fragment

# remove addresses from fragments
fragments_ok_filtered = []
for f in fragments_ok:
    fragments_ok_filtered.append("\n".join(symbol_pattern.findall(f)))

# Read data from a text file for fail case
with open('rough-trace-fail.log', 'r') as file:
```

```
    data_fail = file.read()

# Split data into fragments based on the TEB marker
fragments_fail = fragment_pattern.split(data_fail)
fragments_fail = fragments_fail[1:] # ignore the first empty fragment

# remove addresses from fragments
fragments_fail_filtered = []
for f in fragments_fail:
    fragments_fail_filtered.append("\n".join(symbol_pattern.findall(f)))

# Create overall stack trace collection from both fragment collections
fragments = fragments_ok_filtered + fragments_fail_filtered

# TF-IDF Vectorization
vectorizer = TfidfVectorizer()
tfidf_matrix = vectorizer.fit_transform(fragments)

iso_forest = IsolationForest(contamination=0.1, random_state=42)
labels = iso_forest.fit_predict(tfidf_matrix)

# Print the results
print("Isolation forest labels (1 = normal, -1 = anomaly):", labels)

# Build a simple autoencoder model
tfidf_matrix = tfidf_matrix.toarray()
input_dim = tfidf_matrix.shape[1]  # number of features from TF-IDF
autoencoder = tf.keras.models.Sequential([
    tf.keras.layers.Input(shape=(input_dim,)),
    tf.keras.layers.Dense(64, activation="relu"),
    tf.keras.layers.Dense(32, activation="relu"),
    tf.keras.layers.Dense(64, activation="relu"),
    tf.keras.layers.Dense(input_dim, activation="sigmoid")  # Output layer
])

autoencoder.compile(optimizer="adam", loss="mse")

# Train the autoencoder on the overall stack trace collection
autoencoder.fit(tfidf_matrix, tfidf_matrix, epochs=50, batch_size=2, validation_split=0.1,
verbose=1)

# Calculate reconstruction errors
reconstructions = autoencoder.predict(tfidf_matrix)
mse = np.mean(np.power(tfidf_matrix - reconstructions, 2), axis=1)

# A threshold for anomalies
threshold = np.percentile(mse, 95)  # top 5% reconstruction error
anomalies = mse > threshold
```

```
print("Anomalies:", anomalies)
```

Note: We have the following output:

```
PS C:\EWMDA-Dumps\ML> & C:/Python311/python.exe c:/EWMDA-Dumps/ML/trace-anomalies.py
Isolation forest labels (1 = normal, -1 = anomaly): [ 1  1  1  1  1  1  1  1 -1  1  1  1  1  1
1  1  1  1  1  1  1  1  1  1
  1  1  1  1 -1  1 -1  1  1  1  1  1  1  1  1  1  1  1  1  1 -1  1  1
  1  1  1  1  1  1  1  1  1  1 -1  1  1  1 -1  1  1  1  1  1  1  1  1  1
  1  1  1  1  1  1  1 -1 -1  1 -1 -1  1  1  1  1  1  1  1 -1  1  1  1  1
  1  1  1  1  1 -1  1  1  1  1  1  1  1  1  1 -1  1 -1  1  1  1  1  1  1
  1  1  1  1  1  1 -1  1  1  1  1  1  1  1  1  1  1  1 -1  1  1  1  1  1
  1  1  1  1  1  1  1  1  1  1  1  1  1  1]
Epoch 1/50
71/71 ━━━━━━━━━━━━━━━━━━━━ 4s 9ms/step - loss: 0.2040 - val_loss: 8.2749e-04
Epoch 2/50
71/71 ━━━━━━━━━━━━━━━━━━━━ 0s 4ms/step - loss: 7.9370e-04 - val_loss: 6.8392e-04
Epoch 3/50
71/71 ━━━━━━━━━━━━━━━━━━━━ 0s 4ms/step - loss: 6.8466e-04 - val_loss: 6.4460e-04
Epoch 4/50
71/71 ━━━━━━━━━━━━━━━━━━━━ 0s 4ms/step - loss: 6.8170e-04 - val_loss: 6.2722e-04
Epoch 5/50
71/71 ━━━━━━━━━━━━━━━━━━━━ 0s 3ms/step - loss: 6.3899e-04 - val_loss: 6.0924e-04
Epoch 6/50
71/71 ━━━━━━━━━━━━━━━━━━━━ 0s 4ms/step - loss: 6.3410e-04 - val_loss: 6.1082e-04
Epoch 7/50
71/71 ━━━━━━━━━━━━━━━━━━━━ 0s 5ms/step - loss: 6.1697e-04 - val_loss: 5.9616e-04
Epoch 8/50
71/71 ━━━━━━━━━━━━━━━━━━━━ 0s 4ms/step - loss: 6.2453e-04 - val_loss: 6.1700e-04
Epoch 9/50
71/71 ━━━━━━━━━━━━━━━━━━━━ 0s 5ms/step - loss: 6.2219e-04 - val_loss: 6.0071e-04
Epoch 10/50
71/71 ━━━━━━━━━━━━━━━━━━━━ 0s 5ms/step - loss: 6.3378e-04 - val_loss: 6.0765e-04
Epoch 11/50
71/71 ━━━━━━━━━━━━━━━━━━━━ 0s 6ms/step - loss: 6.0878e-04 - val_loss: 5.8364e-04
Epoch 12/50
71/71 ━━━━━━━━━━━━━━━━━━━━ 0s 4ms/step - loss: 6.1312e-04 - val_loss: 5.8040e-04
Epoch 13/50
71/71 ━━━━━━━━━━━━━━━━━━━━ 0s 5ms/step - loss: 5.8635e-04 - val_loss: 5.8036e-04
Epoch 14/50
71/71 ━━━━━━━━━━━━━━━━━━━━ 0s 4ms/step - loss: 5.8745e-04 - val_loss: 5.9026e-04
Epoch 15/50
71/71 ━━━━━━━━━━━━━━━━━━━━ 0s 3ms/step - loss: 5.5881e-04 - val_loss: 5.5122e-04
Epoch 16/50
71/71 ━━━━━━━━━━━━━━━━━━━━ 0s 4ms/step - loss: 5.5915e-04 - val_loss: 5.1909e-04
Epoch 17/50
71/71 ━━━━━━━━━━━━━━━━━━━━ 0s 4ms/step - loss: 5.3380e-04 - val_loss: 5.1784e-04
Epoch 18/50
71/71 ━━━━━━━━━━━━━━━━━━━━ 0s 4ms/step - loss: 5.3094e-04 - val_loss: 5.3040e-04
Epoch 19/50
71/71 ━━━━━━━━━━━━━━━━━━━━ 0s 3ms/step - loss: 4.9070e-04 - val_loss: 5.2435e-04
Epoch 20/50
71/71 ━━━━━━━━━━━━━━━━━━━━ 0s 5ms/step - loss: 4.9026e-04 - val_loss: 4.9657e-04
Epoch 21/50
71/71 ━━━━━━━━━━━━━━━━━━━━ 0s 4ms/step - loss: 4.6826e-04 - val_loss: 4.9899e-04
Epoch 22/50
71/71 ━━━━━━━━━━━━━━━━━━━━ 0s 4ms/step - loss: 4.7409e-04 - val_loss: 5.4194e-04
Epoch 23/50
```

```
71/71 ━━━━━━━━━━━━━━━━━━━━ 0s 4ms/step - loss: 4.7015e-04 - val_loss: 4.6907e-04
Epoch 24/50
71/71 ━━━━━━━━━━━━━━━━━━━━ 0s 4ms/step - loss: 4.8807e-04 - val_loss: 4.4344e-04
Epoch 25/50
71/71 ━━━━━━━━━━━━━━━━━━━━ 0s 4ms/step - loss: 4.4307e-04 - val_loss: 5.1766e-04
Epoch 26/50
71/71 ━━━━━━━━━━━━━━━━━━━━ 0s 4ms/step - loss: 4.5894e-04 - val_loss: 5.0175e-04
Epoch 27/50
71/71 ━━━━━━━━━━━━━━━━━━━━ 0s 5ms/step - loss: 4.8731e-04 - val_loss: 4.5132e-04
Epoch 28/50
71/71 ━━━━━━━━━━━━━━━━━━━━ 0s 6ms/step - loss: 4.2800e-04 - val_loss: 4.8078e-04
Epoch 29/50
71/71 ━━━━━━━━━━━━━━━━━━━━ 0s 5ms/step - loss: 4.6749e-04 - val_loss: 4.2627e-04
Epoch 30/50
71/71 ━━━━━━━━━━━━━━━━━━━━ 1s 7ms/step - loss: 4.2288e-04 - val_loss: 4.1653e-04
Epoch 31/50
71/71 ━━━━━━━━━━━━━━━━━━━━ 0s 5ms/step - loss: 4.2465e-04 - val_loss: 3.6611e-04
Epoch 32/50
71/71 ━━━━━━━━━━━━━━━━━━━━ 0s 5ms/step - loss: 4.0035e-04 - val_loss: 3.5872e-04
Epoch 33/50
71/71 ━━━━━━━━━━━━━━━━━━━━ 0s 5ms/step - loss: 3.6424e-04 - val_loss: 3.6841e-04
Epoch 34/50
71/71 ━━━━━━━━━━━━━━━━━━━━ 0s 4ms/step - loss: 3.5740e-04 - val_loss: 3.0456e-04
Epoch 35/50
71/71 ━━━━━━━━━━━━━━━━━━━━ 0s 4ms/step - loss: 3.3388e-04 - val_loss: 2.4935e-04
Epoch 36/50
71/71 ━━━━━━━━━━━━━━━━━━━━ 0s 5ms/step - loss: 2.9533e-04 - val_loss: 2.4172e-04
Epoch 37/50
71/71 ━━━━━━━━━━━━━━━━━━━━ 0s 6ms/step - loss: 2.8988e-04 - val_loss: 2.3540e-04
Epoch 38/50
71/71 ━━━━━━━━━━━━━━━━━━━━ 0s 4ms/step - loss: 3.0989e-04 - val_loss: 2.1396e-04
Epoch 39/50
71/71 ━━━━━━━━━━━━━━━━━━━━ 0s 4ms/step - loss: 2.8729e-04 - val_loss: 2.1027e-04
Epoch 40/50
71/71 ━━━━━━━━━━━━━━━━━━━━ 1s 7ms/step - loss: 2.8042e-04 - val_loss: 2.0873e-04
Epoch 41/50
71/71 ━━━━━━━━━━━━━━━━━━━━ 0s 5ms/step - loss: 2.5846e-04 - val_loss: 2.0761e-04
Epoch 42/50
71/71 ━━━━━━━━━━━━━━━━━━━━ 0s 4ms/step - loss: 2.5848e-04 - val_loss: 2.0725e-04
Epoch 43/50
71/71 ━━━━━━━━━━━━━━━━━━━━ 0s 4ms/step - loss: 2.3178e-04 - val_loss: 2.0170e-04
Epoch 44/50
71/71 ━━━━━━━━━━━━━━━━━━━━ 0s 4ms/step - loss: 2.8088e-04 - val_loss: 2.0017e-04
Epoch 45/50
71/71 ━━━━━━━━━━━━━━━━━━━━ 0s 4ms/step - loss: 2.5225e-04 - val_loss: 1.9745e-04
Epoch 46/50
71/71 ━━━━━━━━━━━━━━━━━━━━ 0s 5ms/step - loss: 2.2597e-04 - val_loss: 1.9452e-04
Epoch 47/50
71/71 ━━━━━━━━━━━━━━━━━━━━ 0s 6ms/step - loss: 2.2103e-04 - val_loss: 1.8848e-04
Epoch 48/50
71/71 ━━━━━━━━━━━━━━━━━━━━ 0s 4ms/step - loss: 2.3216e-04 - val_loss: 1.9063e-04
Epoch 49/50
71/71 ━━━━━━━━━━━━━━━━━━━━ 0s 4ms/step - loss: 2.1265e-04 - val_loss: 1.8663e-04
Epoch 50/50
71/71 ━━━━━━━━━━━━━━━━━━━━ 0s 6ms/step - loss: 2.2058e-04 - val_loss: 1.8980e-04
5/5 ━━━━━━━━━━━━━━━━━━━━ 0s 33ms/step
Anomalies: [False  True False False False False False False False False False False
 False False False False False  True False False False False False False
 False False False False False False False False False False False False
```

```
False False False False False False False False  True False  True False
False False False False False False False False False False False False
False False False False False False False False False False False False
False False False False False False False False False False False False
False False False False False False False False False False False False
False False False False False False False False False False False False
False False False False False False False False False False False False
False False False False False  True  True  True False False  True False
False False False False False False False False False False False False
False False False False False False False False False False False False
False False]
```

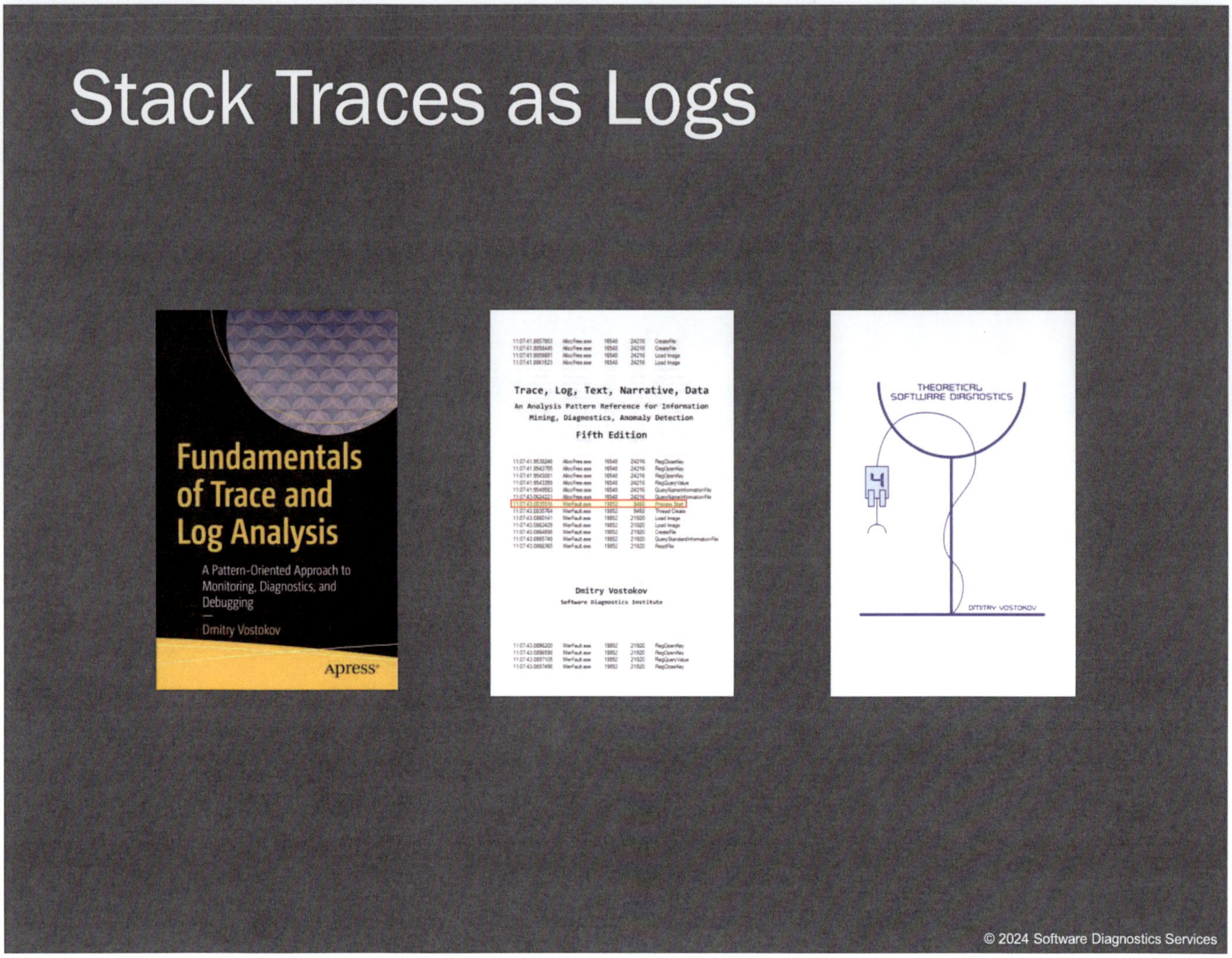

Stack traces and other WinDbg textual data can be considered instances of software traces and logs. The slide shows additional books related to general trace and log analysis.

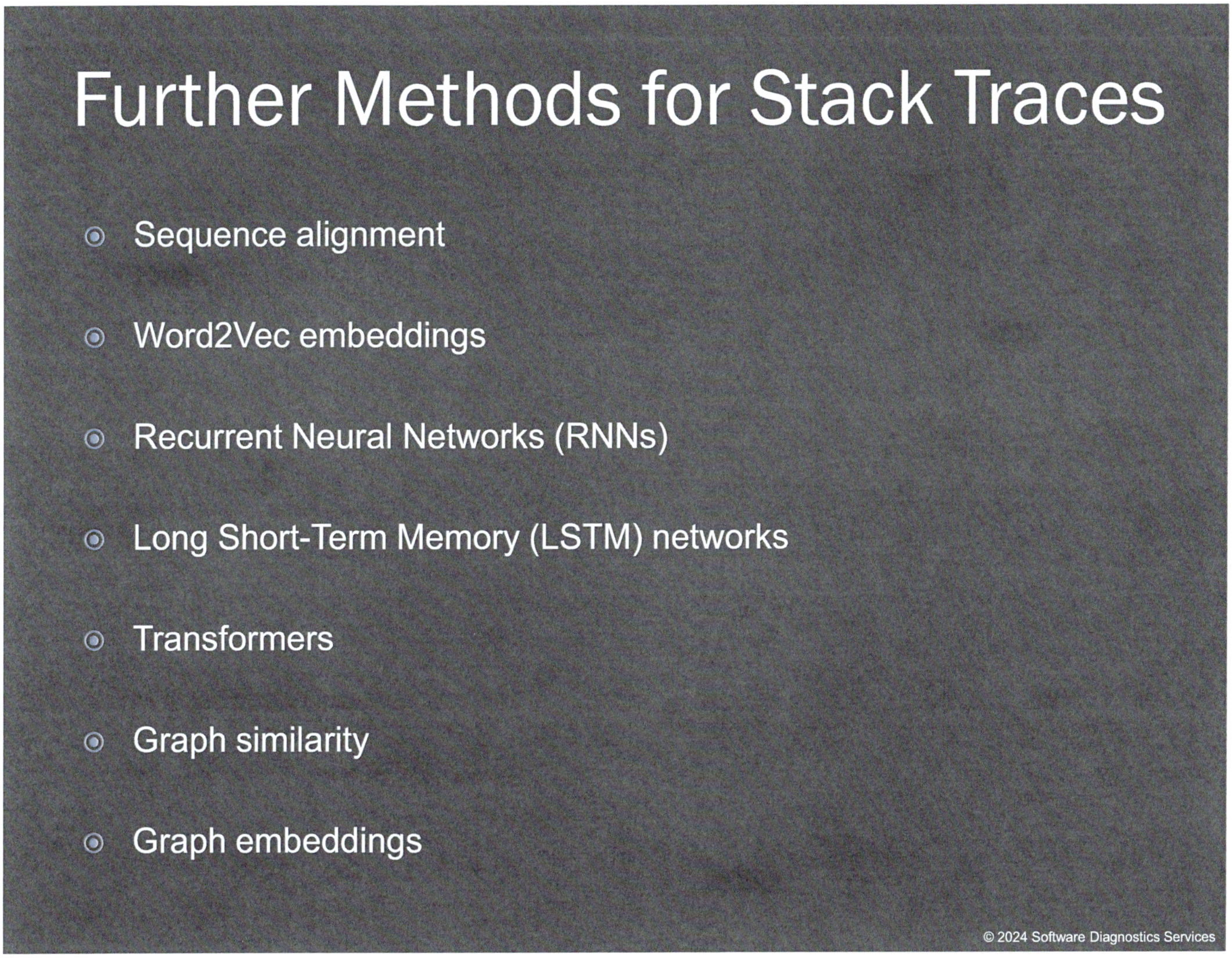
Further Methods for Stack Traces
Sequence alignment
Word2Vec embeddings
Recurrent Neural Networks (RNNs)
Long Short-Term Memory (LSTM) networks
Transformers
Graph similarity
Graph embeddings
© 2024 Software Diagnostics Services

Other ML methods can be used for execution residue and stack trace analysis. We may cover some of them in the next edition.

Further Course

Machine Learning for Software Diagnostics

We plan to provide the thorough introduction to the basics of ML in the additional course.

Conclusion

Memory Analysis Pattern Links

Execution Residue (Unmanaged Space, User)
Execution Residue (Unmanaged Space, Kernel)
Instrumentation Information
Driver Device Collection
Stack Trace Collection (I/O drivers)
Stack Trace Collection (Predicate)
Stack Trace Collection (CPUs)
Handle Limit (GDI, Kernel Space)
Virtualized Process (WOW64)
Stack Trace Collection (Unmanaged Space)
Missing Thread (Kernel Space)
Wait Chain (Window Messaging)
Self-Diagnosis (Registry)
Out-of-Module Pointer
Deviant Token
Patched Code
Step Dumps
Region Profile
Stack Trace Collection (Commands)
Stack Trace (Command)
Rough Stack Trace (Unmanaged Space)
Annotated Stack Trace
Region Summary
Rough Stack Trace Collection (Unmanaged Space)

Zombie Processes
Module Collection
Historical Information
Stack Trace (I/O devices)
Exception Stack Trace
Blocked Thread (Software)
Active Thread
Suspended Thread
Wait Chain (ALPC)
Spiking Thread
System Object
Input Thread
Value References
Environment Hint
Raw Pointer
Context Pointer
Evental Dumps
Region Clusters
Namespace
Structure Sheaf
Analysis Summary
Disassembly Summary
Frame Trace
Thread Cluster

Here are links to pattern descriptions and additional examples:

Execution Residue (Unmanaged Space, User)
http://www.dumpanalysis.org/blog/index.php/2008/04/29/crash-dump-analysis-patterns-part-60/

Zombie Processes
https://www.dumpanalysis.org/blog/index.php/2008/02/28/crash-dump-analysis-patterns-part-54/

Execution Residue (Unmanaged Space, Kernel)
https://www.dumpanalysis.org/blog/index.php/2021/10/03/crash-dump-analysis-patterns-part-60c/

Module Collection
https://www.dumpanalysis.org/blog/index.php/2012/12/24/crash-dump-analysis-patterns-part-190/

Instrumentation Information
https://www.dumpanalysis.org/blog/index.php/2010/09/27/crash-dump-analysis-patterns-part-107/

Historical Information
https://www.dumpanalysis.org/blog/index.php/2007/11/06/crash-dump-analysis-patterns-part-34/

Driver Device Collection
http://www.dumpanalysis.org/blog/index.php/2013/01/20/malware-analysis-patterns-part-10/

Stack Trace (I/O devices)
https://www.dumpanalysis.org/blog/index.php/2017/05/06/crash-dump-analysis-patterns-part-25e/

Exception Stack Trace
http://www.dumpanalysis.org/blog/index.php/2010/08/05/crash-dump-analysis-patterns-part-105/

Stack Trace Collection (Predicate)
https://www.dumpanalysis.org/blog/index.php/2011/12/03/crash-dump-analysis-patterns-part-27c/

Blocked Thread (Software)
https://www.dumpanalysis.org/blog/index.php/2008/02/27/crash-dump-analysis-patterns-part-53/

Stack Trace Collection (CPUs)
https://www.dumpanalysis.org/blog/index.php/2015/08/24/crash-dump-analysis-patterns-part-27e/

Active Thread
https://www.dumpanalysis.org/blog/index.php/2015/10/31/crash-dump-analysis-patterns-part-232/

Handle Limit (GDI, Kernel Space)
https://www.dumpanalysis.org/blog/index.php/2008/04/09/crash-dump-analysis-patterns-part-58a/

Suspended Thread
https://www.dumpanalysis.org/blog/index.php/2008/02/06/crash-dump-analysis-patterns-part-47/

Virtualized Process (WOW64)
http://www.dumpanalysis.org/blog/index.php/2007/09/11/crash-dump-analysis-patterns-part-26/

Wait Chain (ALPC)
https://www.dumpanalysis.org/blog/index.php/2008/12/17/crash-dump-analysis-patterns-part-42e/

Stack Trace Collection (Unmanaged Space)
https://www.dumpanalysis.org/blog/index.php/2007/09/14/crash-dump-analysis-patterns-part-27/

Spiking Thread
https://www.dumpanalysis.org/blog/index.php/2007/05/11/crash-dump-analysis-patterns-part-14/

System Object
https://www.dumpanalysis.org/blog/index.php/2011/12/04/crash-dump-analysis-patterns-part-158/

Wait Chain (Window Messaging)
https://www.dumpanalysis.org/blog/index.php/2010/12/16/crash-dump-analysis-patterns-part-42h/

Self-Diagnosis (Registry)
https://www.dumpanalysis.org/blog/index.php/2011/12/04/crash-dump-analysis-patterns-part-69c/

Value References
https://www.dumpanalysis.org/blog/index.php/2011/12/05/crash-dump-analysis-patterns-part-159/

Out-of-Module Pointer
http://www.dumpanalysis.org/blog/index.php/2013/02/10/malware-analysis-patterns-part-23/

Environment Hint
https://www.dumpanalysis.org/blog/index.php/2010/12/24/crash-dump-analysis-patterns-part-124/

Deviant Token
https://www.dumpanalysis.org/blog/index.php/2012/12/31/crash-dump-analysis-patterns-part-191/

Raw Pointer
http://www.dumpanalysis.org/blog/index.php/2013/02/09/malware-analysis-patterns-part-22/

Patched Code
http://www.dumpanalysis.org/blog/index.php/2013/02/09/malware-analysis-patterns-part-21/

Context Pointer
https://www.dumpanalysis.org/blog/index.php/2020/06/15/crash-dump-analysis-patterns-part-269/

Step Dumps
https://www.dumpanalysis.org/blog/index.php/2013/01/04/crash-dump-analysis-patterns-part-192/

Evental Dumps
https://www.dumpanalysis.org/blog/index.php/2015/10/26/crash-dump-analysis-patterns-part-231/

Region Profile
https://www.dumpanalysis.org/blog/index.php/2019/09/27/crash-dump-analysis-patterns-part-260/

Region Clusters
https://www.dumpanalysis.org/blog/index.php/2019/10/13/crash-dump-analysis-patterns-part-261/

Namespace
http://www.dumpanalysis.org/blog/index.php/2013/02/05/malware-analysis-patterns-part-20/

Structure Sheaf
Stack Trace (Command)
Stack Trace Collection (Commands)
https://www.dumpanalysis.org/blog/index.php/2021/03/03/crash-dump-analysis-patterns-part-275/

Rough Stack Trace (Unmanaged Space)
https://www.dumpanalysis.org/blog/index.php/2014/10/07/crash-dump-analysis-patterns-part-213/

Analysis Summary
https://www.dumpanalysis.org/blog/index.php/2024/03/18/crash-dump-analysis-patterns-part-294/

Annotated Stack Trace
https://www.dumpanalysis.org/blog/index.php/2024/03/14/crash-dump-analysis-patterns-part-291/

Disassembly Summary
https://www.dumpanalysis.org/blog/index.php/2024/03/17/crash-dump-analysis-patterns-part-292/

Region Summary
https://www.dumpanalysis.org/blog/index.php/2024/03/18/crash-dump-analysis-patterns-part-293/

Frame Trace
https://www.dumpanalysis.org/blog/index.php/2020/06/13/crash-dump-analysis-patterns-part-267/

Rough Stack Trace Collection (Unmanaged Space)
https://www.dumpanalysis.org/blog/index.php/2022/06/08/crash-dump-analysis-patterns-part-281/

Thread Cluster
https://www.dumpanalysis.org/blog/index.php/2014/04/18/crash-dump-analysis-patterns-part-204/

Note: all these patterns (and hundreds of others) are also available in **Memory Dump Analysis Anthology** volumes or **Encyclopedia of Crash Dump Analysis Patterns** (see the **References** slide).

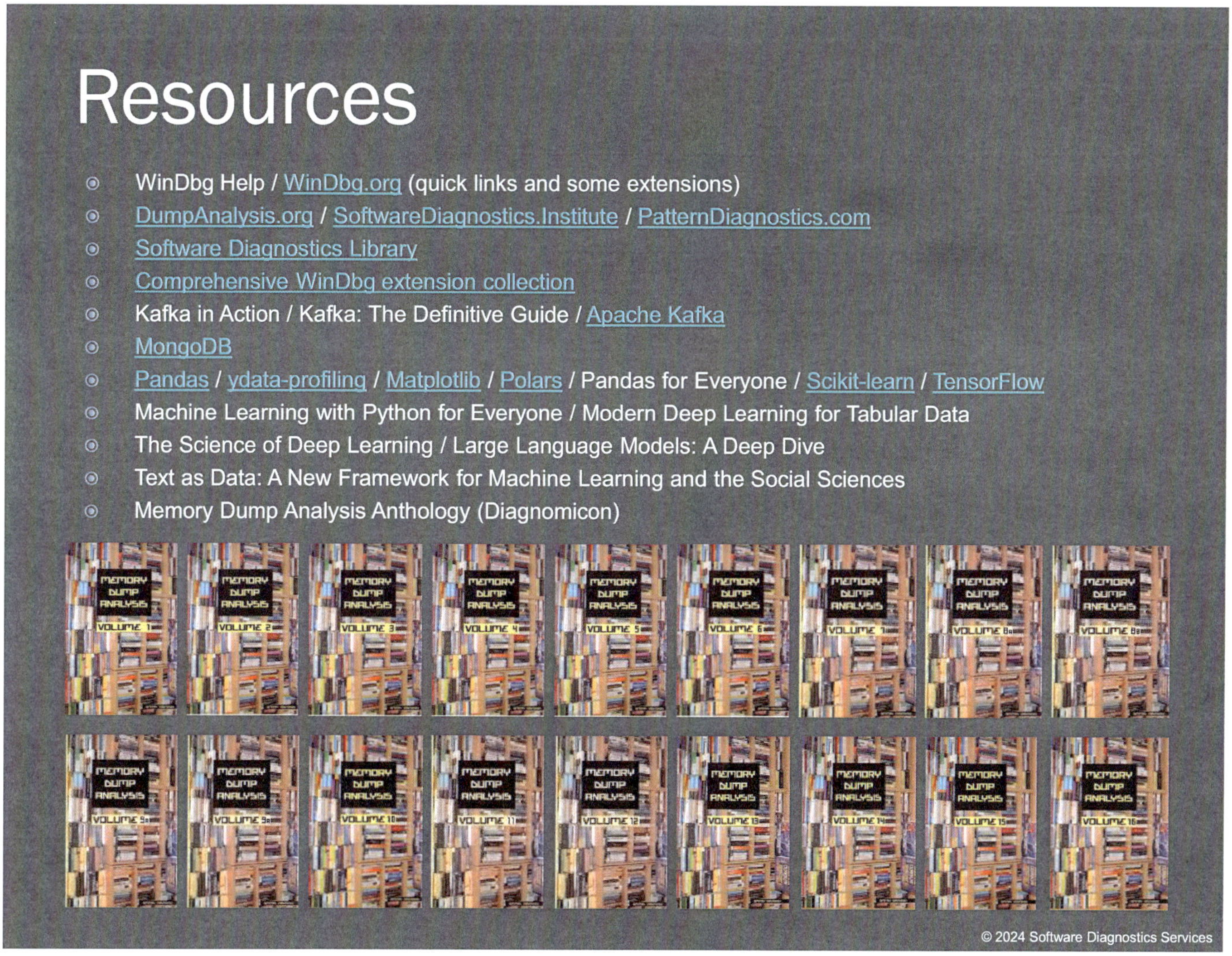

Additional learning and reference resources:

WinDbg quick links
http://WinDbg.org

Software Diagnostics Institute
https://www.dumpanalysis.org

Software Diagnostics Services
http://www.patterndiagnostics.com

Software Diagnostics Library
https://www.dumpanalysis.org/blog

Comprehensive WinDbg extension collection
https://github.com/anhkgg/awesome-windbg-extensions

Apache Kafka
https://kafka.apache.org/

MongoDB
https://www.mongodb.com/

Pandas
https://pandas.pydata.org/

ydata-profiling
https://github.com/ydataai/ydata-profiling

Matplotlib
https://matplotlib.org/

Polars
https://www.pola.rs/

Scikit-learn
https://scikit-learn.org/

TensorFlow
https://www.tensorflow.org/

Memory Dump Analysis Anthology (Diagnomicon)
https://www.patterndiagnostics.com/mdaa-volumes

www.ingramcontent.com/pod-product-compliance
Lightning Source LLC
Chambersburg PA
CBRC091939210326
41598CB00012B/861

* 9 7 8 1 9 1 2 6 3 6 5 1 8 *